DESCRIPTIVE LIST OF MUTINY PAPERS

1. Descriptive List of Mutiny Papers, Vol. I, 1960
2. Descriptive List of Mutiny Papers, Vol. II, 1963
3. Descriptive List of Mutiny Papers, Vol. III, 1971
4. Descriptive List of Mutiny Papers, Vol. IV, 1973
5. Descriptive List of Mutiny Papers, Vol. V, 1979
6. Descriptive List of Mutiny Papers, Vol. VI, 1993
7. Descriptive List of Mutiny Papers, Vol. VII, 2015
8. Descriptive List of Mutiny Papers, Vol. VIII, 2020

DESCRIPTIVE LIST OF MUTINY PAPERS

IN THE NATIONAL ARCHIVES OF INDIA, BHOPAL

Volume IX

EDITED BY
MUZAFFAR-E ISLAM

vaniprakashan.com

Peparback First Edition : 2024

Yatra Books is an imprint of Vani Prakashan Group

Head Office

4695, 21-A, Daryaganj, New Delhi-110 002, India
Phone : +91 11 23273167, 11 23275710

Registered Bookstores and Offices

Ashok Rajpath, Patna-800 004, Bihar
Coffee House Campus, Mahatma Gandhi Marg, Prayagraj-211 001, Uttar Pradesh
Mahatma Gandhi International Hindi University, Wardha-442 001, Maharashtra

sales@vaniprakashan.in
vaniprakashan@gmail.com

Descriptive List of Mutiny Papers
Edited by Muzaffar-E Islam

ISBN : 978-93-48235-86-2
History

₹ 800

Printed and bound in City Press, Delhi-110 095

Contents

Introduction 7
Descriptive List of Munity Papers 9
Illustrations 541

Introduction

It is my pleasure to put before the scholars and the readers, Volume IX of the series of 'Descriptive List of Mutiny Papers'. Spreading over 425 files, these Mutiny Papers, about 10,000 documents in Persian language, are housed in the National Archives of India, Regional Office, Bhopal, which are in the form of letters, news reports, statements, narrations, eyewitness accounts, notifications, etc. exchanged between the then Nawwab of Bhopal, Nawwab Sikandar Begam and the State's Political Agent. Situated on the Vindhyachal Hills of Central India, Bhopal was a small Princely State, comprising only two districts- Bhopal and Raisen. The State was carved out by Amir Dost Muhammad Khan in 1723. Between 1819-1926, the State witnessed four great women or Begams ruling over it. Nawwab Qudsia Begam was the first female ruler of the State, followed by her daughter, Nawwab Sikandar Begam, in whose time the uprising took place. Her daughter Nawwab Shahjahan Begam and grand- daughter, Nawwab Sultan Jahan Begam, ruled over the State till 1926. Nawwab Hamid Allah Khan, son of Nawwab Sultan Jahan Begam was the last ruler of the State, in whose regime the State was merged with the Union of India in 1949.

All the records of erstwhile Bhopal State, which also include the records of 1857-1858, called the mutiny papers, were acquired by the Government of India and preserved in the Regional Office, National Archives of India, Bhopal. These 10,000 mutiny records, mainly in cursive Persian writing, are important source material, pertaining to the great uprising of 1857 which is otherwise also known as the mutiny, the revolt, the rebellion, the upheaval, the first war of independence, etc. These epithets are given by both, British as well as Indian historians.

The study of this record series, a primary source material to history becomes important to understand the great event of 1857. Unfortunately, these records remained almost untouched, possibly because they are in Persian language. In the Oriental Record Division of the National Archives of India, many records of Mughal era are preserved. Besides, the Repository 1 of the National Archives of India holds the regular series of Persian records of the British period. The National Archives of India has been endeavoring to translate and compile these Persian records. The 11 volumes of 'Calendar of Persian Correspondence' and 5 volumes of 'Descriptive List of Persian Correspondence' are the translated and edited works of the Persian correspondences, held between the Indian rulers and the British. The 'Descriptive List of Acquired Documents' in five volumes are the translated and edited works of the Persian documents of Mughal era. Similarly, the mutiny records are also being translated and edited by the National Archives of India. The present volume covers 1433 documents from 93 Files (File No. 251 to 312).

In the previous volume, it was observed that the uprising was completely suppressed. All prominent Indian rebels, the nawwabs, the rajas, the jagirdars, who revolted against the East India Company rule, were captured, gunned down or blown by cannon, or hanged. The documents included in this volume, tell the story of Tantia Tope, Rao Sahab Peshwa, Adil Muhammad Khan, Raja Bhorji (Raja of Narwar) and many others. Although they carried a huge number of *sawars* and foot soldiers with them, had arms and ammunitions and cannon too, they could not stand before the mighty British forces. They fled from one place to another, taking shelter in the mountains and in forests. They attacked British forces in Sironj and captured many villages. They entered the territory of the Bhopal State and made captive the *thanadar* and the *tahsildar* of Bamhuri. There was an apprehension of their attack upon Bhopal also. But their attempt was foiled due to the presence of the large British force. Later, the British Government issued a notification giving amnesty to all its subjects, except those who killed a British man or woman.

The present volume, like the previous one, is a word for word translation of Persian or Urdu documents. I am thankful to Shri Muzaffar-e Islam, former Assistant Director of Archives for editing the IXth volume of the series. I also congratulate the editorial team of Publication Division of the National Archives of India specially, Dr. Devendra Kumar Sharma, Assistant Director of Archives, and Shri Limasashi Aier, Archivist in coordinating and giving shape to this volume. I am also thankful to Dr. Sanjay Garg, Deputy Director of Archives for his valuable suggestions and comments. I am sure this volume too would be of immense value for all those who want to have a better understanding of the great uprising of 1857.

Dated 4.11.2024 **Arun Singhal, IAS**

Director General of Archives

Descriptive List of Mutiny Papers, Vol. IX

File No. 251
Box No. 12
No. of Documents 3

Dispute between Ghulam Muhammad Khan, Risaldar, and Sarfraz Ali,* Kotha-Dafadar*, Expressing Resentment against each other

P 1. Contents

PP 3-5. *Saiyid Sarfraz Ali,* Kotha-Dafadar *to Nawwab Sikandar Begam.* Informs that he has been serving on the post of *kotha-dafadari* under *risala* of orange uniform. The said *risala* was under deputy *madar al-maham.* During the march with deputy *madar al-maham*, Ghulam Ahmad Khan, *jamadar,* brother of Ghulam Muhammad Khan, *risaldar*, *risala* of orange uniform did many things which were against the rule of the government.

i. One such violation of the rule was that every *sawar* was ordered to wear the uniform everyday. While there is no government order that the *sawars* should wear dress uniform everyday.

ii. The official order is that, at the time of guarding, the guard should remain standing. But the *jamadar* performed the duty while sitting.

iii. The *jamadar*, brother of *risaldar*, while on duty remained riding on the horse and the symbol (allotted by the government) was put behind and the *bhanger* sat on the carts, not allowing him to sit on the horse.

iv. He sent his horses to Bhopal and the *bhangers* were asked to perform the duty of *babwan*.

v. The post of *kotha-dafadari* belongs to him and it is his duty to take the services of *sawars*. But the *jamadar* did not allow him to perform his duty, rather took the services of *sawars* for himself.

vi. At the time of his arrival, inspite of the presence of the *dafadar,* he took the work of *Kotha-dafadari* from a *lais* and the job of *lais* from *bhanger*.

vii. For the last three months, all the horses were marked in the office of *bakhshigari,* except one horse and *bhanger*.

viii. Personal works are taken from the *sawars*, especially, from those who are new.

Due to the violation of the rules he not once but many times came in loggerhead with the *jamadar*. The *jamadar* also presented him before Bakhshi Murawwat Muhammad Khan. The *bakhshi*, after coming back from Indore, expressed his anguish. He said he got his salary without performing any duty. It is better to sit in the house. Says it is a matter of concern that an old loyalist and loyal to his salt was abused and asked to sit in his house for the wrong doings of the *jamadar*. There is a need to investigate the case thoroughly.

Further says that the horse of Pratab Singh, *sawar* fell ill but all the *sawars* were threatened. He asked the *jamadar* why all the *sawars* were threatened and questioned on their appointment. The *jamadar* replied, he would not allow anyone to serve in that *risala*. As the answer of the *jamadar* was clear, he made up his mind to go to Bhopal. All the *sawars* expressed their concern to him about their removal from the *risala*. He replied to them that he would meet the *bakhshi* and put the matter before him without any addition or ommission. Whatever would be his reply would be communicated to them. Thus, he came to Bhopal and told the *bakhshi* everything. He said, ok. If all the *sawars* of the *risala* desire to see him as the caretaker of the horses of the *risala*, they should submit their petition to the government, as he is not empowered to appoint him at his own. Whatever order would be given would be followed. The same was conveyed to them. All the *sawars,* as ordered by the *bakhshi*, wrote a petition and put their seals on it. The same was sent to the government. The *jamadar* told the *bakhshi* that the *kotha-dafadar* obtained the petition from the *sawars* by befooling them and by fraud. The *bakhshi* asked him to submit all the petitions of the *sawars*. Says that all the petitions, submitted by the *sawars*, bear their seals. Requests that an investigation should be conducted to know what fraudulence he has committed.

Adds that the *jamadar* during the month of *Shawwal*, sent his younger sister to Shujaálpur to meet her relatives. She was loaded with gold and silver. When he heard about it, the *jamadar* met him and requested not to make it public. Says he replied, he is loyal to the salt and would not hide from the government if happens anything wrong. Not only this, but a notification is also published by the government with regard to not keep secret from the government if anything wrong happens with the government. From that very day, he is afraid of him and developed ill-will against him. The *bakhshi* is in Bhopal, God knows how the *jamadar* would manipulate the things against him. The *bakhshi* told him that the *jamadar* expressed his anguish upon him and humiliated him. Says if the government servants are humiliated by such officers what would be expected from them in the battlefield. Another thing is that the *jamadar* is frequently visiting Sehore which is also a matter of investigation.

Requests that in such circumstances, he may be transferred to other *risala* in view of his loyalty to the government since past, otherwise where he would go then. If it is not possible, he may be posted to where he was posted in the previous order or in any *risala* where the post of *jamadari* is vacant, as it will be a blessing for him. Otherwise, wherever would be posted he would do his best to accomplish the tasks assigned to him.

PP 7-8. *Ghulam Muhammad Khan, Risaldar, Orange Uniform, Deployed at Bheglone to Nawwab Sikandar Begam.* Informs about the Disobedience and Misconduct of Sarfraz Ali, Kotha Dafadar under his Risala.

Some of these are:

i. At the time of the march of the *sawars* to Jabrah Bhotrah, he was commanding a force which was going to Siwans and *jamadar* too was present there. The *jamadar* gave the charge of the *risala* to a *dafadar,* as per the rules. But he took the services of two *lais* and sent the *risala* to Jabrah Bhotrah which shows his disobedience and misconduct. The *dafadar* in every matter creates disturbances.

ii. That the deputy *madar al-maham,* at the time of going to Sehore, stayed in the house of Raja Sahab and ordered that 3 *sawars* should be put on guard there while the rest of the *sawars* of the *risala* should encamp in the garden of Chhtrasal. The *jamadar* due to his harshness purchased a *rauti* for a sum of Rs. 3 and asked one out of three guards, deployed with *madar al-maham* to join him at the *rauti* where he arranged, keeping aside all rules and regulations, a dance party of concubines. Although the *jamadar* tried to stop him from doing any unlawful activity but he paid no attention.

iii. He was not there as he was commanding a *risala.* The *jamadar* without informing the officer in violation of the rules, took the services of *dafadari* from *lais* while this work is done by the *risaldar* and *jamadar*.

iv. Although he was on duty of command, but the *jamadar* was there. The *kotha-jamadar* is troublesome as he, without informing him and without the consent of *jamadar,* created disturbances which is in violation of rules and against the agreement, concluded by every employee not to

> gather at one place. He got prepared a list which bears firstly, his name as *risaldar* followed by the name of *jamadar* and thereafter the name of all the *sawars* of the *risala*. Every *sawar* was asked to affix his seal also, after which the seal of *risaldar* and *jamadar* was sought. As it was a matter of shame, Ghulam Ahmad Khan, *jamadar* took it in his possession through Murawwat Muhammad Khan and sent it to him.

The matter is brought to the notice of the government. It is a matter of concern that at the time of uprising, persons like him in coordination with others are creating disturbances.

File No. 252
Box No. 12
No. of Documents 4

Arrest of Wasil Muhammad Khan, a Disciple of Waris Muhammad Khan

P 2. Content

PP 3-4. *Bhawani Prasad to Nawwab Sikandar Begam.* Informs on 14 *Ziqada* 1274 AH, the army marched from Rahat to *mauza* Mohna. During the journey, Kale Khan informed him that Wasil Muhammad Khan, a disciple of Waris Muhammad Khan, was coming to join the army at Bhir. He immediately, sent Ramden, *Peshdast Wakil* along with Kale Khan, directing him that if he is really a disciple of Waris Muhammad Khan, he should join Rustam Khan, *dafadar* under the battalion of Wazir Ali, *jamadar*, an employee of Bhopal government, who too is coming along with bullock carts and the soldiers and when he arrives there, his statement should be recorded. Says when Ramden and Kale Khan proceeded, they saw that Wasil Muhammad Khan was coming in the company of Rustam Khan, *dafadar*, and the soldiers of the guard. Ramden asked him his name and enquired where he was earlier. Wasil Muhammad Khan said his name was Mirza Raza Beg and earlier he was employed with Waris Muhammad Khan and was going to Bhopal.

Ramden handed him over to Rustam Khan. When he arrived at Mohna, his statement was recorded in the presence of witnesses and informed the Political Agent about the arrest of Wasil Muhammad Khan. The latter said, good. The statement was not sent to her, due to mismanagement of posts at the *chaukis* as it might have lost. Dated 16 *Ziqada* 1274 AH (28 June 1858).

P 5. Parwana *of Nawwab Sikandar Begam to Bhawani Prasad*, Wakil. Refers his letter, dated 16 *Ziqada* 1274 AH (28 June 1858), informing the arrest of the disciple of Waris Muhammad Khan and recording his statement which could not be despatched due to mismanagement of post, and as soon as the postal system is restored, the same will be despatched. But it is not clear from his letter whether he is alive or dead. Directs him to despatch his statement but before that, he should try to gather from him the truth of Waris Muhammad Khan and communicate her. Dated 30 *Ziqada* 1274 AH (12 July 1858).

P 7. *Bhawani Prasad to Nawwab Sikandar Begam*. Refers the *Parwana,* dated 30 *Ziqada* 1274 AH, and says that the disciple would soon be produced before her along with his statement and that the disciple revealed nothing about Waris Muhammad Khan. Says one day, he discussed the matter with the Political Agent who opined that the disciple should be threatened every day unless he revealed the truth about Waris Muhammad Khan. Says due to continuous march, he did not enquire further from him. He could be thoroughly interrogated when would be presented there. The report, as heard from the Agent to the Governor General is that after his humiliating defeat, Waris Muhammad Khan fled from Akbarabad and arrived at Karoli and encamped there. At night, the Raja, *Karoliwala* attacked upon the *sawars* and all dispersed. As a result, Waris Muhammad Khan and two other persons were separated from the group. They went towards the desert and lost their way. Waris

Muhammad Khan paid one *muhr* to a villager to guide him to the route of Khushhalgarh. The farmer took the money from him and asked him to wait as he would come back after taking his cloths and a stick to guide him. Instead, he informed the villagers about those three persons. The villagers surrounded them from all sides and killed Waris Muhammad Khan and one more person. The third one, who had fled from the spot, narrated the story of killing of Waris Muhammad Khan in the presence of his friends. The story passed from one to another and finally, it reached Maula Bakhsh, *jamadar* and thereafter it reached to the Agent to the Governor General, Central India. Says he himself heard from the Agent that Waris Muhammad Khan is killed. Dated 6 *Zilhijja* 1274 AH (18 July 1858).

File No. 253
Box No. 12
No. of Documents 7

Notification that if Anyone Reports Anything on the Basis of a Letter of a Mahajan, it Should Bear Date, Time and Name of the News-Writer

P 1. Contents

P 3. *Madan Mohan,* Naib Wakil, *to Nawwab Sikandar Begam.* Reports that day, Dhanraj Seth, trader, came from Sehore cantonment at the shop of Lakhmi Chand, carrying a letter from a shop in Gwalior, informing that Jiwaji Rao entered Gwalior on 21 June 1858 and the miscreants fled. They were pursued by the army of Sindhia and the British. In the evening, the soldiers of the battalion of 'Abd al-Ali Khan, *jamadar*, deployed to guard the *Khaparyal,* situating in the Naka Bazar engaged in amusement, nearby the *Khaparyal.* Meanwhile all the soldiers ran away upon seeing Sikandar Khan, Agent riding on the cart, walking towards that side. The shopkeepers in the market became afraid, closed their shops and went to their houses. When they came to know the reality, they came out of their houses. Sikandar Khan, Agent, warned the soldiers and prohibited them from doing such acts. There is a rumour in the market that some insurgents assembled and devastated the *qasba* Ichhawar. He tried to know the reality, but still he did not get authentic news. This might have been spread by the smackers. The forces of the *jagirdars* of *pargana* Sehore are yet to come. The deputy *madar al-maham* asked the *chobdar* and a peon to request the *tahsildar* to depute the forces of the *jamadars*. Thus, the *jagirdars* engaged the soldiers and met the *tahsildar*. The soldiers refused to serve for Rs. 3. Finally, they agreed to serve for a sum of Rs. 4. In the *thana* of Sehore, there is too much chaos in the absence of a *thanadar*. Dated 11 *Ziqada* 1274 AH (23 June 1858).

P 5. *Madan Mohan,* Naib Wakil, *to Nawwab Sikandar Begam.* Refers to the letters of traders from Gwalior, informing that Maharaja Jiwaji Rao with the help of the British force entered in *Bara* on 9 *Sudi Jeth,* the insurgents fled from there and the British forces were pursuing them. From the letter of Babu Kishore Mohan, dated 16 June 1858, addressed to Babu Harnath, it comes to light that on that date the British forces entered in Murar cantonment, fought with the insurgents and 60 to 70 persons were killed. The rest fled to Phul Bagh. From the British side, about 8 persons were killed. The number of insurgent forces is still not confirmed. But it seems their number was quite high. The victorious army, about 12000, was in Murar cantonment, contemplating how to deal with the remaining forces of the insurgents. The Maharaja has joined the army. There is a report of the coming of forces from Akbarabad. The letter of Bisheshar Dutt from Kota cantonment brings to light that on 18 June 1858, the insurgents fled and Sindhia captured Gwalior. The letter of Babu Kailash Chand from Indore brings to light that some of the army of Maharaja Holkar raised the banner of revolt after hearing the news of siege of Gwalior by the insurgents. But with the victory of Gwalior their tone changed.

Lala Ram Prasad, *jagirdar* of Dallod came to him and said that all his employees and the employees of other *jagirdars* declined their job and refused to serve on the pretext of low salary. But he id unable to enhance their salary. Though there was pressure from *madar al-maham* to present them. When he failed to persuade them, he conveyed the *tahsildar* about the one who was behind the scene at the time of uprising. He ordered to bring him there and served him an order to oust him along with his wives and children from that place. It will be a lesson for others and then they would present themselves. The message reached to everyone and all of them agreed to serve for a sum of Rs. 3/8 and appeared before the deputy *madar al-maham.*

P 7. *Nawwab Sikandar Begam to Ghulam Murtaza Khan.* Directs him that whenever he sends a letter to the Government, based on the information given by the *mahajans*, it should bear the date and name of the informer and the place of writing, as Madan Mohan, *naib wakil* has brought to her notice through a letter dated 15 *Ziqada* 1274 AH. Directs him that he should adhere to this practice. Dated 18 *Ziqada* 1274 AH (30 June 1858).

P 9. Parwana *of Nawwab Sikandar Begam to Muhammad Raza Husain Khan,* Madar al-Maham. Sends a sample of the notification, addressed to Ghulam Murtaza Khan and directs him to get 160 copies published of that notification from *Matba' Sikandari* which should bear the name of all the *amils, thanadars and nazims* of the State of Bhopal and then it should be sent to the Government along with the original notification. Dated 18 *Ziqada* 1274 AH (30 June 1858).

PP 11-15. *Notification Issued by Nawwab Sikandar Begam to her Officials.* In reference to the letter of Madan Mohan, Naib Wakil, dated 15 *Ziq'ada* 1274 AH (27 June 1858), all are informed that whenever they write a news and send it to the Government which is based on the information given by the Mahajans, it should bear the date and time of writing, besides the name of the news-writer and the place from where he has sent the news. They all should adhere to it. These are 160 notifications which are sent to her 160 officials which include the *nazims* of all three districts; South, West and East, and the Officials of all 4 *Risalas* of Red Uniform and Black Uniform, besides others. Dated 18 *Ziqada* 1274 AH (30 June 1858).

PP 17-18. *Muhammad Raza Husain to Nawwab Sikandar Begam*. Informs in accordance to her *Parwana,* dated 18 *Ziqada* 1274 AH (30 June 1858), which is regarding the instruction to all the officials to mention date, name of the news-writer and the place from where the news is sent, in all their communiqué to the Government, 160 notifications have been prepared and are being sent to her for providing to the *amils*, *thanadars*, *nazims* and other officials of the Government.

File No. 254
Box No. 12
No. of Documents 4

Notifications for the Arrest of Himmat Singh, Munawwar Khan and Jamal Khan, Tthe Fugitives, Responsible for Looting Pathari

PP 1-2. Contents

P 3. *Parwana of Nawwab Sikandar Begam to Muhammad Raza Husain Khan*, Madar al-Maham. Sends him a sample of the notification, addressed to Ghulam Murtaza Khan, *Kamdar,* Deorhi Khas, which is for arresting Himmat Singh, Munawwar Khan and Jamal Khan, the fugitives. Directs that 18 copies of the notification may be published from *Matba' Sikandari* and send to her.

P 5. Parwana *of Nawwab Sikandar Begam to Ghulam Murtaza Khan*, Kamdar, *Deorhi Khas*. The *rubakari* of the Criminal Court, dated 7 *Ziqada* 1274 AH, in the case against Sukhra and five other accused, which is based on the statement of Mukund Aonkhram and on the report given by Chhedu Singh, sepoy of *mahal* Raisen, it is evident that Himmat Singh, Munawwar Khan and Jamal Khan, dwellers of Raisen were involved in the loot of Pathari and capturing the booty. Directs him to make a notification in his jurisdiction. If the above mentioned accused are traced, should be arrested and produced before her under security and challan. Dated 17 *Ziqada* 1274 AH (29 June 1858).

P 7. *Muhammad Raza Husain to Nawwab Sikandar Begam*. Informs in accordance to her *Parwana,* dated 17 *Ziqada* 1274 AH, which is for arresting the accused, Himmat Singh, Munawwar Khan and Jamal Khan, the fugitives, 18 notifications have been published from *Matba' Sikandari* and are sent to her. Dated 3 *Zilhijja* 1274 AH.

File No. 255
Box No. 12
No. of Documents 8

Investigation in Fake News Regarding the Assemblage of Insurgents on Salabaru Mountain

PP 1-2. Contents

P 3. *Bhawani Prasad to Nawwab Sikandar Begam*. Refers to a *Parwana* of the Political Agent, dated .... July 1858, informing that about 500 Gond miscreants have assembled on Salabaru mountain, lying in the Bhopal region, and creating disturbance in the territory of the British Government, and directing that they should be dealt with firmly. The same is presented before her for taking appropriate action. Dated 24 *Ziqada* 1274 AH (6 July 1858).

P 5. *The Political Agent to Bhawani Prasad*. Refers to the *rubakari* of the Criminal Court of Narsinghpur, dated 11 May 1858, which is based on the report of the *thanadar* of Shekhpura that about 500 Gond miscreants have assembled on Salabaru mountain, lying in the Bhopal region and that Basiwala and Salyanwala are moving suspiciously. The same has been received for appropriate action. Directs him to enquire how the miscreants arrived there and if they are creating disturbances in the British territory. Dated 4 July 1858.

P 7. *Daulat Rai,* Nazim-i Mashriq *to Nawwab Sikandar Begam*. Muhammad Abd al-Qadir, *Thanadar* of Solwani, through his letter, dated 8 *Zilhijja* 1274 AH, has informed that he made a thorough search of the insurgents in the mountains of Pratabgarh and Salabaru under *ilaqa* Chhotiya but did not find any sign of theirs anywhere. The dwellers of those *mauzas* told him that for the last 4-5 months, no group of insurgents have entered in the region. On 8th of the month, from dawn till evening, cannon were carried to Sagar. But there is no report further in the matter. As soon as he comes to know anything pertaining to the matter, he would inform him. The said letter of the *Thanadar* is sent to her. Dated 17 *Zilhijja* 1274 AH.

P 9. *Muhammad Abd al-Qadir,* Thanadar *of Solwani to Daulat Rai,* Nazim-i Mashriq. Informs that on 8 *Zilhijja* 1274 AH, he made an extensive search of the insurgents in the mountains of Pratabgarh, Salabaru and Anguranpura under *ilaqa* Chhotiya, but found no indication of theirs anywhere. The dwellers of those *mauzas* told him that for the last 4-5 months, no group of insurgents entered in the region. On 8th of this month, from dawn till evening, cannon were carried to Sagar. But there is no further report in the matter. As soon as he comes to know anything pertaining to the matter, he would inform him. Dated 9 *Zilhijja* 1274 AH.

The letter contains the order for sending it to the Nawwab along with his own letter. Dated 17 *Zilhijja* 1274 AH.

P 11. *Daulat Rai,* Nazim-i Mashriq *to Nawwab Sikandar Begam*. Refers her order, dated 29 *Ziqada* 1274 AH, recorded on the top of the letter of Bhawani Prasad, *wakil*, besides the letter of the Political Agent which is regarding the assemblage of insurgents in *mauza* Salabaru in *pargana* Solwani. Informs he sent the said order to the *thanadar* of Solwani for conducting an enquiry into the matter. That day, he received a letter of the *thanadar* and that of *thanadar* of Shaikhpur, informing that no insurgent has ever entered in *mauza* Salabaru. The said letter along with the letter of the *wakil*, besides her *parwana*, are being sent to her. Dated 19 *Zilhijja* 1274 AH.

P 13. *Muhammad Abd al-Qadir,* Thanadar *of Solwani to Daulat Rai,* Nazim-i Mashriq. Refers to the letter of Bhawani Prasad, *wakil*, dated 29 *Ziqada* 1274 AH, besides the letter of the Political Agent which is regarding the management and to deal with 500 insurgents present on the hills of *mauza* Salabru, *ilaqa* Bhopal and not informing the assemblage of the insurgent as reported by the *thanadar* of Shaikhpur. Informs that at the very moment, he reached the said *mauza* and searched the insurgents. But found no sign of them. The dwellers too informed that no enemy, either of Bhopal or the British Government, came to the hills of the region. If any such group arrives, information would surely be given. He also wrote to the *Thanadar* of Shaikhpur requesting if any report is received by him about the assemblage of the insurgents in the region of Bhopal, the same should immediately be sent to the *Thanadar* of State of Bhopal so that they could be dealt with then and there. In reply, a letter, dated 18 July 1858 of the *thanadar* was received stating that no insurgent has arrived so far. The said letter, along with the letter of the *wakil* and the letter of the Political Agent, are sent to him. Dated 12 *Zilhijja* 1274 AH (24 July 1858).

P 15. Thanadar *of Shaikhpur to the* Thanadar *of Solwani*. Refers to his letter, asking about the assemblage of 500 insurgents of Gond caste in *mauza* Salabaru, *ilaqa* Chhotiya under the territory of Bhopal Government who are the Bahtiwala and Mahalanwala. Informs there is no report of the insurgents of the group of Bahtiwala or Mahalanwala. Informs, earlier on 7 May 1858, one Udit, a dweller of Shaikhpur who had gone to *mauza* Kakribad, *ilaqa* of Raja Patra, was arrested and brought to *mauza* Salabaru. There is no other report of the insurgents. Adds that if any report is received in the *thana*, the information will immediately be sent to him. Dated 18 July 1858.

File No. 256, A
Box No. 12
No. of Documents 13

Staying of Adil Muhammad Khan and Aqil Muhammad Khan, the two Insurgents at Pura Guna, Agra Barkhera and nayapura, the Territory of Sindhia

PP 1-14. Contents

P 17. *Daulat Rai,* Nazim-i Mashriq *to Nawwab Sikandar Begam*. Earlier it was learnt that Jaitgarhwala with a contingent of 500 soldiers was encamping at Pura Guna, *ilaqa* Bhilsa. Says he made an enquiry into the news of the insurgent, and came to know that he has a considerable number of soldiers in his company. It is also famous that Adil Muhammad Khan with a contingent of 3000 soldiers is encamping at Pura. He enquired into it and came to know that Adil Muhammad Khan was in the fort of Narwar where he was employed by Narwarwala. The news that he is encamping at Pura Guna is totally baseless. Some say that the fugitives of Gwalior have gone to Jaipur. Some say they have gone to Kota or Lucknow. But this much is clear that they did not come to that side yet. Dated 27 *Ziqada* 1274 AH.

P 19. *Murawwat Muhammad Khan to Nawwab Sikandar Begam.* Informs as ordered, Abhay Singh and Bhagwant Singh, *sawars* in the company of Thakur Sher Singh were sent to Bhilsa and Pura Guna to know about the assemblage of the insurgents. They came back that day; the 28 *Ziqada* 1274 AH, and said that in *mauza* Madawrah, *ilaqa* Bhilsa, situating at a distance of 9 *curoh* from Bhilsa, some British forces with cannon were encamping and their intention was to march to Bhilsa. There was no sign of insurgents in the region except it was heard that about 300 insurgents were still hiding in the mountains of Pura Guna. Dated 28 *Ziqada* 1274 AH.

P 21. *A Letter in Hindi Devanagari.*

PP 23-4. *Shahzad Rai,* Thanadar *of Mahalpur to Nawwab Sikandar Begam.* Informs that day, Gobardhan Patel of *mauza* Belna, *pargana* Mahalpur came to *thana* and stated that 3 days before he had gone to *mauza* Sangni, *ilaqa* Bhilsa for some work. He happened to meet one of his brothers there, a dweller of Pura Guna. He said with certainty that, 5 days before, Adil Muhammad Khan had arrived in Pura Guna. He himself gave Adil Muhammad Khan provisions like flour, etc. The latter was accompanied with 500 *sawars* and 10, 000 to 12,000 foot-soldiers. Thereafter, they went back. The statement of Patel as stated by him is communicated. The statement is quite right as said by him. There is no doubt about it. Dated 1 *Zilhijja* 1274 AH.

P 25. *Ihsan Ali,* Tahsildar *of Mahalpur to Nawwab Sikandar Begam.* Informs that day, i.e. 1 *Zilhijja* 1274 AH, Gobardhan Patel of *mauza* Belna, *pargana* Mahalpur came and stated that he was from a village of a *mustajir* and had fled to *mauza* Sangni, *pargana* Bhilsa. He met there one of his brothers, a dweller of Pura Guna who said with certainty that, 5 days before, Adil Muhammad Khan had arrived at Pura Guna. He himself gave him the provision of flour, etc. He was accompanied with 500 *sawars* and 10, 000 to 12,000 foot-soldiers. Thereafter, they went back. The statement of Patel, as stated is communicated. The statement is quite right as said by him. There is no doubt about it. Dated 1 *Zilhijja* 1274 AH.

P 27. *'Abd al-Karim Ansari to Nawwab Sikandar Begam.* Informs that on the previous day, Hasan Khan, *muhtamim, chaukiyat* came from Raisen with a contingent of 20 soldiers, following and pursuing Aqil Muhammad Khan.

P 29. *Muhammad Hasan Khan to Nawwab Sikandar Begam.* Informs that day i.e. the 4th of the month, a letter of Sarnam Singh, Sergeant Major came to him from Madawrah, informing about Murdan Singh, Banpurwala and Raja Bakht, Shahgarhwala. The same is presented before her. Dated 1 *Zilhijja* 1274 AH.

P 31. *Captain Sarnam Singh to Hafiz Muhammad Hasan Khan*, Naib Bakhshi. Informs that 3 days before, Raja Murdan Singh of Banpur and Raja Bakht Bali of Shahgarh came and met Sergeant as ordered by the agent. Thereafter, there was no ill-will or difference between the two Rajas. Informs that Imam Ali Khan, *dafadar*, Muhammad Khan, *sawar*, Bhorey Khan, Mast Khan and Hanuman, soldiers of the platoon came. Says that about one month has passed but 5 Sikh soldiers of Sikh platoon have not come from Siwans. Requests to send them.

P 33. *Daulat Rai*, Nazim-i Mashriq *to Nawwab Sikandar Begam.* Informs that Hasan Ali Khan, in-charge of *chaukis* of the district was sent along with 10 persons of the battalion of Balwant Singh, *jamadar* posted at Garhi to the mountains in *mauza* Bharonpur, Morchari, Lakhwi, and Pura Guna, *ilaqa* Bhilsa to enquire about Adil Muhammad Khan and Aqil Muhammad Khan and to search Hattey Singh, *jagirdar*, the fugitive. Says that day, Hasan Ali Khan came back and stated that in Pura Guna, and in the mountains of Bharonpur, Morchari, Lakhwi, *ilaqa* Bhilsa he found no sign of insurgents. He also searched the relatives of Fazil Muhammad Khan and Adil Muhammad Khan but got no information about them. Dated 9 *Zilhijja* 1274 AH.

P 35. *Abd al-Karim Ansari to Nawwab Sikandar Begam.* Sends the letters received from Mattu Khan and Abd al-Aziz Khan, *risaldars,* received from Malthun through the *sawars.*

PP 37-8. *Mattu Khan and Abd al-Aziz Khan,* Risaldars *to Nawwab Sikandar Begam.* Inform that on 2 *Zilhijja* 1274 AH, they reached Malthun and met Major Garson. They also learnt that the Political Agent was not in Lalitpur and Raja Murdan Singh Bundela was in Madawrah to meet the British officer of Shahgarh district to submit his explanation. The sons of Raja were in Lalitpur along with their forces. He asked the Major about Lalitpurwala. The former replied he did not know anything. He requested to enquire about him. He said let them write a letter and wait for the reply. Inform that they have sent a letter to the officer at Madawrah, district Shahgarh. After receiving the reply from him, they would proceed further. Dated 6 *Zilhijja* 1274 AH.

P 39. *Gist of the Letter of Nawwab Shahjahan Begam to Nawwab Sikandar Begam.* It contains the order that this and the letter of the *thanadar*, Ghairatganj, besides the letter of Nawwab Sikandar Begam to Nawwab Shahjahan Begam, dated 12 *Zilhijja* 1274 AH, may be sent to Maulawi Sa'd al-Din, *muhtamim, adalat-i faujdari* for inclusion in the file and after investigation. a report may be submitted with recommendation in the matter. A copy of this letter and copy of the letter of the *thanadar* of Ghairatganj may be sent to Bhawani Prasad to request the Political Agent that the *amil* of Bhilsa may be instructed to arrest Daim Khan, a servant of Adil Muhammad Khan from Ahmadpur. The reply of the Political Agent may be communicated to her. Dated 12 *Zilhijja* 1274 AH.

File No. 256, B
Box No. 12
No. of Documents 23

P 55. *Ganga Ram and Ganga Prasad,* Jamadars *to Nawwab Sikandar Begam.* Inform that day, an order of suba of Bhilsa in the name of Munshi Jan Ali Khan, deputy Political Agent, Bhopal, *muntazim* of Berasia was received, informing that after the defeat of Thakur Chhatrasal at Gwalior, 4 insurgents entered in Agra along with the Nawwab of Garhi. There is a need to be careful. The deputy has sent the information to the Political Agent at Sehore. They too are intimating the said information to her. Dated 27 July 1858.

P 57. *Narain Singh,* Jamadar, Risala *Roop Singh to Nawwab Sikandar Begam.* To the same effect as the foregoing.

P 59. *Nabi La'l to Nawwab Sikandar Begam.* Sends a letter of his uncle, dated 11 *Zilhijja* 1274 AH in his name, informing about the insurgents, particularly about Adil Muhammad Khan and Aqil Muhammad Khan. Dated 17 *Zilhijja* 1274 AH.

P 61. *Abd al-Ghaffar Khan to Nabi La'l.* Informs about a letter received from Tonk, describing that there was a fierce battle on the bank of river Panas. Also informs that on 10th of the month, Adil Muhammad Khan and Aqil Muhammad Khan, the insurgents went to Agra to Thakur Chhatrasal from Itarsi, *pargana* Sironj. There is no report of destruction in Itarsi. They have a contingent of 500 *sawars* and foot-soldiers. Also informs that on 6 *Sudi Jeth* I, Thakur Kishan Prasad expired.

P 63. *Ghulam Muhammad Khan,* Risaldar *to Nawwab Sikandar Begam.* Informs the previous day, Ram Chand Chaudhury came to Bheglone from Agra where he had gone to return the looted grains of Chhatrasal and reported that about 50 soldiers of Adil Muhammad Khan, Garhiwala, came and after his departure from Agra, when he was at a distance of half a *curoh* from Agra, he heard that Adil Muhammad Khan with a contingent of 1,000 well armed soldiers entered Agra and were ready to start a battle. Then that day, Balam Jitu Thakur, a dweller of Saiyidpur, *ilaqa* Basodah came and said it was 5 to 6 days before when he saw from his own eyes that Adil Muhammad Khan with a contingent of 1,000 which included 500 *sawars* and 500 gunners with arms and ammunitions came to Agra. Then came Serwa, barber of Bheglone, who said that Pran Chand of Barkheri, *ilaqa* Sironj, met him and said to convey the *tahsildar* of Bheglone that Adil Muhammad Khan, Garhiwala with a contingent of 1,000, fully armed soldiers, comprised of 500 *sawars* and 500 gunners entered Agra. Raja Chhatrasal gave them the best possible hospitality. Assures he, an obedient to the government would fight with the insurgents as much as possible at the time of need. Dated 17 *Zilhijja* 1274 AH.

P 65. *Lala Ramden*, Peshdast Wakil *to Nawwab Sikandar Begam.* Informs that day, the Political Agent on the letter of *wakil* ordered to write to the *amil* of Bhilsa to arrest the companions of Fazil Muhammad Khan and present them at Pura Guna. Dated 19 *Zilhijja* 1274 AH.

PP 67-8. *Bhawani Prasad to Nawwab Sikandar Begam.* Informs that day, he told the Political Agent that it is heard that Adil Muhammad Khan along with a few hundred *sawars* and foot-soldiers arrived in Agra, *jagir* of Thakur Chhatrasal and that if he too has any information about him. He said that the informers told Jan Ali Khan, *muntazim* of Berasia, about this news who through a *rubakar* brought to his notice that Adil Muhammad Khan with a contingent of 80 Afghan *wilayatis*, 50 Bundelas and others with a total of 300 *sawars* and foot-soldiers arrived in Agra at Thakur Chhatrasal who did not allow him to stay in Agra and he went somewhere else. It is his stupidness. He might have gone to Garhi Ambapani or to some other place. The Political Agent told him to request Nawwab Sikandar Begam that Adil Muhammad Khan, a rebel of the two governments should be traced and where he is encamping by sending faithful informers. If possible to send a gurjar or mewati to kill him, at once that too should be done. Such a person should not be allowed to go scot free at any cost but should be finished. Says after that a copy of the letter of Munshi Jan Ali Khan was given to him which contained the order of the Political Agent that clever informers should be sent to bring authentic news of the insurgents and inform him. The same is presented before her. Dated 19 *Zilhijja* 1274 AH (31 July 1858).

P 69. *Munshi Jan Ali Khan to the Political Agent.* Informs this is authentic news that Adil Muhammad Khan, Aqil Muhammad Khan, Sarfraz Khan, Nawwab of Banda and Wazir Allah Khan along with a contingent of 400 *sawars* and foot-soldiers are in Agra with Thakur Chhatrasal. They are also managing the force. They have also called on the Raja of Narwar who too is about to come. They have a plan to come to Berasia first, then Bhopal and thereafter Sehore. Furthermore, informs that there is not too much arms and ammunitions or requisite force as much as required to fight with such a force. Gajadhar, *jamadar* has come. He has no magazine with him. The soldiers have only daggers. If some magazines and two cannon are sent there from Sehore, it would be good. Dated 30 July 1858.

P 71. *'Abd al-Karim Ansari to Nawwab Sikandar Begam.* Informs that day, Thanu, caste barber, a dweller of Dhamod, *ilaqa* Maharaja in reference to the letter of Suba Sahab, Issagarh in the name of Bhola Nath, *qanungoi*, stated to him that the Peshwa was defeated by the British forces and thereafter he fled. Then again he collected all the forces from everywhere and in conniavance with Bejabai entered Gwalior. Maharaja Jiwaji fled from Gwalior to Akbarabad. Adil Muhammad Khan arrived in Agra, *ilaqa* of Maharaja. What he heard, he communicated. Dated 20 *Zilhijja* 1274 AH.

P 73. *Daulat Rai,* Nazim-i Mashriq *to Nawwab Sikandar Begam.* Informs that day in the night, a letter of Sada Shiv Rao, Suba Bhilsa, dated 18 *Zilhijja* 1274 AH, along with a *rubakar,* issued from the court of suba was recieved which is in regard to the assemblage of Chhatrasal, Adil Muhammad Khan, Patrara, Kaladwala and son of Jamal Muhammad Khan of Bhopal at Agra, having a contingent of 1,500 *sawars* and foot-soldiers with them, besides 2,500 other forces of insurgents are at Khari, *ilaqa* Sironj; the other force under Bhorji, Raja, Narwarwala with one cannon is at *mauza mutallaqa* Itarsi. The intention of the insurgents is to attack upon Bhopal or Bhilsa, etc. The letter as well as the *rubakar* is sent to her. Suba Sahab, Bhilsa, is a very gentle person who communicates everything concerning the safety and security of Bhopal Government. Dated 20 *Zilhijja* 1274 AH.

P 75. *Sada Shiv Rao, Bhao, Suba of Bhilsa to Daulat Rai,* Nazim-i Mashriq. Sends the *rubakar*, dated 18 *Zilhijja*1274 AH, issued from his office which is regarding the prevailing situation and informs that the insurgents are at Agra. Dated 18 *Zilhijja* 1274 AH.

P 77. Rubakar *Issued from the Office of District Bhilsa Under the Session of Sada Shiv Rao, Dated 18 Zilhijja 1274 AH.* Refers to the news-letter, received from Agra in regard to the encampment of insurgents there, as reported by an informer. It is described that on 15th of this month, Chhatrasal, Agrawala, Adil Muhammad Khan, *jagirdar* of Garhi Ambapani, under Bhopal State became unconscious due to drinking so much so that the *jagirdar* with the help of his men was laid down on the bed. Chhatrasal, while going upstairs, fell from the stairs and became unconscious. His back and hand got injured. On 16th of the month, *jagirdar* of Pandara Kaladwala and son of Jamal al-Din, a dweller of Bhopal held a meeting among themselves. But there is no description of their conversation. But it seems that after the rainy season, their intention is to attack upon Bhopal or Sironj or Berasia or Basodah or Bhilsa. In Agra about 1,000 or 1,500 *sawars* and foot-soldiers are encamping. The other group of force is at Khari, *ilaqa* Sironj. Besides 2,000 to 2,500 forces along with Bhorji, Raja of Narwar with one cannon are at Mhow. The information to this effect was sent to everyone, that was must.

It contains the order that the information may be given to the Political Agent, Bhopal, through the *wakil* and to the *sar suba*. A copy of the order may be sent to the Assistant Political Agent, *pargana* Berasia and to the *nazim-i mashriq* at Raisen. They may also be informed that whatever come to their notice, the aftermath is to be communicated.

PP 79-80. *Letter Addressed to* Suba Sahab. Refers to his letter, dated 18 *Zilhijja* 1274 AH along with a *rubakar* which is in regard to the news of Chhatrasal, Agrawala, Adil Muhammad Khan, Garhiwala, Patrara, Kaladwala and son of Jamal Muhammad Khan along with a contingent of 1,500 *sawars* and foot-soldiers, besides the other forces who are at Khari, *ilaqa* Sironj, the encampment of Bhorji Raja, Narwarwala along with one cannon at *mauza, mutallaqa* Itarsi, and the intention of the insurgents is to attack upon Bhopal or Sironj, or Berasia or Basodah or Bhilsa. Expresses pleasure for making him aware of the situation and keeping him informed. Dated 20 *Zilhijja* 1274 AH.

PP 81-2. *Bhao Lal to Lala Chain Rai,* Munib, Daftar-i Bakhshigiri *and Amanat Rai*. Refers his earlier letter to him through a soldier who had come there. Informs of the latest news which is that about 7 to 8 days before, Adil Muhammad Khan, Patrara, kaladwala and son of Jamal Muhammad Khan and Raja Bhorji with one cannon and a contingent of 2,000 were at Agra, having friendly relations with Thakur Chhatrasal, Agrawala. It is a must that they should be dealt with, and inform the Political Agent, Bhopal, and army camp in Gwalior. Daulat Rai, *nazim-i mashriq*, has also been informed and hopes that the *nazim* would present the *rubakar* before the Nawwab. The information to this effect was must which he did. Dated 20 *Zilhijja* 1274 AH.

P 83. *Shaikh Khuda Bakhsh, Deputy* Thanadar, *Debipura* to *Nawwab Sikandar Begam.* Informs that day, Ibrahim Bohra, a dweller of Doraha, who came from Narsingarh stated that the previous day he heard in the court that about 2,000 to 3,000 insurgent forces of Peshwa, comprising of both *sawars* and foot-soldiers arrived at Agra Barkhera, situating at a distance of 18 *curoh* from there. The information to this effect was must which he did. Dated 20 *Zilhijja* 1274 AH.

PP 85-6. *Hazrat Nur Khan to Nawwab Sikandar Begam.* Informs the previous day, Ram Chand Chaudhury, Bazar Bheglone who had gone to Agra to return the looted grains of Chhatrasal, Agarwala came back and stated that 50 soldiers of Fazil Muhammad Khan entered Agra. Besides on his way to Agra, about half a *curoh* away from Agra, he heard that Adil Muhammad Khan with a contingent of 1,000, comprising of 500 *sawars* and 500 foot-soldiers, and gunners with arms and immunitions and gun powders has also reached Agra. Informs that Balam Jeo Thakur, *ilaqa* Basodah stated that it was 5 days before, he saw from his own eyes that Adil Muhammad Khan with a contingent of 1,000, comprising of 500 *sawars* and 500 gunners with arms and ammunitions have come to Agra.

P 87. Parwana *of Nawwab Sikandar Begam to Bhawani Prasad.* Refers to his letter, dated 19 *Zilhijja* 1274 AH along with a copy of letter of Munshi Jan Ali Khan, assistant, *muntazim* of Berasia, addressed to the Political Agent in the matter of assassination of Adil Muhammad Khan. Informs in accordance to that, *parwanas* have been sent to Bakhshi Murawwat Muhammad Khan, Hafiz Muhammad Khan, *naib bakhshi*, Daulat Rai, *nazim-i mashriq,* Munshi Inayat Husain, deputy *nazim-i junub*, and Ghulam Makhdum Khan, *nazim-i maghrib*. The original one along with this *parwana* is sent to him to bring it to the notice of the Political Agent. The reply received from him may be communicated to her. Dated 21 *Zilhijja* 1274 AH.

PP 89-90. *Ghulam Muhammad Khan, Risaldar to Nawwab Sikandar Begam.* Informs that Puran Kunwar of Bheglone who is a clever, attentive and a man of confidence, besides Hargobind, a servant of Seth Nihal Chand and Har Chand Kunwar; they too are clever and attentive, were sent to bring the news of Adil Muhammad Khan at Agra and Sironj. That day, i.e. 21 *Zilhijja* 1274 AH, they came and stated that Adil Muhammad Khan for the last 2-3 days, with a contingent of 700 which comprised of 200 *sawars* and 500 foot-soldiers, and gunners with the goods of soldiery and gun powders is encamping at a distance of one *curoh* from Agra. Raja Chhatrasal, Agrawala, is providing him the best of hospitality. Hargobind and Har Chand Kunwar, coming from Sironj reported that for the last 2-3 days, Adil Muhammad Khan with a contingent of 1,000 *sawars* and foot-soldiers is encamping at Agra, having arms and ammunitions with him. Raja Bhorji, Narwarwala, with a contingent of 1,500 *sawars* and foot-soldiers with two cannon is stationing at a distance of 4 *curoh* from Sironj.

P 91. *Nawwab Sikandar Begam to Bhawani Prasad.* The news of coming of Adil Muhammad Khan is being heard continuously. He has an army of 1,000 and some say they are 1,500. The army of Bhopal is divided at many places. It is heard that in Mhow, a huge British army has come. If the Political Agent asks for an equal number of troops for Sehore as that of Bhopal contingent it would be good. Directs him to bring the matter into the notice of the Political Agent. Dated 21 *Zilhijja* 1274 AH.

PP 93-4. *Nawwab Sikandar Begam to Bakhshi Murawwat Muhammad Khan.* Refers to a letter of Bhawani Prasad, dated 19 *Zilhijja* 1274 AH, informing that he met the Political Agent that day and told him that it is heard that Adil Muhammad Khan with a few hundred *sawars* and foot-soldiers was in Agra, the *jagir* of Chhatrasal.

P 95. *Ramden,* Peshdaht Wakil *to Nawwab Sikandar Begam.* Informs that day, he received a letter of *amil* of Sironj in the name of *wakil* of Sironj with a request to present it before the Political Agent, informing that Aqil Muhammad Khan and Adil Muhammad Khan along with a contingent have arrived at Agra of Thakur Chhatrasal. Thus, the Thakur has become too powerful with the arrival of these forces. Otherwise, there were too many forces in Sironj to deal with the Thakur. Now the intention of Aqil Muhammad Khan and theThakur is to capture *mauza* Luteri, Maras, and Sironj. Presently, there are 500 soldiers and 12 cannon in Sironj. If they dare to come to Sironj, they would be fairly dealt with.

PP 97-8. *Hazrat Nur Khan,* Tahsildar, *of Bheglone to Nawwab Sikandar Begam.* Informs that day, the 21 *Ziqda* 1274 AH, Farangi Lal, trader and a dweller of Bheglone brought news from Sironj that about 400 *wilayati* soldiers are already in Sironj and now 100 *sawars* have come the previous day. All are saying that these are the contingent of Adil Muhammad Khan. The army headed by him is in Agra. They are divided into 3 groups and encamping at a distance of 2-2 and 3-3 *curoh* on the road from Sironj to Bheglone. But Adil Muhammad Khan is still in Agra. Another report is that Fatahyab Khan, *jagirdar* of *mauza* Gatola, *ilaqa* Korwai, situating at a distance of one *curoh* sent a person to him conveying that the *tahsildar* of Bheglone should be attentive as the movement of insurgents seems very active. The people here are very afraid of the news heard by them. Although, he and Ghulam Muhammad Khan, *risaldar* are consoling them and have compassion. But they are not getting pacified. Everyone wants to flee from there. If they are forced to remain in their homes, they would flee from back door. Dated 21 *Zilhijja* 1274 AH.

PP 99-100. *Ghulam Makhdum Khan to Nawwab Sikandar Begam.* Informs that day, he received a letter of Shaikh Khuda Bakhsh, deputy *thanadar*, Debipura, dated 20 *Zilhijja* 1274 AH, informing that Ibrahim Bohra, a resident of Doraha stated that he heard in the court of Narsingarh that around 2,000 to 3,000 insurgent forces of the Peshwa, both *sawars* and foot-soldiers have arrived at Agra of Chhatrasal. The same is presented before her. Dated 21 *Zilhijja* 1274 AH.

File No. 256, C
Box No. 12
No. of Documents 24

P 101. *Shaikh Khuda Bakhsh, Deputy* Thanadar, *Debipura to Ghulam Makhdum Khan.* Informs that day, Ibrahim bohra, a resident of Doraha, who came from Narsingarh, stated that the previous day, he heard in the court of Narsingarh that around 2,000 to 3,000 forces, both *sawars* and foot-soldiers of the peshwa, the insurgent have arrived at Agra of Chhatrasal, situating at a distance of 18 *curoh* from there.

PP 103-4. Parwanas *of Nawwab Sikandar Begam to her Officials; Ghulam Makhdum Khan,* Nazim-i Maghrib*, Munshi Inayat Husain,* Nazim-i Junub*, Daulat Rai,* Nazim-i Mashriq *and Hafiz Muhammad Hasan,* Naib Bakhshi. The letter of Bhawani Prasad, *wakil*, dated 19 *Zilhijja* 1274 AH, informs that he told the Political Agent during his meeting with him that it is heard that Adil Muhammad Khan along with a few hundred *sawars* and foot-soldiers has arrived in Agra, the *jagir* of Thakur Chhatrasal and that if he too has got any information about him. He said the informers informed Jan Ali Khan, *muntazim,* Berasia about this news who through a *rubakar* brought to his notice that Adil Muhammad Khan with a contingent of 80 Afghan *wilayatis*, 50 Bundelas and a total of 300 *sawars* and foot-soldiers have arrived in Agra before Thakur Chhatrasal. He did not allow him to stay in Agra. He went somewhere else. It is his stupidness. He might have gone to Garhi Ambapani or some other place. He should request Nawwab Sikandar Begam that Adil Muhammad Khan, who is a rebel of the two governments should be traced by sending faithful informers and to know about his encampment. If possible to depute a Gurjar or a Mewati to kill him at once. Such a person should not be allowed at any cost to go free but should be finished. Says after that, a copy of the letter of Munshi Jan Ali Khan in his name, dated 30 July 1858, was sent which contains the order of the Political Agent that the *wakil* may be directed to bring the matter into the notice of the Nawwab, requesting that clever informers may be sent to bring accurate news of the insurgents and inform him. Directs them to take notice of the letter of Jan Ali Khan and act as desired by the Political Agent. Dated 21 *Zilhijja* 1274 AH.

PP 105-6. Parwana-i Ishtahari *Addressed to all.* Adil Muhammad Khan, the insurgent came back to Sironj from Gwalior and from the region of *Wazir al-Daulah,* having huge wealth and he is well contended. All the employees of Bhopal State and the inhabitants of Bhopal are informed that if at any moment, these insurgents enter in the territory of Bhopal or in Bhopal proper, all the employees as well as the inhabitants should attack upon them and eliminate them so that they may not go to any other place from there after becoming contended. They sould be dealt with which means that either they should be arrested or killed. The people as well as the soldiers of Bhopal should feel free to loot booty from them. They should not do like the people of Bheglone and the soldiers who did not make loot of booty from them. It has always been the blessings of Almighty upon Bhopal that the soldiers and the people have always earned name and fame. They should not hesitate in looting and killing them. They should not be defamed like the people and the soldiers of Bheglone. They should always endeavour for their master's longevity and for the prosperity of their State. It will enhance the prestige and dignity of Bhopal among all the states. Dated 21 *Zilhijja* 1274 AH.

PP 107-8. *Ghulam Muhammad Khan,* Risaldar *of Bheglone to Nawwab Sikandar Begam.* Informs on 22 *Zilhijja*, Firangilal, merchant came from Sironj and said that in Sironj there was too much pressure of insurgents. They meet everyday there. Then Fatahyab Khan, *risaldar*, *jagirdar* of Katola, *pargana* Korwai, situating at a distance of one *curoh* conveyed to the *tahsildar* to be cautious and alert. There should not be any negligency. It was also conveyed that 100 *sawars* have arrived in Sironj, the previous day. While 400 *wilayatis* are already in Sironj. The contingent of Adil Muhammad Khan which is about 1,000, comprising both *sawars* and foot-soldiers who are on way to Sironj have dispersed at Bheglone. Says he at the very moment sent two informers of confidence to Sironj and two informers of confidence to Agra.

P 109. *Muhammad Sa'd al-Din,* Muhtamim, Adalat-i Faujdari *to Nawwab Sikandar Begam.* Informs as conveyed by Hattey Singh, *jamadar*, he enquired from the traders of the market the news about Sironj and Agra and came to know that no letter or person came in the city. However, from Abd al-Rasul and Tayyab Ali, bohras who came the previous night from Sironj, it was learnt that 200 *wilayatis;* the companions of Adil Muhammad Khan and Aqil Muhammad Khan arrived in Sironj and due to rain stayed at the shops in the market. Although the *amil* tried his best to prevent them from staying in the market but they did not pay any heed to him and did not leave. Adil Muhammad Khan and Aqil Muhammad Khan with a contingent of 400 to 500 insurgents are staying at Agra Barkhera, the *jagir* of Chhatrasal and their meal comes everytime from the house of Wazir Khan, *jagirdar* of Sironj as he is friendly with them and used to go to Agra to meet Adil Muhammad Khan and Aqil Muhammad Khan. Adil Muhammad Khan and Aqil Muhammad Khan are telling in Sironj that they came and would establish *thana* in Sironj. Dated 22 *Zilhija* 1274 AH.

P 111. *Daulat Rai,* Nazim-i Mashriq *to Nawwab Sikandar Begam.* Informs that day, the news-report of *thana* Siwans, dated 20th of this month, was received reporting the arrival of Adil Muhammad Khan in *mauza* Agra of Chhatrasal along with other reports. The same is sent to her. Dated 22 *Zilhijja* 1274 AH.

P 113. *News-Report of* Thana *Siwans, Dated 20* Zilhija *1274 AH, Received From Nur Muhammad,* Thanadar. Reports that Thanu, the hair cutter, *qasba* Dhamnod, *ilaqa* Maharaja Sindhia came in *thana* and stated that three days before, a letter of *Suba Sahab* from Issagarh came in the name of Lala Bholanath, *qanungoi*, *qasba* Sadar which contained the information that before the arrival of the British forces, the Peshwa fled from there. He came to Gwalior and *thanas* were erected and Baijabai too was in his company. Maharaja Jiwaji fled from Gwalior and arrived at Akbarabad. Adil Muhammad Khan was encamping at *mauza* Agra Barkhera, *ilaqa* Maharaja, situated at a distance of 22 *curoh* from there. God knows whether this information is right or wrong. What he heard, he communicated as per the instruction of the government.

PP 115-6. *Nawwab Baqi Muhammad Khan to Nawwab Sikandar Begam.* Refers to a letter received from Maulawi Saiyid Ghulam Shah, deputy *tahsildar* of Gulgaon, dated 20 *Zilhijja* 1274 AH, informing about a letter of Adil Muhammad Khan to *Suba Sahab*, Bhilsa that he is coming there with 6,000 forces who will need *sarbrah-i saman* from the *Suba Sahab*. It is also heard that Adil Muhammad Khan with a contingent of 1,500 troops has arrived at Patan near Chhatrasal. Hearing the news, a person has been sent to know the reality. The same is sent to her. Dated 22 *Zilhijja* 1274 AH.

P 117. *Saiyid Ghulam Shah, Deputy* Tahsildar *of Gulgaon to Nawwab Baqi Muhammad Khan.* Informs it is heard that a few days before a letter of Adil Muhammad Khan came to *Suba Sahab* of Bhilsawala. It is stated that he is coming there with 6,000 forces who will need *sarbrah-i saman* from the *Suba Sahab*. It is also heard that Adil Muhammad Khan with a contingent of 1,500 troops has arrived at Patan near Chhatrasal. Hearing the news, a person has been sent to know the reality. A report will be sent after coming back of that person. Dated 20 *Zilhijja* 1274 AH.

PP 119-20. *Muhammad Abd al-Rahman,* Thanadar *of Garhi to Nawwab Sikandar Begam.* Informs for the last 3-4 days, there is a news of the arrival of Adil Muhammad Khan at Agra of Chhatrasalwala and whosoever comes from the adjoining regions; like Dhamnod, Basodah or Bhilsa describes the arrival of Adil Muhammad Khan at that place. Although it is unbelievable as this might be a rumour. But the previous day, Dhanna Lal, a mahajan sent a letter from Bhilsa in the name of Mehta Lal, another mahajan who informed him that Adil Muhammad Khan has surely arrived at Agra. It is also a definite piece of news that around 4,000 armymen with 6 cannon is with him. The number of insurgents is increasing day by day. The *sarbrah* for Adil Muhammad Khan and his companion is being provided from *mauza* Nateran, *ilaqa* under her government. His eyes are also on that place which is strange. The *thana* of Peshwa was erected in Tonk. The Peshwas earlier had handed over *riyasat-i* Tonk to the Raja of Jaipur. In Gwalior too there is an apprehension of fresh insurgency as since the last 4-5 days, no posts have been received from Gwalior. Hearing such news the traders and the merchants were very perturbed. They were consoled as much as possible and were assured that the *qasba* is being taken care utmost to keep it off from devastation. Tika Singh and Alam Singh, soldiers of this *thana*, were sent to Pura Guna and Bharonpur; villages in Bhilsa to bring the news. They too came back and informed of the arrival of Adil Muhammad Khan in Agra. They also said that in their presence, the bufallows loaded with rice, etc. from Bharonpur and Lakhnoti, *ilaqa* Bhilsa were moving. The inhabitants told that those were meant for Adil Muhammad Khan. Information to this effect was must which he did. Dated 22 *Zilhijja* 1274 AH.

PP 121-2. *Daulat Rai,* Nazim-i Mashriq *to Nawwab Sikandar Begam.* Informs that day, a letter of Hazrat Nur Khan, *tahsildar* of Bheglone, dated the 18th of the month was received, informing the coming of insurgents in and around Sironj and requesting to engage 2 to 3 persons as informers to bring the news. Sends the same to her with a request that if he is allowed to have two informers it would be good. Dated 22 *Zilhijja* 1265 *fasli.*

PP 123-4. *Hazrat Nur Khan to Daulat Rai,* Nazim-i Mashriq. Informs that the number of insurgents in the region has increased manyfold and without having informers, the news of the surroundings would not come. It would be good if he is allowed to appoint 2 to 3 informers. As the salaries of the informers were not received in the past, he dares not to do so at his own expenses. The dwellers while receiving the news of Adil Muhammad Khan are like the deers of the desert. They are consoled but they are horrified as they are the witnesses of what has happened in the past. Dated 18 *Zilhijja* 1273 AH.

P 125. *Daulat Rai,* Nazim-i Mashriq *to Nawwab Sikandar Begam.* Informs of two letters of Hazrat Nur Khan, *tahsildar* of Bheglone, dated 17 *Zilhijja* 1274 AH and dated 19 *Zilhijja* received that day which inform coming of Adil Muhammad Khan, insurgent in Agra of Chhatrasal. The same is sent to her. Informs that some persons attempted to demolish the fort but they were prevented from doing so. That day, they met their fate which was good for them. Dated 22 *Zilhijja* 1274 AH.

P 127. *Hazrat Nur Khan to Daulat Rai,* Nazim-i Mashriq. Informs that Ram Chand Chaudhury of Bheglone came and stated that he had gone to Agra to deliver the looted grains to Raja Chhatrasal, Agrawala, where he came across to see 50 men of Fazil Muhammad Khan, Garhiwala. They informed that by the next day, Adil Muhammad Khan would come. When he was at a distance of half a *curoh,* he heard that Adil Muhammad Khan with an army of 1,000 which included 500 *sawars* and 500 foot-soldiers entered Agra. At the same time, Balam Chand of Saiyidpur, *ilaqa* Maharaja Sindhia, came and stated that Adil Muhammad Khan, Garhiwala with an army of 1,000 which included 500 *sawars* and 500 gunners with arms and ammunitions came in Agra from Gwalior and met Raja Chhatrasal with an intention to gather the other groups of insurgents and also demanded military help from the Raja. It was thought important to inform and to request that the information may be given to the *Nawwab*. Requests to send army to deal with the insurgents. Chhotey Ram, *jamadar*, who is posted there has only 45 soldiers in his battalion and 7 to 8 soldiers of them are ill. Dated 17 *Zilhijja* 1274 AH.

P 129. *Report from* Thana *Bheglone Recorded Before Hazrat Nur Khan*. Statement of Chaudhury Ram Chand of Bheglone. States that he, from his own eyes, saw Adil Muhammad Khan, Garhiwala in Agra and that Raja Chhatrasal did extend extreme hospitality towards him. The army which he is carrying, consists of 500 *sawars* and foot-soldiers.

From Debi Singh Chauhan, a servant of Maharaja, posted at Vishanpur, came in the court of Basodah before Badal Rao, *amil* of Basodah and had brought perfect news of Sironj that the Peshwa with one battalion, 1,000 *sawar* and two cannon had entered Sironj. Some insurgents and *jagirdars* of Sironj welcomed one group of Peshwa and made *sarbrah-i rasad* for them. They are the advisors and councillors of Peshwa.

P 131. *Bhawani Prasad to Nawwab Sikandar Begam.* Refers to the letter of Munshi Jan Ali Khan, Deputy Assistant at Berasia, dated 2 August 1858 which contains the authentic news that Adil Muhammad Khan, brother of *Kamdar* of Pandara and some other persons are at Agra. It contains the order of the Political Agent, dated 3 August 1858, that it should be sent to Bhawani Prasad for communicating to the *Nawwab*. The same is presented to her. Dated 23 *Zilhijja* 1274 AH (4 August 1858).

PP 133-4. *Letter of Jan Ali Khan, Deputy Assistant at Berasia, Dated 2* August *1858*. Refers to his letter, dated 1 August 1858 in reply to his letter, dated 3 July 1858, that there is no authentic news about the army of Agra so as to make preparation accordingly. There is a need to send reliable informer for bringing authentic news. That day, a reliable informer reported that about 300 men were in *mauza* Pura and *mauza* Sariri, *ilaqa* Sironj. Adil Muhammad Khan and *Kamdar* of Pandara with some men were in the fort of Agra. About 500 men including *sawars* and foot-soldiers were outside the fort. Their intention was to reach Bheglone. To inform him of the matter was must, which he did. A copy of *rubakar* of *Suba Sahab*, Bhilsa has also been received in the matter. This is also sent to him.

PP 135-6. Parwana of *Nawwab Sikandar Begam to Nawwab Nazir al-Daulah, Umrao Daulah, Baqi Muhammad Khan*. Refers to his letter, dated 22 *Zilhijja* 1274 AH, along with the letter of Ghulam Shah, deputy *amil* of Gulgaon which is in regard to Adil Muhammad Khan. Hopes that he himself would depute an experienced and clever person to bring the news of insurgents from Bhilsa, Bitton and Agra who may go there and see from his own eyes the prominent figures and rebels of Bhopal who are there, and about the number of army personnel and cannon in their possession. Report by such an eye witness should be sent through his letter. Dated 23 *Zilhijja* 1274 AH.

PP 137-8. *Bhawani Prasad to Nawwab Sikandar Begam*. Refers to her *parwana*, dated 21 *Zilhijja* 1274

AH, received through Shiv Lal, *chobdar*, the orderly in the context that 3,000 or 4,000 or 5,000 of the Peshwa's army has arrived at Agra and that the state army has been deployed at different places in east district and a demand has been made for the army from Mhow. The same was presented before the Political Agent and the *parwana* received from him in reply to his letter is sent to her. Dated 24 *Zilhijja* 1274 AH (5 August 1858).

PP 139-40. *The Political Agent to Bhawani Prasad.* Refers to his letter along with the *parwana* of *Nawwab* Sikandar Begam which is regarding deployment of the Bhopal army at different places and asking for the retreat of the army to deal with the insurgent forces of Peshwa and others. Informs him that, 300 to 400 men and not 3,000 or 4,000 or 5, 000 insurgents entered Agra. It does not seem feseable to call back the state army stationed at different places unless definite news of the insurgents received.

P 141. *Daulat Rai,* Nazim-i Mashriq *to Nawwab Sikandar Begam.* Informs about a letter of Sada Shiv Rao, Bilal, *Suba Sahab*, *Suba* Bhilsa, dated 23 *Zilhijja* 1274 AH, along with the *rubakar,* informing the arrival of Adil Muhammad Khan at Agra with Sarfraz Khan along with a contingent, having bad intention to go to Sironj, Berasia, Bhilsa or Basodah. The same is sent to her. Dated 25 *Zilhijja* 1274 AH.

P 143. *Letter from* Nizamat-i Mashriq *to Sada Shiv Rao,* Suba *Bhilsa*. Refers to the letter, dated 23rd of the month along with the *rubakari*, informing the entry of Adil Muhammad Khan and Sarfraz Khan, the rebels of the two governments in Agra. No doubt, Adil Muhammad Khan is the rebel of the two governments. He is to be arrested or killed and soon, if God willing, would meet his fate. Requests to make a combined effort to kill or arrest him as it would be a pleasure for the British. Dated 25 *Zilhijja* 1274 AH.

P 145. *Sada Shiv Rao,* Suba *Sahab,* Suba *Bhilsa to Daulat Rai,* Nazim-i Mashriq. Sends the *rubakar*, dated 23rd of the month, issued from his office, which is regarding the news that some insurgents are encamping at Agra. Dated 23 *Zilhijja* 1274 AH.

PP 147-9. Rabakar *Issued from the office of Suba, District Bhilsa Under the Session of Sada Shiv Rao,* Suba Sahab. Informs of the recent news from Agra about the encampment of insurgents there as reported by an informer. It has been heard from some insurgent soldiers that Adil Muhammad Khan, *jagirdar* of Garhi Ambapani, *mutallaqa riyasat-i* Bhopal, Sarfraz Khan of Berasia, *Nawwab* Kaladwala with a contingent of 300-400-500 *sawars* and foot-soldiers are at Agra. There is another group of insurgents who are at a distance of two *curoh* from *chauki* Hanota, waiting for Raja Bhorji with an intention to go to Sironj, Berasia, Bhilsa or Basodah. They were persuading the *wilayatis* of Sironj to help them. They were also managing bullocks to bring grains from Bheglone, *riyasat-i* Bhopal. There is also a rumour that they are at Nahtery, *ilaqa* Sironj, Kaladeo and Itarsi. Besides, the insurgents were also going to Gogur Chera, *ilaqa* Tonk. But it seems to be a rumour, unbelievable, as from where this group of insurgents came. If this had been true it would have become clear from the letters of Bajrangarh, as the place is adjacent to Gwalior towards Kota. To know the reality of news, informers are sent.

It contains the order that the letters are in Marathi and the information as given above may be sent to the Political Agent of Bhopal, and to *Sar Suba* Issagarh. Besides, a copy of the *rubakar* may be sent to the Deputy Magistrate of Sagar and Assistant Political Agent of Bhopal, *muntazim* of Berasia and *nazim-i mashriq* directing them to become ready and alert. Other information would follow. Dated 23 *Zilhijja* 1274 AH.

File No. 256, D
Box No. 12
No. of Documents 21

PP 151-2. *Ramden,* Peshdast Wakil, *to Nawwab Sikandar Begam.* Says in his opinion Adil Muhammad

Khan and Aqil Muhammad Khan might be with Thakur Chhatrasal. This is the time of rain. After rains, persons like Thakur Chhatrasal, Adil Muhammad Khan and Aqil Muhammad Khan should be dealt with in such a way that they should remember forever. The order of the officer of the army station at Mhow is to march after the rainy season, wherever is any insurgent and deal with such elements. The Political Agent is also active to deal with the insurgents. It is her graceness that none of the said insurgents dare to enter into the territory of this government and if they would dare, surely meet their fate. The execution of Anjulal was good in the sense that all the insurgents were afraid of being picked up and hanged. Dated 25 *Zilhijja* 1274 AH.

P 153. *Daulat Rai,* Nazim-i Mashriq *to Nawwab Sikandar Begam.* Refers to a letter of *Thanadar* of Garhi informing that Adil Muhammad Khan, the insurgent who was in Agra, has marched from there and there is an apprehension of entering in the mountains of Pura Guna, *ilaqa* Bhilsa, adjoining to Garhi. He has also requested for the arrangement and to blockade the roads, and to depute another battalion on the said mountain. Says that the request of the *thanadar* seems to be genuine. Sends the letter of the *thanadar* and requests for the deployment of another battalion at *thana* Garhi. Not only this, but the presence of *naib bakhshi* at Garhi seems to be a good development. States that the informer has also been sent from Raisen to Bhilsa and Sironj to bring the news of Adil Muhammad Khan. The *Suba Sahab* of Bhilsa has also been written to send the actual news about the said insurgent. The report received from them would be communicated. Dated 25 *Zilhijja* 1274 AH.

P 155. *Muhammad Abd al-Rahman,* Thanadar *of Garhi to Daulat Rai,* Nazim-i Mashriq. Informs the receipt of his letter, dated 22 *Zilhijja* 1274 AH. Besides, from the statement of Pyarelal, *mutasaddi* sair, who came from Bhilsa that day it is evident that Adil Muhammad

Khan along with his contingent has left Agra and has marched to somewhere else. It is quite obvious that if he has marched from Agra then he would surely be hiding in the mountains of Pura Guna, *ilaqa* Bhilsa, situating at a distance of half a *curoh* and would be conspiring to indulge in insurgency in the region. Since the mountaneous range of Pura Guna is in adjacent to Garhi and lies in between the mountains, there is a passage available to the insurgents. The density of hills and mountains is too much and endless in between Pura Guna and Garhi. In such a situation, the erection of posts on the routes and passages of insurgents as guards *bakt* is essential. To make such arrangement requires some strength of contingent. The contingent which is there is quite clear upon him as there is only one battalion of Balwant Singh, *jamadar*, where in 9 soldiers are also less. To make an arrangement of road is not possible by such meagre contingent. If suppose they are deployed on the routes of the insurgents, there would be none for the safety and security of the village. In such a condition, to have one battalion deployed on the routes of the insurgents in *mauza* Pura Guna and Bharonpur, *ilaqa* Bhilsa, and on the passages under the hills is a must. Requests that one battalion may be sent there to blockade the passage of the insurgents. Says although the informers are sent to Agra and *mauza* Pura Guna but the density of mountains in *mauza* Pura, spreading over a large area is a problem. If Adil Muhammad Khan hides there it would be difficult to get information about him. Dated 24 *Zilhijja* 1274 AH.

P 157. *Nawwab Shahjahan Begam to Nawwab Sikandar Begam.* Informs about a letter received from Lala Durga Prasad, *thanadar* of Ghairatganj, dated 23 *Zilhijja* 1274 AH, along with the transliteration of a letter in Hindi of Amar Singh and Balwant Singh, *zamindars* of Lodhi Bagrod, *ilaqa* Sindhia, addressed to Pram Singh Patel, *mustajir*, *qasba* Ghairatganj besides the statement of Pram Singh, a dweller of Bagrod giving information about Adil Muhammad Khan. The letter as well as the statement and transliteration are sent to her. Dated 26 *Zilhijja* 1274 AH.

P 159. *Durga Prasad,* Thanadar *of Ghairatganj to Nawwab Shahjahan Begam.* Informs it has come to the notice from a letter in Hindi of Amar Singh and Balwant Singh, *zamindars* of Bagrod, *ilaqa* Sindhia, addressed to Pram Singh Patel, *qasba* Ghairatganj, that Adil Muhammad Khan, the insurgent with a contingent of 5, 000 men and 5 cannon and 1,500 *sawars* has come to Agra and it is not clear where they would go from there. The transliteration of the letter and statement of Pram Singh Om, who came from Bagrod, are sent to her. Dated 23 *Zilhijja* 1274 AH.

P 161. *Transliteration of a letter in Hindi of Amar Singh and Balwant Singh,* Zamindars *of Lodhi Bagrod,* Ilaqa *Sindhia Addressed to Pram Singh Patel,* Mustajir, Qasba *Ghairatganj.* There is news that *Nawwab Sahab* Garhiwala has come to Agra. But it is not known where he will go thereafter. If any authentic news is received, it will be communicated. But they should remain alert. From Sanchi it is reported that the *Nawwab Sahab* has surely arrived in Agra. After four days, whatever will be the news it will be communicated. The other information will be given by Pran Singh. Dated 9 *Sawan Budi.*

P 163. Statement of Pram Singh, a Dweller of Bagrod, in the Presence of Durga Prasad. States that his name is Pram Singh, his father's name is Amrau, a dweller of Bagrod, caste kurmi, age 22 years.

Q. Asked to tell about Bagrod as he came from there.

R. He heard from some eyewitness, that Nawwab Sahab, Garhiwala has come to Agra.

Q. Asked to tell about the contingent which the Nawwab Sahab had.

R. He is accompanied with 5, 000 armymen, 5 cannon and 1,500 *sawars*. But it is not known where he would go next.

Q. Who are others with him?

R. Raja Chhatrasal and Raja Sejpur are with him.

P 165. *Parbani Shankar,* Jamadar, *to Nawwab Sikandar Begam.* Refers to her order, dated 6 *Zilhijj* 1274 AH informing that from the letter of Daulat Rai, *nazim-i mashriq*, it has come to her notice that Adil Muhammad Khan is at Agra with Chhatrasal along with his contingent and directing him that if Adil Muhammad Khan and Aqil Muhammad Khan come to his jurisdiction, there should not be any hesitation in arresting or killing him. Assures, as directed he would execute the order in letter and spirit. There would be no negligence of duty on his part. From Raisen, dated 26 *Zilhijj* 1274 AH.

P 167. *Husain Khan to Nawwab Sikandar Begam.* Informs that Lal Singh and Nand Kishore, *harkaras*, went to Agra to bring the news about Adil Muhammad Khan. The information as provided by them is sent to her. Dated 27 *Zilhijj* 1274 AH.

PP 169-72. *News-Report as Reported by Lal Singh and Nand Kishore about Adil Muhammad Khan.* Inform that when they arrived at Berasia, they heard that the insurgents have arrived at Jamusar and were accumulating *saman-i rasad.* When they arrived at Jamusar they did not find any sign either of the insurgents or the *saman-i rasad.* When they arrived at Shamshabad, the soldiers at the gate did not allow them to enter in the village and kept them in captivity from dawn to evening and asked if they had come from Agra. They replied no, rather they had come in search of their cows which were lost. In the evening, they were freed. In the morning, they arrived at Barkhera, where the brothers of Chhatrasal were. They were asked if they were the informers. They said they had come on a visit as they came to know that Raja Sahab was going on a tour. So they to came to join him. If there is no tour, then they would engage in work as wage labourers. They were kept in captivity for the whole day and night and freed the next day in the morning. They then arrived at Agra. They found that about 7, 500 army personnel comprising of both *sawars* and foot-soldiers are accompanying Adil Muhammad Khan and staying in the houses of *zamindars* of Agra. Their horses were in the ground. The *sawars* were the *wilayatis*, the Bundelas. The *sawars* were found talking that, Chhatrasal was drinking when suddenly he fell from the stairs and has pain in his arms. The *sawars* were telling that to capture Sironj is not a difficult task. They thought they would establish *thanas* there. About 75 persons were encamping there and Rs. 200 were paid to the cannoners. In Agra there are 50 men, 12 horses and one elephant of Chhatrasal.

P 173. *Ghulam Muhammad Khan to Nawwab Sikandar Begam.* Informs that day, 27 *Zilhijj* 1274 AH, Laxman Singh Thakur, *mauza* Bishanpur, *ilaqa* Sindhia came and stated that one *sawar* of Adil Muhammad Khan came to Bishanpur and then left for Korwai. He said to him that on that day a contingent of 700 gunners had marched and till the evening they would arrive there. He also said that due to rain their army would encamp at Pathari, *mauza* Rusia, *ilaqa* Sindhia situating at a distance of two *curoh* and 1 *curoh* from Rusia. Hearing the news, all the inhabitants of Bheglone became afraid and assembled at *thana*. They were talking that he was destroying them. They also gave a petition. The same was submitted. Says although he persuaded them and consoled as much as possible. But they were not ready to get pacified as they were the witnesses of the devastation which had occurred in the past. Says he is not afraid of the insurgents at all. Whenever they would be in front of him he would deal with them with all his might. It does not seem possible to control the masses unless they are rescued by providing forces by the government. Requests if some soldiers are sent there, it would be most appropriate. Dated 27 *Zilhijj* 1274 AH.

P 175. *Muhammad Hasan Khan to Nawwab Sikandar Begam.* Refers to her *parwana,* dated 21 *Zilhijja* 1274 AH, which is in regard to coming of Adil Muhammad Khan in Agra and the instruction of the Political Agent to send reliable informers to know about Adil Muhammad Khan and even to assassinate him through a Gurjar or a Mewati and directing him to execute the order. Says he called Majid Khan and Hakim Khan, the soldiers, who are very active and deputed them to execute the order.

PP 177-8. *Hazrat Nur Khan,* Tahsildar *of Bheglone, to Nawwab Sikandar Begam.* Informs that day, the 27th of the month, Jogi, *jamadar* of Bishanpur as well as the *zamindars* of Bishanpur conveyed that one *sawar* of Adil Muhammad Khan came from Agra to Korwai while passing through that *mauza*. He stated that day or that night a contingent of about 1,000 would reach Bheglone. Hearing the news, all the inhabitants who had suffered the previous year became afraid. Inspite of all efforts, they closed their doors.

PP 179-80. *Murdan Singh and Mohan Singh to Nawwab Sikandar Begam.* State the previous year, they had requested to provide them arms and ammunitions. But no reply was received from her. They were attacked by the insurgents and suffered a lot at their hands. Moreover, not only thousands of rupees were lost but the humiliation and disregard of women was enormous.

PP 181-2. *Hazrat Nur Khan,* Tahsildar *of Bheglone, to Nawwab Sikandar Begam.* Informs the previous day; the 27th of the month, he sent two persons to Agra for bringing the news of insurgents as there was a report of attack on one or two places. But they were sent back by the *zamindars* of *mauza* Karru, *ilaqa* Sindhia. They said that at night, a contingent of about 700 to 800 would attack upon Bheglone. In view of this news, he along with the contingent was available there under the command of Ghulam Muhammad Khan, *risaldar*, and remained standing for the whole night. The situation would be clear from the letter of *risaldar*. At night, 10 armed soldiers sent by *Nawwab* Rais, Karwanawala, arrived there to enquire about the insurgents. Dated 28 *Zilhijja* 1274 AH.

P 183. Yaddasht, *Containing News Sent by Informers through Nur Muhammad Khan, Dated 28* Zilhijja *1274 AH*. Puran Kunwar came to Agra and stated that the previous day, the son of Ghulam Qadir Khan came and met Adil Muhammad Khan and informed that someone had demanded rupees two lakh from the *amil* of Sironj. Adil Muhammad Khan replied to him to be cautious and save his house. Adil Muhammad Khan along with an army of 1,000 *wilayatis* is present in Agra. About 500 to 600 t oops are present in the mountain. Their horses are verv strong. It is not known where they would go thereafter. Dated 28 *Zilhijja* 1274 AH.

PP 185-6. *Bhawani Prasad to Nawwab Sikandar Begam*. Informs that day in the evening a letter, dated 7 August 1858 of Munshi Jan Ali Khan, Assistant at Berasia, arrived in the office of the Agent. In the letter it is described that an informer, who saw events from his own eyes, came and stated that Adil Muhammad Khan and Aqil Muhammad Khan along with their relatives with 4 to 5 more persons were in Sironj in the house of Ghulam Qadir Khan, son of *jagirdar* of Sironj. The *amil* does not know about this. The family of Adil Muhammad Khan is in *mauza* Kaladeo, Itarsi, which is nearby to Agra and Sironj. A group of 500 *sawars* and foot-soldiers of Bundelas and the *wilayatis* are in different villages, the one is adjacent to Agra and Sironj.

It further contains the order that a *parwana* may be sent to the *amil* of Sironj, communicating him to arrest Adil Muhammad Khan, Aqil Muhammad Khan and Ghulam Qadir. A copy of the letter may be sent to the Agent to the Governor General, Central India. Munshi Jan Ali Khan may be conveyed that he is a wiseman and is doing a good job by sending informers to different places and that if there is any news about the insurgents who have arrived in Berasia, they should be arrested. A copy of the letter may be given to the *wakil* of Bhopal. Says the letter received by him is sent to her. Dated 28 *Zilhijja* 1274 AH (10 August 1858).

P 187. *Munshi Jan Ali Khan, Muntazim of Berasia, Deputy Assistant of Political Agent to the Political Agent, Bhopal*. Informs that day, an informer, who saw things from his own eyes, came and stated that Adil Muhammad Khan and Aqil Muhammad Khan along with their relatives with 4 to 5 more persons were in Sironj in the house of Ghulam Qadir Khan, son of *jagirdar* of Sironj. The family of Adil Muhammad Khan is in *mauza* Kaladeo, Itarsi, which is nearby to Agra and Sironj. A group of 400 to 500 *sawars* and foot-soldiers of Bundelas and the *wilayatis* are in Pura, Sarer and Sariri, which are adjacent to Agra. Says two more informers have also gone and when they come, further information will be given. Informs two persons of Thakur Chhatrasal met him that day, requesting that they want to go to the office of agent through him. They said that two days before they came to the house of Lala Kalyan Rai and that day they came there. As they had no business there, they just came for the sake of coming. They were then exiled from Berasia. They stayed one night at *mauza* Satti. It is not known whether they returned to Agra or not. The rest is fine. Dated 7 August 1858.

PP 191-2. Parwana of *Nawwab Sikandar Begam to Khan Zaman Khan.* Qila'dar. Sends the letter, dated 28 *Zilhijja* 1274 AH (10 August 1858), received from Munshi Bhawani Prasad and the letter received from Munshi Jan Ali Khan, Deputy Assistant, *muntazim* of Berasia, addressed to the Political Agent that would make everything clear. Directs him that the instruction given by the Political Agent to the *amil* of Sironj in the case of Adil Muhammad Khan, Aqil Muhammad Khan and Ghulam Qadir Khan, he too should follow the same line of action in case they come to Bhopal. It would be an act of fedility and bravery. Besides this, from day first, when the uprising errupted in Gwalior, which was 23 *Shawwal* 1274 AH, till date whatever *parwanas*, orders, etc. were issued by the government to him and in the name of *amil* and *thanadar* in regard to arrest or kill or pursue Adil Muhammad and Aqil Muhammad Khan, all such papers should be taken in his possession. Whenever the need would arise in dealing with any matter as mentioned, he should follow the instruction given in any order or *parwana* for combating the situation. The information to this effect should be given to the government. Dated 29 *Zilhijja* 1274 AH.

P 193. Parwana of *Nawwab Sikandar Begam to Hafiz Muhammad Hasan Khan,* Naib Bakhshi. Sends the letter, dated 28 *Zilhijja* 1274 AH (10 August 1858), received from Munshi Bhawani Prasad and the letter received from Munshi Jan Ali Khan, Deputy Assistant, *muntazim* of Berasia, addressed to the Political Agent that would make everything clear. Directs him that the instruction given by the Political Agent to the *amil* of Sironj in the case of Adil Muhammad Khan, Aqil Muhammad Khan and Ghulam Qadir Khan, he too should follow the same line of action in case they come to Bhopal. It would be an act of his fedility and bravery. Besides this, from day first, when uprising errupted in Gwalior which was 23 *Shawwal* 1274 AH till date whatever *parwanas*, orders, etc. were issued by the government to him and in the name of *amil* and *thanadar* in regard to arrest or kill or pursue Adil Muhammad and Aqil Muhammad Khan, all such papers should be taken in his possession. Whenever the need would arise in dealing with any matter as mentioned, he should follow the instruction as given in any order or *parwana* for combating the situation. Whenever he goes on an expedition to deal or arrest or kill Adil Muhammad Khan and Aqil Muhammad Khan, he should take the army of Garhi and Siwans. The information to this effect should be sent to Khan Zaman Khan, *qila'dar*, some time before he starts his expedition so that the *qila'dar* remains standby at Raisen and if the intention of the insurgents appears to go to Rahatgarh, the information should be passed on to the army station there. Dated 29 *Zilhijja* 1274 AH.

P 197. *Daulat Rai to Nawwab Sikandar Begam.* Sends the two letters receieved from *Suba Sahab*, Bhilsa, informing that Adil Muhammad Khan is encamping at Pura in Agra. Dated 29 *Zilhijja* 1274 AH.

File No. 256, E
Box No. 12
No. of Documents 11

P 201. *Sada Shiv Rao to Daulat Rai,* Nazim-i Mashriq. Acknowledges receipt of his letter, dated 26 *Zilhijja,* informing that from the letter of *thanadar,* Garhi Ambapani, it is learnt that Adil Muhammad Khan arrived at *mauza* Pura Guna, *ilaqa* Bhilsa, from Agra. Also refers to his letter, dated 28 *Zilhijja*, informing about the insurgents. Dated 29 *Zilhijja* 1274 AH.

P 203. *Daulat Rai to Sada Shiv Rao.* Refers to his letter, dated 28 *Zilhijja*, expressing the inability to deal with insurgents due to rainy season and difficulties in moving the cannon. Urges him that there should not be any negligence in dealing with the insurgents in his region, particularly in Pura Guna and in the mountains. The forces, deployed in Garhi Ambapani, Siwans, Bheglone should keep watch so that if the insurgents enter in the region, they should be eliminated. Dated 29 *Zilhijja* 1274 AH.

P 205. *Koka Fatah Jang to Nawwab Sikandar Begam.* Informs that Shaikh Kamil Muhammad had sent his servant, Dalil Khan, to enquire about the insurgent forces. He went there and what he stated has been recorded and is sent to her. Dated 20 *Zilhijja* 1274 AH.

PP 207-8. *Statement of Dalil Khan.* States that he went

to Sironj from Bhopal on 25 *Zilhijja* 1274 AH where he met a *darwesh* whom he asked about the insurgent forces. The latter replied that day, the insurgent forces came from Agra and entered Sironj. Says, he then entered in the army camp in disguise. He saw that Adil Muhammad Khan and his nephew with an army of 2,000, both *sawars* and foot-soldiers with 12 cannon, were fully prepared. On the other side Kamdar Khan and Yar Muhammad Khan with an army of 1,200 were encamping. Nawwab Bạndawala, the third group with an army of 1,500, both *sawars* and foot-soldiers was also encamping.

P 209. *Ghulam Murtaza Khan to Nawwab Sikandar Begam*. Refers to her *parwana*, dated 22 *Zilhijja* 1274 AH, informing that Adil Muhammad Khan after devastating Gwalior and the region of *Wazir al-Daulah* and after acquiring a huge wealth, has entered Sironj. If he passes through the region of Bhopal, the general masses and the employees should come together. There should not be any hesitation in looting and capturing the booty, and should not hesitate in arresting or killing Adil Muhammad Khan. Says he made it known to all the inhabitants. Dated 30 *Zilhijja* 1274 AH.

P 211. *Muhammad Abbas Ali*, Thanadar *of Bamhuri, to Nawwab Sikandar Begam*. Refers to her order, dated 14 *Zilhijja*, informing that from the letter of Daulat Rai, *nazim-i mashriq* and Suba Sahab, it was learnt that Adil Muhammad Khan had arrived at Agra and that whenever he entered his region there should not be any hesistation in arresting or killing him. Assures that the order would be implemented in letter and spirit.

P 213. *Koka Fath Jang to Nawwab Sikandar Begam.* Informs that two soldiers, namely Shankar Singh and Nasir Ali, were sent to bring the news of the insurgents. Shankar Singh has come back. His statement has been recorded and is sent to her.

PP 215-17. *Statement of Shankar Singh*. As ordered by Fath Jang, *qila'dar*, he along with Nasir Ali went from Bhopal in search of the insurgents. He reached Sironj and returned via Berasia. He saw that there were no cannon in the possession of Adil Muhammad Khan. He was questioned by the soldiers, who he was. He replied that he was a dweller of Hoshangabad and had come to Sironj where his brother lived. Now he was returning to his home. Says, he came back straight to Bhopal.

P 219. *Muhammad Mughal,* Tahsildar *of Bareilly, to Nawwab Sikandar Khan.* Refers to her *parwana,* dated 22 *Zilhijja,* informing that Adil Muhammad Khan has come to Sironj from Gwalior with a huge booty from the region of *Wazir al-Daulah* and he is well contended. The masses and employees of Bhopal should be directed to kill him and loot his wealth. Says he informed all the inhabitants of the region in the matter.

P 221. *Khan Zaman Khan to Nawwab Sikandar Begam.* Refers to her parwana, dated 29 *Zilhijja* 1274 AH, along with a letter of Bhawani Prasad and the letter of Jan Ali Khan, Assistant of Political Agent, Bhopal, *muntazim* of Berasia, directing him to arrest Adil Muhammad Khan and Aqil Muhammad Khan. Assures that he would do as desired.

PP 223-4. *Muhammad Sa'd al-Din to Nawwab Sikandar Begam.* Refers her parwana, dated 22 *Zilhijja* 1274 AH, informing that Adil Muhammad Khan, the insurgent after devastating Gwalior and the territory of *Wazir al-Daulah* has arrived in Sironj and in case he comes to the State of Bhopal or in Bhopal he should be dealt with by all the inhabitants of Bhopal. Informs that he made the order public in the entire city through the *nazir*. Dated 20 *Safar* 1275 AH.

File No. 257
Box No. 12
No. of Documents 4

Notifications for the Arrest of Kalu Ram, Alias Kallu Manyah, a Fugitive and Jamadar of Fazil Muhammad Khan, the Rebel and Accused For Devastating Sangal

PP 1-2. Contents

P 3. Parwana *of Nawwab Sikandar Begam to Muhammad Raza Husain, Deputy* Madar al-Maham. Sends a notification which is regarding the arrest of Kalu Ram alias Kallu Manyah of Allahanpur, *Pargana* Garhi, addressed to Murtaza Khan, *Kamdar*, Deorhi Khas, directing him to get 18 copies of the notification from *Matba' Sikandari* published. Dated 28 *Ziqada* 1274 AH.

P 5. Parwana *of Nawwab Sikandar Begam to Murtaza Khan,* Kamdar, *Deorhi Khas.* From the *Rubakari* of *adalat-i faujdari*, dated 21 *Sha'ban* 1274 AH, it is evident that Kalu Ram Patel, caste manyah of *mauza* Allahanpur, *pargana* Garhi, was holding the post of *jamadar* under Fazil Muhammad Khan, the rebel. He was also involved in arsoning and loot of *mauza* Sangal. He along with other *manyahis* of *mauza* Pura Guna, *ilaqa* Bhilsa, is absconding. Directs him to search Kalu Ram in his jurisdiction as per his physical description, and if found may be arrested and produced before her under *challan*.

Physical description: name Kalu Ram alias Kallu, caste *manyah*, colour whitish, a healthy person, little beard, average height, age between 50 to 60, a dweller of Allahanpur, *pargana* Garhi. Dated 28 *Ziqada* 1274 AH.

P 7. *Muhammad Raza Husain, Deputy Madar Al-Maham, to Nawwab Sikandar Begam.* Informs that in accordance to the *Parwana*, dated 28 *Ziqada* 1274 AH, which is regarding the arrest of Kalu Ram alias Kallu, caste *manyah*, dweller of Allahanpur, *pargana* Garhi, 18 notifications have been printed from *Matba' Sikandari* which are being sent to her along with the original notification. Dated 6 *Zilhijja* 1274 AH.

File No. 258, A
Box No. 12
No. of Documents 17

Regarding the Payment of Outstanding Installments of Army Contingent for the Year 1265 Fasli

PP 1-6 Contents

P 7. *Bhawani Prasad to Nawwab Sikandar Begam.* Informs that day, the Political Agent asked him whether he knew about the consent given by the Lord in regard to the amount spent from the treasury of the state on the salaries of the disbanded army contingent. He replied that he knew about this and had sent the report of the said amount to the Lord. He said that the consent for the said amount came. He paid his thanks to him. Requests to communicate it to all the employees. Dated 28 *Ziqada* 1274 AH (10 July 1858).

PP 9-10. Yaddasht, *of Major William Henry Richards to Nawwab Sikandar Begam.* Refers to her letter along with the details of the expenditure of the army contingent of Bhopal. The gist of the letter in English was sent to the Agent to the Governor-General of Central India. The reply of that letter has been received from the Secretary I, dated 21 June 1858, addressed to the Agent to the Governor General. From that letter, it came to notice that during the uprising, the amount which was spent by her on account of salaries with effect from 1 August 1857 till January 8, 1858, the Governor-General has given his consent for its adjustment. Dated 12 July 1858.

P 11. Yaddasht *of Major William Henry Richards, the Political Agent to Nawwab Sikandar Begam.* It has become necessary to deposit in the treasury of Sehore Cantonment the amount demanded. Desires that the amount may be deposited in the treasury of agenty Bhopal as per the details.

P 13. Parwana *of Nawwab Sikandar Begam to Bhawani Prasad.* An amount of Rs. 1, 65, 359/9 on account of salary of the army contingent, Bhopal, besides the road and *madarsa* expenses, is outstanding for the current year. There is a demand for the said amount from the office of the Political Agent. He is directed to tell Than Singh, treasurer, Sehore, that the said amount may be deposited in the treasury of agenty Sehore. The said amount will be paid to him in 4 installments with an interest of anna 8% by the State of Bhopal. The reply of the treasurer may be conveyed to her.

PP 15-17. Yaddasht, *of Nawwab Sikandar Begam to Major William Henry Richards, The Political Agent.* Refers to his letter, dated 14 July 1858, demanding a sum of Rs. 1, 42, 519/7 which is the outstanding amount of installment for the year 1265 *fasli* on account of expenses of the army contingent. Informs of a sum of Rs. 1, 42, 444/9/5, the remaining installment for the year 1265 *fasli* on account of expenses of army contingent, whose details are sent to him. Hopes for the receipt of the amount.

PP 21-2. *Bhawani Prasad to Nawwab Sikandar Begam.* As per the order, dated 6 *Zilhijja* 1274 AH, he called Than Singh and discussed with him about the sum of Rs. 1, 65, 359/9, as mentioned in the *parwana*. He replied that whatever amount was there in his shop, it was for the purpose of purchasing opium that will return to the shop after the rainy season. Now he has received the order of the *Nawwab* and he does not want to reply in negative. A *hundawi* of Rs. 15, 000 should be executed in his name and during the month of *Aswaj* and *Kartik*, he would return Rs. 20, 000. Beyond that he is not able to do anything. He also said to convey his well-being and of his nephew, Beni Prasad. This is for information for the employees of the government. Dated 8 *Zilhijja* 1274 AH (20 July 1858).

P 23. *Nawwab Sikandar Begam to Major Willaim Henry Richards, Political Agent.* Refers to his letter, dated 12 July 1858, informing that the Governor General has agreed to pay an amount of Rs. 63, 837/12/7 Bhopali coin, corresponding to 5, 834 Kaldar coin which was spent by her on the army contingent during the uprising, with effect from 1st August 1857 till January 8, 1858, in their salaries. Expresses her thanks to him for his endeavour and also to the Governor General. Dated 8 *Zilhijja* 1274AH (20 August 1858).

P 25. *Karimal*, Gumashta, *Rupmal and Others to Nawwab Sikandar Begam.* Refers to his earlier communiqué, ordering to pay a sum of rupees one lakh to the government as loan and whether the government would like to receive the above amount in cash or in *hundawi* in Kaldar coin. The same may be conveyed. The reply received from the government is that presently an amount of Rs. 50,000 cash, Bhopali coin, out of the sum of rupees one lakh should be deposited. Informs that in a period of 10 days, the goods of Rs. 50,000 are demanded from Indore. The said amount would be deposited thereafter in the treasury. But as requested earlier, the taxes over the finished goods should not be paid by them. Dated 12 *Zilhijja* 1274 AH (24 August 1858).

PP 27-8. *Bhawani Prasad to Nawwab Sikandar Begam.* Refers to the letter of the Political Agent, dated 28 July 1858, desiring that out of Rs. 1, 42, 519/8, owing to the British government, a sum of Rs. 50,000 should be deposited in the treasury within 5 to 6 days. The rest of the amount if deposited after 10 to 15 days will not be a problem. The same is sent to her for orders, as it seems suitable.

P 29. *The Political Agent to Bhawani Prasad.* Refers to his letter, dated 14 July 1858, to *Nawwab* Sikandar Begam desiring to deposit the outstanding amount of Rs. 1, 42, 519 which is still to be deposited. Directs him to request the *Nawwab* to deposit an installment of Rs. 50,000 in a period of 6 days. It will be good as the treasury is empty and it is difficult to meet the expenses. If the remaining amount is deposited after 10 to 15 days it will make no difference. Dated 8 July 1858.

P 31. Parwana *of Nawwab Sikandar Begam to Bhawani Prasad.* An amount of Rs. 50,000, is sent as per the details which includes the installment of army contingent for the year 1265 *fasli*; the expenses of *Madarsa*, Sehore, the road expenses, the meals of the prisoners, and the annual expenses of grass cutters, is sent as per the details. This should be brought to the notice of the Political Agent and the receipt obtained from him may be submitted. Dated 30 *Zilhijja* 1274 AH (11 August 1858).

P 33. *Bhawani Prasad to Nawwab Sikandar Begam.* Refers to her order, dated 20 *Zilhijja* 1274 AH, as recorded on his letter, dated 17 *Zilhijja* 1274 AH, informing that after receiving a sum of Rs. 50,000 from there, he should bring Rs. 15, 350/9/5 from Than Singh, treasurer and thus a total sum of Rs. 65, 350/9/5 should be deposited in the treasury of the agenty and the receipt of the amount obtained from there should be sent to the government. Informs that day, the sum of Rs. 50,000 was received from the royal treasury and after depositing the same in the treasury of the agenty, he informed the Political Agent. Thereafter, *hundawi* of Rs. 15, 350/9/5 was obtained from Than Singh, the treasurer. He wrote it down in the register and handed it over to Than Singh. The next day, the matter will be brought to the notice of the Political Agent and the receipt obtained from him will be sent to the government. Dated 23 *Zilhijja* 1274AH (4 August 1858).

P 35. *Bhawani Prasad to Nawwab Sikandar Begam.* Refers to the order, given through the letter of Karimal, Khamer Mal and Sudarsh Nath Mal, dated 8 *Zilhijja* 1274 AH, which is in regard to a sum of Rs. 1, 65, 000. Says the matter was brought to the notice of the Political Agent. That day, he received a *parwana* of the Political Agent, dated 3 August 1858, informing that there is no money at all in the treasury of the agenty and difficult to execute day-to-day business. The money in demand should immediately be sent. The same is sent to her. Dated 23 *Zilhijja* 1274AH (4 August 1858).

P 37. *The Political Agent to Bhawani Prasad.* Refers his

letter along with the letter of the traders of the city of Bhopal, intimating delay for few days in depositing the sum for army contingent. Says the treasury of the agenty is quite empty and it is difficult to meet the expenses. In view of this, the money in demand should immediately be sent. Dated 3 August 1858.

PP 39-40. *Bhawani Prasad to Nawwab Sikandar Begam.* Refers to her order, dated 12 *Zilhijja* 1274AH, as mentioned on his letter, dated 8 *Zilhijja* 1274AH, informing that in the month of *Kartik,* the revenue realization of the state will be completed and then there will be no need of this money anymore. Says he held a talk with Than Singh in the light of above orders. He replied that the opium was purchased in huge quantity and stored in Indore. In such a situation, no commitment of extra amount is made. The *hundawi* of Rs. 30, 000, Bhopali coin, as per the orders of the government is written and whenever the government may like to collect it from him, he is ready to pay the same. Informs as ordered, a *hundawi* of Rs. 15, 350/9/5 was obtained from Than Singh, treasurer, and deposited in the treasury of agenty along with Rs. 50,000, sent by the government from the royal treasury. For the rest of amount, after exempting Rs. 15, 350/9/5 from Rs. 30, 000, a *hundawi* will be written that day or after 10 days whenever the royal order is received. Further states that he did not mention anything about the interest of the amount and that the government is all powerful and an arbitrator, who may either give equal to all other traders or some less. But no royal *parwana* in the matter is received. If a *parwana* is sent, it will be good. Dated 23 *Zilhijja* 1274 AH (4 August 1858).

P 41. Parwana *of Nawwab Sikandar Begam to Than Singh.* From the letter of Bhawani Prasad, *wakil,* dated 23 *Zilhijja* 1274 AH (4 August 1858), it came to the notice that he has agreed to pay a sum of Rs. 30,000 as loan. The said amount, besides an amount of Rs. 20,

000 for her sake, thus a total sum of Rs. 50,000 may be given as loan. Hopefully, during the next year, the said amount will be paid in 4 installements and an interest of anna 12% will be paid on the amount given as loan in the previous year. The yield against the said amount will be granted in *pargana* Sehore. At the end of the year, after yearly calculation of the yield from the land grants in the said *pargana,* the exceeding amount after the payment of loan amount will be taken back from him. In case, anything is left with the government for payment, it will be paid back. Dated 26 *Zilhijja* 1274AH (7 August 1858).

File No. 258, B
Box No. 12
No. of Documents 20

PP 43-4. *Bhawani Prasad to Nawwab Sikandar Begam.* Informs as ordered, dated 27 *Zilhijja* 1274 AH, besides her *parwana,* to Lala Than Singh, treasurer of the agenty, he presented the *parwana* to the treasurer who heard him and said that the orders of the government were supreme. Earlier, due to scarcity of money he had made an excuse. Now there is no excuse. The amount of Rs. 50,000 will be paid either in cash or in *hundawi.*

P 45. *Bhawani Prasad to Nawwab Sikandar Begam.* Informs that day, he called Pancham Das Seth and asked him to pay a certain amount as loan to the government promising to return the said amount in 4 installments from the realization of the year 1266 *fasli*, and that how much amount he would be able to manage. He replied that an amount of Rs. 15, 000 could be paid by him to the government either through *hundawi* or through cash, provided the interest rate should not be less than Re. 1. Dated 30 *Zilhijja* 1274 AH (11 August 1858).

P 47. *Bhawani Prasad to Nawwab Sikandar Begam.* Informs that Munshi Muhammad Jamal al-Din held talk with Raghunath Seth who agreed to pay Rs. 15, 000. Says he called him and asked if he is ready to pay the said amount. He replied in affirmation agreeing to the orders of the government, provided the government agrees to pay an interest of Re. 1 and that the total amount is paid in one installment from this year's realization of Sehore. Dated 30 *Zilhijja* 1274 AH (11 August 1858).

PP 49-50. *Bhawani Prasad to Nawwab Sikandar Begam.* Informs that day, Lala Than Singh, treasurer of the agenty, met him and gave a letter in reply of her *parwana,* agreeing to pay Rs. 50,000 and requesting for exemption from paying taxes of *dar al-zarb*[1] in regard to Rs. 25,000. The same is sent to her. He further said to enquire from the Political Agent if the payment is required in Kaldar coin. The said quantity of Kaldar coin might be made available from the government with a deduction of Rs. 10 on Rs. 100. If the Political Agent agrees to pay extra Rs. 10 on Rs. 100, the Kaldar coin would be minted from *dar al-zarb.* Says he is unable to communicate anything to the Political Agent in the matter of the Kaldar coin, unless he receives an order of the government. Requests for orders to proceed further. Dated 3 *Muharram* 1275 AH (14 August 1858).

P 51. *Than Singh, Treasurer, to Nawwab Sikandar Begam.* Refers to her *parwana,* dated 26 *Zilhijja* 1274 AH, which states that he has agreed to pay Rs. 30,000 and for her sake he would pay another Rs. 20, 000, and thus, a total amount of 50,000 is to be paid as loan. The rate of interest which was earlier anna 8% would then be anna 12% and the property would be earmarked in *pargana* Sehore for payment. Says he is totally subservient to the government. But there is extreme hardship due to the purchasing of opium. In regard to the orders of the government for payment of Rs. 50,000, he would not make any excuse and would come forward to do whatever would be possible for him to do. Besides, he is not getting any amount from the inhabitants of Bhopal and has asked for Rs. 25,000 in Kaldar coin from Indore. If an order is issued to the *Dar al-Zarb*, Bhopal, for minting the said amount it would be good as

1. Mint.

the amount could be deposited in the treasury. The rest of the amount would be paid either through *hundawi* or in cash. In regard to the rate of interest, he has nothing to say. It is for the government to look into the matter.

P 53. Parwana *of Nawwab Sikandar Begam to Bhawani Prasad.* An amount of rupees one lakh is due for payment of the remaining installment of the army contingent and thus, Than Singh, treasurer may be asked to pay the said amount in the treasury of the agenty. The amount will be returned with the intrest rate of anna 12% in the year 1266 *fasli* in four installments from the realization of *pargana* Sehore. Dated 4 *Muharram* 1275 AH (14 August 1858).

P 55. *Bhawani Prasad to Nawwab Sikandar Begam.* Refers to her *parwana*, dated 4 *Muharram* 1275 AH, which is in regard to the outstanding installment of rupees one lakh of the army contingent, and to tell Than Singh, treasurer to deposit the said amount in the treasury of agenty and that the said amount will be returned to him with an interest of anna 12% in four installments in 1266 *fasli* from the realization of *pargana* Sehore. Says he talked to the treasurer. He said that he replied to the *Nawwab* on 3 *Muharram* 1275 AH and until reply was received he was unable to suggest anything more. Dated 7 *Muharram* 1275 AH (17 August 1858).

PP 57-8. *Bhawani Prasad to Nawwab Sikandar Begam.* Informs as ordered, dated 5 *Muharram* 1275 AH, mentioning on the top of his letter, he tried to know from the Political Agent what is in his mind in regard to the payment of Rs. 2,010. It seems that he wants the payment of Rs. 25,000 in Kaldar coin. A reply would be sent to her after knowing the intention of the Political Agent. Dated 12 *Muharram* 1275 AH (22 August 1858).

PP 59-60. *Bhawani Prasad to Nawwab Sikandar Begam.* Informs on 12 *Muharram* 1275 AH he, as ordered, brought the matter of Rs. 2,010 in Kaldar coin into the notice of the Political Agent. It seems that his intention is to get Rs. 25,000 in Kaldar coin. However, a clear reply would be sent by the next day.

P 61. Parwana *of Nawwab Sikandar Begam to Bhawani Prasad.* The amount of the installment of the army contingent was ready. Meanwhile, an order of the Agent to the Governor General, Central India was received desiring that the amount should be made available in new Bhopali coin. So the new coins of the said amount are being minted. As and when the new coins are made available, the installments of the army contingent will be sent to the Political Agent. Directs him to bring the matter into the notice of the Political Agent and convey her of his reply. Dated 23 *Muharram* 1275 AH (2 September 1858).

PP 63-4. *Bhawani Prasad to Nawwab Sikandar Begam.* Informs the previous day, as ordered, dated 18 *Muharram* 1275 AH, mentioned on his letter, dated 14 *Muharram* 1275 AH, he brought 10 bags, bearing Rs. 2,000 in Kaldar coin from the shop of Than Singh to Garhi and then from Garhi it was loaded upon the elephants after converting the Kaldar coin into Bhopali coin that amounted to Rs. 22, 000 and sent to the Political Agent by Ramden, *Peshdast Wakil*, as per the procedure and deposited in the treasury of the agenty. That day was a holiday. The next day he will submit the receipt obtaining from there. Dated 26 *Muharram* 1275 AH (5 September 1858).

P 65. *Bhawani Prasad to Nawwab Sikandar Begam.* Informs he brought the matter as mentioned in her *parwana*, dated 23 *Muharram* 1275 AH, to the knowledge of the Political Agent. He said, at the moment there is need of money in the treasury of the agenty.

P 67. *Gist of the Letter of Bhawani Prasad to the Government.* Informs that on 25 *Muharram* 1275 AH, an amount of Rs. 20, 000 in Kaldar coin which in terms of Bhopali coin is Rs. 22, 000 @ Rs. 2 upon Rs. 10 was obtained from the shop of Than Singh, treasurer as loan, as ordered by her on his letter, dated 14 *Muharram* 1275 AH, and deposited the same in the treasury of the agenty for the outstanding installements of the army contingent of Bhopal due upon the government for the year 1265 *fasli*. The receipt obtained from the agenty of Bhopal is sent to her. Dated 28 *Muharram* 1275 AH.

It contains the order that the letter along with the receipt may be sent to Lala Gobind Prasad, treasurer to include in the file and keeping in the *daftar*. A copy of the letter as well as the receipt may be sent to Nawal Rai, *Diwan* directing him to submit the details of the amount of Rs. 22, 000 obtained from Than Singh along with date and time. Dated 29 *Muharram* 1275 AH.

P 69. Parwana *of Nawwab Sikandar Begam to Bhawani Prasad.* Haji 'Abd al-Karim, Agent III, is arriving there with the money of installments for the army contingent of Bhopal. Dated 28 *Muharram* 1275 AH.

PP 71-2. *Gist of the Letter of Bhawani Prasad to the Government.* Informs of the receipt of her *parwana,* dated 19 *Zilhijja* 1274 AH, along with a sum of Rs. 50,000 in Bhopali coin. Informs, as ordered a sum of Rs. 15, 359/9/5 was obtained from the shop of Than Singh, treasurer as loan. Thus, a total sum of Rs. 65, 359/9/5 Bhopali coin, the outstanding sum of the army contingent of Bhopal for the year 1265 *fasli* was deposited in the treasury of the agenty as communicated to her through his letter, dated 24 *Zilhijja* 1274 AH. Informs that day the said amount was received from the office of the Political Agent. The same is sent to her.

It contains the order that the letter and receipt may be sent to Lala Gobind Prasad, treasurer to include them in the file and to keep in the *daftar*. A copy of the order may be sent to *mu'tamid al-maham*, directing him that the *wasilbaqi*[2] of the installments of the army

2. Collections and balances; accounts of payments.

contingent of Bhopal may be prepared and submitted to the government so that further orders may be given in this regard. Dated 2 *Safar* 1275 AH.

P 73. *Diwan Kishan Ram to Nawwab Sikandar Begam.* Informs as ordered, the details of *wasilbaqi* of the amount of the army contingent of Bhopal has been prepared, based on the papers of the treasury and the letters of Bhawani Prasad, *wakil-i riyasat*. The same is submitted to the government. Dated 2 *Safar* 1275 AH.

PP 75-6. Yaddasht, *Regarding Wasilbaqi of the Amount of the Army Contingent of Bhopal, Payable by the Government gor the Year 1265* Fasli. *Dated 2* Safar *1275 AH.*

P 77. *Kishan Ram, Diwan to Nawwab Sikandar Begam.* Than Singh, treasurer, Sehore, has agreed to pay to the government an amount of Rs. 50,000 as loan. The *wasilbaqi* paper has been prepared as per the letter of Munshi Bhawani Prasad, *wakil*, for sending it to Lala Paltu Lal. The same is sent to her. Dated 2 *Safar* 1275 AH.

P 79. Yaddasht, *Containing Details of* Wasilbaqi *Amount of Rs. 50,000, to be Paid by Than Singh, Treasurer to the Government Against the Sum Due to the Army Contingent of Bhopal.*

P 81. Parwana *of Nawwab Sikandar Begam to Bhawani Prasad.* From the *wasilbaqi* installments of the army contingent of Bhopal, as prepared by Kishan Ram, Diwan it is clear that till 1265 *fasli* an amount of Rs. 28, 000 is outstanding of the remaining installments of the army contingent of Bhopal which is to be paid. He is directed to obtain the an amount of Rs. 28, 000 from Than Singh, treasurer, agenty Sehore, and deposit the same in the treasury. The receipt of it may be sent to the government. Dated 2 *Safar* 1275 AH.

File No. 259 C
Box No. 12
No. of Documents 8

Disbursement of the Salary of the Contingent of Bhopal Army with effect from July 1857 to January 8, 1858

P 115. *Madan Mohan,* Naib Wakil *to Nawwab Sikandar Begam.* Refers to her order, dated 23 *Rajab* 1274 AH, that he should present himself before her, and after the settlement of salary expenditure of the army contingent with Thakur Prasad, *naib, mu'tamid al-maham*, he should go back to Sehore. Informs by the next day he would be present there. Further says that, since all the expenditure was incurred by Bakhshi Murawwat Muhammad Khan and Sikandar Khan, therefore, all the accounts referred to could be available with Ambika Prasad. Dated 29 *Rajab* 1274 AH (16 March 1858).

PP 117-18. *Bhawani Prasad to Nawwab Sikandar Begam.* Informs as ordered through her *parwana,* dated 22 *Rajab* 1274 AH, which is regarding the payment of the salary of the employees of army contingent, Bhopal, he put the case before the Political Agent. In reply, he received his *parwana,* dated 17 March 1858, informing that the amount of salary of the army contingent for the previous months is pending and unless the amount is paid, no orders will be issued to the agenty for release of the amount. The same is presented before her and requests that the accounts of the army contingent should be settled before asking the Political Agent for payment. Dated 2 *Sha'ban* 1274 AH (19 March 1858).

P 119. *The Political Agent to Bhawani Prasad.* Refers to his letter in reference to the *parwana* of *Nawwab* Sikandar Begam, requesting for orders to the office of agenty for the payment of the amount of salary of the army contingent, Bhopal, earlier paid by the State of Bhopal. Says, earlier, was asked for the payment of the salary of army contingent but still not paid. Unless the amount is received, no further orders will be issued for the payment of the amount.

P 121. *Bhawani Prasad to Nawwab Sikandar Begam.* Says there is some doubt in the accounts of the amounts concerning the expenses of the army contingent, submitted by Lala Than Singh, treasurer. So also with the *wasilbaqi* amount, paid in advance without comparing it with the papers of treasury of agenty. In view of this, a letter has been written to Than Singh to send his *gumashta* with the papers of accounts of the expenditure of army contingent, besides the details of accounts of *dastgardan*. A copy of the same is sent to her. Dated 4 *Sha'ban* 1274 AH (20 March 1858).

P 123. *Bhawani Prasad to Than Singh*. It is the earnest desire of the government to clear the accounts of the army contingent, and the amount of *dastgardan*[3] made from his shop. Thus, as ordered, Madan Mohan, *naib wakil*, and Munshi Kundan Lal are present. But unless his *gumashta* too comes along with the copies of the accounts of distribution of salary of the army contingent and *dastgardan* amount paid from his shop and the expenses of the Political Agent for the month of July are adjusted in the accounts of treasury, the said accounts cannot be cleared. It is desired that his *gumashta* should soon be sent along with the copies of accounts of the said months, beginning from the month of August till the month of November and December so that there should not be any delay in the clearance of the accounts. The delay is only for the arrival of the *gumashta*. Dated 4 *Sha'ban* 1274 AH (20 March 1858).

P 125. *Madan Mohan,* Naib Wakil*, to Nawwab Sikandar Begam.* Informs, as ordered, he along with the Munshi was present at the *deorhi* of Lala Thakur Prasad to give clarification in regard to the accounts of the army contingent, if required. Says firstly, he was asked about the salary of the sargeant, the major and his staff and the soldiers. He gave whatever information he had in the matter. In regard to the adjustment of the accounts of *dastgardan* made by Than Singh and the advance money which he paid, a letter has been sent to him, the treasurer, calling for his *gumashta*. He asked Lala Thakur Prasad if there is any doubt in any other matter that might be

3. A short-term loan to be repaid on a verbal promise.

settled. He said unless the papers of the time of Sikandar Khan, agenty is received, what he would enquire from him and Lala Bijay Lal. Unless Lala Bijay Lal comes, there is no possibility to settle any issue.

P 127. *Bhawani Prasad to Nawwab Sikandar Begam.* Refers to a letter of his own, dated 4th *Sha'ban*, addressed to Than Singh, treasurer requesting him to send his *gumashta* along with the papers of the accounts of the employees of army contingent as there is some doubt regarding the amount paid in advance, and the demand letter for the return of the money. Says that day, he received the letter of Than Singh, treasurer, informing that whatever was the account it was sent to him with his own signature. If there is any discrepancy in the accounts, he should be communicated so that it might be rectified. If it cannot be resolved without going the *gumashta,* then he should wait for 2-3 days and thereafter he would be present there with the copies of the register. The said letter is sent to her. Says, since the *gumashta* was involved in making payment to the employees of the army contingent, it does not seem possible to resolve the issue without the presence of the *gumashta*. Dated 7 *Sha'ban* 1274 AH (23 March 1858).

P 129. *Than Singh, Treasurer, to Bhawani Prasad.* Refers to his letter for sending the *gumashta* with the copies of the accounts of the distribution of salary of the army contingent. Says there is no problem in sending him there. But the accounts of his shop are known to the *bakhshi* and to him also, and his signatures are present on the papers. If there is any discrepancy in the accounts, it may be pointed out so that it may be resolved. If without the presence of the *gumashta,* the queries cannot be removed, then the *gumashta* would be available after 2-3 days, having papers and copy of the register. Dated 29 March 1858.

File No. 259, D
Box No. 12
No. of Documents 18

P 131. *Kishan Ram,* Mu'tamid al-Maham, *to Nawwab Sikandar Begam.* Says it is difficult to calculate the accounts of the army contingent and it is a must that Lala Than Singh, treasurer should come with the papers pertaining to the accounts and *wasilbaqi* of the period between July 1 1857 to January 8, 1858. Requests for orders to call the *gumashta* of Lala with all papers. Dated 12 *Sha'ban* 1274 AH.

P 133. *Kishan Ram,* Mu'tamid al-Maham, *to Nawwab Sikandar Begam.* Calling Bijay Lal to rectify the accounts of army contingent for the month of November and December 1857, and upto January 8 is must as the unarranged papers make the calculation of the accounts of army contingent difficult. Requests for orders to call Lala with all the papers. Dated 12 *Sha'ban* 1274 AH.

P 135. *Bakhshi Murawwat Muhammad Khan to Nawwab Sikandar Begam.* As ordered, the details of the expenditure and salary of army contingent of Bhopal that were sent to Islamgarh and Siwans are sent to her. Dated 16 *Sha'ban* 1274 AH.

P 137. Yaddasht, *Containing Details of Expenditure of Army Contingent, Bhopal, Sent to Garhi Ambapani. Dated 25* Safar *1275 AH.*

P 139. *Kishan Ram,* Mu'tamid al-Maham, *to Nawwab Sikandar Begam.* Pem Chand, *gumashta* of Than Singh, has submitted the papers and documents addressed to the treasurer constituting the accounts of the shop of Than Singh, treasurer and has requested for the receipts of it. The receipts are included in the files which are not to be returned without the orders of the government. Requests for orders in the name of Paltu Lal that the receipts deposited by Than Singh, treasurer, related to the realization from *mahal* Sehore, should be found out for returning it to the *gumashta*.

P 141. *Kishan Ram,* Mu'tamid al-Maham, *to Nawwab Sikandar Begam.* As ordered, dated 16 *Jumada* I, 1274 AH, mentioned on the top of the letter of Bhawani Prasad, the accounts of army contingent of Bhopal are sent to her. Dated 23 *Sha'ban* 1274 AH.

PP 143-4, 145-6, 147, 149, 151, 153, 155& 157. Yaddasht-i Awarjah *of the Distribution of Monthly Salalry of Army Contingent of Bhopal with effect from 1 August 1857 to January 8, 1858.*

PP 159, 161, 163 & 165. Yaddasht, *Containing Details of Accounts Regarding Distribution of Salaries of the Employees of Army Contingent, Bhopal through Sikandar Muhammad Khan, Agenty II, for the Month of November 1857.*

File No. 259, E
Box No. 12
No. of Documents 22

PP 167, 169, 171-72 & 173. Yaddasht, *Containing Details of Accounts Regarding Distribution of Salaries of the Employees of Army Contingent, Bhopal through Sikandar Muhammad Khan, Agenty II, for the Month of December 1857.*

PP 175-76 & 177. Yaddasht, *Containing Details of Accounts Regarding Distribution of Salaries of the Employees of Army Contingent, Bhopal through Sikandar Muhammad Khan, Agenty II, for the Month of January 1858.*

PP 179-80 & 181-2. Yaddasht, *Containing Details of the Amount Paid to the Army Contingent in Excess during the Period July 1857 to January 8, 1858, as Claimed by Pem Singh, Gumashta of Lala Than Singh, Treasurer.*

It contains a note that there is no match between the details of handing over and taking over the amount as there is a difference in the accounts of Munshi Ambika Prasad and accounts of Than Singh, treasurer, agenty. Whereas from the statement of Munshi Kundan Lal, it is clear that at the time of the need, an advance amount was paid. But at the time of distribution of salary, advance money was paid to the treasurer.

P 183. Yaddasht, *Containing Details of Un-Distributed Amount of the Employees of Army Contingent during the Period July 1857 to January 1858.* The deputy sergeant, major and the staff of sergeant are in Hoshangabad and the *babus* of the army contingent have entered the amount of salary from the month of July to the end of November in the register. Bakhshi Murawwat Muhammad Khan did not make a demand from the treasury as the British officers were not present in Sehore. But from the statement of Than Singh, treasurer it appears that the British officers received the amount of salary at Hoshangabad through the Political Agent.

PP 185-6. *List of Letters Written by Bakhshi Murawwat Muhammad Khan, Munshi Bhawani Prasad and Sikandar Muhammad Khan, Agenty II to Than Singh, Treasurer. Dated 23* Sha'ban *1274 Ah.*

P 187. *Murawwat Muhammad Khan,* Bakhshi *to Than Singh, Treasurer.* An amount of Rs. 12, 293/13/10, Bhopali coin, is required for payment of the salaries of the contingent of Bhopal army for the month of August 1857. The said amount may be paid which will be adjusted at the time of calculation.

P 189. *Murawwat Muhammad Khan Bakhshi to Than Singh, Treasurer.* An amount of Rs. 20/3/8 is required for payment of the arrears of a soldier who has resigned. The said amount may be paid which will be adjusted at the time of distribution of the salaries of the month. Dated 11 *Muharram* 1274 AH.

P 191. *Murawwat Muhammad Khan, Bakhshi to Than Singh, Treasurer.* An amount of Rs. 9/9/11 is required for payment of a dismissed soldier. The said amount may be paid which will be adjusted at the time of distribution of the salaries of the month. Dated 22 *Muharram* 1274 AH.

P 193. *Murawwat Muhammad Khan,* Bakhshi *to Than Singh, Treasurer.* An amount of Rs. 640/1/2 is required to make payment of the dismissed platoon of Bhopal contingent. The said amount may be paid which will be adjusted at the time of distribution of the salaries of the employees. Dated 5 *Muharram* 1274 AH.

P. 195. *Murawwat Muhammad Khan,* Bakhshi *to Than*

Singh, Treasurer. An amount of Rs. 221/2/11$^{1/2}$ may be paid to make the payment of dismissed *risalas*. The amount will be paid at the time of distribution of the salaries of employees. Dated 5 *Muharram* 1274 AH.

P 197. *Murawwat Muhammad Khan,* Bakhshi, *to Than Singh, Treasurer.* An amount of Rs. 30 may be paid to meet the expenses of *dussehra* as per the practice. If it is paid by the government then ok, otherwise it will be paid from the amount of fine. Dated 25 *Muharram* 1274 AH.

P 199. *Murawwat Muhammad Khan,* Bakhshi, *To Than Singh, Treasurer.* A sum of Rs. 11, 921/11/10, Bhopali coin, as the salary of the employees of the contingent of Bhopal army for the month of September 1857 may be paid. The said amount will be adjusted at the time of calculation. Dated 5 October 1857.

P 201. *Murawwat Muhammad Khan,* Bakhshi *To Than Singh, Treasurer.* An amount of Rs. 20, Bhopali coin, as the salary for the month of July 1857 of a *sawar* of *risala* IV, Bhopal contingent, may be paid. Dated 7 October 1857.

P 203. *Murawwat Muhammad Khan,* Bakhshi, *to Than Singh, Treasurer.* Informs that Khaman Singh has died on 28 September 1857. An amount of Rs. 3 may be given to Nathu Ram for his funeral. Dated 9 *Safar* 1274 AH.

P 205. *Murawwat Muhammad Khan,* Bakhshi, *to Than Singh, Treasurer.* An amount of Rs. 265 for purchasing the horses may be paid. Dated 10 *Muharram* 1274 AH.

P 207. *Murawwat Muhammad Khan,* Bakhshi, *to Than Singh, Treasurer.* An amount of Rs. 135 for purchasing horse for a *sawar* of *risala* III may be paid. Dated 17 *Safar* 1274 AH.

P 209. *Murawwat Muhammad Khan,* Bakhshi, *to Than Singh, Treasurer.* An amount of Rs. 300 as the cost of *than* and bungalow of the *risaldar* and Arif Shah, *jamadar*, may be paid. Dated 15 *Safar* 1274 AH.

File No. 259, F
Box No. 12
No. of Documents 25

P 211. *Murawwat Muhammad Khan,* Bakhshi, *to Than Singh, Treasurer.* An amount of Rs. 99/4/4 ½ on account of dismissal of the *risala* III may be paid. The said amount will be adjusted at the time of distribution of the salary. Dated 13 *Safar* 1274 AH.

P 213. *'Abd al-Karim Ansari to Than Singh, Treasurer.* An amount of Rs. 74 towards the salaries of the employees, carrying the goods of the British and going to Hoshangabad, is required. The same may be paid and will be adjusted at the time of distribution of the salary. Dated 13 *Safar* 1274 AH.

P 215. *Murawwat Muhammad Khan,* Bakhshi, *to Than Singh, Treasurer.* An amount of Rs. 9, Bhopali coin, is required to meet the expenses of rent of *chholdari*[4] going to Berasia. The said amount may be paid and will be adjusted at the time of clearance. Dated 7 October 1857.

P 217. *Murawwat Muhammad Khan,* Bakhshi, *to Than Singh, Treasurer.* An amount of Rs. 60, Bhopali coin, is required to meet the expenses of rent of *chholdari* which may be paid in advance to Durga Singh, *kotha-havaldar*. Dated 15 *Safar* 1274 AH.

P 219. *Murawwat Muhammad Khan,* Bakhshi, *to Than Singh, Treasurer.* An amount of 4 *annas* towards the expenses of mustard oil, required for polishing nails of cannon of army contingent of Bhopal may be paid. Dated 16 *Safar* 1274 AH.

PP 221-2. Yaddasht, *Containing Details of the Expenditure, Incurred on the Repair of Arsenal.*

P 223. *Murawwat Muhammad Khan, Bakhshi, to Than Singh, Treasurer.* An amount of Rs. 6, the amount of expenditure of the papers is required in the army contingent. Dated 6 *Safar* 1274 AH.

P 225. *Murawwat Muhammad Khan,* Bakhshi, *to Than*

4. A small tent for horses.

Singh, Treasurer. An amount of Rs. 24/4/3, Bhopali coin, in respect of cost of *thans* of horses, daily expenses of the horses, and for the soldiers of *risaldar* of *risala* III may be paid to Narain Singh, *dafadar*, in advance. Dated 9 October 1857.

P 227. *Murawwat Muhammad Khan,* Bakhshi*, to Than Singh, Treasurer.* An amount of Rs. 18, Bhopali coin, is required to pay the salaries of 4 *kahars* who are on command. Their salaries for the month of September have been deposited in the treasury. The said amount may be paid to Shaikh Habib Allah. Dated 8 October 1857.

P 229. *Murawwat Muhammad Khan,* Bakhshi*, to Than Singh, Treasurer.* An amount of Rs. 5 is required to purchase the medicines needed by the *bakhshi* at the time of departure. The said amount will be adjusted at the time of clearance. Dated 8 October 1857.

P 231. *Sikandar Muhammad Khan, Agenty II, to Than Singh, Treasurer.* An amount of Rs. 12/12/7, Bhopali coin, is required to meet the expenses of the goods that will be needed by Bakhshi Murawwat Muhammad Khan at the time of his departure. Dated 12October 1857.

P 233. *Sikandar Muhammad Khan, Agenty II, to Than Singh, Treasurer.* An amount of *5 anna* 3 *pai* may be paid from the deposits of Kanji. The said amount will be adjusted at the time of clearance. Dated 13 October 1857.

P 235. *Sikandar Muhammad Khan, Agenty II, to Than Singh, Treasurer.* An amount of Rs. 145, Bhopali coin, may be paid to select a horse rider, *risala* IV, as made by the selection committee. The said amount will be adjusted at the time of clearance. Dated 5 November 1857.

P 237. *Sikandar Muhammad Khan, Agenty II, to Than Singh, Treasurer.* An amount of Rs. 9/4, Bhopali coin, is required to meet the expenses of the arsenal as per the details. The same may be provided and will be adjusted at the time of clearance. Dated 7 November 1857.

P 239. *Sikandar Muhammad Khan, Agenty II, to Than Singh, Treasurer.* An amount of Rs. 50, Bhopali coin, is required to meet the expenses of bullocks of the arsenal of army contingent Sehore. Directs him to provide the said amount. Dated 18 *Rabi* I, 1274 AH.

P 241. *Sikandar Muhammad Khan, Agenty II, to Than Singh, Treasurer.* An amount of Rs. 2, 892/15/4, Bhopali coin, in respect of salaries of the employees of Bhopal contingent, who are on the command of the Mhow cantonment, for the month of October 1857 is due. The same may be paid to them in advance. The amount will be reimbursed at the time of clearance. Dated 6 November 1857.

P 243. *Sikandar Muhammad Khan, Agenty II, to Than Singh, Treasurer.* An amount of Rs. 20 in respect of monthly salary of Narain Singh, *dafadar*, *risala* III, contingent of Sehore may be paid to him. Although it is against the rule but since he is going to take the command of Mhow, therefore, make full payment to him and nothing should be left. Takes surety that if any one asks, it will be his responsibility to respond to the same. Dated 19 *Rabi* I, 1274 AH.

P 245. *Bhawani Prasad to Than Singh, Treasurer.* An amount of Rs. 150, Bhopali coin, in respect of carrying grass for the bullocks of the arsenal under the *havaldari* of Sikandar Muhammad Khan, agenty II, is due. The same may be paid to him, which will be reimbursed by the government. Dated 11 *Jumada* I, 1274 AH.

P 247. *Bhawani Prasad to Than Singh, Treasurer.* An amount of Rs. 81 in respect of salaries of the employees for the month of October and November 1857 is due. The same may be paid and the said amount will be reimbursed by the government. Dated 24 *Jumada* I, 1274 AH.

P 249. Yaddasht, *Containing Details of the Amount which is Due for Payment of the Month of July 1857, as Reported By Hem Chand,* Gumashta *of Than Singh, Treasurer.*

P 251. *Murawwat Muhammad Khan, Bakhshi, to Than Singh, Treasurer.* An amount of Rs. 23/12/5 in respect of the cost of medicines, incurred during the month of July-September 1857 is due. The same may be reimbursed. Dated 13 *Zilhijja* 1273 AH.

P 253. *Murawwat Muhammad Khan, Bakhshi, to Than Singh, Treasurer.* An amount of Re. 1/14 in respect of rent of the bullocks of carriers of *havaldar* and the soldiers of *risala* II, going to Debipura, commanded by Havaldar Jiwan Singh, *dafadar* of the said *risala*, is due which may be paid to him. Dated 3 *Zilhijja* 1273 AH.

P 255. *Murawwat Muhammad Khan, Bakhshi, to Than Singh, Treasurer.* An amount of Rs. 9/8 is due in respect of rent of carriers of goods of *havaldars* and soldiers going to Berasia. The same may be paid. Dated 24 *Ziqada* 1273 AH.

P 257. *Murawwat Muhammad Khan, Bakhshi, to Than Singh, Treasurer.* An amount of Re. 1/14 in respect of rent of the bullocks of carriers is due which may be paid. Dated 29 *Ziqada* 1273 AH.

P 259. *Murawwat Muhammad Khan, Bakhshi, to Than Singh, Treasurer.* An expenditure of Rs. 5/20 incurred on the contingent of Bhopal army, as reported by Udhar Singh is sent to him. The said amount may be provided to him and the receipt is to be obtained from him. Dated 23 *Ziqada* 1273 AH.

File No. 260
Box No. 13
No. of Documents 13

Notification of Central India Agenty Giving Amnesty to those who Took Part in the Mutiny

PP 1-2. Contents

PP 3-4. *Bhawani Prasad to Nawwab Sikandar Begam.*

Sends a copy of *Rubakar* received from the office of the Agent, Central India, along with a copy of the notification issued by the orders of the Governor-General, giving amnesty to those who took part in the mutiny but they were not the servants of the government or killers of English officials and that they are not the chiefs of Bundelkhand and Central India. Dated 1 *Zilhijja* 1274 AH (13 July 1858).

It contains the order that the letter, the *rubakar* and the notification may be sent to Muhammad Raza Husain, deputy *madar al-maham,* directing him to get published 728 copies from *matba' Sikandari*, the notification issued under the seal of the government to Ghulam Murtaza Khan, *kamdar*, Deorhi Khas, and send them to the government. A copy of the order may also be sent to Bhawani Prasad, *wakil*, for information. Dated 3 *Zilhijja* 1274 AH (15 July 1858).

PP 5-6. Rubakar *Issued from the office of Sir Robert Hamilton, the Agent to the Governor-General, Central India*. The town of Kalpi was the centre of the insurgents which was conquered. The British army, under the command of Major Henderson and Major Wellock, took a round of all the adjoining districts and found no sign of insurgency in the region of Bundelkhand. Although they tried to create disturbances in other places, but with the victory of Gwalior they were totally suppressed. In view of this, a notification is issued that, except some, all others of the region of Bundelkhand and Central India who were involved in insurgency are given amnesty by the Governor-General. All such persons should return to their homes. Dated 4 July 1858.

P 7. *Notification Issued from the office of Agent to the Governor-General, Central India, under the Session of Sir Robert Hamilton*. The Governor-General has sent an order through the Chief Secretary, dated 22 June 1858, in response to the letters of this office that a notification may be issued in the region of Bundelkhand and Central

India, giving amnesty to all who were involved in insurgency except those who were the servants of the government, those who killed any British man, and those who are the notified chiefs of the insurgents. In view of this, a notification is issued that except the above three categories, all others of the region of Bundelkhand and Central India who were involved in insurgency are given amnesty by the Governor-General. All such persons should return to their homes. Dated 4 July 1858.

P 9. Parwana *of Nawwab Sikandar Begam to Ghulam Murtaza Khan.* Informs about the notification and *rubakar* issued from the office of the Agent to the Governor-General, Central India, under the session of Sir Robert Hamilton, dated 4 July 1858. The notification is that Kalpi, which was the center of insurgents, was conqurered. The British army, under the command of Major Henderson and Major Wellock, took a round of all the adjoining districts and found no sign of insurgency in the region of Bundelkhand. Although they tried to create disturbances in other places, but with the victory of Gwalior they were totally suppressed. In view of this, the kindness of the Governor General demanded his foregiveness for all those who though participated in insurgency but did not kill any British nor were the servants of the government or the chiefs of the insurgents and has sent a letter through the Chief Secretary, dated 22 June 1858, for issuing a notification in this connection. So a notification is issued that the Governor-General has given amnesty to all who were involved in insurgency in Bundelkhand and Central India but did not kill any British and that he was not a servant of the government or a chief of the insurgents. Directs him to notify the notification and the *rubakar* in his jurisdiction for compliance by all. Dated 3 *Zilhijja* 1274 AH.

PP 11-12. *Muhammad Raza Husain to Nawwab Sikandar Begam.* Informs as ordered, dated 3 *Zilhijja* 1274 AH, which is regarding the amnesty to those who took part in insurgency but he is not a killer of a British and that he is not a servant of the government, 728 notifications have been published from *matba' Sikandari* and on 125 notifications, names of all the *Jagirdars* are mentioned. All these, besides 583 notifications, are sent to her. Dated 24 *Zilhijja* 1274 AH.

PP 13-14. *Shahzad Rai,* Thanadar *of Mahalpur, to Nawwab Sikandar Begam.* On the previous day a notification was received from the Governor-General issued in accordance to the orders of Queen of England granting amnesty to all the insurgents and miscreants, and about their rehabilitation in their respective places. Informs that all the inhabitants of the region would be informed of the notification. But whether the insurgents who were the servants of Fazil Muhammad Khan and Adil Muhammad Khan should also be rehabilitated as many at the time of battle at Rajghati, Garhi and Rahatgarh had fled to Bhilsa and other places and they are afraid of their arrest whence they enter in the region. Requests for orders in the matter. Dated 17 *Rabi* I, 1275 AH.

PP 15-16. Tahsildar *of Udaipura to Nawwab Sikandar Begam.* Informs as reported by Harchand Singh, *jamadar*, that the buffalows and other goods which were in the company of the army are with *kunjadgars* of qasba Udaipura, who he called and enquired about the goods. First they refused and later accepted that the goods were in their possession but later on they were destroyed and nothing was left with them. His statement is sent to her. Dated 17 *Rabi* I, 1275 AH.

It contains the order that the letter along with the list of goods may be sent to Paltu Lal, *muhafiz-i daftar-i insha*, for inclusion in the register and keeping in the *daftar*. A copy of the papers may be sent to Bhawani Prasad, *wakil*, and to enquire from the Political Agent earlier the practice was that if anyone from the peasants or employees of Bhopal government was found with the insurgent forces and then returned back with the goods of loot, was arrested. But now there is a notification that such persons should not be harassed. So they have not been arrested. Asks him to enquire from the Political Agent whether the goods of loot too should not be recovered from them. Dated 23 *Jumada* I, 1275 AH.

PP 17-18. *Statement of Harchand Singh*, Jamadar. States that after loading grains from *qasba* Udaipura, he was moving forward. On the way, the goods were lost. It is evident that the goods are with *kunjadgars* of Udaipura who should be enquired. Thereafter, Deo Chand, *kunjadgar*, was called but he did not disclose anything. Then he called Ghaman, *kunjadgar*, who stated that he and other *kunjadgars* brought buffalows from the camp of the army besides utensils, like plate, glass, bowls, etc.

PP 19-20. *Daulat Rai,* Nazim-i Mashriq*, to Nawwab Sikandar Begam.* Refers to the letter of Ganga Sahai, *thanadar* of Chhatari, dated 26 *Jumada* II, 1275 AH, informing that Hasan Khan, Chhotey Khan and others, the dwellers of Chhatari who during the uprising went to Bhilsa and joined the services of Raja of Shaikhpur, a rebel of the British territory, came back and settled in their houses, after hearing the notification of the Governor-General which is in reference to the orders of the Queen, giving foregivness. They did not possess any arm. The same is reported to her. Dated 10 *Rajab* 1275 AH.

PP 21-2. *Ganga Sahai,* Thanadar *of* Pargana *Chhatari, to Daulat Rai,* Nazim-i Mashriq. In reference to the notification of the Governor-General, as ordered by the Queen, which is in regard to the forgiveness to those who were involved in the insurgency during the uprising, he has informed through his letter, dated 22 *Jumada* I, 1275 AH, and hopes that those who from the *ilaqa* had fled would come back and settle in their place of residence. Informs that the following persons, the dwellers of this place who had joined the service of the Maharaja of Gwalior in the region of Bhilsa came back and resettled in their houses, as notified. They are Hasan Khan, Chhotey Khan, Imam Khan, Shaikh Khuda Bakhsh, Amir Ali, Munir Khan and others. Dated 11 *Jumada* II, 1275 AH.

P 23. *Shahzad Rai,* Thanadar *of Mahalpur, to Nawwab Sikandar Begam.* Refers to her order, as mentioned in his letter, dated 26 *Jumada* I, 1275 AH in reference to the notification by the Queen that the insurgents, and the companions of Fazil Muhammad Khan and Adil Muhammad Khan, should be allowed to rehabilitate in their place of residence and there should not be any hinderance in their settlement and to inform about their names and their crime. Informs as reffered in the notification, 8 persons of *pargana* Mahalpur who had joined Fazil Muhammad Khan and Adil Muhammad Khan have resettled in their place of residence. The details of their names, the crime they committed, and their place of residence is sent to her. Dated 15 *Rabi* I, 1276 AH/1266 Fasli/1859 CE.

P 25. Fard, *Containing Names of those Dwellers of Mahalpur who during the Uprising Joined Fazil Muhammad Khan and Adil Muhammad Khan and Became their Employees, and as Ordered they were Rehabilitated in the* Pargana. They were Kishan Chand, Chaturbhuj, Khaman Patel, Bajram Patel, Sohna, Pradip Danger, Chirag Ali and Khwaja Bakhsh. Dated 15 *Rabi* I, 1276 AH.

File No. 261
Box No. 13
No. of Documents 17

Captivity of Hyder Muhammad Khan, Nawwab of Pathari

PP 1-3. Contents

PP 5-6. *Bhawani Prasad to Nawwab Sikandar Begam.* Informs, as ordered, recorded on the top of the letter of Ghulam Murtaza Khan, *kamdar,* Deorhi Khas, dated

26 *Shawwal* 1274 AH, he presented the letter before the Political Agent on 10 *Ziqada* 1274 AH at Murar cantonment explaining that in either of the two letters, he did not mention even a word to keep *Nawwab* Hyder Muhammad Khan under house arrest. If the Political Agent desires that the house in which the said *Nawwab* is residing should be put under surveillance. The Political Agent wrote on the letter "*ittala'shud*" (got informed). Meanwhile, a request of the *wakil* of Pathari has been received, expressing concern about the well-being of the *Nawwab* in the fort of Fatahgarh and allowing him to live in the city. The same is presented before her. Dated 4 *Zilhijja* 1274 AH (16 July 1858).

P 7. *The Political Agent to Bhawani Prasad.* Refers to the letter of Chhotey Singh, *wakil* of *Nawwab* of Pathari, in reference to the letter of the *Nawwab* that he is writing him again and again and that he has sent a letter to the *wakil* of Bhopal that *Nawwab* Hyder Khan may be kept in the city of Bhopal and not in the fort of Fatahgarh. But he is still in the fort and is suffering. The *wakil* has requested to make arrangement for the *Nawwab* in the city. Directs him to reply why his order is not executed. Dated 4 July 1858.

PP 11-12. *Murawwat Muhammad Khan to Nawwab Sikandar Begam.* Refers to her order, dated 7 *Zilhijja* 1274 AH, recorded on the letter of Bhawani Prasad, *wakil-i sarkar*, directing that if there is no harm, *Nawwab* Hyder Muhammad Khan, Pathariwala and his family, as per the suggestion of Ghulam Murtaza Khan may be kept in the house of late Muhammad Ali Khan, *jamadar*, situating in the city of Bhopal. Informs though there is no harm in keeping *Nawwab* Hyder Muhammad Khan and his family in the house of late Muhammad Ali Khan, *jamadar*, but her order is to keep him under house arrest which requires putting guards to keep a watch on him. But in that house there is no space to put guards to keep a watch on him. Dated 13 *Zilhijja* 1274 AH.

P 13. *Murawwat Muhammad Khan to Nawwab Sikandar Begam.* Refers to the orders of Bhawani Singh, *chobdar*, that *Nawwab* Hyder Muhammad Khan has not yet been called in the city. Says he replied to him that the house of Muhammad Ali Khan is not too big to accommodate the guards of the *jamadars*. Dated 16 *Zilhijja* 1274 AH.

P 15. *Ghulam Murtaza Khan to Nawwab Sikandar Begam.* Refers to her order asking as to why her order regarding the rehabilitation of *Nawwab* Hyder Muhammad Khan Pathariwala in Bhopal was not executed. Says, it was ordered that *Nawwab* Hyder Muhammad Khan should be kept under house arrest and he is yet to find out a suitable house to keep him there.

P 17. Parwana *of Nawwab Sikandar Begam to Bhawani Prasad. Nawwab* Hyder Muhammad Khan is under house arrest as ordered by the Political Agent. Now the Political Agent has returned to Sehore, it seems not suitable to keep him further in Bhopal. Directs him to bring the matter into the notice of Political Agent and inform her.

P 19. *Bhawani Prasad to Nawwab Sikandar Begam.* Sends the *parwana* of the Political Agent, dated 11 August 1858, received in response to his letter, dated 26 *Zilhijja* 1275 AH, informing that in the matter of *Nawwab* Hyder Muhammad Khan Pathariwala he has written to the Office of the Agent to Central India and has directed that until the reeipt of the reply, the *Nawwab* should be kept there. Dated 1 *Muharram* 1275 AH (12 August 1858).

P 21. Parwana *of Nawwab Sikandar Begam to Bhawani Prasad. Nawwab* Hyder Muhammad Khan Pathariwala, as per the instruction of the Political Agent, Richards is under house arrest in Bhopal. Now the Political Agent has arrived in Sehore, it does not seem fit for her to keep the said *Nawwab* under house arrest in Bhopal. If he desires, he may be sent there and he may do whatever he likes to do in the matter of his house arrest. Directs him to bring the matter into the notice of the Political Agent and his reply may be communicated to her. Dated 26 *Zilhijja* 1274 AH.

P 23. *The Political Agent to Bhawani Prasad.* Refers to his letter in regard to *Nawwab* Hyder Muhammad Khan Pathariwala, who is under house arrest as per the instruction of the Agenty. Now the Political Agent has arrived in Sehore, if desired the said *Nawwab* may be sent to Sehore as it does not seem fit to keep him there. Informs in regard to *Nawwab* Hyder Muhammad Khan Pathariwala, the Office of the Agent, Central India, has been informed. Until a reply is received from there, he may be kept in Bhopal. Dated 11 August 1858.

P 25. *Bhawani Prasad to Nawwab Sikandar Begam.* Sends the *parwana* of the Political Agent, dated 16 August 1858, which is in reference to a letter in English received from the Agent to the Governor-General, Central India, directing that *Nawwab* Pathariwala may be brought to Sehore. Requests for further orders in this regard. Dated 16 August 1858.

P 27. *The Political Agent to Bhawani Prasad.* In accordance to the letter in English, dated 13 August 1858 received from Indore from the Agent to the Governor General, Central India, he is directed to present *Nawwab* of Pathariwala in Sehore. Dated 16 August 1858.

P 29. *Nawwab Sikandar Begam to Murawwat Muhammad Khan.* From the *Parwana* of the Political Agent Richards, to Munshi Bhawani Prasad, dated 16 August 1858, it is learnt that in accordance to the letter in English of the Agent to the Governor General, Central India, *Nawwab* Pathariwala is to be presented in Sehore. Directs him to provide a guard to the *Nawwab* and present him before Bhawani Prasad and inform her accordingly. Dated 7 *Muharram* 1275 AH.

P 31. *Bakhshi Murawwat Muhammad Khan to Nawwab Sikandar Begam.* Informs as ordered, *Nawwab* Hyder

Muhammad Khan has been sent to Sehore under proper security.

P 33. *Murawwat Muhammad Khan to Nawwab Sikandar Begam.* Informs that in accordance to her *parwana,* dated 7 *Muharram* 1275 AH, *Nawwab* Hyder Muhammad Khan Pathariwala under the security of soldiers from the battalion of Alhar Khan, *jamadar*, has been sent to Munshi Bhawani Prasad. Dated 8 *Muharram* 1275 AH.

P 35. *Bhawani Prasad to Nawwab Sikandar Begam.* Refers to her order, dated 11 *Muharram* 1275 AH, as recorded in his letter, dated 9 *Muharram* 1275 AH which is in regard to *Nawwab* Hyder Muhammad Khan Pathariwala. Informs that he met the Political Agent and told him about the secret content of the letter. He said that the *Nawwab* had clearly expressed and what the need was to keep it secret and said to hand it over to his office. He replied, ok. Requests if desired, he may submit it to the Political Agent through his letter. There is also a report that the next day the case of *Nawwab* Hyder Muhammad Khan would be presented before the Political Agent. If he desires, he would put the case before him. Dated 15 *Muharram* 1275 AH (26August 1858).

P 37. *Muhammad Sa'd al-Din,* Muhtamim, Adalat-i Faujdari, *to Nawwab Sikandar Begam.* Refers to the letter of Bakhshi Murawwat Muhammad Khan, dated 13 *Zilhijja* 1274 AH, informing that there is no problem in keeping *Nawwab* Hyder Muhammad Khan Pathariwala in the house of Muhammad Ali Khan, *jamadar*, but there is no space for the soldiers who would keep watch on him and her order to him to explain the matter. Informs when the said *Nawwab* was arrested he was put in the fort of Fatahgarh under house arrest. Thereafter, as desired by the Political Agent, he was sent to Sehore. So there was no requirement of the house of Ahmad Ali Khan to keep him there. Dated 10 *Shawwal* 1275 AH.

File No. 262
Box No. 13
No. of Documents 19

Deployment of Bhopal Army at Lalitpur Khas, a British Territory

PP 1-7. Contents

P 9. *Muhammad Hasan Khan to Nawwab Sikandar Khan*. Informs that day, 8 foot-soldiers and 3 *sawars* who were left behind were sent to Lalitpur, and Mattu Khan and Abd al-Aziz Khan, *risaldars*, were directed to inform the officer after their arrival.

P 15. *Order from the Office of Assistant Superintendent, Shahgarh to Muhamad Sae'd Khan,* Thanadar *of Malthun.* Refers to his letter, dated 14 July 1858, and informs, as ordered by the British at Shahgarh that at Madawrah 100 *sawars* and 200 foot-soldiers of Bhopal army who are going to Lalitpur are staying at Malthun. Directs him to tell the *sawars* and foot-soldiers to reach Mahur before the *tahsildar* of Lalitpur. Dated 1 July 1858.

P 17. *'Abd al-Karim Ansari to Nawwab Sikandar Begam.* Informs that the papers relating to the *sawars* of *risala* IV of the *risala* of Mattu Khan, *risaldar*, who were at Bhopal before going to Lalitpur were left there. Informs the same is being sent to Lalitpur before Mattu Khan to present it before the British which is regarding their distribution of work in the territory of the British. Dated 8 *Zilhijja* 1274 AH.

P 19. Yaddasht, *Containing Names of the* Sawars *of* Risala *IV, under* Risaldar *Mattu Khan, Going to Lalitpur. Dated 6* Zilhijja *1274 AH.*

P 21. *Muhammad Abd al-Aziz Khan and Mattu Khan,* Risaldars, *to Nawwab Sikandar Begam.* Expressing their apology as the letter which they had drafted in the light of the *parwana* of Assistant Superintendent of Madawrah is left behind and other papers were sent instead. The said letter is being sent herewith. Dated 8 *Zilhijja* 1274 AH.

P 23. *'Abd al-Karim Ansari to Nawwab Sikandar Begam.* Informs the previous day, i.e. on 23 *Zilhijjar* 1274 AH (3August 1858), he learnt from the letter of Muhammad Abd al-Aziz Khan, *risaldar*, that the *sawars* and foot-soldiers who are going to Lalitpur as per the orders of British at Shahgarh are still at Malthun. The travellers coming from Malthun say that they would soon leave for Lalitpur. Dated 23 *Zilhijja* 1274 AH (4 August 1858).

PP 25-6. *Bhawani Prasad to Nawwab Sikandar Begam.* Informs that day the Political Agent conveyed him through Lal Singh, *chobdar*, that a letter has been received from the Agent to the Governor General, Central India, from Shahjahanpur who has enquired about the number of *sawars* and foot-soldiers of Bhopal army who have been deployed at Lalitpur under the command of Mattu Khan, *risaldar*. The information to this effect was to be sent immediately directing him to report how many *sawars* and foot-soldiers went to Lalitpur in the company of Mattu Khan. Informs in reply to that he said that from all correspondences of the *Nawwab* it is clear, and also a list containing details of employees of Bhopal State that has been put day before yesterday. It is evident from these sources that about 1,000 soldiers of Bhopal army have been deployed under the British territory as per the orders of the Agent to the Governor General, Central India. But there is no mention of the *sawars* and foot-soldiers separately. Requests if the details of *sawars* and foot-soldiers deployed in Bundelkhand with the name of their chiefs could be made available so that he may be able to put it before the Political Agent. Dated 26 *Zilhijja* 1274 AH (7 August 1858).

P 27. *Jadun Rai to Nawwab Sikandar Begam.* Refers to her order in reference to the request of Bhawani Prasad, *wakil*, dated 26 *Zilhijja* 1274 AH to submit the details of *sawars* and foot-soldiers as per the record. Informs there is no record of the *sawars* and foot-soldiers. Dated 27 *Zilhijja* 1274 AH (8 August 1858).

P 29. Yaddasht, *Containing Details of* Sawars *and Foot Soldiers, Deployed at Lalitpur.* These are *risala* II of Muhammad Abd al-Aziz Khan and *risala* IV of Mattu Khan, *risaldar*, and the battalions of Wazir Khan, *jamadar*, and Chhotey Ram, *dafadar*. Dated 27 *Zilhijja* 1274 AH (8 August 1858).

P 31. *Nawwab Sikandar Begam to Muhammad Abd al-Aziz Khan and Mattu Khan,* Risaldars. From the letter of Bhawani Prasad, *wakil*, it is learnt that the Agent to the Governor-General, Central India, has asked about the number of *sawars* and foot-soldiers of Bhopal army who are deployed at Lalitpur and that the information to this effect is to be sent immediately. Directs them to submit the list of all the details of *sawars* and foot-soldiers of Bhopal army who are deployed there inclusive of their names and place of posting. Dated 28 *Zilhijja* 1274 AH (9 August 1858).

PP 33-4. *Muhammad Abd al-Aziz Khan and Mattu Khan,* Risaldars, *to Nawwab Sikandar Begam.* Informs about the *parwana* of the British in the name of Muhammad Sa'ed Khan, *thanadar* of Malthun, directing him to send 100 *sawars* and 200 foot-soldiers of the Bhopal army stationed at Malthun to Banpur before the *tahsildar* of Lalitpur. A copy of that order obtained from *thana* is sent to her. Informs they, in accordance to the *parwana*, marched to Banpur on 28 *Zilhijja* 1275 AH. The report, thereafter, will be sent from Banpur. Informs the District Collector of Lalitpur has not yet arrived at Lalitpur. Dated 28 *Zilhijja* 1274 AH (9 August 1858).

PP 35-6. *Muhammad Abd al-Aziz Khan and Mattu Khan,* Risaldars, *to Nawwab Sikandar Begam.* Informs on 27 *Zilhijja* 1274 AH, they left Malthun as ordered by the British Officer at Madawrah and arrived at Banpur before the *tahsildar* of Lalitpur. Informs the next day they would reach Lalitpur in the company of *tahsildar* of Lalitpur. The letter issued from the office of Shahgarh, which is regarding their departure, they obtained a copy of it from the *thanadar* and the same is enclosed along with this letter. Dated 29 *Zilhijja* 1274 AH (10 August 1858).

P 37. *Order from the Office of Assistant Superintendent, Shahgarh to Muhammad Sae'd Khan,* Thanadar *of Malthun.* In reference to an order, he is informed that Mattu Khan and Muhammad Abd al-Aziz Khan, *risaldars*, who came from Bhopal to go to Lalitpur are there. Directs him to allow them to go to Banpur where the *tahsildar* of Lalitpur is. Dated 6 August 1858.

PP 39-40. *Bhawani Prasad to Nawwab Sikandar Begam.* Sends the *Parwana* of the Political Agent, dated 11 August 1858, who has enquired about how many personnel of Bhopal army have been deployed at Lalitpur Khas and who is their chief and that the Agent to the Governor General is happy to know about the deployment of the Bhopal army there as the place is good. Dated 1 *Muharram* 1275 AH (12 August 1858).

P 41. *The Political Agent to Bhawani Prasad.* Wants to know how many personnel of Bhopal army have been deployed at Lalitpur Khas and who their chief is. Directs him to make an enquiry into this and inform him accordingly. Also informs that the Agent to the Governor General is happy to know about the deployment of the Bhopal army there as the place is good. Dated 11 August 1858.

PP 43-4. *Muhammad Abd al-Aziz Khan and Mattu Khan,* Risaldars, *to Nawwab Sikandar Begam.* Informs about the insurgent forces that are at a distance of 2 or 3 *curoh* in different *mauzas*. Assures that whenever they would enter in their jurisdiction, they would get a befitting reply.

P 45. *Muhammad Abd al-Aziz Khan and Mattu Khan,* Risaldars, *to Nawwab Sikandar Begam.* Inform that day; the 9th *Muharram* 1275 AH, a letter of *tahsildar* of Lalitpur, dated 20 August 1858 was received. He has communicated that the District Collector would arrive there on 18th of the month and as desired by him they are directed to send 25 *sawars* in the morning so that they may be present at Tahri to welcome him. Inform that 25 *sawars* have been sent to Tahri on 10 *Muharram* 1275 AH. Dated 9 *Muharram* 1275 AH (20 August 1858).

P 47. *Bhawani Prasad to Nawwab Sikandar Begam.* Informs as ordered, dated 28 *Zilhijja* 1274 AH, he put before the Political Agent the details of the *sawars* and artillery deployed at Lalitpur. The *parwana* of the Political Agent, dated 19 August 1858, received in reply is sent to her. Dated 9 *Muharram* 1275 AH (20 August 1858).

File No. 263
Box No. 13
No. of Documents 20

Deployment of Troops on the Police Post at Sanchi Kanakhera

PP 1-3. Contents

P 5. *Gist of the Letter of Bhawani Prasad to the Government.* Refers to her *parwana,* dated 21 *Zilhijja* 1275 AH, which states that about 3,000 or 4,000 or 5, 000 forces of Peshwa have arrived Agra; about the distribution of the royal army in district east; and to request for the commencement of forces from Mhow, etc. received through Shivlal, *chobdar*. Informs the *parwana* was presented before the Political Agent and the reply received from him is sent to her. Dated 24 *Zilhijja* 1275 AH.

It contains the order that the letter along with the *parwana* of the Political Agent, addressed to Bhawani Prasad, dated 21 *Zilhijja* 1275 AH, and her *parwana* to Bakhshi Murawwat Muhammad Khan, dated 26 *Zilhijja* 1275 AH, may be sent to Paltu Lal, *muhafiz- i daftar- i insha*, for inclusion in the register and keeping in the *daftar*. A copy of the order may be sent to Bhawani Prasad, communicating that as peace prevails in the *parganas* of Deori, Chhatari, Solwani and Chhatarpur, the companies of troops deployed in those *parganas* are withdrawn. After the arrival, these companies would be deployed under the command of Ghulam Husain Khan at check posts on the way to Bhilsa in the region of Bhopal so that they could manage the affairs there. Also, communicates that there is no reference in the letter of the Political Agent, dated 4 August 1858, addressed to him about the Bhopal army deployed in the British territory, whether they would remain there or should be dismantled. Directs him to bring the matter into the notice of the Political Agent and his reply may be communicated to her at the earliest. After receiving the reply, she would deploy Bakhshi Murawwat Muhammad Khan in Aunchh or in Ashta. The details of the Bhopal army deployed in the British territory were sent to him on 7 *Zilhijja* 1274 AH. There is no other copy of the aforesaid details in the royal office which could be sent to him. The matter may be brought to the notice of the Political Agent and his reply may be communicated to her. Dated 29 *Zilhijja* 1274 AH.

P 5. Parwana *of Nawwab Sikandar Begam to Murawwat Muhammad Khan*. Directs him to call back the Bhopal army stationed in *parganas* of Deori, Chhatari, Solwani and Mahalpur, as desired by the Political Agent in his *parwana* addressed to Munshi Bhawani Prasad, *wakil*, on 4 August 1858 and inform her accordingly. Dated 26 *Zilhijja* 1274 AH.

P 7. Parwana *of Nawwab Sikandar Begam to the* Thanadars *of District East.* Directs them to send back the battalion of artillery of Bhopal army, stationed at Deori. Dated 5 *Muharram* 1275 AH.

P 9. *Murawwat Muhammad Khan to Nawwab Sikandar Begam.* Informs as ordered, dated 26 *Zilhijja*1274 AH, he wrote a letter to Daulat Rai, *nazim-i mashriq*, to send back all four companies of the troops stationed at Deori, Chhatari, Solwani and Mahalpur under the district east. Informs that Hamir Singh, *jamadar*, stationed at

Mahalpur with his company has arrived with a letter of the *nazim*. Dated 5 *Muharram* 1275 AH.

P 11. *Ghulam Husain Khan, Agenty 1, to Nawwab Sikandar Begam*. Refers to her order as indicated on the top of the letter of Daulat Rai, *nazim-i mashriq,* that the royal army stationed at Deori, Chhatari, Solwani and Mahalpur has been called back to Bhopal, as peace prevails in those places and no danger persists anywhere, and that he should be ready to take these battalions under his command when these forces arrive, and should go to establish check post at Bhilsa on the way to Bhopal and manage the affairs there with these forces. He should be careful as the troops are so disciplined and organised that even a single soldier of the enemy fails to infiltrate inside the Bhopal State. If Adil Muhammad Khan or Aqil Muhammad Khan, the insurgents, fell in his hand he should not hesitate to arrest or kill them. Informs he along with his four battalions of troops is stationing on the police post at Bhilsa on the way to Bhopal, as directed to him to prevent the miscreants. The said place is adjacent to the garden of late Saiyid Sultan which is nearby to the city. If he is ordered to move somewhere else from that place, he would accomplish the order. Dated 6 *Muharram* 1275 AH.

P 13. *Orders of Nawwab Sikandar Begam As Recorded On The Letter of Bhawani Prasad*. A copy of the order may be sent to Bakhshi Murawwat Muhammad Khan communicating that it is known to her that the check post of Bhopal on the way to Bhilsa is at Sanchi Kanakhera, but where the check post of Bhopal on the way to Agra is and directing him to report about that check post and its respective distance from Bhopal. Dated 9 *Muharram* 1275 AH.

P 15. *Shahzad Rai,* Thanadar *of Mahalpur, to Nawwab Sikandar Begam*. Refers to her *parwana*, dated 5 *Muharram* 1275 AH, directing to send back the battalion stationed there to Bhopal. Informs the battalion of Hamir

Singh, *jamadar*, stationed there has been sent back to Bhopal on 1 *Muharram* 1275 AH with the orders of the *nazim* in reference to the order of the *bakhshi*. Hopes that the said battalion would have reached Bhopal. Dated 10 *Muharram* 1275 AH.

The Nawwab orders that the letter may be sent to Paltu Lal, *muhafiz-i daftar-i insha*, for inclusion in the register and keeping in the *daftar*. Besides, Bakhshi Murawwat Muhammad Khan may be conveyed that the moment the battalions of Mahalpur and Solwani arrive in Bhopal, they should be deployed at the check post of Bhopal on way to Bhilsa under the command of Ghulam Husain Khan. The troops of the battalion should be vigilant for the safety and security of that road. Dated 13 *Muharram* 1275 AH.

P 17. *Gist of the Letter of Murawwat Muhammad Khan to Nawwab Sikandar Begam*. Refers to her order as mentioned in the letter of Ghulam Husain Khan in regard to his request to establish check post, as the instruction would be given after the arrival of the battalions from the *mahals*. Further refers to her order, as given on his letter, dated 7 *Muharram* 1275 AH, that as and when the battalions of Solwani and Mahalpur come to Bhopal the post guards should be established on the way to Bhilsa and Ghulam Husain Khan would be the officer commander of that force. Informs that the battalion of Paratab Singh from Solwani and battalion of Hamir Singh from Mahalpur have arrived. Requests for orders as to which battalion should be given the command of Ghulam Husain Khan. Dated 12 *Muharram* 1275 AH.

The letter contains the order of the *Nawwab* that Bakhshi Murawwat Muhammad Khan should be communicated that she is not aware of the roadmap of Bhilsa and thus, she is unable to give any instruction about the deployment of these battalions on that road. Directs him to visit the place and report about the locations where the post guards of the forces are to be established. Dated 14 *Muharram* 1275 AH.

PP 19-20. *Murawwat Muhammad Khan to Nawwab Sikandar Begam*. Refers to her order, dated 14 *Muharram* 1275 AH, as mentioned on his letter directing him to visit the area in Bhilsa and report about the places where the post guard is to be established on the way to Bhopal. Informs he himself observed that the most suitable place to establish post guard is *mauza* Sanchi Kanakhera, situated on the border of Bhopal and also it is enroute to Agra. If allowed, he may go and establish the post guard there as it is the most suitable. Earlier, the order was that Ghulam Husain Khan, Agenty I, would manage the affairs there but then Haji Muhammad 'Abd al-Karim Ansari was given the responsibility to manage the affairs.

The Nawwab orders that the letter may be sent to to Paltu Lal, *Muhafiz-i daftar-i insha*, for inclusion in the register and keeping in the *daftar*. Besides, Bakhshi Murawwat Muhammad Khan may be conveyed that as soon as the battalion of Lal Singh, *jamadar,* arrives from Deori and the battalion of Paratab Singh, *jamadar*, from Solwani, he should carry the two battalions with him and establish police post at Sanchi Kanakhera, and Ghulam Husain Khan should be given the charge of that post. Dated 21 *Muharram* 1275 AH.

PP 21-2. *Murawwat Muhammad Khan to Nawwab Sikandar Begam*. Refers to her order, dated 11 *Muharram* 1275 AH, as recorded on the letter of Bhawani Prasad asking him to tell about the check posts of Bhopal on the way to Agra and about its distance. Explains that there are two ways to reach Agra. One is through Sanchi Kanakhera, a road that goes to Bhilsa. The other is through Harakḥera, a road that goes to Berasia. The distance of Agra via Sanchi Kanakhera is 11 *curoh*, while via Harakhera the distance is 7 *curoh*. Dated 18 *Muharram* 1275 AH.

It contains the order that the letter may be sent to Lala Paltu Lal, *muhafiz-i daftar-i insha*, for inclusion in the register and keeping in the *daftar*. A copy of the order may be sent to Bakhshi Murawwat Muhammad Khan, communicating that the battalion of Pratab Singh, *jamadar,* coming from Solwani and the battalion of Lal Singh, *jamadar*, coming from Deori should be deployed at Sanchi Kanakhera under the command of Ghulam Husain Khan, Agenty 1. The other two battalions coming from Sehore should be deployed at Harakhera, and Haji 'Abd al-Karim, Agenty III, when comes back from Siwans should be given the command of these two battalions and Hafiz Hasan Khan, *naib bakhshi* should be sent back to Sehore. Dated 18 *Muharram* 1275 AH.

PP 23-4. *Murawwat Muhammad Khan to Nawwab Sikandar Begam*. Informs that day, the 24th *Muharram* 1275 AH, as ordered through the letter of Shahzad Rai, *thanadar* of Mahalpur, he accompanying the battalions of Lal Singh and Pratab Singh, *jamadars*, came from Deori and Solwani and left for Sanchi Kanakhera to erect a check post there. Informs as he envisages, he should search a place which would be suitable for the battalion, safe from rain and free from trouble for the platoon of the carriers of buffalos and bullocks and the carts to save them from water and flood. Hopes for guidance in the matter. Dated 24 *Muharram* 1275 AH.

It contains the order that the letter may be sent to Lala Paltu Lal, *Muhafiz-i daftar-i insha* for inclusion in the register and keeping in the *daftar*. A copy of the order may be sent to Bakhshi Murawwat Muhammad Khan communicating that the two battalions carried by him to Sanchi Kanakhera should be stationed in a village adjoining Sanchi Kanakhera and when the roads are dried, the platoon would be sent. Dated 30 *Muharram* 1275 AH.

PP 25-6. *Murawwat Muhammad Khan to Nawwab Sikandar Begam*. Informs as ordered, recorded in his letter, dated 21 *Muharram* 1275 AH, the battalions of Pratab Singh and Lal Singh, *jamadars,* were deployed at check post of Sanchi Kanakhera on the road to Bhilsa. *Fard*, containing names of the soldiers, is presented before her. Dated 26 *Muharram* 1275 AH.

PP 27-8. Fard, *Containing Names of the Soldiers of the Battalions of Pratab Singh and Lal Singh,* Jamadars, *who are Put on Duty at the Check Post Erected at Sanchi Kanakhera on the Road to Bhilsa, Dated 26* Muharram *1275 AH.*

P 29. *Nawwab Sikandar Begam to Umrao Daulah, Baqi Muhammad Khan.* Informs that the battalions of Pratab Singh and Lal Singh, *jamadars*, have reached Sanchi Kanakhera on the road to Bhilsa which is under his jurisdiction. Hopes that he would instruct the *thanadar* of Gulgaon to ensure supply of *sarbrah-i rasad* to the soldiers of the battalions at reasonable rate and there sould be no negligence. Dated 30 *Muharram* 1275 AH.

P 31. *Nawwab Sikandar Begam to Pratab Singh and Lal Singh*, Jamadars. Informs of her letter to Umrao Daulah, Baqi Muhammad Khan, in regard to the supply of *sarbrah-i rasad* to the soldiers who have arrived at Sanchi Kanakhera on the road to Bhilsa. The *thanadar* of the said *Thana* would make supply of *sarbrah-i rasad* to them. Directs them to take from the *thanadar* whatever commodity they need and pay its reasonable price. Dated 30 *Muharram* 1275 AH.

P 33. *Murawwat Muhammad Khan to Nawwab Sikandar Begam*. Submits the list containing names of soldiers of the battalions of Pratab Singh and Lal Singh, *jamadars*, who have been deployed at Sanchi Kanakhera. Dated 2 *Safar* 1275 AH.

PP 35-6. Fard, *Containing Names of the Soldiers of the Battalions of Lal Singh and Pratab Singh,* Jamadars, *Deployed at Sanchi Kanakhera. Dated 27* Muharram *1275 AH.*

P 37. *Umrao Daulah, Baqi Muhammad Khan, to Nawwab Sikandar Begam.* Refers to her *shuqqa*, dated *30 Muharram* 1275 AH, directing him to instruct the *thanadar* of Gulgaon to supply *sarbrah-i rasad* to the soldiers of the battalions of Pratab Singh and Lal Singh, *jamadars*, who have been deployed on the road to Bhilsa and take reasonable price of the goods required by them. Informs as desired, he issued a *parwana* to Ajodhya Prasad, *thanadar* of Gulgaon, to supply *sarbrah-i rasad* to the soldiers of the battalions of Pratab Singh and Lal Singh, *jamadars,* deployed at Sanchi Kanakhera on road to Bhilsa. Hopes he would surely execute the order in the manner as desired. There would be no reluctance or negligence of duty. Dated 5 *Safar* 1275 AH.

PP 39-40. *Ghulam Husain Khan to Nawwab Sikandar Begam*. Informs that as ordered, dated 20 *Muharram* 1275 AH and 4 *Safar 1275* AH, he handed over both the *shahnais* and the magazines to Hasan Khan, *naib bakhshi* at Solwani, and came back. Further refers to her order to him, as recorded in the letter of Munshi Bhawani Prasad, *wakil-i sarkar*, dated 25 *Muharram* 1275 AH, informing that 3 days before, Bakhshi Murawwat Muhammad Khan along with two battalions had gone to establish a post at Sanchi Kanakhera, *ilaqa* Bhopal, which is the police post of Bhilsa and then he would return to Bhopal and Ghulam Husain Khan, Agenty I, would hold the command of that force at Sanchi Kanakhera so that if the insurgents pass through that region from the side of Bhilsa they could be dealt with by him. Besides, at Harakhera, *ilaqa* Bhopal, which is the police post of Berasia and Sironj, Haji 'Abd al-Karim has been deployed with two battalions so that if the insurgents enter from the side of Sironj, Haji 'Abd al-Karim could defeat them. Assures that whatever order he would receive after reaching Sanchi Kanakhera, he would execute it as he is now ready to go there. Dated 16 *Safar* 1275 AH.

It contains the order that the letter may be sent to Lala Paltu Lal, *Muhafiz-i daftar-i insha*, for inclusion in the register and keeping in the *daftar*. A copy of the order may be sent to Ghulam Husain Khan, Agenty I, communicating that there is no need for him to go to Sanchi Kanakhera as Bakhshi Murawwat Muhammad Khan has already gone there. He should stay in Bhopal. If there will be a need to send him elsewhere, he will be sent there. Dated 18 *Safar* 1275 AH.

File No. 264
Box No. 13
No. of Documents 3

Parwanas and Notifications Issued by Nawwab Sikandar Begam During the Month of Zilhijja 1274 AH (July-August 1858)

P 1. Parwana *of Nawwab Sikandar Begam Issued to Bhawani Prasad, Dated 7 Zilhijja 1274 AH (21 July 1858).* Sends a copy of *rubakar* issued from the office of the criminal court, dated 7 *Sha'ban* 1274 AH, which is regarding Lachhman and others, accused of being in the service of Fazil Muhammad Khan, and directs that the same may be presented before the Political Agent and to convey her of his response. The other details of the case would be known through the *rebakari* itself.

P 3. *Copy of the Letter of Nawwab Sikandar Begam Issued to Nawwab Baqi Muhammad Khan, Dated 12* Zilhijja *1274 AH (26 July 1858).* Refers to his letter, dated *5 Zilhijja* 1274 AH (19 July 1858) along with the letters of Ajodhya Prasad, *thanadar*, and Saiyid Ghulam Shah, acting *amil* of Gulgaon, informing that some persons were sent to *mauza* Pura Guna to enquire about the coming of Adil Muhammad Khan, and said that he had certainly come there and then he went to some other place but his relatives were there who were being watched by 10 to 12 artillery. Hopes that the informer who was sent to enquire about the arrival of Adil Muhammd Khan at Pura Guna and thereafter of his move to other place where his relatives were, would be known to her so that 2 or 3 more informers may be sent to enquire about the whereabouts of Adil Muhammad Khan.

P 5. Parwana *of Nawwab Sikandar Begam Issued to Bhawani Prasad, Dated 13* Zilhijja *1274 AH (27 July 1858).* Refers to his letter, dated 11 *Zilhijja* 1274 AH (25 July 1858), along with the *parwana* of the Political Agent, dated 22 *Zilhijja* 1274 AH (5 August 1858), which states that Ja'far Khan, Shaikh Nur Muhammad and Qadir Khan are the accused being in the service of Fazil Muhammad Khan besides other prisoners about whom a letter has been sent to Sagar. The prisoners would be sent there after receiving reply. The Bhopal prisons are over crowded with prisoners. There is no further space and if the Political Agent desires that these prisoners who are accused of committing crime in the territory of the British as proved by the criminal court should be sent there and to be kept in the prison at Sehore, and when they were demanded by the office at Sagar they should be sent there. If they are not demanded by the office of Sagar, the Political Agent would be better suited to decide about them. In that way, there will be no clash among the prisoners of Bhopal prison. Further, directs him to bring the matter into the notice of the Political Agent and communicate her of his reply.

File No. 265
Box No. 13
No. of Documents 3

Mutiny at Tonk and in the Adjoining Areas

PP 1-2. Contents

P 3. *Lala Munni Lal,* Muharrir, *to Nawwab Sikandar Begam.* Informs that day he received a letter of his uncle, Gaya Prasad, through English post. Since the letter pertains to the insurgents, the same is being sent to her. Dated 7 *Zilhijja* 1274 AH.

P 7. *Lala Munni Lal,* Muharrir, *to Nawwab Sikandar Begam.* Informs that day he received a letter from Sironj. The letter is about the battle of insurgents with Wazir al-Daulah, the ruler of Tonk. The same is sent to her. Dated 24 *Zilhijja* 1274 AH.

File No. 266
Box No. 13
No. of Documnets 8

Nawwab's Request to the Maulawis to Pray for the Longevity and Safety of Bhopal State from Trouble During the Uprising

PP 1-2. Contents

P 3. Parwanas *of Nawwab Sikandar Begam to* Maulawi *Abd al-Qayyum,* Maulawi *Zain al-Abedin and* Maulawi *Habib Allah Khan.* Requests them to pray to the Almighty on 13 *Ziqada* 1274 AH, day Friday, after Friday prayer for the safety of people of Bhopal and Bhopal State and for the safety and security of lives and properties of the inhabitants of Bhopal from the atrocities of the time and of the insurgents. Dated 9 *Ziqada* 1274 AH.

P 5. *Muhammad Habib Allah Khan to Nawwab Sikandar Begam.* Refers to her *Parwana*, dated 9 *Ziqada* 1274 AH, urging him to pray to the Almighty after Friday prayer for the safety of Bhopal and for the safety and security of lives and properties of the inhabitants from the atrocities of time and the atrocities of the insurgents. Assures that he would do as desired. May Allah save the State of Bhopal and its ruler as well as all her well-wishers and servants from the atrocities of the time and may keep them all under His protection. Dated 12 *Ziqada* 1274 AH.

PP 7-8. *Abd al-Qayyum to Nawwab Sikandar Begam.* Refers to her *Parwana*, urging him to pray to the Almighty on 13 *Ziqada* 1274 AH, day Friday, after the Friday prayer for the safety of Bhopal and for the safety and security of lives and properties of the inhabitants from the atrocities of time. States that he and all his followers have been praying and would be praying particularly, in these days of troubles for the safety of the Government and State and for all our brothers. Also conveys that on Friday, after Friday prayer, he would pray to Allah as desired. May the Almighty save the Government, the state and lives and properties of people from the atrocities of the time. Dated 12 *Ziqada* 1274 AH.

PP 9-10. *Zain al-Abedin, Son of Muhsin Ansari, to Nawwab Sikandar Begam.* Refers to her *Parwana*, dated 9 *Ziqada* 1274 AH, urging him to pray to the Almighty after the Friday prayer for the safety of Bhopal and for the safety and security of lives and properties of the inhabitants from the atrocities of time and atrocities of the insurgents. Assures that he would do as desired. Dated 10 *Ziqada* 1274 AH.

P 11. Parwanas *of Nawwab Sikandar Begam to* Maulawi *Abd Allah,* Maulawi *Zain Al-Abedin and* Maulawi *Abd-al Qayyum.* Urges them to go to the mosque and pray in the Court of Allah that He may save all the dwellers and the State of Bhopal from all atrocities and mishaps. Dated 12 *Safar* 1275 AH.

P 13. Maulawi *Abd Allah to Nawwab Sikandar Begam.* Informs that day, he went to the mosque of Ibrahim Khan and prayed to the Almighty along with all other prayer performers that He may save the dwellers and State of Bhopal from all mishaps and keep them in peace. Dated 15 *Safar* 1275 AH.

P 17. *Abd al-Qayyum to Nawwab Sikandar Begam.* Refers to her *Parwana* urging him to go to the mosque and pray in the Court of Allah that He may save all the dwellers and the State of Bhopal from the atrocities and mishaps. Informs that he did as desired. He prayed and has been praying to Allah, the Real Saviour, may save the dwellers, State of Bhopal and all brothers from mishaps and keep them in peace. Dated 15 *Safar* 1275 AH.

File No. 267
Box No. 13
No. of Documnets 4

On the Presence of Munna Lal, the Insurgent, Son of Qanungoi of Basodah in Basodah

P 1. Contents

P 3. *Ghulam Muhammad Khan,* Risaldar *from Bheglone, to Nawwab Sikandar Begam.* Informs that Munna, son of *Qanungoi* of *mahal* Basodah, earlier during the uprising was committing atrocities upon the dwellers of *mahal* Bheglone on behalf of Fazil Muhammad Khan. But for the last few months, he has parted ways with the latter due to Adil Muhammad Khan and Aqil Muhammad Khan, and now he is staying in Basodah and appears in some cases in the court at Basodah.

P 5. *Daulat Rai,* Nazim-i Mashriq, *to Nawwab Sikandar Begam.* Sends the letter received from Nur Khan, *tahsildar* of Bheglone, dated 7 *Zilhijja* 274 AH, informing the presence of Munna Lal in Basodah itself who is the son of *Qanungoi* of Basodah, responsible for committing atrocities and destroying *qasba* Bheglone in the company of Fazil Muhammad Khan. He also served Suroor Khan and Mangal Khan, who were the heads of insurgents in Basodah, with the request to arrest him from there. Dated 14 *Zilhijja* 274 AH.

PP 7-8. *Hazrat Nur Khan to Daulat Rai,* Nazim-i Mashriq. Informs that Munna Lal, son of *Qanungoi* of *mahal* Basodah, on behalf of Fazil Muhammad Khan, was a leading figure in *mahal* Bheglone and other villages where he was committing atrocities upon the inhabitants of the State.

File No. 268, A
Box No. 13
No. of Documents 23

Scarcity of Food-Grains in the Sadar Market of Sehore and Supply for Sarbrah-i Fauj Coming from Mhow

PP 1-6. Contents

PP 7-8. *Bhawani Prasad to Nawwab Sikandar Begam.* Sends the *Parwana* of the Political Agent, dated 26 July 1858, directing him to come back to Sehore immediately from Bhopal and secondly, as there is scarcity and price hike of food-grains in Sehore, the *zamindars* of the adjoining areas of Sehore should be asked to bring food-grains. Dated 16 *Zilhijja* 274 AH (27 July 1858).

It contains the order that the letter along with the *parwana* of the Political Agent, besides her letter and *parwana,* addressed to Faujdar Muhammad Khan and Ghulam Makhdum Khan, *Nazim,* dated 16 *Zilhijja* 1274

AH may be sent to Lala Paltu Lal, *muhafiz-i daftar-i insha* for inclusion in the register and keeping in the *daftar*. A copy of the order may be sent to Bhawani Prasad, communicating that as the Political Agent has direcetd him to come to Sehore from Bhopal, he should immediately go there. In regard to the dearness of food -grains in the cantonment and in Sehore, *parwanas* have been issued to Daulat Rai, *nazim-i mashriq*, Munshi Inayat Husain Khan, *nazim-i junub*, and Ghulam Makhdum Khan, *nazim-i maghrib*. The reply received from them would be communicated to him. Dated 16 *Zilhijja* 1274 (27 July 1858).

PP 9-10. *The Political Agent to Bhawani Prasad*. Expresses his concern that staying in Bhopal for him in those days is not good. Instead, he should seek permission from the *Nawwab* and come back to Sehore immediately. Also desires to request the *Nawwab* Begam to notify in and around Sehore in view of shortage of food-grains in those days in the Sadar and in the town of Sehore, the *zamindars* and the farmers would bring their food-grains, either on bullocks or on the heads of their porters. The only thing is that if they are just communicated. Also, urges him to ask Faujdar Muhammad Khan who has many shops in Sehore which are full of food-grains if there is any room available to use as a clinic. Dated 26 July 1858.

P 11. Parwana *of Nawwab Sikandar Begam to her three* Nazims. Refers to the *parwana* of the Political Agent to Munshi Bhawani Prasad, dated 26 July 1858, informing that there is a shortage of food-grains in the Sadar as well as in town of Sehore and if the *Nawwab* notifies in the surroundings of Sehore, the *zamindars* and farmers would bring food-grains on bullocks and on the heads of their porters. The only thing is that they should be communicated. Therefore, they are directed to inform the *zamindars* and farmers of the region. Dated 16 *Zilhijja* 1274 (27 July 1858).

P 13. *Nawwab Sikandar Begam to Faujdar Muhammad Khan.* Refers to the *parwana* of the Political Agent to Bhawani Prasad, dated 26 July 1858, directing him to urge *Faujdar* Muhammad Khan, who in Sehore nearby to his bungalow has many shops which are full of food-grains, if he could provide a room to use as a clinic. Directs him to send his reply to her for communicating the Political Agent. Dated 16 *Zilhijja* 1274 (27 July 1858).

PP 15-16. *Bhawani Prasad to Nawwab Sikandar Begam.* Informs that day in the morning, Major Richards, the Political Agent conveyed him through Ramhan, peon, about the scarcity of flour and gram in the cantonment area and in the town, and that the rate of flour in Sehore per maund is Rs. 16/or Rs. 15. 8, and the rate of gram in Sehore per maund is Rs. 14. But it is not available. Therefore, he is directed to request Nawwab Sikandar Begam to make arrangement of 5 maund flour and gram from *pargana* Bari and that it should not be taken in an informal manner. Says that the grains during the harvesting season reached in less quantity in Sehore and the British forces after a month would cross through this region, hence the arrangement of supply is a must and food-grain in *pargana* Bhawandi and Ichhawar is available in sufficient quantity. If some grains pour in Sehore through the *tahsildars,* it would help lessen the shortage of food-grains. Requests for orders as she may like. Dated 5 *Safar* 1275 AH (14 September 1858).

It contains the order that the letter, besides her letter and *parwana,* addressed to Muhammad Raza Husain, *nazim-i junub*, Ghulam Makhdum Khan, *nazim-i maghrib* and Bibi Sahiba, dated 7 *Safar* 1275 AH, may be sent to Lala Paltu Lal, *muhafiz-i daftar-i insha*, for inclusion in the register and keeping in the *daftar*. A copy of the order may be sent to Mansukh Rai, deputy *muhtamim*, *sair-i kul,* directing him that as soon as he receives her order, he should manage 5 maund flour as well as gram from Bhopal to sell in Sehore and inform her about it. Dated 7 *Safar* 1275 AH.

P 17. *Nawwab Sikandar Begam to Bibi Sahiba.* From the letter of Bhawani Prasad, *wakil*, dated 5 *Safar* 1275 AH, it is learnt that in the Sehore town and cantonment area of Sehore, flour and gram are not available. The Political Agent has ordered for providing 5 maund flour and gram. It is desired that 5 maund flour and gram from *pargana* Ichhawar, her *jagir*, may be sent to Sehore for sale and inform her about the quantity of food-grain which she would be able to arrange. The Political Agent has also said that the order should not be treated as informal but it should be immediately executed. Dated 7 *Safar* 1275 AH.

P 19. *Nawwab Sikandar Begam to Muhammad Raza Husain, Nazim.* From the letter of Bhawani Prasad, *wakil*, dated 5 *Safar* 1275 AH, it is learnt that in Sehore town and cantonment area of Sehore, flour and gram are not available. The Political Agent has ordered for providing 5 maund flour and gram. Directs him to provide 5 maund flour and gram from *pargana* Bharonda and Bari to Sehore for sale. The Political Agent has also said that the order should not be treated as informal but it should be immediately executed. Dated 7 *Safar* 1275 AH.

P 21. *Nawwab Sikandar Begam to Ghulam Makhdum Khan, Nazim.* From the letter of Bhawani Prasad, *wakil*, dated 5 *Safar* 1275 AH, it is learnt that in Sehore town and cantonment area of Sehore flour and gram are not available. The Political Agent has ordered for providing 5 maund flour and gram. Directs him to provide 5 maund flour and gram from *pargana* Doraha and Debipura to Sehore for sale. The Political Agent has also said that the order should not be treated as informal but should be immediately executed. Dated 7 *Safar* 1275 AH.

P 23. *Bibi Sahiba, Wife of Hakim Shahzad Masih, to Nawwab Sikandar Begam.* Acknowledges receipt of her letter, dated 7 *Safar* 1275 AH, issued in reference to the letter of Bhawani Prasad, *wakil*, dated 5 *Safar* 1275 AH, directing her to supply 5 *manasa* flour and gram from Ichhawar, her *jagir*, in Sehore, it is learnt that in Sehore town and cantonment area of Sehore, flour and gram are not available and the Political Agent has ordered for providing five maund flour and grain in Sehore. The Political Agent has also said that the order should not be treated as informal but it should immediately be executed. Informs that she issued a letter on 7 *Safar* 1275 AH to Hakim Khwan Disilva. The reply of Hakim Khwand Disilva, as received from him, is sent to her along with the letter of Seth Ramkishan. Dated 7 *Safar* 1275 AH.

P 25. *Hakim Khwand Disilva to Dulhan Sahiba*. Informs in accordance with her above order for supplying 5 *manasa* flour and gram to Sehore, he issued a letter to Seth Ramkishan. The reply received from him is sent to her. The orders received from her would be executed. Dated 7 *Safar* 1275 AH.

PP 27-8. *Seth Ramkishan of Ichhawar to Hakim Khwand Disilva,* Nazim. Refers his letter, dated 7 *Safar* 1275 AH, for supplying 5 *manasa* flour and gram in Sehore for sale as ordered by Nawwab Sikandar Begam to Dulhan Sahiba. Informs that to the best of his ability, what he could envisage he wants to bring forth. Due to the non-availability of carriers and the problem of paying tax of *sair,* it would be in the best of things to provide carrier and an exemption from paying *sair*. If these conditions are fulfilled, there would be no problem in executing the said order. Otherwise, it would be difficult to procure food-grain from outside, keeping in view the less production or minimum production of flour and gram in her territory (Dulhan Sahiba). Thus, except to procure from outside of the territory, as he thinks, there is no other option. Dated 7 *Safar* 1275 AH.

P 29. *Nawwab Sikandar Begam to Dulhan Sahiba.* Refers to her letter, dated 7 *Safar* 1275 AH, along with the letter of Hakim Khwan Disilva as well as the letter of Seth Ramkishan requesting for an exemption from paying taxes and for providing carrier. Tells her to intimate the Seth that it is not the royal government which is purchasing the food-grains, hence, there is no question of an exemption from the payment of taxes. In regard to providing carrier, it should be clear to the Seth that he should bring the food-grain in the market of Sehore and sell it on the market rate in addition to carriage charges and other taxes. Dated 12 *Safar* 1275 AH (17 September 1858).

P 31. *Bhawani Prasad to Nawwab Sikandar Begam.* Informs that the gram is not arriving in Sehore town or in the cantonment area, whereas the news of the arrival of British forces in Sehore is spreading. Requests that if an order is issued to the *muhtamim, sair i kul,* to providc gram and flour in Sehore immediately it would be good. Also, requests for issuing *parwana* to the *tahsildar* and *thanadar* of Sehore besides all other *tahsildars* for supplying the *saman-i rasad.* Dated 11 *Safar* 1275 AH (20 September 1858).

It contains the order that the letter may be sent to Lala Paltu Lal, *muhafiz-i daftar-i insha,* for inclusion in the register and keeping in the *daftar*. A copy of the order may be sent to Mansukh Rai, deputy *muhtamim, sair-i kul,* besides the *amils* and *thanadars* of Sehore, Doraha, Debipura, Shamshgarh, Dallod, Bharonda and Bari, directing them to send gram and flour i.e. *saman-i sarbrah-i rasad* to Sehore and inform her immediately about the name and quantity of goods. There should not be any delay; otherwise it would not be good for them. Dated 12 *Safar* 1275 AH (19 September 1858).

PP 33-4. *Bhawani Prasad to Nawwab Sikandar Begam.* Informs of the march of the Political Agent, Henry Richards, that day in the morning from Khandoh to Narsingarh, and that he would halt in *mauza* Basoria, *ilaqa* Narsingarh that day, and the next day he would be in Narsingarh. Informs that he with the permission of the *wakil* of government, returned to Sehore from Khandoh. Further adds that by 5. 30 in the morning heavy rain has started falling. There is a report that British army would directly come to Sehore from Narsingarh. Informs that the *Chaudhury* of the market came and said that there was total scarcity of gram in the market which should be managed urgently. There is a rumour that the insurgent forces arrived at Sironj but the *amil* of Sironj is fully prepared to meet any eventuality of the insurgents. Dated 11 *Safar* 1275 AH (20 September 1858).

It contains the order that the letter may be sent to Lala Paltu Lal, *muhafiz-i daftar-i insha*, for inclusion in the register and keeping in the *daftar*. A copy of the order may be sent to Madan Mohan, *naib wakil*, communicating that the Political Agent has not yet conveyed about the arrival of British forces in Sehore. Another copy of the order may be sent to Mansukh Rai, deputy *muhtamim*, *sair-i kul,* besides the *amils*, and *thanadars* of Sehore, Doraha, Debipura, Shamshgarh, Dallod, Bharonda and Bari, directing them to send gram and flour i.e. the *saman-i sarbrah-i rasad* to Sehore and inform her immediately about the name and quantity of goods. There should not be any delay; otherwise it would not be good for them. Dated 12 *Safar* 1275 AH (19 September 1858).

P 35. *Muhammad Abd al-Aziz Ansari,* Tahsildar *of Debipura, to Nawwab Sikandar Begam.* Refers to her order, dated 12 *Safar* 1275 AH, as mentioned on the top of the letter of Madan Mohan, *naib wakil,* directing him to provide flour and gram i.e. the *sarbrah-i rasad* in Sehore and inform her about the details of food-grain and its quantity. Informs that in the villages of *pargana* Debipura, flour and gram possessed by the *sahus* and *mustajirs* is not more than the quantity of seeds required at the time of sowing of the crop. Further informs that in accordance to her letter, dated 16 *Safar* 1275 AH, addressed to Shaikh Khuda Bakhsh, deputy *thanadar* of Debipura, the employees of *thana* and *mahal* are busy in making arrangement of rice and pulses in a quantity of 50 maund besides other items required for the *sarbrah-i rasad* of the forces of the Political Agent. In such a situation, supplying food-grain to Sehore due to non-availability is impossible. Dated 19 *Safar* 1275 AH (24 September 1858).

PP 37-8. *Shaikh Khuda Bakhsh, Deputy* Thanadar *of Debipura to Nawwab Sikandar Begam*. Refers to her order, dated 12 *Safar* 1275 AH, as mentioned on the top of the letter of Madan Mohan, *naib wakil,* directing him to send flour and gram as *sarbrah-i rasad* to Sehore and inform her about the details of food-grain along with its quantity. Informs earlier, food-grains loaded on 5 carriers as desired by Munshi Bhawani Prasad, *wakil-i Sarkar*, were sent to Berasia under the security of policemen of the *thana*. Besides, in accordance to her order, dated 16 *Safar* 1275 AH, he is busy managing the supply of flour, pulses, and garm i.e. *sarbrah-i rasad* for the army of the Political Agent. Besides, this as heard from Abd al-Aziz, *tahsildar* of Debipura, that for the year, the *sahus* and *mustajirs* of the *pargana* are not to hold flour and gram more than the requirement of seedling. Even in some villages the requirement of seedling too would not be fulfilled. There is no other source to obtain food-grain other than the *sahus* and *mustajirs* and thereafter to send them to Sehore. In this condition, due to the non-availability of food-grain, he is unable to send them to Sehore. Requests for orders to proceed further in the matter. Dated 20 *Safar* 1275 AH (25 September 1858).

P 39. *Bhawani Prasad to Nawwab Sikandar Begam.* Informs of a letter of Lala Bisheshar Dayal, *thanadar* of Ichhawar, informing that in accordance to the royal order about the food-grain required for the cantonment, 80 maund flour has been collected, and the merchants should be sent to purchase the food-grain at the rate of

Rs. 13/8. Informs he replied to him that the food-grain which is required for the cantonment may be sent there. The owners would be paid as per the market rate. Dated 25 *Safar* 1275 AH (4 October 1858).

PP 41-2. *Bisheshar Prasad,* Thanadar *of Ichhawar, to Bhawani Prasad.* Refers to the letter of Hakim Khwand Disilva, *nazim,* dated 10 *Safar* 1275 AH, issued in accordance with the royal letter for supplying 5 maund gram and flour in the market of cantonment of Sehore. Informs that he directed all the *sahus* of the *pargana* to make arrangement as ordered. All of them said that they did not possess more than that required for seedling. However, they managed 80 maund flour which is ready to be sent to Sehore. The cost of flour would be Rs. 16/8 to be carried from the *pargana* to Sehore, which will also include the tax and rent of carrier. If the traders come to the *pargana* and purchase directly from the owners, the cost would be Rs. 13/8. Asks if agreed, the grain may be sent to Sehore. Dated 2 October 1858.

PP 43-4. A letter in Hindi.

PP 45-6. *Bilas Rai,* Amil *of Sehore, to Nawwab Sikandar Begam.* Refers to her order, as mentioned on the top of the letter of Madan Mohan, *naib* of Munshi Bhawani Prasad, *wakil-i sarkar,* dated 11 *Safar* 1275 AH (20 September) directing that the letter may be sent to Lala Paltu Lal, *muhafiz-i daftar-i insha*, for inclusion in the register and keeping in the *daftar*. Another copy of the letter may be sent to Lala Mansukh Rai, deputy *muhtamim*, *sair-i kul*, besides the *amils* and *thanadars* of *pargana* Sehore, Doraha, Debipura, Shamshgarh, Dallod, Bharonda and Bari, directing them that as soon as they receive the order, they should send gram and flour i.e. *sarbrah-i rasad* to Sehore and inform her about the details of the commodity and its quantity. In case of any delay, it would be hazardous for them and the consequences would be bad. Says in accordance to her order, he called all the *mahajans* of Sehore proper and of the villages of Sehore and collected 50 maund gram and flour of the same quantity from them. Requests as to where these goods are to be sent and then he may try to collect more goods from other places as the order has been issued to acquire food-grain from other places as well. Informs since there is no government godown where the food-grains are to be stored therefore, no *mahajan* of Sehore proper, due to low price of food-grain, stores it and they say that in case of loss how they would meet the loss. Requests where the food-grains of *mahal* Sehore should to be sent. Dated 20 *Safar* 1275 AH (25 September 1858).

P 47. *Nawwab Sikandar Begam to Bibi Sahiba.* Sends the letter of Madan Mohan, *naib wakil*, dated 25 *Safar* 1275 AH and hopes that she would instruct the *thanadar* of Ichhawar to act as instructed in the letter. Dated 22 *Safar* 1275 AH.

P 49. *Karam Ali Hasan, Deputy* Thanadar, *to Nawwab Sikandar Begam.* Refers to her order, as mentioned on the top of the letter of Madan Mohan, *naib* of Munshi Bhawani Prasad, *wakil-i sarkar,* dated 11 *Safar* 1275 AH (20 September 1858). Informs that the *saman-i rasad,* loaded on the bufalloes and bullocks in consultation with the *tahsildar* of Bari were sent to Sehore to the *wakil*. The remaining goods of *rasad* would be sent later on after the availability of carriers. The details of goods are; flour, flour-garm, mustard oil, pulses, rice, salt, etc.

File No. 268, B
Box No. 13
No. of Documents 17

P 51. *Muluk Chand,* Tahsildar *of Bari, to Nawwab Sikandar Begam.* Refers to her order, dated 12 *Safar* 1275 AH, the *saman-i rasad* as per the details are sent to Sehore, loaded on buffaloes and bullocks. The remaining goods of *rasad* would be sent later on, after the availability of carrier. The details of goods are; flour, flour-garm, mustard oil, pulses, rice, salt, etc. Dated 27 *Safar* 1275 AH (2 October 1858).

P 53. *Saiyid Inayat Ali,* Thanadar *of Bharonda, to*

Nawwab Sikandar Begam. Informs that in accordance to her *parwana,* dated 7 *Safar* 1275 AH addressed to the *nazim* of district South, 189 maund flour and pulses have been sent to Bhawani Prasad through the merchants of the *pargana*. The other merchants are also being pursued to send their commodities there. Dated 1 *Rabi* 1275 AH.

P 55. *Ram Prasad,* Tahsildar *of Bharonda, to Nawwab Sikandar Begam.* Refers to her *parwana,* dated 7 *Safar* 1275 AH, addressed to the *nazim* of district South in reference to the letter of Bhawani Prasad, *wakil*, dated 5 *Safar* 1275 AH, and as desired by the Political Agent for supplying 5 maund flour and pulses from *mahal* Bharonda and Bari. Informs, in accordance to the order, flour and pulses as per the details have been sent to the cantonment of Sehore. The other merchants of the *ilaqa* are also being pursued to send their commodities there. Dated 1 *Rabi* I, 1275 AH.

P 57. *Muluk Chand*, Tahsildar *of* Pargana *Bari, to Nawwab Sikandar Begam.* Informs as ordered, dated 12 *Safar* 1275 AH, *saman-i rasad* as per the details are sent to Karam Ali, *thanadar* of *pargana* Bari, who sent it to Sehore.

P 59. *Karam Ali Husain, Deputy* Thanadar, *to Nawwab Sikandar Begam.* Informs as ordered, dated 12 *Safar* 1275 AH, *saman-i sarbrah-i rasad*, as per the details has been loaded on buffaloes and sent to Sehore to Madan Mohan, *naib wakil*.

P 61. *Muhammad Raza Husain*, Nazim-i Junub, *to Nawwab Sikandar Begam.* Refers to her *parwana,* dated 7 *Safar* 1275 AH, directing him to send 5 maund grain to Sehore cantonment and says that he wrote to the *tahsildar* of *pargana* Chhaner, Bharonda and Mardanpur, that are close to Sehore, to manage the grain. That day, he received the letter of Saiyid Burhan al-Din, *tahsildar* of *pargana* Chhaner, dated 5 *Rabi* I, 1275 AH, informing that he sent 280 maund grain loaded on carriers to Sehore to Bilas Rai, the *tahsildar* of Sehore.

PP 63-4. *Bhawani Prasad to Nawwab Sikandar Begam.* Informs of the receipt of the letter of Muhammad Safdar Ali Khan, *thanadar* of Debipura, dated 10 *Rabi* I, 1275 AH, along with 4 maund 19 *ser* goods of *rasad* like flour, pulses, salt, etc. under the protection of Ghaman Singh. The goods were sent to Bilas Rai, *tahsildar* of Sehore, and Kashiram, *Chaudhury* of the market, and the payment received by Ghaman Singh was sent to Debipura. Says he further stated that an amount of Rs. 3 as tax of goods is being obtained unlawfully from him and some losses incurred to him in respect to the goods. The letter of the *thanadar*, the list containing details of goods, and the letter of Bilas Rai are sent to her. Dated 15 *Rabi* I, 1275 AH (24 October 1858).

It contains the order that the letter and other three papers may be sent to Paltu Lal, *Muhafiz-i daftar-i insha*, for inclusion in the register and keeping in the *daftar*. A copy of the order may be sent to Radhey Kishan, *muhtamim*, *sair-i kul*, asking him to explain whether a sum of Rs. 3, obtained from the carriers in the name of tax, was collected forcibly or under the rules. An order will be issued after his reply. Dated 16 *Rabi* I, 1275 AH (25 October 1858).

P 65. *Bilas Rai to Bhawani Prasad.* Refers to his letter, dated 12 *Rabi* I, 1275 AH, directing him to sell the goods received from *pargana* Debipura on a reasonable price, sent by the *thanadar* through Ganesh and Kishore, the merchants. Informs that the goods like flour were sold through Kashiram, *Chaudhury* of the market, and the receipt was obtained, whereas pulses and salt were sold by the merchants themselves. Dated 13 *Rabi* I, 1275 AH.

PP 67-8. *Muhammad Safdar Ali Khan,* Thanadar *of Debipura, to Bhawani Prasad.* Informs as ordered, 9 bullocks loaded with goods of *rasad* like flour, pulses etc. under the protection of Ghaman Singh and Bakhtawar Singh, soldiers of the *thana*, are sent to him. Hopes for a reasonable payment being made to the merchants. Dated 10 *Rabi* I, 1275 AH.

PP 69-70. *List Containing the Details of Goods of Rasad Sent from* Thana *Debipura to Sehore.* It contains the names of *mauzas*, names of the owners of the goods, and names of goods along with its quantity.

PP 71-2. *Bhawani Prasad to Nawwab Sikandar Begam.* Informs of the receipt of the letter of Karam Ali Husain, *thanadar* of *pargana* Bari, dated 14 *Rabi* I, 1275 AH along with 10 maund and 20 *ser* grain like flour, etc. as *sarbrah-i rasad.* Informs that he immediately sent the grain to Bilas Rai, *tahsildar* of Sehore who sold it to the traders of the market. As the grain was received during the rainy season which caused some damage to the flour so it was sold on lesser price, whereas the other goods were sold on reasonable price. Bilas Rai who helped in the receipt of payment of grains to the merchants, obtained receipt from them and sent to him. The same is sent to her. Dated 15 *Rabi* I, 1275 AH (24 October 1858).

It contains the order that the letter and other two papers may be sent to Paltu Lal, *muhafiz-i daftar-i insha*, for inclusion in the register and keeping in the *daftar*. A copy of the order may be sent to Bhawani Prasad, *wakil*, asking him to explain about the sum of Rs. 10 received as tax from Khub Chand on the grains of *sarbrah-i rasad,* as it is not clear whether the tax was collected in accordance to the rules or it was collected unlawfully. Dated 17 *Rabi* I, 1275 AH.

P 73. *Karam Ali Husain,* Thanadar *of* Pargana *Bari, to Madan Mohan,* Naib Wakil. Informs as ordered, dated 12 *Safar* 1275 AH, the *saman-i rasad* as per the details is sent to him through Khub Chand. The receipt may be sent to him. Dated 14 *Rabi* I, 1275 AH.

P 75. *Bilas Rai to Bhawani Prasad.* Refers to his letter pertaining to selling the goods as per the rate list. Informs the goods were sold through Kashiram, *Chaudhury* of the market at the rate as mentioned. The payment was made to the owner and receipts were obtained from them. Dated 13 *Rabi* I, 1275 AH.

PP 77-8. *Bhawani Prasad to Nawwab Sikandar Begam.* Informs that for the last one week, flour has started to pour in from the *parganas* of Bari, Chhaner and Ichhawar, as urged by the Political Agent in view of the scarcity of food-grains in Sehore. The shopkeepers of Sehore are intending to purchase the grain on a cheap rate and store them in their godown. In that case, there would occur two types of losses. Firstly, after few days the grain would again become costly, and secondly, the loss of the traders of the *parganas* would be more. In views of this, the Political Agent ordered the *kotwal* that the grain should be purchased only by small traders and the people, and not by big traders who have godowns available for hoarding. Also informs of the arrival of grain from Ichhawar sent by Hakim Khwand Disilva. Says that the rate of flour in Sehore is Rs. 16, and rate of gram is Rs. 15. The big traders of Sehore want to purchase flour from the merchants @ Rs. 13 per maund. Dated 15 *Rabi* I, 1275 AH (24 October 1858).

P 79. *Hakim Sahab Disilva to Bhawani Prasad.* Refers to the letter of Bisheshar, *thanadar* of *mahal* Ichhawar, dated 14 *Rabi* I, 1275 AH, which is in regard to the supply of 5 *manasa* grain to Sehore cantonment. Informs that on 6 October 1858, one *manasa* flour was obtained from the traders of Ichhawar and sent to Sehore. Further informs that 2 *manasa* grain bought from *pargana* Ichhawar is lying in the market of Sehore and the owners of the grain who hired room for keeping the grain are puzzled. The price of grain in Sehore market is less in comparison to the the cost incurred on acquiring the grain and expenses occurred for borrowing it from Ichhawar to Sehore. In that sense, the loss of the traders is well understood. In view of this, whatever orders he likes may be issued to be followed. Dated 14 *Rabi* I, 1275 AH.

PP 81-2. *Bhawani Prasad to Nawwab Sikandar Begam.* Informs of the letter of Ram Prasad, *tahsildar*, along with 90 maund flour obtained from the traders of *mauza* Bhaogon, *pargana* Bharonda, Basram and Gobindram for sending it to the Sehore cantonment. Informs that with the permission of the Political Agent, the grain was sold in Sehore cantonment through the *kotwal* of the cantonment and the payment was received by the sellers from the buyers. The receipt of the payment of grain was obtained and sent to the *tahsildar*. Dated 20 *Rabi* I, 1275 AH (29 October 1858).

P 83. *Ram Prasad*, Tahsildar, Pargana *Bharonda, to Bhawani Prasad.* Informs that as ordered, for sending grain to Sehore 90, maund flour obtained from the traders of *mauza* Bhaogaon, *pargana* Bharonda, Basram and Gobindram through Mohan, Moti and other *banjaras*, loaded upon the bullocks has been sent. Hopes for the receipt. The remaining grain would soon reach there. The bullocks of *banjaras* should not be hindered as it would create a hurdle in the timely arrival of the provision. Dated 24 *Safar* 1275 AH.

File No. 269
Box No. 13
No. of Documents 9

Orders for Carrying Money for the Contingent of Bhopal Army

PP 1-2. Contents

P 3. *Nawwab Sikandar Begam to Bakhshi Murawwat Muhammad Khan.* Directs him to obtain camels and elephants from Lala Tikaram, *muhtamim*, *karkhanajat,* and load them with the treasure of salary of the army contingent for the year 1265 *fasli* from the treasury and send them to Sehore, guarded by half a *risala* and half a company of troops. The officials of *risala* and the company may be instructed to hand it over to Munshi Bhawani Prasad at Sehore. The details of the *sawars* and soldiers of the company may be provided to the government. Dated 19 *Zilhijja* 1274 AH.

P 5. *Bakhshi Murawwat Muhammad Khan to Nawwab Sikandar Begam.* Informs that as ordered, dated 19 *Zilhijja* 1274 AH, half a *risala* of Wahid Ali, *risaldar*, and half a company of foot-soldiers of Hashm Nizam are accompanying the treasure being sent to Sehore. The details of *sawars* and foot-soldiers are sent herewith. Dated 23 *Zilhijja* 1274 AH.

P 7. Fard, *Containing Names of the Soldiers of the Company of Hashm Nizam with Wazir Jang,* Subadar, *Accompanying the Treasure Sent to Sehore.* Dated 22 *Zilhijja* 1274 AH.

P 9. Fard, *Containing Names of the* Sawars *of* Risala I *of Wahid Ali,* Risaldar, *Accompanying the Treasure Sent to Sehore.* Dated 22 *Zilhijja* 1274 AH.

PP 11-12. Parwana *of Nawwab Sikandar Begam to Lala Chain Rai,* Munib, Daftar-i Bakhshigiri. To the same effect as P 3. Dated 27 *Muharram* 1275 AH.

P 13. Parwana *of Nawwab Sikandar Begam to Tikaram,* Muhtamim, Karkhanajat. Directs him to provide the royal camels and elephants from his *karkhanajat* to Lala Chain Rai, *munib, daftar-i bakhshigiri* for carrying the salary installment of army contingent for the year 1265 *fasli* to Munshi Bhawani Prasad, *wakil,* guarded by the *sawars* and foot-soldiers. Dated 27 *Muharram* 1275 AH.

P 15. *Bakhshi Murawwat Muhammad Khan to Nawwab Sikandar Begam.* Sends the list containing the names of *sawars* and foot-soldiers going to Sehore guarding the treasure of salary of the contingent of Bhopal army. Dated 29 *Muharram* 1275 AH.

PP 17-18. Yaddasht, *Containing the Names of Sawars and Foot-Soldiers Going to Sehore, Guarding the Treasure of Salary of the Contingent of Bhopal Army.* The *sawars* are from *risala* III, red uniform. The foot-soldiers are from the battalion of Guderji, *dafadar*, and the battalion of Hiralal, *jamadar*. Dated 29 *Muharram* 1275 AH.

File No. 270
Box No. 13
No. of Documents 18

Parwanas of Nawwab Sikandar Begam in Regard to Adil Muhammad Khan who Went to Agra and Staying with Chhatrasal

P 1. Contents

P 3. *Hazrat Nur Khan to Nawwab Sikandar Begam*. The previous day, Ramchand Chaudhary, Bazar Bheglone, had gone to Agra to return the looted grains of Chhatrasal, Agrawala. He came back and told that 50 soldiers of Fazil Muhammad Khan for the last 2-3 days were in Agra. On way to Agra, about 9 *curoh* away, he heard that *Nawwab* Adil Muhammad Khan with an army of 1,000, comprising of 500 *sawars* and 500 gunners with arms and ammunitions arrived at Agra. Further informs that day Balam Jeo Thakur of *ilaqa* Basodah stated that, it was 5-6 days before when he saw from his own eyes that Adil Muhammad Khan with an army of 1,000 comprising of 500 *sawars* and 500 gunners, fully armed with war weapons arrived at Agra. Further informs that Serwa, barber and a dweller of Bheglone, came and stated that Pranchand of Barkheri told him to convey to the *tahsildar* of Bheglone that Adil Muhammad Khan, Garhiwala with an army of 1,000 with arms and ammunitions, comprising of 500 *sawars* and 500 gunners, arrived in Agra. Raja Chhatrasal offered much hospitality to them latter.

PP 5-6. *Ghulam Muhammad Khan*, Risaldar, *to Nawwab Sikandar Begam*. To the same effect as the foregoing, assuring that he would fight with the insugents as much as possible. Further informs that the people, previously harassed by the attack of the insurgents were scared and fleeing from their houses. He is trying his best to pacify them assuring that they need not panic.

P 7. *Khuda Bakhsh, Deputy* Thanadar, *Debipura to Nawwab Sikandar Begam*. Informs that day Ibrahim, a dweller of Doraha, came from Narsingarh and stated that on the previous day he was in the court at Narsingarh where he heard that nearly 2,000 to 3,000 insurgent forces of Peshwa, comprising both the *sawars* and foot-soldiers had gone to Agra Barkhera, Chhatrasalwala, which lies at a distance of 18 *curoh* from there. Dated 20 *Zilhijja* 1274 AH.

P 9. *Daulat Rai*, Nazim-i Mashriq, *to Nawwab Sikandar Begam*. Informs of the letter of Sada Shiv Rao, *Suba Sahab* of Bhilsa, dated 18 *Zilhijja* AH along with the *rubakar* of *kachehri*. He has informed about the encampment of Chhatrasal, Adil Muhammad Khan, Pindara, Kaladwala, son of Jamal Muhammad Khan of Bhopal, and others at Agra. An army of 1,500 *sawars* and foot-soldiers is said to be with them. About 2,500 insurgent forces are at Kheri, *ilaqa* Sironj. The army of Raja Bhorji, Narwarwala, with one cannon is in a village, *ilaqa* Aonarsi, having intention to attack Bhopal or Bhilsa at night. The letter along with the *rubakar* is sent to her. The *Suba Sahab* is a nice person who takes care of the region and the state. Dated 20 *Zilhijja* 1274 AH.

P 11. *Sada Shiv Rao to Daulat Rai,* Nazim-i Mashriq. A copy of the *rubakar* of this office, dated 18 *Zilhijja* 1274 AH, is sent to him which pertains to the encampment of the insurgents in Agra. Dated 18 *Zilhijja* 1274 AH.

P 13. *Letter from the Office of* Nizamat-i Mashriq *to* Suba Sahab, *Bhilsa*. Refers to his letter, dated 18 *Zilhijja* 1274 AH, along with the *rubakar* of his office, informing of the encampment of Chhatrasal, Agrawala, Adil Muhammad Khan, Garhiwala, Pindara, Kaladwala, son of Jamal Muhammad Khan of Bhopal, and others at Agra. An army of 1,500 *sawars* and foot-soldiers is with them. About 2,500 insurgent forces are at Kheri, *ilaqa* Sironj. The army of Raja Bhorji, Narwarwala, along with one cannon is in a village in *ilaqa* Aonarsi, having intention to attack Bhopal or Sironj, or Berasia or Basodah or Bhilsa at night. Expresses his gratitude for taking care of him and the state. Dated 20 *Zilhijja* 1274 AH.

PP 15-16. Rubakar *from the Office of* Suba *of District Bhilsa under the Session of Sada Shiv Rao,* Suba Sahab. The recent news, as reported by an informer is from Agra where the insurgents have assembled. The report is that on 15th of the month Thakur Chhatrasal, Agrawala and Adil Muhammad Khan, *jagirdar*, Garhi Ambapani, State of Bhopal became unconscious so much so that men of *jagirdar* helped him to lie on bed. Chhatrasal who was stepping the stairs fell down due to excessive drinking and an injury occurred to his back and his hand. On 16th of the month, the *jagirdar*, Pandara, Kaladwala, and son of Jamal Muhammad Khan of Bhopal held discussion with each other. But nothing came out from their mouth. But from the discussion of the soldiers it appeared that after the rainy season, they would attack either upon Bhopal or Sironj or Berasia or Basodah or Bhilsa. There are 1,500 forces in Agra. Another army is in Kheri, *ilaqa* Sironj. Besides, Bhorji, Raja of Narwar with an army of 2,000 to 2,500 and one cannon is in a village, *mutallaqa* Aonarsi. The news may be known to all the officers of the district.

Order was issued that through the letters in Marathi the news should be brought to the notice of the Political Agent, and the *Sar Suba* of Issagarh, through the *wakil.* A copy of the *rubakar* may be sent to the Assistant Political Agent at *pargana* Berasia and the *nazim-i mashriq* at Raisen, State of Bhopal. It may also be communicated that anything heard thereafter, would be communicated.

P 17. *Ghulam Makhdum Khan to Nawwab Sikandar Begam.* Informs that day, he received a letter from Shaikh Khuda Bakhsh, *thanadar* of Debipura, dated 6 *Zilhijja* 1274 AH, informing that Ibrahim Bohra of Doraha stated, as he heard in the court of Narsingarh that an army of 2,000 to 3,000, both *sawars* and foot-soldiers led by Peshwa, and others reached Agra Barkhera, Chhatrasalwala. The same is sent to her. Dated 21 *Zilhijja* 1274 AH.

P 19. *Shaikh Khuda Bakhsh,* Thanadar, *Debipura, to Ghulam Makhdum Khan.* Informs that Ibrahim Bohra, a resident of Doraha, came from Narsingarh who in the court heard that the Peshwa with an army of 2,000 to 3,000, both *sawars* and foot-soldiers is in Agra with Chhatrasal, lying at a distance of 18 *curoh* from there. The information has been sent to the government. Dated 20 *Zilhijja* 1274 AH.

P 21. Parwana *of Nawwab Sikandar Begam to Munshi Inayat Husain, Deputy* Nazim-i Junub. Bhawani Prasad, *wakil,* through his letter dated 19 *Zilhijja* 1274 AH, informed her that he told Major Richards, the Political Agent, that it is heard that Adil Muhammad Khan with few hundred *sawars* and foot-soldiers had gone to Agra. If he too got such news, he asked. He said, the informers gave this news to Jan Ali Khan, Assistant *Muntazim*, Berasia. The *muntazim* through *rubakar* informed that Adil Muhammad Khan with 80 Afghan *wilayatis*, 50 Bundelas and others with a total of 300 *sawars* and foot-soldiers, while some are injured and their hoses are fine, arrived at Agra and met Chhatrasal. But Chhatrasal did not entertain him. Thereafter, he went somewhere else. He might be in Ambapani or somewhere else. *Nawwab* Sikandar Begam may be requested that Adil Muhammad Khan, who is a rebel of the two governments, should be traced by sending reliable informers and report to him. If possible, depute someone from the Gurjar community or some *wilayati* and let him be killed. Such insurgents should not be allowed to live but should be finished. Thereafter, he was given a letter of Jan Ali Khan with an order that the letter should be sent to *Nawwab* Sikandar Begam, requesting that authentic news of the insurgents should be sent to him by deputing reliable informers. The letter of Jan Ali Khan is sent to him with an instruction to take action as indicated. Dated 21 *Zilhijja* 1274 AH.

PP 23-4. *Letter of Munshi Jan Ali Khan, Deputy Assistant, Berasia, to the Political Agent of Bhopal.*

Informs this is an authentic news that Adil Muhammad Khan along with Aqil Muhammad Khan, Sarfraz Khan, *Nawwab* of Banda and Wazir Allah Khan along with an army of 400 *sawars* and foot-soldiers are in Agra with Thakur Chhatrasal and are trying to gather more persons. Raja Narwar too has been called and will join that day or the next day. Their plan is to go to Berasia first, then Bhopal and thereafter Sehore. There is not too much arrangement as to fight with a big army. Gajadhar Singh, *jamadar*, has come. They do not have magazine. The soldiers have daggers only. If few magazines and 2 cannon come from Sehore, it will be good. Otherwise, what he thinks may be ordered that will be followed. Dated 3 July 1858.

PP 25-6. Parwana *of Nawwab Sikandar Begam to Munshi Inayat Husain, Deputy* Nazim-i Junub. Adil Muhammad Khan has returned to Sironj with huge wealth from Gwalior and the region of *Wazir al-Daulah*. All the employees and dwellers of Bhopal should come together to fight with them if they enter in the State of Bhopal or in Bhopal, kill them and loot their wealth. They should not be allowed to go elsewhere, carrying their wealth. They should be dealt with, which implies that they should be killed or arrested. Certainly, it will be a pleasure for the employees and dwellers to have booty. They should not be like the people of other regions who concentrate on the loot and forget the responsibility to fight and save the country. God has always saved Bhopal, and Bhopal is proud of his soldiers and the dwellers. They should unite in loot and capturing the booty and should not be ashamed like people of other regions. They should be loyal to their ruler and the country as it will bring name and fame to the State of Bhopal among all the states and countries. Dated 22 *Zilhijja* 1274 AH.

P 27. *Bhawani Prasad to Nawwab Sikandar Begam.* Informs about a letter of Munshi Jan Ali Khan, Deputy

Assistant of Berasia, dated 2 August 1858 which is in regard to a perfect news that Adil Muhammad Khan and brother of *Kamdar* Pindara along with some persons are in Agra. It contains the order of the Political Agent that a copy of this may be provided to Munshi Bhawani Prasad, *wakil* of Bhopal, to inform *Nawwab* Sikandar Begam, State of Bhopal, about it. The same is sent to her. Dated 23 *Zilhijja* 1274 AH.

PP 29-30. *Letter of Munshi Jan Ali Khan, Deputy Assistant of Berasia, to the Political Agent, Dated 2 August 1858*. Refers to his letter, dated 1 August 1858 in reply to his letter, dated 3 July 1858, that there is no authentic news of the insurgent army at Agra as to make an arrangement, and authentic news is to be obtained by sending a reliable informer. Says that the observation made by him is true and perfect. It has come to the notice, through a reliable informer, that around 300 men are in Agra and in *Sarai*, *ilaqa* Sironj. Adil Muhammad Khan and brother of *Kamdar* Pindara along with some more persons are in the fort of Agra and around 500 men, both *sawars* and foot-soldiers are outside the fort. They intend to go to Bheglone. A copy of the *rubakar* has been received from *Suba Sahab*, Bhilsa. The same is sent to him.

P 31. *Karam Ali Husain, Deputy* Thanadar *of* Pargana *Bari, to Munshi Inayat Husain, Deputy* Nazim-i Junub. Refers to a letter of Shaikh Khuda Bakhsh, deputy *thanadar* of Debipura, dated 21 *Zilhijja* 174 AH, bearing the royal order that there should not be any hesitation in arresting or killing Adil Muhammad Khan and Aqil Muhammad Khan, the insurgents, if they enter in his jurisdiction, and that the information of insurgency and suggestion regarding the arrest and killing should be sent. Assures that there would be no negligence in killing or arresting the insurgents and information of the same would be communicated. Dated 3 *Muharram* 1275 AH.

P 33. *Karam Ali Husain, Deputy* Thanadar *of* Pargana *Bari To Munshi Inayat Husain, Deputy* Nazim-i Junub. Refers to the royal *parwana,* dated 22 *Zilhijja* 1274 AH, bearing the royal order to kill and capture the booty of Adil Muhammad Khan, the insurgent, and to circulate a notice to this effect among all the employees and people that by passing through Gwalior and destroying *Wazir al-Daulah,* they have accumulated huge wealth and have entered Sirȯnj. Informs that as ordered, all the employees and people have been acquainted with the news. Dated 2 *Muharram* 1275 AH.

P 35. *Karam Ali Husain, Deputy* Thanadar *of* Pargana *Bari To Munshi Inayat Husain, Deputy* Nazim-i Junub. Refers to the royal *parwana,* dated 21 *Zilhijja* 1274 AH, bearing the royal order to depute clever informers for bringing the news of the arrival of Adil Muhammad Khan, as desired by the Political Agent and to send the real news everyday. Assures that he would do as ordered. Dated 3 *Muharram* 1275 AH.

P 37. *Karam Ali Husain, Deputy* Thanadar *of* Pargana *Bari to Munshi Inayat Husain, Deputy* Nazim-i Junub. Refers to a letter of Daulat Rai, *nazim-i mashriq*, dated 20 *Zilhijja* 1274 AH, bearing the royal order that there should not be any hesitation in arresting or killing of Adil Muhammad Khan and Aqil Muhammad Khan, the insurgents, besides the *rubakar* of *suba* Bhilsa. Assures that he would do as ordered.

File No. 271
Box No. 13
No. of Documents 5

Orders to Conduct Enquiry into the Theft of Goods of the Agent and the Captain from their Bungalows During the Uprising in the Army Contingent

PP 1-2. Contents

PP 3-4. *Murawwat Muhammad Khan to Nawwab Sikandar Begam.* Informs that Shaikh Sa'd Allah, *naik* deployed at the bungalow, came and reported that at a distance of 100 yard from the bungalow is the building of *mistrikhana* of the army. In the evening, the carpenters went to their home and locked the *mistrikhana*. But the bungalow was guarded. At night due to darkness and havoc of heavy rain one was unable to see the other and it was not possible to hear the noise, whence someone entered in the *mistrikhana* and opened the box with the help of the instruments of carpentry. From the carpenter it was heard that there were one dozen instruments, some cloths and 4-5 rupees as well which were stolen. The *naik* was ordered to bring all the goods from there to the bungalow. Dated 8 *Zilhijja* 1274 AH.

PP 5-8. *Gist of the Letter of Munshi Bhawani Prasad.* Informs about a letter of the Political Agent, dated 9 October 1857, which is in regard to the letter of Dr. Tomsen who has communicated that his valuables and goods which were kept in an almirah in his bungalow at Sehore were stolen after breaking the lock. Munshi Husain Bakhsh wrote to him that he knew him who stole the goods. He is directed to make search of goods and that the thief should be arrested. Investigation should be conducted on the clue, provided by Munshi Husain Bakhsh. The same is presented before her.

It contains the order that the letter along with the *parwana* of the Political Agent may be sent to Mirza Imdad Ali Beg, deputy *kotwal* of Sehore, through Bhawani Prasad, communicating him to conduct an enquiry into the theft of goods of Dr. Tomsen and submit the report along with his suggestion in the matter. There should not be any negligence or relectance in the matter. A copy of the order may also be sent to Bijay Lal, *Peshdast Wakil*, through him, communicating that in the matter of theft of goods of Dr. Tomsen, only Mirza Imdad Ali Beg wrote to her and was ordered to conduct an enquiry into the matter. But Munshi Husain Bakhsh did not write anything in the matter at all to her. That day when the *parwana* of the Political Agent was received, she wrote to Mirza Imdad Ali Beg to conduct an enquiry and report to her in the matter. An order will be issued after the report is received and the Political Agent will be informed of the same. Directs him to bring it into the knowledge of the Political Agent and communicate her of his reply. Dated 25 *Safar* 1274 AH.

P 9. *Imdad Ali Beg to Nawwab Sikandar Begam.* Informs that on 15 October, Moti Batterywala, a servant of the Colonel, came and reported of the theft of two sets of battery which should be searched. Says a search was made but no information was received thereto. Information to this effect was must, which he did. Dated 19 October 1857 (30 *Safar* 1274 AH).

PP 11-12. *Imdad Ali Beg to Nawwab Sikandar Begam.* Informs of the receipt of 2-3 letters, directing him to enquire into the matter of theft and submit a report of the stealing away of the goods of the Agenty, the Captain and other British officers. Says investigation was made in the theft of goods, statements of the dwellers were recorded but no sign of theft was found among them. There was none other than the army contingent of Bhopal. Presently, the Bhopal army is deployed at different places. Thus, the investigation process and preparing a *rubakar* is being delayed. Anyone from among the employees of the army who sold anything like cloth, copper or such goods is not heard of. But anything which is not of use for them would have been sold in the market of the cantonment. It is a must that the shopkeepers of the cantonment should be interrogated to unearth the truth. But in this case it is not possible unless permission is granted by the British officers. Requests for a letter containing that if any soldier has sold anything like cloth, copper, gold or anything else to a trader, he should come to the *kotwali* and disclose the same. If it does not happen and anything comes to notice afterwards, he would be considered an accused and would be liable to be punished. A diclaration should also be made in this regard by the traders as it will help in disclosing the theft. Requests for orders to proceed further in the matter. Dated 3 November1857 (15 *Rabi* I, 1274 AH).

File No. 272
Box No. 13
No. of Documents 4

Deploying Nanhey Khan, Imam Khan and Alif Khan of the Battalion of Ghasi Khan to Bring the News About Adil Muhammad Khan, the Insurgent

P 1. Contents

P 3. *Nawwab Sikandar Begam to Bakhshi Murawwat Muhammad Khan.* There is a report that Adil Muhammad Khan is in Agra. There is a conflicting report about the number of troops which he is carrying with him. Some say it is 1,000, some say it is 1,500 and some say it is even more than that. Directs him to send two clever and experienced persons, in disguise to Agra, instructing them to observe everything minutely from their own eyes; the number of troops Adil Muhammad Khan has with him; who are the prominent figures and rebels of the Bhopal government; whether he carries cannon or not, and submit a detailed report to the government after coming back. Dated 22 *Zilhijja* 1274 AH.

PP 5-6. *Murawwat Muhammad Khan to Nawwab Sikandar Begam.* Informs that in accordance to her *parwana*, dated 22 *Zilhijja* 1274 AH, he sent 5 soldiers of the battalions of Asad Khan and Dhani Khan to Agra Barkhera for bringing news of Adil Muhammad Khan, Aqil Muhammad Khan and the number of troops that they are carrying. Names of those soldiers are: Asad Khan, Khwaju Khan, Chhotey Khan, etc. Dated 28 *Zilhijja* 1274 AH.

It contains the order that the letter and *parwana,* addressed to Bakhshi Murawwat Muhammad Khan, dated 22 *Zilhijja* 1274 AH, may be sent to Lala Paltu Lal, *muhafiz-i daftar-i insha*, for inclusion in the register and keeping in the *daftar*. A copy of the order may be sent to Bakhshi Murawwat Muhammad Khan, communicaring that as soon as Asad Khan, Khwaju Khan, Chhotey Khan, etc. come with authentic news of Adil Muhammad Khan and Aqil Muhammad Khan, it may be sent to her. Dated 30 *Zilhijja* 1274 AH.

P 7. *Murawwat Muhammad Khan to Nawwab Sikandar Begam.* Informs that day, he sent Alif Khan, Nanhey Khan and Imam Khan, the employees of the battalion of Ghasi Khan, *jamadar* to Agra Barkhera, Aonarsi and Sironj for bringing the news about Adil Muhammad Khan and Aqil Muhammad Khan. Dated 28 *Zilhijja* 1274 AH.

It contains the order that the letter may be sent to Lala Paltu Lal, *muhafiz-i daftar-i insha*, for inclusion in the register and keeping in the *daftar*. A copy of the order may be sent to Bakhshi Murawwat Muhammad Khan, communicaring that as soon as Alif Khan, Nanhey Khan and Imam Khan come with authentic news of Adil Muhammad Khan and Aqil Muhammad Khan, it may be sent to her. Dated 30 *Zilhijja* 1274 AH.

Deployment of the Battalion of Hattey Khan, Jamadar, the Fugitive at Bamhuri to Deal with the Insurgents and Hattey Singh, Jamadar, the Insurgent

PP 1-2. Contents

PP 3-4. *Chhatar Singh,* Jamadar *At Bamhuri, to Nawwab Sikandar Begam.* Informs as ordered, he is in *mahal* Bamhuri in order to arrest Hattey Singh Thakur, Jaitgarhwala since 18 *Ziqada* 1265 *Fasli.* Every day, he in the company of Abd al-Majid, *muhtamim, chaukiyat* goes in the forest and in the mountains in search of Thakur and to arrest him. But he is still traceless. The battalion of Nanhey Khan did not arrive there as yet and he is alone there for the last one and a half month. Meanwhile, Hattey Singh was arrested from *ilaqa* Bhilsa. The information to this effect was sent to her earlier. Requests for orders whether he should still stay there or should come back to Bhopal. Dated 26 *Zilhijja* 1274 AH.

It contains the order that the letter may be sent to Lala Paltu Lal, *muhafiz-i daftar-i insha*, for inclusion in the register and keeping in the *daftar*. A copy of the order may be sent to Chhatar Singh, *Jamadar,* directing him to stay at Bamhuri. Another order may be sent to Bakhshi Murawwat Muhammad Khan, directing him that no sooner he receives the order he may send the battalion of Nanhey Khan, *jamadar* to Bamhuri. Otherwise, the entire battalion will be dismissed from this very date. Dated 28 *Zilhijja* 1274 AH.

PP 5-6. *Murawwat Muhammad Khan to Nawwab Sikandar Begam.* Refers to her order, as recorded in the letter of Chhatar Singh, *jamadar,* directing that no sooner he gets the order, the battalion of Nanhey Khan, *jamadar,* may be sent to Bamhuri and to inform her immediately; else the order for the suspension of the entire battalion would be issued. Informs that the battalion of Nanhey Khan is at Shahgarh since *Sha'ban* and has sent a letter to Major Thornton, Assistant Superintendent of district Madawrah and Shahgarh, requesting him to send back the battalion and has informed her also. As he received no reply, he sent another letter to this effect. Informs as and when, a reply is received from him and the battalion comes back to Siwans, it would be deployed at Bamhuri. Dated 1 *Muharram* 1275 AH.

P 7. *Muhammad Hasan Khan to Nawwab Sikandar Begam.* Informs that day; the 2nd *Muharram* 1275 AH, the salaries of the soldiers of the battalion of Nanhey Khan, the fugitive, for the month of *Zilhijja* 1274 AH have been sent to Bamhuri. The details of the armymen are sent to her. Dated 2 *Muharram* 1275 AH.

It contains the order that the letter and the *fard* may be sent to Lala Paltu Lal, *muhafiz-i daftar-i insha*, for inclusion in the register and keeping in the *daftar*. A copy of the order may be sent to Ghulam Murtaza Khan, directing him that as soon as the soldiers of the battalion of Nanhey Khan, *jamadar,* arrive at Bamhuri, they should be deployed along with Chhatar Singh. Dated 7 *Muharram* 1275 AH.

P 9. Fard, *Containing Names of the Soldiers of the Battalion of Nanhay Khan,* Jamadar, *who Came from Madawrah and Went to Bamhuri,* Ilaqa *Deorhi Khas, from Siwans*. Their number is forty. Dated 2 *Muharram* 1275 AH.

P 11. *Ghulam Husain Khan to Nawwab Sikandar Begam*. Informs, as ordered, he marched from Siwans on 3 *Muharram* 1275 AH and reached Bamhuri on 5 *Muharram* 1275 AH. Dated 6 *Muharram* 1275 AH.

P 13. *Muhammad Abbas Ali,* Thanadar *of Bamhuri, to Nawwab Sikandar Begam.* Informs that on 5 *Muharram* 1275 AH/1265 *fasli*, day Monday, the battalion of Nanhey Khan, *jamadar*, accompanied by Ghulam Husain Khan, *kotha-dafadar* reached Bamhuri. With the commencement of forces, the dwellers feel happy, if any insurgent enters in the region; he would be dealt with and caught. Dated 7 *Muharram* 1275 AH.

P 15. *Chhatar Singh,* Sipahsalar, *to Nawwab Sikandar Begam.* Informs that on 5 *Muharram* 1275 AH, the battalion of Nanhey Khan, *jamadar*, reached Bamhuri. There is no sign of Hattey Singh Thakur, *Jaitgarhwala,* in the *pargana*. Nobody knows where he has gone. Dated 10 *Muharram* 1275 AH.

It contains the order that the letter may be sent to Lala Paltu Lal, *muhafiz-i daftar-i insha*, for inclusion in the register and keeping in the *daftar*. A copy of the order may be sent to Chhatar Singh, *sipahsalar* of Bamhuri, directing him to stay at Bamhuri along with the battalion of Nanhey Khan, *jamadar*, and keep watch. The moment Hattey Singh Thakur enters in the region, he should be arrested and produced before her, under security. Dated 22 *Muharram* 1275 AH.

PP 17-18. *Ghulam Murtaza Khan to Nawwab Sikandar Begam.* Refers to her order, recorded in the letter of Muhammad Hasan Khan, *naib bakhshi* of the State, dated 7 *Muharram* 1275 AH, and informs that he wrote a letter to Chhatar Singh, *sipahsalar,* to submit the details of attendance of the soldiers of the battalion of Nanhey Khan, *jamadar*. The *sipahsalar* sent a reply along with details of the attendance of the armymen. The details are: the soldiers present are 30, the soldiers who went from Siwans with the permission of *naib bakhshi* are 8, and the soldiers who are on leave with the permission of Shah Muhammad, *amil* of Bamhuri are 6. Besides this, 4 soldiers went to Raisen from Siwans without permission. So far, none of them came back. The letter of the *sipahsalar* is sent to her for information. Dated 5 *Safar* 1275 AH.

P 19. *Chhatar Singh To Ghulam Murtaza Khan.* Refers to his letter, dated 28 *Muharram* 1275 AH which is regarding the name and attendance of the battalion of Natthi Khan. The details of attendance of the soldiers are: the soldiers present are 30. Their names and their fathers's names are submitted separately. From Ghulam Husain Khan it is learnt that 8 soldiers are on leave with the permission of *naib bakhshi*, 6 soldiers are on leave with the permission of Shah Muhammad, and 4 soldiers went to Raisen without permission. They are yet to come back. Dated 23 *Muharram* 1275 AH.

P 21. Yaddasht, *Containing Details of the Attendance of the Soldiers of the Battalion of Natthi Khan, who Came from Madawrah are Posted at* Mahal Bamhuri, Ilaqa *Deorhi Khas*, Dated 22 Muharram 1275 AH.

P 22. Yaddasht, *Containing Details of the Absentee Soldiers as Reported by Ghulam Husain Khan.* It contains the names of those who took permission from *naib bakhshi* and from Shah Muhammad, *tahsildar*, besides the names of those who left without permission. Dated 22 *Muharram* 1275 AH.

File No. 274
Box No. 14
No. of Documents 13

Notification for the Arrest of Tantia Tope and Nephew of Nana Peshwa, the Leader of the Insurgents who Fled from the Battlefield at Rajgarh and Bayawrah

with Awards Worth Rs. 10, 000 for each and Not to Give Rasad to them

PP 1-3. Contents

P 5-6. Parwana *Issued to Muhammad Jamal al-Din Khan,* Madar al-Maham. The notification issued under the seal of the office of the Agent to the Governor-General, Central India, which is further issued with the instruction to Ghulam Murtaza Khan, *Kamdar*, Deorhi Khas, directing him to print 986 copies of the said order from *matba' Sikandari* and send it to the government. Dated 28 *Muharram* 1275 AH (7 September 1858).

The *parwana* contains the order for copying it in the *daftar-i insha* and sending it along with the notification to Lala Lal Chand, *muhafiz-i daftar-i insha*, for inclusion in the register and keeping in the *daftar*. A copy of the *parwana* along with the sample of the notification may be sent to Muhammad Abd al-Wahid, *Muhtamim*, *matba' Sikandari* for printing 986 copies of the notification as ordered in the *parwana* and send it to him so that it may be further sent to the government. Dated 2 *Safar* 1275 AH.

P 7. *Notification Issued from the Office of Agenty, Central India, under the Session of Hamilton Barnout, Agent to the Governor-General.* To arrest Tantia Tope and Rao Sahab, nephew of Nana Peshwa, is a must as they are the leaders of the insurgents and rebels. An award of Rs. 10, 000 has been fixed for the arrest of each of them. This notification is issued and it is proclaimed that everyone should assert to arrest Rao Sahab and Tantia Tope. Those who will arrest them will get the award of Rs. 10, 000 for each. If anybody is found to be reluctant, not interested in arresting them, or heard that they are given shelter, he will be harshly punished. Dated 24 August 1858. [5]

5. A bilingual document, in Urdu as well as in Hindi Devanagari.

PP 9-10. *Orders Issued to Ghulam Murtaza Khan, Kamdar, Deorhi Khas regarding the 'Notification'*. From the notification issued from the Office of Agenty Central India, by the Agent to the Governor-General, dated 24 August 1858, it came to her notice that 'to arrest Tantia Tope and Rao Sahab, nephew of Nana Peshwa is a must, as they are the leaders of the insurgents and rebels. An award of Rs. 10, 000 has been fixed for the arrest of each of them. This notification is issued and it is proclaimed that everyone should assert to arrest Rao Sahab and Tantia Tope. Those who will arrest them will get the award of Rs. 10, 000 for each. If anybody is found to be reluctant or not interested in arresting them or gives shelter to them, he will be harshly punished'. Directs him to make efforts to arrest Tantia Tope and Rao Sahab, as instructed above. Anyone who will arrest them will get the award of Rs. 10, 000. Dated 28 *Muharram* 1275 AH (7 September 1858). [6]

PP 11-12. Parwana *Issued to Muhammad Jamal al-Din Khan,* Madar al-Maham. The notification issued under the seal of the office of the Agent to the Governor-General, Central India, is further issued with instruction to Ghulam Murtaza Khan, *Kamdar* of Deorhi Khas. Directs him to print 137 copies of the said order from *matba' Sikandari* and send it to the government. Dated 28 *Muharram* 1275 AH (7 September1858).

The *parwana* contains the order for copying it in the *daftar-i insha* and sending it along with the notification to Lala Lal Chand, *muhafiz-i daftar-i insha*, for inclusion in the register and keeping in the *daftar*. A copy of the *parwana* along with the sample of the notification may be sent to Muhammad Abd al-Wahid, *muhtamim*, *matba' Sikandari* for printing 137 copies of the notification as ordered in the *parwana* and to send it to him so that it may further be sent to the government. Dated 2 *Safar* 1275 AH.

---

6. A bilingual document, in Urdu as well as in Hindi Devanagari.

P 13. *Notification, Issued From The Office of Agenty, Central India, Under The Session of Hamilton Barnout, Agent to the Governor-General.* The insurgents have adopted a vulnerable technique that before their march they send some sellers of goods in all directions and then they follow them. They send 2 to 4 persons to the *ilaqadars* to convey the message that a huge army of 40, 000 to 50,000 is approaching fast. They should begin the preparation of *rasad*. To prevent the insurgents and to arrest those who come for *rasad* and the mischief mongers who come as sellers of goods is necessary. This notification is issued and it is proclaimed that every *ilaqadar* should ensure that if anyone comes for *rasad* from among the insurgents should be arrested. The sellers of goods, found anywhere, should be killed or arrested. There should not be any reluctance or negligence. If anybody is found acting contrary to this, he will be liable for punishment. Dated 28 August 1858.[7]

P 15. *Orders Issued to Ghulam Murtaza Khan,* Kamdar *of Deorhi Khas, regarding the 'Notification'.* From the notification issued from the Office of Agenty, Central India, by Agent to the Governor-General, dated 28 August 1858, it came to her notice that the insurgents have adopted a policy that before their march, they send some sellers of goods in all directions and then they follow them. They send 2 to 4 persons to the *ilaqadars* to convey the message that a huge army of 40, 000 to 50,000 is approaching fast. They should make preparation of *rasad*. To prevent the insurgents and to arrest those who come for *rasad* and to kill those mischief mongers who come as sellers of goods is necessary. This notification is issued and it is proclaimed that every *ilaqadar* should ensure that if anyone comes for *rasad* from among the insurgents, they should be arrested. The sellers of goods, if found anywhere, should be killed or arrested. There should not be any reluctance or negligence. If anybody

7. A bilingual document in Urdu as well as in Hindi Devanagari.

is found acting contrary to this, he will be liable to be punished. Directs him to issue notification in his region as expressed in the notification. Dated 28 *Muharram* 1275 AH (7 September 1858). [8]

PP 17-18. Parwana *Issued to Muhammad Jamal al-Din Khan,* Madar al-Maham. The notification issued under the seal of the office of the Agent to the Governor-General, Central India, is further issued with instruction to Ghulam Murtaza Khan, *Kamdar* of Deorhi Khas, directing him to print 137 copies of the said order from *matba' Sikandari* and send it to the government. Dated 28 *Muharram* 1275 AH (7 September1858).

The *parwana* contains the order for copying it in the *daftar-i insha* and sending it along with the notification to Lala Lal Chand, *muhafiz-i daftar-i insha*, for inclusion in the register and keeping in the *daftar*. A copy of the *parwana* along with the sample of the notification may be sent to Muhammad Abd al-Wahid, *muhtamim*, *matba' Sikandari* for printing 137 copies of the notification as ordered in the *parwana* and to send it to him so that it may further be sent to the government. Dated 2 *Safar* 1275 AH.

P 19. *Notification Issued from the Office of Agenty, Central India, under the Session of Hamilton Barnout, Agent to the Governor-General.* On 14 August 1858, the insurgents under the leadership of Tantia Tope, Rao Sahab and *Nawwab* of Banda, the rebels, had assembled at Nathdwar. They were badly defeated and they dispersed haplessly. All the cannon and magazines, whatever they possessed, fell into the hands of the powerful rulers. They are fleeing haplessly. It is a must that they are arrested or killed as they are the enemies of peace and danger to mankind. This notification is issued and it is proclaimed that if the *thakurs* or *zamindars* or the villagers attack upon any of the insurgents or arrest or kill him, they will do an incredible work and will be

8. A bilingual document in Urdu as well as in Hindi Devanagari.

awarded. All valued items and horses of the insurgents would be owned by them as booty. It is a must for all to clear the land from those evils and make it pure. Those who will do contrary to this or give shelter to these insurgents will be liable to be punished. Dated 24 August 1858. [9]

P 21. *Orders Issued to Ghulam Murtaza Khan,* Kamdar *of Deorhi Khas Regarding The 'Notification'.* From the notification issued from the Office of Agenty, Central India, by the Agent to the Governor-General, dated 24 August 1858, it came to her notice that on 14th of the month, the insurgents under the leadership of Tantia Tope, Rao Sahab and *Nawwab* of Banda, the rebels had assembled at Nathdwar. They were badly defeated and they dispersed haplessly. All the cannon and magazines, whatever they possessed, fell into the hands of the powerful rulers. They are fleeing haplessly. It is a must that they are arrested or killed as they are the enemies of peace and danger to mankind. This notification is issued and it is proclaimed that if the *thakurs* or *zamindars* or the villagers attack any of the insurgents or arrest or kill him, they will do an incredible work and will be awarded. All valued items and the horses of the insurgents would be owned by them as booty. It is a must for all to clear the land from these evils and make it pure. Those who will do contrary to it or give shelter to these insurgents will be liable to be punished. Directs him to issue notification in his region as expressed in the stated notification. Dated 28 *Muharram*1275 AH (7 September 1858). [10]

P 23. *Muhammad Jamal al-Din Khan,* Madar al-Maham, *to Nawwab Sikandar Begam.* Refers to her order, dated 28 *Muharram* 1275 AH (7 September 1858), and informs that 986 copies of the notification issued under the royal seal to Ghulam Murtaza Khan, *Kamdar* of Deorhi Khas

9. A bilingual document in Urdu as well as in Hindi Devanagari.
10. The notification is in Urdu as well as in Hindi Devanagari.

to arrest Tantia Tope and others, are to be printed from *matba' Sikandari*. These along with the sample of the notification are sent to the government. Dated 13 *Safar* 1275 AH.

P 25. *Muhammad Jamal al-Din Khan,* Madar al-Maham, *to Nawwab Sikandar Begam.* Refers to her order, dated 28 *Muharram* 1275 AH (7 September 1858), and informs that 137 copies of the notification issued under the royal seal to Ghulam Murtaza Khan, *Kamdar* of Deorhi Khas to arrest the insurgents and mischief mongers who come to collect provision, are printed from *matba' Sikandari*. These along with the sample of the notification are sent to the government. Dated 13 *Safar* 1275 AII.

P 27. *Muhammad Jamal al-Din Khan,* Madar al-Maham, *to Nawwab Sikandar Begam.* Refers to her order, dated 28 *Muharram* 1275 AH (7 September 1858), and informs that 137 copies of the notification which is in regard to the defeat of Tantia Tope and Rao Sahab, the insurgents, are printed from *matba' Sikandari* and names of all the *Jagirdars* are also put therein. These along with the sample of the notification are sent to the government. Dated 16 *Safar* 1275 AH.

File No. 275
Box No. 14
No. of Documents 30

Supply of Provision to the Army Accompanying Bakhshi Murawwat Muhammad Khan Deployed at Bhilsa and Berasia to Fight Battle with the Insurgents

PP 1-4. Contents

P 5. Parwana *of Nawwab Sikandar Begam to Mansukh Rai,* Muhtamim, Sair-i Kul. The army of Bhopal State is being deployed under the command of Bakhshi Murawwat Muhammad Khan to suppress the insurgents. It is a must that the goods as listed as *sarbrah-i rasad,* fulfilling the requirement of one month for 1,000 men and 300 horses purchased from Bhopal market may be provided to Ajodhya Prasad, *muhtamim sair* of district east who is accompanying Bakhshi Murawwat

Muhammad Khan. The *muhtamim* would keep the goods with him. The provision and goods of *sarbrah-i rasad,* coming from the *mahals* of the royal state should be sold to the traders on the rate fixed by Bakhshi Murawwat Muhammad Khan in such a manner which gives name and fame to the State of Bhopal. The godown should remain full of provision and available for those who are conducting expedition since one month with 1,000 men and 300 horses to quell the insurgents and to eliminate the insurgency. If any item is required anytime, it should immediately be provided from the market of Bhopal. Whatever item is used in whatever quantity, that item of the same quantity should be made available in the godown from the *mahals* of Siwans, Ghairatganj, Mahalpur and Raisen. Lala Ajodhya Prasad, *muhtamim sair* of district East, should be instructed to tell Bakhshi Murawwat Muhammad Khan to provide one or two battalions of foot-soldiers for the safety and security of the godown. Whatever goods are needed, the soldiers should be sent to the *mahals* to obtain those goods from there. The details of *saman-i rasad* are: flour, pulse, rice, mustered oil, salt and spices. Whatever goods, carriers, the bullocks of banjaras which are managed from Bhopal, the quantity and number, its weight and name of grains and the number of bullocks of banjaras should be communicated to the government. Dated 21 *Muharram* 1275 AH.

P 7. Parwana *of Nawwab Sikandar Begam to Ghulam Makhdum Khan,* Nazim-i Maghrib. The army of Bhopal has been sent under the command of Bakhshi Murawwat Muhammad Khan to the district east. He is directed to instruct the *amils*, *thanadars* and *ilaqadars* to make arrangement of *saman-i rasad* for both the governments and make it available with Uma Prasad, *muhtamim*, *sair* of district east in the army camp. The quantity and weight along with the name of grains may be conveyed to the government. This should be given priority over other tasks. Dated 23 *Muharram* 1275 AH.

P 9. *Nawwab Sikandar Begam to Bakhshi Murawwat Muhammad Khan.* Informs that in regard to make an arrangement of *saman-i sarbrah-i rasad* for the *sawars* who are in his command to march to Sehore, Ghulam Muhammad Khan, *nazim-i maghrib* has been instructed. The *nazim* would provide all essential commodities to him. He may obtain food-grains etc whatever he needs from him and his *ilaqa*. He should also pay the legitimate price of the commodity.

PP 11-12. *Mansukh Rai, Deputy* Muhtamim *of* Sair-i Kul, *to Nawwab Sikandar Begam.* Informs of a letter received from Lala Uma Prasad, *muhtamim* of district east, dated 3 *Safar* 1275 AH, along with the agreement concluded with Muhammad Jamal and Khuda Bakhsh, *banjaras*.

PP 13-14. *Uma Prasad,* Muhtamim *of District East, to Mansukh Rai, Deputy* Muhtamim, Sair-i Kul. Refers to the royal *parwana*, dated 21 *Muharram* 1275 AH, issued to him which is regarding *sarbrah-i rasad* for the army, commanded by Murawwat Muhammad Khan.

P 15. *Agreement Concluded by Muhammad Jamal, Son of Mu'azzam Manik, and Khuda Bakhsh, Dwellers of Bhopal.* That they are ready to provide about 204 bullocks for carrying goods of *rasad* to the godown of the army camp as per the details, and that they are ready to accept the rate for the bullocks and wages for the employees and other allowances as per the previous practice. The bullocks would be available in Bhopal within 7 to 10 days. Due to rainy season, 13 bulloks out of 238 could not be sent. Rest of the bullocks would reach Bhopal well in time. Dated 3 *Safar* 1275 AH.

P 17. *Mansukh Rai, Deputy* Muhtamim *of* Sair-i Kul *to Nawwab Sikandar Begam.* Informs that as ordered, 82 maund 4 *ser* grains, loaded on 204 bullocks managed by Khuda Bakhsh and Muhammad Jamal, *banjaras*, for sending to the army camp are kept ready in the rooms of Fatahgarh. They would be sent to the camp of army led by Murawwat Muhammad Khan, only after the guards are made available. Requests for providing 2 to 4 guards for the protection and safety of the *rasad*. Dated 19 *Safar* 1275 AH.

P 19. Fard, *Containing Details of Goods of* Rasad *Being Sent to Gulgaon near Uma Prasad,* Muhtamim *of District East, Meant for the Army Led by Murawwat Muhammad Khan, Dated 18* Safar 1275 AH.

PP 21-2. *Mansukh Rai, Deputy* Muhtamim *of* Sair-i Kul to *Nawwab Sikandar Begam.* Informs that day; the 20th *Safar,* a letter of Lala Jiwan Lal, *muharrir, sair-i kul* was received, informing that one guard was available at Bhopal and that two guards returned, accompanying the goods, coming from Siwans and that 204 bullocks, loaded with grains guarded by three guards were sent through Uma Prasad, *Muhtamim* of district east, to Bakhshi Murawwat Muhammad Khan, and that there was no need of further guards to take care of the bullocks. The same is sent to her to make the matter clear. On the previous date, the 19th *Safar,* a letter was sent informing that the grains, loaded on the bullocks were made available in Fatahgarh and a request was made for providing 4 guards to accompany the *rasad.* But then there was no further need of guards as the grains were already sent from there. Dated 20 *Safar* 1275 AH.

P 23. *Lala Jiwan Lal,* Muharrir, Sair-i Kul, *to Mansukh Rai, Deputy* Muhtamim, Sair-i Kul. Informs that as ordered the goods of *sarbrah-i rasad* were weighted in Fatahgarh and sent to Uma Prasad, *muhtamim* of district east, loaded on the bullocks with guards. Dated 20 *Safar* 1275 AH.

P 25. *Saiyid Asghar Ali,* Tahsildar, *to Nawwab Sikandar Begam.* Informs that as ordered by Maulawi Muhammad Sa'd al-Din, *muhtamim, adalat-i faujdari*, 300 bullockes of the *banjaras* were captured and sent to him. Dated 21 *Safar* 1275 AH.

P 27. *Mansukh Rai, Deputy* Muhtamim, Sair-i Kul, *to Nawwab Sikandar Begam.* Informs that the next day; the 24th *Safar* 1275 AH, 31 bullocks of Khuda Bakhsh, *banjara,* a dweller of Budkhery, loaded with 10 maund (quintal) 11 *pasery* (a five *ser* weight) pulses, guarded by two soldiers of *sair* Wazirganj were sent through Uma Prasad, *muhtamim* of district east to the godown of the army camp of Bakhshi Murawwat Muhammad Khan. Dated 23 *Safar* 1275 AH.

P 29. *Mansukh Rai Diwan, Deputy* Muhtamim, *Sair-i Kul, to Nawwab Sikandar Begam.* Informs that 100 bullocks of Bhema Bhana, *banjara* sent by Ganesh Singh, *darogha, sair* Mardanpur along with a letter of Kishan Lal, *Muhtamim, Sair-i Kul,* district Junub, dated 28 *Safar* 1275 AH, were received. The bullocks are kept in the police station of Churamali, guarded by Munnu Khan, soldier. Requests for further orders to be followed. The bullocks were brought hungry and the *banjaras* come everyday complaining about it. Dated 28 *Safar* 1275 AH.

P 31. *Kishan Lal,* Muhtamim, Sair-i Kul, District Junub, *to Mansukh Rai,* Diwan, *Deputy* Muhtamim, Sair-i Kul. Informs that 100 bullocks of Bhema Bhana, *banjara* sent by Ganesh Singh, *darogha, sair* Mardanpur, are sent to him through Qasim, *sawar* of *risala* III, as per the royal order. Dated 28 *Safar* 1275 AH.

P 33. *Mansukh Rai,* Diwan, *Deputy* Muhtamim, Sair-i Kul, *to Nawwab Sikandar Begam.* Informs that 1, 505 bullocks of Harchand, Balania and Gobardhan, *banjaras* sent by Lala Bhondi Lal, *darogha, sair* Chabutra Ichhawar, along with a letter of Lala Bahadur Singh, *muhtamim, sair* district west, dated 28 *Safar* 1275 AH, were received, guarded by Amir Beg and Qanoji Lal, soldiers of Chabutra Ichhawar. The bullocks are kept in the police station of Churamali, guarded by the soldiers. The letters of the *muhtamim* and *darogha* of Ichhawar are sent to her. Dated 28 *Safar* 1275 AH.

P 35. *Bahadur Singh,* Muhtamim, *Sair District West, to Mansukh Rai,* Diwan, *Deputy* Muhtamim, Sair-i Kul. Refers to the letter of Bhundi Lal, *darogha sair* Ichhawar, dated 26 *Safar* 1265 *fasli*, in reference to his letter, dated 14 *Safar* 1275 AH in regard to providing bullock carriers.

PP 37-8. A Letter in Hindi Devanagari.

P 39. *Bakhshi Murawwat Muhammad Khan to Nawwab Sikandar Begam.* Informs that the moment his march from Bhopal to Berasia was decided, Lala Bahadur Singh, *muhtamim sair,* district west and Shahbaz Khan, *muhtamim chaukiyat*, district west accompanied him to arrange *saman-i rasad* and to establish a godown. Lala Uma Prasad and Hasan Khan too came to supervise the management. Thereafter, order for march to Sanchi Kanakhera was issued.

P 41. *Bakhshi Murawwat Muhammad Khan to Nawwab Sikandar Begam.* Informs that 30th *Safar* 1275 AH passed with peace in the camp. Informs of the letter received from Baijnath, informing about a letter that came from Thakur of Mangalgarh, intimating that by the next day, army of Neemuch would reach Mangalgarh or Kilokhary, situating at a distance of 8 *curoh* from there and requesting for sending 50 maund rice and 50 maund pulses from his camp to Mangalgarh. Informs that he immediately sent the grains of the same quantity there and also informed the Munshi. Dated 30 *Safar* 1275 AH.

P 43. *Bakhshi Murawwat Muhammad Khan to Nawwab Sikandar Begam.* Informs of the letter of Baijnath that night, expressing his gratitude to the Nawwab, and that the army will be at Berasia after the the next day, and that there is scarcity of grain and thus, provide 50 maund grain from his camp. He replied him in affirmation and that he could also provide rice, if required. Says, he sent a request of 13 maund rice and 12 maund flour through a peon. The same was provided to him. The receipt is with Uma Prasad. This was also informed to Munshi Bhawani Prasad. Dated 1 *Rabi* I, 1275 AH.

P 45. *Baijnath to Bakhshi Murawwat Muhammad Khan.* From the letter of Munshi Bhawani Prasad, it has come to his notice that the Political Agent would be marching through *ilaqa* Bhopal, and that night 50 maund rice and 50 maund pulses were managed which is a matter of pleasure. It is Nawwab Sikandar Begam who for the last 14 months is protecting him and the people from the atrocities of the insurgents, and she is also taking care of the people of Berasia and the people of Bhopal. The army will encamp at Kilokhary by the next day and day after that they will be at Berasia where there is a scarcity of grain. Requests if 25 maund grains are managed for the British army, it will be an act of good gesture. Dated 9 October 1858.

P 47. *Keshav Rai,* Tahsildar *of* Mahal *Mal, to Nawwab Sikandar Begam.* Refers to her *parwana*, dated 21 *Muharram* 1275 AH, received through Muhammad Raza Husain, *nazim-i district junub*, informing that an army of State of Bhopal under the command of Bakhshi Murawwat Muhammad Khan is on march in district east in order to deal with the insurgents and that *saman-i rasad* may be provided to Lala Uma Prasad, *muhtamim*, *sair*, district east. Name of grains along with its quantity and weight may be sent to the government. Informs that as ordered, search of the *banjaras* was made and the goods was loaded on the bullocks and accompanied by the soldiers sent in the camp of Uma Prasad. This is only for her information. Dated 2 *Rabi* I, 1275 AH.

P 49. Yaddasht, *Containing Details of Goods of* Rasad *Sent to the Army Camp.* The goods are; flour, grains, and pulses.

P 51. *Radhey Kishan,* Muhtamim, Sair-i Kul, *to Nawwab Sikandar Begam.* Refers to the letter of Bakhshi Murawwat Muhammad Khan, dated 30 *Safar* 1275 AH bearing the royal order, dated 2 *Rabi* I,

1275 AH. Informs that 50 maund rice and flour and 50 maund pulses against the goods of godown were sent to Neelgarh from Fatahgarh, loaded on the bullocks of Muhammad Jamal, *banjara*, and handed over to Lala Chain Lal, *muhtamim sair*, district west and sent to Beragarh. This is only for her information. Dated 6 *Rabi* I, 1275 AH.

PP 53-4. *Bakhshi Murawwat Muhammad Khan to Nawwab Sikandar Begam.* Informs that he marched from Bhopal and arrived at Eintkhery. There was rain fall the whole night with full force. Due to which goods could not be sent to the godown and *mahajans*. A letter was sent to Hafiz Adil Khan, *qil'dar*, Islamnagar, for providing *rasad*. He informed that the *saman-i rasad* are being carried by the traders on the rates fixed for the goods. As the river Hilali was on full swing, goods were managed to be transported on female elephants and were sold on the rates as quoted and provided by him. The payment was made to the traders then and there. A copy of his letter and the letter of *qila'dar* is sent to her. Dated 9 *Rabi* I, 1275 AH.

P 55. *Bakhshi Murawwat Muhammad Khan to Muhammad Adil Khan, Qila'dar, Islamnagar.* Informs that the previous day, he marched from Bhopal and reached Eitkhery and the next morning wanted to reach Harakhera. But due to heavy rain, the bullock carts and magazines were not able to move further, hence the *saman-i rasad* could not be sent there. Meanwhile, the goods as mentioned would be made available at the earliest. It will be a good gesture from him. Dated 5 *Rabi* I, 1275 AH.

The details of goods are: rice 1 maund, grain 2 maund, mustard oil 10 *ser*, pulses of moong and onion 6 *ser*, salt 12 *ser*, spices as required. The goods are to be sold on the rate fixed by him.

P 57. *Muhammad Adil Khan, Qila'dar, Islamnagar, to Bakhshi Murawwat Muhammad Khan.* Refers to his letter for providing *rasad* at *mauza* Eintkhery. Informs that the *rasad* sent through the soldiers might have received there. The cost of goods could not be made available due to hurry. He himself should fix the rate wherein they should not be a loss to the traders. If there will be too much sand on the way due to rain, the goods should be carried loaded on elephants. Dated 5 *Rabi* I, 1275 AH.

P 59. *Radhey Kishan,* Muhtamim, Sair-i Kul, *to Nawwab Sikandar Begam.* Refers to the letter of Bakhshi Murawwat Muhammad Khan, directing him to provide 13 maund flour and 12 maund gram, *sarbrah-i rasad*, at Berasia, to Baijnath Singh, Assistant. Informs that day, 13 maund flour and 12 maund gram loaded on the bullocks of *banjaras* under the protection of Khub Chand, soldier was sent to Berasia. Dated 9 *Rabi* I, 1275 AH.

P 61. *Radhey Kishan,* Muhtamim, Sair- i Kul, *to Nawwab Sikandar Begam.* Informs that as ordered by *muhtamim, sair* district west, 18 maund gram and 14 maund flour was mananged from Fatahgarh, loaded on the bullocks and sent to the *muhtamim, sair* district west. Dated 14 *Rabi* I, 1275 AH.

File No. 276
Box No. 14
No. of Documents 6

Notification Issued to the Traders and Merchants

P 1. Contents

P 3. Parwana *of Nawwab Sikandar Begam to Muhammad Raza Husain,* Nazim. Sends the notification issued to the traders and merchants of district south and directs him that main notification may be kept in his office and a copy of it may be issued to every trader and merchant and to each *thanadar* and *tahsildar* under his jurisdiction, directing them to act in accordance to the notification. Dated 12 *Muharram* 1275 AH.

P 5. Parwana *of Nawwab Sikandar Begam to Muhammad Raza Husain, Na*zim. Sends him a notification addressed to the traders and merchants of district south and directs him that a copy of that should be provided to all the traders and merchants.

P 7. *Notification Issued to all the Traders and Merchants of District South.* Many dwellers of Bhopal State during the uprising have gone from the Bhopal State to other regions. Most of them are the insurgents and miscreants. Some of them are known but many are unknown, who in connivance of other miscreants, plunder the property of the masses and sell them in other regions, and send the amount of loot through *hundawi* or in cash to their homes or to the homes of their friends through merchants of Bhopal State. The notification is issued that if anyone from the dwellers of Bhopal State or any miscreant who is a dweller of other region sends *hundawi* or cash through mahajans of Bhopal State, to his house or to the house of his friend who is residing in Bhopal State, the mahajan of Bhopal State should inform the *thanadar* through a petition, then the *thanadar* to the *nazim* and the *nazim* to the government. If the *hundawi* or the cash amount was found genuine, order would be issued to deliver it. If the sender of the *hundawi* or the cash is an insurgent, the said amount would be seized till investigation is completed in the matter. If anyone violates the notification and the amount of *hundawi* or cash sent by the inhabitants of Bhopal State or the miscreants of other regions is delivered, it would call stern punishment from the government. Dated 12 *Muharram* 1275 AH.

P 9. *Muhammad Raza Husain,* Nazim-i Junub, *and the Draft of Muquim Ashraf Khan.* Notification is issued by Muhammad Raza Husain to all the traders and merchants. There are many who have gone from Bhopal to other territories. Some of them are very famous. There are others about whom little is known as to where they took part in insurgency and what was their role. The notification is given that if any insurgent sends money though *hundawi* or transfers cash through a merchant or trader to his relatives in Bhopal, it should be brought to the notice of the government, otherwise it will not be good for them.

P 11. *Karam Ali Husain to Muhammad Raz Husain*. Acknowledges the receipt of *parwana* of the *Nawwab*, dated 12 *Muharram* 1275 AH, along with two notifications in regard to the orders issued to the mahajans and to ensure their implementation. Thus, the notification was given to them and their *iqrarnamas* were obtained. Dated 10 *Safar* 1275 AH.

File No. 277
Box No. 14
No. of Documents 8

Notification in Regard to Arrest Sher Khan, Ahmad Sher Khan and Other Wilayatis who Revolted Against the Authority of Khajuri

PP 1-2. Contents

P 3. *Nawwab Sikandar Begam to Murawwat Muhammad Khan.* Directs him to send the report of all the *wilayatis* who have gone with Muhammad Sher Khan and Muhammad Amin Khan, *jamadars* with their physical description and the description of the *jamadars* too. Dated 8 *Muharram* 1275 AH.

P 5. *Murawwat Muhammad Khan to Nawwab Sikandar Begam.* Sends the report as sought through her *parwana,* dated 8 *Muharram* 1275 AH in regard to physical description of the wilayatis who have gone with Sher Khan and Muhammad Amin Khan, *jamadars*. Dated 28 *Muharram* 1275 AH.

PP 7-14. Yaddasht, *Containing Physical Description of the Wilayatis.*

P 15. Parwana *of Nawwab Sikandar Begam to Muhammad Jamal al-Din,* Madar al-Maham. Sends a notification issued in the name of Ghulam Murtaza Khan, *Kamdar,* Deorhi Khas, directing him to get published 141 copies of the notification from *Matba' Sikandari* and send it to the Government. Dated 4 *Safar* 1275 AH.

P 17. *Orders of the Government that the* Parwana *may be Sent to Lala Phul Chand*, muhafiz-i Daftar *to Include in the Register and to Keep in the Daftar*. A copy of the *parwana* and the sample of the notification may be sent to Muhammad Abd al-Wahid, *muhtamim, matba' Sikandari* to print 141 copies and send it to the government. Dated 4 *Safar* 1275 AH.

PP 19-20. *Notification Issued in the Name of Ghulam Murtaza Khan,* Kamdar *of Deorhi Khas*. The following persons during the uprising left the job of the Bhopal government, and went from there and joined hands with the miscreants. It is must that they should be arrested. Thus, he is informed to notify in his entire jurisdiction that if anyone of them comes to Bhopal, he should be arrested and presented under security in the government under challan. Names of such persons and their physical description are as given in the text.

P 21. *Muhammad Jamal al-Din,* Madar al-Maham *to Nawwab Sikandar Begam*. Informs as directed through her *parwana,* dated 4 *Safar* 1275 AH, 141 notifications have been published from *matba' Sikandri* which is regarding those persons who left the job of Bhopal government and went from there and joined hands with other miscreants. The sample of the notification and the *parwana* is sent to her. Dated 16 *Safar* 1275 AH.

File No. 278
Box No. 14
No. of Documents 4

Budh Sen, an Employee of Fazil Muhammad Khan

P 1. Content

P 3. *Bhawani Prasad to Nawwab Sikandar Begam.* Sends the *parwana* of the Political Agent, dated 3 September 1858, issued in reference to the petition of Budh Sen which is that after his arrest an order was issued that until Adil Muhammad Khan and Aqil Muhammad Khan are held, he should not be in captivity. Thus, if there is a proof of his misdeed, he must be in captivity as punishment. Otherwise, to keep one in captivity for the sake of others is unlawful. Dated 25 *Muharram* 1275 AH (4 September 1858).

P 5. *The Political Agent to Bhawani Prasad.* Refers to the letter of Budh Sen arguing that in his case an order was issued that he should not be put either under house arrest or under arrest untill Adil Muhammad Khan and Aqil Muhammad are held. The surety and surety of character (*fe'l-i zamanat*) obtained from him along with the *muchalka* assuring not to serve the insurgents proves his innocence and that he has been held under false charges. A culprit is punishable if misdeeds are proved after investigation, and then such a culprit must be punished. But to keep one under arrest for for the sake of others, as in this case that unless Adil Muhammad Khan and Ail Muhammad Khan are held, is against the law. Dated 3 September 1858.

P 7. Parwana *of Nawwab Sikandar Begam to Bhawani Prasad.* Refers to the *parwana* of the Political Agent in his name, dated 3 September 1858, explaining that a culprit implies that the crime is proved against him. If Budh Sen has committed a crime and it is proved with evidence, then he must be punished. But to put one under arrest for the sake of others, as in this case that unless Adil Muhammad Khan and Aqil Muhammad Khan are held he should remain captive, is unlawful. Says that the observation of the Political Agent is quite right and justified in the eyes of law which means that if there is no proof of crime against a person, such a person is to be freed. But in certain cases, circumstances are also to be taken into consideration. This is a matter of deliberation for the Political Agent that all those soldiers and men of learning who were freed earlier, as there was no prove of crime against them, they joined Adil Muhammad Khan in Sironj and Bhilsa. There is an apprehension that Budh Sen too might join Adil Muhammad Khan. The miscreants are quite aware of the affairs of Bhopal. Besides this, the matter of Fazil Muhammad Khan is still to be settled and Budh Sen is one of them who is aware of the affairs of Fazil Muhammad Khan. He might be required during investigation in the matter. Thus, it is desirable that Budh Sen may be kept in captivity for few more days. He would not be harmed except putting him in captivity. If the Political Agent agrees with the proposal, otherwise order for his release may be issued. Directs him to bring the matter into the notice of the Political Agent and his observation may be communicated to her. Dated 9 *Safar* 1275 AH.

File No. 279
Box No. 14
No. of Documents 4

Nawwab Hyder Muhammad Khan of Pathari under House Arrest

P 1. Contents

PP 3-4. *Bhawani Prasad to Nawwab Sikandar Begam.* Sends the *parwana* of the Political Agent, dated 19 August 1858, asking whether there is a need to keep *Nawwab* Hyder Muhammad Khan under house arrest. Requests for orders as she may like. Dated 9 *Muharram* 1275 AH (20 August 1858).

P 5. *The Political Agent to Bhawani Prasad.* Refers to his letter in the matter of *Nawwab* Hyder Muhammad Khan and the reply received from the agenty, Central India, dated 12 August is that 'the Political Agent of the Bhopal State is instructed to communicate whether there is a need to keep the said *Nawwab* under house arrest and that the Political Agent is free to take decision in the matter'. Directs him to put the matter with valid reason. Dated 13 August 1858.

PP 7-8. *Nawwab Sikandar Begam to Muhammad Sa'd al-Din,* Muhtamim, Adalat-i Faujdari. Sends the letter of Bhawani Prasad, *wakil-i riyasat*, dated 9 *Muharram* 1275 AH, along with the *parwana* of the Political Agent, directing him to include it in the file of *Nawwab* Hyder Muhammad Khan, Pathariwala. Dated 13 *Rajab* 1275 AH.

File No. 280
Box No. 14
No. of Documents 4

Two Harkaras, who During Uprising Came to Bhopal from Indore, Carrying an Envelope with Papers in Hindi

P1. Contents

P 3. Parwana *of Nawwab Sikandar Begam to Bhawani Prasad.* Informs of two *harkaras* who came to Bhopal from Indore, carrying an envelope in Hindi. There is no indication of any government symbol on the envelope. They were not even carrying a *parwana* of the British government. The two *harkaras* along with the envelope are sent to the Political Agent. The Political Agent may take whatever decision he likes in the matter. Directs him to bring the matter into the notice of the Political Agent and his reply may be conveyed to her.

PP 5-6. *Bhawani Prasad to Nawwab Sikandar Begam.* Informs that day, Najib Khan along with two *harkaras* with one envelope in Hindi arrived there. Says he read the outer surface of the letter and came to know that it is the *naib wakil* of Tahri, also called Tikamgarh, who from the Office of Central India has written a letter to *Wazir al-Daulah*, Natthi Khan, *kamdar* of Raja of Tahri. Adds that he also knows Jawar Khan, his sister's son. They are the old servants of Tahri. Says the next day, he would present the *harkaras* and the envelope before the Political Agent.

PP 7-8. *Bhawani Prasad to Nawwab Sikandar Begam.* Refers to her *parwana*, dated 26 *Muharram* 1275 AH, and informs that day, he presented the two *harkaras* before the Political Agent who are held as they do not carry any official document in their favour from any government. Says the Political Agent enquired from them and came to know that they were the servants and informers of the *wakil* of the government of Tikamgarh, who were sent to Tikamgarh by the *wakil* for some official work. The Political Agent ordered for issuing challan of their not being harassed in the region of Bhopal and let them off without any harm. Informs a challan is issued and they are allowed to proceed. Dated 27 *Muharram* 1275 AH (6 September 1858).

File No. 281
Box No. 14
No. of Documents 11

Uprising by Tantia Tope and Others in Jhalra Patan and Other Places

PP 1-3. Contents

PP 5-6. *Bhawani Prasad to Nawwab Sikandar Begam.* Informs that day, he was called by Major William Henry Richards, the Political Agent, and told him about a letter received from the Agent to the Governor-General, Central India, informing that on 27 August 1858, 1,200 insurgents with swords destroyed Jhalra Patan and set on fire the cantonment of the Maharaja Jhalra Patan, situating nearby the city. The cannon and other weapons of warfare were captured and attacked upon the fort where the Maharaja of Jhalra Patan was residing. He is called so that the information may be forwarded to *Nawwab* Sikandar Begam. Informs that the Political Agent was expressing his deep concern as the insurgents for the last 17 months were creating disturbances everywhere. But the chieftains were taking no care of their wealth, dignity and their states. The insurgents were defeated everywhere and fled haplessly. But the chieftains were so afraid of them that they handed over to them their wealth and surrendered before them. They dared not to fight with them. They knew that if they fought with them, they would be defeated. But was it difficult to kill or arrest them? He also said that the reason of the entry of the insurgnets in Jhalra Patan was that a group of the British forces were pursuing them. The insurgents were on the other side of river Chambal whereas the British forces, due to havoc of Chambal river water, stayed on the other side of the river and the distance between the two forces was too long. On 29 August 1858, one group of British forces arrived at Agar from Mhow cantonment. The distance between Jhalra

Patan and Agar is 55 *curoh*. The Agent mentioned very explicitly about the wealth of Jhalra Patan. The Political Agent asked him about it. Says he told him what he had heard or knew about Jhalra Patan. It was the time when with the help of the British, the third share of the territory of Kota which was Rs. 17 lakh, was granted to the grand-son of the Raja Zalim Singh. The *mahals* of Jhalra Patan were part of that share. From Kota, for 3 consecutive days and nights, whatever wealth like jewellery, gold, silver, besides all other valuables were carried away, loaded upon the carriers, camels, horses and bullocks. It was so huge that que of carriers was seen from Kota to Patan upto Jhalra Patan. The people of Jhalra Patan and the traders were very prosperous and happy. The walled city of Jhalra Patan was strong and fortified and situated on such a place that on one side of the city was a river and on the other-side was a nallah. God knows how these insurgents reached there. Dated 25 *Muharram* 1275 AH (4 September1858).

PP 7-8. *Bhawani Prasad to Nawwab Sikandar Begam*. Informs that day, Lala Laxman Narain, *wakil* of Rawat Moti Singh, the ruler of Rajgarh came with a letter of traders of Zirapur Panchalpur, dated, *bhadon budi* 8 (22 *Muharram* 1275 AH) which contained the information that a group of insurgents arrived at Jhalra Patan. The Maharaja was captured in his *haveli* and detained and a sum of Rs. 5 lakh was decided to be paid. Meanwhile, at night, the news from the *haveli* of Riwans came of the birth of a son to the Maharaja. In the morning, Sada Shiv Rao Pandornak, nephew of Peshwa celebrated the occasion. Maharaja made charity of one elephant, besides Rs. 500 and some cloths. Maharaja was permitted to go to Riwans. But Maharaja went to Thania, instead of going to Riwans. The army of Maharaja assembled to fight with Sada Shiv Rao Pandornak. A battle was fought for 9 hours. Around 800 men were killed from both sides. Thereafter, the Muslim employees of Maharana sided with the insurgents. They did not sacrifice their lives. Ultimately, the insurgents succeeded. At Sunil Kothry, *ilaqa* Maharaja Holkar, situating at a distance of 13 *curoh* from Jhalra Patan, the British forces arrived to deal with this group of insurgent forces. From Mhow and Indore too, the British forces marched towards Patan. The intention of the insurgent forces was to devastate Chandkheri, which was already devastated earlier. There is also news that they would go to Khaljipur and Rajgarh. The letter was presented to the Political Agent. There was also a *parwana* of Rawat, addressed to the *wakil*, which contained the information that if the Political Agent helped him with a British force at the moment, it would be good. Informs the traders in Sehore raised their voice after the arrival of that letter. They were telling that, this was totally a false news that the insurgent forces marched from Jhalra Patan and arrived at Khaljipur. If anyone reports such news to her, it should not be relied upon at all. However, alertness and attentiveness should be the priority. On 29 August 1858, the British forces arrived from Mhow cantonment to Agar cantonment. Dated 26 *Muharram* 1275 AH (5 September 1858).

PP 9-10. *Bhawani Prasad to Nawwab Sikandar Begam.* Informs that day, the Political Agent told him that Tantia Tope devastated Patan and the Raja of Patan fled and joined the British army at Agra coming to fight with the insurgents. Tantia Tope, hearing the news of the British forces, fled. But surely he would meet his fate. Says he also told him that Adil Muhammad Khan, Sikandar Khan, Yasin Khan and Chhatrasal were at Agra and then they arrived in a vallage, adjoining to Sironj and that his government was busy in dealing with the insurgents by sending troops. But her priority is to ensure the safety and security of Sehore cantonment. If Sehore cantonment is saved, Adil Muhammad Khan and others could be dealt with effectively. If *sawars* are deployed by him to guard Sehore cantonment, the Bhopal army would not delay a single minute in dealing with the insurgents. He said ok. But he has ordered to the army, deployed at Guna to deal with Adil Muhammad Khan. Not only that, but the army at Guna marched to Sironj. About three days before, there was a skirmish between them and the army led by Tantia Tope at Raghogarh. About 450 insurgents were killed and the rest fled. The said army would soon arrive in Sironj to deal with Adil Muhammad Khan and others. Says, he also told him that in Sironj there were so many relatives of Adil Muhammad Khan who were helping him. He said by that time everything would be settled. There is news that Adil Muhammad Khan came to Ganj Basodah from Sironj and destroyed it. Has he heard about it, he inquired. He said for the last three days he had no information of Adil Muhammad Khan. He said, they arrived at Akbarabad from Banpur and Shahgarh and still they did not stop. He said to him that their management was so good and efficient that in such a hot season carrying a little army, they dealt with the insurgents of Bundelkhand who were huge. Says he expressed his happiness stating that there was too much heat but it was the graceness of *Nawwab* Sikandar Begam as she was regularly sending orange, sweets, fruits and rose water which saved him from the stroke of heat and he came back with all happiness. Dated 27 *Muharram* 1275 AH (7 September 1858).

PP 11-12. *Gobind Prasad, Treasurer, and Madan Mohan,* Naib Wakil *to Nawwab Sikandar Begam.* Informs the previous day; the 26th *Muharram* 1275 AH (6 September 1858), he arrived at Indore. That day, he sought to meet the Agent to the Governor-General, Central India, through Maula Bakhsh, *jamadar*, to deliver the goods purchased as per the order. The Agent has fixed the time of 4 o'clock to meet him. It is heard that Tantia Tope with an army of 3,000 *sawars* and 500 foot-soldiers arrived at Patan and fought a battle with Raja Patan. The two forces fought bravely. Ultimately some employees of Raja Patan who belonged to the Muslim community turned disloyal as they did not fire their ball cannons upon the insurgents. The Raja saw the disloyalty of his employees from his own eyes. He fled from there bare-foot and reached Agra and met Captain Binjis, who was deployed with a column of army to deal with the insurgents. The insurgents devastated and looted all the inhabitants of Patan. They captured the fort and *barah* of Raja. Hearing the news, the Agent to the Governor-General, Central India, sent Benjis with one columnn of army to deal with the insurgents. Hopes the insurgents would soon meet their fate. In both the column of armies, there were 3,000 armymen. All were Britishmen. The insurgent army comprised of 400 men from those who fled from Gwalior, and the army led by Tantia Tope was 300 in strength. A total of 700 personnel attacked upon Balbhat, situating at a distance of 20 *curoh* from Gwalior. A British army appeared to fight with them and 500 of them were killed and about 200 of them fled. Two persons who were sent by Tantia Tope along with his *parwana,* addressed to the British officials of Murar cantonment, arrived there and held talks with them. The *Subedar* gave him the best treatment and informed the officer commander about it. The officer commander soon arrived there and arrested them along with the letters and informed the Agent to the Governor-General, Central India, about the matter requesting for a suitable punishment for them. The Agent to the Governor-General wrote, if they had informed him after their execution he would have been happier as for persons like them, no punishment was more suitable than capital punishment. There is a report from Bundelkhand that some Bundelas have again raised their voice who are being killed by the *tahsildars* and *thanadars*. Dated 27 *Muharram* 1275 AH (7 September 1858).

PP 13-14. *Bhawani Prasad to Nawwab Sikandar Begam*. Informs that day, the Political Agent told him about the content of a letter, received from the Agent to the Governor-General that, at Jhalra Patan a group of 750 insurgents fell prey to Colonel Lockett. There were 450 dead bodies lying on the ground. The rest 300 dispersed and fled. He also said to him to communicate the news to *Nawwab* Sikandar Begam immediately. Dated 1 *Safar* 1275 AH (10 September 1858).

PP 15-16. *Bhawani Prasad to Nawwab Sikandar Begam*. Informs that day, the Political Agent called the *wakil* of Rajgarh who was outside the bungalow and directed him to explain the content of all three letters of Rawat Moti Singh to the *wakil* of Bhopal. The *wakil* read the first letter, dated *bhadon budi amawas,* corresponding to 28 *Muharram* 1275 AH. Its content was, it was heard that around 30,000 insurgent forces attacked Jhalra Patan and made much loot. They took $11^{1/2}$ lakh rupees from the peasants and from the treasury of Maharaja of Jhalra Patan. The destruction caused to the people and the Maharaja was of Rs. 1 crore. Their further intention was to go to Bhopal via Khaljipur, Rajgarh and Narsingarh. It makes him worried. The content of the second letter was, it is heard that the insurgents marched from Patan and devastated many *mauzas* in Raghogarh and set them on fire. Their intention was to go to Indore via Bayawrah. The content of the third letter as he read was, from the letter of Nirbhay Singh, *kamdar* of Khaljipur, it was learnt that the sound of ball cannon was heard in Khaljipur from the side of *qasba* Soyat. Then news reached in Khaljipur that there was a skirmish between the British forces and insurgents at *qasba* Soyat and atleast 800 insurgents were killed and the rest fled. It is not known as to where they went. The Political Agent then let the *wakil* of Rajgarh off and asked him what he learnt from the contents of these three letters; whether the insurgents would go to Indore or to Bhopal. Says he told him that Soyat situating on the bank of river Sind, having the distance of 12 *curoh* from Khaljipur and from Soyat, the distance of Agar cantonment is 12 *curoh*. One battalion of British troops under the command of Captain Robinson has entered in the vicinity of Sumbel under the territory of Holkar.

This was the regiment that fought at Soyat with the insurgents. This is what has been explained in the letter of the Agent to the Governor-General. Colonel Lacket had arrived at Jhalra Patan. The third Regiment of the British troops is at Agra. In such a scenario, it is not possible for the insurgents to go to Rajgarh or Bayawrah or Narsingarh. They know it very well that Bhopal is the place of Afghans. Except war, they will not get anything else from there. Bad fate is waiting for them. If they go towards that side, two companies of the British troops are pursuing them and from this cantonment, 4 companies of troops along with two cannon, besides the troops of Bhopal army of the same number, are enough to deal with them. They would not go to Indore or Ujjain due to fear of Mhow cantonment. But if they go to Sironj or enter in the territory of Maharaja Sindhia or Banpur or Rampura or Mewar that might be possible. Says he said, this is what he also realized. Says he had been the witness of their defeat on two occasions in the past and he remembers the condition of the defeated army. There is a Hindi proverb '*patta kharka, banda bharka*'. For a defeated army of 10, 000 a contingent of only 200 brave soldiers would be able to be victorious upon them and would get huge booty. However, to take precaution is always necessary. Dated 2 *Safar* 1275 AH (11 September 1858).

P 17. *Bhawani Prasad to Nawwab Sikandar Begam*. Informs that day, the Political Agent called Lala Ramden, *Peshdast Wakil*, and asked him to translate the letter of the Agent to the Governor-General in Urdu and sent it to him to communicate all the employees every word of the letter. The content of the letter is, it was two-three days back when there was a skirmish between the British force and the insurgents and 750 were killed. The information is true. But the place of mishap is wrong. It was Bijapur Sipri where this battle was fought. The insurgent forces which were led by Man Singh, Narwarwala, were defeated. Yesterday's news is that the insurgents reached Raipur from Jhalra Patan and on 7 September, they arrived at Soyat. On 9 September, the army led by Colonel reached Susner and the army led by Colonel Bhup reached Agra. On the same day, Colonel Mitchell arrived at Agra from Mhow cantonment to lead the entire army. Rajrana has gone to *pargana* Dig, *ilaqa* Sais Patan. It will be ensured that the insurgents should not cause any harm at all to Khaljipur or Rajgarh. It seems that the insurgents want to join each other. The army which was led by Man Singh and had fled from Bijapur wanted to join the army of Adil Muhammad Khan. Dated 3 *Safar* 1275 AH (12 September1858).

PP 19-20. Parwanas *and Notifications Issued by Nawwab Sikandar Begam to Nawwab Qudsia Begam, Nawwab Shahjahan Begam, Faujdar Muhammad Khan, Nawwab Muiz Muhammad Khan and Nawwab Baqi Muhammad Khan.* Informs of a letter of Bhawani Prasad, *wakil*, dated 3 *Safar* 1275 AH (12 September 1858), informing about the matter as conveyed by Richards, the Political Agent. Hopes that the employees would be instructed to be ready and whatever notifications, issued from day first when a battle was fought at Gwalior till that day which are in regard to fight with the insurgents, all should be kept in mind. The public as well as the army should adhere to it. The public should be ready to make loot of the goods of the insurgents, who are carrying huge wealth with them from Gwalior and elsewhere. We all know very well about Tonk, where the army of *Nawwab Wazir al-Daulah*, Raja of Tonk fought with all courage with the insurgents. Whatever wealth and goods, they had brought from Gwalior, the armymen of Tonk took it from them, killed them or wounded them and became self-sufficient. The thing is that, by bravery and courage, the wealth of others becomes own wealth and if defeated, own wealth goes out.

P 21. *Nawwab Qudsia Begam to Nawwab Sikandar Begam*. Refers to her letter, dated 3 *Safar* 1275 AH, along with the letter of Bhawani Prasad in connection to the employees under her territory that they should be directed to be ready to take on the battle and that they should know about the notification and according to that, the people and soldiers should get prepared and that the people should be made ready to loot the booty and goods of the insurgents. Informs that the public and the army are informed that whenever the insurgents enter in the territory of Bhopal, they should leave no stone unturned in fighting with them and destroying them, and that they should fight with them with courage and bravery. Dated 5 *Safar* 1275 AH.

PP 23-4. *Bhawani Prasad to Nawwab Sikandar Begam.* Informs that day, the Political Agent sent Ahmad, peon, directing that Lal Singh, *chobdar*, is going to *mauza* Pachor for some official work. He should be provided a carrier and *sawars* as per the norm. He conveyed that he is making available the carrier from *thana*. About the *sawars,* the request may be sent to the Agent to the Governor-General. Says he was ordered to provide 4 *sawars* from the *risala* on duty at Sehore.

File No. 282
Box No. 15
No. of Documents 5

Notification for Arresting the Fugitives who are the Culprits, having Committed the Offences During the First Half of 1858, as Issued from Adalat-i Faujdari, Hoshangabad

PP 1-2. Contents

P 3. *Bhawani Prasad to Nawwab Sikandar Begam.* Sends three notifications; one in Persian and others in Hindi, published from *adalat-i faujdari,* Hoshangabad, which are regarding the arrest of the culprits of the first half of 1858. Dated 14 *Muharram* 1275 AH (25 August 1858).

The letter contains the order that all three notifications, issued from the office of *adalat-i faujdari*, Hoshangabad, may be sent to Jamal al-Din, *madar al-maham*, which is addressed to Ghulam Murtaza Khan, directing him to get 140 copies of the notification printed and send it to the government. Information in the matter should also be sent to Bhawani Prasad. Dated 26 *Muharram* 1275 AH (6 September 1858).

P 5. *Bhawani Prasad to Nawwab Sikandar Begam.* Sends 4 notifications in Hindi which are regarding the arrest of the culprits of the first half of 1858, received from Hoshangabad, through the Political Agent. Dated 21 *Muharram* 1275 AH (1 September 1858).

The letter contains the order that all three notifications, issued from the office of *adalat-i faujdari*, Hoshangabad, may be sent to Jamal al-Din, *madar al-maham*, directing him to do as ordered through the letter of Bhawani Prasad. Dated 26 *Muharram* 1275 AH (6 September 1858).

PP 7-8. *Copy of the Notification Addressed to Ghulam Murtaza Khan Issued from the Office of* Adalat-i Faujdari, *District Hoshangabad, which is Regarding the Arrest of the Culprits of the First Half of 1858.*

The notification contains names of 67 culprits along with their father's name, if known; their addresses; the type of crime they committed; place from where they fled; date of fleeing; and their physical description.

P 9. *Muhammad Jamal al-Din*, Madar al-Maham *to Nawwab Sikandar Begam.* Informs that as ordered, dated 26 *Muharram* 1275 AH (6 September 1858), mentioned on the letter of Bhawani Prasad, 137 notifications have been printed from *matba' Sikandari* which is regarding the fugitives who are the culprits of committing the crime during the first half of 1858, issued from the office of *adalat-i faujdari*, Hoshangabad. The same are sent to the government which also bear the name of all the *jagirdars*. Dated 16 *Safar* 1275 AH.

It contains the order that the letter along with the notification may be sent to Bhopal Chand, *muhafiz-i daftar-i insha*, for inclusion in the register and keeping in the *daftar*. A copy of the order may be sent to Abd al-Wahid, *muhtamim, matba' Sikandari,* directing him to print 140 copies of the nitification from *matba' Sikandari* and send it to the government. Dated 2 *Safar* 1275 AH.

File No. 283
Box No. 15
No. of Documents 24

Salary Installments of Army Contingent Due upon the Bhopal Government

PP 1-4. Contents

PP 5-6. *Bhawani Prasad to Nawwab Sikandar Begam.* Refers to the *parwana* of the Political Agent, dated 14 September 1858, which is in reference to the petition of Chetu Lal, *subadar, major* for the salary of one month and eight days outstanding against the army contingent. Hari, Ram Prasad, Niyaz Ali and others who have been acquitted, have submitted a petition for the release of their salary. The Political Agent has urged him to request the government to release their salary. Sends the *parwana* and requests to take action in the matter. Dated 6 *Safar* 1275 AH (15 September 1858).

P 7. *The Political Agent to Bhawani Prasad,* Wakil-i Riyasat. Refers to the earlier letter in his name, written on the basis of the petition of Chetu Lal, *subadar,* major which is about his salary for a month and 8 days outstanding against the army contingent. Now Hari, Ram Prasad and Niyaz, the soldiers who have been acquitted as there is no proof of committing any crime by them, have submitted a petition in this regard. Directs him to get their salary from his government and submit the receipt. Dated 14 September1858.

PP 9-10. *Parwana of Nawwab Sikandar Begam to Than Singh, Treasurer*. A sum of Rs. 37, 352/9/5, as per the details, borrowed from him as loan has been deposited in the treasury of the Agenty, Sehore as installment of the army contingent of Bhopal. Directs him to give another installment of Rs. 28, 000, the arrear of the remaining installment of the army contingent. Further, an interest of anna 12% would be payable from the date of payment. A property yielding a sum of Rs. 65, 352/9/5 has been earmarked in the *tahsil, pargana* Sehore. The amount would be payable in 4 installments in the year 1266 *fasli* from the realization of *pargana* Sehore. At the end of the year, the amount exceeding the loan amount would be taken back from him and if any amount remains payable to him, would be paid by the government. Dated 7 *Safar* 1275 AH.

PP 11-12. *Bhawani Prasad to Nawwab Sikandar Begam.* Acknowledges the receipt of her *parwana,* dated 9 *Safar* 1275 AH, informing that the total amount of salary of the army contingent for the month of December upto January 20, 1858 has been deposited in the treasury of Agenty Sehore and nothing remains to be paid to Hari, Ram Prasad and Niyaz, the former soldiers of the army contingent. Explains that a total sum of Rs 1, 65, 350/9/5 has been deposited in the treasury of the Agenty, as installments of the army contingent, expenses of the Madarsas, feeding of the prisoners, annual expenditure of grass cutters, and for the repair of roads. But a sum of rupees five thousand and a few hundred due as salary of former army contingent has not been deposited in the treasury. The employees of the contingent are demanding their salary from the Political Agent. Requests for orders to be issued for the same. Dated 16 *Safar* 1275 (25 September1881).

P 13. *Madan Mohan,* Naib Wakil *to Nawwab Sikandar Begam.* Informs that he met Captain Maine and asked about his well being and then asked on her behalf where the difference was in the calculation. He said that at Mhow, he spent about Rs. 10, 000 on the employees of the army contingent and this amount was not made available to him. For that matter he has been called to clear it. Says he replied to him that the amount of Rs. 4, 867/7/1 Kaldar coin was received by him at Sehore. He is not aware about any other matter. It would be better to ask the one who maintained the statement of expenditure incurred at Mhow. He replied that the amount was to be spent at Guna. The kind of trouble, he received from him should be pardoned. He said, no mention. Thereafter, he dispersed. He also said that day, he would be going to Berasia with *sawars* and the following day would go to Sehore. Dated 13 *Rabi* I, 1275 AH (20 November 1858).

PP 15-16. *Bhawani Prasad to Nawwab Sikandar Begam.* Informs that day, Lala Than Singh, treasurer, sent her *parwana,* dated 7 *Safar* 1275 AH, addressed to him and conveyed that as per the *parwana,* the realization of *pargana* Sehore is to be sent to him against the amount of loan, borrowed from him and the *tahsildar* of Sehore is to send the first installment of the *hundawi* of the realized sum to the *nizamat-i maghrib*. Says when he asked the *tahsildar* of Sehore about it he said, he did not receive any order so far in the matter. Although in accordance to the order of the *nazim*, the *hundawi* is being sent to him. Dated 19 *Rabi* I, 1275 AH (26 November 1858).

P 17. Parwana *of Nawwab Sikandar Begam to Bhawani Prasad.* The first installment of the army contingent should be received in the treasury of Agenty at Sehore on the first day of *aghan sudi*. That time is about to come. During the last year, the *dastgardan* amount was taken from Than Singh, Treasurer. For its payment in four installments from the realization of *pargana* Sehore, property has been identified in Sehore. According to that the aforesaid amount will be paid to the treasurer's shop in installments from the realization of *pargana* Sehore. Directs him to keep Than Singh in confidence so that the first installment of army contingent for the year 1266 *fasli* is received in the treasury of Agenty at Sehore. The receipt of the payment of the installment by Than Singh, in the treasury of Agenty, Sehore should be obtained and send to the government. The said amount will be paid to Than Singh in due course with an interest of anna 12%. Directs him to reply urgently. Dated 7 *Jumada* I, 1275 AH.

PP 19-20. *Bhawani Prasad to Nawwab Sikandar Begam.* Informs that in accordance to her *parwana*, dated 7 *Jumada* I, 1275 AH, which is in regard to the payment of first installment of army contingent for the year 1266 *fasli* in the treasury of Agenty, Sehore, he called Than Singh and held talk with him in isolation. He said, presently an amount of Rs. 25,000 is available, if said may be paid and that he has no hesitation in obeying the royal order. During the next one and half month, the said amount will be ready for payment and will inform him accordingly. Says he told him that the amount of installment to be paid by *aghan sudi*, *punam*, would be Rs. 57, 000. An amount of mere Rs. 25,000 will not suffice for the purpose. He said that by Sunday, the 12th *Jumada* I, 1275 AH, he himself would go through the accounts of the shop and then would reply to him. Says the next day he would hold a talk with him and then would bring the matter to her notice. Says the previous day, the Political Agent conveyed him through Ramden, *Peshdast Wakil*, that the *Nawwab* may be communicated about the payment of the first installmet of the year 1266 *fasli* in the treasury and when he would tell him of the money required by him. The matter is brought to her notice to be informed to the employees. Dated 11 *Jumada* I, 1275 AH (18 December 1858).

P 21. *Bhawani Prasad to Nawwab Sikandar Begam.* Informs that day, Than Singh, treasurer of Sehore, met him and said that he thoroughly checked the accounts of his shop and that he could manage by that time a sum of Rs. 25,000 to fulfil the orders of the government. After two months whatever amount comes, to his shop, he would inform him. Beyond that it is not possible for him to promise for today or tomorrow. Regarding the amount of Rs. 25,000, if the government is willing, he would deposit it in the treasury of Agenty at Sehore. Says he persuaded him further, he said, he did no have any hesitation in fulfilling the order of the government but presently he has only a sum of Rs. 19, 000 in his shop and by the next day, there would be available another amount of Rs. 6,000. Dated 12 *Jumada* I, 1275 AH (19 December 1858).

PP 23-4. Parwana *of Nawwab Sikandar Begam to Bhawani Prasad.* Refers to his letter, dated 11 *Jumada* I, 1275 AH, informing that Than Singh, treasurer Agenty Sehore is saying that at the moment he is able to pay a sum of Rs. 25,000 towards the payment of first installment of army contingent and by one and half month he would inform him further in the matter. Explains the thing is that normally the amount of installment of army contingent is to be deposited in the treasury at Bhopal, before falling due date, and the amount of installment whatsoever it is, should be deposited without reduction even a single rupee. So also it is her desire that the amount of installment should be in totality without deduction. Directs him to tell the treasurer that the amount of Rs. 57, 000; the first installment of army contingent which also includes the installment of expenditure of road repairing, should be kept ready and whenever the Political Agent demands the said amount, it should be deposited in the treasury of Agenty. For the next installment, there would be no compulsion upon the treasurer as the amount would be realized from the mahajans of Bhopal. In nutshell, the amount of Rs. 57, 000, which is one installment of army contingent which also includes the amount of road construction should be deposited by the treasurer in the treasury. Dated 13 *Jumada* I, 1275 AH (20 December 1858).

P 25. *Bhawani Prasad to Nawwab Sikandar Begam.* Informs that as desired in the *parwana*, dated 13 *Jumada* I, 1275 AH, he explained the matter to Than

Singh, treasurer. He emphasized upon him as much as possible towards making the payment of Rs. 57, 000, the first installment of army contingent for the year 1266 *fasli*. But in reply, he only said that he did not have any hesitation in obeying the royal order. But at the moment, he is unable to manage more than Rs. 25,000 from all sources inspite of his best efforts. He said that the amount of Rs. 25,000 is kept ready and would be deposited in the treasury with the orders of the government. The remaining balance of Rs. 57, 000 would be deposited with the second installment. If he could manage the said amount even before the said time, he would inform him. Says he tried to know about the balance sheet of the treasury of Agenty and came to know that that day a sum of Rs. 4,000 Bhopali coin was available in the treasury. But the expenses meant for the distribution of salary of the Regiment No. 9 and the expenses, incurred upon the army marching with Major Teller also needs to be kept in mind. Dated 15 *Jumada* I, 1275 AH (22 December 1858).

P 27. *'Abd al-Karim Ansari to Nawwab Sikandar Begam.* Informs that day, he arrived at Sehore and informed Munshi Bhawani Prasad about the treasure which he brought. The Munshi said to Ramden, *peshdast* to hand over the treasure to the treasurer of the Agenty and inform the Political Agent. Ramden took him along to the treasurer and deposited the treasure in the treasury. He and the companion were allowed to go and take rest. He went to the Political Agent to inform him that the treasure was deposited in the treasury. The Political Agent said that this was not the way to take the treasure. Have the treasure with him and come in the morning with it to hand it over. So, he came with the treasure to the room and by the next day in the morning he would hand over the treasure to the treasurer as directed by the Political Agent. He would deposit the treasure and would be back to have her glance.

PP 29-30. *Bhawani Prasad to Nawwab Sikandar Begam.* Informs that, as desired in the *parwana*, dated 11 *Rajab* 1275 AH, he talked to Than Singh about a sum of Rs. 50,000-the third installment. He said that he did not have any hesitation in obeying the royal order. But an amount of Rs. 17, 000 is outstanding against the government and a similar amount has also been taken from various agencies of the British government. Presently, the sum of the third installment would not be possible to manage from his shop. The second installment is deposited at Sehore, and an amount of Rs. 7,000 only, has been received in his shop. As a result, he stopped this year's purchase of opium. Till the time of 4th installment, due in the month of *Baisakh*, he would make payment whatever amount would be possible for him to manage. But regarding the 3rd installment, he is helpless to make any commitment. This is for information of the employees of the government. Dated 19 *Rajab* 1275 AH (23 February 1858).

P 31. Parwana *of Nawwab Sikandar Begam to Bhawani Prasad.* By the grace of God, he would be able to deposit two installments of the salary of army contingent, Bhopal for the year 1266 *fasli* in the treasury of Agenty, Sehore. For the payment of 3rd installment of their salary, she would require to borrow Rs. 50,000 from Than Singh, treasurer. An interest of anna 12% would be paid to him till the debt is cleared. Directs him to talk to Than Singh, treasurer, in the matter of Rs. 50,000 and convey to her what is his opinion. Dated 11 *Rajab* 1275 AH.

PP 33-4. *Bhawani Prasad to Nawwab Sikandar Begam.* Refers to the order, dated 26 *Rajab* 1275 AH, recorded in his letter and says that he held talk with Than Singh about the 4th installment of the expenditure of army contingent. He said, these days the need of money is everywhere, particularly, in the month of *Baisakh*, the need of money becomes more vulnerable for the *sahus*. It is difficult for him to commit the payment of

4th installment of the army contingent, as presently he has no plan to purchase opium. If during this period, the installment amount due upon the government paid to him, he would do his own business from that money and would be able to pay the 4th installment of army contingent and would not hesitate at all regarding making the payment. Dated 8 *Sha'ban* 1275 AH (14 March 1859).

P 35. Yaddasht, *Containing the Details of Wasilbaqi Amount Incurring on Army Contingent in their Salary and the Expenditure of Sehore Cantonment for the Year 1266 Fasli.* It contains the order that it may be sent to Lala Paltu Lal, *muhafiz-i daftar-i insha*, for inclusion in the register and keeping in the *daftar*. A copy of this along with the *yaddasht* of the *Nawwab,* dated 20 *Ramazan* 1275 AH may be sent to Captain William Gardon Cumming, Deputy Political Agent of Bhopal. Dated 20 *Ramazan* 1275 AH.

P 37. *Gist of the Letter of Kishan Ram,* Mu'tamid al-Maham, *to the Government.* As ordered in regard to prepare the accounts of income and expenditure for the year 1266 *fasli* and the amount owed to Than Singh, treasurer of Sehore, informs that he called Lala Gobind Prasad, treasurer and prepared the said account. Requests that the *wakil* may be asked to get the amount of debt borrowed from Than Singh, treasurer, verified.

The letter contains the order to send it to Bhawani Prasad, *wakil* to do the needful as mentioned in the letter. Dated 16 *Ziqada* 1275 AH (18 June 1859).

P 39. *Bhawani Prasad to Nawwab Sikandar Begam.* Informs that in accordance to the letter of Kishan Ram, *mu'tamid al-maham*, dated 12 *Ziqada* 1275 AH regarding the verification of the amount of debt of Than Singh, treasurer of Sehore, the *wasilbaqi* signed by Than Singh, treasurer and the *tahsildar* is submitted. Dated 16 *Ziqada* 1275 AH (18 June 1859).

P 41. Yaddasht, *Containing the Details of Royal Accounts of the Shop of Ram Singh Das Jaipal, for the Date 15* Ziqada *1275 AH, as Submitted by Bilas Rai,* Tahsildar, Mahal *Sehore.* An amount of Rs. 43, 715 realized from *mahal Sadar* for the year 1266 *fasli* was deposited at the shop of Than Singh, treasurer. Dated 15 *Ziqada* 1275 AH.

P 43. *Diwan Kishan Ram,* Mu'tamid al-Maham, *to Nawwab Sikandar Begam.* As ordered, dated 20 *Ziqada* 1275 AH, recorded in the letter of Munshi Bhawani Prasad, *wakil-i riyasat,* the details of Rs. 250 which includes the principal as well as the amount of interest due to be paid to Than Singh, treasurer till the end of *Ziqada* 1275 is submitted. But due to non-availability of anyone from the side of Than Singh, treasurer, the amount of interest could not be verified. Three months are left in the year of 1266 *fasli* to come to an end. If a representative of Than Singh is called, the amount of interest could be calculated accurately that would set a precedent in regard to the payment of interest by the government. Dated 4 *Zilhijja* 1275 AH.

PP 45-6. Yaddasht, *Containing Details of the Amount Paid by Than Singh, Treasurer, Sehore, in Installments for the Army Contingent till the End of* Ziqada *1266* Fasli/*1275 AH/* Mati Asarh, Sudi II, Samvat *1216* Fasli.

P 47. Parwana *of Nawwab Sikandar Begam to Lala Kishanram, Amil-i Sehore.* From the letter of *mu'tamid al-maham*, Diwan Kishan Ram, dated 4 *Zilhijja* 1275 AH, communicating the details of amount due to Than Singh, treasurer of Sehore, it is learnt that an amount of Rs. 46, 647/10$^{1/2}$ owes to Than Singh, treasurer. Directs him to collect the said amount from the *tahsil* of *pargana* Sehore in the year 1267 *fasli* and deposit the same in the shop of Than Singh, treasurer, and obtain the receipt from him for submitting it to the government. Dated 11 *Zilhijja* 1275 AH.

P 49. Parwana *of Nawwab Sikandar Begam to Lala Kishanram,* Amil-*i Sehore.* An amount of Rs. 43, 227½ is outstanding to Than Singh, treasurer of Sehore, which is to be paid. Directs him to collect Rs. 14, 400-the 1st installment, Rs. 14, 400- the 2nd installment, Rs. 14, 427 1/2-the 3rd installment for the year 1267 *fasli* from the *tahsil* of *pargana* Sehore and deposit the same in the shop of the treasurer and obtain the receipt from him for submitting it to the government. Dated 4 *Rabi* I, 1276 AH.

File No. 284
Box No. 15
No. of Documents 3

Dismissal of Ramden Tilanga, Former Employee of Bhopal Army Contingent, After the Punishment of 15 Cane by Deputy Commissioner of District Chanderi

PP 1-2. Contents

P 3. *Murawwat Muhammad Khan to Nawwab Sikandar Begam*. Refers to the letter of Deputy Commissioner, district Chanderi, dated 3 September 1858, informing that Ramden Tilanga was given the punishment of 15 canes and thereafter he was removed from the service. He belongs to Bhopal and his stay in this city is no more required. He is being repatriated to Bhopal via Shahgarh and Sagar. He is directed to keep him in Bhopal. Informs that from the statement of the said Tilanga, it is revealed that he was in the company VI of Bhopal Contingent. He was heading the company in Lalitpur and was dismissed from service due to the crime of hiding. He is sent there under challan with the security of soldiers. Sends the letter of the Deputy Commissioner and the statement of the said Tilanga and requests for further orders in the matter. Dated 17 *Safar* 1275 AH.

P 9. *Deputy Commissioner, District Chanderi, to Murawwat Muhammad Khan*. Informs that Ramden Thakur Tilanga was given the punishment of 15 cane and dismissed from service. Since he had come from Bhopal, so he is being sent back there. Dated 3 September 1858.

File No. 285
Box No. 15
No. of Documents 2

Papers Relating to the Culprits who Committed Crime During the Uprising in the Territory of the British

P 1. Contents

PP 3-4. *Bhawani Prasad to Nawwab Sikandar Begam.* Informs that day, Aesri Prasad, as directed by the Political Agent told him that whatever papers, relating to 124 prisoners are in the possession of Bhopal government, who committed crime under the British territory should immediately be sent back so that orders for the displacement of these prisoners could be issued. Requests for orders, as she may like, in the matter. Dated 6 *Safar* 1275 AH (15 September 1858).

File No. 286, A
Box No. 15
No. of Documents 23

Insurgency of Adil Muhammad Khan, Waging War, and his Defeat by the Amil of Sironj

PP 1-5. Contents

PP 7-8. *Ghulam Muhammad Khan,* Risaldar, *to Nawwab Sikandar Begam.* Informs that day; the 2nd *Safar* 1275 AH, Kalwa and Balkishan, informers came and reported that the previous day, *mauza* Mau, *ilaqa* Sindhia, situating at a distance of 2 1/2 *curoh* from *mauza* Nekan towards Bheglone, was destroyed by the insurgent forces. While fighting, 3 persons of the village were wounded and 2 were killed and 4 persons from among the *zamindars* were captured. Half of the insurgent army is encamping in *mauza* Imlai, nearby *mauza* Mau, and half of the army led by Adil Muhammad Khan has gone four days before from *mauza* Nekan to *mauza* Lutery, *ilaqa* Sironj. *Mauza* Lutery is a big village and the insurgents demanded Rs. 10, 000 from the *zamindars*. Dated 2 *Safar* 1275 AH.

P 9. *Hazrat Nur Khan, Tahsildar of Bheglone, to Nawwab Sikandar Begam.* Refers to a report of the insurgents sent by Ghulam Muhammad Khan, *Risaldar*, as reported by Kalwa and Balkishan, the informers, and hopes that it would make everything clear upon her. Dated 2 *Safar* 1275 AH.

P 11. *Hattey Singh*, Jamadar, *to Nawwab Sikandar*

Begam. Refers to the letter of Murdan Singh, requesting that he should be engaged as he has the speed to travel 25 *curoh* a day which bears her order that he should be sent before Hattey Singh, *jamadar* to judge his ability. If found suitable, he may be engaged. Says he appeared before him. He was examined and has agreed to serve for Rs. 15 a month. Dated 2 *Safar* 1275 AH.

It contains the order that the letter may be sent to Paltu Lal, *muhafiz-i daftar-i insha*, for inclusion in the register and keeping in the *daftar*. A copy of the order may be sent to Hattey Singh, *jamadar,* communicating that giving a salary of Rs. 15 a month to Murdan Singh is accepted. Directs him to send him to bring the news of Adil Muhammad Khan. He should be directed that he himself should see that how much *sawars* and foot-soldiers are being carried by Adil Muhammad Khan and the place where he is encamping.

PP 13-14. *Ghulam Muhammad Khan,* Risaldar, *to Nawwab Sikandar Begam.* Informs that day, Kalwa, the informer came from Sironj and reported that the army led by Adil Muhammad Khan entered Sironj, surrounded it from all sides and captured it. Babu, *muhtamim* of English post, was captured and his house was also destroyed. Lachhman Singh, *jamadar, chaukiyat* was also arrested. Says he has sent another informer to Sironj to bring the latest news. Dated 4 *Safar* 1275 AH.

PP 15-16. *Muhammad Hasan Khan to Nawwab Sikandar Begam.* Informs that the previous day, a letter of Ghulam Muhammad Khan, *risaldar*, was received from Bheglone, informing of the insurgency, committed by the insurgents like Adil Muhammad Khan, besides two other letters, addressed to her and requesting for one or half battalion of troops. The letters at that very moment were sent to her through the post. In reply to the letter of the *risaldar,* he wrote to him that his letter as well as the letter of Hazrat Nur Khan were sent to the *Nawwab*. A contingent of 25 soldiers led by Baldev

Singh, *jamadar*, as requested by him has been sent on 28 *Muharram* 1275 AH which might reach there after writing this letter. A copy of the letter is enclosed herewith. Dated 4 *Safar* 1275 AH.

P 17. *Muhammad Hasan Khan to Ghulam Muhammad Khan* Risaldar. Refers to his letter, dated 3 *Safar,* informing of the insurgency, committed by the insurgents like Adil Muhammad Khan and his request for one or half battalion of troops. Informs that his letter as well as the letter of Hazrat Nur Khan were sent to the *Nawwab*, at that very moment through post. A contingent of 25 soldiers, led by Baldev Singh, *jamadar,* as requested by him has been sent on 28 *Muharram* 1275 AH which might reach there after writing this letter. A copy of the letter is enclosed herewith. Dated 4 *Safar* 1275 AH.

P 19. *Ghulam Muhammad Khan*, Risaldar, *to Hafiz Muhammad Hasan Khan*. Informs that day, Kalwa and Balkishan, the informers came and stated that the insurgents devastated *mauza* Mau. Adil Muhammad Khan who was in *mauza* Nekan, lying at a distance of 3 *curoh* from Sironj and at a distance of 9 *curoh* from Bheglone, has now moved to other place. There is also news of the arrival of Raja Bhor there. Requests to send one or half of the battalion to help him meet the challenges of the insurgent forces. Dated 2 *Safar* 1275 AH.

PP 21-2. *Bhawani Prasad to Nawwab Sikandar Begam.* Refers to her order, dated 3 *Safar* 1275 AH, recorded on his letter and informs that he brought every matter into the notice of the Political Agent whether it is regarding the management of *dandah* or about Bheglone or the proposal to depute Bakhshi Murawwat Muhammad Khan with 200 *sawars* and 500 foot-soldiers under a British officer to wage war against the insurgents. Dated 5 *Safar* 1275 AH (14 September 1858).

It contains the order that the letter may be sent to Paltu Lal, *muhafiz-i daftar-i insha*, for inclusion in the register and keeping in the *daftar*. A copy of the order may be sent to Bhawani Prasad, *wakil* to communicate the Political Agent that the arrangement of *rasad* under other's territory should be made by the Political Agent himself. He should also ask the Political Agent about the British officer who would lead the army of Bhopal State in dealing with Adil Muhammad Khan.

P 23. *Faiz Muhammad,* Thanadar *of* Qasba *Dallod, to Nawwab Sikandar Begam.* Refers to the order of *madar al-maham* that reliable soldiers should be deputed to bring the news of the insurgents. So Chhotey Khan, soldier of *thana* Dallod, was sent to Bhilsa and Shamshabad to bring the news of the insurgents. Informs the previous day, he came back and what he saw he reported. His statement is recorded and is sent to her. Dated 6 *Safar* 1275 AH.

It contains the order that the letter and the statement may be sent to Paltu Lal, *muhafiz i daftar-i insha*, for inclusion in the register and keeping in the *daftar*. A copy of the statement may be sent to Bhawani Prasad, *wakil* for presenting it before the Political Agent and his reply may be conveyed to her. Dated 9 *Safar* 1275 AH.

P 25. *Statement of Chhotey Khan, the Informer, a Soldier at* Thana *Dallod.* States as ordered he as a traveller went to Shamshabad, *ilaqa* Bhilsa, to enquire about the insurgents. He came to know that a group of insurgents is in Ujarkhera. One day before, they had looted a village. He went there to learn further in the matter. But he was arrested and brought before Adil Muhammad Khan and Aqil Muhammad Khan. He saw that Adil Muhammad Khan was carrying a contingent of 3,000, comprising of 1,000 *sawars* besides the foot-soldiers. They had three small cannon. On 14 *Muharram,* they looted *qasba* Bhonrasi. They arrested the *amil* of Bhonrasi, who was a Pundit, and Harilal Seth. The *amil* of Bhonrasi was killed and Harilal Seth was made captive.

PP 27-8. *Bhawani Prasad to Nawwab Sikandar Begam.*

Sends the *parwana* of the Political Agent, Henry Richards, dated 13 September 1858, informing that Adil Muhammad Khan is at the pond of Lutery, as mentioned in the letter of the *wakil* of Sironj and to deal with him, the combined forces of Sironj, Bhilsa and Bhopal should be sent there, and directing him to inform the *Nawwab* to send the forces of Bhopal to Sironj to fight with the insurgents. Dated 6 *Safar* 1275 AH (15 September 1858).

It contains the order that the letter along with the *parwana* of the Political Agent, Henry Richards may be sent to Paltu Lal, *muhafiz-i daftar-i insha*, for inclusion in the register and keeping in the *daftar*. A copy of the order may be sent to Bhawani Prasad to communicate the Political Agent that earlier she urged him to manage the *rasad* for the army of Bhopal State if sent to other's territory, and that one or two British officials should accompany to lead army of the State. But no reply has been received from him so far. Directs him to bring the matter into the notice of the Political Agent and his reply may be conveyed to her. Dated 10 *Safar* 1275 AH (19 September 1858).

P 29. *The Political Agent to Bhawani Prasad*. Refers to the letter of *wakil* of Sironj, communicating the presence of Adil Muhammad Khan at the pond of Lutery and that the combined forces of Sironj, Bhilsa and Bhopal should come to fight with him. Directs him to communicate the *Nawwab* to send the army of Bhopal State to Sironj as requested by the *amil* of Sironj. Dated 13 September 1858.

P 31. *Muhammad Hasan Khan to Nawwab Sikandar Begam*. Refers to the letter of Ghulam Muhammad Khan, *risaldar* from Bheglone, informing about the atrocities of the insurgent forces in Sironj and demanding arms and ammunitions. The same is sent to her. Says in reply, he told him that soon arms and ammunitions would be sent there. Meanwhile, a contingent of 25 soldiers under the command of Baldev Singh, *jamadar*, is sent there. Dated 6 *Safar* 1275 AH (15 September 1858).

P 33. *Ghulam Muhammad Khan,* Risaldar, *to Muhammad Hasan Khan*. Informs that Kalwa, the informer came and stated that Adil Muhammad Khan came to Sironj and captured it. The houses of Lachhman Singh, *jamadar* and Babu of post were destroyed. It is also reported that Raja Bhor too has arrived in Sironj. Says that another informer has been sent to report the truth. Once he comes, the report will be sent to him. Dated 4 *Safar* 1275 AH (13 September 1858).

P 35. *Ganga Prasad*, Jamadar*, to Nawwab Sikandar Begam.* Informs that day, Hasan Khan, soldier sent by the *amil* of Sironj, came and said that Adil Muhammad Khan created disturbances in Sironj and captured the city. In the skirmish, 7 insurgent soldiers were killed but the Fort of Sironj was safe. He came to report to the Political Agent, Bhopal of the matter. Dated 10 September 1858.

P 37. *Muhammad Hasan Khan to Nawwab Sikandar Begam.* Sends the letter received from Ghulam Muhammad Khan, *risaldar,* informing about the atrocities of Adil Muhammad Khan, and requesting for arms and ammunitions. Dated 6 *Safar* 1275 AH (15 September 1858).

It contains the order that the letter may be sent to Paltu Lal, *muhafiz-i daftar-i insha*, for inclusion in the register and keeping in the *daftar*. A copy of the letter may be sent to Bhawani Prasad to communicate the Political Agent and his reply may be conveyed to her. A copy of the order may also be sent to Hafiz Muhammad Hasan Khan, *naib bakhshi*, directing him that if at any moment it is learnt that the insurgent forces are coming to Bheglone he should immediately send half of the battalion, stationed in Siwans to Bheglone and he himself should call half of the battalion, stationed in Garhi Ambapani and half of the battalion, stationed in

Raisen to Siwans. A copy of the order may be provided to Wazir Khan and Thakur Sher Singh for execution.

PP 39-40. *Muhammad Hasan Khan to Ghulam Muhammad Khan,* Risaldar Refers to his letter informing about the insurgent forces. Says soon the insurgents would meet their fate. Informs that he has been provided 1,000 cartridges which should be distributed among the soldiers. The other installment of the arms and ammunitions would soon be sent there. Further informs that the next day, his salary, besides the battalion of Chhotey Ram, the *sawars* and 25 soldiers of the battalion of Baldev Singh, would reach there. Dated 6 *Safar* 1275 AH (15 September 1858).

PP 41-2. *Ghulam Muhammad Khan,* Risaldar, *to Muhammad Hasan Khan.* Informs that day, Kalwa, the informer came and stated that about 5 or 6 groups of insurgent forces were encamping at places as mentioned in the *fard* enclosed. Besides, all the villages under *ilaqa* Sindhia, from Bheglone to Nekan are ruined. The insurgent forces were planning to go to Basodah. There were 3,000 insurgent forces with 6 cannon in Basodah. Dated 3 *Safar* 1275 AH (12 September 1858).

P 43. Fard, *Containing Names of the Villages where the Insurgents were Encamping.* There were about 300 gunners in *mauza* Budankheri, situating at a distance of 4 *curoh* from Bheglone, about 700 gunners with 100 *sawars,* in *mauza* Imlai, situating at a distance of 5 *curoh* from Bheglone and on the mountains in *mauza* Uber, there were 200 gunners situating at a distance of 4 *curoh* from Bheglone. In *mauza* Nekan and *mauza* Lutery, the insurgent forces assembled and then dispersed to other places, situating at a distance of 6 *curoh* from Bheglone. In *mauza* Lutery, Adil Muhammad Khan was present along with his clan and contingent.

PP 45-6. A letter in Hindi Devanagari.

PP 47-8. *Murdan Singh*, Harkakra, *to Nawwab Sikandar Begam.* Informs that on 3 *Safar* 1275 AH, he started his journey from there, stayed at night in Eintkhery and reached Lutery, the next day. He heard there that Adil Muhammad Khan along with his contingent would go to *mauza* Nekan, the next day. He further enquired about his next plan and that whether he would go to Bhopal. He was told that Adil Muhammad Khan depends in every matter on Tantia Tope. He would go where Tantia Tope would tell him to go. He enquired about the intention of Tantia Tope. He was told that he would go to Mumbai or Poona. He has a contingent of 20, 000 or 25,000 with him. Adil Muhammad Khan was waiting for the arrival of Raja Bhor, Narwarwala. After his arrival, he would decide his future plan of action. Dated 7 *Safar* 1275 AH (16 September 1858).

P 49. *Bhawani Prasad to Nawwab Sikandar Begam.* Informs that on 4 *Safar* 1275 AH, there was a skirmish in Sironj between Adil Muhammad Khan and the *amil* of Sironj for the whole day. In the evening, he established a *thana* there. Dated 7 *Safar* 1275 AH (16 September 1858).

File No. 286, B
Box No. 15
No. of Document 19

PP 51-2. *Bhawani Prasad to Nawwab Sikandar Begam.* Informs that day, the Political Agent said, it is strange that the insurgents have arrived in the vicinity. They have too many *sawars* and they travel 25 *curoh* a day. But the *Nawwab* is unaware about this. Why she is not sending the informers here and there to collect the news of the insurgents and keep him informed as well? If the insurgents fall all of sudden, then what will happen? It is a must that the *Nawwab* should be informed and there should not be any negligence in the matter. She should send the informers, and the news received from them should immediately be passed on to him. What is the use of such news if given after a week or after 10 days! What remedy by then would be possible to find out. Dated 8 *Safar* 1275 AH (17 September 1858).

It contains the order that the letter may be sent to Paltu Lal, *muhafiz-i daftar-i insha*, for inclusion in the register and keeping in the *daftar*. A copy of the order may be sent to Bhawani Prasad to communicate the Political Agent that she sent the news about Adil Muhammad Khan to him on 22 *Ziqada* when there was no news about him with anyone. From then till now, how many times, the news of the insurgents was sent to him is on record. But every time the Political Agent did not rely upon such news, and conveyed that these were not reliable news. Dated 11 *Safar* 1275 AH (20 September 1858).

P 53. *'Abd al-Karim Ansari to Nawwab Sikandar Begam.* Informs that evening Bhura Singh, soldier of the battalion of Gudar, *jamadar,* stationed at Berasia, came and reported what he heard from Fatah Ali, *bohra*, who came from Sironj that after a battle, Adil Muhammad Khan entered in Sironj, captured it and half of the city of Sironj was devastated. Dated 8 *Safar* 1275 AH (17 September 1858).

P 55. *Niyaz Ali*, Thanadar, *to Nawwab Sikandar Begam.* Informs that on 22 *Muharram* 1275 AH, he sent Moti Singh, soldier to Agra Barkhera to bring the news of the insurgent forces. He came back that day with the information of Chhatrasal, Adil Muhammad Khan and others. His statement is recorded and is sent to her. Dated 8 *Safar* 1275 AH (17 September 1858).

PP 57-8. *Statement of Moti Singh, Soldier at* Thana *Sehore, in the Presence of Niyaz Ali,* Thanadar. States that his name is Moti Singh, his father's name is Aesri Singh, caste Rajput, a dweller of Sehore, and is in service.

As he was sent to Agra Barkhera to bring the news of Chhatrasal and Adil Muhammad, the rebels, he is asked to tell what he saw there. States that he left Sehore on 22 *Muharram* and reached Agra Barkhera on 26th of the month. He saw that in Agra, 1,000 foot-soldiers and 400 *sawars* were with Chhatrasal who were fully armed and alert. He did not see Adil Muhammad Khan there.

He was asked to tell whether he enquired about their further move. He replied that his further plan was to go to Sironj.

PP 59-60. *Ghulam Muhammad Khan,* Risaldar, *to Nawwab Sikandar Begam.* Refers to his letter, informing about the entry of the insurgent forces in Sironj. Informs about a letter received from Fatahyab Khan, *jagirdar*. The same is sent to her. Requests for providing one battalion of the army to fight with the insurgents. Dated 17 *Muharram* 1275 AH.

It contains the order that all three letters, including this, may be sent to Paltu Lal, *muhafiz-i daftar-i insha,* for inclusion in the register and keeping in the *daftar*. A copy of the order may be sent to Bhawani Prasad to communicate to the Political Agent. A copy of the order may be sent to Ghulam Muhammad Khan, *risaldar*, communicating that he has written about the insurgency in Bheglone whereas the British forces have already defeated the insurgents, who after the defeat fled from there. If he feels any threat from them, he should ask Hafiz Muhammad Hasan, *naib bakhshi*, to provide him half of the battalion, stationed at Siwans.

P 61. . . *to Ghulam Muhammad Khan,* Risaldar. Informs that on 2 *Safar* 1275 AH, Adil Muhammad Khan along with his army reached in Sironj and surrounded the Fort. For a day and night, the sound of guns and cannons was heard. Thereafter, all the chiefs, dwellers and *jagirdars* assembled and fought together with full force with the insurgent forces. Ultimately, they fled from the city. In that skirmish, 100 or even more insurgents were killed. Dated 7 *Safar* 1275 AH (16 September 1858).

P 63. Letter in Hindi Devanagari.

P 65. *Transliteration of the Letter of Balkishan to Hazrat Nur Khan*. There is a report pertaining to the coming of Garhiwala in Bheglone. He has distributed arms and ammunitions amongst the armymen. Amanat Khan, Bakhshi and Muhammad Sher Khan, *jamadar* will come first. Their intention is to capture four prominent persons of Bheglone. They are; Babaji, Lamberdar, Seth Nihal Chand and Chaudhury Ramchand. He too should be careful and alert. Dated 9 *Mati Bhadon Sudi* 1266 *fasli*.

PP 67-8. *Gangaram and Ganga Prasad*, Jamadars, *to Nawwab Sikandar Begam.* Informs on 17 September 1858, they heard that Adil Muhammad Khan along with his contingent entered in Sironj and fought a battle with the *jagirdars* and *amil* of Sironj. In that battle, 125 insurgents were killed and 2 men of the *jagirdars* were also killed. Thereafter, Adil Muhammad Khan fled to some other place. Other news is that Tantia Tope along with his contingent marched from Jhalra Patan and reached Rajgarh. Due to fear, the chief of Rajgarh hid himself. Meanwhile, the British army marched from Mhow and reached Bayawrah. From Guna too, the British army has arrived. All the British army then reached Rajgarh and attacked upon the insurgent army. For two days, a battle was fought. But what happened to the insurgent army thereafter, is not known.

PP 69-70. *'Abd al-Karim, Ansari, to Nawwab Sikandar Begam.* Informs that day, Gangaram, *jamadar*, stationed at Berasia reported as told by Bhawani Singh, soldier that after the defeat at the hands of the *amil* of Sironj, Adil Muhammad Khan went to Basodah. In the battle, 2 persons from the side of the *amil* were killed but from the side of Adil Muhammad Khan, 50 men were killed. It is reported that the insurgent forces would travel that day from Khajner to Narsingarh and that the British army is at Bayawrah. Dated 9 *Safar* 1275 AH (18 September 1858).

P 71. *Bhawani Prasad to Nawwab Sikandar Begam.* Informs about the authentic news that came from Sironj to the Political Agent that *Nawwab* Wazir al-Daulah has sent an army contingent to Sironj from Tonk, as requested by the *amil* of Sironj. Hearing the news, Adil

Muhammad Khan fled from Sironj to Manohar *Thana*. Dated 9 *Safar* 1275 AH (18 September 1858).

P 73. *Paltu Lal, Muhafiz-i Daftar-i Insha, to Nawwab Sikandar Begam.* Sends a separate list of the papers and orders issued from the royal office to the office of the Political Agent during the last two and half months or from 22 *Ziqada* 1274 AH to 7 *Safar* 1275 AH which are in regard to the insurgency of Adil Muhammad Khan and about his encampment.

PP 75-83. Yaddasht, *Containing Details of Papers which are About the Encampment of Adil Muhammad Khan Issued from the Royal Office to the Office of the Political Agent During the Last Two and Half Months; from 22* Ziqada *1274 AH to 7 Safar 1275 AH.*

PP 87-8. *Muhammad Hasan Khan to Nawwab Sikandar Begam.* Refers to her order, dated 23 *Muharram* 1275 AH, mentioned on the letter of Bhawani Prasad, *wakil*, directing him that when Bakhshi Murawwat Muhammad Khan moves from Bhilsa he should reach there along with his forces stationed in the district east. Informs that whenever he would be called by the *bakhshi,* he would reach there with all promptness. Dated 10 *Safar* 1275 AH (19 September 1858).

PP 89-90. *Muhammad Hasan Khan to Nawwab Sikandar Begam.* Refers to her order, dated 27 *Muharram* 1275 AH, mentioned on the letter of Bhawani Prasad, dated 25 *Muharram* 1275 AH, which is regarding arresting and killing of Adil Muhammad Khan, Aqil Muhammad Khan and other insurgents and blockading the roads to prevent them, and that he should be ready to deal with them, if they pass through the region where he is posted. Assures that he would do as desired and that he would give a befitting reply to the insurgents if they pass from the place where he is posted. Dated 10 *Safar* 1275 AH (19 September 1858).

PP 91-2. *Bhawani Prasad to Nawwab Sikandar Begam.* Refers to her order, dated 6 *Safar* 1275 AH, mentioned on the letter of Ghulam Muhammad Khan, *risaldar*, deployed in Bheglone to present it before the Political Agent that contained the news of insurgency of Adil Muhammad Khan in the region of Sindhia. The Political Agent rejected the letter and returned the same. The same is sent to her. Dated 14 *Safar* 1275 AH (23 September 1858).

It contains the order that the letter as well as the other letters may be sent to Paltu Lal, *muhafiz-i daftar-i insha*, for inclusion in the register and keeping in the *daftar*. A copy of the order may be sent to Bhawani Prasad, to communicate to the Political Agent that whatever news she receives, now or then, is sent to him without any delay. The Political Agent's concern is about the delay of the news. The reply was sent to him on 13 *Safar* 1275 AH, and unless it is brought to his notice, his objection would remain persisting. Expresses her anxiety that it is his negligence that he did not bring the content of that letter to his notice. Dated 16 *Safar* 1275 AH.

P 93. *Bhawani Prasad to the Political Agent.* As ordered by the *Nawwab*, dated 6 *Safar* 1275 AH, presents before him a letter of Ghulam Muhammad Khan, *risaldar,* posted at Bheglone, informing about Adil Muhammad Khan, the insurgent who is in the region of Sindhia, Dated 12 *Safar* 1275 AH.

The letter contains the order of the Political Agent to return it as it is worthless. It was expected from the *Nawwab* that she would bring into his notice the news of the attack of insurgents in the territory of State of Bhopal. Only such news which is new and not known to him should be brought to his notice. Dated 22 September 1858.

PP 95-8. *Ghulam Muhammad Khan,* Risaldar, *to Nawwab Sikandar Begam.* Informs that day; the 2nd *Safar* 1275 AH, Kalwa and Balkishan, the informers came and stated that the previous day, the insurgents destroyed a village near Bheglone. They further stated that the insurgent forces were encamping in *mauza* Imlai. An army led by Adil Muhammad Khan has encamped in *mauza* Lutery in Sironj. Dated 2 *Safar* 1275 AH.

It contains the order that the letter may be sent to Paltu Lal, *muhafiz-i daftar-i insha*, for inclusion in the register and keeping in the *daftar*. A copy of the letter may be sent to Bhawani Prasad to communicate to the Political Agent. Ghulam Muhammad Khan, *risaldar* may be communicated to remain alert from the possible attack of Adil Muhammad Khan. Dated 6 *Safar* 1275 AH.

P 99. *Ghulam Muhammad Khan,* Risaldar, *to Nawwab Sikandar Begam.* Informs that day; 21st *Safar* 1275 AH, Kalwa and Balkishan, the informers came and stated that Adil Muhammad Khan along with his forces went to Issagarh. They went with that army upto Sarai Na'l, situating at a distance of 6 *curoh* from Sironj towards Issagarh.

File No. 287
Box No. 15
No. of Documents 6

To Create Disturbance in the Army of Tantia Tope and Adil Muhammad Khan in Exchange of Surety of Life

PP 1-2. Contents

PP 3-4. *Bhawani Prasad to Nawwab Sikandar Begam.* Informs that day Bakhshi Murawwat Muhammad Khan told him that some persons of the army of Adil Muhammad Khan left him and started living in Sironj in a rented house. But the *amil* of Sironj exiled them. They again joined Adil Muhammad Khan. If such persons are given amnesty by British government, it would be good. Says, one day he talked to the Political Agent in reference to a notification that if anyone who is not the chief and is willing to part ways from the insurgents, if such persons could be pardoned. He replied to search such persons. Requests to send someone to Sironj to enquire about such persons. Dated 15 *Safar* 1275 AH (27 September 1858).

P 7. *Nawwab Sikandar Begam to Murawwat Muhammad Khan.* From the letter of Munshi Bhawani Prasad, dated 15 *Safar* 1275 AH, it has come to her notice that many insurgents of the army of Tantia Tope and Adil Muhammad Khan have requested that if they are given amnesty by the office of Agent of Bhopal they could leave the services of the army of insurgents. Directs him to see if it is possible to create disturbances or dig a ditch in the army of insurgents by sending someone secretly and expressing himself as a friend and pursue them that whosoever from the army of insurgents is desiring to be pardoned, they should submit their petitions, either through him or through a *wakil* of their own to the office of the Agent. The latter might be pardoned. Otherwise after that there is no chance for them to escape from hardships. Dated 23 *Safar* 1275 AH.

P 9. *Nawwab Sikandar Begam to* Madar al-Maham. To the same effect as the foregoing. Dated 23 *Safar* 1275 AH.

PP 11-12. *Nawwab Sikandar Begam to Maulawi Muhammad Sa'd al-Din,* Muhtamim, Adalat-i Faujdari. To the same effect as the foregoing. Dated 23 *Safar* 1275 AH.

P 13. *Murawwat Muhammad Khan to Nawwab Sikandar Begam.* Refers to her *parwana,* dated 23 *Safar* 1275 AH, informing that the companions of Tantia Tope and Adil Muhammad Khan are desiring for surety of life and ready to abandon the insurgency, and directing him that if possible to send someone from the army to pursue them that whosoever desires to be pardoned, they should submit their petitions either through him or through their *wakil* to the Agent of Bhopal. Informs presently, none among the armymen is available of the required quality. So the order is kept pending. Dated 2 *Rabi* I, 1275 AH.

File No. 288 A
Box No. 15
No. of Documents 21

Insurgency by Tantia Tope and Brother of Nana Sahab in Rajgarh, Victory of the British Forces Led by Captain Hutchinson Over the Insurgent Forces and Forced to Flee

PP 1-6 Contents

PP 9-10. *Captain Hutchinson to Nawwab Sikandar Begam.* Informs that day, the British forces captured 28 cannons, magazines and other weapons of warfare of the insurgent forces in between Rajgarh and Bayawrah. They were pursued and killed, and many of them fled in different directions. It is not known where they went. The information is given to her, as the friendship of the two governments demands so. Hopes for her well-being and that she may execute the duty as the head of the state. Dated 15 September 1858 (6 *Safar* 1275 AH).

It contains the order that the letters and *parwanas* of *Nawwab* Sikandar Begam issued to her officials may be sent to Paltu Lal, *muhafiz-i daftar-i insha,* for inclusion in the register and keeping in the *daftar*. Dated 9 *Safar* 1275 AH (18 September 1858).

PP 11-12. *Husain Bakhsh,* Thanadar *of* Pargana *Doraha, to Nawwab Sikandar Begam.* Informs that day, Khuda Bakhsh, Shah Darwesh, dweller of Doraha, came to *thana* and said that he had gone for some work to Rahatgarh where he heard that the insurgents marched from Jhalra Patan and reached Khalji on 2nd *Safar* and devastated it. Hearing this news, he himself went to Khaljipur and saw from his own eyes that Tantia Tope along with Laxmi Rani, Jhansiwali, *Nawwabs* of Bareilly and Jawrah with an army of 80, 000 were encamping there. Raja Sher Singh, Khaljipurwala was busy in their hospitality and in making arrangement of *saman-i sarbrah* for them. Sweets were distributed among the armymen, the beggars and the Brahmins. He too was given one *laddu*. There were 62 cannons. On 3rd *Safar,* Tantia Tope asked an astrologer about his march to Rajgarh. They then marched from Khaljipur to Rajgarh. Raja Sher Singh, Khaljipurwala, his son and Raja Jhalra Patanwala too went along with them to Rajgarh. The physical description of four chiefs of insurgent forces are:

Tantia Tope, white complexion with beard; Laxmi Rani Jhansiwali, colour brown, average height; Nawwab Jawrahwala, colour brown, broad forehead, tall figure; and Nawwab Bareillywala, white complex, broad forehead. Dated 7 *Safar* 1275 AH (16 September 1858).

PP 13-14. *Bhawani Prasad to Nawwab Sikandar Begam.* Refers to her order, dated 3 *Safar* 1275 AH, as mentioned on his letter, dated 29 *Muharram* 1275 AH which is in regard to dealing with the insurgents, to protect and safeguard the territory of Bhopal State, and the deployment of Murawwat Muhammad Khan. Informs he brought the matter into the notice of the Political Agent through his letter. In reply, a *parwana* of the Political Agent, dated 15 September was received, informing that the *Nawwab* is free to deploy Murawwat Muhammad Khan wherever she thinks him better to be deployed. The same is presented to her. Dated 7 *Safar* 1275 AH (16 September1858).

It contains the order that the letter, the *parwana* of the Political Agent, and the *parwana* of *Nawwab* Sikandar Begam addressed to Bakhshi Murawwat Muhammad Khan may be sent to Paltu Lal, *muhafiz-i daftar-i insha*, for inclusion in the register and keeping in the *daftar.* A copy of the order and *parwana* issued to the *bakhshi* may be sent to Bhawani Prasad which is regarding the proposed march of the *bakhshi* with the Bhopal army. The same may be presented before the Political Agent and his reply may be conveyed to her. Dated 10 *Safar* 1275 AH (19 September 1858).

P 15. *The Political Agent to Munshi Bhawani Prasad.* Refers to his letter and the letter of *Nawwab* Sikandar Begam which is in regard to dealing with the insurgents, to protect and safeguard the territory of Bhopal State, and the deployment of Murawwat Muhammad Khan. Directs him to convey to the *Nawwab* that she is free to deploy Murawwat Muhammad Khan wherever she thinks suitable. Dated 15 September 1858.

PP 17-18. *Orders of Nawwab Sikandar Begam as Mentioned in the Letter of Bhawani Prasad.* The *Nawwab* orders that the letter and *parwana* of the Political Agent may be sent to Paltu Lal, *muhafiz-i daftar-i insha,* for inclusion in the register and keeping in the *daftar.* A copy of the order may be sent to Munshi Bhawani Prasad, informing that that day the letters of *thanadar* and *tahsildar* were received, describing that 500 *sawars* reached Narsingarh. A copy of the letter may be given to the Political Agent. It seems reasonable to send Bakhshi Murawwar Muhammad Khan with 500 foot-soldiers, 100 *sawars* and 2 cannon to Satan Bari, situated at a distance 2 to 3 *curoh* from Narsingarh.

PP 19-20. *Bhawani Prasad to Nawwab Sikandar Begam.* The Political Agent asked him as to how many armymen *Nawwab* Sikandar Begam could provide if such need arose. He further said to convey the *Nawwab* to manage 2 cannons with magazines, explosives, strong bullocks, musketeers, *sawars* and foot-soldiers as much as possible and keep them ready at Bhopal so that there should not be any kind of delay or negligence when the need arose. Dated 7 *Safar* 1275 AH (16 September 1858).

It contains the order that the letter may be sent to Paltu Lal, *muhafiz-i daftar-i insha*, for inclusion in the register and keeping in the *daftar.* A copy of the order may be sent to Bhawani Prasad, communicating that after the distribution of the employees, there remained 200 *sawars* and 500 foot-soldiers as mentioned in her letter to the Agent to the Governor-General, who could be sent under the command of Murawwar Muhammad Khan. Hopes that the contingent would be led by the Political Agent himself. Expresses her inability to commit more than that. She is not like the other chiefs who have contradiction in their sayings and deeds. This army, as mentioned, is ready to march. The only thing is the management of carts of carriers. If the

Political Agent wants to keep this contingent under his command, it may be sent there. If he does not want to carry it, then it may be sent to Debipura as there is news of the arrival of insurgents in Narsingarh and the road to Debipura from Narsingarh is connected. Directs him to bring the matter into the notice of the Political Agent and convey his opinion to her. Dated 10 *Safar* 1275 AH (19 September 1858).

PP 21-2. *Bhawani Prasad to Nawwab Sikandar Begam.* Informs of the letter of Rawat Moti Singh to his *wakil*, dated 13 September 1858, informing that there is news of coming of the insurgents in Rajgarh. He wanted to go and meet Captain Hutchinson. But it seems difficult to reach the camp, as the roads are blocked due to the presence of the insurgents. He started his journey from Rajgarh and reached a village, situating at a distance of 8 *curoh* from Rajgarh where he received a message that about 2,000 insurgents had entered in Rajgarh. The *wakil* brought the matter to the notice of the Political Agent who said that he did not rely upon such news as the British army blocked all the roads of the insurgents. It is not possible for them to enter Bayawrah.

Further informs that to confirm the fact he sent Ramden, the *wakil*. He met a *harkara* who said that till then the insurgents had not entered Rajgarh and the British forces arrived in Bayawrah via Garhi. The telephone and telegraph lines as well as the postal system are fully in operation. On 15th September, day Wednesday, the army led by Hutchinson fought a battle with the insurgents who were encamping at Khaljipur. He himself heard the sound of cannon.

News from Sironj is that, though the *amil* of Sironj did not commit any mistake in fighting with the insurgents, even then Adil Muhammad Khan succeeded. He also made the *bohras* captive and demanded money from them. Hope the insurgents would be finished in one or two days as they have been surrounded from all sides by the British forces. Further, it is heard that Adil Muhammad Khan set an English post office in Sironj on fire. A British army led by General Mitchell entered in *mauza* Pachor. Dated 7 *Safar* 1275 AH (16 September 1858).

PP 23-4. *Muhammad 'Abd al-'Aziz Ansari,* Tahsildar *of Debipura, to Nawwab Sikandar Begam.* Reports that Khaman Singh and Muhkam Singh, the soldiers at *thana* Debipura came back from Narsingarh. They stated that they went to Narsingarh as permitted. But the servants of Raja Narsingarh did not allow them to enter into the walled city. When they were returning to Debipura, they heard 9 ball cannon fires. Meanwhile, some persons of the city came who said that 500 *sawars* of the Peshwa arrived in Narsingarh and to welcome them, ball cannons were fired. The *sarbrah-i rasad* is being collected in the city for the army of Peshwa for the last few days. They also heard that the Peshwa along with Adil Muhammad Khan and some other chieftains were encamping in Bayawrah. Says he reported as he heard from the soldiers who reported as they heard at Narsingarh. Dated 8 *Safar* 1275 AH (17 September1858).

It contains the order that the letter may be sent to Paltu Lal, *muhafiz-i daftar-i insha*, for inclusion in the register and keeping in the *daftar.* A copy of the letter may be sent to Bhawani Prasad to present it before the Political Agent, and his observation may be communicated to her. Dated 9 *Safar* 1275 AH (18 September 1858).

P 25. *Shaikh Khuda Bakhsh, Deputy* Thanadar *of Debipura, to Nawwab Sikandar Begam.* To the same effect as the foregoing PP 23-4. In addition to that, Narsingarh is situated at a distance of 8 *curoh* from Debipura and from *chauki* Goa the distance is 3 *curoh.* Dated 8 *Safar* 1275 AH (17 September 1858).

PP 27-8. *Bhawani Prasad to Nawwab Sikandar Begam.* Informs that day in the morning, the Political Agent called him. First, he read before him the letter of Shore, informing that he had sent Adil Beg, *dafadar* of Holkar, to Tachpur to bring the news of the insurgents. From him it was heard that the army of insurgents comprised of 5, 000 with 9 cannon. But they were too afraid of the British army. In that army there were Tantia Tope, Rao Sahab, Nawwabs of Banda, and Kanod, Muhammad Saed Khan, Tonkwala and one *darogha,* famous as Arham *darogha*. A letter of Nawwab of Rahatgarh or Adil Muhammad Khan came in the name of Tantia Tope, informing that he is fully ready and has managed 10, 000 armymen. He should soon come to Sironj.

The Political Agent enquired about Adil Muhammad Khan and how he managed 10,000 armymen. He further said that an army has marched from Shivpuri to Sironj to deal with Adil Muhammad Khan. Meantime, the *wakil* of Narsingarh presented a letter of Diwan Bhup Singh. The letter contained the information that the insurgent army was encamping at Khaljipur and Captain Hutchinson came with a huge army. As the dwellers had fled and there was no arrangement of *saman-i rasad,* the Captain ordered the armymen to collect the *rasad* wherever it was found. The letter received from the office of Assistant at Berasia was also shown to him. In that letter, it was mentioned that on 4th *Safar,* Adil Muhammad Khan attacked Sironj. He faced resistance from the *amil* of Sironj and 3 to 5 persons of Adil Muhammad were killed. Adil Muhammad Khan, however, entered Sironj and arrested *bohras*. *Amil* of Sironj was ready with cannon at the court and Adil Muhammad Khan was yet to take control of court and the arsenal. Dated 8 *Safar* 1275 AH (17 September 1858).

P 29. *Bhawani Prasad to Nawwab Sikandar Begam.* Informs of the *parwana* of Rawat Moti Singh to his *wakil*, dated 16 September 1858, for bringing the matter to the notice of the Political Agent, describing the crushing defeat of the insurgents and fleeing towards

Sironj, leaving behind 23 cannon and magazines, etc. . A copy of the said *parwana* has been obtained and presented before her. Dated 9 *Safar* 1275 AH (18 September 1858).

P 31. *Rawat Moti Singh to Lala Laxman,* Wakil. Refers to his earlier communiqué, informing about the activities of the insurgent forces and coming to Khaljipur and hopes that he would have informed the Political Agent about it. The recent news about the insurgent forces is that they have arrived at Rajgarh. He was unable to face them so he along with his family went to the mountains in the north of Rajgarh. The insurgent forces entered Rajgarh, doors and locks were broken and everything in the house was destroyed. They stayed there for two days. Buildings and houses were demolished. Goods worth lakhs of rupees were destroyed. Also refers to the letter of the Captain from Sanesar, informing of his arrival at Rajgarh and directing him to make arrangement of essential commodities. But as all the roads were closed due to the presence of the insurgent forces everywhere, and the spies and the informers were moving round the clock, it was not possible to send the essential commodities to him. He had no option but to take shelter in the mountains, hiding all the goods of his house. Although the insurgents made so much effort to find him but they did not succeed. On the third day, the Captain launched an attack on Rajgarh. Hearing the news of the arrival of the Captain, he too went to meet him. From there, they moved together, crossed the river and reached Bayawrah and erected *morchhal.* From the other side, the insurgent forces too moved towards Bayawrah and erected *morchhal* at Kishangarh Ghati. Thereafter, the two forces started throwing cannon balls on each other. The insurgent forces could not stand before the mighty forces and fled from the battlefield, leaving behind one cannon. He, in the company of the Captain, pursued them and fought the battle. They were defeated and fled from there, leaving some cannon there as well. Although they were 30,000 but could not stand before the British army. About 100 insurgents were killed in the battle and their 23 cannon fell in the hands of the British army. It is heard that the insurgents have gone to Sironj. Directs him to bring all happenings to the notice of the Political Agent. Dated 6 September 1858.

P 33. Parwana-i Ishtahari *of Nawwab Sikandar Begam to Ghulam Muhammad Khan,* Risaldar, *Sikandar Khan, Agenty II, Hafiz Muhammad Hasan Khan,* Naib Bakhshi, *'Abd al-Karim Ansari and Wazir Khan,* Qila'dar. That day, i.e. 9 *Safar* 1275 AH, a letter of Captain Hutchinson, dated 15 September 1858, was received in her name. The content of the letter, word for word along with her *parwana* is sent to them. The message as given in the letter should be conveyed to all their employees. They themselves should remain alert and attentive so that in case of any eventuality, they could be able to give a befitting reply to the insurgents, in case they enter into their jurisdiction. If the number of insurgents is high, information should immediately be passed on to the government. They should intimate the receipt of the *parwana* through their letters so that the *harkara* carrying the letter is to be awarded. Dated 9 *Safar* 1275 AH (18 September 1858).

P 35. *Nawwab Sikandar Begam to Muhammad Abd al-Aziz Khan and Mattu Khan,* Risaldars. That day, i.e. 9 *Safar* 1275 AH, a letter of Captain Hutchinson, dated 15 September 1858, was received in her name. The content of the letter, word for word, along with her *parwana* is sent to them. The message as given in the letter should be conveyed to all the armymen of the State of Bhopal, deployed under the British territory. They should intimate the receipt of the *parwana* through their letters so that the *harkara,* carrying the *parwana* is awarded by the government. Dated 9 *Safar* 1275 AH (18 September 1858).

P 37. *Nawwab Sikandar Begam to Bakhshi Murawwat Muhammad Khan.* That day; 9 *Safar* 1275 AH, a letter of Captain Hutchinson, dated 15 September 1858, was received in her name. The content of the letter, word for word, along with her letter is sent to him. The message, as given in the letter, should be conveyed to all the armymen of the State of Bhopal, stationed at Bhopal to make them happy. Dated 9 *Safar* 1275 AH (18 September1858).

P 39. *Nawwab Sikandar Begam to Koka Fatah Jang Khan.* That day; 9 *Safar* 1275 AH, a letter of Captain Hutchinson, dated 15 September 1858 was received in her name. The content of the letter, word for word, along with her *parwana* is sent to him. The message, as given in the letter, should be conveyed to all the employees under his jurisdiction to make them happy. Dated 9 *Safar* 1275 AH (18 September 1858).

PP 41-2. *Nawwab Sikandar Begam to the* Thanadars *of all Three Districts.* That day; 9 *Safar* 1275 AH, a letter of Captain Hutchinson, dated 15 September 1858, was received in her name. The content of the letter, word for word, along with her *parwana* is sent to them. The message, as given in the letter, should be conveyed to all the employees of *thanas* and *mahals* under them. They themselves should remain alert and attentive so that in case of any eventuality, they should be able to give a befitting reply to the insurgents if they enter in their jurisdiction. If the number of insurgents is high, information should immediately be passed on to the government. They should intimate the receipt of the *parwana* through their letters so that the *harkara* carrying the *parwana* is awarded by the government. Dated 9 *Safar* 1275 AH (18 September 1858).

P 43. *Nawwab Sikandar Begam to Bakhshi Murawwat Muhammad Khan.* That day, the letters of *thanadar* and *tahsildar* of *mahal* Debipura, dated 8 *Safar* 1275 AH (17 September 1858) is received, communicating that 500 *sawars* of the insurgent forces has reached at Narsingarh. Directs him to rush to Satan Bari, *ilaqa* Bhopal, situating at a distance of 2 *curoh* from Narsingarh with the army of State of Bhopal with two cannon and encamp there. The moment the insurgents move further of Satan Bari, he too should move side-by-side the insurgents along the border of State of Bhopal upto the end of the territory and if they fell in front of them, he should fight with them. Dated 10 *Safar* 1275 AH (18 September 1858).

P 45. Yaddasht, *of Nawwab Sikandar Begam Addressed to Captain Hutchinson, Agent at Bhupader.* Acknowledges the receipt of his letter, dated 15 September 1858, informing the fleeing of insurgents leaving behind 28 cannon, besides magazines and other weapons of warfare, killing a large number of insurgents and fleeing of the remaining in all directions. Expresses her pleasure and congratulates him and the Agent to the Governor-General, Central India, for this victory. May God bless him to give her the news of assassination of all the miscreants from his hand and that no insurgency remains anywhere. Informs, with the receipt of his letter, everything in the State of Bhopal was set right. The copies of his letter were sent to the officers and *thanadars* of the State of Bhopal to communicate to all. It is heard that the insurgents have fled to Narsingarh, while some say to Maqsudangarh. Dated 10 *Safar* 1275 AH (19 September 1858).

P 47. Parwana *of Nawwab Sikandar Begam to Bhawani Prasad.* A letter of Captain Hutchinson has been received in her name. A copy of the reply, as given by her, is sent to him. The same may be presented before the Political Agent and his reply may be conveyed to her. Dated 10 *Safar* 1275 AH (19 September 1858).

P 49. *Muhammad Abd al-Aziz Ansari,* Tahsildar *of Debipura to Nawwab Sikandar Begam.* Informs on 9th of the month, he had sent Khaman Singh and Basharat

Khan, soldiers to Narsingarh to know the situation there. That day, they came back and stated as told them the dwellers of Narsingarh that on 7th of the month, there was a skirmish between the British forces and the forces of Peshwa at Bayawrah wherein many of the Peshwas's forces were killed and some British forces were also killed. 20 cannon of the insurgent forces were captured by the British forces. The defeated insurgent forces fled to Chachura. In that battle, Bayawrah and Rajgarh were destroyed. The Raja of Rajgarh and the people of Narsingarh also fled. An army of 2000 British forces is encamping at Narsingarh. The report as reported by the soldiers is sent to her. Dated 11 *Safar* 1275 AH (20 September 1858).

File No. 288, B
Box No. 15
No. of Documents 23

PP 51-2. *Shaikh Khuda Bakhsh, Deputy* Thanadar *of Debipura to Nawwab Sikandar Begam.* Refers to his earlier letter, dated 8th of the month, informing of the arrival of 500 Peshwa *sawars* at Narsingarh, giving 9 ball cannon salute to him and arrangement of *sarbrah-i rasad* by Raja of Narsingarh for the army of Peshwa. On 9th of the month, he sent Khaman Singh and Basharat Khan, soldiers of *thana* to know about the situation at Narsingarh. That day they came back to *thana* and said that the news of the arrival of *sawars* of Peshwa at Narsingarh was incorrect. But from the servants of the English and people of Narsingarh, it was heard that there was a skirmish between the forces of Peshwa and the British at Bayawrah which led to the killing of many of the Peshwa's army and some of the British soldiers were also killed. The defeated army of Peshwa fled to Chachura, a territory of Sindhia, leaving behind 20 cannon which were captured by the British and they went to Mhow. In that battle, *qasba* Bayawrah and Rajgarh were completely ruined and devastated. Raja of Rajgarh and the dwellers of Narsingarh fled from Narsingarh and closed their doors. An army of 2,000 British and tilangas reached Narsingarh after the vicrory. Dated 11 *Safar* 1275 AH (20 September 1858).

PP 53-4. *Bhawani Prasad to Nawwab Sikandar Begam.*

Informs that after a great difficulty, he arrived at Dhanora from Khandoh, *ilaqa* Berasia situating at a distance of 4 *curoh* from Berasia, to join the army led by General Mitchell. He called on him who said that for the safety of Bhopal 2-2, 3-3 groups of army marched from Mhow and reached Rajgarh. The insurgents were defeated. But the British army was still encamping in two *thanas* of Rajgarh in pursuit of the insurgents. In Rajgarh, Rawat Moti Singh is not liked by him. It is strange that he did not receive a single news of insurgency from Nawwab Sikandar Begam. That day, Captain Maine himself enquired about the insurgents. He was reported that the insurgents fled from Maqsudangarh and crossed the river at *ghat* Paruti and went to Sironj. Meanwhile, news arrived that Tantia Tope and Adil Muhammad Khan were in Sironj.

PP 55-6. *Orders of Nawwab Sikandar Begam, as Recorded in the Letter of Bhawani Prasad.* The Nawwab orders that the letter may be sent to Paltu Lal, *muhafiz-i daftar-i insha*, for inclusion in the register and keeping in the *daftar.* A copy of the order may be sent to Bhawani Prasad to communicate to the Political Agent that on 13 *Safar* 1275 AH, the letters received from Ghulam Muhammad Khan, *risaldar*, and Hazrat Nur Khan, *amil* of Bheglone were sent to him, informing that the insurgents went to Sironj. The statement of the Political Agent that he was not informed of the activities of insurgents is wrong. Besides, he did not inform her about the *chaukis* of posts established to carry the posts to the camp of the Political Agent. Directs him to immediately convey her of the details of *chaukis,* established so that the posts could be sent to him through that route. There is no information about the place where the Political Agent's camp is. From the letter of the *amil* of Debipura it was learnt that the army of General Mitchell entered in Berasia. So Qalander Khan, *tahsildar*, was directed to meet the General and convey her good wishes to him. The *saman-i sarbrah-i rasad* for the army of the

Political Agent was loaded on bullock carts and donkeys, and sent to him. Efforts are on to manage carriers and wherever carriers would be available it would be sent there. The elephants of *jagirdars* of Bhopal have been sent to him earlier. Two more elephants have been found which are sent to him. Says she does not know about the army of Captain Hutchinson, at which place they are. Directs him to inform her about that army. Bakhshi Murawwat Muhammad Khan is ready to march. But due to rain, he is yet to start his march. As soon as the flow of river and *nalla* comes to a standstill, he would start his march. This is because he is carrying the carts of carriers and due to overflowing of river and *nalla,* he is unable to march. The bullocks and donkeys, whatever became available, carrying the *saman-i rasad* were sent to the Political Agent. If the Political Agent desires, Bakhshi Murawwat Muhammad along with his army would be sent to Bhilsa. If he desires that the *bakhshi* and the army may be sent to Berasia before his arrival, they would be sent there. Directs him to bring the matter into the notice of the Political Agent and his reply may be conveyed to her. Dated 14 *Safar* 1275 AH (23 September 1858).

P 57. *Muhammad Ali,* Thanadar *of Jawar, to Nawwab Sikandar Begam.* Refers to her *parwana*, dated 9 *Safar* 1275 AH, along with the letter of Captain Hutchinson, Agent of Bhupader, directing him to make all the employees of *thana* and *mahal* aware of the content of the letter of Captain, and that he himself should remain ready so that if the insurgents pass through that region they should be dealt with firmly. If their number is huge, the information should be sent to the government. Information of the receipt of the *parwana* should also be sent so that the *harkara* of the post should be awarded by the government. Says, as he is in Bhopal he sent the royal *parwana* to Munshi Narain Swarup, *munsarim-i thana,* with the orders of the *nizamat*, instructing him to obey the orders as mentioned in the *parwana*. Besides, the contingent of *thana* and *jagirdars* led by the *jamadar* should be deployed on probable routes of the insurgents so that if they pass through that region they should be dealt with in accordance to the royal orders; Hashmat Khan, *sipahsalar* and Shaikh 'Abd al-Rahman, *jamadar*, should be instructed that one guard should be kept on duty on the routes, keeping watch on the insurgents; and he too should keep himself ready with his battalion so that in case, the insurgents pass through that region they should be given a befitting reply. Dated 12 *Safar* 1275 AH (21 September 1858).

P 59. *Qasim Ali to Nawwab Sikandar Begam.* Informs that the previous day, 12 *Safar* 1275 AH, 'Abd al-Ali, soldier, an employee in the *tahsil* of *qasba* Debipura told him, as narrated by Moti Singh, an employee of *thana* qasba Debipura adjoining to Jama Masjid that the insurgent forces went to Narsingarh after they fled from Rajgarh. Meanwhile, the news reached that the British forces pursued and killed them, their 20 cannon were captured, and the victorious British army entered Narsingarh. Dated 13 *Safar* 1275 AH (22 September 1858).

P 61. *Shahzad Rai*, Thanadar *of Mahalpur, to Nawwab Sikandar Begam.* Informs of the receipt of her *parwana*, dated 9 *Safar* 1275 AH, along with the letter of Captain Hutchinson, Agent of Bhupader, directing him to make all the employees of *thana* and *mahal* aware of the content of the letter of Captain and that he himself should remain ready to deal with the insurgents who fled after the defeat in between Rajgarh and Bayawrah, and 28 cannon of the insurgents fell in the British hands. Informs that he immediately notified among all the employees of *thana* and *mahal*. Dated 13 *Safar* 1275 AH (22 September 1858).

P 63. *'Abd al-Rahman*, Thanadar *of* Mahal *Tal, to Nawwab Sikandar Begam.* Refers to her *parwana*, dated 9 *Safar* 1275 AH, along with a copy of the letter of the Agent at Bhupader, informing of the news of capturing

28 cannon of the insurgent forces, killing many of them and their disbursement in different directions after their defeat by the British forces in between Rajgarh and Bayawrah and directing him to inform about it to all the employees of *thana* and *mahal* and instructing him to deal with them if they pass through the *pargana*. Informs as mentioned in the *parwana,* he notified the news among all the employees of *thana* and *mahal*. Informs that hearing the news all expressed their happiness. Assures, as ordered, he would deal with the insurgents if they pass through the *pargana*. Dated 14 *Safar* 1275 AH (23 September1858).

P 65. *Muhammad Abd al-Aziz, Ansari,* Tahsildar, Munsarim-i Kar, Thana *Debipura, to Nawwab Sikandar Begam*. Refers to her *parwana*, dated 9 *Safar* 1275 AH, along with a copy of the letter of Captain Hutchinson, Agent at Bhupader, directing him to inform the content of the letter of Captain Hutchinson to all the employees of *thana* and *mahal*, and that he too should remain alert and attentive to deal with the insurgents. Also refers to the order, as mentioned in the *parwana*, to inform the receipt of the letter so that the *harkara* of the post could be rewarded. Hence, reports the receipt of the *parwana* on 14 *Safar* 1275 AH (23 September 1858).

P 67. *Karam Ali Husain, Deputy* Thanadar, Pargana *Bari to Nawwab Sikandar Begam.* Informs that day, he received her *parwana*, dated 9 *Safar* 1275 AH, along with a copy of the letter of Captain Hutchinson, Agent at Bhupader, dated 15 September 1858, informing that every word of the content of the letter of the Captain is sent to him. The same may be communicated to all the employees of *thana* and *mahal* of his region and that he himself should remain ready and alert so that in case the insurgents pass through that region, they should be dealt with firmly. If their number is high, information should immediately be passed on to the government. He should also intimate the receipt of the *parwana* through his letter so that the *harkara* of the post, carrying the *parwana* could be awarded. Informs that all the employees of *thana* and *mahal* were communicated of the content of the letter of the Captain through a notification and that he too is ready and attentive to meet any challenge of the insurgents. If their number would be more, information would be given to her. Dated 14 *Safar* 1275 AH (23 September 1858).

P 69. *Saiyid Imtiaz Ali,* Thanadar *of Jogigarh, to Nawwab Sikandar Begam.* Informs that day; the 14th *Safar* 1275 AH, he received her *parwana*, dated 9 *Safar* 1275 AH, directing him to communicate all the employees of *thana* and *mahal* about the content of the letter of Captain Hutchinson, and that he himself should remain ready to deal with the insurgents and to inform the receipt of the letter of Captain Hutchinson, Agent at Bhupader, communicating about the victory of the British forces and crushing defeat of the insurgents, their dispersion and fleeing, and capturing of 28 cannon of the insurgents in between Rajgarh and Bayawrah. Informs that he immediately conveyed the message to all the employees of *thana* and *mahal* of the content of the letter of the Captain, and that he too is ready, as desired, to meet any challenge of the insurgents if they pass through his region. Dated 14 *Safar* 1275 AH (23 September 1858).

P 71. *Muhammad Hasan Khan to Nawwab Sikandar Begam.* Informs that day; 14th *Safar* 1275 AH, he received her *parwana*, dated 9 *Safar* 1275 AH, along with a copy of the letter of Captain Hutchinson, Agent at Bhupader, communicating about the crushing defeat of the insurgents, capturing of 28 cannon along with magazines and killing a large number of insurgents, and their dispersion and fleeing to unknown destination and directing him to inform all the employees under him about it, and that he himself should remain ready to meet the challenges of the insurgents. If their number is high, information should immediately be passed on to the government. Informs, as directed he informed all those who were accompanying him and also the inhabitants about this happy news. Assures that he as well as his entire companions are fully ready to deal with the insurgents. If their number would be large, information would immediately be passed on to the government. Dated 14 *Safar* 1275 AH (23 September 1858).

P 73. *Abd al-Rahman,* Thanadar *of Garhi Ambapani, to Nawwab Sikandar Begam.* Informs of the receipt of her *parwana*, dated 9 *Safar* 1275 AH, along with a copy of the letter of Captain Hutchinson, Agent at Bhupader, communicating about the capturing of 28 cannon along with magazines of the insurgents in between Rajgarh and Bayawrah, their dispersion and fleeing to other places, and that he himself should remain ready and alert so that in case the insurgents pass through that region they should be dealt with firmly. Assures that there would be no deviation from the royal orders in dealing with the insurgents if they pass through his region. Dated 15 *Safar* 1275 AH (24 September 1858).

P 75. *Muhammad Abbas Ali*, Thanadar *of Bamhuri*, *to Nawwab Sikandar Begam.* Informs that day; 15th *Safar* 1275 AH, he received her *parwana,* dated 9 *Safar* 1275 AH along with a copy of the letter of Captain Hutchinson, Agent at Bhupader, dated 15 September 1858, communicating every word of the letter of the Captain; capturing of 28 cannon of the insurgents in between Rajgarh and Bayawrah; their dispersion and fleeing to anywhere; to inform all the employees of his *thana* and *mahal* about the same; and that he himself should remain ready and alert so that in case the insurgents pass through that region, they should firmly be dealt with. If their number is huge, information should immediately be passed on to the government. He should also intimate the receipt of the *parwana* through his letter so that the *harkara* of the post, carrying the *parwana* should be awarded. Informs that all the employees of *thana* and *mahal* were communicated of the content of the letter of the Captain, and that he too as well as the *tahsildar* are ready with the forces present at *thana* to meet any challenge posed by insurgents. If their number would be more, information would be given to her immediately. Dated 15 *Safar* 1275 AH (24 September 1858).

P 77. *Husain Bakhsh,* Thanadar *of Doraha to Nawwab Sikandar Begam.* Refers to her *parwana*, dated 9 *Safar* 1275 AH, along with a copy of the letter of Captain Hutchinson, Agent at Bhupader, dated 15 September 1858, informing the killing of the insurgents, receiving their 28 cannon along with magazines, and their dispersion haplessly after the defeat in between Rajgarh and Bayawrah from the hands of the British, and instructing that they should be dealt with if they pass from his *thana* of the *pargana*. If their number is high, information should immediately be passed on to the government. The intimation of the receipt of the *parwana* should be sent through the letter so that the *harkara* of the post is awarded. The information is made available to her as ordered. Dated 16 *Safar* 1275 AH (25 September 1858).

P 79. *Munshidhar,* Thanadar *of Raisen, to Nawwab Sikandar Begam.* Refers to her *parwana*, dated 9 *Safar* 1275 AH, along with a copy of the letter of Captain Hutchinson, Agent at Bhupader, ordering to communicate all the employees of *thana* and *mahal* of the content of the letter, he himself should remain alert and attentive to deal with the insugents who after the defeat in between Rajgarh and Bayawrah have fled, and that 28 cannon of the insurgents also fell in the hands of the British. Informs that the message was immediately conveyed to all the employees of *thana* and *mahal* and that he himself would execute as ordered. Dated 16 *Safar* 1275 AH (25 September1858).

P 81. *Abd al-Qadir,* Thanadar *of Solwani, to Nawwab*

Sikandar Begam. Refers to her *parwana*, dated 9 *Safar* 1275 AH, along with a copy of the letter of Captain Hutchinson, Agent at Bhupader, informing the victory of British forces, capturing 28 cannon of the insurgent forces, and to intimate the receipt of *parwana* to her. The information, as ordered, was given to all the employees and the information of the receipt of the *parwana* is sent to her. Dated 16 *Safar* 1275 AH (25 September 1858).

P 83. *Shaikh Nur Muhammad,* Thanadar *of Siwans to Nawwab Sikandar Begam.* Refers to her *parwana*, dated 9 *Safar* 1275 AH, along with a copy of the letter of Captain Hutchinson, Agent at Bhupader, received on 15 *Safar* 1275 AH. Assures that he would do as ordered, and whenever the insurgents enter in his region, they would be given a befitting reply. Dated 16 *Safar* 1275 AH (25 September 1858).

P 85. *Ghulam Muhammad Khan,* Risaldar, *to Nawwab Sikandar Begam.* Refers to her *parwana*, dated 9 *Safar* 1275 AH, along with a copy of the letter of Captain Hutchinson, Agent at Bhupader. Expresses his happiness, which is beyond description, on the victory over the insurgent forces. Informs that as ordered, all the employees of the government were informed of the happy news. The information of the coming of the Peshwa in Sironj has been given to her through his letters. Informs that he along with his contingent is fully ready to fight with the insurgents and that she is aware of the number of contingents in the *mahal*. Dated 16 *Safar* 1275 AH (25 September 1858).

P 87. *Muhammad Mustaquim Khan,* Thanadar *of Bareilly to Nawwab Sikandar Begam.* Refers to her *parwana*, dated 9 *Safar* 1275 AH, along with a copy of the letter of Captain Hutchinson, Agent at Bhupader, which is in regard to capturing 28 cannon of the insurgents by the British forces in between Rajgarh and Bayawrah, along with the magazines, killing of many insurgents, pursuing them by the British forces and fleeing of the defeated ones to unknown destination, ordering him to communicate all the employees of *thana* and *mahal* of the content of the letter, and that he himself should remain alert and attentive to prevent and deal with them. Says that he informed all the employees of *thana* and *mahal* of the happy news. Besides, her further order is to intimate the receipt of the *parwana* so that the *harkara* of the post, carrying the *parwana* should be awarded. The same is communicated to her and that he along with all his staff is fully ready to meet any challenge posed by the insurgents. Dated 16 *Safar* 1275 AH (25 September 1858).

PP 89-90. *Saiyid Abd al-Rahman,* Thanadar *of Ashta, to Nawwab Sikandar Begam.* Refers to her *parwana*, dated 9 *Safar* 1275 AH, along with a copy of the letter of Captain Hutchinson, Agent at Bhupader, dated 15 September 1858, ordering to communicate all the employees of *thana* and *mahal* of the content of the letter and that he himself should remain alert and attentive to deal with the insurgents. If their number is high, information should immediately be passed on to the government. The intimation of the receipt of the *parwana* should be sent through the letter so that the *harkara* of the post should be awarded. Informs that the message was conveyed to all the employees of *thana* and *mahal*, and that he himself along with the employees is fully ready and surely the insurgents would be dealt with effectively. Dated 15 *Safar* 1275 AH (24 September1858).

PP 91-2. *Bhawani Prasad to Nawwab Sikandar Begam.* Refers to her order, as mentioned on his letter dated 7 *Safar* 1275 AH, and the content of the letter received from *thana* and *tahsil* of Debipura regarding entering of the insurgents in Narsingarh, sending Murawwat Muhammad Khan with an army of 500 foot-soldiers and 100 cavalrymen with 2 cannon to Satan Bari, coming of the *wakil-i sarkar,* Madan Mohan, *naib wakil*, and Ramden, *peshdast*, the encampment of the Political Agent at Debipura, and stationing of the Agent to the Governor-General at Bhopal, besides other matters. Says he deliberated upon the content of the letter whether it will be good or not to inform the Political Agent about it as the information of entering the insurgents in Narsingarh is incorrect. The insurgents after the defeat at Rajgarh became hapless and fled to Sironj. The British forces were in that region. As he did not think it wise to present it to the Political Agent, so he kept the letter in his possession. Dated 17 *Safar* 1275 AH (26 September 1858).

P 93. *Ganga Sahai,* Thanadar *of* Pargana *Chhatari to Nawwab Sikandar Begam.* Refers to her *parwana*, dated 9 *Safar* 1275 AH, along with a copy of the letter of Captain Hutchinson, Agent at Bhupader, which is in regard to capturing 28 cannon of insurgents and the magazines, and fleeing of the insurgents and directing him to deal with them and arrest them. Assures that the insurgents would be dealt with if they enter his region. Dated 17 *Safar* 1275 AH (26 September 1858).

P 95. *Saiyid Abbas Ali,* Thanadar *of Bharonda to Nawwab Sikandar Begam.* Refers to her *parwana*, dated 9 *Safar* 1275 AH, along with a copy of the letter of Captain Hutchinson, Agent at Bhupader, which is in regard to capturing 28 cannon of the insurgents in between Rajgarh and Bayawrah, killing of the insurgents by the British forces, and fleeing of some insurgents. As ordered, all the employees of *thana* and *mahal* were informed of the content of the letter enclosed with the *parwana*. Assures that he is fully ready to arrest or kill the insurgents. The information of the insurgents, entering in the region, would be given immediately and that they would surely be arrested and presented before her. Dated 23 *Safar* 1275 AH (2 October 1858).

File No. 289, A
Box No. 15
No. of Documents 19

Deployment of the Contingents of the Jagirdars of Bhopal, in Ashta, Siwans and Kalyakhery During the Uprising

PP 1-7. Contents

PP 9-12. Yaddasht, *Containing Details of* Sawars *and Foot-Soldiers of the* Jagirdars *of the State of Bhopal.* Dated 6 *Safar* 1275 AH.

P 13. Parwana *of Nawwab Sikandar Begam to Ghulam Makhdum Khan,* Nazim. Directs him to call all the contingents of the *jagirdars* of district west, as mentioned in the agreement, and send them to Ashta and Jawar. The details of the *jagirdars* are sent to him. Dated 6 *Safar* 1275 AH.

P 15. Parwana *of Nawwab Sikandar Begam to Sikandar Khan.* The details of the contingents of *the jagirdars* of district west are sent to him. Directs him to call all *jagirdars* of the district. Dated 6 *Safar* 1275 AH.

P 17. Parwana *of Nawwab Sikandar Begam to Hafiz Muhammad Hasan Khan.* The details of *jagirdars* of district east are sent to him. Directs him to call all *jagirdars* of the district. Dated 6 *Safar* 1275 AH.

P 19. Parwana *of Nawwab Sikandar Begam to Daulat Rai.* Directs him to call all the contingents of *the jagirdars* of district east, as mentioned in the agreement, and send them before Hafiz Muhammad Hasan Khan in Siwans. The details of the contingents of *the jagirdars* are sent to him. Dated 6 *Safar* 1275 AH.

P 21. Parwana *of Nawwab Sikandar Begam to Muhammad Raza Husain.* Directs him to call all the the contingents of *the jagirdars* of district south, as mentioned in the agreement, and send them to Kalyakhery. Dated 7 *Safar* 1275 AH.

P 23. *Dildar Ahmad Khan,* Jagirdar, Mauza *Bhanpur, to Nawwab Sikandar Khan.* Refers to his petition for the renewal of *sanad* of his *jagir mauza* Bhanpur, *pargana* Bhanpur. Now, he has received an order to go to Siwans before Hafiz Muhammad Hasan Khan. So he is going there. Requests for renewal of *sanad* of the said *mauza*, which is his *jagir*.

P 25. Jagirdar *of Garhi Ambapani to Nawwab Sikandar Khan.* Refers to the order to go to Siwans and that he has no objection to it. But it was promised that he would be paid @ Re. 1 per daim which was not paid to him. Requests for payment. Dated 8 *Safar* 1275 AH.

P 29. *Muhammad Hasan Khan to Nawwab Sikandar Begam.* Refers to her *parwana,* directing him to call all the of district east in Siwans. Informs that the order has been executed and details of the contingent are sent to her. Dated 24 *Safar* 1275 AH.

PP 31-2. Yaddasht, *Containing Details of the Soldiers of* Jagirdars *Under* Nizamat-i Mashriq, *who are Present in Siwans.*

PP 33-4. *Wazir Khan,* Qila'dar *to Nawwab Sikandar Begam.* Informs that Raja Madhekar sent 37 soldiers to Siwans on 12 *Rabi* I, 1275 AH. On 14 *Rabi* I, 1275 AH, he called back 20 soldiers on the pretext of sowing seeds. The details of the soldiers are enclosed. Dated 16 *Rabi* I, 1275 AH.

It contains the order that the letter may be sent to Paltu Lal, *muhafiz-i daftar-i insha*, for inclusion in the register and keeping in the *daftar*. A copy of the order may be sent to Wazir Khan, directing him to reach Garhi with all the forces available in Siwans immediately, as the insurgent forces have arrived in Garhi Ambapani.

PP 35-6. Fard, *Containing Details of the Soldiers of Raja Madhekar, who after Coming to Siwans Returned Back.*

P 37. *Wazir Khan,* Qila'dar, *to Nawwab Sikandar Begam.* Informs of the *jagirdars* who are present before Hafiz Muhammad Hasan Khan, *naib bakhshi* in Siwans. Their details have been sent to her by the *bakhshi*. Since then, details of all the *jagirdars* who came in Siwans till date are sent to her. For rest of the *jagirdars,* a letter has been sent to Daulat Rai, requesting him to send their details.

PP 39-40. Fard, *Containing Details of the Soldiers of the* Jagirdars, Ilaqa Nizamat-i Mashriq, *who Came in Siwans*.

P 41. *Wazir Khan,* Qila'dar, *to Daulat Rai,* Nazim-i Mashriq. Refers to the order of the Nawwab, as mentioned on the letter of Muhammad Hasan Khan, *naib bakhshi,* directing that all the remaining soldiers of the *jagirdars* should come to Siwans soon. Requests for the execution of the order.

PP 43-4. *Wazir Khan,* Qila'dar, *to Nawwab Sikandar Begam.* Informs that the following *jagirdars* on the pretext of sowing and distribution of seeds and manure have returned from Siwans. They are: Nae'm Muhammad Khan, Karam Khan and others.

P 45. *Wazir Khan, Qila'dar, to Nawwab Sikandar Begam.* Informs that Raja Madhekar who had gone to his *jagir* village on the pretext of sowing seeds has returned back to Siwans. Dated 19 *Rabi* I, 1275 AH.

P 47. *Muhammad Raza Husain to Nawwab Sikandar Begam.* Refers to her *parwana*, dated 7 *Safar* 1275 AH, directing him to call all the *jagirdars* of the district and send them to Kalyakhery. Sends the details of the contingents of the *jagirdars* of the district who came there.

File No. 289, B
Box No. 15
No. of Documents 8

PP 50-7. *List Containing Details of the Contingents of the* Jagirdars *Under* Nizamat-i Junub.

P 61. *Muhammad Raza Husain to Nawwab Sikandar Begam*. Informs that the day, Meharban Singh, *jamadar* of Raja Mardan Singh, Bariwala, reported that 12 soldiers to among 30 soldiers have voluntarily left. Says, he has written to Mardan Singh to recruit other soldiers in their place and send them there. Dated 29 *Rabi* I, 1275 AH.

P 63. *Muhammad Hasan Khan to Nawwab Sikandar Begam*. Informs that day passed calmly in the camp.

Informs that Majid Khan and other *jagirdars* have gone back from Bhopal without informing him. Dated 16 *Rabi* II, 1275 AH.

P 65. *Petition of Jugal Kishore,* Tahsildar *of* Thana *Deori, Requesting for Stopping Boats at Narmada Ghat.* It contains the order that Jugal Kishore, *amil* of Deori, may be conveyed that in the matter of boat, he should do as directed by district Narsinghpur. If there will be any deviation, it will not be good for him. A copy of the papers may be sent to Bhawani Prasad to bring the matter into the notice of the Political Agent. Dated 26 *Rabi* II, 1275 AH.

P 67. *Daulat Rai,* Nazim-i Mashriq, *to Nawwab Sikandar Begam.* Informs that Raja Ajmer, *jagirdar* of Gorakhpur, *pargana* Deori, along with his contingent besides other *jagirdars* are in Siwans as ordered. Jugal Kishore has requested for the deployment of the said Raja in Deori and some other contingent should be deployed in Siwans in his place. Sends his letter and requests that until the other contingent is sent there, the Raja should remain there.

P 69. *Report from* Thana *Deori by Jugal Kishore.* Informs that day, Mukund Singh, soldier came from Raisen and said that a huge army of the insurgents is encamping in Pura Guna and intending to come to that side. Hearing the news, the dwellers of *pargana* Bamhuri and other *parganas* have fled. Requests that if Raja Ajmer Singh is deployed in this region it would be good to prevent the entry of the insurgents.

P 71. *Muhammad Hasan Khan to Nawwab Sikandar Begam.* Informs that he has asked Abd al-Rahman, *thanadar* of Garhi Ambapani, to explain why some *jagirdars* went to Bhopal without order. If they are present there, they should be questioned. The report received from him will be sent to her.

P 73. *Muhammad Hasan Khan to Nawwab Sikandar*

Begam. Refers to her order, directing him to send Ajmer Singh, Gorakhpurwala from Siwans and Deori before Jugal Kishore, *amil* of Deori. Says the order will be executed in letter and spirit.

File No. 290
Box No. 15
No. of Documents 8

Notification Regarding the Number of Gunners Among the Dwellers and the Zamindars, to Remain Ready at the Time of Eventuality

PP 1-2. Contents

P 3. *Madan Mohan,* Naib Wakil, *to Nawwab Sikandar Begam.* Informs that day, the uprising started and all the *malguzars* deployed 5 to 10 gunners for the safety of villages. Says, in his opinion it would be good if all the *tahsildars* and *thanadars* of the State of Bhopal are instructed to prepare a list of gunners, who they are and where they are deployed, so that at the time of urgency they could be called and made ready to fight with the insurgent forces along with forces of the *thana* and *mahal*. Dated 17 *Safar* 1275 AH (26 September 1858).

P 5. Parwana-i Ishtahari *Issued by Nawwab Sikandar Begam to Her Three* Nazims. In view of the letter of Lala Madan Mohan Lal, *naib wakil,* dated 17 *Safar* 1275 AH, it is notified that the *malguzars* of the villages of *parganas* of Bhopal State should ensure the safety of life and property of the dwellers from insurgency. Thus, it is a must that in every village there should be 10 or 5 gunners who should always be ready. In view of this, the *amils* and *thanadars* of their respective regions are instructed that a list of gunners of every village may be prepared and taken in their possession. A copy of the same may be sent to the government along with their letters. At the time of insurgency, the sepoys of *thana* and *mahal* and gunners of the dwellers of villages should come together to fight with them collectively and defend the State of Bhopal from the insurgents. Dated 19 *Safar* 1275 AH.

PP 7-8. *Narain Saroop to Nawwab Sikandar Begam.* Refers to her *parwana* to Ghulam Makhdum Khan, *nazim*, dated 19 *Safar* 1275 AH, informing that in view of the letter of Lala Madan Mohan Lal, *naib wakil,* dated 17 *Safar* 1275 AH, it is notified that the *malguzars* of the villages of the *parganas* of Bhopal State should ensure the safety of life and property of the dwellers from insurgency. Thus, it is a must that in every village there should be 10 or 5 gunners who should always be ready. In view of this, the *amils* and *thanadars* of their regions are instructed that a list of gunners of every village should be prepared and taken in possession. A copy of the same may be sent to the government along with their letters. At the time of insurgency, the sepoys of the *thana* and *mahal* and gunners of villagers should come together to fight with them collectively and defend the State of Bhopal from the insurgents.

It contains the order that the letter may be sent to *muhafiz-i daftar-i insha* to include in the register and keep it in the *daftar*. A copy of the letter may be sent to all the *amils* and *thanadars* of seven *mahals* of the district, directing them to act in accordance with the orders of the government, received in his office on 7 *Rabi* I, 1275 AH. Says, he made a survey of all the gunners of the *mahal junub* and prepared a list in duplicate. One copy of the list is retained in his office and another copy is sent to her. Dated 7 *Jumada* II, 1275 AH.

PP 9-19. *List of Gunners in the* Mahal *of Jawar.*

PP 25-6. *Hazarilal,* Tahsildar *to Nawwab Sikandar Begam.* Refers to the letter of the *nizamat*, dated 7 *Jumada* II, 1275 AH, in reference to the royal order, dated 17 *Safar* 1275 AH, informing that in accordance with the letter of Lala Madan Mohan Lal, *naib wakil,* dated 17 *Safar* 1275 AH, it is informed that the *malguzars* of all the villages of the *parganas* of Bhopal State should ensure that for the safety of life and property of the dwellers from insurgency, it is must that in every village there should be 10 or 5 gunners who should always be ready. In view of this, every *amil* and *thanadar* of their regions may be instructed to prepare a list of gunners in every village and take them in their possession. A copy of the same may be sent to the government along with the letters. At the time of insurgency, the sepoys of the *thana* and *mahal* and gunners of villagers should deal with them firmly and defend the sate of Bhopal from the insurgents. Reports, after interacting with the *zamindars* of these villages, it came to the notice that Jitu Patel in *mauza* Himmatgarh, Kamud Patel in *mauza* Mutheri, and Hulas Patel in *mauza* Bhelkhari are capable and worthy. They are able to employ and bear the expenses of the gunners. A list of gunners available with these three *zamindars,* as explained is submitted.

P 27. Yaddasht, *Containing Names of the Soldiers Employed by* Mustajirs *of Villages in* Mahal *Raisen.* Dated 28 *Sha'ban* 1266 *Fasli*.

P 29. *Muhammadi Lal,* Tahsildar, *and Tafazzul Husain,* Thanadar, *to Nawwab Sikandar Begam.* Dated 11 *Zilhijja* 1275 AH.

File No. 291
Box No. 15
No. of Documents 3

Insurgents in Hoshangabad

P 1. Contents

P 3. *Nawwab Sikandar Begam to Umrao Daulah, Baqi Muhammad Khan.* Refers to his consent given in regard to the dismissal of Ghulam Nabi Khan, *risaldar*, that the opinion of *Madar al-Maham*, *Mu'tamid al-Maham* and Maulawi Sa'd al-Din, *muhtamim, adalat-i faujdari* is justified. While the fact is that the date on which he has recorded his consent, there is no record of any statement given by *Madar al-Maham* and *Mu'tamid al-Maham.* It means that he has given his consent without going through the *rubakar*. Dated 14 *Safar* 1275 AH.

PP 5-6. *Baqi Muhammad Khan to Nawwab Sikandar Begam.* Refers to her *shuqqa,* dated 14 *Safar* 1275 AH, raising objection on his consent to the opinion given by *madar al-maham, mu'tamid al-maham and Muhammad* Sa'd al-Din, *muhtamim, adalat-i faujdari,* pertaining to the dismissal of Ghulam Nabi Khan, *risaldar*, whereas the fact is that the date on which he gave his consent there was no record of any statement given by *madar al-maham* or *mu'tamid al-maham.* It seems he gave his consent without going through the *rubakar*. Explains that when he had received the *rubakar* for giving his opinion, he had studied the entire *rubakar* from the beginning to the end minutely. He remembers that it carried the opinion of *madar al-maham* and *mu'tamid al-maham* and Muhammad Sa'd al Din, *muhtamim*, *adalat-i faujdari*. The official procedure is that if an order is recorded on the top of a letter, it is understood that it is officially binding to all. So, when he received an order which had consent of all the three, he too gave his consent. Says he is unable to understand as to why his constent is being objected. If he followed the rules he should be appreciated, if he committed a mistake he should be pardoned. Dated 7 *Jumada* II, 1275 AH.

File No. 292
Box No. 15
No. of Documents 5

Quick Arrangement to Deal with the Insurgents

PP 1-2. Contents

PP 3-4. *Bhawani Prasad to Nawwab Sikandar Begam.* Informs of the news that the Agent to the Governor General has ordered Smith, who is coming from Gwalior, to go to Bhopal along with his forces. Meanwhile, General Mitchell ordered him to go to Sironj as there is no requirement as such of the forces in Bhopal. Dated 17 *Safar* 1275 AH (26 September 1858).

P 5. *Nawwab Sikandar Begam to Bhawani Prasad.* Refers to his letter, dated 17 *Safar* 1275 AH, in the matter that it is the opinion of all the officers of the Political Agent that she should make arrangement in such a way that the insurgents who are on the bank of river Narmada should not even think of Bhopal. Asks if the British officials want that the insurgents on the bank of river Narmada should not be seen. If so she should be informed or it means *nakabandi* by the combined forces of Bhopal State, Maharaja Sindhia and the British.

P 7. *Nawwab Sikandar Begam to Madan Mohan Lal,* Naib Wakil. Informs about her letter to Bhawani Prasad regarding making arrangement of *dandah* on the bank of the river. The same is sent to him, directing to bring the matter into the notice of the Political Agent at Sehore before sending it to Bhawani Prasad. The reply of Political Agent may be conveyed to her through his letter. Dated 20 *Safar* 1275 AH (29 September 1858).

P 9. *Madan Mohan Lal to Nawwab Sikandar Begam.* Informs as ordered, dated 20 *Safar* 1275 AH, through her letter addressed to Bhawani Prasad, the matter regarding the management of *ghats* of Narmada and arrangement of *dandah* in Bhopal State through the forces of state, the Sindhia's and British forces, was brought first into the notice of Major Ayuns, Commander of Regiment 9, deployed at the cantonment and then into the notice of the Political Agent. Both of them said that the Nawwab's opinion was justified and that her opinion and the opinion of the General would be the same. The *parwana* of Nawwab should be sent to the army camp as it is the responsibility of the General to make arrangement and deal with the insurgents. Dated 21 *Safar* 1275 AH (30 September 1858).

File No. 293
Box No. 15
No. of Documents 6

Role of Muhammad Yasin Khan, Son of Namdar Khan, During the Uprising

P 1. Contents

P 3. *Bhawani Prasad to Nawwab Sikandar Begam.* Sends the petition of Muhammad Yasin Khan, son of Nawwab Namdar Khan, received from the Political Agent, asking to inform about the role of the petitioner in the uprising from the beginning till that day and about his character. Requests to enquire from the office of *Bakhshigari* about him. Dated 7 *Safar* 1275 AH(16 September 1858).

PP 5-6. *Muhammad Yasin Khan, Son of Nawwab Namdar Khan, to Nawwab Sikandar Begam.* Refers to his petition, requesting the release of the arrear of his pension and order of the government to prove his innocence. Explains that his father, late Namdar Khan, was in the service of the government. After his death half of his salary was fixed for him, and for his other brothers and his mother. Says, after the death of his mother, the amount was divided amongst his four brothers which did not include Kamdar Khan due to the insurgency. Meanwhile, the uprising erupted. Says, he was not involved in the mutiny at all. He was in the company of the army contingent which was deployed at Sehore for ensuring the safety and security. He was also in the company of the contingent who escorted the British to Hoshangabad. Dated 13 September 1858.

PP 7-8 *Murawwat Muhammad Khan to Nawwab Sikandar Begam.* Refers to her order, dated 9 *Safar* 1275 AH, recorded on the letter of Bhawani Prasad which is about the character of Muhammad Yasin Khan, son of Nawwab Namdar Khan. Informs that it was Lala Lakhpat Roy who was looking to the *sawars* and according to his description, Muhammad Yasin Khan was appointed on 2 June 1856 in *Risala* I, red uniform and even after the change of colour of horses with effect from 1 January 1867/4 *Jumada* I, 1273 AH, he remained serving the *Risala* I, red uniform.

P 9. *From Lakhpat Roy.* Informs that Yasin Muhammad Khan, son of Nawwab Namdar Khan, *risala,* red uniform was appointed on 2 June 1856/28 *Ramazan*, 1272 AH in place of Kamdar Khan, son of Namdar Khan under *risala* IV, red uniform and remained there in that capacity till the end of December 1856 and after the change of colour of horses on 1 January 1857/4

Jumada I, 1273 AH, he was recruited under *Risala* I, red uniform and held the same post till date. Dated 24 *Safar* 1275 AH.

PP 11-12. *Murawwat Muhammad Khan to Nawwab Sikandar Begam.* Refers to her order asking about the character of Muhammad Yasin Khan, son of Nawwab Namdar Khan. Informs that he was appointed in *risala* IV, red uniform, and deployed at Sehore. He was also in the company of the contingent which went to Hoshangabad, escorting the British officers. There is no report of his involvement in the insurgency. Dated 18 *Rabi* I, 1275 AH.

File No. 294, A
Box No. 15
No. of Documents 18

Uprising and Siege of Sironj by Tantia Tope, Adil Muhammad Khan and Others, the Arrest of the Amil and Devastation of Sironj. Fleeing of the Insurgents to Issagarh Via Lonjhar, Hearing the News of the Commencement of the British Forces

PP 1-9. Contents

PP 11-12. *Hazrat Nur Khan,* Tahsildar*, Bheglone, to Nawwab Sikandar Begam.* Informs that the insurgents entered Sironj, captured it and sieged the city and made fortification of the court. But the dwellers of the city came together and ousted them from the city by ball-cannoning and gun firing. Around one hundred of them were killed and many of them wounded. About 6-7 soldiers of Sironj were also killed. The insurgents remained there for a day. Some say they want to retreat and attack Sironj. It is also said that they would go to Bheglone. They destroyed and set 4-5 villages of Sironj on fire after their return. The detailed description of the situation would be known through the letter of Ghulam Muhammad Khan, *risaldar*, and the letter of *jagirdar* and through a letter in Hindi of Balkishan, the informer. Dated 9 *Safar* 1275 AH.

PP 13-14. *Ghulam Muhammad Khan,* Risaldar, *to*

Nawwab Sikandar Begam. Informs that after sending the post, Hira Singh, the informer, came and told the previous day that the Peshwa with an army of 4,000 and 4 cannon came and encamped at a place lying at a distance of 1 *curoh* from Sironj. That day, the camp of Peshwa was installed there. Dated 10 *Safar* 1275 AH.

It contains the order that the letter may be sent to Lala Paltu Lal, *muhafiz-i daftar-i insha*, for inclusion in the register and keeing in the *daftar*. A copy of the letter may be sent to Bhawani Prasad, *wakil*, for presenting it before the Political Agent and convey his observation to her. Dated 13 *Safar* 1275 AH.

PP 15-16. *Ghulam Muhammad Khan,* Risaldar, *to Nawwab Sikandar Begam.* Informs that day, i.e. 10th *Safar* 1275 AH, Balkishan and Hira Singh, the informers, came and stated that day before the previous day an army of 10, 000 of Peshwa with 4 cannon came in Sironj and encamped at Bijilya Kondal, adjoining to Sironj. The previous day the said army reached near the fort and installed 4 cannon around the fort. The contingent of Sironj, due to fear of this army, fled from there. The *amil* and *kamdar* with 4 cannon were captured. Later on, the *amil* and *kamdar* were released. All the *jagirdars* and *bohras* of Sironj and their relatives fled from there. Adil Muhammad Khan along with his army is staying at the court. All the people of Korwai are inside the fort. It is also heard that *amil* of Basodah and the dwellers have fled. The informers also said that another army of Peshwa was too coming. It is also heard that 200 *sawars* of Peshwa have gone to Basodah. Dated 10 *Safar* 1275 AH.

It contains the order that the letter may be sent to Lala Paltu Lal, *muhafiz-i daftar-i insha*, for inclusion in the register and keeing in the *daftar*. A copy of the letter may be sent to Bhawani Prasad, *wakil* for presenting it before the Political Agent and conveying his observation to her. Dated 17 *Safar* 1275 AH.

PP 17-18. *Ghulam Muhammad Khan, Risaldar, to Nawwab Sikandar Begam.* Informs that day, i.e. 11th *Safar* 1275 AH, Udairam, the informer and an employee under the battalion of Hattey Singh, *jamadar,* came and stated that he was sent to bring the news from Sironj where he found that an army of 1,000 of the Peshwa, 1,000 of Raja Bhor, and 2,000 of Adil Muhammad Khan, were encamping in *mauza* Nekan. Dated 11 *Safar* 1275 AH.

PP 19-21. *Ghulam Muhammad Khan,* Risaldar, *to Nawwab Sikandar Begam.* Informs that day, i.e. 13th of the month, Kallu and Balkishan, the informers came and stated that an army of 40, 000, both *sawars* and foot-soldiers of Peshwa with 20 cannon and 14 elephants, besides a large number of camels, were encamping at three places in Sironj; at Bijilya Kondal, on the mountains of Murtaza Ali, and at Bhoripur, situating at a distance of 2 to 3 *curoh* from Sironj. The previous day, an army of 5, 000; both *sawars* and foot-soldiers were ready to march to Korwai, Bheglone and Basodah. In the meantime, they heard the news of the arrival of British forces. But it was the army of Raja Bhor. Thereafter, their plan became stronger and they strategized to capture first Bhilsa and thereafter Bhopal. From Issagarh, one battalion and 2 cannon were coming to Basodah. Dated 13 *Safar* 1275 AH.

PP 23-4. *Bhawani Prasad to Nawwab Sikandar Begam.* Informs that day, through a letter of *suba* of Bhilsa, dated 11 *Safar* 1275 AH, a report reached to Major Richards, the Political Agent, that Tantia Tope and other insurgents entered Sironj, arrested the *amil* of Sironj and captured his cannon. Their further programme was to go to Bhopal via Lutery and Bhilsa. There is news that a British army has marched from Sipri to Sironj. The post from Sehore did not come to the Political Agent due to overflowing of river Naroti. Informs that three days before he wrote to Madan Mohan, *naib wakil*, for the disposal of posts of Sehore, Khandoh and Bhopal.

Hopes that Madan Mohan would do so, and the orders are issued to deploy *sawars* at the post offices in the State of Bhopal. Says, he has sent 4 *sawars* to Berasia and 4 *sawars* to Beragarh to bring the post. Might be the *sawars* were carrying the posts from Sehore and Khandoh via Bhopal and Berasia due to overflowing of river and *nallas*. General Mitchell for the last two days has stopped sending the post via Bayawrah and directed to send it via Sehore and Bhopal. The previous day, an order was received by General Mitchell from the Agent, Central India, to go to Bhopal along with his forces. If they reach after the loss, what is the use of it; and that two battalions of *sawars* and two other companies are despatched from Mhow. It is heard that the said army has reached Bayawrah and would join at Berasia. Due to continuous and heavy rainfall since the previous day, the march of the army did not take place. There is no way to move the arsenal, bullock carts and camels. Even the posts were not carried away by the *sawars* to Berasia. The arrangement of *rasad* at Gulgaon, Diwanganj, Dallod, Debipura, Doraha and in Bhopal should be made by her orders for the army, that would be coming soon. The daily expenses of that army have been communicated through his letter as well as by the *parwana* of the Political Agent. The *suji* as much as possible should be prepared and kept ready in Bhopal for the British and that the bullocks from *banjaras* should be made available. Dated 14 *Safar* 1275 AH.

PP 25-6. *Madan Mohan,* Naib Wakil, *to Nawwab Sikandar Begam.* Informs that day, at the time of meeting Hutchinson, he expressed his gratitude to her and stated that management of the Nawwab was beyond expression. The arrangement of Bhopal State during the uprising was such that no other state of Hindustan did like the Bhopal State, the assistance which the British received from Bhopal was not received from any other state. The Agent, Central India, has clealy instructed that the Nawwab of Bhopal State should be given all possible help. The arrangement should be made in such a manner that no insurgent ever dares to enter Bhopal. Thus, the British army has marched from Bayawrah to Narsingarh and would soon arrive at Berasia. Dated 14 *Safar* 1275 AH.

PP 27-8. *Banilal to Nawwab Sikandar Begam.* Refers to her order regarding the news of the insurgents. Says, he sent a person to Sironj, who will bring the news after 5 or 6 days. To manage a quick receipt of news from Sironj, he thinks that three persons should be deployment from Bhopal to Bhilsa and three persons in Sironj and that he himself at Bhilsa. Those who are in Sironj should report everyday to him and, thereafter, he should report to her everyday. The salary of three persons would be Rs. 4 and for another 3 persons would be Rs. 5. Requests for orders to proceed further. Requests for providing a 'babu' for his riding and some money to manage the things. If ordered, he may proceed the next day. Also requests that Lamba Prasad, *sawar* under *risala* Roop Singh, *risaldar* is fairly a clever person. If allowed, he may be sent to Sironj to write the news of the insurgents. Dated 15 *Safar* 1275 AH.

P 29. *Bhawani Prasad to Nawwab Sikandar Begam.* Informs that day he arrived at Berasia and hired two persons and sent them for bringing the news of the insurgents. Besides, two soldiers of the battalion of Gangaram; Gosain Gangagur, and Bihari were sent for spying on the insurgents. Two others were also engaged who too would be sent. They have been paid Rs. 5 for the expense of the journey. Dated 15 *Safar* 1275 AH (24 September 1858).

PP 31-3. *Chain Rai to Nawwab Sikandar Begam.* Informs that day, the 15th *Safar* 1275 AH, day Friday, a letter of Bhao, his father-in-law came from Bhilsa. Apart from personal matters, he describes the siege of Sironj by Adil Muhammad Khan, the rebel. He was attacked by Aonarsiwala, which led to the killing of 50 to 100 persons. Then the army of Bhor, Raja of Narwar, and the army of Tantia Tope came together and attacked once again. They captured the *amil* and made him captive and caused devastation in the city so much so that no one was left even with one cloth, and made a pundit of the said place the ruler of that place. Then, they marched from there and came to *mauza* Kandeh, *ilaqa* Bhilsa. That *mauza* too was devastated. Many women fell in the well to save their dignity and died. Those who remained, they endangered their dignity. They and their officers, in groups of 800 or 700, encamped at places like Nekan, Shamshabad and Shiv. The army of the insurgents was 10, 000 in number, including both *sawars* and foot-soldiers. They have managed everything very well. They have installed cannon on every tower. It was Wednesday when they heard the news of the arrival of British forces at Shamshabad. The people of Tiran and Basodah were very afraid and fled. Let us see how the Almighty saves the dignity of the people. If one looses his life, it does not matter but if the dignity is lost, it matters. May God save the dignity of the people. Says, whatever he wrote to him he wrote word for word to her. Dated 15 *Safar* 1275 AH.

P 35. Parwanas *and Letters of Nawwab Sikandar Begam to Nawwab Muiz Muhammad Khan, Faujdar Muhammad Khan, Nawwab Shahjahan Begam, Nawwab Umrao Daulah, Dulhan Sahaba and Sarkar-i Buzurg.* A copy of the letter of Lala Chain Rai, *munib, daftar-i bakhshigari*, dated 15 *Safar* 1275 AH, is sent to them. The details would be known through the letter. Hope they would instruct the people of their region to remain alert and attentive. Dated 15 *Safar* 1275 AH (24 September 1858).

P 37. *Daulat Rai,* Nazim-i Mashriq, *to Nawwab Sikandar Begam.* Informs of the report, received from *thana* Raisen, dated 14 *Safar* 1275 AH (23 September 1858), regarding insurgency in Bhilsa and coming back of Jankar Rao Charnayak, a dweller of Bhilsa who had gone to manage the affairs there along with 200 *sawars* and 300 foot-soldiers. Dated 16 *Safar* 1275 AH (25 September 1858).

P 39. *News-Report from* Thana *Raisen, Sent by Bansidhar,* Thanadar. Reports that day, Chandu Singh, caste Brahmin, a dweller of Raisen who had gone to Bhilsa, came back and stated that Jankar Rao Charnayak, a dweller of Bhilsa who had gone to manage the affairs of *mauza* Natran, *pargana* Bhilsa, along with 200 *sawars* and 300 foot-soldiers, came back to Bhilsa on 16 *Safar* 1275 AH (25 September 1858). Bawan Bao Pandit, *gumashdar* of Basodah, and Nahta Sahab, *gumashdar* of Shamshabad, were sent to Bhilsa. Jankar Rao Charnayak told *Sarsuba*, Bhilsa, about the intention of the insurgents in Bhilsa. The army of insurgents comprises of 3,000 *sawars* and 5, 000 foot-soldiers and is encamping at Anjad Agarha, *pargana* Bhilsa. Dated 14 *Safar* 1275 AH (23 September 1858).

P 41. *Ghulam Muhammad Khan, Risaldar, to Nawwab Sikandar Begam.* Informs that day, i.e. 16th *Safar* 1275 AH, Kalwa and Sohanram, the informers came and reported that about 500 *gosains*, 200 camels, 1000 *sawars* and foot-soldiers of Raja Bhor came and encamped in the mountains of Murtaza Ali. There were atleast 25 soldiers who were injured. It is heard that these forces would march after Dussehra. There is a report of the coming of the British forces. There was a battle between the two forces. Thereafter, they went to some other direction. A penalty of Rupees three lakh was imposed on the *amil* of Sironj and the Peshwa took Rs. 50,000 from that amount. There is peace everywhere in the entire State of Bhopal. Dated 16 *Safar* 1275 AH (25 September 1858).

PP 43-4. *Madan Mohan,* Naib Wakil, *to Nawwab Sikandar Begam.* Refers to a letter of Chain Rai, *munib bakhshigari,* dated 15 *Safar* 1275 AH, which contains the report of devastation of Sironj and *mauza* Kandaha, the captivity of the *amil* of Sironj, and the news of the arrival of an insurgent army at Tateran which bears her order to inform the content of the letter to Hutchinson and other British officials, stationed at Sehore cantonment. Says, he in the early morning appeared before Major Ayuns where Hutchinson and Walker were also present. He brought each and every word of the letter into the notice of all three officials. They looked at the map and said General Mitchell was in Berasia along with his forces, blockading the route of the insurgents. They would not be able to come to Bhopal. General Mitchell is in Berasia with the orders of Central India, besically to make arrangement in that perspective. An army from Neemuch is pursuing the insurgents, wherever they would go. From Siwans too the troops are pursuing the insurgents. In Sagar, an army with arsenal is ready to take on the battle with the insurgents and there too everyone is almost ready and prepared. In Bhopal too, the Nawwab has fully prepared herself. The platoons of 5 companies, stationed at Mhow, have been asked to move to that cantonment. But due to continuous rain, their march is in abeyance but soon they would arrive. They said to him to convey the Nawwab their many good wishes and convey that there is no need to worry as General Mitchell is on duty to eliminate the insurgents. The above-mentioned forces are also pursuing the insurgents wherever they would go. Soon they would be dealt with. Thanks to the Nawwab for giving information of the insurgents, they said. Dated 16 *Safar* 1275 AH (25 September 1858).

P 45. *Madan Mohan,* Naib Wakil, *to Nawwab Sikandar Begam.* There was calm in the cantonment and in Sehore. Captain Hutchinson with a contingent of 200 *sawars* has entered Bhilsa. Suba Sahab with an army of 4,000, besides cannon and arsenal, is fully prepared in Issagarh to eliminate the insurgents. The army from Neemuch has arrived at Bayawrah and will go to Sironj.

4 platoons of the Bengal troops, deployed in Punjab, had raised the banner of revolt. Dated 16 *Safar* 1275 AH (25 September 1858).

PP 47-8. *Bakhshi Murawwat Muhammad Khan to Nawwab Sikandar Begam*. Informs that day, Piranshah, a *faqir* and dweller of Diwanganj, came from Sironj and stated that Adil Muhammad Khan sieged Sironj and was defeated by the *amil* of Sironj. In the meantime, Man Singh son of Raja Bhor came with 2 battalion forces from Kota. Adil Muhammad Khan, when he heard this news, thought it was the British forces and fled from there. But Man Singh himself let him know about him, who then retreated. They demanded compensation from the *amil* which he did not accept. The Raja then prepared himself to fight with him. He installed 2 cannon, entered within the walled city, and captured the arms and ammunitions. Tantia Tope too has arrived there after his defeat and loosing 200 men at Rajgarh by the British forces. The British army is pursuing them. About 2,000 British forces are present at Berasia. The British forces are in their pursuation from many places. The army of Tantia Tope has a strength of 25,000. They also have cannon with them. Dated 18 *Safar* 1275 AH (27 September 1858).

PP 49-50. *Bhawani Prasad to Nawwab Sikandar Begam.* Informs that on 15 *Safar* 1275 AH, he sent 4 informers; 2 from the battalion of Gangaram, *jamadar*, and 2 new recruits to Sironj. The two who were from the battalion of Gangaram came and what they stated was recorded and put before the Political Agent. The same is sent to her. Says, although there is no need to worry but they should remain alert. This is a firm intention of the British that the insurgents should not enter Bhopal at any cost. On 3 October 1858, a British army from Mhow would come to Bhopal. From the letter of Baijnath, it is learnt that another British army would reach Berasia via Narsingarh. Requests that in the matters of post, Madan

Mohan, *wakil*, should be instructed to take care and remain cautious, and that posts from Bhopal to Berasia are carried on smoothly by the *sawars*. He too is taking care of the posts from the cantonment to Berasia. One *chauki* of post with 2 *sawars* at Lalarya, *ilaqa* Berasia, situating at a distance of 4 *curoh* from Berasia, and another *chauki* of post at Sabilgarh, *ilaqa* Bhilsa, have been identified. Dated 18 *Safar* 1275 AH (27 September 1858).

File No. 294, B
Box No. 15
No. of Documents 24

PP 51-2. *Statement of Gangagar, an Employee of the State of Bhopal, Deployed at Berasia Under the Battalion of Gangaram, Jamadar.*

Q. He was sent to Sironj. He is asked to tell what he saw there or heard.

R. He reached Sironj on 25 September 1858 and stayed in the house of Eknath. From there he saw that 5 cannon were at one place on the road of Bhilsa, another 5 cannon at some distance from there, and 5 more cannon were also at some other place. A large number of *sawars* and foot-soldiers were in Sironj and all were contended. The troops were in the surroundings of the city on the west, south and north sides. There were fewer troops on the eastern side. The name of Narwarwala was very often heard there. On Saturday, more troops also joined from outside. They were 25,000 armymen and telling that their goal was Bhopal and had there been no rain, they would have been in Bhopal. They were talking about the salary and borrowed Rs. 50,000 from the people. They were demanding Rs. 50,000 from the *bohras* and rupees one lakh from the *amil* of Tehri. If all the money was received, they would be able to pay the salaries of the soldiers. The names of Rao Sahab and Tantia Tope were popular. There were 4 *nawwabs* who were the chiefs of these forces. In the evening, he came in a village where his other companions also came. Water from the river was overflowing on to the streets. There was news of the coming of British forces. They were talking even if the British forces come, they would fight battle with them and then they would go to Bhopal. Two *sawars* of insurgents were on guard everywhere.

PP 53-4. *Hazrat Nur Khan,* Tahsildar *of Bheglone to Nawwab Sikandar Begam.* Sends the letter received from Nawwab Sahab, Mahbubpur, desiring that if need arises he should not hesitate to take the help of the army contingent. Dated 18 *Safar* 1275 AH.

P 55. *Muhammad Najaf Khan, Nawwab of Mahbubpur To Hazrat Nur Khan.* It is heard from the people that the insurgents and miscreants are in the vicinity of Sironj, hiding in mountains and forests. He, for the last few days, is in Sehore. Nizam Ali, *jamadar* and the *qila'dar* of Mahbubpur have been directed to remain alert and attentive and if need arises, he should rush to Bheglone to help the people with his contingent as both the governments are one. There should not be any negligence or reluctance in giving help to them. A copy of that is enclosed, so that if there is need he should not hesitate to take the help of the *jamadar*. Dated 5 *Safar* 1275 AH.

P 57. *Muhammad Najaf Khan to* Jamadar, Qila'dar *of Mahbubpur.* It is heard from the people that the insurgents and miscreants are in the vicinity of Sironj, hiding in mountains and forests. He is in Sehore for the last few days. Instructs him to be cautious and help the people of Bheglone if the need arises. Dated 5 *Safar* 1275 AH.

P 59. *Ghulam Muhammad Khan*, Risaldar, *to Nawwab Sikandar Begam.* Informs that day, 18 *Safar* 1275 AH, Hira Kotwar came from Korwai and stated that 200 *sawars* of Peshwa arrived there. They demanded cash, 2 cannon and horses from Nawwab of Korwai. Dated 18 *Safar* 1275 AH.

P 61[11]. *Refers to his Letter and Says that he is Happy to Know of the Situation*. Says, he should always write and keep him informed of the situation. It is heard that some Bundela forces are in *mauza* Bairi and their intention is to cross the river in *mauza* Deoli and come to that side. Directs him to be aware and attentive. Dated 17 January 1266 *Fasli*.

P 63. *Bhawani Prasad to Nawwab Sikandar Begam.* He had sent two soldiers of the battalion of Gangaram, *jamadar*, from Berasia to Sironj in disguise. The previous day, they came back at Sabilgarh from Sironj. Bihari, the soldier, was not an experienced person. He was sent back in the battalion of Gangaram, *jamadar*. Gangagar, another soldier, was retained to accompany him to Sironj the next day. Dated 19 *Safar* 1275 AH (28 September 1858).

P 65. *Daulat Rai,* Nazim-i Mashriq, *to Nawwab Sikandar Begam.* Enquiring about the insurgents in Bhilsa, he wrote a letter to the Suba Sahab of Bhilsa. That day, he received the reply of his letter, dated 16 *Safar* 1275 AH, informing that the insurgents are in Sironj. The same is presented before her.

P 67. *Sada Shiv Rao,* Suba *of Bhilsa, to Daulat Rai,* Nazim-i Mashriq. Refers to his letter, dated 1 *Safar* 1275 AH, informing the defeat of the insurgents, and their encampment in Shamshabad and Sironj. Informs that infact the chief of the insurgents, Tantia Tope, after the defeat at Rajgarh and Bayawrah, fled and took shelter in Sironj. Adil Muhammad Khan, the insurgent is also present in his company. There is no clarity about their actual number. Some say they are 10, 000 to 12,000, and some say they are 20, 000 or 25,000. But the British forces have arrived at Berasia and surely the insurgents would meet their fate. Dated 16 *Safar* 1275 AH.

PP 69-70. *Murawwat Muhammad Khan to Nawwab*

---

11. Name of the writer or the addressee is not clear.

Sikandar Begam. Himmat Khan, a dweller of Balya, *ilaqa* Diwanganj, came from Sironj and reported that firstly Adil Muhammad Khan sieged Sironj with an army of 2,000 but later on he was defeated by the *amil* of Sironj. He informed Tantia Tope who after having defeated at Rajgarh came to Sironj and arrested the *amil* and extracted rupees one lakh from him in compensation and a pundit was chosen as their *mukhtar*. On Thursday, they arrived in Bhilsa. Meanwhile, news was heard that Hira Singh, *sipahsalar* of the dismantled army of Kota, fought a battle with the British forces. Tantia Tope sent two *risalas* and two platoons to bring him from Kota. Tantia Tope was angry with Adil Muhammad Khan for the devastation of the villages of Sironj. Everyone says if the Nawwabs of Banda, and Bareilly, and Rao Sahab are arrested, others would not be able to stand before the mighty forces. The Nawwabs of Bareilly, Banda and Jawrah, Rao Sahab and Adil Muhammad Khan and their families are with Tantia Tope, carrying a huge army. The army which was sent to Malhargarh came back and is encamping at Sironj. The British army is at Lalarya, *ilaqa* Bhilsa. Dated 19 *Safar* 1275 AH (28 September 1858).

P 71. *Ghulam Muhammad Khan,* Risaldar, *to Nawwab Sikandar Begam.* Informs that day, the 19 *Safar,* Udairam, an informer and an employee under the battalion of Hattey Singh, *jamadar,* came and said that in the army of Peshwa, new recruitments were being made and thus 4,000 to 5, 000 new recruits were employed. The total number of insurgents would be around 22, 000 who are professional soldiers. The servants and *sais*[12] are in addition to the army personnel. Besides, the soldiers of Tonk and Sironj are engaged in Sironj. Those who possessed royal guns were told by the Peshwa that either they surrender or become his servants. All entered the service of Peshwa. The Peshwa increased

12. Horse-keepers.

their salary to Rs. 5. Their guns also remained in their possession. The Peshwa also got 200 guns, besides arms and ammunitions and Rs. 5, 000 from Sironj. They were further demanding Rs. 10, 000 from them. The *amil* of Sironj was still captive with them. Every house in Sironj was imposed a fine of Rs. 4 or Rs. 5. Two persons were arrested on the suspicion of spying on the British. There is also news of the division of the army in three groups. One group left for Korwai Bhonrasa, other group to Bheglone and Basodah, and the third group to Bhilsa. They have also heard the news of the arrival of the British forces. So they were very alert. They have collected 20 bullocks from *mauza* Eklod for carrying cannon. Says, he with this small group of troops is ready to fight with the insurgents. Dated 19 *Safar* 1275 AH (28 September 1858).

P 73. *Ghulam Muhammad Khan,* Risaldar*, to Nawwab Sikandar Begam.* Informs that day, the 19 *Safar,* Hira, the informer came and stated that upon hearing the news of the arrival of the British forces, the army of the Peshwa was intending to go from Sironj. Adil Muhammad Khan asked the Peshwa, if allowed, he might go to either Korwai or Bheglone or Bhilsa. The Peshwa told him to wait till the next day. Says, Kalwa and Balkishan Dhanraj, the informers who are in Sironj send news everyday. If anyone is suspected as informer, he is caught by them. Hira, the informer, escaped from their hands. About the other two informers, there is no news, whether they are caught by the insurgents or hiding. Kalwa has also conveyed to him to be careful for another one or two days. Says, he and all his men are ready to meet any eventuality. Dated 19 *Safar* 1275 AH (28 September 1858).

P 75. *Madan Mohan,* Naib Wakil*, to Nawwab Sikandar Begam.* Informs that day, Major Ayuns and Hutchinson took attendance of the soldiers of Regiment 9. They were all the time ready and attentive. There is peace in

Yohran. The insurgents yet did not come from Sironj to that side. Many of them are hiding in the houses. Otherwise, all are encamping in the north of Sironj. Dated 19 *Safar* 1275 AH (28 September 1858).

PP 77-8. *Bhawani Prasad to Nawwab Sikandar Begam.* Informs that day, Lal Singh and Ghanshyam, the informers brought the news from Sironj. Their statement was recorded and presented before the Political Agent. The same is presented before her. The informers also stated that Adil Muhammad Khan came out of Sironj and followed the insurgent forces. The actual news will be received by next day. Dated 20 *Safar* 1275 AH (29 September 1858).

PP 79-80. *Statement of Lal Singh, the Informer*. He was sent to Sironj. He is asked to tell what he saw or heard there. States that on 27 September 1858, he along with Ghanshyam reached the house of Chhotey Ram, the stone cutter, and that very night he heard the sound of drum beating to march. They started the preparation and on 28th, they were marching on the road of Gwalior. He asked the people as to where the army was going. They said, they were apprehending the attack by British forces that had arrived in Sehore. They said they would go to Balhargarh to capture two cannon which were there. Besides, they had 4 cannon of the *amil* of Sironj, promised to be returned to him afterwards. If the British forces attacked them, they would flee leaving behind the cannon. They were demanding huge money from the *amil* of Sironj and took Rs. 18, 000 from him but it was left in Sironj. Nana Sahab and Nawwab Sahab all left Sironj. They hired 4 mechanics from Sironj for 4 cannon. Chhotey Ram said there were 17, 000 to 18, 000 forces; some with arms, some without arms. The *sawars* were more in comparison to foot-soldiers. Chhatrasal was called by Nana Sahab by sending 15 *sawars*. He fled from Agra and did not come back. Adil Muhammad Khan was also there along with 4,000 forces and 2 elephants. His ladies were on elephants and palanquine.

P 81. *Madan Mohan*, Naib Wakil, *to Nawwab Sikandar Begam*. Informs that as ordered, dated 19 *Safar* 1275 AH, recording on his letter, dated 14th *Safar,* he brought the matter to the notice of Hutchinson and put before him two possibilities; one if the insurgent forces come to Bhopal then one has to take care of Bhopal, and the other is to guard river Narmada. He said to convey to the Nawwab that he had no authority to call the army. He was simply following the order of the Agent to the Governor-General, Central India, that the arrangement was such that the insurgents did not enter Bhopal. This is conveyed to the Nawwab in view of the friendship. The insurgents would surely be dealt with. They would not be able to go to Bhopal or Hoshangabad. A large army is coming from different places. He said it is heard that 4,000 insurgents fled from Sironj. He asked in what direction they went. He said it is not known. But certainly they would have gone to Bundelkhand as there is no other place for them to hide. Dated 20 *Safar* 1275 AH (29 September 1858).

PP 83-4. *Statement of Akhtar Khan Wilayati*. On 25 September 1858, he left Bhopal and on 26th reached Sironj. On 27th he was there and went to the camp of the insurgents. He heard that around 4,000 forces marched from there on the orders of Nana Sahab and the rest of the army, around 10, 000 to 12,000, was outside the city. There were 1,000 *wilayatis*, others were *purbias*. There were English rules and regulations which were followed. There were 4 cannon which were captured from the *amil* of Sironj. There was no other cannon. The *sawars* were posted at a distance of every 2 *curoh* in order to keep a watch. The *amil* was in captivity of Peshwa. The *azhar* of people of Sironj is collecting money from Sironj and depositing it with Peshwa.

P 85. *Muhammad Jamal al-Din Khan,* Madar al-Maham, *to Nawwab Sikandar Begam*. On 13 *Safar* 1275 AH (22 September 1858), Mohan Lal, *harkara*, was sent to Sironj to know about the insurgents and their encampment. That day, he came back and what he stated was recorded and sent to her. Dated 20 *Safar* 1275 AH (29 September 1858).

P 87. *Statement of Mohan Lal*, Harkara. On 22 September 1858, he reached Sironj. The next day, he went to the camp of Peshwa, encamping at a distance of half a *curoh* from Sironj towards west. This was a huge army beyond his imagination. There were 12 cannon which he saw from his own eyes. He heard that there were 4 cannon of Sironj. States that if there was any stranger, he was searched before he was released by the men of Peshwa. All the cannon were installed on the mountains of Maula Ali. The Maula Ali mountain is situated towards south of Sironj. The army of Peshwa was within a diameter of one *kos*. The army of Adil Muhammad Khan was encamping at a distance of half a *kos* from the army of Peshwa. Says, he did not go in the camp of Adil Muhammad Khan. He also heard that Khair Allah Khan, *amil* of Sironj, was arrested by the men of Peshwa. There was complete rule of Peshwa in Sironj what he himself felt. He also heard that the foot-soldiers were being recruited. The 4 cannon which he took from Sironj were small. But 8 cannon of Peshwa were big. He also heard that 12 *sawars* of Adil Muhammad Khan came to see the *ghats* at Betwa river. River Betwa flows beneath Bhilsa. On 24 September 1858, he returned to Bhopal. Dated 20 *Safar* 1275 AH (29 September 1858).

P 89. *Ghulam Yar Khan,* Sawar *to Nawwab Sikandar Begam.* Informs that day, the 20th *Safar* 1275 AH, Balkishan, informer came from Sironj and stated that since the previous day, the army of Peshwa was moving from Sironj. They formed two groups; one group, consisting of 1,200 men went to Biladargarh, and the other group, consisting of 500 *sawars* along with the *bakhshi* of Adil Muhammad Khan went to Berasia as they heard the news of the arrival of British forces.

The rest of the army of Peshwa went to Issagarh. Only Adil Muhammad Khan remained in Sironj, having a contingent of 1,500 men with him. They did not have big cannon. Says, he is ready all the time to fight with the insurgent forces. Dated 20 *Safar* 1275 AH (29 September 1858).

P 91. *Parwana of Nawwab Sikandar Begam to Bhawani Prasad*. The news-report about the insurgents, dated 29 September 1858, received from *madar al-maham* is sent to him. The same may be presented before the Political Agent and what he says may be communicated to her. Dated 21 *Safar* 1275 AH (30 September 1858).

PP 93-5. *Ranjit Singh*, Harkara *to Nawwab Sikandar Begam*. On 15 *Safar* 1275 AH, he started his journey and arrived in *mauza* Narela, adjoining Berasia. The British army was marching from Berasia to Sabilgarh. He too joined the army and arrived in *mauza* Sanagal. In the morning, he arrived in *mauza* Imlai, lying at a distance of two and half *curoh* from Sironj. He heard from a Brahmin that Raja Bhor, Tantia Tope, Adil Muhammad Khan and Nawwab Bandawala were in Sironj. Next day, he secretly reached *mauza* Sironj. He entered the camp of the insurgents and found that they had erected big tents. The soldiers of Bengal, the *wilyatis* and Hindustanis were on guard and others were inside the tents.

Chandu, a dweller of Bhopal, was also there. He was at a shop where some men of Adil Muhammad Khan also came for medicine. A Brahmin asked them about the strength of their army. They said they were 14, 000 to 15, 000 commanded by Tantia Tope, Sada Shiv Rao, nephew of Nana, the insurgent, Nawwab Bandawala. Raja Bhorji of Narwar was about to come. Adil Muhammad Khan was encamping nearby a pond with an army of 3,000. They captured the cannon of Sironj and *amil* was made captive. They were demanding thousands of rupees from them. They took

Rs. 5, 000 from *bohras* and were still demanding that much amount from them. Every house of *bohras* was under the surveillance of guards. He asked a *wilayati* about the cannon. He said there were 18 cannon with Tantia Tope. He also heard that 50 soldiers had gone to bring Hira Singh who is known as one of the chiefs and a famous warrior. All the weapons and arms of *bohras* were brought from their houses and auctioned. Raja Bhorji was not in Sironj. It was heard that the *sawars* were sent to bring him. At noon, he saw that Aqil Muhammad Khan, nephew of Adil Muhammad Khan, came out from his camp along with 50 *sawars* and went in the camp of Nana. Thereafter, son of Chhatrasal also joined him. In the meantime, 2-3 *purbias* came who were eating sweets, whom he asked where they would go from there. They said first they would go to Bhilsa and then to Bhopal. Then he heard that the *sawars* of Adil Muhammad Khan would go to blockade the roads at a distance of 3 *curoh* from Bhilsa. There was too much danger. He retuned from there and reached Bhopal. On the way, he heard that the British army was at Dholikhera and then it arrived in Sonkutchh. Dated 21 *Safar* 1275 AH (30 September 1858).

P 97. *Murawwat Muhammad Khan to Nawwab Sikandar Begam*. Kamale Khan and Akbar Khan, soldiers of the battalion of Dhani Khan, the suspended *jamadar* were sent to Sironj to bring the news about the insurgents. The previous day; date 20 *Safar* 1275 AH, they came back. Their statements were recorded and sent to her. Dated 21 *Safar* 1275 AH (30 September 1858).

P 99. *News-Report of the Insurgents Encamping at Sironj as Reported by Kamale Khan and Akbar Khan, Soldiers of the Battalion of Dhani Khan, Dated 17* Safar *1275 AH*. Report that Adil Muhammad Khan, carrying an army of 2,000, both *sawars* and foot-soldiers is encamping at a pond in Sironj and the son of Bhor with an army of 9, 000, both *sawars* and foot-soldiers is encamping outside the city near river Khanan and on the mountain called Fakhr al-Din mountain. The army of the insurgents is very alert. There is a report that they have 25 cannon with them but they did not see those from their own eyes. Adil Muhammad Khan devastated some villages of Sironj and made a proclamation in the name of Peshwa. 4 cannon of Sironj fell in the hands of the insurgents. An agreement was concluded with the *amil* of Sironj who had to pay Rs. 50,000 or Rs. 60, 000. They looked contended. But the arrangement of *rasad* was difficult. They were pressurizing the *bohras* of Sironj to provide them gunpowder. But the *bohras* instead of providing it to them preferred to hide it in the wells of their houses. It was heard that they also had magazines but they did not see them from their eyes. The *wilayatis* of Bhopal were also with them. They were talking among themselves that soon they would be able to have control over Bhilsa. Thereafter, they would capture Bhopal. Dated 21 *Safar* 1275 AH (30 September 1858).

File No. 294, C
Box No. 15
No. of Documents 19

PP 101-02. *Bhawani Prasad to Nawwab Sikandar Begam.* Informs that on 19 *Safar* 1275 AH, he had sent Ganesh to Sironj giving him 6 plain papers to report. He reached there the same day and found no insurgent. His statement was recorded and presented before the Political Agent. A copy of that is sent to her. Surely, Adil Muhammad Khan has fled from Sironj along with Tantia Tope to Issagarh. Dated 21 *Safar* 1275 AH (30 September 1858).

P 103. *Statement of Ganesh, Informer who Came from Sironj*. He was asked to tell what he saw or heard in Sironj about the insurgents. He replied that on 19 *Safar*, he left Sabilgarh and arrived in Sironj in the evening. The armies of the insurgents had left Sironj that day in the morning and went to Malhargarh and Korwai. He met the *amil* who said that his 4 cannon were taken away by the insurgents, besides Rs. 15, 000 from him, Rs. 10, 000 from the *bohras* and Rs. 25,000 from the traders.

They also took the utensils of *bohras*. They destroyed the crops. They were telling that the army of General Mitchell arrived at *mauza* Sewavir and certainly they would attack them so they were going to Malhargarh and Issagarh. One battalion of British army arrived at Arwal where Bhorji, Narwarwala, was hiding in the fort. The British army fired ball cannon on the fort and Narwarwala fled from there. About 500 men were killed there. About 1,000 to 1,100 Afghans of Sironj went with the insurgents. The insurgents had no cannon with them. Two sons of Chhatrasal went in the company of Tantia Tope from Sironj. Dated 21 *Safar* 1275 AH (30 September 1858).

P 105. Rubakar *from the Office of Assistant of Berasia Under the Session of Baijnath, Deputy Assistant of Political Agent, Bhopal*. Ghanshyam, musketeer under the battalion of Gangaram, an employee of Bhopal State who was sent by Bhawani Prasad to Sironj to bring the news of the insurgents, came back to Berasia. He stated that on 28 September 1858, day Tuesday, all the insurgents went to Malhar. They also carried with them the *amil*. Adil Muhammad Khan too was in the company. Now no one was left in Sironj. The court ordered that the *rubakar* may be sent to Major Richards, the Political Agent of Bhopal. A copy of this may also be sent to Nawwab Sikandar Begam. Dated 1 October 1958.

P 107. *Madan Mohan*, Naib Wakil*, to Nawwab Sikandar Begam.* Informs that day he brought to the notice of Major Ayuns, the two letters of Bhawani Prasad and the statement of Lal Singh, informer, besides the letter of *sarsuba*, Bhilsa. He said the previous day, he received the letter of *suba sahab* which contained the information that all the insurgents fled from Sironj. It did not contain a detailed report as received from the agency of the Nawwab. He further said to convey his greetings to her and communicate her that sooner all the insurgents would be dealt with. If Adil Muhammad Khan is in

Sironj, he will be arrested soon. Benson said, earlier Regiment 9 was ordered to come to Sehore from Mhow. But it was later on postponed as the General realized that the insurgents were not daring to come before them. They were fleeing so there was no need of foot-soldiers. However, a Regiment of *sawars* is coming from Poona to deal with the miscreants. Another company of the *sawars* was coming from Gujarat via Ujjain. Soon the army would be available to Major Mitchell. Though the insurgents have gone to Arwal where the royal forces are also present. Infact, no place is left for them to go and soon they would be dealt with. Says he asked him about the Regiment which was supposed to come on 1 October but had not come yet. He expressed ignorance in the matter. Dated 22 *Safar* 1275 AH (1 October 1858).

P 109. *Ghulam Husain Khan and 'Abd al-Karim Ansari to Nawwab Sikandar Begam.* Madah Khan and Yar Khan and four soldiers of the battalion of Asad Khan were sent to Sironj by Chain Rai on 16 *Safar* 1275 AH to bring the news of insurgents. They came back and stated that they reached *talluqa* Noka situating at a distance of 10 *curoh* from Sironj. They saw an army of 10, 000 to 15, 000 of Tantia Tope with 10 to 12 cannon, was staying near the fort. They heard that they devastated *mauza* Bagrod and Bhuri, *ilaqa* Sironj. Dated 23 *Safar* 1275 AH.

PP 111-13. *Lal Singh and Navnit Ram*, Harkaras, *to Nawwab Sikandar Begam*. Lal Singh reports that on 10 *Safar* 1275 AH, he started his journey. There was heavy rainfall on the way. The rivers and nallas were overflowing and it was difficult to cross the river. However, he reached Bhilsa, the next day and stayed there for three days due to rain. He heard the news of the arrival of the Peshwa in Bhilsa. The suba of Basodah and Tetran and the *sawars* of Issagarh were removed. On day six, he resumed his journey and reached *mauza* Indma, *ilaqa* Bhilsa and sent Navnit Ram, *harkara* to Sironj from there. The next day, he came back and described the situation there. But he was not satisfied with the description. He himself, along with Navnit, secretly went to Sironj. He reached near Adil Muhammad Khan and saw an army of 1,000 with him, comprising both *sawars* and foot-soldiers, on the bank of a pond. It was heard that Rao Sahab, nephew of Peshwa, along with an army of 20, 000 besides Nawwab of Banda, Sikandar Muhammad Khan, Amanat Khan, son of Nanhey Khan, was encamping in a village. The tents and *rautis* were erected. It was also heard that Nawwab of Rampur and Bareilly were accompanying him as well. He did not hear the presence of Tantia Tope and Raja Bhor in their camp. It was only heard that Raja Bhor would soon join them. Adil Muhammad Khan had deployed some persons for spying so that if anyone from Bhopal was seen he had to be killed. People say about 200 men of Adil Muhammad Khan were killed so far. If Adil Muhammad Khan had come, he too would have been killed. When this army reached Sironj, they demanded Rs. 50,000 from the *amil* of Sironj. They collected the said amount from all the inhabitants except the labourers. It is heard that the *bohras* objected to the realization of the said amount. But later on, they paid. The soldiers told the *amil* to provide 200 *begars*. Says, he and Navnit Ram were also captured and sent to the camp of Nawwab Bandawala. In the night, drum was beaten to march from there. They marched from Sironj and reached Sarai Mughal, situated at a distance of 8 *curoh* from Sironj. Says, he also saw Adil Muhammad Khan with his army who too was going along with the army. They were not aware where they were going. Some say they would go where Rao Sahab would tell them to go. There were 35 elephants with them and a lot of camels. There were only 4 cannon which were captured from Sironj. Says he came to Sironj. It is heard that a large number of arms and ammunitions were captured from the *bohras*. Says, he then left Sironj. On the way he saw a British army of 1,000. It was learnt that that army was going from Imlai to Sironj to assess the situation as a huge army was behind that army. He reached Imlai, then Berasia and finally came back to Bhopal on Sunday. Dated 24 *Safar* 1265 *Fasli.*

P 115. *Daulat Rai*, Nazim-i Mashriq, *to Nawwab Sikandar Begam.* Sends the letter received from Sada Shiv Rao, *suba* of Bhilsa, dated 20 *Safar* 1275 AH along with the *rubakar,* informing the fleeing of insurgents from Sironj as they were unable to face the British army. Dated 24 *Safar* 1275 AH.

P 117. *Sada Shiv Rao, to Daulat Rai*, Nazim-i Mashriq. Sends him the *rubakar* of that office, dated 20 *Safar* 1275 AH, which is about the fleeing of thc insurgents from Sironj. Dated 20 *Safar* 1275 AH.

PP 119-20. Rubakar *of the Office of* Suba *of Bhilsa Executed Under the Session of Sada Shiv Rao,* Suba. When the insurgent army reached Sironj, the British army came pursuing them. General Mitchell divided the army into three groups. One group led by the Political Agent and General Mitchell reached Sabilgarh, the other group reached Shiv and the third group was behind the two groups in order to help these two groups. The *sarsuba* of district Issagarh also arrived at Sabilgarh to make arrangement of *rasad.* The insurgent army, realising it impossible to stand before the British army, fled from Sironj and reached Devalpur, lying at a distance of 3 *curoh* from Sironj, surrounded by forests and mountains. To keep Rai Kishan Narain, deputy magistrate district Sagar and the *nazim-i mashriq* Bhopal informed in the matter is a must.

The order was issued that it may be sent to the deputy magistrate, Sagar and also to send a copy to the *nazim-i mashriq*, Bhopal. Dated 20 *Safar* 1275 AH.

PP 121-2. *Nizam Ali Khan, Risaldar*; *to Nawwab Sikandar Begam.* Informs that day from the report of Nandram, Balwant Singh and Kumbh Singh, soldiers of the battalion of Umrao Singh, *jamadar* who were sent to

Sironj to bring the news of the insurgents, it is clear that Tantia Tope, popular as Peshwa, and Adil Muhammad Khan with an army of 40, 000 came to Sironj and held discussion with the *amil* of Sironj to come to a compromise and accept his lordship. The *amil* agreed with him. They demanded rupees three lakh from the *amil*. On 19 *Safar,* a *harkara* came with some papers and entered the camp of Tantia Tope who after reading the papers, ordered to fire 22 ball cannon. On 20 *Safar,* hearing the news of the arrival of the British forces at Aron, *ilaqa* of the Maharaja, lying at a distance of 9 *curoh* from Sironj, he sent 4,000 *sawars* to destroy the market of Aron and to arrest the *amil*. While they were destroying everything in the market, in the meantime, the British army came to deal with them. There was a fighting between the two forces involving guns and swords. Thereafter, the British army and the *sawars* returned to its camp at Sironj after the defeat. On 21 *Safar,* Tantia Tope marched from Sironj and reached Sarai Mughal situating at a distance of 4 *curoh* from Sironj and wanted to go to Issagarh. On 23 *Safar,* Adil Muhammad Khan too left Sironj. Dated 25 *Safar* 1275 AH.

PP 123-4. *Baqi Muhammad Khan to Nawwab Sikandar Begam.* Informs that Ilahi Bakhsh, his attendant, had gone to Sironj on 10 days leave to attend the marriage of his brother. He had told him at the time of his departure to come with authentic news of the insurgents from Sironj. That day he came back and his statement about the insurgents in Sironj is recorded and sent to her. Dated 25 *Safar* 1275 AH.

PP 125-9. *News Report from the Camp of Adil Muhammad Khan and Others who Seiged Sironj.* Ilahi Bakhsh, the attendant of Baqi Muhammad Khan, stated that he had gone to Sironj on 10 days leave for the marriage of his cousin brother. When he was proceeding, the Nawwab had told him to watch the activities of the insurgents and come back with authentic news. He arrived in Sironj and stayed for four days in the house of his brother. Thereafter, he thought to come back to Bhopal. In the morning, what he saw was that Adil Muhammad Khan and other insurgents with an army of 5, 000-both *sawars* and foot-soldiers, came from Imlai. An army of 4,000 was encamping in Neemuch cantonment and an army of 1,000 arrived at Sironj and seiged it. The *amil* of Sironj fought with them for three days. On last day of the battle, three soldiers of the insurgents were killed; one was Mewati, others were *wilayatis*. On day fourth, Adil Muhammad Khan made a proclamation in the name of Peshwa. The *amil* then asked the *jagirdars* and *shurafa* of the city if they would participate in the battle. Thereafter, Akbar Ali Khan, maternal uncle of Sikandar Muhammad Khan Agenty, Naiyer Khan, Karam Sher Khan, and others came with their armed forces and met the *amil* who was fighting with the guards of the insurgents at the outskirts of the city. They all fought with valour and courage with the insurgent forces for two consecutive days and killed many of them. On day third, Akbar Ali Khan, Naiyer Khan, Karam Sher Khan and Ahmad Khan, *jamadar*, took the *amil* in their company and went towards the pond to fight with the insurgents. Suddenly, Akbar Ali Khan attacked the insurgent forces with his sword and killed many of them. When counted, there were 300 dead bodies. Among them there was a *subadar*, an officer and many Mewatis and *wilayatis*. In a nutshell, Akbar Ali pursued Adil Muhammad Khan upto 3 *curoh*. On their side, only one *golandaz* was wounded. Adil Muhammad Khan was badly defeated. They also devastated a village in *ilaqa* Korwai. On day third, after the counting of the dead bodies, Doran Khan, *risaldar*, Rao Sahab, nephew of Nana Sahab, and others threatened the *amil,* to either provide them provision or else they would destroy the city. The *amil* told them to stay in Lal Bagh where they would be provided with provision. The *amil* ordered all the shopkeepers of the city to make arrangement of provision. Day fourth, Rao Sahab came with a huge army. It is said there were 20, 000 Tilangas and 20, 000 Mewati and *wilayati sawars*. They were occupying fields in an area of 7 *curoh*. Says, he took a round of the army of Rao Sahab and he saw from his own eyes its huge strength. He counted the elephants which were 150. There were many arms and ammunitions. On day fifth, Rao Sahab had his control over Sironj. He demanded 3 cannon from the *amil*. The four companies which were deputed on the security of the city had cartridges, loaded over 5 camels. About their arsenal, he has no knowledge. Rao Sahab had taken oath from the entire army that if the British army attacked them, they would not turn their back. But they would fight with them firmly. On day sixth, Adil Muhammad Khan with 1,500 armymen came and requested Rao Sahab to allow him to join his camp. Rao Sahab told him to stay at the pond. He personally came to meet Rao Sahab. Rao Sahab was very angry upon him as he had devastated many villages and killed many people. Adil Muhammad Khan lamented his mistake. Rao Sahab expressed his anguish and said that he wrote to Nana Sahab in the matter. Let us wait for his reply that will be communicated to him. Thereafter, Adil Muhammad Khan put before Rao Sahab the matter of those soldiers who were killed by *bohras*. Rao Sahab sent one company and one *risala* to bring the *bohras* and asked them the reason for killing men of Adil Muhammad Khan. They replied that Adil Muhammad Khan had fled, leaving behind 25 *sawars* who entered in their houses and made loot and destroyed their houses. So they killed them. All the *bohras* were made captive for one night. Thereafter, they were released. Rao Sahab searched the houses of *bohras* and collected cash, jewellry and war weapons. He gave Rs. 12,000 to Adil Muhammad Khan for distribution among his armymen as their salary.

Says he then came back from the camp of Rao Sahab to his house. When he was in the market, Muhammad

Ali Khan, *risaldar* and Abd al-Rauf, nephew of Qazi Hanif were returning from the camp of Rao Sahab. One of his attendant told Abd al-Rauf about him that he was in the service of Umrao Daulah. Muhammad Ali Khan then asked him why he came. He replied, in search of livelihood. Thereafter, Bhondu Khan, *havaldar*, Ram Bharosey, and Debi Den, soldiers, the fugitives of the company of army of Nawwab Shahjahan Begam and 4 other persons came to his house, arrested him and brought him before Adil Muhammad Khan. He asked him if he was employed with Umrao Daulah and why he came there. He replied to him that his brother was there, who had died. He came to collect his belongings. He said he was telling a lie. Muhammad Ali Khan, *risaldar* told Adil Muhammad Khan that he was an employee of Umrao Daulah and infact came there for spying. Adil Muhammad Khan tied both his hands, with a saddle to a mango tree. He remained like this for a day. He was in captivity for 10 days. One day, an armyman told that he had been in Sironj for the last five to six months and he was not an employee of Umrao Daulah. Thereafter, he was released.

Sardar Khan, Muhammad Ali Khan, *risaldar*, Abd al-Rauf, *kamdar*, and Amanat Khan, *Bakhshi* were the companions of Adil Muhammad Khan. Amanat Khan, son of Bathey Khan Banarsi, was the *risaldar*, his other sons were *sawars*, Hashim Ali Khan was the *kotha-dafadar* who was from the battalion of Mama Qahar Khan, *jamadar*. *Wilayatis* and Mewatis who were ousted from Bhopal were in his company. Adil Muhammad Khan asked him about Bhopal. He said a huge British army with *mandraji*, cannon and arsenal came for the management of Bhopal. The Bhopal army too is managing the affairs of Bhopal with cannon from all sides. Muhammad Ali Khan reacted and said 'So what!'. He also said 'He would capture fort Islamnagar'. Amanat Khan said he would capture Fort Rajgarh. Abd al-Rauf said he would capture the fort of Raisen.

Adil Muhammad Khan said he would capture Bhopal. Rao Sahab was intending to come to Bhopal. But due to havoc of the British forces he lost his hope. They all went to Issagarh. He came to Bhopal. The people accompanying Adil Muhammad Khan passed through extreme hardships. They hardly got bread once in three days. He was with them for a week on one pretext or the other. He sold his horse, his babu and 2 sets of his cloths. Sarfraz Khan too was with Adil Muhammad Khan along with one babu, facing harships. Rao Sahab told Adil Muhammad Khan that he was not able to serve the country. He was unnecessarily wasting the lives of his soldiers. 23 *Safar* 1275 AH (24 Ocrober 1858).

P 131. *Transliteration of the Letter of Pandit Beni Ram, a Dweller of Sironj, Addressed to* Madar al-Maham. Refers to his letter, asking him to tell about the army of the insurgents. Informs that they have 10, 000 *sawars*, 2,000 *tattu*, 12,000 foot-soldiers, 50 elephants and 300 camels. Peshwa Rao Sahab is the chief leader of all the groups. Nawwabs of Char Bandiwala, Bareillywala, Jawrahwala and Garhiwala are other leaders of the insurgents. The total number of troops with them is 30, 000. Earlier they were planning to go to Bhopal. But later on, they postponed the program and went to Issagarh which was captured. Dated 25 *Safar* 1275 AH (4 Ocrober 1858).

PP 133-4. *Ramden*, Peshdast Wakil, *to Nawwab Sikandar Begam.* Says, his opinion about General Mitchell is that he is a fickle minded person. He does not have the stability of mind. Says, pursuing the insurgents in the night when they were fleeing was kept pending. Had they been pursued in Baywarah, they would not have reached Sironj and thus, there would not have been any destruction. Secondly, he does not take rest for a while. Otherwise, to rest for a while and then to attack is not without dividend. In his opinion, the British officers think that capturing the cannon, wealth, bullocks, etc.

of the chiefs of the region by the insurgents was fairly a good job what they were doing as when they were pursued, all items would automatically fall in the hands of the British forces. But they do not see that this act of insurgents weakened the chieftains of the region. Wherever the insurgents go they are dealt with such mindset. The armies of the chieftains are unable to fight with the insurgents in the manner as is required. See, if the army would have fought in the manner as required, the insurgents would not have dared to enter in Issagarh. What to say of the foolishness of the employees of Sindhia. Says, the wrong decisions of the Political Agent are a matter of concern. May God not give such a Political Agent to any Agenty. It is heard that on the route to Bombay, the telegraph line is disrupted. So Captain Cumming, Agent at Bhilwara, was called back from the camp by the Agent, Central India. The insurgents are at Issagarh and the British forces have started to come in from all the sides. But he thinks the road to Bhilsa is free. The distance of Issagarh from Bhilsa would be around 15 *curoh*. Though the insurgents might go from Issagarh to Lalitpur and Chanderi. But to remain alert and attentive is the foremost consideration. The deployment of the *bakhshi* in other regions is not a wise thing. If he takes care of his own state, it would be good as unless and until Adil Muhammad Khan is killed or arrested there would be no peace. He is pursuing Tantia Tope and Rao Sahab to prevent them from coming to Bhopal. Says, the Political Agent is too coward and afraid to be explained. Dated 26 *Safar* 1275 AH.

PP 135-6. *Madan Mohan*, Naib Wakil, *to Nawwab Sikandar Begam.* Informs that as ordered, dated 24 *Safar* 1275 AH, recorded on the letter of the *wakil,* besides the statement of Ganesh, the informer, he reported the news of the insurgents to the Political Agent. He said that was old news. He told him that that might be an old news but there were three things which were new; one, the fleeing of Bhorji Raja, Raja of Narwar from Arwal, due to fear of the arrival of the British forces; two, the joining of the Afghans of Sironj to Tantia Tope; and third, the sons of Thakur Chhatrasal joining the camp of the insurgents. He said it is a fact that he did not find such elaborate information in any writing. He said to convey his greetings to the Nawwab and convey his thanks too. Dated 27 *Safar* 1275 AH (6 October 1858).

P 137. *Baqi Muhammad Khan to Nawwab Sikandar Begam.* Sends the letter, dated 25 *Safar* 1275 AH, received from Saiyid Ghulam Shah, deputy *tahsildar* of Diwanganj, informing about the insurgents, encamping in Sironj. Dated 27 *Safar* 1275 AH (6 October 1858).

P 139. *Saiyid Ghulam Shah to Nawwab Nazir al-Daulah, Baqi Muhammad Khan.* Informs that as ordered he sent Himmat Khan Mewati, a resident of the *pargana*, to bring the news of the insurgents. On 19 *Safar* 1275 AH, he came back and stated that the Peshwa and Tantia Tope were in Sironj along with their forces. Their number would be 60, 000. But there was no cannon with them. They captured Sironj. Adil Muhammad Khan also joined them. Apart from Adil Muhammad Khan, there were three Nawwabs; Nawwab Bareillywala, Nawwab Bandawala and Nawwab Jawarahwala. On last Thursday, they were intending to go to Bhilsa. In the meantime, a letter of Hira Singh, the insurgent, was received, informing that he too was coming to join them and they should wait for him. Bakhshi Murawwat Muhammad Khan who was also there called Himmat Khan and enquired about him and engaged him as informer. Says, if he is not engaged by the *bakhshi* he should engage him. Dated 25 *Safar* 1275 AH (46 October 1858).

PP 141-2. *Bekaji and Ashraf Khan*, Harkaras, *to Nawwab Sikandar Begam.* Informs that on 25 *Safar* 1275 AH, they marched from there, reached Berasia and secretly entered Sironj. They heard that the insurgent forces were at Jarwar and went to Issagarh. Then, they went to Hajipura and saw that the army of Adil Muhammad

Khan had devastated it. But the *shurafa* of Sironj fought with them and killed them. As a result, Adil Muhammad Khan and his companions fled from there. The *shurafa* of Sironj pursued them upto two *curoh*. But when they heard of the arrival of Peshwa and Tantia Tope, they returned to Sironj. When Adil Muhammad Khan joined the insurgent forces, he was abused as his act of devastation was not liked by them. Thereafter, they heard that the British forces would soon march. The *suba* of Issagarh was also accompanying them. They heard that when the insurgents moved near Issagarh, the servants of Maharaja closed the gates and fought with them with guns. The insurgents broke the gate of Issagarh by their cannon that was brought from Sironj.

On Tuesday, they left Sironj. On their way to Berasia, they saw the brandy, loaded on *babwan* and bullocks, coming from Mhow was going to the camp of the British officers. When they reached Berasia, they saw that Bakhshi Murawwat Muhammad Khan with his forces was encamping there. They also asked the *zamindars* about Chhatrasal who replied that they did not know anything. He then left Berasia and reached Bhopal on 28 *Safar* 1275 AH.

PP 143-4. *Murawwat Muhammad Khan to Nawwab Sikandar Begam.* Informs of the letter of Bhawani Prasad, *wakil*, along with the statement of Lal Singh, the informer, dated 26 *Safar* 1275 AH, directing him to inform about the place of his encampment and that the statement of Lal Singh should be brought to the notice of the Political Agent. Says, the insurgents are encamping at Issagarh. The statement of Lal Singh, also contains the information that Chhatrasal along with Thakur of Barkhera and Patel Khera has gone to Uditwara. Earlier there were 200 men in the company of Chhatrasal. His brothers; like Kokaji, Jugalji, Debji and Gulabji, who are the *jagirdars* are the *risaldars*. There is no information where they have gone. Dated 26 *Safar* 1275 AH.

It contains the order that the letter may be sent to Lala Paltu Lal, *muhafiz-i daftar-i insha*, for inclusion in the register and keeping in the *daftar*. A copy of the letter may be sent to Bhawani Prasad, *wakil* to inform the Political Agent and his reply may be communicated to her. Dated 1 *Rabi* I, 1275 AH.

File No. 295
Box No. 15
No. of Documents 3

Notification: Not to Spread Rumour of Cutting Nose and Hands of those who are on Duty by Nana Sahab's Forces

P 1. Contents

P 3. *Bhawani Prasad to Nawwab Sikandar Begam.* Sends a copy of the notification issued by the office of Agenty Bhopal, dated September 1858, under the signature of the Political Agent. It is heard that the servants of the State of Rajgarh, deployed at English posts in Bayawrah, advised the *sawars* and *khochars* of the *chauki* to run away from there as the forces of Nana Sahab were about to reach who would cut off their noses and hands. In view of this, it is notified that whosoever will talk like this will be punished. Dated 5 *Safar* 1275 (14 September 1858).

P 5. *Notification Issued Under the Session of William Henry Richards*. It has been heard that the servants of the State of Rajgarh, deployed at English posts in Bayawrah, said to the *sawars* and *khochars* of the *chauki* to run away from there as the forces of Nana Sahab were about to reach who would cut off their noses and hands. In view of this, it is notified that whosoever will talk like this will be punished. Dated 13 September 1858.

File No. 296, A
Box No. 15
No. of Documnets 39

Arrival of Colonel Pitcher along with Regiment 1, of the Nizam Contingent, and the Arrangement of Sarbrah-i Rasad

PP 1-10. Content

PP 11-12. *Gist of the Letter of Bhawani Prasad to the Government which is in Regard to a* Parwana *Received from the Political Agent, Dated 25 September 1858.*

This is in reference to an order received from the office of the Agent to Governor-General, Central India, dated 20 September 1858, which informs that the Regiment of the cavalry which comprises of 600 *sawars*, 600 men, 600 horses, 300 *tattus*, 100 bullocks and 25 camels has marched from Mhow Cantonment on 23 September 1858. On 28th it will reach Gajna, on 29th it will be at Ashta, on 30th at Imlai, on 1st October at Sehore, on 2nd at Pinda and on 3rd at Bhopal. It is a must that the goods of *rasad* should immediately be managed as per the details. These include flour, rice, pulses, mustard oil, grains, etc. Directs him to inform his government. Dated 16 *Safar* 1275 AH.

It contains the order that the letter along with the *parwana* of the Political Agent may be sent to Maulawi Muhammad Sa'd al-Din, *muhtamim*, *adalat-i faujdari*. Besides, one copy each to *madar al-maham*, Lala Mansukh Rai, *muhtamim*, *sair-i kul*, *amil* and *thanadar* of Ashta, Jawar and Sehore, directing them to make arrangement of the goods of *rasad* as mentioned in the *parwana* of the Political Agent in their own jurisditions for the regiment of *sawars*. There should not be any negligence. It should be given top priority and *suji* should be prepared in huge quantity. A copy of the order may be sent to Bhawani Prasad, *wakil*. Dated 17 *Safar* 1275 AH.

PP 13-14. *Bhawani Prasad to Nawwab Sikandar Begam.* Informs of the march of the said army that day from Berasia, who encamped at Lalarya, *ilaqa* Berasia, situating at a distance of 4 *curoh* from there. The Political Agent called him and asked about the route to Shiv, *ilaqa* Bhilsa. River Bina is lying at a distance of 6 *curoh* from Lalarya and in between lies Ganj Basodah. It is heard that the insurgents are on the other side of river Bina. The intention of the General is to cross river Bina. The insurgents are intending to go to Bhilsa or Bhopal. But they might be thinking that they would be caught. A report from Indore came that day, that a

Regiment of 600 *sawars* marching from Indore and Mhow via Ashta and Sehore would reach Bhopal for the security and safety of Bhopal. Dated 16 *Safar* 1275 AH (25 September 1858).

It contains the order that the letter may be sent to Lala Paltu Lal, *muhafiz-i daftar-i insha*, for inclusion in the register and keeping in the *daftar*. A copy of the letter may be provided to Maulawi Muhammad Sa'd al-Din, *muhtamim adalat-i faujdari*, besides the *amils*, the *thanadars* of *pargana* Ashta, Jawar and Sehore-directing them that at the time of the arrival of the said regiment in their respective jurisdiction, the arrangement of *sarbrah-i saman-i rasad* should be made as per the practice. There should not be any negligence in the matter. A copy of the order may be sent to Bhawani Prasad, *wakil*, for information. Dated 18 *Safar* 1275 AH.

P 15. *Parwana of Nawwab Sikandar Begam to Madan Mohan,* Naib Wakil. Refers to the report of the arrival of the Regiment 1 at Imlai, dated 30 September 1858. Directs him to send one *sawar* to Imlai and inform her as soon as the regiment arrives there. Dated 19 *Safar* 1275 AH.

PP 17-18. *Madan Mohan*, Naib Wakil, *to Nawwab Sikandar Begam.* Informs that day, Wahid Ali, *attar*, caste *bohra*, a shopkeeper in Sehore, met him and said in reference to a letter of his brother received from Sironj that the insurgents like Tantia Tope and others arrested the *amil* of Sironj and captured his 6 cannon which were in Sironj, besides Rs. 50,000 that were demanded from him. An amount of Rs. 5, 000 was, however, paid to him.

PP 19-20. *Madan Mohan, Naib Wakil*, *to Nawwab Sikandar Begam.* Refers to her *parwana*, dated 19 *Safar* 1275 AH, regarding a report that the Regiment 1 will arrive at Imlai on 30 September 1858 and directing him to send one *sawar* to Imlai and inform her as soon as the Regiment arrives there. Says the previous day, he sent 'Abd al-Sattar Khan, *sawar, risala* 1, red uniform to Imlai, and that day a letter was received from him, communicating that the Regiment 1 did not yet arrive at Imlai. The letter is sent to her. Further informs that the *sawar* is still in Imlai to bring the information of the Regiment when it arrives there. Dated 21 *Safar* 1275 AH (30 September 1858).

It contains the order that the letter may be sent to Lala Paltu Lal, *muhafiz-i daftar-i insha*, for inclusion in the register and keeping in the *daftar*. A copy of the order may be sent to Madan Mohan, *naib wakil,* informing that from the letter of Bhawani Prasad, dated 16 *Safar* 1275 AH (25 September 1858), the date of the arrival of regiment is learnt and in view of that she ordered to depute the *sawar* at Imlai to bring the news. There is no report why the regiment did not come yet. Directs him to enquire into it and inform her. Dated 23 *Safar* 1275 AH (2 October 1858).

PP 21-2. *Abd al-Sattar,* Risala *1, Red Uniform, to* Madan Mohan, Naib Wakil. Informs that till then there is no report of the arrival of the Regiment 1, neither in Imlai nor in Tappa. Dated 21 *Safar* 1275 AH (30 September 1858).

PP 23-4. *Bilas Rai, Amil of Sehore, to Nawwab Sikandar Begam.* Refers to the letter of Bhawani Prasad, *wakil* to the government, dated 16 *Safar* 1275 AH (25 September 1858), which contains her order that a copy of the letter along with the *parwana* of the Political Agent may be sent to Maulawi Muhammad Sa'd al-Din, *muhtamim, adalat-i faujdari*, besides, the *madar al-maham*, Lala Mansukh Rai, *muhtamim*, *sair-i kul*, the *amils*, and *thanadars* of *pargana* Ashta, Jawar and Sehore, directing them that at the time of the arrival of the said regiment in their respective jurisdiction, the arrangement of *sarbrah-i saman-i rasad* should be made as per the practice. There should not be any negligence in the matter and that *suji* should be made in huge quantity. A copy of the order may be sent to

Bhawani Prasad, *wakil*, for information. Informs that he is fully ready in making arrangement of *saman-i rasad* and that by 30th September 1858, he managed 10, 000 to 12,000 *polas*[13] of green grass, besides grains like flour, etc. the *sarbrah-i rasad,* as mentioned in the *parwana* of the Political Agent and kept ready for the regiment coming from Mhow. But the arrangement of gram could not be made as in Sehore no gram is available at any shop. Dated 26 *Safar* 1275 AH (5 October 1858).

It contains the order that the letter may be sent to Lala Paltu Lal, *muhafiz-i daftar-i insha*, for inclusion in the register and keeping in the *daftar*. A copy of the order may be sent to the *amil* of Sehore through *madar al-maham*, and Ghulam Makhdum Khan, *nazim*, communicating that if gram is not available in *pargana* Sehore, it should be managed from *pargana* Ichhawar and kept ready for the *sarbrah-i lashkar* of the British. There is no use of writing senseless and useless things. If the arrangement of the *saman-i sarbrah-i rasad* for the Regiment 1 is not made and the British army devastates the *pargana* and the *amil* and *thanadar* are harassed, who will be responsible. That should not happen. A copy of the order may also be provided to all three *nazims*, through *madar al-maham*, directing them to instruct the *amils* and *thanadars* of their respective jurisdiction in the matter. Dated 1 *Rabi* I, 1275 AH.

PP 25-6. *Madan Mohan,* Naib Wakil, *to Nawwab Sikandar Begam.* Refers to her order, dated 23 *Safar* 1275 AH, as mentioned on his letter that the message of the arrival of the Regiment1was received from the letter of Bhawani Prasad and so she directed him to send a *sawar* to Imlai to bring a report about it. It was till then not known why the Regiment did not come and, therefore, he was directed to know the reason for it and inform her. Says, meanwhile, a letter of Haji 'Abd al-Sattar, *sawar*, dated 25 *Safar* 1275 AH, was received

13. A small bundle of grass.

informing that the said regiment did not yet arrive in Imlai. The said letter is sent to her. Says, he also tried to know the reason from other sources and came to know that the said regiment went to Bayawrah via other route. Dated 26 *Safar* 1275 AH (5 October 1858).

PP 27-8. *'Abd al-Sattar,* Risala *1, Red Uniform, to Madan Mohan,* Naib Wakil. Informs that 5 days have passed after arriving in *mauza* Imlai and he has no business except to enquire about the arrival of the British forces. He asks everyone who comes from Indore and Mhow. They say that from Mhow to that place, there is no British or Indian army; neither the *sawars* nor foot-soldiers. Says, he had borrowed one rupee from Khair Allah, *dafadar*, for his expenses and now he is overburdened of his expenses. Also informs of the amount of salary lost by him during the journey in between Malthun and Jhansi, that was deducted from his salary. Dated 25 *Safar* 1275 AH.

P 29. *Haji Abd al-Sattar Khan,* Sawar *and* Sais, *Red Uniform from Sehore to Madan Mohan*, Naib Wakil. Informs that as ordered, he stayed in Imlai and enquired about the arrival of the British Regiment. But there is no report of the arrival of the regiment. Says he is performing his duty with all dedication, and all the time he is waiting for the news of the arrival of Regiment1. Dated 27 *Safar* 1275 AH (7 October 1858).

PP 31-2. *Madan Mohan,* Naib Wakil, *to Nawwab Sikandar Begam.* Informs that day, a letter of Colonel Pitcher, Commander of the Regiment 1 of the *sawars* who was expected to arrive in Sehore on 1st October 1858, was received in the name of Post Master, post office cantonment, Sehore from Pipilya, dated 5 October 1858, informing that he along with the regiment would reach Sehore on 10 or 11 October 1858. The same is sent to her. That day the regiment would be at Patta. If there is no rain, the regiment would be at Sehore on 10 October. Dated 27 *Safar* 1275 AH (7 October 1858).

PP 33-4. *Bhawani Prasad to Nawwab Sikandar Begam.* Informs of the letter of Saiyid 'Abd al-Rahman, *thanadar* of Ashta, informing of the arrival of Banda Ali Khan, *jamadar*, Regiment 1 at Ashta and who misbehaved with the *thanadar*. He immediately brought the matter to the notice of the Political Agent. Says he, thereafter, wrote to the *thanadar*, Ashta that he should not do any negligence in providing *saman-i sarbrah-i rasad* to the regiment and evolve a strict mechanism that there should not be any mismanagement in the *rasad*. Dated 20 *Safar* 1275 AH (9 October 1858).

It contains the order that the letter may be sent to Lala Paltu Lal, *muhafiz-i daftar-i insha*, for inclusion in the register and keeping in the *daftar*. A copy of the order may be sent to Bhawani Prasad, *wakil*, to communicate to the Political Agent and communicate her about his reply. Dated 3 *Rabi* I, 1275 AH.

PP 35-6. *Saiyid 'Abd al-Rahman,* Thanadar *of Ashta, to Bhawani Prasad, Wakil.* Informs that day, Banda Ali Khan, *jamadar*, Regiment 1 of 600 British *sawars* came to make arrangementof *sarbrah-i rasad* and that the regiment would arrive the next morning.

P 37. *Rate-List of Goods in Hindi Devanagari Under the Territory of Bhopal State of Nawwab Sikandar Begam.*

P 39. *Transliteration of the Rate List of Goods in Hindi Devanagari Under the Territory of Bhopal State of Nawwab Sikandar Begam.* The goods are: flour, gram, rice, gurr, ghee, salt, edible oil and grass.

PP 41-2. *Rate-List of Goods in Hindi Devanagari of Bazar Ashta.*

PP 43-4. *Transliteration of Rate-List of Goods in Hindi Devanagari, Bazar Ashta, Date 23 Safar 1265 Fasli.*

PP 45-6. *Rate-List of Goods in Hindi Devanagari.*

P 47. *Transliteration of Rate-List of Goods in Hindi Devanagari, as Required by the Armymen.* The goods are: flour, rupa brand, gram, rupa brand, pulses; masoor and urad, rice, rupa brand, gurr, rupa brand, ghee, rupa brand, salt, rupa brand, edible oil, rupa brand, salt normal, sugar from Ichhawar, rupa brand, sugar banarsi, rupa brand and grass. The rates are in *Bhopali ser*, the total requirement, and rates given by the armymen.

P 49. *Bhawani Prasad to Nawwab Sikandar Begam.* Refers to his letter to the *thanadar* of Ashta, directing him to communicate of the arrival of Regiment 1 at Gajna. Informs that, from the letter of the *thanadar,* it is clear that on Friday the *sawars* would be at Gajna, on Saturday they would be at Ashta and after staying for a while at Imlai, they would be at Sehore. Dated 20 *Safar* 1275 AH (9 October1858).

P 51. *Saiyid 'Abd al-Rahman*, Thanadar *of Ashta, to Bhawani Prasad, Wakil.* Informs that day, day Friday, 600 *sawars* of the Regiment 1 were at Gajna. Next day, day Saturday, in the morning, they would be at Ashta. After staying for a while at Imlai, they would be at Sehore. Bullock carts were also with them. The roads were to be cleared and goods of *rasad* also to be managed. As per the royal order, for the total number men and the animal, 20 quintal flour, 40 quintal pulses, 16 quintal rice, and 5 quintal mustard oil, besides green grass and other items are required. Requests for orders to fulfil the demand. Dated 29 *Safar* 1275 AH.

P 53. *Madan Mohan,* Naib Wakil*, to Nawwab Sikandar Begam.* Informs that day he instructed the *thanadar* and *tahsildar* of Sehore to arrange all goods of *rasad* and the traders of the market before arrival of the caravan of *sawars* at the place of their encampment and that they too should encamp there. Accordingly, the *tahsildar* and *thanadar* along with the goods of *rasad* along with the shops of traders of the market reached the garden of Dussehra, Sehore. He also sent Dalsingh, peon before the *kotwal* of Sehore cantonment, to request him for 10 shops of traders who can provide flour, pulses etc. to the *thanadar* and *tahsildar* at the place of army camp in the market. Dated 1 *Rabi* I, 1275 AH (10 October 1858).

PP 55-6. *Madan Mohan,* Naib Wakil, *to Nawwab Sikandar Begam.* Informs that day, Colonel Pitcher called him by his orderly, the *havaldar*, in his bungalow and told that till the nexy day they would be staying there. Thereafter, they would go to Sironj via Berasia. The *rasad* should be managed at the places of encampment as per the requirement. Says, he has sent letters to the *tahsildar* and *thanadar* of Sehore to make arrangement of *rasad* at Sehore. Requests for orders for the arrangement of *rasad* at other places where the army would encamp.

P 57. *Madan Mohan,* Naib Wakil, *to Nawwab Sikandar Begam.* Informs that there was no negligence in making arrangement of *rasad* for Regiment 1 by the *tahsildar* and *thanadar*. All the armymen were happy and at ease. There was no report of atrocity of the armymen upon the people in the market.

P 59. *Madan Mohan,* Naib Wakil, *to Nawwab Sikandar Begam.* Informs that as described by Bilas Rai, *tahsildar,* he brought the matter to the notice of the Colonel that *kabaris* who came along with the armymen were accumulating grass from the mountains who should be prevented from doing so as they would provide the grass as much as they would require.

P 61. *Bilas Rai,* Amil *of Sehore, to Bhawani Prasad.* Informs that from Hurmat Khan and Faiz Khan, the soldiers, it was learnt that the *kabaris* who came with the armymen were accumulating grass from the mountains. They were prevented from doing so but they did not heed. Requests to tell the Colonel to prevent them from doing so. The soldiers too were sent there to explain the situation. Dated 3 *Rabi* I, 1275 AH (12 October 1858).

P 63. *Madan Mohan,* Naib Wakil, *to Nawwab Sikandar Begam.* Informs that day too, the *tahsildar* and *thanadar* of Sehore made a very good arrangement of goods of *rasad* for Regiment 1 for the *sawars* of Nizam of Hyderabad. There was no negligence at all. Next day too, they would encamp there. There was some scarcity of gram. But the *tahsildar* and *thanadar* of Bari arranged gram as well as flour at a distance of 2 *curoh* from that place. He immediately sent the soldiers of the *mahal* to bring goods from there before dawn, the next day.

P 65. *Madan Mohan,* Naib Wakil, *to Nawwab Sikandar Begam.* Informs that day, he sent a soldier of the state to Pinda to know about the arrangement of *rasad* there. He after having a look at the goods of *rasad* there, met Ramden, *peshdast wakil,* and brought a letter from him in his name about the arrangement of *rasad* at Pinda. He told the Colonel about it who said that he did a good job by sending a *sawar* to bring the news from there. He was really happy and that till the next day, they would encamp there and then they would march from there. Dated 4 *Rabi* I, 1275 AH (13 October 1858).

PP 67-8. *Madan Mohan,* Naib Wakil, *to Nawwab Sikandar Begam.* Informs that as ordered through her *parwana,* dated 3 *Rabi* I, 1275 AH (12 October 1858), he met Colonel Pitcher to inform him about the march of the army to Berasia via Harakhera and about the arrangement of *saman-i rasad* at Harakhera where there was also a godown of the army of Bhopal government, besides the arrangement of 2,000 bullocks of *banjaras*. The Colonel expressed his happiness and told him to convey his good wishes to her.

P 69. *Madan Mohan,* Naib Wakil, *to Nawwab Sikandar Begam.* Informs that day the arrangement of *sarbrah-i rasad* for the Regiment 1 was very nice and there was no negligence at all.

P 71. *Bhawani Prasad to Nawwab Sikandar Begam.* Sends the *parwana* of the Political Agent, dated 15 October 1858, informing of the march of Colonel Pitcher along with the *sawars* of Regiment 1 from there to Pinda, and day after the next day, they would reach Bhopal. He and other officials are intending to meet Nawwab Sikandar Begam and directed him to inform the Nawwab. Dated 6 *Rabi* I, 1275 AH (15 October 1858).

It contains the order that the letter along with the *parwana* of the Political Agent and her *parwanas* to Muhammad Sa'd al-Din and Husain Khan, dated 7 *Rabi* I, 1275 AH (16 October 1858), may be sent to Lala Paltu Lal, *muhafiz-i daftar-i insha*, for inclusion in the register and keeping in the *daftar*. A copy of the order may be sent to Bhawani Prasad, informing that the meeting with Colonel Pitcher will take place as indicated in the *parwana* of the Political Agent. Dated 15 October 1858.

P 73. *The Political Agent to Bhawani Prasad.* Says that the Colonel has informed that the following day Pitcher along with the *sawars* of Regiment 1 would march from there to Pinda and day after tomorrow they would reach Bhopal. He and other officials are intending to meet Nawwab Sikandar Begam. He should inform the Nawwab. Dated 15 October 1858.

P 75. Parwana *of Nawwab Sikandar Begam to Maulawi Muhammad Sa'd al-Din, Muhtamim, Adalat-i Faujdari.* From the *parwana* of Richards, the Political Agent, addressed to Bhawani Prasad, dated 15 October 1858, she came to know that the following day, Colonel Pitcher along with the *sawars* of Regiment 1 would march from there to Pinda, and day after the next day, they would reach Bhopal. He and other officials are intending to meet her. Directs him that when Colonel Pitcher arrives in Bhopal, he should be welcomed by him and Husain Khan, *muhtamim, ta'mirat* and scot him to her at 4 o'clock. Dated 7 *Rabi* I, 1275 AH (16 October 1858).

P 77. Parwana *of Nawwab Sikandar Begam to Husain Khan,* Muhtamim, Ta'mirat. Refers to the above letter of the Political Agent in the name of Bhawani Prasad. Directs him to welcome him along with Maulawi Muhammad Sa'd al-Din at his arrival in Bhopal, the next day, i.e. the 8th *Rabi* I and scot him to her at 4 o'clock.

PP 79-80. *Bhawani Prasad to Nawwab Sikandar Begam.* Informs of the complaint of *rasad* to the *sawars* of the regiment, accompanying Colonel Pitcher at Ashta and Imlai, as heard from the armymen. A letter of Banda Ali Khan, an employee of the regiment, complaining from Ashta and Imlai, is sent to her. Next day, the Regiment and Banda Ali Khan would encamp at Bhopal. The reason might be the negligence and utterances of the *amil* and *thanadar* of Ashta and Imlai and poor quality of *rasad*. Dated 7 *Rabi* I, 1275 AH (16 October 1858).

It contains the order that the letter may be sent to Lala Paltu Lal, *muhafiz-i daftar-i insha*, for inclusion in the register and keeping in the *daftar*. A copy of the order may be sent through *madar al-maham* to Ghulam Makhdum Khan, *nazim*, informing that the *thanadar* committed negligence in providing the *sarbrah-i saman-i rasad* to the army of Colonel Pitcher and he himself was not present at Imlai to make the arrangement of *sarbrah-i saman-i rasad*. Due to this crime, the salaries for 15 days may be deducted from the salaries of the *amil* and *thanadar* and deposited in the treasury.

PP 81-2. *A Report Sent by Banda Ali Khan,* Jamadar *of the Regiment of the Colonel, from* Mauza *Imlai,* Ilaqa, Thana *Ashta.* Reports that when Colonel Pitcher reached Ashta he was sad to see the arrangement of *rasad* which showed the negligency of the *thanadar* and *amil*. In *mauza* Imlai, he noticed many shortcomings in the *saman-i sarbrah-i rasad*.

P 83. *Gist of the Letter of Mirza Abu al-Hasan,* Thanadar *of Sehore, to Nawwab Sikandar Begam.* Informs of the encampment of the army of Colonel Pitcher at Sehore for 4 days, expressing happiness on the arrangement of *rasad,* made by the royal government, in sufficient quantity, and giving an appreciation letter. The same is presented before her.

It contains the order that the letter along with the letter of appreciation may be sent through *madar al-maham* to Mirza Abu al-Hasan, *thanadar*, Sehore for keeping it with him. A copy of the order may be passed on to Lala Gopal Sahai, *sarishta-nigar*, *daftar-i insha*, for entering it in the book of letters and *parwanas* of appreciation. Dated 10 *Rabi* I, 1275 AH (19 October 1858).

PP 85-7. *Ramden,* Peshdast Wakil*, to Nawwab Sikandar Begam.* Informs that he while accompanying the army of the Colonel reached *mauza* Hinda, *ilaqa sarkar buzurg*, and in cooperation of the *thanadar*, the management of *rasad* was made so efficiently that nobody complained of anything. The Colonel was so happy that he gave Rs. 2 to the *jamadar*. The *thanadar* was paid the price of every item. The next day, the army will march to Bhopal. The Colonel is above 50 years of age. His beard is white. There are 4 officials in this army. First is the Colonel, the second is the Captain, the third is Walker and the fourth is the Agenty. There are 50 *sawars* in Sehore. They carry their families along and have settled in the rented houses in Sehore. Some of them are to keep their families in Bhopal. The Colonel has firm intention to join the forces of General Mitchell. The horses of the Colonel's army look very weak. There are 4 *risaldars*. The salary of the *risaldar* is Rs. 100 with 4 *naib risaldars* whose salary is Rs. 80. The salary of the *jamadars* of the *risala* is Rs. 60. The consumption of gram in the army is 80 maund, the consumption of flour is 30 maund, and the consumption of grass is 40 *pola* per diam. Besides, other items like pulses, mustard oil, black pipper, etc. are as per the requirement. The harbinger *sawars* have left for Bhopal. The army of the Colonel demanded too many *begars* and bullock carriers. He told them that it was a small village. Let him go to Bhopal where the *begars* would be available in abundance and the change of bullocks too could be made there.

File No. 296, B
Box No. 15
No. of Documents 16

P 89-90. *Muhammad Sa'd al-Din,* Muhtamim, Adalat-i Faujdari *to Nawwab Sikandar Begam.* As ordered, dated 7 *Rabi* I, 1275 AH (16 October 1858), he along with Husain Khan, *muhtamim, ta'mirat-i* Moti Masjid asked Colonel Pitcher in regard to his meeting with her. The Colonel told him that even that day he could go to meet her. Thereafter, he conveyed through Banda Ali Khan, *jamadar*, that if the Nawwab was willing he would like to meet her along with his officials like the *risaldars* and *naib risaldars*, etc. If the Nawwab was not willing, he would come alone to meet her. Dated 7 *Rabi* I, 1275 AH (16 October 1858).

It contains the order that the letter may be sent to Lala Paltu Lal, *muhafiz-i daftar-i insha*, for inclusion in the register and keeping in the *daftar*. A copy of the order may be sent to Maulawi Muhammad Sa'd al-Din, *muhtamim*, *adalat-i faujdari*, to communicate the Colonel that he is free to take as many officials as he may like during his meeting with her. The reply of the Colonel may be conveyed to her. Dated 8 *Rabi* I, 1275 AH (17 October 1858).

P 91. *Bhawani Prasad to Nawwab Sikandar Begam.* Informs as said by the Colonel Pitcher, that only 4 officials out of 25 would come to meet her. Dated 8 *Rabi* I, 1275 AH (17 October 1858).

P 93. *Muhammad Sa'd al-Din,* Muhtamim, Adalat-i Faujdari, *to Nawwab Sikandar Begam.* Informs that Banda Ali Khan, *dafadar* came to him and said that the Colonel was carrying a big tent with him and wanted to sell it and have two small tents and two *rautis*[14]. Requests for orders in the matter. Dated 8 *Rabi* I, 1275 AH (17 October 1858).

It contains the order that the letter may be sent to

14. A small gable tent.

Lala Paltu Lal, *muhafiz-i daftar-i insha*, for inclusion in the register and keeping in the *daftar*. A copy of the order may be sent to Maulawi Muhammad Sa'd al-Din, *muhtamim*, *adalat-i faujdari,* directing him that two tents, brought from Jabalpur for the Colonel, may be presented before him. Both the tents should be installed in the garden for inspection of the Colonel and whichever tent is liked by him it should be handed over to him and that his own big tent may be kept there. The cost of both the tents should be estimated. The amount exceeding the cost of the tent of the Colonel from the tent should be paid to him. The message may be conveyed to him and his reply may be conveyed to her. Dated 8 *Rabi* I, 1275 AH (17 October 1858).

P 95. *Tikaram,* Muhtamim, Karkhanajat, *to Nawwab Sikandar Begam.* Refers to a letter of Maulawi Muhammad Sa'd al-Din, *muhtamim*, *adalat-i faujdari,* dated 8 *Rabi* I, 1275 AH (17 October 1858), informing that Ankit Rao, *kotwal*, has demanded 2 *shamianas* and 2 *jajims*[15] for the Colonel that carries her order in his name to fulfill the demands. Says in the *farashkhana,* neither is the *shamiana* nor the *jajim* so as to be provided to the Colonel.

It contains the order that the letter may be sent to Lala Paltu Lal, *muhafiz-i daftar-i insha*, for inclusion in the register and keeping in the *daftar*. A copy of the letter may be sent to Ramden, *peshdast wakil,* to inform Ankit Rao, *kotwal* of the army of Colonel Pitcher about the content of the letter and his reply may be conveyed to him. Dated 9 *Rabi* I, 1275 AH (18 October 1858).

P 97. *Ramden,* Peshdast Wakil, *to Nawwab Sikandar Begam.* Informs that milk has been presented by *sarkar buzurg* (Nawwab Qudsia Begam) to Colonel Pitcher, the Captain, Walker and the Agenty. Says the Colonal has asked for the arrangement of as many horses as possible in Sehore. Also informs that the arrangement

15. A chequered-lined cloth spread over a carpet.

of *sarbrah-i rasad* for the army of the Colonel is made in sufficient quantity by Maulawi Muhammad Sa'd al-Din, *muhtamim*, *adalat-i faujdari*. There is no shortage of anything nor has any negligence been noticed.

P 99. *Radhey Kishan to Nawwab Sikandar Begam.* Informs that as directed by Maulawi Muhammad Sa'd al-Din, *muhtamim, adalat-i faujdari,* 15 maund, 16 passery flour, 12 maund 16 passery gram, besides mustard oil have been sent from Wazirganj, Bhopal, as *sarbrah-i lashkar* in the camp of Colonel Pitcher. Dated 8 *Rabi* I, 1275 AH (17 October 1858).

P 101. Darogha *to Radhey Kishan,* Muhtamim, Sair-i Kul. Informs that 16 *passery* flour and 16 *passery* gram, obtained from Fatahgarh, have been sent to Sehore through Umed Rai, peon. Dated 8 *Rabi* I, 1275 AH (17 October 1858).

PP 103-04. *Ramden,* Peshdast Wakil, *to Nawwab Sikandar Begam.* Informs that day, Colonel Pitcher and other British officers came to see the garden and expressed their happiness, seeing the royal buildings and the garden. They also expressed their appreciation for the management and behavior of the Nawwab and then they returned in the camp via Budhwara. They were happy to see the *sawars* and foot-soldiers, besides the places of entertainment and roads. Dated 9 *Rabi* I, 1275 AH (18 October 1858).

P 105. Parwana *of Nawwab Sikandar Begam to Bhawani Prasad.* Conveys that whatever *saman-i sarbrah-i rasad,* Colonel Pitcher would require for himself and the bullock carts of carriers needed to be replaced, they should be ready by the time of his arrival. Directs him to enquire from the Colonal and inform her so that the same may be provided to him during his journey. Besides, the carts of carriers are needed to be replaced as the bullocks managed by the *banjaras* are in great trouble due to long span of time. The message should be conveyed to the Colonel and his reply may be conveyed to her. Dated 9 *Rabi* I, 1275 AH (18 October 1858).

PP 107-08. *Ramden,* Peshdast Wakil, *to Nawwab Sikandar Begam.* Informs that he presented the dishes before the Colonal who was very happy to eat them and expressed his thanks to her. Says, he told him that the dishes were meant for the British officers.

PP 109-10. *Bilas Rai,* Amil *of Sehore to Nawwab Sikandar Begam.* Refers to the letter of Bhawani Prasad, dated 16 *Safar* 1275 AH (25 September 1858), which contains her order that a copy of the order may be provided to Maulawi Sa'd al-Din, *muhtamim, adalat-i faujdari*, besides *madar al-maham* and Mansukh Rai, *muhtamim, sair-i kul*, and the *amils* and *thanadars* of Ashta, Jawar and Sehore, directing them, as ordered by the Political Agent that the *saman-i sarbrah-i rasad* should be managed at their own places. There should not be any negligence and it should be given top priority. A copy of this should also be sent to Bhawani Prasad. Informs that as ordered by the Political Agent, the *saman-i rasad* was kept ready. The Regiment 1 did not reach Sehore due to rains on the date as mentioned. The green grass went waste. On 2nd *Rabi* I, 1275 AH, day Monday, the *sawars* of Regiment 1 entered *mahal* Sehore and after staying for 5 days, they marched from there to Bhopal on 7th of the month. The Colonel and his army happily passed 6 days there. Hope there would be no complaints against him. Dated 9 *Rabi* I, 1275 AH (18 October 1858).

It contains the order that the letter may be sent to to Lala Paltu Lal, *muhafiz-i daftar-i insha*, for inclusion in the register and keeping in the *daftar*. A copy of the letter may also be sent to Bhawani Prasad for informing the Political Agent and convey to her as to what he says. Dated 14 *Rabi* I, 1275 AH (23 October 1858).

P 111. *Gist of the Letter of Ramden*, Peshdast Wakil, to *Nawwab Sikandar Begam*. Refers to her order, dated 9 *Rabi* I, 1275 AH, which is regarding the carriers and *saman-i sarbrah* required by Colonel Pitcher. Says, he talked to Colonel Pitcher who said that by the evening whatever carriers he needed, he would ask for and that the Nawwab should send *saman-i sarbrah* through bullock carts as much as that would be sufficient to meet the requirement for two or three days. The details of one day requirement includes flour, gram, mustard oil, pulses, salt, rice. Requests for the orders to proceed further.

It contains the order that it may be sent to *madar al-maham*, Radhey Kishan, *muhtamim, sair-i kul*, for immediate fulfillment of the requirements, and inform her about the number and quantity of food-grains. Dated 9 *Rabi* I, 1275 AH (18 October 1858).

PP 113-14. *Tikaram,* Muhtamim, Karkhanajat *to Nawwab Sikandar Begam.* Informs that as ordered, dated 9 *Rabi* I, 1275 AH, the tent purchased from Jabalpur for Rs. 225 was sent to Colonel Pitcher through Ramden, *peshdast wakil*. He asked about its cost. He told him that it was purchased for Rs. 225 from Jabalpur. He said that for him it would cost Rs. 250. The extra amount of Rs. 25 should be the expenses which would have incurred for carrying the tent, and that he does not want that the cost of the tent should be borne by the Nawwab. Instead, it should be exchanged from his tent which is fairly big and difficult to carry. While the other tent was small. Says, there is not too much difference between the two tents except that this tent was less used while the tent of the Colonel was frequently used. Secondly, there was difference of colour. The Colonel asked for the reply of the Nawwab so that he may retain that one for himself and hand over his own tent to him, to be handed over to the Nawwab. Requests for orders to proceed further. Dated 9 *Rabi* I, 1275 AH (18 October 1858).

It contains the order that the letter may be sent to Lala Paltu Lal, *muhafiz-i daftar-i insha*, for inclusion in the register and to keep in the *daftar*. A copy of the order may be sent to Naval Rai, communicating that Colonel Pitcher has retained the tent that costs Rs. 225 and has handed over his own tent against a sum of Rs. 250. He should submit a letter, demanding Rs. 25 from the treasury to pay the same to the Colonel. A copy of the order may be sent to Lala Gobind Prasad, treasurer, to hand over Rs. 25 to Ramden, *peshdast wakil*, to give it to the Colonel along with the tent.

P 115. *Muhammad Sa'd al-Din to Nawwab Sikandar Begam.* Refers to her order, dated 6 *Rabi* I, 1275 AH, mentioned on the letter of this office. Informs that both the tents brought from Jabalpur were put in the garden of Ganjlal, which were inspected by four British officers. The Colonel chose one of the two for himself and the second was returned. About the price of the tent, he said let it be decided by others who were present there. Although he was valuing it to Rs. 250.

It contains the order that the letter may be sent to Lala Paltu Lal, *muhafiz-i daftar-i insha*, for inclusion in the register and to keep in the *daftar*. Maulawi Muhammad Sa'd al-Din, *muhtamim, adalat-i faujdari* may be communicated that in regard to the tents Colonel Pitcher chose two tents for himself as Tikaram, *muhtamim, karkhanajat*, informed her so the order was issued to the Lala for execution. Dated 9 *Rabi* I, 1275 AH (18 October 1858).

P 117. *Ramden,* Peshdast Wakil, *to Nawwab Sikandar Begam.* Refers to the letter of Lala Radhey Kishan, *muhtamim, sair-i kul,* which is in regard to *saman-i sarbrah* required for the army of Colonel Pitcher and his repy to him. A copy of that is sent to her that would make everything clear. Dated 9 *Rabi* I, 1275 (18 October 1858).

P 119. Parwana *of Nawwab Sikandar Begam to Ramden,* Peshdast, Wakil. Refers to his letter, dated 9 *Rabi* I, 1275 AH, and informs that the grains of *sarbrah-i rasad* as mentioned required for *sarbrah-i lashkar* of Colonel

Pitcher are sent there through Kaluram, Mukund Lal, *mutasaddis,* and Gangu Rao Bolaqi. Hopes that the owners would be facilitated to sell their grains in the camp at a suitable price.

Insurgency in Garhi and Bamhuri by Tantia Tope and Other Groups of Insurgents, and Crossing River Narmada at Ghat Patrora, Pargana Udaipura

PP 1- 32. Contents

PP 33-4. *Bhawani Prasad to Nawwab Sikandar Begam.* Informs that Major Richards, the Political Agent, called him and told about the content of the letter of the Bregadier from Sagar, dated 24 October 1858. He also told him to convey the Nawwab that on 23rd the insurgents returned and arrived at Khimlasa. A personal letter from Malthun contains the information that General Mitchell entered Malthun and went to Khorai after a march of 18 *curoh*. It seems that the insurgents are going to Bhilsa. That day, at dawn, a letter of a Thakur came which contains the information that 12,000 insurgent forces along with 17 elephants encamped in a village called Dhara situating at a distance of 3 *curoh* from Khimlasa. But why the letter bears the signature of Bregadier is not understandable. The Political Agent also advised that the Nawwab should abandon her plan to go to Ichhawar for a change of climate, and should immediately call back Bakhshi Murawwat Muhammad Khan along with his forces to Bhopal. The management of the fort and walled city should be given priority and the movement of the insurgents should be resrtricted. The British forces are pursuing them from two sides. The insurgents, if they enter Bhilsa they would certainly enter Bhopal. Surely, the Brititsh forces pursuing the insurgents would enter Bhopal. But to remain alert and attentive is a must until the British forces arrive. The informers should be sent to Bhilsa and Khorai to make an enquiry about the insurgents, and inform the Nawwab. The Political

Agent also said to him to call back the British *sangian* stationed in Berasia. The Political Agent earlier had said to him that the arsenal and *sawars* deployed at Sehore should be sent to Bhopal. But that day in the meeting he said that the arsenal and *sawars* should not be sent to Bhopal. If they are required in Bhopal, he would think of it. Thus, Wajid Ali, *risaldar* and *suba* of arsenal, were retained. It is doubtful that the insurgents would enter Bhopal if General Mitchell is present at a short distance from the camp of the insurgents. The Political Agent was hopeful that in case the insurgents enter Bhopal, they would be resisted from the side of Bhopal. He explained that the prestige of Bhopal had always been lying upon the Almighty. This time too, it is his belief that the Almighty will save the dignity and honour of Bhopal. If someone thinks contrary to it, he would be ashamed. Indeed alertness and confidence is always required. Dated 17 *Rabi* I, 1275 AH (26 October 1858).

It contains the order that the letter, the *parwanas* and letters of Nawwab Sikandar Begam, addressed to her officials and others may be sent to Lala Paltu Lal, *muhafiz-i daftar-i insha*, for inclusion in the register and keeping in the *daftar*. A copy of the order may be sent to Bhawani Prasad, *wakil*, communicating that Bakhshi Murawwat Muhammad Khan was immediately ordered to come back with his forces stationed at Beragarh. The *bakhshi* communicated that as soon as the carriers become available, he would return to Bhopal. The contingent, coming from Beragarh, should be retained in Bhopal or it should be sent to Sanchi Kanakhera is not clear. In the letter it is mentioned that, one group of insurgents is coming via Khorai, Khimlasa and the other group is going to Bhilsa. Directs him to bring the matter into the notice of the Political Agent and his reply may be communicated to her. The informers have also been sent to bring the news of the insurgents. If any news comes, it would be sent to the Political Agent. Dated 17 *Rabi* I, 1275 AH (26 October 1858).

P 35. *Nawwab Sikandar Begam to Ghulam Husain Khan.* From the letter of Bhawani Prasad, dated 17 *Rabi* I, 1275 AH, it is learnt that a group of insurgents after fleeing, has reached Khorai and Khimlasa. Directs him to count the *sawars* and foot-soldiers and cannoners present in the lane and that they should remain alert. The order should be notified in the Urdu book to make every employee aware. Dated 17 *Rabi* I, 1275 AH (26 October 1858).

P 37. *Nawwab Sikandar Begam to Koka Fatah Jang Khan.* From the letter of Bhawani Prasad, dated 17 *Rabi* I, 1275 AH, it is learnt that a group of insurgents, after fleeing, has reached Khorai and Khimlasa. Directs him to count all the soldiers, present at different *chaukis* and that they should remain alert. The order should be notified in the Urdu book to make every employee aware. Dated 17 *Rabi* I, 1275 AH (26 October 1858).

P 39. *Nawwab Sikandar Begam to Nawwab Begam Sahiba.* From the letter of Bhawani Prasad, dated 17 *Rabi* I, 1275 AH/26 October 1858, it is learnt that a group of insurgents after fleeing has reached Khorai and Khimlasa, and British army under the command of General Mitchell is pursuing them. Desires that all her employees should remain alert. Dated 17 *Rabi* I, 1275 AH (26 October 1858).

P 41. Khutut-i Ishtihari *of Nawwab Sikandar Begam to Nawwab Shahjahan Begam, Umrao Daulah Baqi Muhammad Khan, Nawwab Muiz Muhammad Khan, Mian Faujdar Muhammad Khan, and Dulhan Sahiba.* From the letter of Bhawani Prasad, dated 17 *Rabi* I, 1275 AH, it is learnt that a group of insurgents after fleeing has reached Khorai and Khimlasa, and British army under the command of General Mitchell is pursuing them. Directs them that all their employees should remain alert. Dated 17 *Rabi* I, 1275 AH (26 October 1858).

P 43. *Husain Khan,* Munsarim-i Dak, *to Nawwab Sikandar Begam.* Informs that on 17 *Rabi* I, 1275 AH, as ordered, Mankuran and Pancham, *harkaras*, were sent to Khorai, Khimlasa and Malthun to bring the news of the insurgents, and Lal Singh was sent to Bhilsa as he was willing to go there. Dated 17 *Rabi* I, 1275 AH (26 October 1858).

P 45. *Abd al-Ali, Muhammad Abd al-Rahman, and Chandulal to Nawwab Sikandar Begam.* Inform that day, Husain Ali, sepoy and Bhimram, shopkeeper came from *mauza* Aradmau and Jaitpur and said that, they saw from their own eyes that 4,000 insurgent forces, both *sawars* and foot-soldiers, commanded by Tantia Tope, were encamped just at a distance of two *curoh* from that place and received food-grains from the said village. Dated 17 *Rabi* I, 1275 AH (26 October 1858).

P 47. *Wazir Khan,* Qila'dar, *to Nawwab Sikandar Begam.* Informs that a Balahi of *mauza* Barkheri, falling under the *jagir* of Karamat Khan, *jagirdar,* situating at a distance of one *curoh* from Siwans came and said that about 500 *sawars* of Peshwa arrived in the said village and were demanding *begari-i rahnuma*. They also enquired about the route of Basodah. Dated 17 *Rabi* I, 1275 AH (26 October 1858).

P 49. *Wazir Khan,* Qila'dar, *to Nawwab Sikandar Begam.* Informs that on 17 *Rabi* I, 1275 AH, he sent Parsuram, sepoy at *thana* Siwans, an intelligent and clever person, to bring the news of the insurgent forces. The said person came back and his statement was recorded on the situation. The same is sent to her. Dated 18 *Rabi* I, 1275 AH (27 October 1858).

PP 51-2. *Statement of Parsuram, an Employee at* Thana *Siwans, Before Wazir Khan,* Qila'dar.

Q. Explain what he saw as he was sent to bring the news of insurgent forces.

R. He reached Dhampur, dressed as a begger and putting mud on his entire body. He heard there that the soldiers of the insurgent forces looted the provision managed for the

British forces. The *sawars* destroyed the peasants. Some foot-soldiers looted 2 to 3 houses of the villagers. Some forces with cannon went to Gayaraspura. Thier number is not known. He asked them about the commander of that force. He was told that Tantia Tope was the chief of that force. Adil Muhammad Khan too was in their company. Then, he enquired about two persons; one of them was on a white horse, and the other was on foot. He was told that it was Adil Muhammad Khan who was riding on the white horse. About the other he came to know nothing.

Q. Explain if he knows where they were intending to go.

R. From the people of Dham, he learnt that the British forces were encamping at Bagrod and left for Gayaraspura, after hearing the news of the insurgent forces.

P 53. *Wazir Khan,* Qila'dar, *to Nawwab Sikandar Begam.* Informs that day, i.e. 17th *Rabi* I, 1275 AH, the insurgents arrived at Bagrod, falling under Sindhia's territory, situating at a distance of 5 *curoh* from Siwans and were continuously pouring in as stated by Nadaf, Kanhai Brahmin and Ratiram Onkar, the soldiers. Their statements as recorded are sent to her. Says, he has also sent someone there to inquire into the reality. Dated 17 *Rabi* I, 1275 AH (26 October 1858).

PP 55-6. *Statement of Ratiram, a Dweller of Gotkha,* Ilaqa *Ghairatganj Under the* Jagir *of Nawwab Shahjahan Begam.* States that his name is Ratiram, his father's name is Rajaram, caste clad, dweller of Gotkha, *ilaqa* Ghairatganj and his profession is *zamindari.*

Q. Tell what he saw at Bagrod where he had gone.

R. On the previous day, he was in Bagrod. At the end of the day, the army of Peshwa reached there and looted the entire village and encamped there.

Q. Tell how many forces were with the Peshwa and whether he was assaulted by them?

R. There were about 10, 000 to 12,000 forces with him. He was far away from the army, so he was not caught by them.

Q. Is he sure, that the forces were at Dhampur that day?

R. He saw from his own eyes and came back as fast as possible.

Q. How many cannon were with them?

R. He did not notice any cannon with them, either at Bagrod or anywhere on the way.

PP 57-8. *Statement of Kanhai Barhmin, Dweller of Siwans, Before Wazir Khan,* Qila'dar. States that his name is Kanhai Brahmin, his father's name is Sewakram, a dweller of Siwans, caste Brahmin and his profession is *panditi*.

Q. Tell what he heard or saw at Dhampur where he had gone?

R. A servant of Bholanath, *qanungoi*, said that the army of Peshwa arrived at Bagrod. Hearing this, brother of Bholanath came hurriedly and said to him why he was going there. So he fled and reached there.

Q. Has he heard anything about the number of forces?

R. People were telling that there were about 10, 000 to 12,000 men in the forces. But they did not mention any number of cannon with them. Thereafter, all the inhabitants of Dhampur fled.

PP 59-60. *Statement of Bahadur Nadaf, Dweller of Siwans, in the Presence of Wazir Khan,* Qila'dar. States that his name is Bahadur and his father's name is Khansi, caste nadaf, a dweller of Siwans and he is a shopkeeper. Further stated that, he was going to Bagrod for shopping. On the way, nearby *nalla* Bhargwan, two Rajputs met him and told not to go further as the insurgent forces were at Dhampur. Hearing this, he came back and informed that old Bagrod was destroyed.

File No. 297, B
Box No. 16
No. of Documents 29

PP 61-2. *Letter of Lal Singh,* Jamadar, *Dated 17 Rabi I, 1275 AH (26 October 1858), Informing the Arrival of the British Forces in Bhilsa. (A letter in Hindi).*

PP 63-4. *Letter of Pratab Singh,* Jamadar, *Dated 17 Rabi I, 1275 AH (26 October 1858), Informing the Arrival of the British Forces in Bhilsa (a letter in Hindi).*

PP 65-6. *Daulat Rai,* Nazim-i Mashriq, *to Nawwab Sikandar Begam.* Sends the letters received from Shaikh Abd al-Rahman, *thanadar*, Saiyid Abd al-Ali and Lala Chandulal, *tahsildar* of *pargana* Garhi, dated 17 *Rabi* I, 1275 AH besides the statements of Hemraj, *gumashta* and Haridas Mahasangh, informing of the arrival of 3,000 insurgents in Jaitpur, *ilaqa* Garhi, situating at a distance of 2 *curoh* from Garhi and demanding additional forces. Informs that earlier 40 soldiers, posted at *chaukis* in Garhi, were called back to Raisen and 15 of them were sent to Bhopal which made a total of 50 soldiers. The remaining 25 soldires were immediately sent to Garhi. The statement of Hemraj, *thanadar* of Garhi, clarifies the movement of the insurgent forces, their atrocities upon the inhabitants and their loot of the *mustajir*. Haridas Mahasangh has requested for half a dozen horses. Requests that in such a situation, 50 soldiers of the *chaukis* who are in the *mahal* of this district and in Bhopal should be sent back immediately. Hira Paras Singh, *jamadar*, who is in Raisen should also be sent there. Dated 18 *Rabi* I, 1275 AH (27 October 1858).

PP 67-8. *Abd al-Rahman,* Thanadar, *Garhi Ambapani, to Daulat Rai,* Nazim-i Mashriq. The news of the insurgents, entering in the region and his march to suppress them would have come to his notice through the letter of Lala Chandulal, *tahsildar*. Says whether it is the statement of the sepoys, who came from villages, or the statement of *balahis* coming from Jaitpur and Mhow, it might be ascertained that the group of insurgents is not large enough to be noticed. The informers from among the sepoys and *balahis* said that the insurgents were 3,000 or more than that. Meanwhile Hemraj, *gumashta* of Sethji Gopal, who had gone to Jaitpur for the distribution of grain, returned hurriedly when he noticed the insurgents there. His statement is recorded and sent to him. Dated 17 *Rabi* I, 1275 AH (26 October 1858).

PP 69-70. *Statement of Hamraj, Gumashta of Sethji Gopal*. States that his name is Hemraj and his father's name is Suratram, caste Brahmin, a dweller of Garhi Ambapani, aged about 40 years, and by profession is a *sahu*. States that he had gone to Jaitpur, *pargana* Garhi, for the distribution of seeds and came to report what he saw there.

P 71. *Nawwab Sikandar Begam to Bhawani Prasad.* Informs that *balahi* of *mauza* Chura, having two letters, came in the office of *adalat-i faujdari* in Bhopal Khas. He also stated that the forces of Tantia Tope arrived at Diwanganj *ilaqa* of Bhopal State. The two letters are sent to him along with her *parwana* to present it before the Political Agent and convey his response to her. The tetters are in Hindi, written by two *jamadars,* the employees of State of Bhopal and posted in the battalion, stationed at Sanchi on way to Bhilsa. Dated 18 *Rabi* I, 1275 AH (27 October 1858).

P 73. *Nawwab Baqi Muhammad Khan to Nawwab Sikandar Begam.* Sends the letters received from Ajodhya Prasad, *thanadar,* and Maulawi Saiyid Ghulam Shah, deputy *tahsildar, pargana* Gulgaon, dated 17 *Rabi* I, 1275 AH (26 October 1858).

PP 75-6. *Ajodhya Prasad,* Thanadar *of Gulgaon, to Nawwab Baqi Muhammad Khan.* Informs that he was in Kanakhera to distribute the seeds of grain and came back only in the evening. In Gulgaon, people came from Bhilsa and said that the dwellers of Bhilsa were fleeing to any direction and the British army was encamping at Neon river, 3 *curoh* away from Bhilsa while the insurgent forces had assembled in village Hinda, situating at 7 *curoh* from Bhilsa and waging war there. Hearing the news, he came to the *thana* to make arrangement of flour and pulses as *sarbrah-i rasad* for the British army. Dated 17 *Rabi* I, 1275 AH (26 October 1858).

It contains the order that the letter may be sent to Nawwab Sikandar Begam. A copy of the order may be sent to Ajodhya Prasad, *thanadar* of Gulgaon, directing him to take care of the people and the state and make arrangement of *saman-i rasad* for the British army.

P 77. *Saiyid Ghulam Shah to Nawwab Baqi Muhammad Khan.* Informs that Lala Ajodhya Prasad, *thanadar* who had gone to Kanakhera for the distribution of seeds of grain, came back and reported about the disturbances in Bhilsa. The British forces were encamping at river Betwa, situating at a distance of 3 *curoh* from Bhilsa while the insurgent forces were at *mauza* Hinda, situating at a distance of 7 *curoh* from Bhilsa and waging war there. The *thanadar* has already written him in the matter. He too thought it necessary to inform him of the matter. He is also busy in the arrangements of food-grain as *sarbrah-i* rasad for the army to come. Dated 17 *Rabi* I, 1275 AH (26 October 1858).

It contains the order that the letter may be sent to Nawwab Sikandar Begam. A copy of the order may be sent to Saiyid Ghulam Shah, deputy *tahsildar* of Gulgaon, directing him to take care of the people and the state and make arrangement of *saman-i rasad* for the British army.

PP 79-80. *Daulat Rai,* Nazim-i Mashriq, *to Nawwab Sikandar Begam.* Sends the report received from *thana* Siwans, informing that the Peshwa's army reached *mauza* Qasba, situating at a distance of 5 *curoh* from Siwans and devastated the entire village and then they fled to Dahanipur. Dated 18 *Rabi* I, 1275 AH (27 October 1858).

It contains the order that the letter along with the newsletter may be sent to Lala Paltu Lal, *muhafiz-i daftar-i insha*, for inclusion in the register and keeping in the *daftar*. A copy of the order may be sent to Wazir Khan, *qila'dar*, informing, it is learnt that some insurgent forces have reached Ghayaspur and Bhilsa and the British forces are pursuing them. Bakhshi Murawwat Muhammad Khan is sent there so that if the insurgents pass through Bhopal they should be prevented.

P 81. *News-Report of Shaikh Nur Muhammad,* Thanadar *of Siwans.* Informs that day, Kanhaya Lal Brahmin a dweller of Siwans returned to *qasba* Dahanipur and stated, as he heard, that the army of Peshwa reached *qasba* Bagrod, situating at a distance of 5 *curoh* from there and devastated the said *qasba*. The inhabitants of Bagrod fled and reached Golyan. Even the *qanungoi* of Dahanipur fled. The said Brahmin was then sent to Wazir Khan, *qila'dar* to report. The *qila'dar* sent two *sawars* to enquire into the matter. The report will be sent after the *sawars* come back. Dated 17 *Rabi* I, 1275 AH (26 October 1858).

P 83. *Harshai,* Tahsildar *of Bamhuri, to Nawwab Sikandar Begam.* Informs the receipt of the letter of Chandulal, *tahsildar* of Garhi Ambapani, stating that the insurgent forces have devastated *mauza* Aradmau and Jaitpur and the *thanadar* has gone to enquire about them. It is must that he should take care of his region and help him with men and material. Says, he immediately sent 20 soldiers of *thana* and *tahsil* with arms and ammunitions along with two *jamadars* of *thana* and *mahal* there. He himself is busy in managing the affairs there. He has also sent letters to the *thanadars* and *tahsildars* of Udaipura and Bareilly and has asked each of them to provide 15 soldiers. Dated 18 *Rabi* I, 1275 AH (27 October 1858).

PP 85-6. *Chandulal,* Tahsildar *to Abbas Husain Khan,* Thanadar *and Lala Harsahai,* Tahsildar *of Bamhuri.*

Informs that a person came to *mauza* Aradmau, Jaitpur, *pargana* Garhi and stated that the insurgent forces entered *mauza* Aradmau and Jaitpur, and devastated these villages. It is therefore, required that they all should remain alert and attentive. Dated 17 *Rabi* I, 1275 AH (26 October 1858).

PP 87-8. *Harsahai,* Tahsildar *of Bamhuri, to Nawwab Sikandar Begam.* Informs that as requested by the *tahsildar* of Garhi Ambapani, he sent 20 soldiers to help and assist the *tahsildar*. Says in the evening, Multan, a dweller of Garhi Ambapani, came to Bamhuri who said that the previous day the insurgents captured Garhi Ambapani. The statement of Multan has been recorded and is sent to her. Dated 18 *Rabi* I, 1275 AH (27 October 1858).

PP 89-90. *Statement of Multan*. States that his name is Multan Chand and his father's name is Jaitmal, he is a dweller of Garhi Ambapani, by profession he is a *sahu*, and his age is 22 years.

Q. What he wants to tell about Garhi Ambapani?

R. The situation in Garhi is such that the previous day the insurgent forces entered *mauza* Aradmau, *pargana* Garhi. In that village, Mahasangh Seth had his shop of seeds opened. The insurgents filled up 40 bags with seeds as a tribute and then entered in the village. The villagers went to the *thana* to report. The *thanadar* consoled them. The *thanadar* went to see the insurgents who were in huge number and returned to Garhi, and said, the people might flee wherever they would like to. States that day the insurgents captured Garhi. The *thanadar* and *tahsildar* fled as the insurgents were in a huge number.

Q. Was he at that time in Garhi?

R. He was then in *mauza* Malarmatya.

PP 91-2. *Wazir Khan,* Qila'dar, *to Nawwab Sikandar Begam.* Informs, upon hearing the news that the insurgents have gathered at Dhampur, Shaikh Nur Muhammad, *thanadar* of Siwans, Shaikh Ghulam Muhammad, *qila'dar* of Siwans, and Waris Ali, *tahsildar*, sent their families and goods to the villages adjoining Siwans. Says, he told them that if they would do like that, then people would be scared. But they did not pay heed to him. As a result, the people fled too. Although he made his best effort to prevent them from fleeing, but the people did not pay heed to him. Dated 18 *Rabi* I, 1275 AH (27 October 1858).

It contains the order that the letter may be sent to Lala Paltu Lal, *muhafiz-i daftar-i insha*, for inclusion in the register and keeping in the *daftar*. A copy of the order may be sent to Wazir Khan, *qila'dar,* intimating that it is the habit of the people that they run away if they get the news of any disturbance or of the arrival of the insurgents. But it is not his duty to pacify and keep them calm. His duty is to prevent the insurgency. He is directed to inform as to who of his region fought with the insurgents and how many insurgents were killed or wounded, and how many from their side were killed or wounded, and who from amongst them fled and how many insurgents were arrested. Dated 26 *Rabi* I, 1275 AH (4 November 1858).

P 93. *Wazir Khan,* Qila'dar, *to Nawwab Sikandar Begam.* Informs when he heard that the insurgent forces were at a distance of 3 *curoh* from there, he along with Nizam Ali Khan, *risaldar*, Majeed Muhammad Khan, son-in-law of Sher Muhammad Khan, besides the relatives of Sardar Khan, Asif Khan, along with the contingent present at Siwans became ready to take on battle with them. Later on, it was heard that the insurgent forces went to Basodah. Since Basodah does not fall under the jurisdiction of Bhopal government, he left pursuing them. Dated 18 *Rabi* I, 1275 AH (27 October 1858).

P 95. *Saiyid Imtiaz Ali,* Thanadar, *and Rahim Bakhsh,* Tahsildar, Pargana *Jogigarh to Nawwab Sikandar*

Begam. Inform that Shaikh Chand, soldier of Mahalpur and Najaf Khan of Chandpur, who were with Chandulal, *tahsildar* of Garhi Ammbapani, came back that day, the 19th *Rabi* I, 1275 AH, and stated that the insurgents left Garhi Ambapani and encamped at Dehgaon. The informers hurriedly left the place and through the mountains reached Bhalariya, situating at a short distance from Mahalpur. Khaplal, son of Bhogach and *qanungoi* of Mahalpur, told them that the insurgents devastated Mahalpur and made the *tahsildar* and *thanadar* captive. They were afraid that wherever they go through the mountains, the insurgents reached there. It is not known where the insurgents went after capturing Mahalpur. The information as received is communicated as it was must. Dated 19 *Rabi* I, 1275 AH (28 October 1858).

P 97. *Husain Khan,* Munsarim-i Dak, *to Nawwab Sikandar Begam.* Sends the report submitted by Sharif Khan, *harkara dak*, who was sent to Bhilsa to bring the news of insurgents. Dated 19 *Rabi* I, 1275 AH (28 October 1858).

P 99. *Sharif Khan,* Harkara Dak, *to Nawwab Sikandar Begam.* Informs that he and Sumer, *harkaras dak,* were sent by Husain Khan, *munsarim-i dak*, to bring the news of the insurgents. Informs in Bhilsa he saw that there were 4,000 British forces. The people were also saying that more forces were coming from Inayatpur. The essential commodities required by the British army were being supplied from Bhilsa. The dwellers of Bhilsa were happy in their houses. In Bhilsa, he also heard from the soldiers that the insurgent forces were hiding in the forests of Dhaturia, situating at a distance of 5 *curoh* from Basodah and 7 *curoh* from Bhilsa. About their number, some say they are 7,000 some say they are 8,000 and some say they are 10, 000. From there Sumer went further to enquire about the insurgents. Dated 19 *Rabi* I, 1275 AH (28 October 1858).

PP 101-02. *Baqi Muhammad Khan to Nawwab Sikandar Begam.* Sends the report received from Hidayat Ali, *jamadar, thana* Gulgaon, dated 19 *Rabi* I, 1275 AH, which is regarding the coming of the insurgent forces from Bhilsa, at a distance of 4 *curoh* and challenging the British forces who reached Bhilsa on 18th of the month, and the dwellers of Bhilsa fled due to fear. Dated 19 *Rabi* I, 1275 AH (28 October 1858).

PP 103-04. *Hidayat Ali to Baqi Muhammad Khan.* Says that he is not unaware of his responsibilities towards maintaining safety and security at the *chaukis* and as he takes round after round and the soldiers are ready at every post. Informs on 14 *Rabi* I, 1275, he was taking round of Garhighat. He remained there for 3 days. On the last day, 7 thieves entered in the *mauza* and took away 24 cows. He, however, recovered all the cows of the *mauza* and handed them over. The *thanadar* was in Sanchi Kanakhera for the distribution of seeds among the peasants. He came back and reported that the insurgent forces were encamping at a distance of 3 to 4 *curoh* from Bhilsa. On 18th of the month, the British army entered Bhilsa. The dwellers of Bhilsa were fleeing due to fear. With the grace of God and due to her blessings, there is peace in the region. But people hearing the news of Bhilsa were scared. Dated 19 *Rabi* I, 1275 AH (28 October 1858).

The letter contains the order that the letter along with his letter may be sent to Nawwab Sikandar Begam.

PP 105-06. Parwana *of Nawwab Sikandar Begam to Bhawani Prasad.* Sends the two letters received from some British officials without name, and directs him to bring the matter into the notice of the Political Agent. The letters, thereafter, may be returned to her and inform her about the name of the writer. The observation of the Political Agent may also be communicated to her. Dated 19 *Rabi* I, 1275 AH (28 October 1858).

PP 107 & 109-10. *Letter of Major to Nawwab Sikandar*

Begam. Informs that he was in village Bagrod when suddenly at 3 pm, he heard about the arrival of 300 *sawars*. Hearing the news, he became ready, attacked and defeated them. Some of them were killed, some wounded and two others were arrested. It is heard from the informers that 10, 000 insurgent forces have marched towards Bhopal via Saras to fight battle there. Desires that she should manage the affairs of her state. Informs that his and other forces are coming to suppress the insurgents. Dated 27 October 1857.

PP 111-12. *Bhawani Prasad to Nawwab Sikandar Begam.* Acknowledges receipt of her *parwana*, dated 18 *Rabi* I, 1275 AH, and the report of *balahi* of *mauza* Chhola that Tantia Tope's troops have entered Diwanganj, *ilaqa* Bhopal, besides two letters in Hindi of Lal Singh and Pratab Singh, *jamadars,* delivered by a horse rider of the post Sanchi Khera. Says he immediately went to the bungalow of the Political Agent, awoke him up and told him about the *parwana* and the two letters. The Political Agent replied if Tantia Tope, after the defeat at Bhilsa, went to Diwanganj it would not be a surprise. If he entered Diwanganj as a defeated one, it would be an easy task for the *Bakhshi* to eliminate him completely. In that way, Bhopal's name would come into prominence. Dated 19 *Rabi* I, 1275 AH (28 October 1858).

PP 113-14. *Bhawani Prasad to Nawwab Sikandar Begam.* Acknowledges the receipt of her *parwana* along with two unnamed letters of a British addressed to her, delivered by a camel rider, directing him to ascertain the name of the writer through the Political Agent and communicate the same to her. Says he immediately presented it before the Political Agent who, inspite of all efforts, could not ascertain the name of the writer of the letter. However, he verbally told that it might be Major's letters who on 24 October had attacked upon the insurgents. Dated 19 *Rabi* I, 1275 AH (28 October 1858).

PP 115-16. *Baqi Muhammad Khan to Nawwab Sikandar Begam.* Sends the two letters received from Lala Durga Prasad, *thanadar* of Ghairatganj, dated 17 *Rabi* I, 1275 AH (26 October 1858). The first one is in reference to the letter of *tahsildar* of Garhi, which is about the insurgency there. The other is in regard to devastation of *mauza* Bagrod, *ilaqa* Bhilsa, on the previous day by 10, 000 insurgent forces as narrated by Pyare, *mustajir* of Khairgarh, *pargana* Garhi. The insurgents again entered *mauza* Dardu, *ilaqa* Garhi, situating at a distance of 3 *curoh* from Ghairatganj and were intending to come to Siwans and Ghairatganj. Dated 19 *Rabi* I, 1275 AH (28 October 1858).

P 117. *Lala Durga Prasad,* Thanadar *of Ghairatganj, to Nawwab Shahjahan Begam.* Informs that day it was heard from a *mustajir*, *pargana* Garhi, that on the previous day about 10, 000 insurgent forces came in Bagrod, *ilaqa* Bhilsa, and destroyed it. It was also heard that they were going to Siwans. Harchandar reported that the insurgent forces were encamping at a distance of 3 *curoh* from there and they were intending to go to Ghairatganj. Says, hearing the news he became alert along with his forces at the *thana*. Whatever happens afterwards will be reported. Dated 17 *Rabi* I, 1275 AH (26 October 1858).

The letter contains the order to send it along with her letter to Nawwab Sikandar Begam. A copy of the order may be sent to Lala Durga Prasad, *thanadar,* Ghairatganj, directing him to remain alert and attentive along with the forces of *thana*, *tahsil* and *chaukis*. If the insurgents pass through that region, they should be dealt with firmly. Authentic information of the insurgent forces; about the place of their encampment and their strength may be sent to the government. Dated 19 *Rabi* I, 1275 AH (28 October 1858).

P 119. *Lala Durga Prasad,* Thanadar *of Ghairatganj, to Nawwab Sikandar Begam.* Refers to a letter of *tahsildar* of Garhi, directing him to reach there along with the forces of *tahsil* and *thana* in view of the insurgency in Garhi. Informs he, thus, marched to Garhi along with 15 soldiers. The rest of the soldiers and *jamadar* are in the *thana* as ordered. Dated 5 *Muharram* 1275.

File No. 297, C
Box No. 16
No. of Documents 30

PP 121-2. *Daulat Rai,* Nazim-i Mashriq, *to Nawwab Sikandar Begam.* Informs that day, hundreds of dwellers of Bhilsa fled and took shelter in *pargana* Raisen and in the town itself. There have also been reports of the *thanadars* of Siwans and Garhi that the insurgents are at Bagrod. The information to this effect has been sent to the government. Also refers to a letter of Nawwab Khan, *sawar* to the suba of Bhilsa, requesting him to pacify the dwellers from fleeing and about the encampment of the insurgents. The Suba Sahab informed that a group of insurgents- their number is not known- was encamping at Bagrod, *ilaqa* Bhilsa. Meanwhile, the British forces arrived at Basodah in Gayaraspur. The forces, stationed at Korwai would reach Bhilsa that day via Basodah. Hearing the news of the British forces, the insurgent forces fled to Muhammad Garh and Siwans. The letter of Suba Sahab is sent to her. The distance of Bagrod from Siwans is 5 *curoh* and the distance of Siwans from Muhammad Garh is 3 *curoh*. The march of insurgents towards Siwans and Muahammad Garh is understood from the letters of Suba Sahab and from the report of the *thanadar*. It is important to deal with the insurgents firmly and to remove fear from the minds of peasants who are fleeing due to fear of insurgents. This is the season of sowing seeds by the farmers and *mustajirs* that came to a standstill, thereby, the loss of the government is also visible. Says he thinks that the *naib bakhshi* should be deputed with a considerable number of troops to deal with the insurgents as the British forces are ordered to pursue them immediately. In this situation, the deployment of *naib bakhshi* would be a step in the direction of suppression of the insurgents and in restoring confidence of the peasants.

It contains the order that the letter may be sent to Lala Paltu Lal, *muhafiz-i daftar-i insha*, for inclusion in the register and keeping in the *daftar*. A copy of the order may be sent to Daulat Rai, *nazim-i mashriq*, informing him that the forces which are in Siwans are enough to fight with the insurgents and no other force will be sent there.

P 123. *Sada Shiv Rao,* Suba *of Bhilsa to Daulat Rai,* Nazim-i Mashriq. Refers to his letter in regard to the insurgents. Informs that the number of insurgents who are encamping at Bagrod, *ilaqa* Bhilsa, is not known. At the same time, the British forces encamping at Basodah have arrived at Gayaraspur. The forces which are stationed at Sasurdan, coming via Basodah, are still there. Hearing the news of the British forces, the insurgents fled to Muhammad Garh Basodah and Siwans. Whatever happens in future will be communicated. Dated 19 *Rabi* I, 1275 AH (28 October 1858).

P 125. *Baqi Muhammad Khan to Nawwab Sikandar Begam.* Informs about a letter of Ajodhya Prasad, *thanadar* of *pargana* Gulgaon, which is under his *jagir*, dated 18 *Rabi* 1275 AH, along with a letter in Hindi of Gulab Patwari of *mauza* Kanakhera, informing that 700 British forces are coming soon and behind them are the insurgent forces of Peshwa. The British army is encamping at Bhilsa while the insurgent forces are encamping at Ghayaraspur. In the afternoon, the British forces will leave Bhilsa and will go to Bhopal. A copy of the letter of the *thanadar* along with translation of the Hindi letter is being sent to her. Dated 19 *Rabi* 1275 AH (28 October 1858).

P 127. *Ajodhya Prasad,* Thanadar *of* Pargana *Gulgaon, To Baqi Muhammad Khan.* Informs about a letter of Gulab Patwari of Kanakhera, dated 18 *Rabi* I, 1275 AH, informing that 700 British forces are coming soon and behind them are the insurgent forces of Peshwa. The British forces are encamping at Bhilsa while the forces of Peshwa are at Gayaraspur. The same is presented to him. In the afternoon, all 700 British forces would leave Bhilsa and would go to Bhopal. Dated 18 *Rabi* I, 1275 AH (27 October 1858).

P 129. *Transliteration of a Hindi Letter Written by Gulab Patwari of* Mauza *Kanakhera*. The report of Bhilsa is that 700 British forces have arrived in Bhilsa. They will march in the night and will stay at Bhopal. The army of Peshwa, as heard, is at Gayaraspur. The British army is advancing while the army of Peshwa is behind that army. The dwellers have fled from Bhilsa. Only the soldiers are left there. The Suba Sahab is in Bhilsa and has closed the door very carefully. There are 4 cannon at the doorstep and too much precaution is being maintained in Bhilsa. Dated *Kartik Budi Panchmi* 1266 *Fasli*.

PP 131-2. *Bhawani Prasad to Nawwab Sikandar Begam*. Acknowledges the receipt of the letter of Nawwab Baqi Muhammad Khan, along with other two letters addressed to her, which is the translation of the letter of Gulab Rai Patwari, *mauza* Kanakhera, directing him to present it before the Political Agent. Informs that the previous day the matter was brought to the notice of the Political Agent who heard him carefully and said that General Mitchell who was at Sandorah killed many insurgents and gave them a crushing defeat. There were no cannon with them and there is no possibility of their advancement towards Bhopal after such a humiliating defeat. But still one should be careful and the soldiers should be kept on high alert, he said. Dated 19 *Rabi* I, 1275 AH (28 October 1858).

P 133. *Parwana of Nawwab Sikandar Begam to Daulat Rai,* Nazim-i Mashriq. Refers to his letter, informing the coming of the insurgents and the arrest of *amil* and *thanadar*. The news of the arrest of the *amil* and *thanadar* is really perturbing her. Hafiz Hasan Khan, *naib bakhshi*, is sent there along with some forces, besides the British forces who entered Bhopal. Have patience and be calm as the British forces would be coming to Bhopal, the contingent of Bhopal army will be sent to him in that quantity.

PP 135-6. Parwana *of Nawwab Sikandar Begam to Hafiz Muhammad Hasan Khan, Naib Bakhshi.* Sends him the papers of distribution of the *sawars* and foot-soldiers of the State of Bhopal and directs him to reach Sanchi Kanakhera along with the *sawars*, foot-soldiers and cannoners as per the description given in the papers of distribution, and inform the British officer at Bhilsa after reaching Sanchi Kanakhera, and request him for orders to be executed by him. Dated 19 *Rabi* I, 1275 AH (28 October 1858).

PP 137-8. *Baqi Muhammad Khan to Nawwab Sikandar Begam.* Sends the letter received from Shamsh al-Din from Raisen, dated 19 *Rabi* I, 1275 AH, informing that the insurgent force has arrived at Siwans, Garhi Ambapani and Mahalpur, and have arrested the *amil*, the *thanadar* and *muharrir* of that place.

PP 139-40. *Shamsh al-Din Ansari To Baqi Muhammad Khan.* Informs that the previous day, he met Ahmad Ali who told him that hearing the news of a contingent of 4,000 *sawars* and foot-soldiers of insurgent forces he along with Abd al-Ali and Abd al-Rahman, *thanadar* and *tahsildar* of Mahalpur besides the *thanadar* and *tahsildar* of Garhi Ambapani reached nearby Garhi. Says, he stayed at Jogi where he enquired about the situation from Situ Rajput, an employee at Dehgaon. From Ahmad Ali it was learnt that, the insurgents arrested Abd al-Ali and Abd al-Rahamn and took them along. Dated 19 *Rabi* I, 1275 AH (28 October 1858).

The letter contains the order to send it along with his letter to Nawwab Sikandar Begam. A copy of the order may be sent to Shamsh al-Din, directing him to report whatever news he receives about the insurgents.

He should reach Ghairatganj and manage the affairs there efficiently.

PP 141-2. *Letter of Maulawi Muhammad Sa'd al-Din, Muhtamim, Adalat-i Faujdari*. Informs that Major Teller said to him after hearing the news of the insurgents that, he along with some *sawars* should reach Bhopal that day as desired by General Mitchell. Says, he left Bhilsa and reached Raisen and in the night itself reached Bhopal. But on the way he did not hear any news of insurgents anywhere. Even in Bhopal there was no news of the insurgents. General Mitchell too would reach Bhopal with a huge army in the morning. It might be that the insurgents enter Bhopal by evening that very day. It is a must that the Nawwab should be informed to make arrangement accordingly. Dated 19 *Rabi* I, 1275 AH (28 October 1858).

P 143. *Nawwab Sikandar Begam to Nawwab Begam Sahiba.* There is news that the insurgents would enter Bhopal that day. Requests that all her *sawars* and foot-soldiers should be directed to remain ready along with arms and ammunitions at her *deorhi*. Dated 19 *Rabi* I, 1275 AH (28 October 1858).

PP 145-6. *Muhammad Raza Husain to Nawwab Sikandar Begam.* Refers to the letter of the *thanadar* of *pargana* Jogigarh, dated 19 *Rabi* I, 1275 AH, informing that the insurgents have devastated Garhi Ambapani and Mahalpur. The same is sent to her. The *thanadar* did not write anything about the number of insurgents. So 5 informers were sent to Kalyakhery to bring the news. Requests for orders to be issued to recruit new soldiers for deployment at *mahal* Jogigarh, Tal and other *mahals*. Dated 19 *Rabi* I, 1275 AH (28 October 1858).

It contains the order that the letter may be sent to Lala Paltu Lal, *muhafiz-i daftar-i insha*, for inclusion in the register and keeping in the *daftar*. A copy of the order may be sent to Muhammad Raza Husain, *nazim-i junub*, informing him that the forces which are in Siwans are enough to fight with the insurgents and that no other force will be sent there.

P 147. *Saiyid Imtiaz Ali,* Thanadar *of* Pargana *Jogigarh to Muhammad Raza Husain.* Reports that Shaikh Chand, soldier at *thana* Mahalpur and Najaf Khan of Chandpura, reported that the insurgents reached Garhi Ambapani and devastated it and made the *thanadar* and *tahsildar* captive. Thereafter, the insurgents went to Dehgaon. Information to this effect was a must which he did. Dated 20 *Rabi* I, 1275 AH (29 October 1858).

P 149. *Daulat Rai,* Nazim-i Mashriq, *to Nawwab Sikandar Begam.* Sends the news-report, pertaining to the destruction caused by the insurgents and the treatment meted out to the *tahsildars* and *thanadars* of Garhi and Mahalpur. It is clear that the insurgents have arrived in Garhi and went upto *mauza* Dehgaon, situating at a distance of 8 *curoh* from Raisen. Their firm intention is to reach Raisen by that night itself. The contingent which is there is known to her. Assures, in case the insurgents come to that place he would do whatever would be possible for him to do. But if a good number of armymen are provided to him, it will be good. Dated 19 *Rabi* I, 1275 AH (28 October 1858).

PP 151-2. *News-Report of Saiyid Ahmad Ali.* Reports that day Saiyid Ahmad Ali, cousin brother of Saiyid Abd al-Ali, came and stated that on 17 *Rabi* I, 1275 AH a person came to Garhi and said to Abd al-Ali and Shaikh Abd al-Rahman, *thanadar* of Garhi, that the insurgents arrived in Jaitpur and Aradmau through the mountains and devastated those villages. The insurgents were searched but not found. The guards were deployed everywhere. The bundles of official papers were sent to Raisen. On 18th of the month, Shaikh Ihsan Ali, *tahsildar*, and Lala Shahzad Rai, *thanadar* of Mahalpur, came to Garhi. They decided to go to Raisen. In the meantime, Adil Muhammad Khan and Rao Sahab along with an army of 2,000 *sawars* arrived in Garhi and destroyed the houses there. Meanwhile, about 400 *sawars* of insurgent forces entered *mauza* Badhnagarh, *pargana* Mahalpur, and arrested Saiyid Abd al-Ali, Shaikh Muhammad Abd al-Rahman, *thanadar*, Lala Chandulal, *tahsildar*, and Lala Chaturbhuj. Shaikh Ihsan Ali, *tahsildar*, and Lala Shahzad Rai, *thanadar*, who had fled from there were arrested from *mauza* Dehgaon, *pargana* Mahalpur.

P 153. . . . *to Nawwab Sikandar Begam.* Hopes that the description given by Saiyid Ahmad Ali about the insurgents, who came from Garhi Ambapani, and the report of the *thanadar* and *tahsildar* of Mahalpur and Garhi would make everything absolutely clear. Besides a huge British army has marched from Bhilsa and will be in Bhopal the next day. Dated 19 *Rabi* I, 1275 AH (28 October 1858).

P155. *Muhammad Raza Husain to Nawwab Sikandar Begam.* Sends the letter received from Saiyid Imtiaz Ali, *thanadar* of *pargana* Jogigarh, along with the statement of Abu Karar of *mauza* Sangal, informing about the insurgent forces. Dated 19 *Rabi* I, 1275 AH(28 October 1858).

It contains the order that the letter may be sent to Lala Paltu Lal, *muhafiz-i daftar-i insha*, for inclusion in the register and keeping in the *daftar*. A copy of the order may be sent to Muhammad Raza Husain, *nazim-i junub* through *madar al-maham,* directing him that the contingent which is with him, besides the contingent of *jagirdars* and the soldiers employed by the people, should be called and kept with him and pursue the insurgent army. If their number is large, the information should immediately be give to the government. Dated 20 *Rabi* I, 1275 AH (29 October 1858).

P 157. *Imtiaz Ali*, Thanadar *of Jogigarh, to Muhammad Raza Husain,* Nazim-i Junub. Informs that day; the 20th *Rabi* I, 1275 AH, Abu Karar of *mauza* Sangal, *pargana* Mahalpur, came and whatever he stated was recorded and presented before him. Dated 20 *Rabi* I, 1275 AH (29 October 1858).

It contains the order that the letter and statement may be sent to Nawwab Sikandar Begam.

P 159. *Statement of Abu Karar of* Mauza *Sangal Recorded in the Presence of Imtiaz Ali,* Thanadar *of Jogigarh.* States that his name is Abu, his father's name is Dharmun, caste karar, and he is a dweller of *mauza* Sangal. Further states that the army of peshwa came in *mauza* Dehgaon, *ilaqa* Mahalpur, and had fully intermingled with the inhabitants of that place. They were making loot and destruction there. They captivated the *thanadar* and *tahsildar* of Garhi Ambapani and the *thanadar* and the *tahsildar* of Mahalpur. Some of his forces went to Bhilsa, the rest of the forces were there and were intending to go to Raisen. When he went further, he saw that a huge army was encamping in Mahalpur. He then fled from there. He did not know where they went from there. A soldier was saying that there were 14, 000 armymen and 7,000 went to Kalyakhery.

P 161. Qila'dar *of Jogigarh to Nawwab Sikandar Begam.* Informs that day; the 19th *Rabi* I, 1275 AH, he received a letter from Shaikh Rahim Bakhsh, *tahsildar* of *pargana* Jogigarh, informing that as soon as he heard the news of the arrival of insurgent forces in Garhi Ambapani and *pargana* Mahalpur, he sent the information to the government. Informs he has made all possible arrangements in the fort and he is fully alert. Dated 19 *Rabi* I, 1275 AH (28 October 1858).

P 163. *Bhawani Prasad to Nawwab Sikandar Begam.* Refers to the receipt of the letter of Umrao Daulah along with the letter of Hidayat Ali, *jamadar* of Gulgaon, informing the arrival of insurgent forces at a distance of 4 *curoh* from Bhilsa creating hinderances for the British forces and directing him to bring the matter into the notice of the Political Agent. Informs that the Political Agent has been informed and as ordered, the copies of the letters would be presented before him. Dated 19 *Rabi* I, 1275 AH (28 October 1858).

P 165. *Bhawani Prasad to Nawwab Sikandar Begam.* Informs of the receipt of the letter of Umrao Daulah along with the letter of *thanadar* and *tahsildar* of Diwanganj, informing about the fleeing of the inhabitants of Bhilsa, the arrival of British forces on the bank of river Neon at a distance of 3 *curoh* from Bhilsa, and encamping of insurgent forces at Hinda, *pargana* Bhilsa, and directing him to bring it to the notice of the Political Agent. Informs that he immediately went to the bungalow of the Political Agent to inform him in the matter. He heard and asked him to present the gist of these papers before him. Dated 19 *Rabi* I, 1275 AH (28 October 1858).

PP 167-8. *Madho Kishan,* Amil, *and Saiyid Harhar Ali,* Thanadar *of* Mahal *Udaipura, to Nawwab Sikandar Begam.* Informs that on the previous day; 18th *Rabi* I, 1275 AH, a letter of Harsahai, *tahsildar* of Bamhuri was received informing that as desired by the *tahsildar* and *thanadar* of Garhi Ambapani, all the forces of *thana* and *mahal* were sent to him as the insurgent forces had devastated the *mauzas* of Aradmau, Jaitpur, *pargana* Garhi Ambapani, and has requested for 20 soldiers for managing the *chauki* and for the management of *mahal* Bamhuri by the soldiers of *mahal* and *thana* Udaipura. Informs, as requested by him, 20 soldiers of his mahal were sent to Bamhuri. Informs that day Karim Khan and Mangal Beg, soldiers who were sent to Bhilsa to purchase horses, came back and stated that the British forces arrived in the adjoining region of Bhilsa and from the other side the insurgent forces were coming. They, thereafter, reached Garhi Ambapani and saw that the insurgent forces had devastated Garhi Ambapani. The houses of *mahal* and *thana* were set on fire. The insurgent forces had 2,000 *sawars,* besides the foot-soldiers. Says although the dwellers of the *mahal* after hearing the news, were scared he was trying to pacify them. He would do whatever would be possible for him to do, he assures. Dated 19 *Rabi* I, 1275 AH (28 October 1858).

P 169. *Bhawani Prasad to Nawwab Sikandar Begam.* Informs of the receipt of the letter of Daulat Rai, *nazim*, along with the letter of *tahsildar* and *thanadar* of *pargana* Garhi besides the statement of Hemraj *gumashta* and Premdas Mahasangh, to bring it into the notice of the Political Agent. Informs, he brought the matter into the notice of the Political Agent who heard it passionately but remained silent and asked fo[illegible]e gist of these papers. Dated 19 *Rabi* I, 1275 AH (28 October 1858).

PP 171-2. *Bhawani Prasad to Nawwab Sikandar Begam.* Informs that day, the Political Agent told him to convey the Nawwab on his behalf that the insurgents were defeated and would be defeated further. It is certain that they, in a group of 5 or 10, would disperse in different directions. Thus, it should be notified in the entire State of Bhopal that wherever the insurgents are found, they should be killed without any hesitation and none should be left alive. It is to be notified that the forces of the *thana* and *tahsil* would be required to eliminate the insurgents and so they should do accordingly. Dated 19 *Rabi* I, 1275 AH (28 October 1858).

PP. 173 & 175-6. Parwana-i Ishtahari *of Nawwab Sikandar Begam to all her Jagirdars and Other Officials.* Refers to the letter of Bhawani Prasad, dated 19 *Rabi* I, 1275 AH (28 October 1858), informing that day the Political Agent told him that the insurgents were defeated and would be defeated further. It is certain that they, in a group of 5 or 10, would disperse in different directions. Thus, it should be notified in the entire State of Bhopal that wherever the insurgents are found, they should be killed without any hesitation and none should be left alive. It is notified that the forces of *thana* and *tahsil* are required to eliminate the insurgents and so they should do accordingly. Dated 20 *Rabi* I, 1275 AH (29 October 1858).

P 177. *Muhammad Jamal al-Din Khan,* Madar al-Maham, *to Nawwab Sikandar Begam.* Informs that as ordered, dated 20 *Rabi* I, 1275 AH, mentioned on the top of the letter of Bhawani Prasad, 160 notifications are published from *Matba' Sikandari* and sent to her. Dated 20 *Rabi* I, 1275 AH (29 October 1858).

P 179. *Muhammad Sa'd al-Din, Muhtamim, Adalat-i Faudari, to Nawwab Sikandar Begam.* Informs that Hafiz Sadr al-Din, *muhtamim, chaukiyat*, was sent to Bhilsa to inquire about the insurgents. A letter was received from him, informing that he went upto Diwanganj where the army was led by General Mitchell. He heard from some armymen that few insurgent forces went to Ghyaspur and others to Siwans. So, he came back from that place. Dated 20 *Rabi* I, 1275 AH (29 October 1858).

File No. 297, D
Box No. 16
No. of Documents 26

P 181. *Hafiz Sadr al-Din to Muhammad Sa'd al-Din.* Informs, as directed, he was going to Sanchi Khera to get the news of the insurgents. When he reached Diwanganj, he saw a huge British army, entering Diwanganj and encamping there. He heard from a *sawar* that some insurgents are in Ghyaspur and some have gone to *mahal* Raisen. Dated 19 *Rabi* I, 1275 AH(28 October 1858).

PP 183-4. *Daulat Rai,* Nazim-i Mashriq, *to Nawwab Sikandar Begam.* Refers to her *parwana,* dated 19 *Rabi* I, 1275 AH, which is regarding the deployment of Hafiz Hasan Khan, *naib bakhshi*, to deal with the insurgents and have passion as the royal army is about to come. Says, everything belongs to her and she is taking utmost care of everyone. He too is fully ready to serve her in the best possible manner. Informs upon hearing the news of the arrival of insurgents in Dehgaon, he reached there along with the forces and is present in Raisen. Dated 20 *Rabi* I, 1275 AH (29 October 1858).

It contains the order that the letter may be sent to Lala Paltu Lal, *muhafiz-i daftar-i insha*, for inclusion in the register and keeping in the *daftar*. A copy of the order may be sent to *Daulat Rai, nazim-i mashriq*, through *madar al-maham,* expressing anxiety that insurgents are ruining inhabitants and he is writing in view of safety of the inhabitants. He did not go to launch attack on the insurgents which means he is befooling her. Dated 22 *Rabi* I, 1275 AH (31 October 1858).

PP 185-8. *Daulat Rai,* Nazim-i Mashriq, *to Nawwab Sikandar Begam.* Informs, that day Saiyid Abd al-Ali came and stated that on 18th of the month, Tantia Tope and Rao Sahab along with a huge army entered Garhi. He along with others went to fight with them. He and others like Shaikh Ihsan Ali, *tahsildar*, Shahzad Rai, were arrested by men of Tantia Tope and were brought before him. He told them to make arrangement of *sarbrah-i rasad* or they all would be killed. The insurgents have destroyed Dehgaon and they intend to go to Bamhuri and Deori. Dated 20 *Rabi* I, 1275 AH (29 October 1858).

PP 189-90. *Muhammad Sa'd al-Din to Nawwab Sikandar Begam.* Refers to the letter of Daulat Rai, *nazim-i mashriq,* addressed to the government with the instruction to inform the General about the content of the letter. But the General does not know Urdu at all. Hence, the letter is sent back. Dated 20 *Rabi* I, 1275 AH (29 October 1858).

P 191. Parwana *of Nawwab Sikandar Begam to Daulat Rai,* Nazim-i Mashriq. Expresses anxiety that for the last three days no post has been received from the *mahals* of district east, although it is true that due to the presence of insurgents in Garhi Ambapani, the posts from Garhi Ambapani and Mahalpur might not come. But the posts not coming from other *mahals* of district east reflects his negligence. Directs him to report immediately the reasons behind no posts being received from these *mahals*. Also, inform about the forces of Peshwa, Adil Muhammad Khan and others. Dated 20 *Rabi* I, 1275 AH (29 October 1858).

P 193. *A Letter in Devanagari.*

P 195. *Transliteration of a Hindi/Devanagari Letter of Pratab Singh and Lal Singh,* Jamadars, *Commanding at Sanchi Kanakhera*. Informs, it is heard that the insurgents after fleeing from Muhammad Garh, Basodah have gone to Qila Garhi and the British forces have arrived at Bhilsa. Dated 20 *Rabi* I, 1275 AH (29 October 1858).

PP 197-8. Parwana *of Nawwab Sikandar Begam to Bhawani Prasad.* Sends the report submitted by Shams al-Din, dated 19 *Rabi* I, 1275 AH, received from Baqi Muhammad Khan, informing that the insurgent forces have reached Garhi Ambapani and Mahalpur, besides the letter of the *nazim* sent to him earlier to bring it into the notice of the Political Agent. It is also added that as per the description of Mir Ahmad Ali, the insurgents of Bishankhera having cannon and arrows with them are at Barkheri with 5 cannon. The matter may be brought to the notice of the Political Agent and his reply may be communicated to her. Dated 20 *Rabi* I, 1275 AH (29 October 1858).

P 199. *Bhawani Prasad to Nawwab Sikandar Begam.* Refers to a letter of Lala Daulat Rai, *Nazim-i Mashriq*, along with a news-report of Ahmad Ali, informing that the insurgents have entered Garhi Ambapani, besides the letter of Munshi Dhar, *thanadar* of Raisen. Informs that the matter was immediately brought to the notice of Political Agent. A copy of the news-report was submitted to the office of the Political Agent. The original one is sent back to her. Dated 20 *Rabi* I, 1275 AH (29 October 1858).

P 201. *Tika Ram to Nawwab Sikandar Begam.* Informs that, as directed, he sent a bullock rider to *mauza* Kolhwa, *pargana* Ramgarh, to bring the news of the insurgents. He came back and reported that he visited the said village, besides other two villages and asked the people and farmers about the insurgents. But found no sign of the insurgents there. Dated 20 *Rabi* I, 1275 AH

(29 October 1858).

P 203. *Husain Khan to Nawwab Sikandar Begam.* Sends the report about the insurgents who have entered Garhi Ambapani, submitted by Khubchand who was at Garhi Ambapani and has come to Bhopal.

PP 205-09. *News-Report of Garhi Ambapani by Khubchand*, Mutasaddi. Reports that on 17 *Rabi* I, 1275 AH, Balahi reported in the *thana* that the insurgents arrived in *mauza* Aradmau. Meantime, Hemraj, a dweller of Garhi, came and stated that he had gone to *mauza* Aradmau for the distribution of seeds and manure where he heard that 2,000 or 2,500 *sawars* and foot-soldiers of the insurgent forces have entered in the said *mauza*. They demanded gram from him. He gave them 40 maunds of gram for their horses. The dwellers of Garhi, when they heard about the insurgents, fled from their houses. The *thanadar* tried his best to pacify them. But they did not pay heed to him. The *thanadar* and *tahsildar* of Mahalpur were arrested by the insurgents. On 19th of the month, he arrived in Raisen where he saw that the people were fleeing from there.

PP 211-12. *Harsahai,* Tahsildar, *to Nawwab Sikandar Begam.* Refers to his earlier letter, informing the crossing of the insurgents from the *naka* of Garhi Ambapani and devastating *mauza* Aradmau and Jaitpur, *mahal* Garhi. Says, he has asked for 20 soldiers from *thana* Udaipura for the safety of the *qasba*. In the meantime, Tantia Tope and Rao Sahab with an army of 10, 000 to 12,000 arrived and seiged Bamhuri. The soldiers fled leaving him alone. He and the *thanadar*, besides others, were made captives by them. He and the *muharrir* freed themselves from their captivity. The insurgent army, whatever they found; edible oil, flour, salt, rice, gram, etc. looted it. It is also heard that the insurgents arrested the *thanadar* and *tahsildar* of Garhi and Mahalpur. They did not have cannon with them. Says, in a few days he would come to know about the situation in Chhatari,

Solwani, Udaipura, Deori and Bareilly and would bring it to her notice. Dated 20 *Rabi* I, 1275 AH (29 October 1858).

PP 213-14. *Wazir Khan,* Qila'dar, *to Nawwab Sikandar Begam.* Informs on 17 *Rabi* I, 1275 AH he heard that about 4,000 insurgents arrived at Dhampur, situating at a distance of 3 *curoh* from Siwans and they have firm intention to come to Siwans. Says, hearing the news, he ordered the army to get ready. Dated 20 *Rabi* I, 1275 AH (29 October 1858).

PP 215-16. *News-Report of Rao Sher Singh.* The report given by Rao Sher Singh is that on 17th *Rabi* I, 1275 AH the army led by Tantia Tope arrived in Aradmau, situating at a distance of 3 *curoh* from Garhi. Hearing the news, he along with others like Abd al-Rahamn, *thanadar*, and Abd al-Ali, *tahsildar*, reached Ambapani. Further reports that he did not dare to stand before the insurgent forces as their number was too large while they were only a few. Dated 19 *Rabi* I, 1275 AH (28 October 1858).

PP 217-18. *Wazir Khan,* Qila'dar, *to Nawwab Sikandar Begam.* Informs that Raja Budhkar Sai Sirmauwala has conveyed through his *wakil*, Hafiz Muhammad, that the insurgent forces have arrived at Bamhuri and they are intending to go to *qasba* Solwani the next day. Due to this, the dwellers of Solwani fled from Sirmau and took shelter in the mountains of Sirmau. Even the *thanadar* and *tahsildar* of Solwani and Sirmau have fled. The gonds of the district are with the insurgents. The insurgents further plan to go to Siwans. Dated 20 *Rabi* I, 1275 AH (29 October 1858).

PP 219-20. *Saiyid Yad Ali,* Tahsildar, *to Nawwab Sikandar Begam.* Informs it is heard that the insurgents have gone to Siwans. They have also entered in Garhi and Bamhuri. Hearing the news, all the dwellers of Bamhuri and Udaipura fled and hid in the mountains. In view of this, he sent letters to the *tahsildar* and *thanadar* of Deori to be cautious and alert. Says that, she is aware about the contingent which is in *thana* and *mahal* as they are not more than 21 soldiers. Assures that he would not hesitate in fighting with the insurgents if the situation demands so. Requests for providing assistance. Dated 20 *Rabi* I, 1275 AH (29 October 1858).

PP 221-22. *Saiyid Qadir Ali,* Thanadar *of Deori, to Nawwab Sikandar Begam.* Informs that day, the 20th *Rabi* I, 1275 AH, it is heard that the army led by Adil Muhammad Khan devastated the market in Siwans and then reached Garhi Ambapani. They intend to come to Deori. Hearing the news of fleeing of the dwellers of Bamhuri and Udaipura, all the dwellers of Deori are scared. Though he is pacifying them but they do not listen to him, and rather ask as to how many forces are in *tahsil* and *thana* who would protect them. Expresses apprehension that if they enter in the *pargana*, there would be great trouble. Dated 20 *Rabi* I, 1275 AH (29 October 1858).

PP 223-4. *Daulat Rai,* Nazim-i Mashriq*, to Nawwab Sikandar Begam.* Refers to her *parwana*, dated 20 *Rabi* I, asking about the insurgents and expressing anxiety on his negligence. Says he is so perturbed for the last two or three days that he forgot even his meal, what to talk of negligence. About the news of the insurgents, he has already informed her on 20 *Rabi* I, through a camel rider. Says, due to hinderances and as the insurgents have blocked the roads, the posts from Solwani Bamhuri, Deori and Chhatari have completely stopped. From the letter of Durga Prasad, *thanadar* of Ghairatganj, it is learnt that the insurgents have set on fire the *thana* and *mahal* of Garhi and destroyed it. Dated 21 *Rabi* I, 1275 AH (30 October 1858).

PP 225-6 & 295-6. *Statement of Tika Singh, Soldier,* Thana *Garhi.* States that his name is Tika Singh, his father's name is Nihal Singh, caste Rajput, and aged 25 years. States the day the insurgents reached Garhi he along with the *thanadar*, *tahsildar* and others fled from the *thana*. They reached *mauza* Nadyakhera, *pargana* Mahalpur, where the *thanadar* and *tahsildar* of Mahalpur also joined them. Meantime, the insurgent forces reached there and arrested them. They kept them in captivity for the whole night. They released the soldiers but took away the *thanadar* and *tahsildar*. He was with them upto Rajghati. Thereafter, he sneaked from there. About the number of insurgents, he said there were 6,000 *sawars* and 10 elephants. Their intention was to go across river Narmada or to Deccan or Bhopal. Dated 20 *Rabi* I, 1275 AH (29 October 1858).

P 227. *Letter of Abd Ali*, Naib Nazim, *Dated 21 Rabi I, 1275 AH which is in Regard to Execute the Order Given in the Matter of Abd al-Rauf, Through the Letter of the* Wakil.

PP 229-30. *Muhammad Raza Husain Khan to Nawwab Sikandar Begam.* Sends the letter received from the *tahsildar* of *pargana* Jogigarh, dated 21 *Rabi* I, 1275 AH, along with the transliteration of the letter of Gori Lal, *mustajir* of *mauza* Khamarya, *pargana* Jogigarh, and the statement of Nanhey Khan and Khushhal Singh, the soldiers, accompanying Lala Chandulal, *tahsildar, pargana* Garhi Ambapani, informing that the insurgents have devastated Bamhuri and the *sawars* of the insurgents have arrived at *mauza* Patya, *pargana* Mahalpur, and *mauza* Aradmau, *pargana* Jogigarh, under the jurisdiction of *Sarkar Buzurg*. Dated 21 *Rabi* I, 1275 AH (30 October 1858).

P 235. *Rahim Bakhsh,* Tahsildar, *and Saiyid Imtiaz Ali,* Thanadar *to Muhammad Raza Husain*. Sends a report of the happenings from dawn till night which pertains to the news of destruction of Bamhuri, the arrival of *sawars* of insurgents in *mauza* Patya, *pargana* Mahalpur, and in *mauza* Aradmau, *pargana* Jogigarh, the arrest of *thanadar* and *tahsildar* of Mahalpur and fleeing of *tahsildar* and *thanadar* of Garhi. Dated 21 *Rabi* I, 1275 AH (30 October 1858).

P 237. *Transliteration of the Letter of Gorelal,* Mustajir

of Khamarya Sonepur, and Khubchand, Mustajir *of Amrai*. Khubchand of Amrai reports that he had gone to *mauza* Dehgaon where he saw that the *tahsildar* and *thanadar* of Mahalpur were imprisoned and the weapons of the soldiers were snatched. On Thursday, there will be more forces in Dehgaon and it is heard that the forces have reached Mahalpur.

P 239. *Muhammad Raza Husain to Nawwab Sikandar Begam.* Sends the letter received from Lala Manik Chand, *tahsildar, pargana* Bari, dated 21 *Rabi* I, 1275 AH, along with a letter of Ganga Ram, *malguzar* of *mauza* Dobahi, addressed to the *tahsildar,* informing about the disturbances in Bamhuri and Mahalpur and arresting of the *thanadar*. Dated 21 *Rabi* I, 1275 AH (30 October 1858).

File No. 297, E
Box No. 16
No. of Documents 26

PP 242-3. *Nanakchand*, Tahsildar, Pargana *Bari to Muhammad Raza Husain*. Informs that on 20 *Rabi* I, 1275 AH, Puran Kotwar, *pargana* Bari, along with 4 soldiers came in the *thana* and presented a letter of Gangaram, *malguzar*. In the letter, it is mentioned that the insurgent forces entered Bamhuri and destroyed it and arrested the *thanadar* of Mahalpur. Says, to know the reality he has sent Shaikh Ramazan and Akbar Khan, the soldiers. A report will be sent after their return.

PP 245-6. *Bhawani Prasad to Nawwab Sikandar Begam.* Refers to her *parwana,* received through Lala Ramden, dated 20 *Rabi* I, 1275 AH, which is regarding the insurgents who are in Garhi Ambapani with 5 cannon and that a huge army is in Siwans. Informs that every matter was brought to the notice of the Political Agent. Dated 21 *Rabi* I, 1275 AH (30 October 1858).

It contains the order that the letter may be sent to Paltu Lal, *muhafiz-i daftar-i insha*, for inclusion in the register and keeping in the *daftar*. A copy of the order may be sent to Bhawani Prasad informing that any news about the insurgents which arrives there is communicated first to the Agent to the Governor-General and then to the Political Agent.

P 247. *Muhammad Mustaqim to Nawwab Sikandar Begam.* Informs, it is heard that the insurgents have entered Bamhuri and captured it. That day they came in *mauza* Bareilly. Says, there are only 4 soldiers and there is apprehension as to how to face the insurgent forces. Requests for providing forces to fight with the insurgents. Dated 21 *Rabi* I, 1275 AH (30 October 1858).

P 249. Parwana-i Ishtahari *Issued to her three* Nazims. Directs them to inform her every day and every hour about the activities of the insurgents. There should not be any negligence. The report of the insurgents should bear the information about the place of their stay and to be communicated to her every hour.

P 251. *Ramden,* Peshdast Wakil*, to Nawwab Sikandar Begam.* Says, the Political Agent that day told Aesri Prasad that the ruler of Bhopal knows the tricks as to how to make fools. This is the time to work fast. Sends a letter in English received from the Political Agent for notification in the State of Bhopal.

It contains the order that the letter may be sent to Paltu Lal, *muhafiz-i daftar-i insha*, for inclusion in the register and keeping in the *daftar*. A copy of the order along with the notification addressed to *Bakhshi* Murawwat Muhammad Khan may be sent to *madar al-maham* for printing 738 notifications from *matba' Sikandari* and send it to the government. Dated 29 *Rabi* I, 1275 AH.

P 253. *Baqi Muhammad Khan to Nawwab Sikandar Begam.* Informs of a letter from Ajodhya Prasad, *thanadar* of Gulgaon, dated 20 *Rabi* I, 1275 AH, as reported by Gulab Patwari of *mauza* Kanakhera which informs that about 1,000 *sawars* and foot-soldiers of the British army have gone to Bhopal.

P 255. *Ajodhya Prasad,* Thanadar *of Gulgaon, to Baqi Muhammad Khan.* Says, that day he received a letter from Gulab Patwari of *mauza* Kanakhera from Madwai, informing that about 1,000 British soldiers, comprising of *sawars* and foot-soldiers are encamping at Bhilsa and will go to Bhopal. Besides, Seth Hirday Chand who along with all his goods was going to Bari was looted at Narwar Khera by the insurgents and, thus, he came back. It is also heard that Adil Muhammad Khan has devastated Sanched, Mahalpur and Dehgaon. Dated 20 *Rabi* I, 1275 AH (29 October 1858).

P 257. *Transliteration of a Hindi Letter of Wazir Khan,* Jamadar *of* Thana *Gulgaon, to Ajodhya Prasad,* Thanadar *and* Tahsildar. Informs the situation is that the British forces are encamping at Bhilsa and are intending to go to Bhopal. Their number is 1,000 to 1,500. It is also heard that Seth Hirday Chand of Bhilsa was going to his shop at Bari. At Narwar Khera, some miscreants looted him. It is heard that he had about one lakh cash in his possession. It is also heard that Adil Muhammad Khan has devastated Siwans, Mahalpur and Dehgaon.

P 259. *Muhammad Lal,* Tahsildar *of Bareilly, to Nawwab Sikandar Begam.* Refers to a letter received from *mahal* Bamhuri asking for 15 soldiers from *mahal* Bareilly for the safety of *mahal* Bamhuri. Says, he was preparing to send the soldiers, meanwhile, he heard that the insurgent forces entered in Bamhuri and intend to come to Bareilly. The dwellers of Bareilly upon hearing the news fled from their villages and *qasba*. Requests that his *pargana* and other *parganas* should be taken care of and should be saved from the hands of the insurgents. Dated 21 *Rabi* I, 1275 AH (30 October 1858).

P 261. *Daulat Rai,* Nazim-i Mashriq, *to Nawwab Sikandar Begam.* Informs that the insurgents reached Garhi. The houses of *thanadar* and the *tahsildar* were set on fire and Abd al-Rahman, *thanadar* and Chandulal, *tahsildar* of Garhi, Lala Chaturbhuj, Munshi Abd al-Ali, *naib nazim*, Shaikh Ihsan Ali, *tahsildar*, Lala Shahzad Rai, were arrested and taken away. Munshi Abd al-Rahman, *naib nazim,* and Lala Chaturbhuj were released who came to meet him in Raisen. Their statement is sent to her. The *thanadar* and *tahsildar* of Garhi and Mahalpur are yet to be released from the captivity of the insurgents. Dated 21 *Rabi* I, 1275 AH (30 October 1858).

PP 263-4. *Muhammad Sa'd al-Din to Nawwab Sikandar Begam.* Informs that General Pitcher is getting angry as he is not yet receiving the news about the insurgents and inquiring again and again about such news. Dated 21 *Rabi* I, 1275 AH (30 October 1858).

It contains the order that the letter may be sent to Paltu Lal, *muhafiz-i daftar-i insha*, for inclusion in the register and keeping in the *daftar*. A copy of the order may be sent to Muhammad Sa'd al-Din, *muhtamim, adalat-i faujdari,* communicating that the *thanadars* and *tahsildars* of Garhi and Mahalpur were captured by the insurgent forces, hence, no news was received from those *mahals* about the encampment and movement of the insurgent forces.

PP 265-6. *Shaikh Nur Muhamad,* Thanadar *of Siwans, to Nawwab Sikandar Begam.* Informs the previous day, on 20 *Rabi* I, 1275 AH, it was heard from Ghasi, soldier, that a huge army of the insurgents has arrived at Lakhnauti, *ilaqa* Bhilsa, situating at a distance of 9 *curoh* from there. To know the reality he sent Lal Singh, peon, to Lakhnauti. That day he came back and reported that presently, Amanat Khan, *bakhshi*, with a large number of *sawars* and foot-soldiers is encamping, waiting for the arrival of Adil Muhammad Khan from Bundelkhand. It was also heard that Hattey Singh, *Chokawala*, with a contingent of 2,000 is hiding in the mountains. Informs that he has prepared himself to arrest Hattey Singh. Dated 21 *Rabi* I, 1275 AH.

PP 267-71. *Chaturbhuj to Nawwab Sikandar Begam.*

Informs about the atrocities of the insurgent forces in Garhi and Dehgaon and says that, on 17 *Rabi* I, 1275 AH, an informer came in the *thana* and reported that the insurgents entered in the village and destroyed it. Hearing the news, he along with Saiyid Abd al-Ali, *naib nazim*, Chandulal and Abd al-Rahman are taking rounds of the *qasba*. Says, in the meantime, a letter of Wazir Khan, *qila'dar*, came from Siwans asking for two battalions, hence, the battalion was sent to Siwans by the *thanadar* of Garhi.

PP 273-4. *Muhammad Abbas Ali,* Thanadar *of Bamhuri, to Nawwab Sikandar Begam.* Informs that on 18 *Rabi* I, 1275 AH, 20 soldiers were sent to Garhi to help the *tahsildar* of Garhi. On 19th, they came back and stated that Garhi was devastated by the insurgents. Meanwhile, when he was in the mosque for prayer, some papers of the *thanadar* of Ghairatganj came through the post from Ghairatganj informing about the destruction of Bamhuri by insurgent forces who were 10, 000 and about the fleeing of the *thanadar* and *tahsildar* of Garhi, setting on fire the building of *kachehry*, and the intention of the insurgent forces to go to Bari. Meanwhile, a noise was heard that warned to be aware as the insurgent forces have entered. Thus, the soldiers and dwellers as well fled from there. Some *sawars* came towards him. He was caught besides the *jamadar* and Hukum Chand Seth. They were brought to Bamhuri where he saw that thousands of *sawars* and foot-soldiers, just like ant and locust, are spread everywhere. Then, he was presented before Tantia Tope. In the evening, he was presented before Rao Sahab. Dated 22 *Rabi* I, 1275 AH (31 October 1858).

PP 275-6. *Wazir Khan to Nawwab Sikandar Begam.* Informs of a letter of Ali Ahmad, *tahsildar*, and Muhammad Abd al Qadir, *thanadar* of Solwani, informing that the insurgents have reached Bamhuri and arrested the *thanadar* and has demanded forces from him. Informs that as requested by him, he sent Raja Badankar there. Dated 22 *Rabi* I, 1275 AH(31 October 1858).

It contains the order that the letter may be sent to Paltu Lal, *muhafiz-i daftar-i insha*, for inclusion in the register and keeping in the *daftar*. A copy of the order may be sent to Wazir Khan, *qila'dar,* intimating him that for the last two years he has been demanding arms and ammunitions. But when time came to fight, he was not seen anywhere except under the fort or over the mountains. God knows what happened to his bravery and loyalty to the salt. He did not yet write which *parganas* of Bhopal State were destroyed by the insurgent forces and where the insurgent forces were encamping. It will not be good for him if he did not reply to all these questions satisfactorily and promptly. Dated 25 *Rabi* I, 1275 AH (3 November 1858).

P 277. *Muhammad Sa'd al-Din to Nawwab Sikandar Begam.* Refers to a letter of Kishan Rai, *madar al-maham* in reference to the letter of Munshi Raza Husain, *nazim-i junub* from Kalyakheri, informing that the insurgents are presently in and around Garhi Ambapani, Mahalpur and Dehgaon, and to bring the news into the notice of the British officials is a must. Informs that the previous day, when General Pitcher and other British officials were to meet the Political Agent, he met them and communicated the content of the letter of *mutamid al-maham* to the General. The General asked whether the insurgents were still there. He replied that till the writing of the letter they were there. The General heard him and said nothing. To inform her in the matter was a must which he did. Dated 22 *Rabi* I, 1275 AH (31 October 1858).

P 279. *Bhawani Prasad to Nawwab Sikandar Begam.* Informs of a letter from Captain Comming, dated 30 October 1858 to Richards from the army headed by General Mitchell who entered Bhilsa, informing that there is a report that the insurgents have marched from Ghairatganj and reached Bhojpur, Kalyakhery and Deep and there is a need to be cautious. The Political Agent said everything was okay as the Nawwab did not yet say anything about it. Says he told him that if the insurgents had reached Deep which is 6 *curoh* from Bhopal, the Nawwab would have been aware about it and the news would have reached there too. It seems to be a false news unless a *parwana* of Nawwab is received in this regard. The Political Agent said, whether the news is right or wrong, it should be confirmed by the Nawwab and she should inform him accordingly. Dated 22 *Rabi* I, 1275 AH (31 October 1858).

P 281. *Saiyid Mustafa,* Qila'dar *of Jogigarh, to Nawwab Sikandar Begam.* Informs that the previous day, Lala Chandulal, *tahsildar*, *pargana* Garhi, who fell prey to the insurgent forces got himself freed from their captivity and came to him. He stated about the story of his captivity. He further said that the leaders of the insurgent forces were Tantia Tope and Rao Sahab. The statement of the *tahsildar* is recorded and sent to her. Dated 22 *Rabi* I, 1275 AH (31 October 1858).

P 283. *Ghulam Murtaza Khan to Nawwab Sikandar Begam.* Sends the letter received from Muhammad Lal, *tahsildar*, and Muhammad Mustaquim Khan, *thanadar* of Bareilly, dated 19 *Rabi* I, 1275 AH, informing about the insurgency in Garhi and the devastation of *mauza* Aradmau as reported by Chandulal, *tahsildar* of Garhi.

P 285. *Muhammad Mustaquim Khan to Ghulam Murtaza Khan,* Kamdar, *Deorhi Khas*. Refers to the letter of *thanadar* and *tahsildar* of *pargana* Bamhuri, dated 18 *Rabi* I, 1266 *fasli*, informing that the insurgent forces destroyed *mauza* Aradmau and Jaitpur. It is must that he should immediately send 15 soldiers there. Says, he immediately executed the orders given by the *tahsildar* and *thanadar*. Dated 19 *Rabi* I, 1275 AH.

P 287. *Daulat Rai,* Nazim-i Mashriq, *to Nawwab*

Sikandar Begam. Informs that day, he received a letter of Lala Chandulal, *tahsildar* of Garhi, who fell prey to the insurgent forces who informs that on 20 *Rabi* I, 1275 AH he fled from *mauza* Nayagaon, *pargana* Bareilly, along with Shaikh Ihsan Ali, *tahsildar*, Shahzad Rai, *thanadar*, Abd al-Rahman, *thanadar* of Garhi and Saiyid Abbas Ali, *thanadar* of Bamhuri and reached *mauza* Bajni, *pargana* Bareilly. As they were being pursued by the insurgent forces, he further ran away and reached Jogigarh near Saiyid Mustafa, *qila'dar* of Jogigarh. The said letter is sent to her. Dated 22 *Rabi* I, 1275 AH.

PP 289-90. *Lala Chandulal,* Tahsildar *to Daulat Rai,* Nazim-i Mashriq. Informs that on 20 *Rabi* I, 1275 AH he fled from *mauza* Nayagaon, *pargana* Bareilly, along with Shaikh Ihsan Ali, *tahsildar*, Shahzad Rai, *thanadar*, Abd al-Rahman, *thanadar* of Garhi and Saiyid Abbas Ali, *thanadar* of Bamhuri and reached *mauza* Bajni, *pargana* Bareilly. As they were being pursued by the insurgent forces, he further ran away and reached Jogigarh near Saiyid Mustafa, *qila'dar* of Jogigarh. Dated 21 *Rabi* I, 1275 AH.

P 291. *Nawwab Shahjahan Begam to Nawwab Sikandar Begam.* Sends the two letters received from Durga Prasad, *thanadar* of Ghairatganj; one is dated 19 *Rabi* I, 1275 AH, along with the statement of Tika Singh, a soldier at Garhi, informing about the insurgents and that there is peace in Ghairatganj. Dated 22 *Rabi* I, 1275 AH.

P 293. *Durga Prasad,* Thanadar *of Ghairatganj, to Nawwab Shahjahan Begam.* Refers to his previous two letters, informing about the arrival of the insurgent forces and setting on fire the buildings of *tahsil* and *thana* of Bamhuri and that there is peace in *pargana* Ghairatganj. Perhaps due to the insurgency, letters would not have been delivered to her. Hence, two soldiers, carrying the letter are sent there, besides the statement of Tika Singh, soldier of *thana* Garhi, who too was captured by the insurgent forces and later got released from their captivity. His statement has been recorded and sent to her. Dated 20 *Rabi* I, 1275 AH.

P 297. *Durga Prasad,* Thanadar *of Ghairatganj, to Nawwab Shahjahan Begam.* Informs, that day about 1,000 insurgent *sawars* went via Garhi to Dehgaon to join the insurgent forces there. From Lallu, coming to Siwans, it was heard that all the dwellers of Siwans have fled. It is also heard that other 10, 000 force is also coming. It is also heard that 2,000 British forces have arrived at Bagrod in Bhilsa. Requests to send some forces there. Dated 19 *Rabi* I, 1275 AH.

PP 299-300. *Wazir Khan to Nawwab Sikandar Begam.* Informs that day Roshan Khan, *jamadar*, former employee of Thana Ashta, said that the insurgents who were about 3,000, arrested him and others like Abd al-Ali *tahsildar*, Abd al-Rahman, *thanadar* of Garhi, Shahzad Rai, *thanadar* and Nisab Ali, *tahsildar* of Mahalpur, from *qasba* Dehgaon and *pargana* Mahalpur and took them along. At Bamhuri, he was freed after giving him one *angrakha* and they took away all his goods. The *thanadars* and *tahsildars* are still in their custody. Dated 22 *Rabi* I, 1275 AH.

File No. 297, F
Box No. 16
No. of Documents 28

PP 301-02. *Ganaga Sahai,* Thanadar, *to Nawwab Shahjahan Begam.* The information about the coming of insurgents, as communicated by different *thanas* of *mahals* of Solwani and Deori, has been communicated to her through his letter. It is her blessing that there is peace in his region and the dwellers are persuaded not to migrate from their houses due to fear. However, some have fled. He along with the forces of *thana* and *mahal* are performing day-night duty in the court of Garhi in *qasba* Chhatari. Informs that on the previous day he heard from Nandram, *mahajan*, a dweller of *qasba* Udaipura who came from Udaipura that the insurgent forces have gathered at *mauza* Aotha Jiyarah, *ilaqa* Udaipura, situating at a distance of 10 to 12 *curoh* from there. However, with her graceness there is peace in the region of Udaipura, Chhaner, Deori and Chhatari. Although many inhabitants of Udaipura, Deori and Solwani have fled. Some took shelter in the hills, others have taken shelter in the villages across river Narmada. Also, refers to his request to provide relief to the dwellers and he is performing his duties as directed to him. Dated 22 *Rabi* I, 1275 AH.

PP 303-04. *Muhammad Raza Husain to Nawwab Sikandar Begam.* Informs about a letter of Muhammad Mustaquim Khan, *thanadar, pargana* Bareilly, dated 21 *Rabi* I, 1275 AH, informing about the atrocities of the insurgents in *pargana* Bamhuri and intending to enter *pargana* Bareilly and the request of the dwellers to come to their rescue. The same is presented to her for further clarification. Also informs that he is waiting for the arrival of General Pitcher and Major Heman to accompany them as directed through her letter, dated 21 *Rabi* I, 1275 AH. Also refers to the request of *thanadar* and *tahsildar* of *pargana* Jogigarh for providing 50 soldiers for the rescue of the dwellers of *mahal* Bareilly, and informs that the request has been fulfilled. Dated 22 *Rabi* I, 1275 AH.

PP 305-06. *Muhammad Mustaquim Khan,* Thanadar *of Bareilly, to Muhammad Raza Husain.* Informs it is heard that the insurgent forces reached Bamhuri and captured it. That day it was heard that they entered Bareilly. Hearing the news, the people of the region fled and in *thana* except four soldiers none was left. Requests him to come to that place along with more forces. Dated 21 *Rabi* I, 1275 AH.

PP 307-08. *Bhawani Prasad to Nawwab Sikandar Begam.* Refers to the letter of Daulat Rai, *nazim-i mashriq*, dated 20 *Rabi* I, 1275 AH, informing about Tantia Tope and Rao Sahab, the insurgents, as reported by Saiyid Abd al-Ali, *naib nazim*. Says, he brought the matter into the notice of the Political Agent. The Political

Agent said that it was the only news which reached to him promptly. He also said that such news should be sent to General Mitchell. Dated 22 *Rabi* I, 1275 AH (31 October 1858).

It contains the order that the letter may be sent to Paltu Lal, *muhafiz-i daftar-i insha*, for inclusion in the register and keeping in the *daftar*. A copy of the order may be sent to Bhawani Prasad, *wakil*, communicating that there is no information of the place of encampment of General Mitchell, hence, no report was sent to him whereas reports were sent to Major Teller and others. Directs him to inform the Political Agent about it.

PP 309-10. *Bhawani Prasad to Nawwab Sikandar Begam.* Refers to the letter of Daulat Rai, *nazim-i mashriq*, dated 22 *Rabi* I, 1275 AH, informing that Shaikh Ihsan Ali, Chandulal, *tahsildar*, Saiyid Abbas Ali, *thanadar*, Sehore and Shahzad Rai freed themselves from the captivity of the insurgent forces. Says the matter was brought to the notice of the Political Agent. Dated 23 *Rabi* I, 1275 AH (1 November 1858).

PP 311-12. *Bhawani Prasad to Nawwab Sikandar Begam.* Informs that day, he brought the content of the letter of Daulat Rai, *nazim-i mashriq*, dated 21 *Rabi* I, 1275 AH, which is regarding the march of Tantia Tope from Garhi Ambapani towards Bamhuri, and coming of Adil Muhammad Khan in Garhi Ambapani. The Political Agent told that such news should be first brought to the notice of General Mitchell. Dated 22 *Rabi* I, 1275 AH (31 October 1858).

It contains the order that the letter may be sent to Paltu Lal, *muhafiz-i daftar-i insha*, for inclusion in the register and keeping in the *daftar*. A copy of the order may be sent to Bhawani Prasad, *wakil*, communicating that the Political Agent asks everytime about the authentic news of Tantia Tope whereas she always sends authentic news. But since the news about the insurgents comes from different sources, sometimes it becomes difficult to distinguish as to which new is more authentic.

P 313. *Muhammad Raza Husain to Nawwab Sikandar Begam.* Sends the letter received from the *thanadar* and *tahsildar* of Jogigarh, dated 22 *Rabi* I, 1275 AH, informing about the insurgency in Bamhuri.

P 315. *Rahim Bakhsh,* Tahsildar *and Saiyid Imtiaz Ali, to Muhammad Raza Husain.* The report received from an informer is sent to him. Also informs that the people from Chandpura and other villages of the *pargana* have fled. Dated 22 *Rabi* I, 1275 AH.

PP 317-18. *Statement of Balli in the Presence of Imtiaz Ali,* Thanadar. He is asked to tell as to what he saw in Mahalpur. He replied that there were 4 or 5 soldiers in the *tahsil* and *thana*. He was also asked to tell as to who told him that Tantia Tope had gone to Bamhuri. He replied that, he heard that news from his son who had gone to Siwans. He said that Saiyid Abd al-Ali, Shaikh Ihsan Ali, *tahsildar*, Shahzad Rai, *thanadar* of Bamhuri, Abd al-Rahman and Siayid Abbas Ali were arrested by the insurgent forces.

PP 319-20. *Daulat Rai,* Nazim-i Mashriq, *to Nawwab Sikandar Begam.* Refers to her *parwana,* dated 21 *Rabi* I, 1275 AH, directing him to report every hour the news of the insurgents. Informs that for the date 20 *Rabi* I, 1275 AH, the authentic news is that the insurgents are at Bamhuri and destroyed the *mahal* and villages there. Bamhuri is situated at a distance of 18 *curoh* from Raisen. Since it is a distant place and there is no postal system, hence it is not possible to send the news every hour. It seems that the insurgents have left Bamhuri and after passing through Udaipura and Deori, they went across the river Narmada. Dated 22 *Rabi* I, 1275 AH.

PP 321-2. *Chandulal to Nawwab Sikandar Begam.* Informs that on 18 *Rabi* I, 1275 AH, he along with Saiyid Abd al-Ali, Shaikh Ihsan Ali, *tahsildar*, Shahzad Rai, *thanadar* of Bamhuri, Abd al-Rahman and Siayid Abbas Ali were arrested by the insurgent forces, headed by Tantia Tope and Rao Sahab who were more than

10, 000 in number. They also looted their goods. They, however, managed to escape from their captivity. Dated 22 *Rabi* I, 1275 AH.

PP 323-4. *Saiyid Muhammad Akbar Ali,* Tahsildar, *and Saiyid Abbas Ali,* Thanadar *to Nawwab Sikandar Begam.* Refers to his letter, informing about the arrival of the insurgent forces at Nazarganj and their march to Hoshangabad and the destruction of *pargana* Bari. Further informs about the coming of the insurgent forces in the territory of Bhopal and the destruction of *mauzas* in *pargana* Bamhuri. Dated 22 *Rabi* I, 1275 AH.

P 325. *Muhammad Mustaquim Khan,* Thanadar *of Bareilly, to Nawwab Sikandar Begam.* Refers to his earlier letter, dated 21 *Rabi* I, 1275 AH, informing the coming of the insurgent forces in Bamhuri and their intention to come to Bareilly, and fleeing of the people of the region, and the request for help to deal with these insurgent forces. Informs that day, i.e. 22nd *Rabi* I, the insurgent forces marched from Bamhuri. They crossed the river Narmada at *ghat* Patrora, *ilaqa* Udaipura. They intend to go to Hoshangabad. Their number is about 25,000. Dated 23 *Rabi* I, 1275 AH.

PP 327-8. Parwana *of Nawwab Sikandar Begam to Muhammad Raza Husain.* Directs him that as soon as he receives the *parwana*, he should deploy the *sawars* from Kalyakhery to Udaipura from the *sawars* under the jurisdiction of *nizamat-i junub*, and keep her informed every moment about the news of the insurgents as the Political Agent puts the blame of not getting the news of the insurgents upon her. Warns if there will be any delay in sending the news of the insurgents, it would harm his position. If the insurgent forces move from Udaipura to Deori before the arrival of the *sawars* of posts, they too should move forward and erect *chaukis* at the place where the insurgents are encamped. He himself should erect *chaukis* of posts on those places. The *sawars* of the posts should also be instructed to take rounds looking for the insurgents and should come to know about the exact place of their encampment. If the *thanadar* and *amil* are there, they should try to get confirmation of the place of their encampment and communicate the same to her. If the *thanadar* and *amil* are not there, the confirmation about the place should be taken from the *patwari* in Hindi and the report should be sent regularly.

PP 329-30. *Gangaram,* Muhtamim Karkhanajat, *to Nawwab Sikandar Begam.* Says, he was sent by Abd al-Rahman to bring news of insurgent forces. He went upto Mahalpur where he saw that about 5, 000 forces were there. They stayed at Garhi for a day. They arrested the *thanadar* and *tahsildar* of Mahalpur and looted their goods. Later, they released *thanadar* and *tahsildar.* They came to Dehgaon and devastated it. They did not have cannon, they had only *sawars* and foot-soldiers and the *sawars* were more. They also had elephants and camels in large number.

PP 331-2. *Muhammad Raza Husain to Nawwab Sikandar Begam.* Refers to her *parwana*, received that evening through a camel rider, directing him to deploy the *sawars* present in the *nizamat-i junub* from Kalyakhery to Udaipura for bringing the news of the insurgents at that very moment. In case, the insurgents move further, the other *sawars* of the post should be deployed there. Informs as directed the *chaukis* of the posts of *sawars* were erected from Kalyakhery to Udaipura or at places where the insurgents were encamped and they were instructed, as directed in the *parwana*. Dated 23 *Rabi* I, 1275 AH.

P 333. *Bhawani Prasad to Nawwab Sikandar Begam.* Sends ten letters pertaining to the activities of the insurgents, and the Political Agent himself wrote his comments on them. Dated 23 *Rabi* I, 1275 AH (1 November 1858).

PP 335-6. *Muhammad Raza Husain to Nawwab Sikandar Begam.* Sends the letter received from

Manik Chand, *tahsildar*, *pargana* Bari, along with the transliteration of the letter of Moti. There is no doubt about it that the insurgent forces have arrived in Bareilly situating on the bank of river Narmada. This is also clear from the letter of *tahsildar* and *thanadar* of Mardanpur. There is apprehension that either they would cross river Narmada or they would loot and destroy the adjoining *mauzas*. Suggests that if all the *ghats* are managed by deploying 100 or 200 persons, the insurgent forces could be prevented from crossing the river Narmada and thus, the *parganas* of Jogigarh, Tal and Mardanpur could be saved.

PP 337-8. *Nanak Chand,* Tahsildar, Pargana *Bari, to Muhammad Raza Husain.* Informs that Bijay Singh, soldier of *mahal* Bari, was sent to *mauza* Jangpur to bring the news of the insurgents. On the way, Moti, a soldier, stopped him to go to Jangpur. He came back and stated that the insurgent forces were in Bareilly, Jamgarh and other places. The letter of Moti is sent to him.

PP 339-40. *A Letter in Hindi/Devanagari.*

P 341. *Transliteration of a Hindi/Devanagari Letter of Moti Panda, to Nanak Chand,* Tahsildar. Informs that the insurgents looted Bamhuri and went to Bareilly. The people have fled from their villages. He too is trying to flee. He should remain alert.

PP 343-4. *Statement of Amar Singh, a Soldier and a Servant of Raja Marwan Sai, Bariwala, Recorded Under the Session of Munshi Muhammad Raza Husain.* States that four days before, he had gone with a letter from the *nizamat* to Raja Marwan of Bari. On the previous day, day Sunday, he left for Kalyakhery. One *bhand*, who lived in Bari had gone to Udaipura for beggary, came back from Udaipura and described to the villagers what happened to him there. He said that he was caught by the armymen and asked as to where he came from. He replied that he was a beggar. The armymen said, no, he was an informer of someone and came to assess their position. He was caught by the armymen between Tonga and Begnan, situating at a distance of 4 *curoh* from Udaipura. The armymen did not listen to him and said that he was an informer and not a begger. Meantime, one *wilayati* attacked him with dagger and said if he was a *bhand* he should say some sayings of *bhand*. He recited some slogans of *bhand*. He was then freed and returned hurriedly. He did not know where the forces then went. There were many horses and foot-soldiers with them. He cannot say about their exact number. What he heard there, he said. He was then asked whether he saw from his own eyes the wound of dagger on his body. He replied he saw some scratches of some weapon on his leg. It was not so deep.

PP 345-6. *Radhey Kishan,* Muhtamim, Sair-i Kul, *to Nawwab Sikandar Begam.* Informs that day, i.e. 23rd *Rabi* I, 1275 AH, he received a letter of Mohanlal, *nakedar* of Narwar, *ta'lluqa* Sair Mahalpur, district east, dated 21 *Rabi* I, 1275 AH, addressed to Balaram, *mutasaddi* of the said *sair.* Reports that on Wednesday in the month of Kartik-Jeth Budi, the forces reached Dehgaon and the entire village was looted. The horse and sword of the *darogha* were destroyed. This news reached him through Ram Chandra, soldier, and that he was on the hills. All the dwellers fled and in the *pargana*, riot erupted and it became deserted. The army then went to Bamhuri and it was also devastated. Other reports will be sent as and when it will be received. Dated 23 *Rabi* I, 1275 AH/1 November 1858.

P 347. *Transliteration of a Hindi/Devanagari Letter of Mohan Lal,* Nakedar, Ilaqa *Sair Mahalpur, to Balaram,* Mutasaddi *of the Said Sair.* Reports that the insurgent forces entered Dehgaon and looted all the villages. He too was looted. He reported the matter to the *darogha* of *thana* Dehgaon. He was in the mountains. The villagers have fled. The insurgents then went to Bamhuri. Further report will be sent thereafter.

PP 349-50. *A Letter in Hindi.*

PP 351-2. *Statement of Narsingh, Banjara in the Office of Lala Radhey Kishan,* Muhtamim, *Sair-i Kul.* States that his name is Narsingh, his father's name is Budsingh, caste rajput, guwar rathore, aged 30 years. He was asked to tell as to how many bullocks he had which were loaded with grains from Seth Shiv Das and how many bullocks were taken away by the insurgent forces. He replied that there were 100 bullocks which were loaded with gram from Seth Shiv Das, and 60 bullocks loaded with gram were looted by the insurgents.

PP 353-4. *Saiyid Inayat Ali,* Thanadar *of Mardanpur, to Nawwab Sikandar Begam.* Refers to his letters sent to her earlier, informing about the march of the insurgent forces from Hoshangabad. It has also been reported that the chiefs of the insurgent forces are Tantia Tope, his nephew and Nawwab of Jawra having an army of 15, 000 and 30 elephants. They are yet to cross the river Narmada. Dated 23 *Rabi* I, 1275 AH/1 November 1858.

PP 355-6. Parwana *of Nawwab Sikandar Begam to Daulat Rai,* Nazim-i Mashriq. Directs him that as soon as he receives the *parwana,* he should deploy *sawars* from Raisen to Bamhuri from the *sawars* who are there in the jurisdiction of *nizamat-i mashriq* to bring the posts and keep her informed at every moment about the news of the insurgents as the Political Agent puts the blame on her for not getting the news of the insurgents. Warns if there will be any delay in sending the news of the insurgents, it will harm his position. If the insurgent forces went to Udaipura from Bamhuri before the arrival of the *sawars* of the posts, they too should move forward and erect *chaukis* at the place where the insurgents are encamped. He himself should erect *chaukis* of posts at these places. The *sawars* of the posts should also be instructed to take rounds and should come to know of the exact place of their encampment. If the *thanadar* and *amil* are there, they should get confirmation of the place of their encampment and communicate it to her. If the *thanadar* and *amil* are not there, confirmation about the place should be taken from *patwari* in Hindi and report to be sent regularly.

File No. 297, G
Box No. 16
No. of Documents 29

PP 361-2. *Munammad Hasan Khan to Nawwab Sikandar Begam.* Informs, that day there was peace in the army camp. First, it was heard that a group of insurgents has arrived on low land, then it was heard that they reached on the bank of river Narmada or they crossed the river. To inquire about the coming of the second group of insurgents, he sent two Mewati soldiers of the battalion of Hasan Khan, *jamadar,* accompanying the army to Pura Guna. The information received from them would be passed on to her. In case, the insurgents try to enter in this region, he would take on battle with them. Dated 23 *Rabi* I, 1275 AH/1 November 1858.

PP 363-6. *Muhammad Abd al-Rahman,* Thanadar *of Garhi Ambapani, to Nawwab Sikandar Begam.* Says, through the letter of *naib nazim* she would have come to know about his arrest and the others, and about the release of Saiyid Abd al-Ali, *naib nazim,* and Lala Chaturbhuj. He and Chandulal and Shahzad Rai were brought before Rao Sahab, nephew of Nana Sahab, the chief of the insurgent forces. He ordered to keep them under arrest and take them to Bamhuri. They devastated the entire *qasba* and set it on fire. The *thanadar* of Bamhuri too was arrested and kept with him. They, however, freed themselves from their captivity after a long struggle. The insurgent forces were on the bank of river Narmada and intending to go across the river. Dated 23 *Rabi* I, 1275 AH/1 November 1858.

PP 367-8. *Harsahai,* Tahsildar *of Bamhuri, to Nawwab Sikandar Begam.* Informs that on 20th of the month, Tantia Tope and Rao Sahab, the insurgents marched from Bamhuri and via Khajwara reached *mauza* Chhapara, *pargana* Bareilly. They arrested the *thanadar* and took him along, who at *mauza* Nayagaon got himself freed from their captivity and came back to *mauza* Padarya on 21st *Rabi* I. He described what he saw in the camp, Rao Sahab was the chief of the army and Tantia Tope was his *kamdar*. The Nawwabs of Banda and Bareilly, Muhammad Ali Khan, *risaldar*, and Sikandar Muhammad Khan were also accompanying them.

P 369. *Diwan Daulat Rai to Nawwab Sikandar Begam.* Informs that on 23 *Rabi* I, 1275 AH, Shaikh Muhammad Abd al-Rahman, *thanadar*, Garhi, Shaikh Ihsan Ali, *tahsildar* of Mahalpur, and Lala Shahzad Rai, *thanadar*, *pargana* Sadar, freed themselves from the captivity of the enemy by their own wisdom and in the evening they reached there. They described their army and wrote two letters to the government. The same is sent to her. Dated 24 *Rabi* I, 1275 AH/2 November 1858.

PP 371-2. *Saiyid Inayat Ali,* Thanadar, Pargana *Mardanpur to Nawwab Sikandar Begam.* Informs, that day Ram who was sent by him, came back and informed that one *sawar*, sent by the British officer of the army for suppressing the insurgents in Suhagpur, came and said that a battle was still being fought with the insurgents by the British forces. But the insurgents fled hearing the news of the arrival of the British forces and went to the mountain called Mahadev. In the morning, the British army would reach there to suppress the insurgents. Everyone of them is afraid that if this time they are traced, then where they would go to hide. Also, informs that through Goyal Balahi of *mauza* Khushipur it is heard that one soldier came to the *ghat* of river Narmada called Drapur who said that about 50 rebel *sawars* came to the *zamindars* of *ilaqa* Chhaner and asked for the *rasad* of salt. As a result, many inhabitants of the villages have fled. The insurgents have formed three groups; one group is encamping at Sohanpur, *ilaqa* of the British on the other side of river Narmada; the other group has occupied a part of river Narmada; and the rest is staying on this side and by her grace there is peace.

Dated 24 *Rabi* I, 1275 AH/2 November 1858.

PP 373-4. Parwana *of Nawwab Sikandar Begam to Madho Kishan,* Tahsildar *of Udaipura.* From the letter of Lala Chandulal, *amil* of *pargana* Ambapani, dated 22 *Rabi* I, 1275 AH/31 October 1858, it is heard that on 21 *Rabi* I, 1275 AH, the insurgents entered *mauza* Aontha Chitwara, *pargana* Udaipura, and through the letter of *jamadar* of *thana* Suhagpur, addressed to the British officer at Hoshangabad, an information to this effect has been given by the *amil* and *thanadar* of Murdanpur. It is evident from these references that the insurgents and mischief mongers have entered the British territory from the side of Suhagpur. But in his writing, there is no reference to the date and time whence the insurgents entered there and when they crossed over from his region. Directs him to inform her immediately about the date and time when the insurgents entered in the British territory or the insurgents are still encamping in his jurisdiction. Dated 24 *Rabi* I, 1275 AH/2 November 1858.

PP 375-6. Parwana *of Nawwab Sikandar Begam to Lala Jugal Kishore, Amil of* Pargana *Deori.* To the same effect as the foregoing. Dated 24 *Rabi* I, 1275 AH/2 November 1858.

P 377. Parwana *of Nawwab Sikandar Begam to Daulat Rai,* Nazim-i Mashriq. Expresses anxiety that for the last two years he has been continuously demanding gun powder. But when time came to fight with the enemy, he was not seen anywhere but in the forts or on the mountains. It is really a matter of concern as to what anxiety of God has fallen upon him that he lacks bravery, honesty and sacrifice. He has not informed so far as to how many *parganas* under his jurisdiction have been devastated by the insurgents and what are the places where the insurgents are still encamping. If he considers it good for himself, he should immediately submit the details of all the happenings. There should not be a single minute delay. He should inform about those people of his *ilaqa* who fought with the insurgents and how many insurgents were killed or wounded. Likewise, whether the dwellers were killed or wounded by the insurgents and who were those rebels and culprits arrested by him. Dated 24 *Rabi* I, 1275 AH/2 November 1858.

P 379. Parwana *of Nawwab Sikandar Begam to Three* Nazims *of East, West and South.* These days it is time for all the loyal servants of the government to fight with the insurgents, no matter wherever they are and what is their number. If they die for the royal cause of the government it is as good as this world has to finish one day after all. Then, where is the need to be afraid of and become a cause of anxiety for his master. If he holds a higher office, he would be appreciated. A soldier does nothing except to flee. It is not an act of bravery to have a group of officers or to hold the post of *thanadari* or *tahsildari* or *nizamat* or *risaldari* or *jamadari* and search ways to escape from the insurgents while their hands and legs are tied. It is a known fact that no one would come to rescue such a person. It is strange if a *thanadar* or *tahsildar* or *risaldar* or *jamadar* or *nazim* is caught by the enemy without fighting and nobody is killed by him. Dated 24 *Rabi* I, 1275 AH /2 November 1858.

P 381. *Muhammad Raza Husain to Nawwab Sikandar Begam.* Informs, that day he received a letter of Lala Nanak Chand, *tahsildar* of *pargana* Bari, dated 23 *Rabi* I, 1275 AH/1 November 1858, informing that about 7,000 insurgent forces have crossed river Narmada at the *ghat* in *mauza* Patrora, *pargana* Udaipura, and encamping at *mauza* Sandia, *ilaqa* Hoshangabad, and that about 2,000 insurgents are still in *mauza* Patrora and are intending to cross it. The letter received is being sent to her. Dated 24 *Rabi* I, 1275 AH/2 November 1858.

PP 383-4. *Nanak Chand to Muhammad Raza Husain,* Nazim-i Junub. Informs about the receipt of his letter, dated 23 *Rabi* I, 1275 AH, expressing concern that for the last two days he did not write anything to him. He should inform about the arrangement in the region and about the insurgent forces. Informs that on 21 *Rabi* I, 1275 AH, he sent a report to the *tahsildar* of Bamhuri about the coming of the insurgent forces and the destruction of Bamhuri.

P 385. *Muhammad Akbar Ali,* Tahsildar *of* Pargana *Murdanpur, to Nawwab Sikandar Begam.* Informs that the dwellers are so afraid after hearing the news of the arrival of insurgents that they are intending to flee. However, they were pacified by him and by the grace of God and with her blessings there is peace and calm in his region. Information to this effect was a must which he did. Informs that he is managing the affairs of his region promptly by himself and with the soldiers present there. The information in regard to the affairs of Nudebi would have been communicated to her through the letter of Mir Inayat Ali, *thanadar* of Murdanpur. Dated 24 *Rabi* I, 1275 AH/2 November 1858.

P 387. *Daulat Rai,* Nazim-i Mashriq, *to Nawwab Sikandar Begam.* Informs that Daddu Thakur, a servant of *thana* Bamhuri who brought *dak* from there, said that the insurgent forces crossed river Narmada at the *ghat* in *mauza* Patrora which is under the *mahal* of Udaipura and encamped in *mauza* Chhapara. Some say they are intending to go to Fatahpur and Sohagpur, falling under the territory of the British. The insurgents brought black rice from Bamhuri. They stood on their elephants on the side where there was less water in order to pass the goods and other items. Dated 24 *Rabi* I, 1275 AH/2 November 1858.

PP 389-90. *Statement of Daddu Thakur in the Criminal Court of* Nizamat-i Mashriq *Under the Session of Daulat Rai.* States that his name is Daddu and his father's name is Ganesh, he is a dweller of Bamhuri, and an employee of the government. States that the insurgent forces crossed the river Narmada at *ghat* Patrora and went to the other side of the river.

PP 391-2. *Diwan Daulat Rai,* Nazim-i Mashriq, *to Nawwab Sikandar Begam.* Refers to her *parwana,* dated 23 *Rabi* I, 1275 AH, directing him to establish the posts of *sawars* from Raisen to Bamhuri. Says, there is no *sawar* in the *nizamat*. The *sawars* who are in Siwans and Bheglone are yet to come inspite of his writing to Wazir Khan, *qila'dar*, and Nizam Ali Khan, *risaldar*. Requests if 16 *sawars* are provided to him for deputing at different *chaukis*. Dated 24 *Rabi* I, 1275 AH/2 November 1858.

PP 393-4. *Baqi Muhammad Khan to Nawwab Sikandar Begam.* Sends the letter of Munshi Shamsh al-Din, dated 23 *Rabi* I, 1275 AH/1 November 1858, received from Raisen which is in regard to the activities of insurgents. Dated 24 *Rabi* I, 1275 AH/2 November 1858.

PP 395-6. *Shamsh al-Din Ansari to Baqi Muhammad Khan.* Informs, that day Shaikh Ihsan Ali, *tahsildar*, Shahzad Rai, *thanadar*, and Abd al-Rahim came in Raisen and told Daulat Rai that the insurgent forces have reached Bamhuri. They destroyed 4 shops, including the shop of Seth Kunwar Chand. Abbas Ali, *thanadar*, was arrested and was taken away. It is not known where Chandulal is. The insurgents went to Garhi and Dehgaon. Dated 23 *Rabi* I, 1275 AH/1 November 1858.

P 397. *Bhawani Prasad to Nawwab Sikandar Begam.* Refers to her order as mentioned in the letter of Daulat Rai, *nazim-i mashriq*, and the statement of Matka Singh which is in regard to the activities of the insurgents. Says, he brought the matter into the notice of the Political Agent and the reply received from him is sent for her perusal. Dated 24 *Rabi* I, 1275 AH/2 November 1858.

P 399. *The Political Agent to Bhawani Prasad.* Refers to his letter along with the statement of Matka Singh, soldier, which is in regard to the insurgent forces. Says it is the time of war and what is the use of 4 days old news. Directs him to inform him after seeking a reply from his own government. Dated 2 November 1858.

P 401. *Diwan Daulat Rai,* Nazim-i Mashriq *to Nawwab Sikandar Begam.* Refers to a letter of Shaikh Nur Muhammad Khan, *thanadar* of Siwans, and that he came to know that the insurgent forces have crossed from that place. Dated 24 *Rabi* I, 1275 AH/2 November 1858.

PP 403-04. *Ranjit Singh, Peon to Nawwab Sikandar Begam.* Says as directed, he went to Bhilsa to bring the news about the British forces. When he reached Bhilsa he saw the British forces were encamping there. He also heard that the insurgent forces have gone to Garhi. He immediately moved to Garhi Ambapani. The next day, he reached Garhi where he found none of the inhabitants whom he could ask anything. He then went from there to Dehgaon and found that the insurgents had totally devastated Dehgaon and the shops were looted. He heard from the dwellers that the number of insurgent forces would be about 10, 000. It was also heard that insurgents sent some of their *sawars* from Dehgaon to Mahalpur, who destroyed Mahalpur. Thereafter, he started pursuing them and reached a place which was at a distance of 3 to 4 *curoh* from Rajghati.

P 405. *Bhawani Prasad to Nawwab Sikandar Begam.* Refers to a letter of *tahsildar* and *thanadar* of Bamhuri, dated 20 *Rabi* I, 1275 AH, besides the letter of *nazim-i mashriq* along with a statement of Daddu Thakur which are in regard to the activities of the insurgents. Informs he brought all the matters mentioned therein into the notice of the Political Agent. All the letters are now returned to her. Dated 24 *Rabi* I, 1275 AH/2 November 1858.

PP 407-8. *Bhawani Prasad to Nawwab Sikandar Begam.* Refers to a letter, dated 21 *Rabi* I, 1275 AH, received from Shaikh Nur Muhammad, *thanadar* of Siwans, as he heard from Ghasi, the soldier, which is in regard to a huge insurgent army that has gathered in Lakhnauti, *ilaqa* Bhilsa. Informs that the content of the letter was brought to the notice of the Political Agent who said that was a dead news and since it was not live news, how could it be believed. The said letter is returned to her. Dated 24 *Rabi* I, 1275 AH/2 November 1858.

P 409. *Nawwab Shahjahan Begam to Nawwab Sikandar Begam.* Sends the letter, dated 21 *Rabi* I, 1275 AH, received from Durga Prasad, *thanadar* of Ghairatganj, pertaining to the insurgent activities. Dated 24 *Rabi* I, 1275 AH/2 November 1858.

P 411. *Durga Prasad,* Thanadar *of Ghairatganj, to Nawwab Shahjahan Begam.* Informs that day, it was heard from Naubat Rai Tiwari of Khamarya, Ghairatganj, who had gone to Bhilsa, that a huge British army has arrived at Bhilsa and about 2,000 forces are stationed at Khery, situating at a distance of 9 *curoh* from Naini. Earlier this was reported about the insurgent forces. But it was incorrect as the report was about the British forces. About 2,000 insurgent forces are at Bharonpur, situating at a distance of 3 *curoh* from Naini and encamping in the valley. There is also a report of the arrival of other insurgent forces. A group of insurgent forces who had gone to Bamhuri via Garhi and Dehgaon have now proceeded towards Narmada. There is peace in his region. But the inhabitants have fled. As a result, seedling of crop has come to a standstill. Says, he visited two or three villages and persuaded them to start the process of crop seedling. Further adds that, from Amir Khan and Brij Lal, who were coming from Garhi, it was heard that Mewatis were devastating the said *qasba* and the blame was put on Adil Muhammad Khan. Dated 21 *Rabi* I, 1275 AH.

P 413. *Bhawani Prasad to Nawwab Sikandar Begam.* Refers to a letter received from Mankaram, *muhtamim* of the royal *karkhana,* dated 23 *Rabi* I, 1275 AH/1

November 1858, informing about the insurgents as said by Abd al-Rahman, *kochwan,* a loyal servant for communicating to the Political Agent. Informs that the said letter is sent to her after informing the Political Agent in the matter. Dated 24 *Rabi* I, 1275 AH/2 November 1858.

P 415. *Baqi Muhammad Khan to Nawwab Sikandar Begam.* Sends the letter, dated 24 *Rabi* I, 1275 AH/2 November 1858, received from Munshi Shamsh al-Din Ansari from Raisen which is in regard to the insurgents. Dated 25 *Rabi* I, 1275 AH/3 November 1858.

PP 417-18. *Shamsh al-Din Ansari to Baqi Muhammad Khan.* Informs that he asked Zorawar, gond of Bamhuri and Brijlal, about the insurgent forces and about the destruction of Bamhuri. They reported that the insurgents arrested Abbas Ali, *thanadar*, and demanded *rasad* from him. As there was nothing in the shop of Kapur Chand Seth so they set it on fire, besides other shops. Dated 24 *Rabi* I, 1275 AH/2 November 1858.

PP 419-20. *Bhawani Prasad to Nawwab Sikandar Begam.* Informs that day in the evening, the Political Agent called him and told that the British officer at Hoshangabad has sent him a letter informing that Tantia Tope crossed river Narmada and entered Hoshangabad. On 30th September and 1st October, the British army attacked Tantia Tope. The Political Agent told him to inform the Nawwab in the matter. Dated 25 *Rabi* I, 1275 AH/3 November 1858.

Filea No. 297, H
Box No. 16.
No. of Documents 27

P 421. *Bhawani Prasad to Nawwab Sikandar Begam.* Sends the letter of *thanadar* of Bareilly, informing about the march of insurgent forces from Bamhuri and crossing river Narmada, after informing the Political Agent about it. Dated 25 *Rabi* I, 1275 AH/3 November 1858.

P 423. *Bhawani Prasad to Nawwab Sikandar Begam.* Sends the letter received from Daulat Rai, *nazim-i mashriq,* dated 24 *Rabi* I, 1275 AH/2 November 1858, which is in regard to the insurgents, after informing the Political Agent about it as desired. Dated 25 *Rabi* I, 1275 AH/3 November 1858.

PP 425-6. *Bhawani Prasad to Nawwab Sikandar Begam.* Refers to the letter of Lala Chaturbhuj, dated 22 *Rabi* I, 1275 AH, and the letter of Lala Daulat Rai, *nazim-i mashriq,* dated 24 *Rabi* I, 1275 AH, as written by Abd al-Ali, *naib,* which is about the insurgents and their atrocities upon the inhabitants. Informs that the matter has been brought to the notice of the Political Agent, Major Richard, the Agent of Bhopal and the letters are returned to her. Dated 25 *Rabi* I, 1275 AH/3 November 1858.

P 427. *Lala Daulat Rai,* Nazim-i Mashriq, *to Nawwab Sikandar Begam.* Refers to her *parwana*, dated 24 *Rabi* I, 1275 AH, asking him about the villages that were destroyed by the insurgent forces, about their encampment, about those who fought with the insurgents, and those who were wounded, and also those who were wounded by them or ran away. Informs that it is known to her about the cities which were destroyed by the insurgent forces and about their defeat at Gwalior, Tonk, and Jhalra Patan, inspite of the fact that they were in large number. Says, whatever news he receives about the insurgent forces are sent to her right then and there. The *mahals* like Raisen, Mahalpur, Ghairatganj, etc. remained safe from the destruction caused by the insurgent forces. Dated 25 *Rabi* I, 1275 AH/3 November 1858.

P 429. *Bhawani Prasad to Nawwab Sikandar Begam.* Refers to a letter of Muhammad Raza Husain, *nazim-i junub*, which is in regard to the insurgents. Informs that the information has been brought to the notice of the Political Agent and the same is returned to her. Dated 25 *Rabi* I, 1275 AH/3 November 1858.

PP 431-2. *Saiyid Inayat Ali,* Thanadar *of Murdanpur, to Nawwab Sikandar Begam.* Informs as it is heard from

Idi Khan, peon of the *thana*, that the insurgents are still in the mountains of Mahadev and the British officers are pursuing them.

PP 433-4. *Diwan Daulat Rai,* Nazim-i Mashriq, *to Nawwab Sikandar Begam.* Informs about a report of *thana* Mahalpur, dated 24 *Rabi* I, 1275 AH, stating that the insurgent forces crossed *ghat* Patrora at noon and went to Sohagpur and about 100 *sawars* were encamping there. Dated 25 *Rabi* I, 1275 AH/3 November 1858.

PP 435-6. *Report from* Thana *Mahalpur, Dated 24* Rabi I, *1275 AH/2 November 1858, Sent Through Shahzad Rai,* Thanadar. Reports that Bhora, peon, and Sethu *Banjara* sent by him have returned from *ghat* Patrora at noon and told that the insurgent forces crossed *ghat* Patrora at noon and went to Sohagpur and about 100 *sawars* were encamping at *ghat* Patrora. From them it was also heard that two companies of troops are behind them and two to three *sawars* have gone to call them back. As soon as they come, they would leave this place. From a *harkara* of Ghairatganj, it is heard that about 400 to 500 insurgents are encamping at *mauza* Nironpur, *ilaqa* Bhilsa.

P 437. *Muhammad Raza Husain to Nawwab Sikandar Begam.* Informs that day, Jafar Ali, a former soldier of the battalion on duty in this *nizamat* who came from Chhaner, *pargana* Udaipura, has reported about the insurgents. His statement has been recorded and is sent to her. Dated 25 *Rabi* I, 1275 AH/3 November 1858.

PP 439-40. *Statement of Jafar Ali, Soldier.* States that his name is Jafar Ali, his father's name is Latafat Ali, caste Saiyid, and does a job. He was asked to tell about Chhaner and Udaipura. He replied that when he reached Chhaner, he saw that there were 20 soldiers. They entered in a shop and purchased goods and made payment. One shop that was closed, was opened and looted by them.

PP 441-2. *Muhammad Mughal,* Tahsildar, Pargana *Bareilly, to Nawwab Sikandar Begam.* Informs about the insurgents and says that the *tahsildar* and *thanadar* of Bamhuri asked for help. Says, he sent 15 soldiers from Bamhuri to Garhi. Says, he is busy in managing the things. Also informs of his letters to Ghulam Murtaza Khan and Raza Husain Khan, pertaining to the insurgents who suddenly fell in Bamhuri and arrested Abbas Ali, *thanadar*. Hearing this news, all the dwellers fled from Bareilly and hid in the mountains.

P 443. *Muhammad Mughal,* Tahsildar, Pargana *Bareilly, to Nawwab Sikandar Begam.* Informs it was learnt that some people of *pargana* Bareilly who had gone to *mauza* Sandia, the British territory, were caught by insurgent forces. They asked them whether they were spies of the British. The latter refused. All were arrested and later, they were released. Dated 26 *Rabi* I, 1275 AH/4 November 1858.

PP 445-6. *Bhawani Prasad to Nawwab Sikandar Begam.* Informs that he just met the Political Agent to convey him about the content of the letter of Saiyid Inayat Ali, *thanadar* of Murdanpur, dated 24 *Rabi* I, 1275 AH, He heard the content of the letter and said he was ill since the previous night. Says, he said that looking at his face it appears that he was suffering from fever. He then said, due to his illness, he would go to Sehore by the next day and that day in the evening he would go to meet the Nawwab in Moti Mahal. The letter of *thanadar* of Murdanpur is sent to her

PP 447-8. *Daulat Rai,* Nazim-i Mashriq, *to Nawwab Sikandar Begam.* Informs about the receipt of the letter of Durga Prasad, *thanadar* of Ghairatganj, informing that the insurgent forces devastated Bamhuri and other *mauzas*. The news about Garhi is that, they also destroyed many villages there. Dated 26 *Rabi* I, 1275 AH/4 November 1858.

PP 449-50. *Durga Prasad,* Thanadar *of Ghairatganj, to Daulat Rai,* Nazim-i Mashriq. Informs that day Kanhai Singh of Keel Kutchh, *ilaqa* Bareilly, came and said to him that on Friday the insurgent forces, after devastating Bamhuri and *mauza* Bhasra, marched farther and encamped in *mauza* Chhapara, *ilaqa* Udaipura. In the morning, the places like Aonia, Balya, Kanu *ghat* and Chhaner, etc. were destroyed.

PP 451-2. *Kishan Ram to Nawwab Sikandar Begam.* Informs as ordered, he wrote to Munshi Muhammad Raza Husain, *nazim-i junub*, about the movement of insurgent forces. Informs that day, he received the reply of the letter from Muhammad Raza Husain that is being sent to her. Dated 28 *Rabi* I, 1275 AH/6 November 1858.

P 453. *Muhammad Raza Husain to Kishan Ram.* Refers to his letter reporting the presence of insurgent forces in Chhaner, *pargana* Udaipura. But there is no report from the *amil* or *thanadar* of that *pargana* for the last week. Even in his letter there is no report except the destruction of *mahalat* there. But the previous day one person named Jafar Ali, who was earlier employed in the battalion of the *nizamat* and who does not report false news, came from Chhaner to Kalyakhery and his statement was recorded and sent to the govenmnet. From that statement everything would become clear. The gist of his letter is that till 22 *Rabi* I, 1275 AH, Chhaner and Udaipura were entirely saved from the destruction from the hands of the insurgents. Some *sawars* of the insurgents came from Chhapara, *pargana* Udaipura, and purchased provision, whatever was available, from the merchants and paid the amount. One shop which was closed, was broken into and the grain was destroyed. Dated 25 *Rabi* I, 1275 AH/3 November 1858.

P 455. Parwana-i Ishtahari *of Nawwab Sikandar Begam to her Three* Nazims *and Munshi Dhar,* Mutasaddi. Notifies that whatever news they receive about the insurgents, firstly, it should be brought to the notice of the Political Agent and then, it should be conveyed to her. Dated 26 *Rabi* I, 1275 AH/4 November 1858.

PP 457-8. Parwana-i Ishtahari *of Nawwab Sikandar*

Begam to the Tahsildars *and* Thanadars *of Mahalpur, Bheglone, Deori, Bamhuri, Solwani, Siwans, Chhatari, Garhi Ambapani, and Raisen.* Expresses anxiety that for the last two years there was a continuous demand of gunpowder and cartridges by them. But when time came to fight a battle, they were not seen anywhere except in the forts and mountains. It is really a matter of concern as to what anxiety of God has fallen upon them or do they lack bravery, honesty and sacrifice. So far, they did not inform as to how many *parganas* under their jurisdiction were devastated by the insurgents and what are the places where the insurgents were still encamping. If they consider it good for themselves, they should immediately submit the details of all the happenings. There should not be a single minute delay. They should inform about those who, from their *ilaqa*, fought with the insurgents and how many insurgents were killed or wounded. Likewise, details of the dwellers who were killed or wounded by the insurgents, and the rebels and culprits arrested by him. Dated 24 *Rabi* I, 1275 AH/2 November 1858.

P 459. . . *to Nawwab Sikandar Begam.* Informs as ordered, he after handing over the charge of the court to the *thanadar* of Bamhuri came to Bhopal. Says, he is a loyalist of the government and it is Ajodhya Prasad who complained against him. Further says that, an army of 12,000 under the command of Tantia Tope entered Bamhuri and 4 or 5 *mauzas* were destroyed. The *tahsildar* and Ajodhya Prasad fled to the mountains before coming of these forces. Says, if he had committed such a crime God knows what would happen to him. Dated 27 *Rabi* I, 1275 AH/5 November 1858.

P 461. *Bhawani Prasad to Nawwab Sikandar Begam.* Sends back the letters, whose contents were brought to the notice of the Political Agent before he left for Sehore.

P 463. *Muhammad Raza Husain to Nawwab Sikandar*

Begam. Informs as ordered, the arrangement of the posts of *sawars* was made from Kalyakhery to that place in such a manner that the news of the insurgents from the *thanadar* and *amil* should reach her every hour. Dated 27 *Rabi* I, 1275 AH/5 November 1858.

P 465. *Nazar Muhammad Khan, Sawar to Nawwab Sikandar Begam.* From Puran, a servant of Jawaharmal Seth, it is heard that Abbas Ali, *thanadar* who was made captive by the insurgents, has been freed.

P 469 & 471. *Nawwab Sikandar Begam to Paltu Lal,* Muhafiz-i Daftar-i Insha. Directs him to submit details of the army, accompanying Tantia Tope from the date they entered in the territory of Bhopal till the date they left the region as per the details given by the *amils* and *thanadars* through their letters. Dated 28 *Rabi* I, 1275 AH/6 November 1858.

PP 475-6. *Daulat Rai,* Nazim-i Mashriq, *to Nawwab Sikandar Begam.* Informs that when he was at Bhilsa, General Mitchell and Comming, Assistant Leiutenant of Governor General, Central India, asked him about the captivity of the *thanadar* and *tahsildar* by the insurgents and then how they were freed. Says in reply, he said that, there was a report that the insurgents were encamping around Tahri and through the mountains of Basodah and Muhammad Garh, they suddenly arrived at Garhi and held the *tahsildar* and *thanadar* captive and the number of *sawars* of insurgents was about 8,000. Then they asked about the number of soldiers in the *thana*. He replied that there were 10 to 12 soldiers at that time in the *thana*. They said it means that they were very few and due to less number of soldiers in the *thana* and lack of information about the coming of the insurgents they were arrested. Then they asked as to how they were freed. He replied, Tantia Tope had put them under the guards. They persuaded the guards to free them by offering jewellery as bribe.

PP 477-8. Parwana-i Ishtahari *of Nawwab Sikandar*

Begam to the Tahsildars *and* Thanadars *of Mahalpur, Bheglone, Deori, Bamhuri, Solwani, Siwans, Chhatari, Garhi Ambapani, and Raisen.* From outside agencies it has been heard that, the army of Tantia Tope after being dispersed are hiding in small groups in the districts towards east and south. Directs them to have authentic and accurate news of these insurgents and either kill them or produce them before her under arrest along with proper security. As there is a proverb *bhagte ki langoti*. If they did not fall in their hands then it is a matter of shame for her servants and employees. For the last two and half years, she is regularly writing to either kill or arrest the insurgents but not a single order was executed. Even this much is not remembered by them as to what methods were to be adopted. She is saying so because they have become adept to feel free. Why they did not ever think that a matter of bravery will give happiness to their Master and it will lead to longevity of the State of Bhopal! Dated 28 *Rabi* I, 1275 AH/6 November 1858.

P 479. *Munshi Dhar, Mutasaddi to Nawwab Sikandar Begam.* Refers to her order, dated 26 *Rabi* I, 1275 AH/4 November 1858, that whatever news they receive about the insurgents, firstly, it should be brought to the notice of the Political Agent and then, to be conveyed to her. Assures that the order would be executed in letter and spirit. Dated 28 *Rabi* I, 1275 AH /6 November 1858.

Filea No. 297, I
Box No. 16.
No. of Documents 25

PP 481-2. *Muhammad Raza Husain to Nawwab Sikandar Begam.* Sends the letter of Saiyid Jawwad Ali, *muhtamim*, *chaukiyat*, dated 26 *Rabi* I, 1275 AH /4 November 1858, informing that the insurgent forces crossed river Narmada at *ghat* Patrora, *ilaqa* Hoshangabad, and none of them are left in Patrora and Chhatara. One copy of the letter is also being sent to Haji 'Abd al-Karim and Munshi Dhar, *mutasaddi*, to bring it into the notice of the British officers and the reply received from them, may be sent to the government. Dated 28 *Rabi* I, 1275 AH/6 November 1858.

P 483. *Saiyid Jawwad Ali,* Muhtamim, Chaukiyat, *to Muhammad Raza Husain.* Refers to his letter, dated 25 *Rabi* I, 1275 AH/3 November 1858, which informs that the report about the movement of the insurgent forces and about their encampment as he saw from his own eyes or heard from the relible informers has been sent to the government. The recent news is that the insurgent forces on 21 *Rabi* I, day Saturday, have marched from Chhatara and crossed *ghat* Patrora, *pargana* and *ghat* Sandia, situating on the bank of river Narmada under the territory of the British. Now there is none in Chhatara or Patrora or in the entire region of *nizamat-i junub* which is to be reported. There is complete peace in the region. If anything new happens in the region which he may notice from his own eyes, it will be reported. Dated 26 *Rabi* I, 1275 AH/4 November 1858.

PP 485-6. *Muhammad Abbas Ali to Nawwab Sikandar Begam.* Informs that when Tantia Tope crossed Narmada at the *ghat* in *mauza* Sandia, there was a rumour among the insurgents that Rajas of Sohnapur and Fatahpur were also accompanying them. But this was just a rumour. Sarangdhar Seth, a shopkeeper of Bamhuri who had gone a few days ago to Khaperkhera, situating on the other side of Narmada, was hiding in the mountains of Fatahpur for three days along with some other traders and inhabitants of Fatahpur. He came back to Bamhuri that day from there. From him it was heard that the forces of Tantia Tope had gone to Nagpur from the places of Sandia, Khaperkhera, Fatahpur and Dudakhera and devastated these villages. Raja of Fatahpur and other *ilaqadars* on the other side of river Narmada fled due to fear of the British and look shelter in the mountains. After two days, the officer at Hoshangabad reached Fatahpur with 200 *sawars* and asked for help from the Rajas for pursuing the insurgent forces. But the Rajas expressed their excuse as they had no force of their own. The Rajas of Fatahpur and Sohnapur were imposed fine, being the culprit of helping the insurgents. What he heard he communicated. Dated 29 *Rabi* I, 1275 AH/7 November 1858.

P 487. *Hazarilal,* Tahsildar *of Raisen, to Nawwab Sikandar Begam.* Refers to her *parwana*, dated 26 *Rabi* I, 1275 AH/4 November 1858, directing him to inform as soon as he receives the *parwana,* about those villages of his *ilaqa* Raisen which have been devastated by the insurgents, the places where they are encamping, battle that was fought with them, how many of them wounded or arrested, likewise, those who were killed or wounded from his side. Informs that it is a fact that none of the villages of *pargana* Raisen, by her graceness, was devastated by the insurgents. Besides, the insurgents have not yet entered in this *pargana*. If they enter, surely a battle would be fought with them. Then it would cause killing and wounding. With the help of Allah and with her blessings, the insurgents would be killed and wounded and arrested and then no question would arise of his loyalty to the salt. Meanwhile, no village has been harmed from the hands of the insurgents. Dated 29 *Rabi* I, 1275 AH/7 November 1858.

PP 489-90. *Bhawani Prasad to Nawwab Sikandar Begam.* Informs that day, Major Richards conveyed him through Ramhans, peon, that it was day three when the news of insurgents in Garhi Ambapani, Dehgaon and Bharot was reported to him. There is no further report of the insurgents, whether they went to the other side of Narmada or fled to some other side or they were still there. Urges him to get latest information from the Nawwab and communicate to him. Dated 29 *Rabi* I, 1275 AH/7 November 1858.

PP 491-2. *Muhammad Abbas Ali to Nawwab Sikandar Begam.* Informs that the previous day, he had sent a letter to the *thanadar* of Garhi through Inder Singh, soldier for informing about the movement of insurgents in Garhi and Nagchari. In reply, he has received the letter of the *thanadar,* informing that at the moment some 300 forces were present in the desert of Nagchari and then they fled from there to somewhere else. Informs that he too has sent two informers to Bharonpur and on the mountains of Tans, situating towards Jasnagar to enquire and bring the news of the insurgents. The information as received would be communicated. Also, sends the letter sent to the *thanadar* of Garhi. Dated 29 *Rabi* I, 1275 AH/7 November 1858.

P 493. *Muhammad Abd al-Rahman to Saiyid Abbas Ali,* Thanadar *of Bamhuri.* Informs that at the moment, some 300 forces were present in the desert of Nagchari and then they fled from there to somewhere else. Informs that he has sent the informers here and there. The information, as received, would be communicated to him. Says, he is not aware about the reason behind the retreat of the British forces. This much was heard that hearing the news, the insurgents were going to Hoshangabad, these forces were pursuing them. Dated 29 *Rabi* I, 1275 AH/7 November 1858.

P 494. *Saiyid Abbas Ali,* Thanadar *of Bamhuri, to Muhammad Abd al-Rahman*, Thanadar *of Garhi.* Informs that through the letter of *thanadar,* Ghairatganj, it is heard that about 300 insurgents have gathered at Nagchari. He requested him to inform immediately about the situation there, so that he may be in peace. Also urges him to inform the reason behind the retreat of British forces to Raisen. Dated 28 *Rabi* I, 1275 AH/6 November 1858.

P 495. *Notification Issued in the Name of Bakhshi Murawwat Muhammad Khan.* Notifies that the employees of the Bhopal army should be ready all the time so that at the time of need and when a call is given by the government, they should not waste a single minute in obeying the royal order. Any kind of negligence or laziness on part of any employee, if noticed, will not be good for him. It is a must that all the employees under his jurisdiction should be instructed to follow the order. Dated 29 *Rabi* I, 1275 AH/7 November 1858.

PP 497-8. *Shahzad Rai,* Thanadar *of Mahalpur, to Nawwab Sikandar Begam.* Refers to her *parwana,* dated 28 *Rabi* I, 1275 AH/6 November 1858, informing that it has been heard from the outside agencies that the army of Tantia Tope when dispersed, hid in small groups in the districts towards east and south. It is directed to have authentic and accurate news of those insurgents and either kill or produce them under arrest before her with proper security. For the last two and half years, she is regularly instructing them to either kill or arrest the insurgents but not a single order is executed. She is saying so because he has become adept to feel free and run away from responsibility. Why he did not ever think that a matter of bravery will give happiness to his Master and it will lead to longevity of the State of Bhopal. Argues that, as ordered, he is relentlessly obeying the orders in regard to arresting or killing the insurgent forces of Tantia Tope. Assures, the moment he gets such news he would execute her order. Also says that he did not show any reluctance in obeying her command or directives, as he immediately reached Garhi, the moment he got the news of the insurgents to suppress them. Although it was the will of God and an order from the above that just the opposite happened. She is good enough to judge as it occurred due to insufficient number of army personnel. Dated 1 *Rabi* II, 1275 AH.

PP 499-500. *Bhawani Prasad to Nawwab Sikandar Begam.* Informs that day, during the discourse, Walker Charles Tomsen asked him whether he knew as to when General Mitchell would be questioned from the office of Agent that inspite of having a huge army how did the insurgents reach on the other side of Narmada and why they were not prevented. Not only this, but the British officers of that district raised objection on the performance of General Mitchell. The General, in his defence, would say that he was not informed by the Nawwab or anyone else about the insurgents. In his view, the reason of the resenment of General Mitchell was that the Political Agent, Bhopal, never intimated him about the news of the insurgents. Due to this, the Political Agent looked perturbed that day. Not only that, but when the *wakils* presented their petitions, he got up from the chair and went outside. Even a letter which was delivered by the 9th Regiment by an orderly, the Political Agent took the letter from his hand and threw it outside the door. Dated 1 *Rabi* II, 1275 AH/8 November 1858.

PP 503-4. *Harsahai*, Tahsildar, *to Ghulam Murtaza Khan*. Refers to his letter, dated 22 *Rabi* I, 1275 AH, expressing concern for not sending the report of the insurgents and happenings of Garhi while *mahal* Garhi is adjacent to his *mahal*. Informs that on 18th of this month, he received a letter of Lala Chandulal, *tahsildar* Garhi Ambapani, requesting for help and informing about the destruction of *mauza* Aradmau and Jaitpur. The information was immediately passed on to the government along with the letter of the *tahsildar* and 20 soldiers from *thana* and *mahal* were sent there to help him. The information of this mishap was also given to the *tahsildar* and *thanadar* of Bareilly, Udaipura and Solwani. As 20 soldiers of this mahal were sent to Garhi, a very few number of soldiers were left in this *mahal*. On 19th of this month, an army of 10, 000 to 12,000 including both *sawars* and foot-soldiers cordoned Bamhuri and encamped there. As he was unable to face this huge army, he sneaked and hid in the mountains. The insurgents arrested the *thanadar* and took him along with them. Another letter, informing the devastation of Garhi, as heard from Kalyan Chand Seth, was received on 18th of this month. His statement was recorded and sent to the government. Hopes that all those letters would have been seen by him. Dated 26 *Rabi* I, 1275 AH.

PP 505-6. *Muhammad Abbas Ali,* Thanadar *of Bamhuri to Ghulam Murtaza Khan.* Refers to his letter, dated 22 *Rabi* I, 1275 AH, complaining for not sending the report of the insurgents and happenings of Garhi while *mahal* Garhi is just adjacent to his *mahal*. Informs that on 18th of this month, he was on a visit to Ausra. On that very day, the *tahsildar* of Garhi Ambapani sent a letter, requesting for help and informing about the destruction of *mauza* Aradmau and Jaitpur. The *tahsildar* of Bamhuri gathered 20 soldiers from *mahal* and *thana* with their *jamadars* and sent to Garhi. He himself came back to the *mahal* as informed the *tahsildar*. It was noon of 19th *Rabi* I, when the insurgents cordoned Bamhuri. The army of the insurgents was about 10, 000 to 12,000 comprising of the *sawars* and foot-soldiers.

P 507. *Lachhman Singh, Peon to Nawwab Sikandar Begam.* Informs that he along with Ranjit Singh, *harkara* went to bring the news of the insurgents. What Ranjit Singh saw at Garhi Ambapani and Dehgaon, he reported to her. He himself pursued the insurgents and reached Chhapara in their camp, wearing the dress of a beggar. The forces of insurgents crossed the river at *ghat* Patrora on 22 *Rabi* I, 1275 AH and reached Sohnapur. He too was in the company of the insurgents. When they reached Sohnapur, Raja Chhatar Shah, Sohnapurwala, arranged one day meal for them and provided *saman-i sarbrah-i rasad* of all types. The Raja himself along with two elephants, 25 horses and 200 men joined the insurgent forces. The army of insurgents is comprised of 40 elephants, 3,000 horses, and 4,000 to 5, 000 soldiers. They were well off, fully armed. But they did not have cannon with them. Some from the camp of insurgents said that the intention of Rao Sahab and Tantia Tope was to go to Hoshangabad. Says, he himself saw Tantia Tope. He was blackish, medium height, and aged around 40 years. He was wearing a golden chain. Some say that Aqil Muhammad Khan, son of Fazil Muhammad Khan, was also in the camp. But he did not see him from his own eyes. The army was about to march to Fatahpur, therefore, he left the camp. Dated 1 *Rabi* II, 1275 AH/8 November 1858.

P 509. *Muhammad Raza Husain to Nawwab Sikandar Begam.* Sends the letter received from Lala Harsahai, *tahsildar* of *pargana* Bamhuri, dated 26 *Rabi* I, 1275 AH, informing that the insurgents reached Bamhuri on 19 *Rabi* I, 1275 AH, arrested the *thanadar* of that place and destroyed two maunds of golden *zira,* three maunds of edible oil and one *tola biranji*. Dated 1 *Rabi* II, 1275 AH/8 November 1858.

PP 513-14. *Muhammad Raza Husain to Nawwab Sikandar Begam.* Sends the undated letter received from Nazar Muhammad Khan and Jangbaz Khan, *risaldars,* from Bareilly, informing that the insurgents left three horses there, and the *thanadar* of Bamhuri captured one horse along with *sawar* and *sais* and two camels died near *mauza* Chhapara. Dated 1 *Rabi* II, 1275 AH/8 November 1858.

PP 515-16. *Nazar Muhammad Khan to Muhammad Raza Husain.* Informs that, as ordered, he went in search of the insurgents and reached Bamhuri via Bareilly. At that very moment, a person sent by Saiyid Abbas Ali, *thanadar* of Bamhuri, reached there from Garhi. He said that from Garhi to Siwans no insurgent had any existence. Further informs that day, i.e. 27 *Rabi* I, 1266 *Fasli*, day Friday, he reached Bareilly and would report what he would see there. Reports that in Bareilly he heard that the insurgents reached Garhi, so he went to Garhi to know about them. There were three horses which were left by the insurgents as they had become too weak. Says he went on foot to *mauza* Kondani. The horses along with their *sawars* were arrested by the *thanadar* of Bamhuri. Also, informs that two camels died near *mauza* Chhapara. The report, as seen, is sent. Further informs that now he is in Bareilly and whatever order is given to him, it would be followed. Dated 1 *Rabi* II, 1275 AH.

P 517. . . . . to *Nawwab Sikandar Begam.* Refers to her *parwana,* dated 28 *Rabi* I, 1275 AH /6 November

1858, informing that from outside agencies it has been heard that the army of Tantia Tope after becoming disorganized is hiding in small groups in the districts of east and south, and directing them to have authentic and accurate news of these insurgents and either kill or produce them under arrest before her with proper security. Informs, no insurgent has entered in this region so far so as to arrest him and to produce him before her. Assures if any insurgent enters in the region, he would surely be arrested or killed. There will be no negligence in executing the order. Dated 1 *Rabi* II, 1275 AH.

P 519. *Bansidhar*, Thanadar *of Raisen, to Nawwab Sikandar Begam.* Refers to her *parwana*, dated 26 *Rabi* I, 1275 AH/4 November 1858, directing him to inform as soon as he receives the *parwana* about those villages of his *ilaqa* Raisen which were devastated by the insurgents and about the places where they were encamping, battle that was fought with them; and how many of them were wounded or arrested. Likewise, how many were killed or wounded from his side. Informs that till then, by her graceness, neither any battle was fought between the forces of his *thana* and the insurgent forces nor was any village in *pargana* Raisen destroyed by the insurgents, nor was there any insurgent in any village who might indulge in the activities of insurgency, destruction or loot. Assures that if any battle takes place with the insurgents or there is any information of the presence of the insurgents in any village, he would not hesitate to fight with them and kill them. If any insurgent takes shelter in any village of his jurisdiction, the information would soon be communicated to the government. Further assures that there will be no reluctance on his part in executing the order given to him. Dated 1 *Rabi* II, 1275 AH.

PP 521-3. *Shahzad Rai,* Thanadar *of Mahalpur*, to *Nawwab Sikandar Begam.* Refers to her *parwana,* dated 26 *Rabi* I, 1275 AH, expressing anxiety that for the last two years, he had been demanding arms and ammunitions but when time came to fight with the enemy, he was not seen except in the fort or on the mountains, and set the lesson of bravery and loyalty to the salt totally aside. He did not write as to how many villages were destroyed by the insurgents. If he thinks it good for himself, he should immediately write to her about it. He did not write as to who among the dwellers of his region fought with the insurgents. How many insurgents were killed and how many were wounded. How many insurgents were arrested by the dwellers of his region and how many fled. Informs that it is known to her that he did not take shelter in the mountains or in any fort. But as soon as he received the letter of the *thanadar* and *tahsildar* of Garhi for help, he came forward and Shaikh Ihsan Ali, *tahsildar*, was sent to Garhi along with 6 soldiers of *thana* and 20 soldiers of *mahal* In Garhi, there was nobody except the *tahsildar*, *thanadar*, and Abd Ali, *naib nazim*. No contingent was present there. Their number was not too much that they could fight with the insurgents who were 10, 000 to11, 000 in strength, comprising of both *sawars* and foot-soldiers. Then, they came back to Mahalpur. The *thanadar* and *tahsildar* of Garhi went to Raisen. The *thanadar*, *tahsildar* and *naib nazim* were arrested by the insurgent forces. There was no battle with the insurgent forces as they were less in number. So, there was no killing or wounding. They freed themselves from the hands of the insurgents. At the time of fighting with the insurgents, the orders of the government would be executed in letter and spirit. *Mauza* Dehgaon, where the insurgents were encamping, was fully destroyed. The insurgents also entered In *mauza Mondia,* and the grain was destroyed there. Dated 1 *Rabi* II, 1275 AH.

P 527. *Hazarilal,* Tahsildar, *Raisen, to Nawwab Sikandar Begam.* Refers to her *parwana*, dated 28 *Rabi* I, 1275 AH, informing that it is heard that the army of Tantia Tope is perturbed and has spread in groups in the districts of east and south. It is a must that authentic information about them should be collected and that they should be killed or arrested and produced under proper security in the court. Informs that the fact is that no insurgent has yet entered in his region. If he enters, he would be arrested and produced before her. Assures that if any insurgent ever enters in his region, he would not deviate from the orders in killing or arresting him. He is all the time busy in gathering such information.

PP 533-4. . . . . to *Nawwab Sikandar Begam.* Ganesh, peon, and Chhatar Khan, soldier, were sent to bring the news of crossing of the river by the insurgent forces at the *ghat* in *mauza* Paharkatchh, *pargana* Bari. That day, they came back and stated that they saw from their own eyes that the insurgent forces crossed the river at the said *ghat* and encamped on the other side of river Narmada. Colonel Pitcher had sent an informer through the *thanadar* of Murdanpur to bring the news. But he gave the wrong news. Hence, he sent two persons to bring authentic news. A report was sent to the British officer about the incorrect news. Dated 3 *Rabi* II, 1275 AH.

P 535. *Ali Ahmad Khan,* Tahsildar *of Solwani, to Nawwab Sikandar Begam.* Refers to her *parwana*, dated 28 *Rabi* I, 1275 AH, directing him that the insurgents have spread and it is heard that they have entered in his region. They should be arrested or killed. Informs that the informers have been sent upto river Narmada. After receiving the information, action would be taken. Dated 3 *Rabi* II, 1275 AH.

P 537. *Ali Ahmad Khan,* Tahsildar *of Solwani to Nawwab Sikandar Begam.* Refers to her *parwana*, dated 26 *Rabi* I, 1275 AH, directing him to inform about the villages which were destroyed by the insurgents in his region and how many of them were killed or wounded. Informs that the army of Tantia Tope entered from the territory of Sindhia and encamped in Garhi, Dehgaon,

Bamhuri, Jiyara and Autia, *ilaqa* Udaipura, and crossed river Narmada. The entire *pargana* Solwani is safe and no mishap has ever happened there. Dated 3 *Rabi* II, 1275 AH.

P 539. *Muhammad Abd al-Qadir,* Thanadar *to Nawwab Sikandar Begam.* Refers to her *parwana,* dated 26 *Rabi* I, 1275 AH, enquiring from him about the villages which were destroyed by the insurgents in his region and the places where the insurgents encamped, how many insurgents were wounded and arrested. Informs that he has sent news-report to her everyday. However, it is again stated that the army of Tantia Tope marched from Bagrod, *ilaqa* Sindhia, and reached *pargana* Mahalpur. On 19 *Rabi* I, 1275 AH, they came back to Bamhuri and reached on the bank of river Narmada. By her blessings, there was peace in *pargana* Solwani, Chhatari, and Deori. Although the insurgent army was 10, 000 to 12,000 in strength, but they were scared so they did not stay here. Dated 3 *Rabi* II, 1275 AH.

File No. 297, J
Box No. 16
No. of Documents 26

PP 543-8. Parwana *of Nawwab Sikandar Begam to Bhawani Prasad.* Refers to his letter, dated 1 *Rabi* II, 1275 AH, informing that day, during the discourse, Walker Charles Tomsen asked him, whether he knew as to when General Mitchell would be questioned from the office of the Agent that, inspite of having a huge army how the insurgents reached other side of the Narmada and why they were not prevented. Not only this, but the British officers of that district had raised objection on his performance. The General in his defence would say that he was not informed by the Nawwab or anyone else about the insurgents. Informs, that time she too did not know where the army of General Mitchell was. Directs him to clarify to Walker Charles of having no information of the army of Mitchell to her so that he should not be punished for that reason. About the entry of insurgents, three letters were sent by the *thanadar*, *tahsildar* and *nazim* to Brigadier Bark who was in

Bhopal. The Brigadier hearing the news said that, for the last three or four days it is heard that the insurgents are active in an area of 60 to 65 *curoh*. In the State of Bhopal, the post of footers have been increased two-fold which means if a news reached in five days it will now reach in two and half days. Walker Charles should himself judge that Tantia Tope did not dare to enter Bhopal, relying on his weapons. He was coming only to destroy the treasure of Bhopal. Had there not been the British forces everywhere, Tantia Tope would have destroyed all the treasures and the State of Bhopal. Besides this, she herself had told to the Brigadier upon meeting him that Tantia Tope destroyed *mahal* Garhi Ambapani and *mahal* Mahalput and then went to *mahal* Bamhuri. It is her opinion that the forces should be divided into three groups. One group should be in Bhopal for pursuing the insurgent forces. The other group should be behind the first group to keep a watch. The third group should fall upon the insurgents via Raisen as the first group has gone to Bamhuri. The group coming via Kalyakhery should cross river Narmada at the *ghat* in *mauza* Patrora, *pargana* Udaipura, before the first group of insurgents reach there. The British officer appreciated the suggestion and went to his camp. It is not known as to what happened to the departure of the forces. Directs him to bring the matter into the notice of Walker Charles and his observation may be communicated to her. Dated 3 *Rabi* II, 1275 AH.

PP 549-50. Parwana *of Nawwab Sikandar Begam to Muhammad Raza Husain.* The most important work what the British officers want from her is that there should be clever informers present in two-fold, who should go everywhere and report whatever they see from their own eyes in respect of the insurgents. The first point of movement of the insurgents is Garhi Ambapani and the end of their movement is *ghat* Patrora. The day the insurgents have crossed *ghat* Patrora, not a single letter has been received from the *amil* or *thanadar* of

Udaipura. Directs him to enquire about the reason and inform her. Dated 3 *Rabi* II, 1275 AH.

P 551. *Muhammad 'Abd al-Karim to Nawwab Sikandar Begam.* Well known news is that the insurgents have reached Amraoti and are intending to go to Poona. The British forces are pursuing them wherever they go. Ultimately, they will meet their fate as no one has the courage to stand before this mighty force. Dated 4 *Rabi* II, 1275 AH.

PP 553-4. *Wazir Khan*, Qila'dar, *to Nawwab Sikandar Begam.* Refers to her order, as mentioned on his letter dated 22 *Rabi* I, 1275 AH, expressing anxiety that for the last two years, he was demanding arms and ammunitions but when time came to fight with the enemy, he hid in the fort or on the mountains and forgot the lesson of bravery and loyalty to the salt. He did not write as to how many villages were destroyed by the insurgents and what were those places where the insurgents were encamping, how many insurgents were killed and how many were wounded, and how many fled and how many insurgents were arrested by the servants of the government. Explains that the demand for the arms and ammunitions was for the purpose of arresting or killing the insurgents. Further explains that on 17th *Rabi* I, 1275 AH, the report about the insurgents was that they were encamping at Dhampur, *ilaqa* Gwalior. He and his staff were ready in Siwans to fight with them. On 18th, it was heard that they were in Garhi Ambapani. Later, it was heard that they did not stay for a while in Garhi Ambapani but stayed at Dehgaon and went to Bamhuri. Dated 4 *Rabi* II, 1275 AH.

PP 555-6. *Ganaga Sahai,* Thanadar, Pargana *Chhatari to Nawwab Sikandar Begam.* Refers to her *parwana* in regard to the news that the contingent of Tantia Tope was very perturbed and harassed, some were in the district of east and some were in the district of south, if found they should be killed or arrested. Also refers to her anxiety that if he ever thought to do something extraordinary which may give him name and happiness to his master and the name of Bhopal State becomes famous. Says, her observation is quite right. But at the same time, he and the *tahsildar* along with the staff of *thana* and *tahsil* remained firm at the time of insurgency by Tantia Tope and never turned their back. They would not have hesitated in' sacrificing their lives had the situation demanded so. But the insurgents went to Bamhuri via *ilaqa* Udaipura, crossed the river and entered the British territory. But due to fleeing of the *amils* and *thanadars* of other *mahals*, other people also got bad name. She is all powerful and she is the best judge. Dated 4 *Rabi* II, 1275 AH.

PP 557-8. *Shaikh Nur Muhamamd,* Thanadar *of Siwans*. Refers to her *parwana,* dated 26 *Rabi* I, 1275 AH, expressing anxiety as no report was sent about the killing of the insurgents, the details of villages destroyed by those forces and about their encampment. Expressing his fedility, says that for the last 30 years of his service there is not a single instance of his disloyalty. He was holding the post of *tahsildari* of *pargana* Jogigarh where peace was prevailing but preffered to go to *thana* Siwans where during the uprising too much disturbance was witnessed. One month before, Murdan Singh, Raja Chokawala, destroyed 2 to 3 villages in *mauza* Nayankru and *mauza* Mundla. Though he pursued them, but they fled. One horse of theirs was captured. Prasram, informer of Adil Muhammad Khan was captured and his challan was sent. Dated 4 *Rabi* II, 1275 AH.

PP 559-61. *Ganaga Sahai,* Thanadar, Pargana *Chhatari to Nawwab Sikandar Begam.* Refers to her *parwana*, dated 26 *Rabi* I, 1275 AH, expressing anxiety that he did not write about those villages which were destroyed by the insurgents and where the insurgents were encamping, and that if he did not inform the receipt of the *parwana* it would not be good for him. He also did not write about those of his *ilaqa* who fought with the insurgents, and how many of them were killed or wounded, and how many of his *ilaqa* were killed or wounded, and how many fled from there, and who were those who were captured and arrested. Informs that prior to the receipt of the *parwana*, he has sent a letter on 22 *Rabi* I, 1275 AH that would have made everything clear. The fact is that the insurgent army entered in Bamhuri via Udaipura, *ilaqa nizamat-i junub* and after staying for one day in *mauza* Autia Chhapara, *ilaqa* Udaipura, they crossed river Narmada at *ghat* Patrora and through the territory of the British went towards the mountains of Mahadevpur. The insurgents did not destroy any village in the region. He and *tahsildar* along with the staff of *thana* and *tahsil* stood up in the *kachehri* to fight with the insurgents. Had they entired in their jurisdiction, they would not have hesitated in sacrificing their lives. There is peace in the region. The inhabitants of Bamhuri, Deori, Solwani and Udaipura were so scared that they fled. Now they were coming back. Dated 4 *Rabi* II, 1275 AH.

PP 563-6. *Harsahai*, Tahsildar *of Bamhuri, to Nawwab Sikandar Begam.* Refers to her *parwana*, dated 26 *Rabi* I, 1275 AH, expressing anxiety that when it was time to fight with the enemies he was not seen anywhere except in the fort or on the mountains. He totally forgot the loyalty to the salt, the bravery and sacrifice which was required. He did not yet write about the *pargana* and the villages which were destroyed by the insurgents, and where the insurgents were encamping. He must inform immediately about those who fought with the insurgents, as to how many insurgents were killed or wounded, and how many of his *ilaqa* were killed or wounded, and how many fled from there, and who were captured and arrested. Expresses his repentance that he went to the mountains when it was the time to fight with the insurgents. The mistake which he committed was not knowingly committed, but due to extreme situation he took such an extreme step. The report to this effect has been sent on 20 *Rabi* I, 1275. It is again repeated that when the insurgent forces who were 10, 000 to 12,000 in number, comprising both *sawars* and foot-soldiers arrived in Bamhuri and seiged it, he was sitting in the *kachehri* and distributing arms and ammunition. The soldiers upon hearing the news of the siege of Bamhuri ran away leaving him, the *muharrir* of *thana* in the *kachehri*, and the *thanadar* who had gone to perform the prayer in the mosque. The *thanadar* was arrested. After sunset, Khushhal Chand, peon of *thana*, and Natthi Khan, Dud Singh, Panchram, soldiers came to meet him. On 21 *Rabi* I, 1275 AH, the camp of insurgent forces was in *mauza* Chhapara, *pargana* Bareilly, situating at a distance of 5 *curoh* from Bamhuri. He sought the help of the *amil* of Bamhuri who said that, the day the insurgents arrived in Bamhuri, the *amil* and *thanadar* of Bareilly took refuge in the mountains. The *thanadars* and the *amils* of *mahal* Solwani, Chhatari, Deori, Udaipura and Bareilly situating at a distance of 7 or 8 or 12 *curoh,* fled and hid in the mountains or crossed the river Narmada. In such a situation what kind of bravery was expected from an individual who was helpless when the insurgent army was 10, 000 to 12,000 in strength. The insurgents reached Dehgaon, *ilaqa* Mahalpur, and devastated it. The distance of Dehgaon and Raisen is 6 *curoh*.

The news of the villages of Bamhuri is that no village in Bamhuri was destroyed by the insurgents. In *mauza* Kondani, Bharya Bhesra, the insurgent forces looted the flour, pulses, gram, mustard oil, rice etc. whatever they found there. Except that nothing like the utensils or jewellery or cash of the people fell in their hands as they had carried those items with them to the mountains. So the villages remained safe from destruction.

P 567. . . . . *To Lala Harsahai,* Tahsildar, *and Abbas Ali,* Thanadar, Pargana, *Bamhuri*. Refers to a letter, without stamp, dated 21 *Rabi* I, 12785 AH, requesting to come over there along with the *Thanadar*. Informs that there are only 15 soldiers in the *maha*l besides the guards. Says, if desired, he may reach there along with his soldiers. Says that day; the 24 *Rabi* I, 25 soldiers came from Kalyakhery *nizamat* and reached *mauza* Chainpur and by the evening, they would reach the *kachehry*. It is heard that some *sawars* have reached in his *mahal* sent by the government. It is must for them to inform what they would hear about the insurgents in Garhi and other places, Dated 24 *Rabi* I, 1275 AH.

P 569. *Paltu Lal to Nawwab Sikandar Begam.* As mentioned in her *parwana,* dated 28 *Rabi* I, 1275 AH, a list containing the number of troops, carried by Tantia Tope has been prepared from the files of the uprising and is being sent to her. The number of forces which differ from one file to other would be noticed by her. Dated 4 *Rabi* II, 1275 AH.

PP 571-2. Yaddasht, *Containing Details of the Troops of Tantia Tope and Other Insurgents*. On 17 *Rabi* I, 1275 AH, they arrived from Bhilsa in *mauza* Aradmau, *pargana* Garhi, *ilaqa* Bhopal and via Garhi, Rajghati and Bamhuri, they entered in *mauza* Patrora, *pargana* Udaipura and on 22 *Rabi* I, 1275 AH, they crossed the river Narmada and entered the British territory. Dated 4 *Rabi* II, 1275 AH.

P 573. *Paltu Lal to Nawwab Sikandar Begam.* As directed by her *parwana* of 28 *Rabi* I, 1275 AH, the information about staying of Tantia Tope and other insurgents in Bhopal and the date of crossing the river Narmada is submitted herewith. Dated 4 *Rabi* II, 1275 AH.

P 575. Yaddasht, *Containing Dates of Encampment of Tantia Tope and Other Insurgents in the State of Bhopal.*

P 577. *Saiyid Baqar Ali,* Tahsildar, Pargana *Chhatari, to Nawwab Sikandar Begam.* Refers to her *parwana,* dated 26 *Rabi* I, 1275 AH, informing that the forces of Tantia Tope have dispersed in small groups in the districts of east and south. It is a must that the perfect news of the insurgents should be gathered, and either they should be killed or arrested and their challan should be presented under security. For the last two and half years, she is continuously writing as how to arrest or kill the insurgents but no action has yet been taken. She is again asking him, as he is intending to flee, as to why there is no intention to become brave and gather courage to be his own master. Informs that the insurgents, by the grace of God, did not come in Chhatari so as to fight with them or to kill or arrest them. But they reached Udaipura via Bamhuri and at *ghat* Patrora crossed river Narmada and fled. Information to this effect has been sent to her through the letters, dated 20 and 22 of this month. He and Ganaga Sahai, *thanadar*, along with the staff of the *thana* and *tahsil* are in Garhi Chhatari. He did not go to the mountains or other place. She may make an enquiry into it. Assures whenever there will be a battle, he will prove his fedility and loyalty to the salt. Dated 5 *Rabi* II, 1275 AH.

PP 579-80. *Muhammad Abbas Ali,* Thanadar *of Bamhuri, to Nawwab Sikandar Begam.* Refers to her *parwana*, dated 26 *Rabi* I, 1275 AH, expressing her anxiety that wherever was a fight with the enemy he was not seen except in the fort or on the mountains and that he totally forgot the lesson of bravery and sacrifice and loyalty to the salt. He did not yet write as to how many villages were destroyed by the insurgents and what were those places where the insurgents were encamping. Who fought with the insurgents? How many insurgents were killed, and how many were wounded? Who were killed or wounded by the insurgents, and who fled? It is a must that as soon as he receives the *parwana*, he should submit all the details. Submits that whatever has been said it is a reality. There is nothing wrong in it. He does not have the courage to reply. But at the same time, he had informed through a letter, dated 22 *Rabi* II,

1275 AH, about the details of the *mahal*; how he got rid from the hands of insurgents, and how two insurgents with one big horse were captured. It is again explained that the day the insurgent forces who were 10, 000 to 12000 in strength both *sawars* and foot-soldiers entered Bamhuri and sieged it. He and the *tahsildar* of Bamhuri distributed arms and ammunitions among 20 soldiers who came from Udaipura to fight with the insurgents. Meanwhile a sudden noise was heard and Bamhuri was sieged. He saw that none of the soldiers was there as all had fled. He was helpless without the soldiers. The insurgent forces took him along. What bravery he would show before a huge army? From the letter of Chandulal, *tahsildar* of Garhi, it would have become clear that the insurgents devastated *mauza* Udaipura and Jaitpur, *ilaqa* Garhi. Upon hearing the report from the *tahsildar* of Garhi, about the happenings in Udaipura and Jaitpur, he immediately sent 20 soldiers for their help. Had the *thanadar* of Mahalpur and the *nazim* informed him about the situation, it would not have happened in Bamhuri. The insurgents collected the edibles; like flour, pulses, salt, mustard oil, rice, gurr besides cash and jewellery. No village was destroyed. No one from the village fought with the insurgents. No insurgent was killed or wounded. Likewise, no one of the village was killed or wounded from the hands of the insurgents. All the forces fled from the region and went to the other side of river Narmada. One *sawar* and one foot-soldier besides one horse from amongst the insurgent forces were captured by him and the *tahsildar* of Bamhuri, and sent them to the *nazim-i mashriq* along with the goods. Dated 5 *Rabi* II, 1275 AH.

P 581. *Saiyid Baqar Ali,* Tahsildar *of* Pargana *Chhatari, to Nawwab Sikandar Begam.* Refers to her *parwana,* dated 26 *Rabi* I, 1275 AH, expressing anxiety that for the last two years, he was demanding arms and ammunitions but when time came to fight with the enemy, he took shelter in the fort or in the mountains and forgot the lesson of bravery and loyalty to the salt. He did not yet write as to how many villages were destroyed by the insurgents? What were those palces where the insurgents were encamping? How many insurgents were killed and how many were wounded? How many fled and how many insurgents were arrested by the people of his region, and who were those who fought with the insurgents?

Informs that in the month of *Rabi* I, he was appointed to the post of *tahsildari* of *pargana* Chhatari. On 20th of the month, he arrived in the *pargana*. On 22nd, the news of fleeing of the dwellers of *pargana* and Bamhuri and Udaipura was heard in Chhatari and the people there also started to send their families to the mountains. He, besides Gori Shankar and Ganga Sahai, *thanadar*, along with a contingent of 4 soldiers of the *thana* and 12 other soldiers prepared themselves to fight with the insurgents. Finally, it was heard that the insurgents crossed the river Narmada at *ghat* Patrora and went to the other side of Narmada. No insurgent was wounded nor was anyone from this side wounded. The staff of this *mahal* is wrongly implicated with the staff of other *mahals*. Assures, that at the time of fighting they would stand firmly before the enemy forces.

P 583. *Harsahai*, Tahsildar *of Bamhuri, to Nawwab Sikandar Begam.* Informs of the statement of Shaikh Qasim which is in regard to fleeing of the insurgent forces of Tantia Tope across river Narmada and arriving in *mauza* Fatahpur and even 12 *curoh* beyond Fatahpur. The statement of Shaikh Qasim is recorded and is sent to her. The statement would make everything clear to her. Dated 5 *Rabi* II, 1275 AH.

P 585. *Statement of Shaikh Qasim, an Employee of the Government.* States that he is a soldier and a servant of the government and performs duty at *mahal* Udaipura. He further stated that he was carrying a letter of Madho Kishan, *amil* of Udaipura in the name of the *thanadar* of Bamhuri enquiring about the situation. He was asked whether the insurgents passed through his *pargana.* He replied that the insurgent army came from Bamhuri, passed through the villages of *pargana* Udaipura, encamped at Chhapara and then crossed the river Narmada at *ghat* Patrora. It created havoc among the masses as they thought that the insurgents night enter Udaipura and, therefore, they started fleeing. He was asked to tell when the *tahsildar* and *thanadar* fled from the *thana* and where the insurgent army was on that day. He replied, that day the insurgent army was at Chhapara, situating at a distance of 4 *coss* from Udaipura. He was asked to tell when the *tahsildar* and *thanadar* came back. He replied they came back on day 6.

P 587. *Jugal Kishore,* Tahsildar, *and Saiyid Qadir Ali,* Thanadar, *to Nuwwub Sikundur Begum.* Refers to her two *parwanas*; one dated 26 *Rabi* I, 1275 AH, expressing her anxiety that for the last two years, he was continuously demanding arms and ammunitions so much so that she became tired of his demand. But when time came to fight a battle he was seen nowhere except in the fort or in the mountains. God knows what happened to his courage and that he totally forgot the loyalty to the salt. He did not yet write as to how many villages were destroyed by the insurgents and what were those palces where the insurgents were encamping. Directing him to send the reply as soon as he receives the *parwana*, informing of those who fought with the insurgents, how many insurgents were killed and how many were wounded, how many fled and how many insurgents were arrested by the people of his region.

The other letter, dated 28 *Rabi* I, 1275 AH, tells that the army of Tantia has spread over the district of east and south and is staying there and directing him that they should be arrested or killed. Besides, for the last $2^{1/2}$ years, instructions have been issued in regard to arresting or killing the insurgents, that too was not remembered. Expresses his repentence and says that it was an unexpected situation that appeared from the side of Garhi Ambapani, a negligible number of soldiers whereas the insurgent army was 7,000 to 8,000 in strength, both *sawars* and foot-soldiers. The former did not dare to stand before the latter, and vacated their houses in the *kachehry* and took shelter under the forts or the mountains. This is really an act of disloyalty and liable to be punished. But a foot soldier is helpless before a *sawar*. Dated 7 *Rabi* II, 1266 *Fasli*.

It contains the order that the letter and *parwanas* of Nawwab Sikandar Begam, dated 26 and 28 *Rabi* I, 1275 AH, addressed to the *amil* and *thanadar* of Deori may be sent to Lala Paltu Lal, *muhafiz-i daftar-i insha*, for inclusion in the register and keeping in the *daftar*. A copy of the order may be sent to Daulat Rai, *nazim-i mashriq*, informing that Jugal Kishore, *amil*, and Saiyid Qadir Ali, *thanadar* of Deori, who sent their reply in a combined letter responding to her two *parwanas,* have committed a crime as it is against the rule. A fine of Re. 1 upon each is imposed which may be obtained from them and deposited in the treasury. They should also be instructed that in future, reply of every *parwana* should be submitted separately by the *amil* and the *thanadar*. Dated 11 *Rabi* II, 1275 AH.

PP 589-90. *Muhammad Abbas Ali,* Thanadar *of Bamhuri, to Nawwab Sikandar Begam.* Refers to her *parwana*, dated 26 *Rabi* I, 1275 AH, directing him to pursue the insurgents, by carrying the forces of *thana* Bamhuri and the *jagirdars* together. Says, as directed, the forces of *thana* and *tahsil* are put together except Jawahar Singh, *jagirdar* of *mauza* Guthi Hamirpur, who is standing at *mahal* Siwans along with his forces. Requests that the said *jagirdar* may be discharged from the present assignment to join him there along with the *bakhshi*. Dated 5 *Rabi* II, 1275 AH.

It contains the order that the letter may be sent to Lala Paltu Lal, *muhafiz-i daftar-i insha*, for inclusion in the register and keeping in the *daftar*. A copy of the order may be sent to Saiyid Abbas Ali, *thanadar* of Bamhuri, through Ghulam Murtaza Khan, informing that Jawahar Singh, *jagirdar* of *mauza* Guthi Hamirpur falls under the territory of the *riyasat* and he has nothing to do with his contingent. That contingent would remain in Siwans and would not come to Bamhuri. The battalion which is sent earlier will remain there. If he depends more upon that battalion, he should call back the said battalion from Siwans and this battalion may be sent to Bamhuri. Dated 8 *Rabi* II, 1275 AH.

PP 591-2. *Harsahai,* Tahsildar *of Bamhuri, to Nawwab Sikandar Begam.* Refers to his two letters sent to her on 18th *Rabi* I, 1275 AH, informing about the devastation of *mauza* Udaipura and Jaitpur, *pargana* Garhi. The other letter that related to the siege of Garhi by the insurgent forces, contained her order to clarify the reason for the delay in sending the letters. Says on 3 *Rabi* II, 1275 AH, he wrote to Saiyid Abbas Ali, *thanadar* of Bamhuri, asking him to explain the reasons for the delay. The *thanadar* gave his explanation for the delay at the back of his letter. On 19th of the month, the inhabitants of Bamhuri, hearing the news of the attack of insurgents upon Garhi fled and none was left. All such papers were tied together and reached Padarya as the insurgents had sieged Bamhuri. Due to this, the delay occurred in sending the letters. Dated 8 *Rabi* II, 1275 AH.

P 593. *Muhammad Abbas Ali,* Thanadar *of Bamhuri, to Nawwab Sikandar Begam.* Refers to his letter, dated 18th of the month, and informs that he immediately became ready and called Ramkishan to carry the post. But he did not come. On 19th of the month, when the people of the *qasba* heard about the attack of the insurgent forces on Garhi, no one remained in the *qasba* as all had fled. He also folded all official papers and came to *mauza* Padarya. The insurgent forces surrounded Bamhuri and arrested one person. There was nobody to carry the posts. In this way, the papers were not sent for two days. On day third, the posts were sent to the government. Dated 4 *Rabi* II, 1275 AH.

P 594. *Harsahai,* Tahsildar *of Bamhuri, To Saiyid Abbas Ali,* Thanadar *of Bamhuri.* Refers to the two letters, dated 18 *Rabi* I, 1275 AH, informing the devastation of *mauza* Udaipura and Jaitpur, *ilaqa* Garhi, by the insurgent forces as reported by Chandulal, *tahsildar* of Garhi. The other letter which was in regard to capturing of *mahal* Garhi by the insurgents, as stated by Kalyan Chand Seth, reached to the Nawwab after 6 days. The Nawwab has asked for the reason of this delay. Urges him to reply for the reason and convey the same to the government. Dated 3 *Rabi* II, 1275 AH.

P 595-6. *Harsahai,* Tahsildar *of Bamhuri, to Nawwab Sikandar Begam.* Informs that day, as demanded by the *tahsildar* of Garhi Ambapani, 20 soldiers were sent to help him fight with the insurgent forces. Thereafter, Munyan Chand Seth of Garhi came and stated that Garhi Ambapani was captured by the insurgents. His statement was recorded and sent to her.

P 597. *Harsahai,* Tahsildar, *to Nawwab Sikandar Begam.* Informs, that day a letter from Lala Chandulal, *tahsildar* of *mahal* Garhi Ambapani, addressed to him and the *thanadar* was received, informing that the insurgents devastated *mauza* Aradmau and Jaitpur. The *thanadar* has gone to deal with them and he is in Garhi. Informs that as soon as he received the letter of the *tahsildar* of Garhi, he sent 20 armed soldiers of the *thana* along with two *jamadars* of the *thana* and *mahal* to help the *tahsildar* of Garhi. He himself is fully attentive for the safety of the region. He has also sent letters to the *thanadar* and *tahsildar* of *mahal* Udaipura and Bareilly. Requests for providing 15 soldiers to each region for the sake of safety as after sending 18 soldiers to help the *tahsildar* of Garhi, less number of soldiers has left in the region. The region of Garhi is nearby to this region. Dated 18 *Rabi* I, 1275 AH.

P 599. *Muhammad Jamal al-Din*, Madar al-Maham, to *Nawwab Sikandar Begam.* Informs that as ordered, 738 notifications have been printed from *matba' Sikandari* in regard to giving order to all the employees of the army to remain ready and alert and the same are sent to the government. Dated 8 *Rabi* II, 1275 AH.

File No. 297, K
Box No. 16.
No. of Documents 12

P 601. *An Order was Issued that the Letter may be Sent to Lala Paltu Lal,* Muhafiz-i Daftar-i Insha, *for Inclusion in the File and Keeping in the* Daftar. A copy of the order along with the notification, carrying royal stamp addressed to *Madar al-Maham* to publish 738 copies from *Matba' Sikandari* and to send it to the government. Dated 28 *Rabi* I, 1275 AH.

P 603. *Saiyid Abbas Ali,* Thanadar *of Bamhuri, to Nawwab Sikandar Begam.* Refers to her *parwana,* dated 3 *Rabi* II, 1275 AH, for not sending the letter by the *amil* and *thanadar* of Udaipura from the day the insurgent forces crossed the *ghat* in *mauza* Patrora. Explains as soon as the news of the arrival of the insurgent forces was heard, he conveyed through Hyder Muhammad, *jamadar* of *thana* Garhi Ambapani, and requested for sending 20 soldiers for help, and as desired by the *tahsildar* of Bamhuri to gaurd the *chaukis* he gave him Rs. 2 to reach Kalyakhery under *nizamat-i junub* and then send it by post to the government. Thereafter, on 21st, 4 soldiers came back and stated that the previous day, the insurgent forces reached *mahal* Bamhuri and devastated it. The *tahsildar* fled from there but the *thanadar* was captured. Hearing this news, everyone fled. He too started collecting official papers and came along with his family members in *mauza* Basodah in Bamhuri, situating at 1/2 curoh distance from Udaipura towards south in the house of *malguzar*. He then along with the *jamadar* of *thana* and *mahal*, and 5 to 6 soldiers came to Udaipura and distributed arms and ammunitions among the soldiers of *malguzars* and prepared themselves to fight with the insurgent forces. But some soldiers, after taking the arms and ammunitions, disappeared. Except 5 or 6 soldiers and the *jamadar* of the *thana* and *mahal*, nobody remained in his company. Another news about the insurgent forces is that they reached *mauza* Tunga, *ilaqa* Bareilly, and Chhaner and Chhapara, *ilaqa* Udaipura. By the evening or early in the morning, they would reach Udaipura. It was not possible to fight with them with just 5 or 6 soldiers, therefore, he came to Basodah, Bamhuri.

P 605. *Shahzad Rai,* Thanadar *of Mahalpur, to Nawwab Sikandar Begam.* Refers to her order, dated 6 *Rabi* II, 1275 AH, directing him to explain the technique with which he got himself released from the hands of the insurgents. Informs that he has already communicated about the technique which he adopted with all the details about his arrest and then his release from them in his letter, dated 23 *Rabi* I, 1275 AH. Dated 9 *Rabi* II, 1275 AH.

PP 607-8. *Order of the Nawwab as Indicated on the Letter of Shahzad Rai,* Thanadar *of Mahalpur.* Orders that the letter along with the royal *parwana,* addressed to Shahzad Rai, *thanadar* of Mahalpur, dated 26 *Rabi* I, 1275 AH may be sent to Lala Paltu Lal, *muhafiz-i daftar-i insha*, for inclusion in file and to keep it in *daftar*. A copy of the order may be sent to *thanadar* of Mahalpur through Lala Daulat Rai, *nazim-i mashriq,* directing him to explain the technique with which he got himself released from the hands of insurgents. Reiterates that it is a must to write to the government about the technique which led to his release from captivity, as an order to this effect would be issued only after receiving an elaborate reply from him. Dated 9 *Rabi* II, 1275 AH.

P 609. *Ghulam Murtaza Khan to Nawwab Sikandar Begam.* Sends the statement of Nand Lal, dated 7 *Rabi* II, 1275 AH, addressed to Muhammad Inayat Ali, *thanadar* of *pargana* Bamhuri, informing that the insurgents captured 12 persons; some from Gond and some from Karar. Dated 12 *Rabi* II, 1275 AH.

It contains the order that the letter and statement may be sent to Paltu Lal, *muhafiz-i dafar-i insha*, for inclusion in the register and keeping in the *daftar*. A copy of the statement may be sent to Bhawani Prasad, *wakil* to inform the Political Agent and his reply may be communicated to her. Dated 13 *Rabi* II, 1275 AH.

PP 611-12. *Report of* Thana *Bamhuri*. The report of 7 *Rabi* II, 1275 AH is that there is peace in the region. Durga Prasad, *thanadar* of Ghairatganj, came there. From him it was heard that in the battle held between the British and insurgent forces, the latter got defeated and became hapless and divided themselves into three groups. One group led by Adil Muhammad Khan, went towards the Narmada. The second group went to Madawrah. They wanted to loot in the region and join the first group. From him it was also heard that Tantia Tope told Adil Muhammad Khan that he was creating nuisance in the army and he should not, be with them. Adil Muhammad Khan told him that he too did not want to remain with them and would join Nana Sahab. From Nand Lal of *mauza* Aotya, *ilaqa* Udaipura, it was heard that insurgent forces captured 12 persons of Gond and Karar and engaged them as *begar* (forced labour). At Fatahpur their noses were wounded and thereafter, released them to return to their homes. The statement of Nand Lal is enclosed for further clarification. He then returned to his house with chopped nose. Dated 8 *Rabi* II, 1275 AH.

It contains the order that the news-report may be sent to Paltu Lal, *muhafiz-i dafar-i insha*, for inclusion in the register and keeping in the *daftar*. A copy of the news-report may be sent to Bhawani Prasad, *wakil* to report the Political Agent and his reply may be communicated to her.

PP 613-14. *Statement of Nand Lal in the Presence of*

Saiyid Abbas Ali, Thanadar *of Bamhuri*. States that his name is Nand Lal and his father's name is Hariram, caste *teli*, and a dweller of Aotya, *ilaqa* Udaipura. He is a shopkeeper and a farmer.

Q. Why did he come to *qasba* Bamhuri?

R. He came to meet Shyam of Bamhuri, his father-in-law.

Q. Has the insurgent army passed through the village which has gone towards Narmada?

R. The camp of the said army was in *mauza* Chhapara, *ilaqa* Udaipura. Some *sawars* entered *mauza* Aotya and destroyed it. They also made 12 persons and some gond captive. They took them along upto *mauza* Fatahpur, where they chopped their noses and then freed them. When they came back to their houses, people of the village met them and noticed that their noses were chopped.

Q. Did he ask them, why their noses were chopped?

R. They were asked by the people. But they did not reply anything.

Q. Did he see himself that the insurgent army had chopped their noses?

R. It was his village. He saw himself and heard from none.

PP 615-16. *Madho Kishan,* Amil *of Udaipura, to Nawwab Sikandar Begam.* Refers to his earlier letter, dated 10 *Rabi* II, submitting the statement of Aman Ali, *sawar,* deployed at *chauki* Bamhuri, who stated what he heard from a person coming from Chhapara. He stated that the insurgent forces crossed river Narmada at *ghat* Patrora and were coming. To check its authenticity, 4 *sawars* have gone from Chhaner to that place. Hearing this news, he immediately sent two soldiers to Chhaner from there. The said letter has been sent through the post. The soldiers just came back and stated that the *sawars* of the British government were guarding *ghat* Patroda of Narmada. The dwellers of village of the other side of river Namada are saying that the insurgent forces have returned back and that the *sawars* of the British government are on guard. They have seen the mobility of insurgent forces on the other side of the river. Information to this effect was a must which he did. Dated 8 *Rabi* II, 1275 AH.

PP 617-18. *Madho Kishan,* Amil *of Mahal Udaipura, to Nawwab Sikandar Begam.* Refers to her order, dated 8 *Rabi* I, 1275 AH, as mentioned on his letter, for not giving information of the arrival of the insurgents in Udaipura. Informs that he has already sent her a letter on 9 *Rábi* I, 1275 AH, giving explaination of not receiving letters from the *amil* and *thanadar* of *mahal.* A copy of that is again sent to her. Hopes that he would be pardoned as the insurgent forces had overpowered the people of the region. As a result, they had fled as they were scared of their honour and dignity. Nobody was there to carry the letter. So, this was the reason for not sending the report of the insurgents. It had become impossible to save his life. Those who were nourished the whole life, they too became strangers. If the employees of *mahal* would have been with him, the information would have been communicated through them. The difficulties through which he passed in those days, others should never. Dated 21 *Rabi* II, 1275 AH.

PP 619-20. *Copy of the Letter Explaining the Reason for Not Sending the Letters, Dated 9 Rabi* II, *1275 AH.* Refers to the royal *parwana,* dated 3 *Rabi* II, 1275 AH, which is regarding not sending the letters by the *amil* and *thanadar* of Udaipura from the day the insurgents went from there after crossing the *ghat* at *mauza* Patrora and the reasons behind this. Explains that, on 20 *Rabi* I, 1275 AH, he had sent a letter, informing the coming of insurgent forces at Garhi Ambapani and at *mauza* Dehgaon, and providing 20 soldiers for the safety of the *chauki,* as desired by the *tahsildar* of Bamhuri. Thereafter, on 21st of the month, 4 soldiers from among the soldiers who were sent to Bamhuri came back. They stated that the previous day, the insurgent forces arrived at *mahal* Bamhuri and devastated it. The *tahsildar* fled from there and the insurgents arrested the *thanadar*. Hearing the news, everyone fled from there. He too came out of his house to know about his people, and started collecting the official goods and goods of his house. Thereafter, the people of his house were shifted to Basodah, Bamhuri, situating at a distance of half a *curoh* from Udaipura towards south in the house of a *malguzar* of the said *mauza*. He then, along with the *jamadar* of *thana* and *mahal* besides 5 to 6 soldiers, came to Udaipura for the distribution of cartridges and arms and decided to fight with the insurgents. But some soldiers did not receive arms and disappeared. Except 5 to 6 soldiers, and the *jamadar* of *mahal,* no one remained in his company. Another news, as heard, is that the insurgent forces have arrived at *mauza* Tunga, *ilaqa* Bareilly Chhaner, and Chhapara, *ilaqa* Udaipura, and that they would capture Udaipura by the evening or in the morning. Hearing this news, these 5 or 6 soldiers did not dare to face the insurgents. He then went back to Basodah Bamhuri. From there, the siege of insurgent forces from *mahal* Bamhuri to *mahal* Bareilly and the surrounding villages of *qasba* Udaipura, deploying the guards everywhere and sending the informers and *sawars* to search the *amil* was planned. Besides, the news of the arrival of other group of insurgents behind this group and due to fear of interception of these letters, he did not send the letters to the government. Another large group of insurgents arrived in Udaipura on 24th of month. In order to pacify and console the inhabitants, he wrote letters to the *nizamat* and wanted to convey all these details to the government but in the meanwhile he received the royal *parwana* ordering him to provide *rasad* to the British army at Chhapara. No sooner he received the *parwana*, he became busy in arranging the *rasad* for the British army by sending the soldiers and *jamadar* in the villages. Thus, he forgot to send the reply of the *parwana*. In the meantime, he received the letter of Muhammad Raza Husain, *nazim-i junub* from Jogigarh, informing the return of the British army from Raisen to Hoshangabad. Thereafter, on 26th *Rabi* I, 1275 AH, he came to *qasba* Udaipura, wrote the letter of all the happenings and sent it through Chand Khan.

P 621. Tahsildar *of Bareilly to Nawwab Sikandar Begam.* Refers to a letter, dated 26 *Rabi* I, 1275 AH, informing the release of Saiyid Abbas Ali, *thanadar* of Bamhuri from the captivity of insurgents by adopting a technique. In reply an order, dated 28 *Rabi* I, 1275 AH was received, directing that the order may be passed on to Shaikh Muhammad Lal, *tahsildar* through Ghulam Murtaza Khan, communicating that he has written about the release of Saiyid Abbas Ali, *thanadar* of Bamhuri from the captivity of the insurgent forces due to some technique. But he did not mention about the technique which he adopted that led to his release. It is a must that the technique should be made clear so that an order may be issued in that light. Informs he wrote a letter on 8th of the month to the *tahsildar* of Bamhuri to explain the method which was adopted regarding the release of the said *thanadar*. In reply, he wrote to him on 4 *Jumada* I and it came to his notice that there was a person who was a Haji whom he met in the days when the forces reached Nayagaon. Someone from the army asked why he was sitting. He replied he was ill. When all the armymen reached in their camps and none was left behind, the said Haji told him to run away. Thus, the *thanadar* and *tahsildar* ran away. This was the technique which let them to flee by her grace without any harm. What was said was written down. The story of the release of Saiyid Abbas Ali, *thanadar* of Bamhuri, from the captivity of insurgent army as written by Lala Hersahai, *tahsildar*, is communicated to her word-by-word. Dated 19 *Jumada* I, 1275 AH.

P 623. *The Statement of Madari Khan* Chaudhury *of Panch Farhat Bakhsh,* Qasba *Bamhuri.* It is that it was 2 pm when Tantia Tope along with 15, 000 forces came to Bamhuri via Rajghati. The army remained standing at Kondani but 50 *sawars* came to Bamhuri. From them, 25 *sawars* went to Panch Farhat Bakhsh and 25 *sawars* were on the gate of Dulhari and captured both the post of Bamhuri. At that time, Kamuda, soldier of *mahal*, called while standing at *kachehri* that the forces entered the Bagh. Hearing this, Hersahai, *tahsildar* of Bamhuri, and Ajodhya Prasad, *mutasaddi* of *thana,* brother of *tahsildar*, fled riding on horse. Thereafter, Abbas Ali, *thanadar*, asked where *tahsildar* was. People told that he fled. *Thanadar* said, he did a wrong thing. *Thanadar* went towards Dulhari while riding on horse. Meanwhile, *thanadar* was caught by the *sawars* of Tantia Tope. The soldiers who were with him fled. So did the soldiers of *tahsil*. Jamiat Khan, *jamadar*, and Gorelal, soldier went to the Bagh. Meanwhile, the *sawars* of Tantia Tope asked him who he was. He said he was the caretaker of the Bagh. Jamiat Khan, *jamadar*, and Gorelal, soldier said that they were on duty at the Bagh. The *sawars* of Tantia Tope asked them for their weapons. *Jamadar* said, 'He is a Muslim and he too is a Muslim, he should not snatch his weapon. Better he may take him along'. The *sawars* did not accept and snatched his weapon. The *jamadar* and soldier were caught and presented before Tantia Tope and informed that they had snatched their weapon. Tantia Tope asked to return their weapons and free them. The army reached sometime after the arrival of *sawars* and cordoned off entire Bamhuri. In the entire army, there is one *rauti* wherein Tantia Tope encamps. This *rauti* is guarded by 40 soldiers with swords. It stands in the middle of the army and the army is around him. Tantia Tope came in the market and forced open the shop of Asaram Seth.

File No. 298, A
Box No. 16
No. of Documents 21

A False Report About Adil Muhammad Khan, the Insurgent, that he is Encamping at Garhi Ambapani and Cleaning Valleys in Mauza Sakunian

PP 1-6. Contents

P 7. *Daulat Rai,* Nazim-i Mashriq, *to Nawwab Sikandar Begam.* Refers to the statement of Khub Chand, *harkara,* posted at *thana* Mahalpur, who was sent by Lala Ajodhya Prasad, *thanadar* of Mahalpur to Garhi Ambapani to carry the *dak*. From that, it is clear that he reached Garhi with the *dak* papers and then went to *mauza* Kareta. There, he met 6 *sawars* and some foot-soldiers who enquired from him as to who he was. He replied that he came in search of his lost cattle. The army of the insurgents is in *mauza* Budhya Langra, *ilaqa* Muhammad Garh, situating at a distance of 5 *curoh* from Garhi. The statement is sent to her. One group of insurgents led by Tantia Tope has gone to Udaipura coming from Garhi, Dehgaon, Bamhuri and Bareilly. Dated 22 *Rabi* I, 1275 AH.

It contains the order that the letter along with the statement of Khub Chand, *harkara*, may be sent to Lala Paltu Lal, *muhafiz-i daftar-i insha*, for inclusion in the register and keeping in the *daftar*. A copy of the order may be sent to Daulat Rai, *nazim-i mashriq*, through Muhammad Jamal al-Din Khan, *madar al-maham*, directing him to enquire about the encampment of other group of insurgents and send a report immediately. Dated 24 *Rabi* I, 1275 AH.

PP 9-10. *Statement of Khub Chand,* Harkara, *Posted at* Thana *Mahalpur*, Dated 21 Rabi I, 1275 AH. States that his name is Khub Chand, his father's name is Kesri, and he is a dweller of *pargana* Sangal, Mahalpur. States that he is carrying the *dak* to hand it over to the *harkara* at Garhi. If the *harkara* is not available there, he should carry it to Siwans. Says, he reached Garhi but found nobody in Garhi. On the way, he saw 6 *sawars* and some foot-soldiers in the jungle. They asked him who he was and from where he came. He replied that he had lost his cattle and came in search of it. They followed him. He fled and entered in the field of *juar* and through the forests he came back. The army of the insurgents is in *mauza* Budhya Langra, *ilaqa* Muhammad Garh, situating at a distance of 5 *curoh* from Garhi.

PP 11-12. *Daulat Rai,* Nazim-i Mashriq *to Nawwab Sikandar Begam.* Refers to the letters of Shaikh Muhammad Abd al-Rahman, *thanadar* of Garhi, and Shaikh Ihsan Ali, *tahsildar*, and Lala Shahzad Rai, *thanadar* of Mahalpur, dated 22 *Rabi* I, 1275 AH, intimating of their arrival at Mahalpur after the release from the captivity of the insurgent forces and proceeding of the first group of insurgents towards river Narmada and the arrival of next group at Garhi till the previous day, and requesting to prevent them. Informs that just after the arrival of the letter, it was sent to Hafiz Muhammad Hasan, *naib bakhshi*, requesting him to prevent the insurgents who would do the needful. The letter is sent to her for her perusal. It is clear that one group of insurgents reached Narmada via Garhi and Dehgaon. The second group in which Adil Muhammad Khan, the insurgent, is also present might enter Garhi, the next day. After the arrival of the *tahsildar* and *thanadar*, a detailed report would be submitted. Dated 22 *Rabi* I, 1275 AH.

P 13. *Shaikh Muhammad Abd al-Rahman,* Thanadar *of Garhi, and Shaikh Ihsan Ali,* Tahsildar, *and Lala Shahzad Rai,* Thanadar *of Mahalpur to Daulat Rai,* Nazim-i Mashriq. Inform that by the grace of God and blessings of the govennment, on 29th of the month, they by their wisdom and strategy got themselves freed at Chhapara, situating adjacent to Narmada, and reached Mahalpur on foot after travelling through the mountains. As two groups of insurgents are following them and Adil Muhammad Khan is also among them, if an attempt is made to cordon him it would be good. A *harkara* of *thana* Chandpura, who was sent to Garhi by the *thanadar* to enquire about the insurgents, came back and stated that another army would reach Garhi, the next day, and then he left for Chandpura. The first group of insurgents has crossed river Narmada. The second group which is approaching, could be cordoned. Dated 23 *Rabi* I, 1275 AH.

P 15. *Muhammad Raza Husain,* Nazim-i Junub*, to Nawwab Sikandar Begam.* Informs about the letter received from the *tahsildar* and *thanadar* of *pargana* Jogigarh, dated 24 *Rabi* I, 1275 AH, informing the crossing of river Narmada by the insurgents, the rest of army along with Adil Muhammad Khan is at Garhi Ambapani and Dehgaon, and cleaning the *valley* Sagotia for cannon. Sends the same to her, as it would make everything clear. Dated 22 *Rabi* I, 1275 AH.

PP 17-18. *Imtiaz Ali and Shaikh Rahim Bakhsh,* Thanadars *of Jogigarh, to Muhammad Raza Husain,* Nazim-i Junub. Inform that they had sent Baliram, peon to *mauza* Khamarya and other villages. He came back that day and stated as told him Gorilal, *mustajir* of *mauza* Khamarya, that one person of the said *mauza* had gone to Dehgaon, *ilaqa* Mahalpur. He came and said that Adil Muhammad Khan was in Gathi Ambapani. That day, i.e. 23rd *Rabi* I, he marched from Garhi and encamped at Dehgaon. He is having in his company about 16, 000 forces. Out of these, 7,000 forces are at *mauza* Dehgaon, 1,000 at Rajghati, 2,000 forces with cannon are still at Garhi Ambapani and 6,000 forces are at Hardor. Baliram, peon saw from his own eyes that the dwellers of villages like Kamrora, Satra and Khuti were fleeing due to fear of this force. Ganga of *mauza* Kandhela said to Gorilal that he was sent by Kharagram for spying in Garhi Ambapani and was arrested by the insurgents, suspecting him as an informer. The situation is that the valley of Sagotia is being cleared. An army of 10, 000 with Adil Muhammad Khan was at Garhi Ambapani. Shaikh Nur Muhammad, former *tahsildar* of Chandpura was in cativity. Says, what he heard he conveyed. Dated 24 *Rabi* I, 1275 AH.

P 19. *Muhammad Raza Husain,* Nazim-i Junub, *to Nawwab Sikandar Begam.* Informs about a letter in Hindi received from the *tahsildar* and *thanadar, pargana* Jogigarh, dated 23 *Rabi* I, 1275 AH along with a letter of Gorilal, *mustajir* of *mauza* Khamarya and Baliram, peon of the said *thana,* informing the presence of Adil Muhammad Khan along with 1,000 *sawars* and foot-soldiers, besides 14 cannon at Garhi. The same, besides the letter in Hindi, along with its transliteration is sent to her so that things may become clear after going through these correspondences. *Mauza* Khamarya in *pargana* Jogigarh is situating on the border of the said *pargana* which is at a distance of 4 to 5 *curoh* from Garhi Ambapani. Dated 22 *Rabi* I, 1275 AH.

P 21. *Saiyid Imtiaz Ali and Rahim Bakhsh,* Thanadars, *to Muhammad Raza Husain,* Nazim-i Junub. Sending a letter in Hindi received from Gorilal, *mustajir, mauza* Khamarya, and Baliram, peon, which contains the news of the insurgent forces. Dated 23 *Rabi* I, 1275 AH.

P 23. *Transliteration of the Hindi Letter of Gorilal, Mustajir,* Mauza *Khamarya,* Pargana *Jogigarh*. Reports that day, the date is 22nd, day Sunday in the afternoon Ganga, cobbler, *mauza* Khadela, came from Garhi Ambapani. He stated that Adil Muhammad Khan with a contingent of 1,000 *sawars* and foot-soldiers with 22 elephants and 14 cannon along with magazine is present. He is intending to go to Raisen and thus, the *valley* Sagotia is being cleared. In the night, one *balahi* came from *mauza* Pilkasiri, *pargana* Bari, and said that the army of Tantia Tope was encamping at Tonga, *pargana* Bareilly. His intention is to arrest Thakur Das Patel, Autiawala and to devastate Udaipura and Chhaner. But Patel has fled and the army is encamping there. Reports that one person has gone to Garhi, as and when he returns the report will be sent. The two should be careful and alert as the army movement is continuous. Dated 23 *Rabi* I, 1275 AH.

PP 25-6. *The Letter in Hindi Devanagari.*

P 27. *Order of the Nawwab as Mentioned in the Letter of 'Abd al-Karim Ansari.* The letter may be sent to Lala Paltu Lal, *muhafiz-i daftar-i insha*, for inclusion in the file and keeping in the *daftar*. A copy of the order may be sent to Haji 'Abd al-Karim, Agenty III, communicating that from the newspaper and other sources, it has come to her notice that a group of other insurgents is in east district of Bhopal State. Some have written that Adil Muhammad Khan is also in that group along with a contingent of 7,000 to 8,000, comprising of both *sawars* and foot-soldiers with 12 cannon and the way to valley Sagotia is being cleared. Directs him to make an enquiry into it. It is also to be ascertained that whether the insurgents have crossed river Narmada or a group of insurgents is in Bhopal. If so, then at what place. Also, sends 100 pieces of soap, and 50 Shatranji as desired by General Mitchell may be provided to him. Dated 23 *Rabi* I, 1275 AH.

P 29. *Daulat Rai,* Nazim-i Mashriq, *to Nawwab Sikandar Begam.* Refers to her order as mentioned on the top of his letter, directing to enquire and inform about the second group of insurgents as to where it is. Whatever news from the *mahals* and *thanas* is received in his office, should be immediately sent to her. Says there is still no news of the second group of insurgents as to communicate her. The true news after the assessment without any deletion or addition would be communicated to her. Informs that day from the writings of Durga Prasad, *thanadar* of Ghairatganj, it is learnt that there is no second group of insurgents in the region which has already been communicated through his letter. Dated 26 *Rabi* I, 1275 AH.

P 33. *Daulat Rai,* Nazim-i Mashriq, *to Nawwab Sikandar Begam.* Informs about a letter received from Shaikh Abd al-Rahman, *Thanadar* of Garhi, dated 27 *Rabi* I, 1275 AH, informing of the arrival of Adil Muhammad Khan along with a contingent of 7,000, comprising of both *sawars* and foot-soldiers at Bagrod with an intention to come to Bhopal, and preparation of 50 maund sweets (*sherini*) for *fatiha* on the graveyard of his father at Muhammad Garh. In view of this, he has requested for help. The same is sent to her. Informs that day the *qila'dar* of Raisen along with the battalion of *qila'* has gone to Garhi where his son is ill. Now in Raisen no force is left, neither of *jagirdar* nor that of the *qila'dar*. Dated 28 *Rabi* I, 1275 AH.

PP 35-6. . . . *To Diwan Daulat Rai,* Nazim-i Mashriq. Gharibdas Patel of *mauza* Sank through Shamsher, soldier of this *thana* who was sent in disguise to enquire about the gathering of insurgent forces in the desert of Aradmau and Jaitpur, has conveyed that Adil Muhammad Khan, having a contingent of 7,000 comprising of both *sawars* and foot-soldiers has reached Khorai and thereafter reached Bagrod and intending to come to this side, and to make 50 maund *sherini* from Muhammad Garh for performing *fatiha* on the graveyard of his father. The coming of Adil Muhammad Khan has been seen by the reporter with his own eyes. This has also been reported by 2 to 3 other persons. On the basis of that, two soldiers with a letter addressed to the *thanadar* of Basodah has been sent. Whatever news is received from there would be conveyed thereafter. It should also be clear upon him that nobody is ready to serve as an informer. Resquests if some forces are sent there, it would not be less than a blessing for him. Three insurgents who had come earlier, were hanged. Two of them were on way to Basodah and another one was found hanged from a tree in the desert of Aradmau. The other news, as heard, would be communicated in due course. Dated 27 *Rabi* I, 1275 AH.

P 37. Parwana-i Ishtahari *of Nawwab Sikandar Begam to Her Officials Like The* Bakhshi, Naib Bakhshi, Nazim-i Mashriq. It is heard that one group of insurgents along with a contingent of 8,000 soldiers and 12 cannon is in Garhi Ambapani. Some say that Adil Muhammad Khan too is in that group. God's anger fell on the *tahsildar*, and *thanadar* of east district as their negligence was as much as that they did not make an enquiry into it and inform the government. Directs them to choose 4 clever informers and send them to Garhi Ambapani. They should hide themselves and see if Adil Muhammad Khan is in the second group of insurgents and inform the government about them and their chiefs. The distance of Garhi Ambapani from that palce is 55 mile or $27^{1/2}$ *curoh*. The informers would come within two days from there. Dated 28 *Rabi* I, 1275 AH.

P 39. Parwana *of Nawwab Sikandar Begam to Diwan Daulat Rai,* Nazim-i Mashriq. Refers to his letter, dated 28 *Rabi* I, 1275 AH, along with the letter of Shaikh Abd al-Rahman, *thanadar* of Garhi Ambapani, informing the arrival of Adil Muhammad Khan in *mauza* Bagrod. But it is not clear whether he is carrying cannon or not. It is not understandable if Adil Muhammad Khan, after separating his ways from Tantia Tope, is staying there as he is not in a strong position or his fate has brought him there. Directs him to enquire into the matter and report to her. Dated 29 *Rabi* I, 1275 AH.

PP 41-2. Parwana *of Nawwab Sikandar Begam to Hafiz Muhammad Hasan Khan,* Naib Bakhshi *of Murawwat Muhammad Khan.* From the letter of Daulat Rai, *nazim-i mashriq,* dated 28 *Rabi* I, 1275 AH and from the letter of Shaikh Abd al-Rahman, *thanadar* of Garhi Ambapani, it is learnt that Adil Muhammad Khan has come to Bagrod. He is directed that he along with his force and cannon should remain in Raisen and make proper arrangement there. Whenever Khan Zaman Khan, *qila'dar*, needs his help he should go there to rescue him. If the *qila'dar*, asks for cannon he himself go there with the cannon and deploy his forces at the *qila'* of Raisen and manage the affairs of *qila'* at his own. Dated 29 *Rabi* I, 1275 AH.

P 43. Parwana *of Nawwab Sikandar Begam to Shaikh Abd al-Rahman,* Thanadar, *Garhi Ambapani.* From the letter of Daulat Rai, *nazim-i mashriq,* dated 28 *Rabi* I, 1275 AH, it is learnt, that 3 persons have been hanged; two on way to Basodah and one in the desert of Aradmau. But he has not mentioned as to who were those three persons and what were their name. Directs him to enquire about their names and communicate the same to her. Authentic news about Adil Muhammad Khan, may be conveyed to her. The authenticity of the news should be gathered only from the *zamindars* and soldiers. The news sent by the *zamindars* and soldiers should also be verified and then only it should be sent to the government at the earliest. Dated 29 *Rabi* I, 1275 AH.

P 45. *Nand Kishore, Peon to Nawwab Sikandar Begam.* Informs that as directed, he went to Garhi Ambapani to see the developments at valley Sagotia adjoining Garhi Ambapani and to know about the insurgents. Says, when he reached Garhi Ambapani he found no sign of the insurgents there. The dwellers of Garhi and the villages adjoining to it were happy and at ease. Dated 29 *Rabi* I, 1275 AH.

PP 47-50. *Muhammad Salar Khan to Nawwab Sikandar Begam.* Informs that after his departure from there, he arrived in the camp of Bregadier on 28 *Rabi* I, 1275 AH. He called on him in the morning and conveyed him of her well-being. He too told him to convey his well-being to her. He asked him to enquire whether Adil Muhammad Khan is in Garhi Ambapani or not. If he is there, how much army contingent is with him, as after knowing this, the strategy to combat him would be formulated. He then asked about the roads of every *mauza* and village from Bhilsa to Bhopal. He explained to him everything very elaborately. He was well-aware of all the *mauzas* in and around Bhopal falling on the roadside and every *nalla*, river and ponds that fell on the way. The officer expressed his happiness after getting satisfactory reply of every question and praised the ability and wisdom of the Nawwab who has no match as far as the selection of the employees are concerned. Thereafter, the Civil Officer who knew the Hindustani language played a role of mediator between him and the Bregadier who said that he had been deployed to manage the affairs of Bhilsa and Bhopal. He should ask his government if any insurgent is anywhere towards Garhi the same should be reported. Says the soldiers who are accompanying him are totally ignorant has there is none who should be well aware, except one Umrao Singh, a dweller of Rahatgarh he hired at Rs. 3 and sent him to Garhi to bring the news of the insurgents. Says whatever the news he gets from him, would be sent to her and to the Bregadier. He has also sent letters to the *thanadar* of Dallod and the *nazim-i mashriq* for providing persons of ability. The reply received from them would be communicated to her. Second thing is that the *sawars* who are on duty at the *chauki* to transmit posts have been deployed to Sanchi Kanakhera. Informs that there is no *sawar* in the camp as without a *sawar* it is difficult to perform the task quickly. The Bregadier also urged to provide 2 to 3 good *sawars* who should be aware of the roads of Garhi. It has also been heard from the armymen that, the previous day, 500 *sawars* of the British *risala,* coming from Baroda have joined the army under the Brigadier. The British forces are about 1,500 in number which include both the *sawars* and foot-soldiers. Dated 29 *Rabi* I, 1275 AH.

File No. 298, B
Box No. 16
No. of Documents 20

P 51. *Daulat Rai,* Nazim-i Mashriq, *to Nawwab Sikandar Begam.* Informs about the letter received from Ihsan Ali, *tahsildar*, and the letter of Shahzad Rai, *Thanadar* of Mahalpur, informing the arrival of Adil Muhammad Khan at *mauza* Agarya and Bhanpur, *pargana* Garhi, situating at a distance of 2 *curoh* from Garhi with a contingent of 8,000 including both cavalry and infantry, and going of *tahsildar* and *thanadar* of Garhi to the mountains of Sugotia, village *jagir* of Naji Khan. The same is sent to her. The *tahsildar* and *thanadar* of Mahalpur, due to fear of the insurgents, came to Raisen and locked themselves in the office of *nizamat*. Dated 29 *Rabi* I, 1275 AH.

PP 53-4. *Shahzad Rai,* Thanadar *of Mahalpur, to Daulat Rai,* Nazim-i Mashriq. Informs that day, Joya, *harkara*, went to Garhi, carrying the posts coming from Raisen and came late in the evening. He stated that he met the *thanadar* of Garhi, the *tahsildar* and soldiers at Sugotia in the mountains of Garhi. Says, he handed over the posts and also he came to know from the soldiers that the army of Adil Muhammad Khan is encamping at Bagrod and Bhanpur. Says, he has also sent an informer to Garhi to enquire into the matter. Information as received from him, would be communicated. Dated 28 *Rabi* I, 1275 AH.

P 55. *Ihsan Ali,* Tahsildar, *to Daulat Rai,* Nazim-i Mashriq. To the same effect as the foregoing. Dated 28 *Rabi* I, 1275 AH.

P 57. Parwana-i Ishtahari *of Nawwab Sikandar Begam to Nawwab Shahjahan Begam, Nawwab Umrao Daulah, Nawwab Muiz Muhammad Khan and Faujdar Muhammad Khan.* Refers to the letter of Daulat Rai, *Nazim-i Mashriq*, dated 28 *Rabi* I, 1275 AH, and the letter of the *amil* and *thanadar* of Mahalpur addressed to the *nazim* which is in regard to the arrival of Adil Muhammad Khan with a contingent of 8,000 inclusive of both cavalry and infantry in the region of Garhi. The same is sent to them to make things clear. Dated 1 *Rabi* II, 1275 AH.

P 59. Parwana *of Nawwab Sikandar Begam to Bhawani Prasad.* Sends the letter of Daulat Rai, *Nazim-i Mashriq*, dated 29 *Rabi* I, 1275 AH, the letter of Ihsan Ali, *tahsildar* of Mahalpur, and the letter of Shahzad Rai, *thanadar* of Mahalpur, and directs him to present these letters before the Political Agent and his reply may be communicated to her. Also informs that Daulat Rai, *nazim-i mashriq,* has informed about it to the Brigadier and she too has sent the copies of the letter to the Brigadier. Dated 1 *Rabi* II, 1275 AH.

PP 61-2. *Bhawani Prasad to Nawwab Sikandar Begam.* Refers to her *parwana,* dated 1 *Rabi* II, 1275 AH along with the letters of Daulat Rai, *nazim-i mashriq*, and that of Shaikh Ihsan Ali, *tahsildar* of Mahalpur, and the letter of Shahzad Rai, *thanadar* of Mahalpur, which are regarding the arrival of Adil Muhammad Khan with a contingent of 8,000, comprising of cavalry and infantry at Agarya and Bhanpur, *pargana* Garhi in the mountains of Sogotia, *jagir* of Munjay Khan. Says, he at the very moment sent Lala Ramden, *peshdast*, before Major Rachards, the Political Agent, to communicate to him about the content of these letters. The Political Agent heard it and kept mum. In the morning, he would present all the letters to him.

P 63. *Daulat Rai,* Nazim-i Mashriq, *to Nawwab Sikandar Begam.* Refers to her *parwana,* dated 29 *Rabi* I, 1275 AH, asking whether he knows about the number of cannon which Adil Muhammad Khan is carrying and to make an enquiry into this besides his communiqué about Adil Muhammad Khan's separation from Tantia Tope. Informs that it came to his notice through the *tahsildar* and *thanadar* of Mahalpur and Garhi and from Saiyid Abd al-Ali, deputy *Qazi*, who fell prey into the hands of the insurgents and then they fled from there at a suitable time, besides from the *zamindars* that Adil Muhammad Khan is not in the company of Tantia Tope and that he is at Jhaklone, *ilaqa* Bundelkhand near Lalitpur. He does not have any cannon with him. He had only an army which comprised of *sawars* and foot-soldiers. The *thanadar* and *tahsildar* of Mahalpur and Garhi reported that the number of artillery carrying by Adil Muhammad Khan was 7,000 to 8,000 but it does not seem to be a correct figure. Most of them are farmers of Pura Guna and Bharonpur. It is further learnt that, he is injured. Definitely, his end is near. He is separated from the army of Tantia Tope. Thus, the army of Tantia Tope, is harassed and hapless, fled and crossed the river Narmada. The royal forces led by *naib bakhshi* are stationed at Siwans. If an attack is launched on the insurgents and many are killed, it will not be a matter of surprise. If the British forces also join them, it will be the finest thing. Dated 1 *Rabi* II, 1275 AH.

It contains order that the letter may be sent to Lala Paltu Lal, *muhafiz-i daftar-i insha*, for inclusion in the register and keeping in the *daftar*. A copy of the order may be sent to Daulat Rai, *nazim-i mashriq*, through *madar al-maham*.

P 65. *Daulat Rai,* Nazim-i Mashriq, *to Nawwab Sikandar Begam.* Informs that the previous day, he communicated to her, as reported by the *tahsildar* and *thanadar* of Mahalpur, the arrival of Adil Muhammad Khan at *mauza* Bhanpur situating at a distance of 2 *curoh* from Garhi. That day, he received a letter of Shahzad Rai, *thanadar* of Mahalpur, dated 29 *Rabi* I, 1275 AH, informing the arrival of the insurgents at *mauza* Bharonpur, Agarya and Bhanpur and then they went to some other place. The same is presented to her. Also reports that due to reporting false news about Adil Muhammad Khan that he has arrived at Muhammad Garh, a fine was imposed upon the *thanadar* and warned if any news without proof and authentication is reported. Dated 1 *Rabi* II, 1275 AH.

P 67. *Shahzad Rai to Daulat Rai,* Nazim-i Mashriq. Reports that the previous day, he sent Ratiram, the informer, to *mauza* Bharonpur, Jambani, Agarya, and Bhanpur to bring the news of encampment of the insurgents. He came back that evening and stated that the insurgents were surely encamping at *mauza* Bharonpur, Agarya and Bhanpur. But from the previous night, they have been vacating those places and it is not known as to where they are going; whether they are hiding in the mountains or have gone to any other place. Says, what he stated has been communicated to her. Dated 29 *Rabi* I, 1275 AH.

P 69. *Daulat Rai,* Nazim-i Mashriq, *to Nawwab Sikandar Begam.* The prevous day, he sent letters of the *tahsildar* and *thanadar* of Mahalpur, informing the arrival of Adil Muhammad Khan, the insurgent with a contingent of 8,000 forces including both *sawars* and foot-soldiers at *mauza* Bhanpur situating at a distance of 2 *curoh* from Garhi. To know the reality, he has sent the informers who are yet to come. But a letter of Shaikh Muhammad Abd al-Rahman, *thanadar* of Garhi, along with the letter of *thanadar* of Basodah besides the statement of Shamsher Khan, soldier at Garhi who in disguise had gone to Basodah to bring the news of insurgents, have been received in his office. After going through these letters, it came to notice that a dweller of Basodah who was the servant of Adil Muhammad Khan came to Basodah and said to the *thanadar* of Basodah that Adil Muhammad Khan on 27 *Rabi* I, 1275 AH, along with 8,000 forces was at Bagrod, carrying 7 cannon with him and due to a wound received from an arrow he was unable to ride on the horse. Thus, he sat behind the *sawar*. All those letters besides the statement of Shamsher Khan are sent to her and also to the British Officials through Muhammad Salar Khan, deputy *muhtamim, adalat-i faujdari*, who is in Bhilsa in the service of the British. Says, he does not believe that Adil Muhammad Khan is carrying 7 cannon or any number of cannon with him. It will be ascertained only after the return of the informers and authentic news would be communicated to her. However, as the *tahsildars* and *thanadars* of Mahalpur and Garhi, and Saiyid Abd al-Ali, deputy *qazi*, have reported, as said by the companions of Tantia Tope that there was no cannon with Adil Muhammad Khan and described his haplessness. Thus, to rely upon the statement of the soldier is difficult. Dated 1 *Rabi* II, 1275 AH.

P 71. *Muhammad Abd al-Rahman,* Thanadar *of Garhi, to Daulat Rai,* Nazim-i Mashriq. Informs that Shamsher Khan, the soldier who was sent to Basodah to enquire about the encampmenmt of the insurgent forces, has returned with a letter of the *thanadar* of Basodah. The letter of the *thanadar* as well as the statement of Shamsher Khan, soldier is sent to him which will make things clear about the insurgents. Informs that day in the morning, he sent Amir Khan, soldier, and Lal Muhammad Kahi to Basodah. They have also been instructed to go to Bagrod. The insurgents do not stay more than a day in one place due to the fear of attack. They might march to some other place in the morning or in the evening. Requests for sending another force as the battalions of Ghulam Rasul Khan and Balwant Singh, *jamadars*, do not have more than 30-30 soldiers each. Besides, the soldiers of the *thana* who are in Bhopal have not come back yet. Dated 29 *Rabi* I, 1275 AH.

P 73. *Janki Prasad,* Thanadar *of* Thana *Basodah, to Muhammad Abd al-Rahman,* Thanadar *of Garhi Ambapani*. Refers to his letter informing that he has heard that Adil Muhammad Khan along with 8,000 forces, inclusive of both cavalry and infantry, has marched from Khorai and reached Bagrod and intending to come to that side. Bagrod is nearby to Basodah. If the news is true, information may be given immediately. The information given by him about the insurgents is also heard there. The need is that one should be careful. A description of the situation would be known to him through the bearer of this letter. Dated 29 *Rabi* I, 1275 AH.

PP 75-6. *Statement of Shamsher Khan, Soldier at* Thana *Garhi, Before Abd al-Rahman,* Thanadar.

Q. He was sent to Basodah to enquire about the insurgent

forces and the *thanadar* of Basodah mentioned in his letter that the story of the insurgents would be known from the bearer of the letter. He is asked to tell about the encampment of the insurgent forces and about their numbers.

R. The previous day, a person of Basodah employed with Adil Muhammad Khan came to Basodah and said that Adil Muhammad Khan along with a contingent of 8,000 forces and 7 cannon arrived at Bagrod on 27th of the month. He had wound of anarrow in his right leg and thus, was unable to ride on the horse.

Q. Asked to explain why the *thanadar* did not mention in his letter what he has described.

R. The said person came to Basodah from the camp of Adil Muhammad Khan after writing the letter. But he stated this before the *thanadar*. When the said person left, the *thanadar* told him to describe to the *thanadar* what he has heard from him.

Q. He was asked to go to Bagrod and report what he saw from his own eyes. But he did not go there. Why?

R. The roads were closed and whosoever went there was hanged without investigation. Due to this, he did not go there and the *thanadar* too prevented him to go there.

Q. Asked to tell whether the said person, who came to Basodah, did say anything else about their army?

R. He said that the British army came from Sagar to fight with them. But when they heard about the number of the army of Adil Muhammad Khan, they returned back.

Q. Asked to tell where the dwellers and the *kamdar* of Basodah were?

R. The dwellers fled from the village as they were scared of the army of Adil Muhammad Khan. The *kamdar* took shelter in the fort.

Q. Whether the said person also said that, the insurgent forces were intending to go somewhere else from there.

R. He did not know anything about their march from Bagrod to elsewhere.

Q. What is the distance of Bagrod from Basodah?

R. The distance is 3 *curoh* and distance of Bagrod from that place is 9 *curoh*.

P 77. *Muhammad Abd al-Rahman,* Thanadar *of Garhi Ambapani, to Nawwab Sikandar Begam.* Refers to her order, conveyed through Hukumat Singh and Genda Singh, *sawars* of *risala* Rup Singh, enquiring about the number of the insurgent forces who passed through that region, besides the situation in and around there. Informs that on 24 *Rabi* II, 1275 AH, a letter containing information about the number of insurgents who marched from that region, besides other details of the said force, has been sent to her. However, as desired, the information is again submitted. The insurgent forces who marched earlier, carried no cannon with them. There were around 8,000 *sawars* and 3,000 foot-soldiers. Thus, the army had a total strength of 11,000. A report is sent to the *nizamat* everyday. The news of the region is as reported by the informers and the *thanadar* of Basodah, that Adil Muhammad Khan reached Bagrod situating at a distance of 9 *curoh* from there. He has a deep wound of arrow on his right leg. About the number of troops, accompanying him, some say it is 8,000 with 7 cannon whereas some informers put their number to 12,000, comprising both the *sawars* and foot-soldiers with 22 cannon. Meanwhile, Jumman Khan, soldier under the battalion of Ghulam Rasul Khan, *jamadar*, who had gone to Basodah came back and stated that indeed Adil Muhammad Khan reached Bagrod and destroyed Tondi and Bagrod. In Basodah, it is an established fact that there are 12,000 armymen and 32 cannon in the company of Adil Muhammad Khan and that Raja Bhor, Narwarwala, is also accompanying him. The informers are regularly sent to Basodah and Bagrod. The information received from them would soon be communicated to her. It would not have been hidden from her that if an unknown person is arrested, he is immediately hanged or shot from a gun. Thus, the informers are afraid to enter in the army of the insurgents. To inform her about all these happenings was a must, which he did. Dated 1 *Rabi* II, 1275 AH.

PP 79-82. *Muhammad Salar Khan to Nawwab Sikandar Begam.* Refers to her order, dated 29 *Rabi* I, 1275 AH, along with a letter of Nand Kishore, peon, in his name and the royal order, delivered by Appa Rao, camel rider of *risala* Ghulam Muhammad Khan, *risaldar*. Says, he immediately went to meet the Brigadier and conveyed him the content of the letter of the peon. He said the insurgents did not fall in front of him, otherwise they would have been dealt with. Meanwhile, a representative of Suba Sahab, Bhilsa, came with a letter from Lakholi, *ilaqa* Bhilsa which lies at a distance of 4 *curoh* from Garhi Ambapani. In that letter it is mentioned that on 27 *Rabi* I, 1275 AH, Adil Muhammad Khan, the insurgent along with his clan and Amanat Khan, *Bakhshi*, and a contingent of 500 *suwars* and 300 soldiers besides, 700 *wilayatis* have marched towards river Narmada. Khatla Khan Bahadur Bareillywala, is also accompanying him. The Brigadier is intending to go to Bhopal by the next day or day after that. As soon as he comes to know the exact time of his march he would convey her at the very moment. Captain Main has marched for Hoshangabad from there. The letter received from Munshi Husain Bakhsh, *munsarim-i dak*, has been sent to Hoshangabad. Dated 1 *Rabi* II, 1275 AH.

PP 83-5. *Muhammad Salar Khan to Nawwab Sikandar Begam.* Refers to the letter of Daulat Rai, *nazim-i mashriq*, in his name and the royal order besides two other letters, delivered by Imdad Ali Khan, camel rider. Informs that the content of the letter, as desired was communicated to the Brigadier. He said, if the insurgents went towards Narmada, the royal army would deal with them. The army with 4 cannon carrying by him would defend the territory of Bhopal State on the outskrits of Bhopal. Thus, the next day, they would march for Bhopal from there. He also said that during the next 3 to 4 days, he might encamp at Gulgaon. Says that day, *naib suba,* Issagarh met Civil Sahab where he too was present and held talk with him. The *naib* talked to him in Marathi as he was well versed in the Marathi language. The *naib* said it was heard from outside that a group of 7,000 to 8,000 insurgent was at Jalone and to deal with them, Shakespear, son-in-law of the Agent, Central India, was in the battlefield along with his forces. The Civil Sahab said that it might be that on 4th of this month, the British forces who were in Hoshangabad, pursued Tantia Tope who crossed the river Narmada along with a huge army. It might be that a battle took place between the two forces. The next day or after that, everything would be clear after receiving a letter from there. Dated 1 *Rabi* II, 1275 AH.

It contains the order that the letter as well as her letter addressed to Niwwab Qudsia Begam may be sent to Lala Paltu Lal, *muhafiz-i daftar-i insha*, for inclusion in the file and keeping in the *daftar*. A copy of the order may be sent to Salar Khan communicating that she has sent a letter to Nawwab Qudsia Begam regarding the arrangement of *sarbrah-i rasad* for Bregadier at Gulgaon. If they ask him for *sarbrah-i rasad*, he should not hesitate at all in making arrangement of *sarbrah-i rasad* for them. He should see that the Bregadier is not hurt at all by his attitude and behaviour. Dated 2 *Rabi* II, 1275 AH.

P 87. *Muhammad Abd al-Rahman,* Thanadar *of Garhi Ambapani, to Nawwab Sikandar Begam.* Refers to her *parwana*, dated 29 *Rabi* I, asking the name of those three persons of the insurgent forces who were hanged, besides, the report of Adil Muhammad Khan. Informs that even before receiving her *parwana,* Najju Khan and Lal Muhammad, the soldiers, were sent to enquire about them who were hanged from amongst the insurgent forces. All were from the Hindu community and one of them was a *zunnar*. They were not from the adjoining areas of this region. Although the dwellers of the adjoining villages tried to identify them, but they were unable to identify them by their place of dwelling and their name. They were brought by the insurgent forces from Khorai. It is also heard from the insurgent forces that they were the informers of the British and due to giving wrong information, they were arrested and hanged on the road.

In regard to the report of Adil Muhammad Khan, it is stated that he is not unaware at all about the news of the insurgents. Whatever news he receives through the informers or soldiers, he sends it to her through the *nizamat*. Day before yesterday, Lal Muhammad and Najju Khan, soldiers, and on the previous day, Chhanka, *harkara*, and Ganga Ram and that day Gulab Singh and Murdan Singh, son and nephew of Raja Mustajir, were sent to enquire into the matter of the insurgents. They were instructed that they themselves should see the insurgents. Hopes that they would come back soon and the information received from them would soon be sent to her. Informs that everyday 2 or 3 persons are sent to get the news of the insurgents and whenever they come back, information is sent to her.

It is heard that Khan Zaman Khan, *qila'dar* of Raisen, with 40 soldiers is coming to this side and day before yesterday they were at Narwar. It is possible that they might leave Narwar that day and arrive there. Hopes that with his arrival, he with her consent would block the valley of *mauza* Aradmau which is a difficult route and at the same time it is a safe passagae for the insurgents. Hopes that the enemies would meet their fate. It is his earnest desire that God bless him to prove his loyalty to the salt and to die for the royal cause and become victorious in both the worlds. Dated 2 *Rabi* II, 1275 AH.

It contains the order that the letter may be sent to Lala Paltu Lal, *muhafiz-i daftar-i insha*, for inclusion in the file and keeping in the *daftar*. A copy of the order may be sent to Bhawani Prasad, *wakil*, to bring the matter into the notice of the Political Agent and his reply may be conveyed to her. Khan Zaman Khan, *qila'dar*, may be directed to explain as to why he has been in Garhi for the last three days as it came to her notice through the letter of Shaikh Abd al-Rahman, *thanadar* of Garhi.

P 89. *Daulat Rai,* Nazim-i Mashriq, *to Nawwab Sikandar Begam.* Says about 8 days before he had requested to depute an army in Garhi Ambapani, where the mountains and uneven land and the dense forest with trees after trees are the safe heaven for the robbers and the insurgents. But still no officer along with forcc and arms and ammunitions has been deployed in Garhi. If there will be any negligence, the insurgents might create hinderance in the movement of the British forces on their route which falls in that region. Although the contingent of *thana* and *mahal* are performing their duties, busy in the arrangement of *sarbrah-i rasad,* in making challan of the prisoners and the miscreants of the villages, in the management of works of *chaukis,* in keeping watch on the houses and resources of *thana* and *tahsil,* in bringing the *begars* and the carts and in providing grass, etc. But many of them are coward. Thus, the soldiers of *mahal* and *tahsil* of Garhi Ambapani had fled when they heard about the coming of the insurgent forces. They did not cooperate with the *tahsildar* and *thanadar*. In view of this, it is his request to her to pay attention. Hopes if orders are issued to the royal forces, the insurgents would be killed in large numbers that would certainly give her name and fame and the region would be free of the insurgents. Dated 2 *Rabi* II, 1275 AH.

It contains the order that the letter may be sent to Lala Paltu Lal, *muhafiz-i daftar-i insha*, for inclusion in the file and keeping in the *daftar*. A copy of the order may be sent to Daulat Rai, *nazim*, through *madar al-maham*, communicating that till then nothing came to her notice which may prove his bravery and it is not possible to send the army to Garhi Ambapani just on his mere statement. The instruction would certainly be issued to Bakhshi Murawwat Muhammad Khan whatever would be thought feasible in regard to managing the affairs of Garhi Ambapani. Dated 4 *Rabi* II, 1275 AH.

P 91. *Gopal, the Peon, to Nawwab Sikandar Begam.* Informs that, as ordered, he went to Garhi Ambapani to know about the insurgents there. He arrived there and found no sign of the insurgents either in Garhi or in its adjoining areas and then he left for Basodah and went upto Ganj Basodah. He took round 2 to 3 *curoh* around Basodah and asked the dwellers. But they said nothing about the presence of the insurgents. They said that there was peace everywhere. Thereafter, he returned to Garhi and stayed in Garhi Ambapani for a while and enquired about the insurgents. There was peace in Garhi as well as in the adjoining villages of Garhi Ambapani. Somewhere farmers were sowing seeds in their fields. On Monday; date 1 *Rabi* I, 1275 AH, he left Garhi and reached Raisen in the evening. Next day; day Tuesday, he would be in Bhopal. Dated 3 *Rabi* II, 1275 AH.

PP 93-4. *Bakhshi Murawwat Muhammad Khan to Nawwab Sikandar Begam.* Informs that day; the 3rd *Rabi* II, 1275 AH, day Saturday, Daulat Rai, *nazim*, conveyed through Bhola Lal, *munshi nizamat-i mashriq*, that the news about the destruction of Basodah was wrong. The *sawars* who came from Bagrod also said that no insurgent was either in Bagrod or in Garhi Ambapani. The *sawars* who were sent by him also said that there was no news of insurgents from anywhere. Dated 3 *Rabi* II, 1275 AH.

P 95. *Koka Fatah Jang Khan, Qila'dar, to Nawwab Sikandar Begam.* Informs that as desired, he sent Kalyan Singh to Garhi Ambapani on 29 *Rabi* I, 1275

AH to enquire about the insurgents. He came back on 5 *Rabi* II, 1275 AH, and reported that he entered Garhi Ambapani via Raisen and stayed overnight there but nowhere found any insurgent nor heard anything about them. Dated 6 *Rabi* II, 1275 AH.

File No. 299
Box No. 16
No. of Documents 26

News About the Encampment of Adil Muhammad Khan, the Insurgent, with Muhip Singh at Jhaklone and Lalitpur Khajurya

PP 1-3. Contents

P 5. *Bhawani Prasad to Nawwab Sikandar Begam.* Sends the letter, received from the *thanadar* of Mahalpur, informing that Adil Muhammad Khan got injured in his leg, and due to this, he is staying at Lalitpur Khajurya, and that there is peace and calm in Ghairatganj and Siwans. Dated 24 *Rabi* I, 1275 AH.

It contains the order that the letter may be sent to Lala Paltu Lal, *muhafiz-i daftar-i insha*, for inclusion in the file and keeping in the *daftar*. A copy of the letter may be sent to Mattu Khan and Abd al-Aziz Khan, *risaldras*, directing them to know the whereabouts of Adil Muhammad Khan from the Bhopal army who are deployed at many places under the British territory like Lalitpur Khajurya, etc. and report to her. There should not be any delay in this. Dated 29 *Rabi* I, 1275 AH.

P 7. Parwana *of Nawwab Sikandar Begam to Bhawani Prasad.* Indeed it is a reality and has also been learnt from Bakhshi Murawwat Muhammad Khan as the informers told the *bakhshi* that Adil Muhammad Khan was in *mauza* Jhaklone along with Muhip Singh, *jagirdar*. He has 200 soldiers with him. But there is no information about the army of Muhip Singh. Directs him to enquire from the Political Agent if he permits to enter in others' territory. If so, *Bakhshi* Murawwat Muhammad Khan may go with the army of Bhopal along with two cannon and if Adil Muhammad Khan fights, he may be killed or if he can be arrested, he may be arrested. The Political Agent should also send a British officer to make the arrangement of *sarbrah-i rasad* under the others' territory and to allow the *bakhshi* so that he may be ordered to proceed. Adil Muhammad Khan wherever he goes in others'territory, the *bakhshi,* accompanying the British officer may enter there and with his orders kill or arrest Adil Muhammad Khan. Directs him to bring the matter into the notice of the Political Agent and what he says may be conveyed to her. Dated 29 *Rabi* I, 1275 AH.

P 9. *Bhawani Prasad to Nawwab Sikandar Begam.* Informs, that day he met Major Richards, the Political Agent, and brought into his notice the matter described in her *parwana,* dated 29 *Rabi* I, 1275 AH in regard to the news that Adil Muhammad Khan along with a contingent of 200 or so is in Jhaklone, a village *jagir* of Muhip Singh, *ilaqa* Banpurwala, and Bakhshi Murawwat Muhammad Khan, having 2 cannon with him, is to kill or arrest him. Being the other's territory, an English officer should accompany him to execute the order to manage the provision, etc. He said earlier he told him to send Bakhshi Murawwat Muhammad Khan to Agra of Chhatrasal and he gave an unwise reply. All informations reached to the Agent to the Governor-General, Central India, who gave the same reply. He further said that he asked *Sarsuba*, Bhilsa, if Bakhshi Murawwat Muhammad Khan comes to Agra to deal with Chhatrasal whether he would like it or not. The reply of *Sarsuba* was that he would be the happiest man if that time help comes to him from the State of Bhopal. Not only that, he would also provide him a confidant to accompany him. But the reply of Nawwab Sikandar Begam was not a favourable one. This time too the situation is the same. He then asked where Bakhshi Murawwat Khan was at that time. He replied that he might have returned to Bhopal and Hafiz Muhammad Hasan Khan was at Chiklod with the General. About him the General said, his presence was not required as

Haji 'Abd al-Karim was enough for him. He kept mum and did not say anything. Thereafter, he was told by Kesri Prasad that the Political Agent gave his remarks on his letter as keep it in the *daftar* due to the reason that he ordered several times to *bakhshi* to march which was not understood by the Nawwab. Now she has urged to provide a companion to the *bakhshi* which is against the tradition. It is strange that the army of Bhopal cannot do anything on its own. Dated 1 *Rabi* II, 1275 AH/8 November 1858.

It contains the order that the letter along with the *parwana* of Nawwab Sikandar Begam, addressed to Bhawani Prasad, *wakil*, dated 29 *Rabi* I, 1275 AH may be sent to Lala Paltu Lal, *muhafiz-i daftar-i insha*, for inclusion in file and keeping in *daftar*. A copy of the order may be sent to Bhawani Prasad, informing that Bakhshi Murawwat Muhammad Khan would be staying at Garhi Ambapani coming from Raisen and Hafiz Muhammad Hasan Khan, *naib bakhshi*, would encamp in Siwans. If Adil Muhammad Khan enters the State of Bhopal, he would be dealt with. Directs him to bring the matter into the notice of the Political Agent and his reply may be conveyed to her. A copy of the order may be provided to Bakhshi Murawwat Muhammad Khan and Hafiz Muhammad Hasan Khan, *naib bakhshi*. Dated 4 *Rabi* II, 1275 AH.

PP 11-12. *Ghulam Muhammad Khan, Son of Gauhar Muhammad Khan, to Nawwab Sikandar Begam.* Refers to his earlier letter, dated 1 *Rabi* II, 1275 AH, informing about the news there. That day, Nanhey Khan, informer who had gone to Bundelkhand returned from *qasba* Mongawali, *ilaqa* Sindhia and stated that the insurgent forces were at Jhaklone situating at a distance of 6 *curoh* from the range of mountains. All the chieftains of the insurgent forces like Rao Sahab, nephew of Nana Sahab Peshwa, Tantia Tope, Muhip Singh Bundela, Adil Muhammad Khan, Garhi Ambapaniwala and others were there. Adil Muhammad Khan is injured. One of his legs got injury from cannon and the other has an injury from an arrow. He is unable to walk or ride a horse. He is intending to devastate the *qasba*. Due to this, the British forces have arrived there. The insurgents upon getting the news of the arrival of the British forces dispersed and fled to hide in the mountains and jungle. The news of Bheglone is that there is only one *sawar* and 30 soldiers. Says, the orders of the British officials regarding the arrangement of *rasad* are clear to him and surely he would execute the orders in letter and spirit. Dated 5 *Rabi* II, 1275 AH.

It contains the order that the letter may be sent to Lala Paltu Lal, *muhafiz-i daftar-i insha*, for inclusion in the file and keeping in the *daftar*. A copy of the letter may be sent to Ghulam Muhammad Khan, son of Gauhar Muhammad Khan, who wrote about the presence of the army of Rao Sahab and Tantia Tope in Jhaklone, and that they were in the mountains of Jhaklone. But it is not clear from which place under the territory of Bhopal State they entered the mountains. Warns him to report such false news. Further, he is not concerned to provide *sarbrah-i rasad* to the British. It is the duty of the *amil* of *pargana* Bheglone to see how the needs of *sarbrah-i rasad* for the British army are met. His concern is only to fight with the insurgents who come to his *pargana*. If he is able to meet the challanges of insurgents, he should do at his own by pursuing and arresting them. If the number of insurgents is high, then he should inform her through his letter. Dated 11 *Rabi* II, 1275 AH.

PP 13-14. *Daulat Rai* Nazim-i Mashriq *to Nawwab Sikandar Begam.* Informs that 6 days before, he had sent two informers to Khorai, Chehla and Jhaklone for bringing the news of the insurgents. But they did not come back yet. It is not known whether they are arrested or where they are. That day he sent Khamaney Khan Mewati, a dweller of *pargana* Raisen, and Daley, a dweller of *pargana* Mahalpur to Jhaklone to bring the news of Adil Muhammad Khan by giving them one rupee each. Jhaklone from Raisen lies at a distance of 7 *manzil* and in between falls the territory of others. While entering in others' territory, the informers are interrogated and searched which causes delaying of the news. While the government emphasises everytime to send authentic news of the insurgents. Says, he is not unaware of his responsibility in obtaining the news of the insurgents and deputing the informers. But the distance where the insurgents are encamping is too far, besides falls in others' territory, which causes delay. Had they been encamping nearby, there would not have been so much delay. How it is possible to send a daily report from such a long distance. The *thanadars* too have been instructed that there is no need to send news on the basis of hearsay. But the news should be authentic, should have seen from one's own eyes and then only it should be reported. If he reports anything based on hearsay, he would surely be punished. Dated 8 *Rabi* II, 1275 AH.

It contains the order that the letter may be sent to Lala Paltu Lal, *muhafiz-i daftar-i insha*, for inclusion in the register and keeping in the *daftar*. A copy of the order may be sent to Lala Daulat Rai, *nazim-i mashriq*, who has written that the distance of Jhaklone from there is 7 *manzil* and in between falls the others's territory and how it is possible to send a report within one or two days. But what is the use of such an excuse and writing uncalled for things. Directs him to send clever and reliable informers to bring the news and submit it to the government. Dated 10 *Rabi* II, 1275 AH.

P 15. *Bakhshi Murawwat Muhammad Khan to Nawwab Sikandar Begam.* Refers to her *parwana*, dated 28 *Rabi* I, 1275 AH, directing him to submit perfect news about the group of insurgents, and Adil Muhammad Khan and that he has entered Garhi Ambapani. Informs when he reached Raisen and searched them, he found no sign of theirs. He enquired thoroughly into the matter that how such news reached to the government. But as Abd al-Rahman, *thanadar*, has gone to his village, a report would be sent to her after enquiring from him. Presently, he has arrived along with the royal army, where is the need to give importance to the news circulating among the general masses. In Bhopal, it was also famous that Adil Muhammad Khan along with an army of 12,000 and 12 cannon was in Garhi. In Garhi, it is said that he is in Chehla or in Khorai or Khimlasa or Jhaklone. To know the reality he has sent Gulab, informer to Jhaklone, and Ghulam Husain and Fatah Khan, *sawars* to Chehla and Khorai and Khimlasa. The actual news, whatever it is would be communicated. Although, there are not too much informers, even then he would try his best to know about the movement of the insurgents in the region. Dated 8 *Rabi* II, 1275 AH.

It contains the order that the letter may be sent to Lala Paltu Lal, *muhafiz-i daftar-i insha*, for inclusion in the file and keeping in the *daftar*. A copy of the order may be sent to Bakhshi Murawwat Muhammad Khan, directing him that as soon as he receives the news of the insurgents from Gulab, informer, and Ghulam Husain and Fatah Khan, *sawars*, whom he has sent to Jhaklone, Chehla, Khorai and Khimlasa to bring the actual news of the insurgents, he should immediately pass it on to the government. Dated 14 *Rabi* II, 1275 AH.

PP 17-18. *Daulat Rai,* Nazim-i Mashriq, *to Nawwab Sikandar Begam.* Informs from the report received from *thana* Mahalpur, dated 12 *Rabi* II, 1275 AH, it is clear, as reported by Ratya, the informer who had gone to enquire about the insurgents that there is no sign of insurgents upto Harbhat and that about 2,000 British forces are encamping there. Besides, Adil Muhammad Khan and Raja Bhor along with an army of 7,000 to 8,000 are in Jhaklone. It was also heard that one of the insurgents along with a contingent of 400 to 500 *sawars* arrived in *mauza* Bhatharya, situating at a distance of 4 *curoh* from Sagar. The entire *mauza* has been devastated. The British forces are pursuing them. The said report is sent to her. Dated 13 *Rabi* II, 1275 AH.

PP 19-20. *News-Report Sent by Shahzad Rai,* Thanadar *of Mahalpur.* Informs that day Ratya, the informer came back and stated that he went upto the *qasba* Harbhat, the distance from there is 4 *manzil*, to know about the insurgents where there were also 2,000 British army. There, he heard that Adil Muhammad Khan and Raja Bhor, having an army of 7,000 to 8,000 were encamping at Jhaklone situating at a distance of 10 to 12 *curoh* from Harbhat. In Harbhat, it was also heard that one of the insurgents along with a contingent of 400 to 500 has arrived in *mauza* Tapharya, situating at a distance of 4 *curoh* towards Sagar. The entire *mauza* has been devastated. Hearing the news, the British forces are pursuing them. The information as given by the informer is reported without any manipulation. The other two *harkaras* have not yet returned. The moment they return, their report would be sent. Dated 12 *Rabi* II, 1275 AH.

P 21. *Daulat Rai,* Nazim-i Mashriq, *to Nawwab Sikandar Begam.* From the report received from *thana* Garhi, dated 12 *Rabi* II, 1275 AH, it is clear that there is no sign of insurgents, as reported by Udit, the *harkara* who was sent by Lala Tikaram, *muhtamim, karkhanajat*, to enquire about the insurgents who reached Khorai via Chehla. He moved further to Jhaklone, as it was heard that Adil Muhammad Khan is in Jhaklone. The same is sent to her. Dated 13 *Rabi* II, 1275 AH.

P 23. *News-Report Sent by Abd al-Rahman,* Thanadar *of Garhi Ambapani, Dated 12* Rabi *II, 1275 AH.* Informs, by the grace of God and by her blessings, there is peace and calm in this *qasba* and in all the villages. That day, Udit, *harkara*, who was sent by Tikaram, *muhtamim, karkhanajat*, as ordered by the Nawwab to enquire about the insurgents came back. He stated that he reached Khorai via Chehla and nowhere saw any sign of the insurgents. About Adil Muhammad Khan, he heard that he is in Jhaklone. So he is going to Jhaklone.

P 25. *Daulat Rai,* Nazim-i Mashriq, *to Nawwab Sikandar Begam.* Informs of the report received from *thana* Siwans, dated 17 *Rabi* II, 1275 AH, stating that Adil Muhammad Khan and Aqil Muhammad Khan are in the mountains of *mauza* Murdanpur, *jagir* village of Muhip Singh Bundela, which is the adjoining region of Jhaklone and that Muhip Singh is in the company of Adil Muhammad Khan, carrying an army of 7,000 to 8,000 with him who are the Bundelas, and that Raja Bhor is encamping at a distance of 2 *curoh* from Adil Muhammad Khan, having an army of 7,000 to 8,000 with him. The same is sent to her that would make everything clear. Dated 20 *Rabi* II, 1275 AH.

It contains the order that the letter and report may be sent to Lala Paltu Lal, *muhafiz-i daftar-i insha*, for inclusion in the register and keeping in the *daftar*. A copy of the report may be sent to Bhawani Prasad, *wakil* to bring the matter into the notice of the Political Agent and convey his comments. Dated 22 *Rabi* II, 1275 AH.

PP 27-30. *Report from* Thana *Siwans Sent by Shaikh Nur Khan,* Thanadar, *Dated 17* Rabi *II, 1275 AH, Day Wednesday*. Reports that, as ordered on 5 *Rabi* II, 1275 AH, Khaman Singh Khagar and Rahim Nadaf, the informers, were sent to Jhaklone situating nearby to Lalitpur to bring the true news of Adil Muhammad Khan and Aqil Muhammad Khan, the insurgents. That day, they returned and stated that on their way to Jhaklone, they met Ishaq, a soldier, who was earlier employed in Siwans. They met each other and discussed amongst themselves. Firstly, he did not disclose anything. Thereafter, they said that they had come to know of the news of the insurgents. The soldier said that he was an employee of Adil Muhammad Khan. But then, he left his job. He was staying with the consent of Muhib Singh in the mountains of *mauza* Mardanpur, *jagir* village of Muhib Singh situating at a distance of 4 to 5 *curoh* from Jhaklone. He was not having any bullet injury. They did not believe him and went further in search of the news and reached *mauza* Murdanpur and on the pretext of searching his son, he wanted to enter in the camp of the army of insurgents. But the guards prevented them and did not allow their entry. But from a distance of half a *jarib*, they saw Adil Muhammad Khan from their own eyes and noticed that his leg was wounded. They came closer to the camp and asked about Adil Muhammad Khan. He had a contingent of around 7,000 to 8,000 *sawars* and foot-soldiers that also included the contingent of Muhip Singh. He then returned from there. On the way, he was arrested by Saiyid Bilal of *mauza* Dongasara, suspecting him as an informer. After two days, he was released and came to *mauza* Sipri where he heard authentic news of Raja Bhor who along with a contingent of 7,000 to 8,000 was encamping at a distance of 1or 2 *curoh* from the army of Adil Muhammad Khan and Muhip Singh. Then, they left for Sironj.

P31. *Daulat Rai,* Nazim-i Mashriq, *to Nawwab Sikandar Begam.* Informs that Khaman Khagar and Rahim Nadaf, dwellers of Bundelkhand were sent to Jhaklone to bring autnetic news about Adil Muhammad Khan and Aqil Muhammad Khan. They reached Jhaklone but seeing no sign of the insurgents there, they went to *mauza* Murdanpur, *jagir* of Muhip Singh, the insurgent. They saw Adil Muhammad Khan and Aqil Muhammad Khan and their army from their own eyes. They came back that day. Their statements about the insurgents and their contingents were recorded. The same is sent to her to make everything clear. Dated 21 *Rabi* II, 1275 AH.

It contains the order that the letter and statement may be sent to Lala Paltu Lal, *muhafiz-i daftar-i insha*, for inclusion in the register and keeping in the *daftar*. A copy of the statement may be sent to Bhawani Prasad, *wakil* to bring the matter into the notice of the Political Agent and convey his comments.

PP 33-4. *Statement of Khaman Khagar and Rahim Nadaf, Informers of Qasba Siwans, Before Daulat Rai,* Nazim-i Mashriq. They were sent by Shaikh Nur Muhammad, *tahsildar*, to bring the news of Adil Muhammad Khan.

Q. Asked to tell what the news is.

R. He, as well as Rahim Nadaf, were sent by the *thanadar* of Siwans. Firstly, they went to Khorai and then to Malthun. As the roads were closed, they came back to Khimlasa and in the company of a known person they via Devalgarh, reached Murdanpur, village *jagir* of Muhip Singh, Jhaklonewala, situating at a distance of 11 *coss* from Devalgarh and Jhaklone the distance is 5 *coss*. They saw that Adil Muhammad Khan having an army of 800 to 900 with 8 to 9 *sawars* and the rest being foot-soldiers along with Muhip Singh Bundela is present there. From Mehrab Khan, who met him at Devalgarh, they came to know that he had injury of bullet in his head and was unable to ride a horse. He was carried by his soldiers on a cot. Thereafter, he was ousted from the camp. So they came back.

Q. Asked to tell what they were carrying.

R. He replied there were guns with them. There was no cannon with them.

Q. Asked to tell where they were going then.

R. He heard that they were intending to go to Tehri adjoining to Sironj.

Q. Asked to tell about their community.

R. They were either Muslims or Bundelas. But the latter was more acceptable in comparison to the former.

Q. Did he see Adil Muhammad Khan from his on eyes?

R. He saw him from a distance of 15 to 20 feet.

Q. Was the British army in front of him?

R. The British was not there. But it was heard that the British army was at Lalitpur or Jhaklone.

P 35. *Daulat Rai,* Nazim-i Mashriq, *to Nawwab Sikandar Begam.* Informs about the two letters of Hazrat Nur Khan, *amil* of Bheglone, dated 1 and 2 *Jumada* I, 1275 AH, informing that some insurgents are in Jhaklone and the attack of the British forces upon the insurgent forces and about their dispersal and the presence of Raja Bhutra along with his army at Chanchur and the arrival of Umrao Singh, *jamadar*, with his battalion from Bheglone to Hafiz Hasan Khan, *naib bakhshi*, as directed by him. The same is sent to her which would make everything clear. Dated 5 *Jumada* II, 1275 AH.

P 37. *Hazrat Nur Khan to Daulat Rai,* Nazim-i Mashriq. Informs that day, the 2nd *Jumada* I, day Friday, Kallu, the informer, came and stated that towards the hills in *mauzas* Bangan, etc. there is no sign of the insurgents at all. There is information about the presence of the army of Raja Bhotra in Chachura. The distance of Chachura from Bangan is 8 *curoh*. Rest everything is ok. On that day, as ordered by *Naib Bakhshi*, Umrao Singh, *jamadar* along with his battalion has marched towards Siwans from there. A copy of the letter of *Naib Bakhshi* is also sent. Further, asks about the directives in regard to sending news in the future. Whether it should be sent everyday or if there is perfect news about the insurgents then only it should be communicated, and everyday news of the well-being should be stopped as it only increases the quantity of material of post. Whatever directives may be considered fit, may be communicated to him. Dated 2 *Jumada* II, 1275 AH.

P 39. *Muhammad Hasan Khan to Hazrat Nur Khan,* Tahsildar, *Bheglone.* Refers to his two letters sent to him earlier which were in regard to sending the battalion of Umrao Singh, *jamadar* to him as the said battalion is still to be sent to him which is a matter of concern and also what has happened. Reiterates that the said battalion may soon be sent there by the time this letter arrives to him. There should not be any further delay. Dated 29 *Rabi* II, 1275 AH.

P 41. *Hazrat Nur Khan to Daulat Rai,* Nazim-i Mashriq. Informs that day, i.e. 1st *Jumada* I, day Wednesday, Lal Singh, the informer, came and stated that he had gone to Mogawali to bring the news of the insurgents where he found no sign of the insurgents at all. Lala Kallu Ram, a dweller of Mogawali, told him that at Jhaklone there was a gathering of insurgents and the British forces had attacked upon them and devastated the village, and the insurgents had fled and dispersed and took shelter in the hills and bushes. Dated 1 *Jumada* I, 1275 AH.

P 43. *Bakhshi Murawwat Muhammad Khan to Nawwab Sikandar Begam.* Informs that Jumman, the informer, and Chandan, the soldier of the battalion of Balwant Singh, were sent by him to Jhaklone to bring the news of Adil Muhammad Khan. That day, they returned and described what they noticed. The report submitted by them is sent to her. Dated 16 *Jumada* I, 1275 AH.

P 45. *News-Report as Heard from Jumman, the Informer, and Chandan Singh, the Soldier, Son of Balwant Singh,* Jamadar. State that when they reached Issagarh from Korwai and Kanchiamogawali, they got the news of insurgents there. They travelled 3 *curoh* from Issagarh towards Chanderi. They met a guard of the army of Adil Muhammad Khan in the mountain range surrounded by trees and found Chhoga Lal, son of Kishan Ram, *kamdar* of Adil Muhammad Khan. He was known to them. Through him it came to notice that Adil Muhammad Khan, Aqil Muhammad Khan and Raja Bhor along with an army of 10,000 to 12,000 were present there. They would soon come to that side.

P 47. *Nizam Ali Khan,* Risaldar, *to Nawwab Sikandar Begam.* Informs that day; the 18th *Jumada* I, 1275 AH, passed with calm in the army camp encamp at Siwans.

Amir Khan who was assigned the duty of an informer by Hafiz Muhammad Hasan Khan, *naib bakhshi*, for bringing the news about Adil Muhammad Khan came back. He stated that he heard about the staying of Adil Muhammad Khn in the fort of Shergarh, *ilaqa* Jalone. Says, he tried his best to enter in the fort but failed in his mission as the insurgents arrest and kill whoever is found there. Says on the way, he met Karamat Khan, son of Ahmad Khan Bhuria, who is a servant of Adil Muhammad Khan.

P 49. *Daulat Rai,* Nazim-i Mashriq, *to Nawwab Sikandar Begam.* Informs that day a report was received from *thana* Solwani, dated 21 *Jumada* I, 1275 AH, stating as heard that Nana Peshwa is at Patankhera, situating at a distance of 8 *curoh* from Issagarh, and Adil Muhammad Khan is at Jhaklone and Bangawali. The same is sent to her. The *Thanadar* of Solwani has sent the informers to know about the presence of Peshwa. When they will come back, information will be sent. Dated 24 *Jumada* I, 1275 AH.

P 51. *News-Report from* Thana *Solwani.* Reports that day, Bhawani, the informer, and Wazir Khan, the soldier of *thana*, had gone to Jhaklone and Bangawali, hearing the news of Adil Muhammad Khan being there. They came back and stated that there was no sign of Adil Muhammad Khan's presence. When they arrived at *mauza* Bangawali, they heard about the arrival of the army of Nana Peshwa at Patankhera, situating at a distance of 8 *curoh* from Issagarh. Says, that day the informers are sent to Patankhera and Issagarh to bring the perfect news about Nana. A report will be sent once they come back.

P 53. *Daulat Rai,* Nazim-i Mashriq, *to Nawwab Sikandar Begam.* Sends the letter received from Nur Khan, *tahsildar* of Bheglone, dated 30 *Jumada* I, 1275 AH, informing that Jhaklone is now a deserted and vacant place, fleeing of Muhip Singh after an attack by the British forces, and hiding of Adil Muhammad Khan in the jungles of *mauza* Dudmai, situating at a distance of 3 *curoh* from Jhaklone. Dated 3 *Jumada* II, 1275 AH.

P 55. *Hazrat Nur Khan to Daulat Rai,* Nazim-i Mashriq. Informs that day; the 30th *Jumada* I, day Thursday, Muhammad Khan and Nanhu Shah, *jamadar,* came and stated that they had gone to Jhaklone to bring the news. In Jhaklone, none of them was there. It was completely deserted. Muhip Singh, after an attack by the British forces, fled from the village and reached Manik Chawk, situating at a distance of two and half *curoh* from Jhaklone and hid in the mountains. Adil Muhammad Khan is hiding in the bushes in *mauza* Dudhai, situating at a distance of 3 *curoh* from Jhaklone. The distance between *mauza* Manik Chawk and *mauza* Dudhai is about 2 *curoh*. The Bundelas have devastated 4 *mauzas*, namely Harkal, Bhangarh, Bedahti and Plasri. The insurgency on that side is too much. Dated 30 *Jumada* I, 1275 AH.

File No. 300, B
Box No. 16
No. of Documents 25

P 53. *Bhawani Prasad to Nawwab Sikandar Begam.* Informs that the Political Agent in respect to the receipt of a letter of the Agent to the Governor General, Central India, who in reference to the request of General Mitchell has communicated that Bakhshi Murawwat Muhammad Khan may report to the General along with his forces. Thus, he is informed that, after the following day, General Mitchell would be at Dehgaon and Bakhshi Murawwat Muhammad Khan should march along with his forces and join the General. He told him that he would convey the same to the Nawwab. Thereafter, he complained of not providing a reliable person to the General. Says, he told him that who could be more reliable and familiar than Daulat Rai, *nazim-i mashriq* who is present here. He listened and kept mum. The matter, as described by the Political Agent, is sent to her. Dated 26 *Rabi* I, 1275 AH/3 November 1858.

It contains the order that the letter may be sent to Lala Paltu Lal, *muhafiz-i daftar-i insha*, for inclusion in the register and keeping in the *daftar*. A copy of the order may be sent to Bhawani Prasad, informing that Bakhshi Murawwat Muhammad Khan was sent to General Mitchell and two days before Hafiz Muhammad Hasan Khan, *naib bakhshi*, was sent to the camp of General Mitchell. As the *bakhshi* was suffering from fever, he came back from there after staying for two days and Hafiz Muhammad Hasan Khan, *naib bakhshi*, would remain with him. Directs him to bring the matter into the notice of the Political Agent and convey to her of his reply. Dated 26 *Rabi* I, 1275 AH/3 November 1858.

P 55. *Bakhshi Murawwat Muhammad Khan to Nawwab Sikandar Begam*. Refers to the letter of Hafiz Hasan Khan, *Naib Bakhshi* from Khujuri, dated 20 *Rabi* I, 1275, stating that in accordance to the distribution of the employees under Roop Singh, *risaldar,* there are 5 *sawars* of *risala* III, red uniform, but he did not yet report to him. Their joining him would be a matter of appreciation. In view of this, Roop Singh, *risaldar*, was instructed to send 5 *sawars* before him. The *risaldar* replied that he received a royal order in regard to not despatching the *sawars* and thus, thereafter, as per the royal order, he sent the *sawars* to Sanchi Kanakhera. Then he received an order to dismantle them from Sanchi Kanakhera and in accordance to that, the *sawars* were called to Bhopal. But the *naib bakhshi* has got *sawars* more than the norms, formulated under the system of distribution of employees from *risala* III, black uniform. Thus, the *naib bakhshi* has 53 *sawars* who, as per the norms of the distribution of employees was compensated from *risala* III, black uniform. As he got 2 *sawars* more than the norms that were returned to him. Information to this effect was a must, which he did. Dated 25 *Rabi* I, 1275 AH.

It contains the order that the letter may be sent to Lala Paltu Lal, *muhafiz-i daftar-i insha*, for inclusion in the register and keeping in the *daftar*. A copy of the order may be sent to Bakhshi Murawwat Muhammad Khan communicating that *sawars* of *risala* Roop Singh, *risaldar*, the soldiers of the Sikh battalion and the *sawars* of gond battalion should not be deployed outside without her order. If anyone is posted anywhere in accordance to the distribution system, information should be given to her. Dated 29 *Rabi* I, 1275 AH.

P 57. *Muhammad Hasan Khan to Nawwab Sikandar Begam.* Informs of his letter, communicating that he, in the early morning, would be coming to meet Cumming. On his way, Daulat Rai, *nazim* brought back the *sawar*, the bearer of the letter who was coming back from Raisen. Says he called him and said that there was no need for him to go to Bhilsa at the moment as the British army would be at Ahmadpur in the morning. So he should go to Ahmadpur from there. A letter addressed to the officer was handed over to him. Thus, he left the idea of going to Bhilsa. Says, that day, he arrived Ahmadpur from Raisen. Everything concerning *sarbrah* was made available there. However, the British army is yet to arrive. Informs that as he did a long journey and nothing of the army has come, he would go to Bhilsa in the morning. He has sent a letter to the British at Bhilsa about his arrival at Ahmadpur from Raisen. A copy of the same is enclosed. Dated 25 *Rabi* I, 1275 AH.

It contains the order that the letter may be sent to Lala Paltu Lal, *muhafiz-i daftar-i insha*, for inclusion in the register and keeping in the *daftar*. A copy of the order may be sent to Bhawni Prasad, *wakil* to convey to the Political Agent and his reply may be conveyed to her.

PP 59-60. *Hafiz Muhammad Hasan Khan to the British Officer*. Refers to the letter of Nawwab Sikandar Begam, in his name, directing him to report to Cumming as soon as he receives her order along with all his *sawars* and foot-soldiers. Says, he was preparing to march and to reach Bhilsa before him in the morning. Meanwhile, he got a message from Daulat Rai who had just come to Raisen after meeting him that early in the morning the forces would march from Bhilsa for Ahmadpur. Thus, he arrived at Ahmadpur from Raisen along with all the *sawars* and foot-soldiers. But the British army is yet to arrive. Requests for orders to proceed further. He has with him 27 elephant *sawars* and 115 elephant soldiers. Dated 25 *Rabi* I, 1275 AH.

P 61. *Bhawani Prasad to Nawwab Sikandar Begam.* Informs that as ordered, dated 26 *Rabi* I, 1275 AH, he informed the Political Agent about the departure of Bakhshi Murawwat Muhammad Khan to the camp of General Mitchell who had no carriers with him. Says he said, very well. Dated 26 *Rabi* I, 1275 AH/4 November 1858.

P 63. Parwana *of Nawwab Sikandar Begam to Muhammad Hasan Khan,* Naib Bakhshi. Directs him that the soldiers of *mahals* under the district *nizamat-i mashriq* who are under his command should be sent to Daulat Rai, *nazim-i mashriq*. The battalion of *wilayatis* is being sent to him. Dated 26 *Rabi* I, 1275 AH/4 November 1858.

PP 65-6. *Muhammad Hasan Khan to Nawwab Sikandar Begam.* Refers to his letter, informing that he is going to report to General Mitchell at Ahmadpur. In Ahmadpur, it so happened that the camp of the General was not located by him. Then it was heard that the army has not yet marched from Bhilsa. Hearing this he, on 26th of this month in the early morning arrived in Bhilsa leaving aside all his carriers and belongings. He observed that the General had gone to Raisen along with the army. He then left for Raisen at the very moment. After reaching there, he conveyed of his well-being to Captain Cumming. He conveyed him that the next day, he would meet him. Says in Bhilsa he authorized Qadir Bakhsh, *jamadar*, along with one *sawar* to come along with all other forces and belongings. The next day, the army of Captain Cumming would march to Chiklod and he too would be accompanying him. Assures that he would obey whatever order, would be given to him. Dated 26 *Rabi* I, 1275 AH.

It contains the order that the letter may be sent to Lala Paltu Lal, *muhafiz-i daftar-i insha*, for inclusion in the register and keeping in the *daftar*. A copy of the order may be sent to Bhawni Prasad, *wakil* to convey to the Political Agent and his reply may be conveyed to her.

P 67. *Bakhshi Murawwat Muhammad Khan to Nawwab Sikandar Begam.* Informs that the previous day ; 27th *Rabi* I, 1275 AH, as ordered, he along with Ghulam Husain Khan, agent I, besides both the diwans, the *sawars* and foot-soldiers, in accordance to the distribution of the employees, marched from Jahangirabad and reached at river Betwa in the night itself. When the light of the day spread, it was heard that Hafiz Muhammad Hasan, *naib bakhshi*, was accompanying the British army. As it was not clear where they would go, so he reached Raisen and came to know that, that day Cumming and General Mitchell were at *mauza* Chiklod situating at a distance of 6 *curoh* from Raisen. He ordered all his companions to take rest and to take their meals and to relax from the night's tiredness. At the end of the day, they left the place to join the army of Cumming and met Hafiz Hasan Khan there. Informs that early in the morning, he would be before her. Dated 27 *Rabi* I, 1275 AH.

P 69. *Muhammad Hasan Khan to Nawwab Sikandar Begam.* Informs that day Cumming gave him permission to go, but due to a long journey the foot-soldiers and bullocks of carriers that are coming with the royal army are yet to reach. Therefore, the next day, he would march from there and encamp at Penchhor. Day after the next day, after collecting the entire contingent which is left behind would reach Raisen from Penchhor. Requests for orders to be followed by him after his arrival at Raisen as where to encamp and where to go. Dated 27 *Rabi* I, 1275 AH.

It contains the order that the letter may be sent to Lala Paltu Lal, *muhafiz-i daftar-i insha*, for inclusion in the register and keeping in the *daftar*. A copy of the order may be sent to Hafiz Muhammad Hasan Khan, *naib bakhshi*, directing him to go to Garhi Ambapani and Khan Zaman Khan may be sent back to the fort of Raisen along with his army. Dated 29 *Rabi* I, 1275 AH.

PP 71-2. *Muhammad Hasan Khan to Nawwab Sikandar Begam.* Informs that day, i.e. 17th *Rabi* I, 1275 AH, he accompanying General Mitchell and Cumming came from Raisen to Chiklod. He got an appointment with Cumming. He asked about her well-being and deliberated upon fighting with the insurgents at Gwalior and Bundelkhand and capturing 27 cannon of the insurgents at Rajgarh. He then said that, earlier it was thought that they would to go from Bhilsa via Ahmadpur and Dehgaon. But it was heard that the insurgents have crossed the river Narmada. Thus, the march of his army was postponed to that side and they marched to Raisen to go to Hoshangabad. As the *sawars* are too many in Hyderabad, Deccan, the insurgents would be dealt with effectively. He also said that 200 camels rided by the Britishers are coming soon from Ajmer. Then he said to him that he was ordered by the Nawwab to join Cumming with all his *sawars* and foot-soldiers. Thus, he has arrived with 27 elephant riders and 115 elephents led by foot-soldiers. Whatever orders he likes, may give to be implemented by him. He replied that Haji *Sahab* is also accompanying him. He is very attentive and hopes that there will be no problem for them. Thus, he is not required to give him company. The only thing is that the roads from Raisen to Hoshangabad should be cleaned and cleared. Thereafter, he expressed his desire to meet the General. Cumming himself took him along to the General. The General told him to convey his good wishes to the Nawwab. It was his earnest desire to personally meet the Nawwab. But as the insurgents have fled he has to march via other routes outside Bhopal to pursue them. Says, he left the British officials and called the *thanadars* of Kalyakhery and Raisen who were present there and instructed them to clean the road. The *thanadars* who were busy in cleaning the roads also called others to perform the duty. Dated 27 *Rabi* I, 1275 AH.

P 73. *'Abd al-Karim Ansari to Nawwab Sikandar Begam.* Informs that day, i.e. 27th *Rabi* I, 1275 AH, the army of General Mitchell marched from Raisen and encamped at Chiklod. The *thanadar* of Kalyakhery provided essential commodities needed by the army. The *tahsildar* and *thanadar* of Raisen provided flour and gram, at Chiklod to the army. All the commodities were weighted and handed over to the army as ordered by Cumming. The *tahsildar* and *thanadar* returned to Raisen from Chiklod. Abd al-Rahman, *thanadar* of Kalyakhery, is accompanying the army for providing commodities needed by the army and for the cleaning the roads. In the evening, Muhammad Hasan Khan, *Naib Bakhshi*, met the General and Cumming and said that he, as ordered was present and should be ordered the way he liked. They said there was no need for him to be there. He would unnecessarily be put in trouble. 'Abd al-Karim, who is accompanying him, is enough for them. Cumming expressed his deep desire to meet the Nawwab. But what to do as the insurgents have crossed river Narmada and to pursue them is a must. Dated 27 *Rabi* I, 1275 AH.

It contains the order that the letter may be sent to Lala Paltu Lal, *muhafiz-i daftar-i insha*, for inclusion in the register and keeping in the *daftar*. A copy of the letter may be sent to Bhawani Prasad, *wakil* to present it before the Political Agent and convey his reply to her.

A copy of the order may be sent to Hafiz Hasan Khan, *naib bakhshi*, informing him that General Mitchell has allowed him to go, so he should take the army along with him and go.

P 75. *'Abd al-Karim Ansari to Nawwab Sikandar Begam.* Informs that, as desired by Hafiz Muhammad Hasan Khan, *naib bakhshi*, he informed Cumming of the arrival of Ghulam Husain Khan, Agenty with two battalions, one company and *risala* of Pir Ma'sum with two cannon at Chiklod to accompany the General. In reply, he said if his march would be to Bamhuri there is no harm in having the cannon with him. Presently, there seems to be no need to carry these cannon to the other side of Narmada. If these cannon as well as the troops are kept in Garhi, it would be good. Information to this effect was communicated to Hafiz Muhammad Hasan Khan. Dated 24 *Rabi* I, 1275 AH.

It contains the order that the letter may be sent to Lala Paltu Lal, *muhafiz-i daftar-i insha*, for inclusion in the register and keeping in the *daftar*. A copy of the order may be sent to Haji 'Abd al-Karim Ansari, Agenty III, communicating that even before the orders of General Mitchell she ordered Hafiz Muhammad Hasah Khan, *naib bakhshi*, to go to Garhi Ambapani along with the army and cannon. The information should be given to General Mitchell and his reply may be conveyed to her. Hafiz Muhammad Hasan Khan should also be communicated that he should immediately rush to Garhi Ambapani along with his army and cannon and inform her of the same. Dated 29 *Rabi* I, 1275 AH.

P 77. *Muhammad Hasan Khan,* Naib Bakhshi, *to Nawwab Sikandar Begam.* That day, i.e. 28 *Rabi* I, 1275 AH, he along with his army, the *sawars* and foot-soldiers, as ordered by Cumming and the General has marched from Chiklod and is going to Raisen. On the route in between Chiklod and Penchhor, he met Ghulam Husain Khan, Agenty I, who was accompanying with

2 cannon, magazine, 2 battalions and *sawars* of *risala* Pir Ma'sum. The agenty explained to him that all these things; the cannon, the army were sent for him and to join the General. Says it does not seem wise to go back to the General without his permission. Says, he wrote a letter to Haji 'Abd al-Karim Ansari asking whether he should come back from Raisen or he should stay at Chiklod along with all the forces and cannon. He should seek the reply of Cumming and the General and inform him so that he may do accordingly. Informs, he would do as directed by Cumming and the General. Dated 26 *Rabi* I, 1275 AH.

It contains the order that the letter may be sent to Lala Paltu Lal, *muhafiz-i daftar-i insha*, for inclusion in the register and keeping in the *daftar*. A copy of the order may be sent to Hafiz Muhammad Hasan Khan, *naib bakhshi*, directing him to immediately go to Raisen from Chiklod as it is heard that Adil Muhammad Khan has arrived in Garhi Ambapani. If there is skirmish between him and Adil Muhammad Khan, he should kill him. Asks why he went back to Chiklod when he received all the things; the cannon and the army on the route. God knows what has happened to his wisdom. Dated 1 *Rabi* II, 1275 AH.

P 79. *Daulat Rai,* Nazim-i Mashriq, *to Nawwab Sikandar Begam.* Informs that Hazarilal, *tahsildar*, who had gone with the army to Chiklod with *rasad* in apprehension that the scarcity of *rasad* in Chiklod might occur and that he conveyed her order to both the *nizamat*. Says that Hazarilal, *tahsildar*, came back from Chiklod, and stated that the British had marched from there and the *naib bakhshi* too was allowed to go back. Requests if the *naib bakhshi* stays for few days in Garhi along with his forces and cannon, otherwise as she may like. Dated 28 *Rabi* I, 1275 AH.

It contains the order that the letter may be sent to Lala Paltu Lal, *muhafiz-i daftar-i insha*, for inclusion in the register and keeping in the *daftar*. A copy of the order may be sent to Daulat Rai, *nazim-i mashriq*, through *madar al-maham,* conveying that General Mitchell has himself ordered to Hafiz Muhammad Hasan Khan, *naib bakhshi*, to remain stationed at Garhi Ambapani. Dated 1 *Rabi* II, 1275 AH.

P 81. *Muhammad Hasan Khan,* Naib Bakhshi, *to Nawwab Sikandar Begam*. Acknowledges the receipt of her *parwana,* dated 26th of the month, directing that the forces of *mahal* of the *nizamat-i mashriq* which are under him should be sent to Daulat Rai, *nazim-i mashriq*. Informs that none of the soldiers of *mahals* of *nizamat-i mashriq* has come with him. The names of the foot-soldiers along with the name of battalion has been communicated to her from Raisen. The names of the battalion who are with him are being sent to her. The details of the battalion are; battalion of Mangal Das, *jamadar*, battalion of Hasan Khan, *jamadar*, battalion of Ghasi Khan, *jamadar* and others. Dated 28 *Rabi* I, 1275 AH.

P 83. *Muhammad Hasan Khan,* Naib Bakhshi, *to Nawwab Sikandar Begam*. Informs that day, i.e. 29 *Rabi* I, 1275 AH, he is encamping at Chiklod as ordered by Cumming. Ghulam Husain Khan, Agenty, has been sent to her. Dated 29 *Rabi* I, 1275 AH.

P 85. Parwana *of Nawwab Sikandar Begam to Muhammad Hasan Khan,* Naib Bakhshi. Directs him to inform as to when he was separated from the camp of Mitchell and presently where he is. Information to this effect may be sent immediately. Dated 1 *Rabi* II, 1275 AH.

P 87. Parwana *of Nawwab Sikandar Begam to Muhammad Hasan Khan,* Naib Bakhshi. A very good opportunity has arrived as the first group of insurgents, which is the group of Tantia Tope, has gone to the other side of Narmada. The group of Adil Muhammad Khan which is about 8,000 but carries no cannon has arrived the previous day at Garhi Ambapani. The army led by Brigadier is in Bhilsa and has closed the road to Bhilsa and Bhopal. The *suba* of Bhilsa has sent a letter to Daulat Rai, *nazim-i mashriq*, that he should not move until he arrives along with his forces to deal with the insurgents. Khan Zaman Khan, *qila'dar* of Raisen, is in Garhi with one battalion of troops and Sher Singh and Wazir Khan, *qal'dars*, along with their troops are at Siwans. Directs him to rush to Raisen with his troops and if the insurgents try to flee, he should pursue them. The time demands quick action and immediate performance. There should not be any negligence or laziness. May God bless if anything great happens from the hands of the people of Bhopal to prove the proverb that '*bhagte bhut ki langoti hi'*. If these insurgents are killed or arrested by them. Dated 1 *Rabi* II, 1275 AH.

PP 89-90. *Muhammad Hasan Khan,* Naib Bakhshi, *to Nawwab Sikandar Begam*. Informs that he wrote a letter to 'Abd al-Karim Ansari from Chiklod, stating that 2 cannon were coming with Cumming. Sends the letter received from him, communicating as directed by Cumming, that if his army's march is to Bamhuri, he would not mind, carrying the cannon with him. But he thinks if these cannon were sent to Garhi, it would be better. Says the following day, i.e. 2nd *Rabi* II, 1275 AH, he would be at Raisen after marching from Chiklod and would wait for her order so that it may be carried out.

It contains the order that the letter may be sent to Lala Paltu Lal, *muhafiz-i daftar-i insha*, for inclusion in the register and keeping in the *daftar*. A copy of the order may be sent to Hafiz Muhammad Hasan, *naib bakhshi*, directing him that in accordance to the order of Cumming, as communicated through Haji 'Abd al-Karim, Agenty III, he should go to Garhi Ambapani along with his forces and two cannon. She would pray to Allah that Tantia Tope may meet the fate of Fazil Muhammad Khan, who was arrested by the servants of

Bhopal government. Adil Muhammad Khan and Aqil Muhammad Khan, the two tails of Tantia Tope, may meet their fate. It might be that by the graceness of God, the army of Bhopal may arrest and kill both the tails of Tantia Tope. If so happens, it will be an act of bravery of the army of Bhopal in the eyes of the British officers. It is a must that every effort should be made to arrest and kill the two evils. A copy of the order may be sent to Daulat Rai, *nazim-i mashriq*, to communicate the order to all the *thanadars* of his *ilaqa*. Dated 2 *Rabi* II, 1275 AH.

P 91. *'Abd al-Karim Ansari to Muhammad Hasan Khan,* Naib Bakhshi. Refers to his letter, informing of the arrival of Ghulam Husain Khan along with the *risala* of Pir Ma'sum, besides one company and two battalions along with two cannon and magazine to give company to the army of General Mitchell and to communicate Cumming about his arrival along with cannon to give company to the British army and about his stay at Chiklod till the reply is received. Says with the receipt of his letter he brought every matter mentioned in the letter in to the notice of Cumming. In reply, the officer said that if he was to go to Bamhuri then there was no problem in carrying those cannon there. But carrying the cannon across Narmada is not required. In his opinion, it will be good if these cannon or the forces, carrying these cannon are sent to Garhi. What he said, he conveyed. Dated 29 *Rabi* I, 1275 AH.

PP 93-4. *Muhammad Hasan Khan,* Naib Bakhshi, *to Nawwab Sikandar Begam*. Informs of his arrival at Raisen after his march from Chiklod along with cannon and the forces and sent letters to Khan Zaman Khan, *qila'dar*, and 'Abd al-Rahman, *thanadar* of Garhi, for sending the true news of Adil Muhammad Khan, as directed. Assures that after getting the news, they would be dealt with firmly and effectively. It is also heard that Bakhshi Murawwat Muhammad Khan would arrive there by the evening that day itself. After his arrival, action would be taken under his guidance and instructions. Dated 2 *Rabi* II, 1275 AH.

It contains the order that the letter may be sent to Lala Paltu Lal, *muhafiz-i daftar-i insha*, for inclusion in the register and keeping in the *daftar*. A copy of the order may be sent to Hafiz Muhammad Hasan, *naib bakhshi*, directing him that there is no need to wait for the news from the *amil* and *thanadar* but he should deploy his own reliable and confident informers to bring authentic news of the insurgents and deal with them firmly. Pursue them, arrest or kill them. Dated 2 *Rabi* II, 1275 AH.

P 95. *Daulat Rai,* Nazim-i Mashriq, *to Nawwab Sikandar Begam.* Refers to her order, dated 2 *Rabi* II, 1275, as recorded in the letter of Hafiz Muhammad Hasan Khan sent through a bullock rider, directing that the *naib Bakhshi* should go to Garhi Ambapani along with the forces and two cannon to kill and eliminate Adil Muhammad Khan and Aqil Muhammad Khan. Informs that, as ordered, Bakhshi Murawwat Muhammad Khan and *naib bakhshi* arrived the previous day along with their forces. But due to carriers of goods, overflow of the *nallas* and weaknesses of the bullocks for carrying loads had failed to move further. They would march that day from there along with all their belongings. Day after the next day, they would be at their destination. May Allah give His blessings to her. The peasants too are praying that the two tails of Tantia Tope; Adil Muhammad Khan and Aqil Muhammad Khan, may meet their fate as they are trouble makers for the people since past two years. They have been seperated from Tantia Tope. Hope they would meet their fate in that region. Dated 3 *Rabi* II, 1275 AH.

P 97. *Muhammad Hasan Khan,* Naib Bakhshi, *to Nawwab Sikandar Begam.* Informs that day, i.e. 3rd *Rabi* II, 1275 AH, day Wednesday, he received her order as recorded in his letter sent by a camel rider of the *risala* Ghulam Muhammad Khan, *risaldar* at Raisen, directing him to go to Garhi with cannon and the royal army and kill or arrest Adil Muhammad Khan and Aqil Muhammad Khan at any cost. Informs that the previous day in the evening, the *Bakhshi* also arrived there. The next day, the royal forces would march for Nerakhari. Assures that the insurgents would be dealt with, as desired, after getting the news about them. Dated 3 *Rabi* II, 1275 AH.

It contains the order that the letter may be sent to Lala Paltu Lal, *muhafiz-i daftar-i insha*, for inclusion in the register and keeping in the *daftar*. A copy of the order may be sent to Hafiz Muhammad Hasan, *naib bakhshi*, directing him to explain what he means by secret news as the time does not allow to rely upon his mere sayings. Dated 6 *Rabi* II, 1275 AH.

P 99. *Bakhshi Murawwat Muhammad Khan to Nawwab Sikandar Begam.* Informs that after meeting her, he started his march to Chiklod and in the night itself he was just one and half *curoh* away from Chiklod when he heard that the General granted permission to Hafiz Muhammad Hasan Khan, *naib bakhshi*, to go to Raisen. Thus, from there he turned his march towards Raisen and reached there by the evening and sent the *sawars* here and there for the news of the insurgents. He also enquired from the *nazim*. For the arrangement of carts of carriers, he has sent the soldiers in the villages. Thus, for the day he would stay there, waiting for the news of the insurgents and for the arrangement of carts of carriers. Early in the morning, he would march from there for Garhi. He would stay at Aradmau and the next day, he would be at Dehgaon and by the third day, he would be at Garhi. Dated 3 *Rabi* II, 1275 AH.

It contains the order that the letter may be sent to Lala Paltu Lal, *muhafiz-i daftar-i insha*, for inclusion in the register and keeping in the *daftar*. A copy of the order may be sent to Bakhshi Murawwat Muhammad informing him that he did not write his name nor fixed his seal on his letter, dated 3 *Rabi* II, 1275, and due to this negligence he should deposit one day's salary in the treasury. Besides, her *parwanas* addressed to him and Hafiz Muhammad Hasan Khan, *naib bakhshi*, were sent through a camel rider. He, at Gobarya, took the *parwanas* from the camel rider and said to him that he would deliver the *parwanas* addressed to *naib bakhshi* at Chiklod. The camel rider was sent back from Gobarya. He was not allowed to go to Chiklod to deliver the letter to Hafiz Muhammad Hasan Khan, *naib bakhshi*. He is directed to explain as to why he returned the camel rider without delivering the letter to Hafiz Muhammad Hasan Khan. Dated 6 *Rabi* II, 1275 AH.

PP 101-2. *Bhawani Prasad to Nawwab Sikandar Begam.* Informs that day Major Richards, the Political Agent, called him and said that an officer was asking him as to why the Nawwab sent Bakhshi Murawwat Muhammad Khan to Garhi Ambapani. He replied to him that from those places, tales, right or wrong were frequently heard due to the uncalled activities by the people of Pura Guna, Bharonpur etc. *ilaqa* Bhilsa. The *mahals* of Garhi, Ghairatganj and Bamhuri, *ilaqa Riyasat* Bhopal are the adjoining *mahals* of Raisen. Thus Bakhshi Murawwat Muhammad Khan was sent there and the *naib Bakhshi* was in Siwans with his forces. Says he heard him and kept mum. Dated 10 *Rabi* II, 1275 AH/17 November 1858.

It contains the order that the letter may be sent to Lala Paltu Lal, *muhafiz-i daftar-i insha*, for inclusion in the register and keeping in the *daftar*. A copy of the order may be sent to Bhawani Prasad, *wakil,* communicating that the reason for staying of Bakhshi Murawwat Muhammad Khan at Garhi Ambapani is that an area of 10 to 20 *curoh* in the surrondings of Garhi Ambapani, Pura Guna and Bharonpur, *ilaqa* Bhilsa, were the hiding and residing place of the insurgents. This was the place of eruption of insurgency. The deployment of Bhopal army at Garhi Ambapani was to ensure the safety and security of *mahals* of the State of Bhopal adjoining Garhi Ambapani. Besides this, General Mitchell allowed Hafiz Muhammad Hasan Khan, *naib bakhshi*, to go to Garhi Ambapani from Chiklod. At that time, Bakhshi Murawwat Muhammad Khan was at Bhopal. The *Bakhshi* with the contingent of Hafiz Muhammad Hasan Khan, and the contingent carrying from Bhopal reached Garhi Ambapani with the orders of General Mitchell. Directs him to bring the matter into the notice of the Political Agent and covey his comments to her. Dated 22 *Rabi* II, 1275 AH.

PP 103-04. *Bakhshi Murawwat Muhammad Khan to Nawwab Sikandar Begam.* Refers to her order, dated 6 *Rabi* II, as mentioned in his letter, that her *parwanas* to him and Hafiz Muhammad Hasan Khan were sent to them through a camel rider. At Gobarya, he took the *parwanas* from the camel rider and said to him that the *parwana* addressed to Hafiz Muhammad Hasan Khan would be delivered by him. He is directed to explain as to what was in his mind when he returned back the camel rider. Says, as he himself was going to Chiklod so he took the *parwana* to deliver it to him. He did not say the *sawar* to return. If he was going to Chiklod, why he returnd it would be known to him. Dated 24 *Rabi* II, 1275 AH.

It contains the order that the letter may be sent to Lala Paltu Lal, *muhafiz-i daftar-i insha*, for inclusion in the register and keeping in the *daftar*. A copy of the order may be sent to Bakhshi Murawwat Muhammad khan, communicating him that, if the camel rider gave him the *parwana* addressed to Hafiz Muhammad Hasan Khan, *naib bakhshi,* why he took the *parwana* from him and why he did not refuse and that he himself should deliver the *parwana* to Hafiz Muhammad Hasan Khan. If he would not have taken the *parwana* from him, he would have dared not to go to Hafiz Hasan Khan. It is clear that the statement of camel rider is correct. Warns him that this should not happen in the future. Dated 3 *Jumada* I, 1275 AH.

File No. 301
Box No. 16
No. of Documents 23

News-Report of Adil Muhammad Khan who Along with Hattey Singh and Raja of Choka are Encamping in the Mountains of Tans and in the Deserts of Bharonpur and Nakchari

PP 1-4. Contents

PP 5-6. *Harsahai,* Tahsildar *of Bamhuri, to Nawwab Sikandar Begam.* Informs that day, from the letters of *thanadar* of Garhi and Ghairatganj to the *thanadar* of Bamhuri, it came to notice that around 300 insurgents are in Nakchari. It is also heard from someone that the insurgents like Hattey Singh, Chokawala, Jaitgarhwala and Narwar Singh along with some forces are staying in the mountains of Tans and in the forest of Bharonpur. The danger of their attack always persists in the region. But he does not have a gun. Requests to provide him a flint gun worth of Rs. 35 from the weaponry. The said amount will be paid by him to the government. To carry a gun by him is a necessity of the time. Dated 29 *Rabi* I, 1275 AH.

It contains the order that this letter and the letter of Nawwab Sikandar Begam, addressed to Baqi Muhammad Khan, may be sent to Paltu Lal, *muhafiz-i daftar-i insha*, for inclusion in the register and keeping in the *daftar*. A copy of the order may be sent to Lala Harsahai, *tahsildar* of Bamhuri, through Ghulam Murtaza Khan, asking him that in which *pargana, mauza* Nakchari and the mountains called Tans and *mauza* Bharonpur are situated. Are these under the territory of Bhopal State or under the territory of other state? An order will be issued thereafter. Dated 4 *Rabi* II, 1275 AH.

PP 7-8. *Harsahai,* Tahsildar *of Bamhuri, to Nawwab*

Sikandar Begam. Says that Gulab, caste *khagar* and a dweller of *mauza* Bamhuri, was sent to mountains of Tans, adjoining to Siwans and Bharonpur, *ilaqa* Bhilsa to bring news of insurgents. That day, he came back and stated that Hattey Singh, *Chokawala,* with a contingent of 125 soldiers was hiding in the mountains called Tans and due to this, road to that side was closed. Any traveller, if happens to go there, is looted by them. Thereafter, he left for Bharonpur. When he reached Siwans, he heard that about 10,000 to 12,000 insurgent forces have arrived at Bagrod, situating at a distance of 7 to 8 *curoh* from Siwans. The statement of Gulab is recorded and sent to her. Dated 3 *Rabi* II, 1275 AH.

It contains the order that the letter, the statement and *parwana* of Nawwab Sikandar Begam, addressed to Bhawani Prasad may be sent to Paltu Lal, *muhafiz-i daftar-i insha*, for inclusion in the register and keeping in the *daftar*. A copy of the letter may be sent to Bakhshi Murawwat Muhammad Khan, communicating him to send reliable and experienced informers to the mountains of Tans, *mauza* Bharonpur and Bagrod, to bring authentic news as might have seen by them. Also directs him that if Hattey Singh and other insurgents enter the State of Bhopal, there should not be any hesitation in killing or arresting them. A copy of the order may be sent to Lala Harsahai, *tahsildar* of Bamhuri, directing him to report at the earliest the name of *pargana* and region where the mountains of Tans are situated. Dated 7 *Rabi* II, 1275 AH.

PP 9-10. *Statement of Gulab, a Dweller of Bamhuri, in the Presence of Harsahai,* Tahsildar *of Bamhuri*. States that his name is Gulab, his father's name is Lalan, and he is a dweller of *qasba* Bamhuri. His age is 25 years.

Q. Asked to tell honestly what he saw in Bharonpur where he was sent to bring the news of insurgents.

R. Firstly, he went to the mountains of Tans where *Chokawala* with a contingent of 125 was hiding. Due to this, the road to that side was closed. If any traveller was seen there, he was looted by them. Thereafter, he went to Bharonpur from there and inquired about the insurgents. Some said that the army of the Peshwa had come to that side but by then they had gone from there. It is not known where they went. When he was in Siwans, he heard that around 10, 000 to 12,000 forces arrived in Bagrod situating at a distance of 7 to 8 *curoh* from Siwans and in between there is also a range of mountains and vallys. What he heard, he stated. There is nothing further to be stated.

P 11. Parwana *of Nawwab Sikandar Begam to Bhawani Prasad,* Wakil. Refers to the letter received from Harsahai, *tahsildar* of Bamhuri, dated 3 *Rabi* II, 1275 AH, communicating that Gulab, caste *khagar*, and a dweller of *mauza* Bamhuri was sent to the mountains of Tans adjoining Siwans and Bharonpur, *ilaqa* Bhilsa to bring the news of insurgents. That day, he came back and stated that Hattey Singh, *Chokawala*, along with a contingent of 125 soldiers was hiding in the mountains called Tans and due to this the road to that side was closed. If any traveller happens to be there, was looted by them. Thereafter, he left for Bharonpur. When he reached Siwans, he heard that about 10,000 to 12,000 insurgent forces arrived at Bagrod situating at a distance of 7 to 8 *curoh* from Siwans. Directs him that the same may be presented before the Political Agent and his observation may be communicated to her. Dated 7 *Rabi* II, 1275 AH.

PP 13-14. *Harsahai,* Tahsildar *of Bamhuri, to Nawwab Sikandar Begam.* Refers to her order, dated 4 *Rabi* II, 1275 AH, as mentioned in his letter, directing him to inform that in which *pargana*, *mauza* Nakchari and the mountains called Tans and *mauza* Bharonpur are located. Informs that *mauza* Nakchari is situated in *pargana* Himmatgarh, the mountain called Tans is a mountain range located between Sagar and Siwans, and *mauza* Bharonpur is situated in *ilaqa* Bhilsa. The *mauza* Bharonpur and *mauza* Nakchari are adjoining regions. Dated 28 *Rabi* II, 1275 AH.

PP 15-16. *Orders of Nawwab Sikandar Begam, as Recorded in the Letter of Harsahai,* Tahsildar *of Bamhuri.* Orders that the letter along with the copy of letter of Nawwab Sikandar Begam, addressed to Nawwab Nazir al-Daulah Umrao Daulah Baqi Muhammad Khan may be sent to Paltu Lal, *muhafiz-i daftar-i insha* for inclusion in the register and keeping in the *daftar*. A copy of the order may be sent to Harsahai, *tahsildar* of Bamhuri, through Ghulam Murtaza Khan, *kamdar,* Deorhi Khas, directing him to tell that in which *pargana*, *mauza* Nakchari and the mountains called Tans, besides *mauza* Bharonpur are situated. Whether these are under the State of Bhopal or are located under the territory of others. Directs him to reply, before any order in the matter is further given. Dated 29 *Rabi* II, 1275 AH.

P 17. *Harsahai,* Tahsildar *of Bamhuri, to Nawwab Sikandar Begam.* Refers to her order, as recorded in his letter, directing him to inform that in which region the mountain called Tans is situated. Says to know about it, he wrote a letter to the *tahsildar* of *pargana* Siwans. In reply, he wrote that the mountain called Tans is the range of mountains from Sagar to Siwans. The same is presented to her. Dated 29 *Rabi* II, 1275 AH.

PP 19-20. *Harsahai,* Tahsildar *of Bamhuri, to Lala Gori Shankar,* Tahsildar of *Siwans.* Refers to the order of the Nawwab, mentioned in his letter to explain in which *pargana,* the mountain of Tans is situated. Requests him to reply whether Tans is situated in Siwans or Sagar or it is the range of mountains from Bhopal to Sagar, on what side of Siwans it is situated and what is its distance from Siwans. Dated 12 *Rabi* II, 1275 AH.

P 21. *Orders of the Nawwab as Mentioned in the Letter of Harsahai,* Tahsildar *of Bamhuri.* Orders that the letter along with the copy of the *parwana* of Nawwab Sikandar Begam, addressed to Bhawani Prasad, dated 7 *Rabi* II, 1275 AH, may be sent to Paltu Lal, *muhafiz-i daftar-i insha*, for inclusion in the register and keeping in the *daftar*. A copy of the letter may be sent to Bakhshi Murawwat Muhammad Khan, directing him to send experienced and clever informers to the mountains of Tans, Bharonpur and Bagrod with clear instructions that only the news seen by their own eyes should be reported and that Hattey Singh or any other insurgent, if enters Bhopal at any point of time, there should not be any hesitation in killing or arresting him. A copy of the order may be sent to Lala Harsahai, *tahsildar* of Bamhuri, through Ghulam Murtaza Khan, directing him to report that in which *pargana,* the mountains of Tans lie and in whose region is located. Dated 7 *Rabi* II, 1275 AH.

PP 23-4. *Daulat Rai,* Nazim-i Mashriq, *to Nawwab Sikandar Begam.* Informs about a letter of Ramchand, *patwari*, *mauza* Maujpur, *pargana* Siwans, dated 22 *Jumada* II, 1275 AH, informing that the army of Adil Muhammad Khan along with the Raja of Choka and Raja Hamir Singh has entered in the mountains of Tans, situating at a distance of 3 *curoh* from Siwans. Informs that he immediately went to the mountains of Tans to deal with the insurgents after receiving the letter sent by *Bakhshi* Nizam Ali along with the forces, present in Siwans, in *thana*, *tahsil* and the forces of *jagirdars*. A report will be sent after the return of the *bakhshi*, if any battle is fought with the insurgents or not. A report on the apprehension of devastation of the villages along with translation of the letter of the *patwari* is sent herewith. Besides, the nomads present in the hills are reporting the entry of the insurgents in the mountains. But there is no report of the presence of their forces in the hills. Dated 23 *Jumada* I, 1275 AH, from Siwans.

PP 25-6. *Letter of Ramchand Patwari in Hindi Devanagari.*

PP 27-8. *Letter of Ramchand Patwari in Urdu.*

P 29. *Muhammad Faiyaz Khan,* Munsarim *of Measurement of* Dandah *In Siwans, to Nawwab Sikandar Begam.* Informs that day, day Thursday, date 23 *Jumada* I, 1275 AH early in the morning, a *balahi* of *mauza* Choka came and stated that the Raja of Choka and Adil Muhammad Khan with 2,000 *sawars* and foot-soldiers had encamped in the mountains of Tans. A letter has also been received in this connection. Informs that after hearing this news, as per the royal order to him, he asked the soldiers of the *thana* and *mahal* to be ready and taking them and Nizam Ali Khan in his company marched to the place of their encampment which was 4 *curoh* or so away from Siwans. There he heard that they left the place that day in the morning and through the routes of mountains went to Pura Guna. Dated 23 *Jumada* I, 1275 AH.

P 31. *Daulat Rai,* Nazim-i Mashriq, *to Nawwab Sikandar Begam.* Refers to his earlier letter, informing that Nizam Ali Khan, *bakhshi*, district east along with the forces of Siwans and the forces of *jagirdars* went to the mountains of Tans to fight with the forces of Adil Muhammad Khan and Raja of Choka. The *bakhshi* reached the mountains of Tans and found the signs of armymen and their horses but they had moved from there. The *bakhshi* then returned to Siwans at night. Hazari Gond, the informer sent by the *patwari* of Bhojpur to the mountains of Tans to bring the news of the insurgents came back and described the presence of Adil Muhammad Khan and Raja of Choka in the mountains till that evening and that they moved from the mountains to the other side at night. He himself remained there to get his statement recorded and send it to her along with the report of *thana* Siwans. It is clear that the mountains of Tans are the range of mountains of Pura Guna falling in *ilaqa* Bhilsa. The route is always used by the insurgents and Pura Guna is the place of their shelter and encampment.

Hence, the informers have been sent to Pura Guna. A report will be sent after their coming back. Dated 24 *Jumada* I, 1275 AH.

P 33. *A Report of* Thana *Siwans Sent by Shaikh Nur Muhammad,* Thanadar, *Dated 23* Jumada *I, 1275 AH.* Reports that the previous day, hearing the news of Hattey Singh, *Chokawala*, in the mountains of Tans, at a distance of 3 *curoh* from the plains, Parsuram, and Husain Khan, soldiers of the *mahal* were sent to know the reality. Reports that day they returned and stated that the previous day they could not reach to that place as the distance was too much and stayed at night in *mauza* Simra, *pargana* Siwans. In the morning, before they reach there the said Raja had marched towards some other direction.

P 35. *Statement of Hazari Gond, a Dweller of* Mauza *Mohnanagar,* Pargana *Siwans*. States that his name is Hazarilal, his father's name is Sukhlal Singh, caste gond, a dweller of *mauza* Himmatnagar, *pargana* Siwans, engaged in the profession of daily wage-labourer, and is aged around 19 years. Further states, that day before yesterday he was called by Ramchand, *patwari* in *mauza* Bhojpur, *pargana* Siwans and said that it is heard that the insurgent forces had arrived in the mountains of Tans and so he should go to bring the perfect news. States that as said to him, he went to the mountains of Tans where he confronted with Adil Muhammad Khan who had 50 *sawars* with him. He was caught by him and asked as to who he was and where he was going. He replied that he was sent by Asaram from Bhanger to Mohna to meet his relative. He was caught and Adil Muhammad Khan ordered to kill him. He was in captivity till the evening when Raja Choka came and freed him from captivity.

Q. Asked to tell who were with Adil Muhammad Khan and how much army was with him.

R. He replied that many were Muslims but he did not know the name of anyone. There were 50 horses with him. They were scattered in the mountains so about their number, nothing can be said definitely.

Q. He was asked about the physical features of Adil Muhammad Khan and how he recognized him.

R. He was whitish, average height and his one leg was injured and tied with cloth. People were calling him Nawwab. So he thought, he was Adil Muhammad Khan.

Q. Asked to tell if he knew where they went from the mountains of Tans.

R. He did not know about it as when he was freed, he came directly to the *patwari* in Bhojpur. They did not discuss about their plan of movement. Till evening they were there. Thereafter, where they did go it is not known.

Q. Asked to tell what Adil Muhammad Khan or his colleagues discussed when he was in their captivity till the evening.

R. They did not discuss anything.

P 37. *Bakhshi Murawwat Muhammad Khan to Nawwab Sikandar Begam.* Informs that day, i.e. 25th *Jumada,* I 1275 AH, there was calm in the camp. Refers to a letter of Nizam Ali Khan, *bakhshi*, *nizamat-i mashriq,* informing as it was heard that Adil Muhammad Khan and Raja Choka along with an army of 2,000 *sawars* and foot-soldiers arrived in the mountains of Tans which is at a distance of 3 *curoh* from Siwans. He immediately, along with the forces present, marched there. Meanwhile, it was heard that he moved to Kalyanpur, *ilaqa* Joga, and taking some force and *gajand* went to the mountains of Bagrod. He followed them upto two *curoh*. In the meantime, Dilip Singh, a servant of *jagirdar* of *mauza* Barargaon who had gone to bring the news of insurgents, said that at night in the moonlight, he moved further. Says the report of Ghairatganj and the report of informers would be sent separately. Dated 25 *Jumada* I, 1275 AH.

P 39. *News-Report as Heard from Najib Nadaf, a Dweller of Rampura and Kadhu Kunwar, Dated 25* Jumada *I.* Reports that 300 *sawars* who met Amanat Khan earlier, went to bring Raja Choka in the mountains of Halandhar situating in Rahatgarh. Aqil Muhammad Khan and Amanat Khan went to the hills of Danmari with 25 *sawars* and 400 foot-soldiers and arrested the *mustajir* of *mauza* Tarawli, *ilaqa* Bhilsa and his wife and devastated *mauza* Nurja, *ilaqa* Bhilsa. Adil Muhammad Khan went to Sironj. Kallu Patel, *mauza* Rampura, Gulab Patel, Basarthi Patel of Pura Guna, and Patel of *mauza* Lagdhi, *ilaqa* Bhilsa, went to meet Amanat Khan to get Dhanraj Seth released and agreed that they would manage *sarbrah-i rasad* for them and Dhanraj should be released. It has also been heard that they intend to arrest Jas Patel of *mauza* Hirankhery, *ilaqa* Rahatgarh. There is also a rumour of the coming of another group of insurgents. Kadhu Patel who was sent by Jas Patel, *mustajir* of *mauza* Hirankhery, reported that Raja Choka was encamping in *ilaqa* Rahatgarh with some forces. Amanat Khan has arrived in Pura Guna. The report as received from *thana* Ghairatganj is sent to her.

PP 41-2. *Nizam Ali Khan* Bakhshi, Nizamat-i Mashriq, *to Murawwat Muhammad Khan,* Bakhshi. Informs that it was reported that Raja Choka and Adil Muhammad Khan along with an army of 2,000, inclusive of both *sawars* and foot-soldiers arrived in the mountains of Tans situating at a distance of 3 *curoh* from Siwans and were staying there since the last night. Hearing the news, he rushed to the mountains and came to know that they marched from there and reached *mauza* Kalyanpur and then went towards the mountains of Bagrod. They were pursued upto two *curoh* but no trace of them was found and then, he returned. From Dushyant Singh, a servant of *jagirdar* of Barkren who was sent to bring the news, it was heard that Adil Muhammad Khan and Raja Choka were moving together. They stayed there for a while and then they marched towards Pura Guna. Also, informs about a *parwana* of the Nawwab, stating that he has been alleviated to the post of *bakhshi* of *nizamat-i mashriq* from the post of *risaldari* with effect from 1 *Jumada* I.

It contains the order that the letter may be sent to the government. The Nawwab orders that the letter may be sent to Paltu Lal, *muhafiz-i daftar-i insha*, for inclusion in the register and keeping in the *daftar*. A copy of the letter may be sent to Bhawani Prasad, *wakil* to present it before the Political Agent and his reply may be conveyed to her. Another copy may be sent to Lala Mansukh Rai to report to James, Deputy Commissioner, Hoshanagabad, and his reply may be conveyed to her. Dated 29 *Jumada* I, 1275 AH.

P 43. *News-Report as Heard from Pirthi*. An army of 500 of Adil Muhammad Khan is encamping at *mauza* Baryayi, *ilaqa* Muhammad Garh, for the last three days and some forces are at Pura Guna with Amanat Khan, *kamdar* of Adil Muhammad Khan.

It contains the order that the news-report may be sent to Paltu Lal, *muhafiz-i daftar-i insha*, for inclusion in the register and keeping in the *daftar*. A copy of the news-report may be sent to Bhawani Prasad, *wakil*, to present it before the Political Agent and his reply may be conveyed to her. Another copy may be sent to Lala Mansukh Rai to report to James, Deputy Commissioner, Hoshanagabad, and his reply may be conveyed to her. Dated 29 *Jumada* I, 1275 AH.

P 45. *Daulat Rai,* Nazim-i Mashriq, *to Nawwab Sikandar Begam*. Informs about the news-report received from *thana* Siwans sent by Khwaja Muhammad Daim, *thanadar*, dated 23 *Zilhijja,* reporting that he along with *Bakhshi* Nizam Ali Khan went, pursuing the insurgents, as reported by Jai Singh, Balahi of *mauza* Devalapur *ilaqa* Siwans, that about 200 insurgent forces were encamping at *mauza* Choka, *jagir* of Raja Hattey Singh. In *mauza* Choka, situating at a distance of 4 *curoh* from

Siwans, it was heard that Firoz Shah with an army of 200 *sawars* and foot-soldiers entered the territory of the British and went to *mauza* Tura. Finally, he came back with the *bakhshi* and reported that there was no harm in the territory of the Nawwab. The same is sent to her. Dated 28 *Zilhijja*1275 AH.

It contains the order that the letter and news-report may be sent to Paltu Lal, *muhafiz-i daftar-i insha*, for inclusion in the register and keeping in the *daftar*. A copy of the letter and news-report may be sent to Bhawani Prasad, *wakil* to present it before the Political Agent and his reply may be conveyed to her. Dated 3 *Muharram* 1276 AH.

P 47. *News-Report from* Thana *Siwans Sent by Khwaja Muhammad Daim,* Thanadar, *Dated 23* Zilhijja *1275 AH.* Informs, as reported by Jai Singh, Balahi of *mauza* Devalapur, he arrived in *mauza* Choka of Raja Hattey Singh to deal with the insurgents. He came to know that Firoz Shah along with an army of 200 *sawars* and foot-soldiers entered in the British territory and went to *mauza* Tura, *ilaqa* of the British. They were surrounded from all sides. But no trace was found of them. He along with Bakhshi Nizam Ali Khan came back to Siwans. Reports that there was peace in the *pargana*.

File No. 302
Box No. 16
No. of Documents 14

Wazir Khan, Qila'dar, Sipahsalar of Siwans, and Sher Singh, Sipahsalar of Garhi, Accused of Not Attacking the Group of Tantia Tope and Displacing Sher Singh by Wazir Khan from Garhi to Siwans when the Group of Insurgents Entered Garhi.

PP 1-3. Contents

P 5. *Orders of Nawwab Sikandar Begam as Recorded in the Letter of Wazir Khan,* Sipahsalar. Orders that the letter may be sent to Paltu Lal, *muhafiz-i daftar-i insha*, for inclusion in the register and keeping in the *daftar*. It also contains the order for Wazir Khan, *qila'dar,* that as the insurgents have entered Garhi Ambapani, he should immediately attack on them along with the forces of Siwans without any delay. Dated 19 *Rabi* I, 1275 AH/26 November 1858.

P 7. Parwana *of Nawwab Sikandar Begam to Daulat Rai,* Nazim-i Mashriq. Refers to his letter, informing about the insurgent forces in Garhi Ambapani. Directs him to write immediately to Wazir Khan, *qila'dar*, to pursue them along with the forces of Siwans. Dated 19 *Rabi* I, 1275 AH/26 November 1858.

P 9. Parwana *of Nawwab Sikandar Begam to Daulat Rai,* Nazim-i Mashriq. Wazir Khan, *qila'dar*, is on duty at Siwans and Thakur Sher Singh is on duty at Garhi Ambapani. It is strange that others are reporting the devastation of Siwans and Garhi Ambapani. But Wazir Khan, *qila'dar*, and Thakur Sher Singh are reporting nothing. It is not known as to where they are and why he too is not aware about them. Directs him to look into the matter and report as soon as he receives the *parwana*. Dated 23 *Rabi* I, 1275 AH.

P 11. *Thakur Sher Singh to Nawwab Sikandar Begam.* Informs that on 17 *Rabi* I, 1266 *Fasli*, it came to his notice through some dwellers of Garhi that the insurgent forces who are about 10,000 in strength, coming from Aradmau have encamped in between Siwans and Garhi. Hearing the news of the insurgent forces, Abd al-Rahman, *thanadar*, Abd al-Ali, *tahsildar*, and Shafi Muhammad Khan, *jagirdar*, came together and decided to follow the insurgents and when they would be in Garhi, they would fight battle with them. They strengthened as many *chaukis* and posts as possible all around Garhi.

Says the safety and security of Fort Garhi Ambapani was given to him. It was midnight, when he was called by the *thanadar* and *tahsildar* and told him about the letter of Wazir Khan, *qila'dar,* directing to send the battalions of Balwant Singh and Ghulam Rasul Khan, *jamadars* to Siwans. He then prepared himself and left for Siwans along with the battalion of Balwant Singh, *jamadar*, and arrived at Siwans, as directed by the *qila'dar*. Informs that he is in Siwans whereas the *thanadar* and *tahsildar* have gone somewhere else. Dated 24 *Rabi* I, 1275 AH.

P 13. *The Content, as Recorded in the Letter of Lala Daulat Rai,* Nazim-i Mashriq. There is an order for Wazir Khan, *qila'dar*, to suppress the insurgents having with him the forces, station at Siwans. In addition to this, he should also be instructed to firmly deal with Raja Chokawala. Dated 25 *Rabi* I, 1275 AH.

P 15. *Balwant Singh,* Jamadar, *to Nawwab Sikandar Begam.* Refers to a letter of Wazir Khan, *qila'dar* to the *thanadar* of Garhi Ambapani, dated 15 *Rabi* I, 1274 AH, directing that his battalion may be sent there. The *thanadar* called him and directed to go there. He said ok. In the meantime, two nomads came and reported that the army of Peshwa had arrived at Aradmau. He asked what his order was then. He ordered him to remain with his battalion. Then, Rao Sher Singh came and said that he was going to Siwans in order to manage the affairs there, he too should go with him. He asked the *thanadar* in the matter. He said ok. Ultimately, it is Allah who will take care of him. So, he came to Siwans. He was performing all the duties assigned to him faithfully without fear and would remain performing his duties as desired by the *qila'dar* unless he is assigned other duty. Dated 25 *Rabi* I, 1275 AH.

P 17. *Daulat Rai,* Nazim-i Mashriq, *to Nawwab Sikandar Begam.* Refers to her *parwana,* dated 23 *Rabi* I, 1275 AH, in regard to Wazir Khan, *qila'dar*, who is on duty at Siwans and Thakur Sher Singh who is on duty at Garhi Ambapani. It is strange that others are reporting the devastation of Siwans and Garhi Ambapani but Wazir Khan, *qila'dar*, and Thakur Sher Singh are reporting nothing. Where they are and why he is not aware about them and directing him to respond to it by reporting in the matter. Informs that he had sent Kasrat Singh, a peon in his office to Siwans to bring news from there. The report submitted by him was sent to her on 24 *Rabi* I, 1275 AH. The battalions of Balwant Singh and Sher Singh on duty at Garhi, were sent to the *thanadar* of Garhi before such a situation arose as desired by Wazir Khan, *qila'dar.* Informs that Wazir Khan, *qila'dar*, Balwant Singh, Sher Singh and Nizam Ali Khan, *risaldar*, besides 8 *sawars* and Majid Muhammad Khan along with the forces of *jagirdars* are in Siwans by that time. Dated 25 *Rabi* I, 1275 AH/2 December 1858.

It contains the order that the letter and *parwana* of the Nawwab to Daulat Rai, *nazim-i mashriq,* dated 23 *Rabi* I, 1275 AH, may be sent to Lala Paltu Lal, *muhafiz-i daftar-i insha,* for inclusion in the register and keeping in the *daftar*. A copy of the order may be sent to the *nazim-i mashriq* through *madar al-maham,* directing him to deploy the battalions of Balwant Singh and Sher Singh in Garhi, calling them back from Siwans, who due to their foolishness went from Garhi to Siwans with the orders of Wazir Khan, *qila'dar*. Also directs him to report about the place of encampment of another group of insurgents. Dated 28 *Rabi* I, 1275 AH/5 December 1858.

P 19. *Daulat Rai,* Nazim-i Mashriq, *to Nawwab Sikandar Begam.* Informs of the letter of Wazir Khan, *qila'dar*, dated 25 *Rabi* I, 1275 AH in reply to his letter, directing him to attack upon the insurgents coming via Jaitpur and Aradmau in Garhi Ambapani. The same is presented to her. Rao Sher Singh, who was in Garhi, went to Siwans with both the battalions, inspite of having the information of the coming of the insurgents in Garhi. The information about the soldiers of *mahal* and *thana* of Garhi who had fled and did not accompany the *thanadar* and *tahsildar* would be communicated after receiving the report. Dated 28 *Rabi* I, 1275 AH/5 December 1858.

P 21. *Wazir Khan*, Qila'dar, *to Daulat Rai,* Nazim- i Mashriq. Refers to his letter informing about the arrival of the insurgent forces in Garhi Ambapani and launching attack on the dwellers. Says that before receiving his letter, the insurgents were at Dhampur on 17 *Rabi* I, 1275 AH. There is continuous news of the arrival of insurgents in Siwans. Not only that but on that date, they intended to come to *mauza* Barkheri and Mand, *pargana* Siwans, situating at a distance of 1$^{1/2}$ *curoh* from there. He managed all the forces of Siwans and was ready to fight. Meanwile, the news reached that insurgents had fled to Basodah. On 18 *Rabi* I, 1275 AH, Sher Singh came from Garhi to Siwans. He said that the intention of the insurgents was to come to Garhi. Immediately, an informer was sent to Garhi to know the reality. He reported that no insurgent was in Garhi as they had fled from there. There is a report that Amanat Khan, *bakhshi* of Adil Muhammad Khan, along with an army of 4,000 to 5,000 insurgents arrived at Bharonpur, *ilaqa* Gwalior, situating at a distance of 4 *curoh* from there. Raja Chokawala with an army of 3,000 insurgents, as reported by a *balahi*, is in the mountains of Tans, *ilqa* Siwans situating at a distance of 2 to 3 *curoh* from there. Dated 25 *Rabi* I, 1275 AH/2 December 1858.

P 23. *Daulat Rai,* Nazim-i Mashriq, *to Nawwab Sikandar Begam.* With the receipt of her order, dated 1 *Rabi* II, 1275 AH, he sent a letter to Wazir Khan, *qila'dar,* to pursue insurgents and to launch attack on them, as ordered in her *parwana,* dated 19 *Rabi* I, 1275 AH. Besides, the letter of Wazir Khan, *qila'dar*, to Thakur Sher Singh to come to Siwans along with his battalion and battalion of Balwant Singh and Rasul Khan. Thus, Thakur Sher Singh arrived at Siwans from Garhi with his battalion. All these letters are sent to her. Dated 9 *Rabi* II, 1275 AH.

P 25. *Orders of Nawwab Sikandar Begam as Recorded in the Letter of Daulat Rai,* Nazim-i Mashriq. Orders that the letter may be sent to Paltu Lal, *muhafiz-i daftar-i insha,* for inclusion in the register and keeping in the *daftar*. A copy of the order may be sent to *Daulat Rai, nazim-i mashriq,* through *madar al-maham,* directing him to present the letter written by him to Wazir Khan, *qila'dar*, which was regarding attacking the insurgents, besides the letter of Wazir Khan, *qila'dar*, to Sher Singh. Dated 1 *Rabi* II, 1275 AH.

P 27. *Letter from the Office of* Nizamat-i Mashriq *to Wazir Khan,* Qila'dar. Directs him to immediately rush to Garhi Ambapani, pursuing the insurgents who are advancing towards Garhi Ambapani with the forces stationed at Siwans as per the royal order, dated 19 *Rabi* I, 1275 AH/26 November 1858.

P 29. *Wazir Khan*, Qila'dar, *to Thakur Sher Singh*. There is a report that about 10, 000 insurgent forces have arrived at Bagrod which is at a distance of 3 *curoh* from Siwans. Directs him to reach Siwans to save Garhi Ambapani with the battalions of Ghulam Rasul Khan and Bhup Singh, *jamadars,* leaving the forces of *tahsil* and *thana* there. There should not be any delay in executing the order. Dated 17 *Rabi* I, 1275 AH/24 November 1858.

File No. 303
Box No. 16
No. of Documents 27

Arresting of Dilawar Khan, Shaikh Alfu and Other Culprits by Thana Bamhuri who were the Companions of Tantia Tope, Chief of the Insurgents

PP 1-3. Contents

PP 5-6. *Muhammad Abbas Ali,* Thanadar *of Bamhuri, to Nawwab Sikandar Begam.* Informs that after enquiry it was found that the insurgent army of Tantia Tope, due to meagreness and tiredness and injury on their back and in the legs left behind 6 horses of Mandia brand besides one more horse. The dwellers captured and kept them in their houses. Then they were handed over to the *thana*. Among those, one big horse was too weak and tired, unable to walk. If someone takes care and makes arrangement of food and water, it might be able to ride after two months. Requests, if allowed, a person may be given the responsibility of taking care of it and keeping it for riding. Says, the big horse of Mandia brand which was under his riding and had been purchased for Rs. 50

was injured by the insurgents, besides all other things of his house were devastated. The information to this effect was made to him. The challan of a big horse and two persons was made through Daulat Rai, *nazim-i mashriq*. The other horses which are too weak and have deep wounds, their challans are not made. Dated 26 *Rabi* I, 1275 AH.

It contains the order that the letter may be sent to Lala Paltu Lal, *muhafiz-i daftar-i insha,* for inclusion in the register and keeping in the *daftar*. A copy of the order may be sent to Saiyid Abbas Ali, *thanadar* of Bamhuri, through Ghulam Murtaza Khan, communicating to him to send all six horses besides one more horse captured from the insurgents as it is not good to keep the horses there. If the horses are too weak to walk they after halting at every two *curoh*, should be sent to Bhopal. Dated 4 *Rabi* II, 1275 AH.

P 7. *Daulat Rai,* Nazim-i Mashriq, *to Nawwab Sikandar Begam.* Refers to a letter received from Saiyid Abbas Ali, *thanadar* of Bamhuri, besides two persons namely Dilawar Khan and Shaikh Alfu, the dwellers of Sarangpur, who are the culprits being the companions of Tantia Tope with one horse of red color besides other goods. Informs that as per the royal order, issued for the investigation of the cases of the time of uprising, all were sent to the Maulawi Muhammad Sa'd al-Din, *muhtamim*, *adalat-i faujdari*, under proper security and in chain. Dated 25 *Rabi* I, 1275 AH.

It contains the order that the letter may be sent to Lala Paltu Lal, *muhafiz-i daftar-i insha,* for inclusion in the register and keeping in the *daftar*. Copies of all the papers may be sent to Bhawani Prasad, *wakil* to request the Political Agent, if allowed, both the captives may be sent there. Dated 4 *Rabi* II, 1275 AH.

PP 9-10. *Muhammad Abbas Ali,* Thanadar *of Bamhuri, to Daulat Rai,* Nazim-i Mashriq. Informs that from the insurgent army of Tantia Tope, two insurgents with one horse of red colour were captured. There is a rumour of the arrival of other group of insurgents in the region. Due to this, the dwellers are scared. It was not thought good to keep them there. Their challan was made under security of the soldiers. Hopes that they would safely reach there and that the two would be kept in the Fort. Information to this effect may be given to the Nawwab. Requests that statements may be recorded there and a copy may be sent to him as well. Dated 23 *Rabi* I, 1275 AH.

P 11. Parwana *of Nawwab Sikandar Begam to Lala Harsahai,* Tahsildar *of Bamhuri.* Says if God gives him courage, he should produce the culprits arrested by the *thanadar* of Bamhuri before her, under proper security and in chain. Dated 26 *Rabi* I, 1275 AH.

PP 13-14. *Harsahai,* Tahsildar *of Bamhuri, to Nawwab Sikandar Begam.* Informs that on 20 *Rabi* I, 1275 AH two persons; one *sawar* and one foot soldier from amongst the insurgent forces, with one big horse, red colour, came in *mauza* Kondali and stayed there. He and the *thanadar* arrested them and on 23rd of the month they were sent to her through Daulat Rai, *nazim-i mashriq,* under proper security. The horse which was with them was very big but very weak and tired, it looked ill and was unable to ride. Says, he does not have a big horse to ride. It was her assurance that if an insurgent enters in the royal territory, whoever pursues him and loots his goods, he would not be questioned. But he is not willing to take anything for free. Requests if the horse is auctioned, he should be given preference for a reasonable price. It should be sent to him through the *nazim* and *madar al-maham*. The cost of the horse would be sent to her. The horse which is about to die would be nourished by him. The cost of the horse due to illness seems to be not more than Rs. 10 or Rs. 12. Dated 29 *Rabi* I, 1275 AH.

It contains the order that the letter may be sent to Lala Paltu Lal, *muhafiz-i daftar-i insha,* for inclusion in the register and keeping in the *daftar*. A copy of the order may be sent to Daulat Rai, *nazim-i mashriq* through *madar al-maham,* communicating to him to send both the captives one *sawar* and one foot soldier; there, sent to him by the *thanadar* and *tahsildar* of Bamhuri. A copy of the order may be sent to Harsahai, *tahsildar* of Bamhuri , through Ghulam Murtaza Khan, communicating to him that if the horse is auctioned, he would be given due consideration. Dated 4 *Rabi* II, 1275 AH.

P 15. *Harsahai,* Tahsildar *of Bamhuri, to Nawwab Sikandar Begam.* Refers to her *parwana*, dated 26 *Rabi* I, 1275, directing that the *sawar* of the insurgent forces captured by the *thanadar* of Bamhuri should be put in chains and his challan should be made to her. Says, one *sawar* and one foot soldier were captured by him and the *thanadar* from *mauza* Kondali. Both of them along with a horse and two swords were sent to her through the *nazim* of *mashriq* under proper security and hopes that they would have reached there. Dated 4 *Rabi* II, 1275 AH.

It contains the order that the letter may be sent to Lala Paltu Lal, *muhafiz-i daftar-i insha,* for inclusion in the register and keeping in the *daftar*. A copy of the order may be sent to Lala Harsahai, *Tahsildar* of Bamhuri, through Ghulam Murtaza Khan directing him to communicate the name of the *sawar* and foot soldier of the insurgent forces captured by him. Dated 9 *Rabi* II, 1275 AH.

P 17. *Muhammad Mustaquim Khan,* Thanadar *of Bareilly, to Nawwab Sikandar Begam.* Informs that on 16 *Rabi* II, 1275 AH, when he heard that the insurgent forces have arrived in Rajghati, he immediately made the arrangement of *dak* from Bareilly to Bamhuri and wrote to the *thanadar* of Bamhuri to inform him about the present position of the insurgents. He too became busy in making arrangements in his jurisdiction.

Says, he has received a letter from the *thanadar* of Bamhuri. The same is presented to her. Dated 10 *Rabi* II, 1275 AH.

It contains the order that the letter may be sent to Lala Paltu Lal, *muhafiz-i daftar-i insha,* for inclusion in the register and keeping in the *daftar*. A copy of the order may be sent to Abbas Ali, *thanadar of Bamhuri*, through Ghulam Murtaza Khan, directing him to send all three insurgent soldiers captured by him, besides the description of the two *sawars* of the insurgent forces who were killed. The statement of both the foot-soldiers of the insurgent forces who are wounded may be recorded and sent to her. Dated 21 *Rabi* II, 1275 AH.

PP 19-20. *Muhammad Mustaquim Khan,* Thanadar *of Bareilly, to Muhammad Abbas Ali,* Thanadar *of Bamhuri.* Informs that as he heard that the insurgent forces have arrived in Rajghati, he immediately made the arrangement of *dak* from Bareilly to Bamhuri by deputing 16 persons across the entire route and deputing Zaman Khan for writing the news. He too should watch the situation and inform him about all the developments. Dated 10 *Rabi* II, 1275 AH.

P 20. *Muhammad Abbas Ali,* Thanadar *of Bamhuri, to Muhammad Mustaquim Khan,* Thanadar *of Bareilly.* Informs that the previous day, a battle was fought with the insurgent forces at *mauza* Dokri in the mountains wherein two *sawars* were killed, two others were wounded and other three were captured of the insurgent forces. Besides, 4 horses were also captured. In the evening, they returned to the *morchal*[16]. The insurgent forces who were hiding in the mountains fled towards Narmada. Hearing the news they were pursued, but found nowhere. Informs that day he received a letter of Durga Prasad, *thanadar,* informing that about 2,000 insurgent forces are at Pura Guna. Either that day or the next day, they would go towards Narmada.

16. Line of entrenchment.

P 21. *Bakhshi Murawwat Muhammad Khan to Nawwab Sikandar Begam.* Informs that on 18th *Rabi* II, 1275, when he was returning from Bamhuri, he heard that a *sawar* of the insurgent forces was amongst them. A search was made for him and finally a female horse was found in the field of sugarcane which was sent to *thana* Garhi. Then a letter of Abbas Ali, *thanadar* of Bamhuri, came, informing that a *sawar* too has been captured from the field of sugarcane by the men of *thana* and *mahal* of Bamhuri. The letter received from him is sent to her. Dated 20 *Rabi* II, 1275 AH.

It contains the order that the letter may be sent to Lala Paltu Lal, *muhafiz-i daftar-i insha,* for inclusion in the register and keeping in the *daftar*. A copy of the order may be sent to Muhammad Sa'd al-Din, *muhtamim, adalat-i faujdari,* directing him that as soon as the *sawar* of the insurgent forces, captured by the *thanadar* of Bamhuri is brought to him, he should send him immediately to Bhawani Prasad, *wakil*, under proper security to present him before the Political Agent. Information to this effect may be given to her. Dated 22 *Rabi* II, 1275 AH.

P 23. *Muhammad Abbas Ali,* Thanadar *of Bamhuri, to Bakhshi Murawwat Muhammad Khan.* Refers to a female horse of the insurgent forces, captured by the *sawars,* accompanying him from the field of sugarcane. Informs that the *sawar* of the horse was also hiding in the field of sugarcane who was traced by him and the *tahsildar* of Harsahai. He was captured and made captive in the *thana*. His challan would be made after taking his statement. Dated 18 *Rabi* II, 1275 AH.

P 25. *Muhammad Abbas Ali,* Thanadar *of Bamhuri, to Nawwab Sikandar Begam.* Informs that day, i.e. 21st *Rabi* II, 1275 AH, the challan of Ganga Misr, an enjured soldier, besides 4 others along with 2 big horses and 3 small horses was made by *thana* Bamhuri to Ghulam Murtaza Khan, *kamdar*, Deorhi Khas, to present before her. Hopes for the receipt of the same. Dated 21 *Rabi* II, 1275 AH.

It contains the order that the letter may be sent to Lala Paltu Lal, *muhafiz-i daftar-i insha,* for inclusion in the register and keeping in the *daftar*. A copy of the letter besides all 5 *sawars* along with their 5 horses may be sent to Bhawani Prasad for presenting them before the Political Agent and his reply may be communicated to her. Dated 29 *Rabi* II, 1275 AH.

P 27. *Ghulam Murtaza Khan to Nawwab Sikandar Begam.* Refers to the receipt of the letter of Saiyid Abbas Ali, *thanadar* of Bamhuri, dated 20 *Rabi* II, 1275 AH, informing of the challan of Jhabwa, Shiv Barat, Raghunath and Debi Den from amongst the insurgent forces, along with their statements. Informs that it was only the letter received, in his office without the captives. After enquiry, it was heard that the challan of the captives was made through the office of *adalat-i faujdari* to Sehore. Information to this effect was a must which he did. The statements of the captives are also enclosed. Dated 27 *Rabi* II, 1275 AH.

It contains the order that the letter and all three statements may be sent to Lala Paltu Lal, *muhafiz-i daftar-i insha,* for inclusion in the register and keeping in the *daftar*. A copy of the letter and the statements may be sent to Bhawani Prasad for presenting it before the Political Agent and his reply may be communicated to her. Dated 29 *Rabi* II, 1275 AH.

PP 29-30. *Statement of Jhabwa, the Insurgent, in the Presence of Abbas Ali,* Thanadar. States that his name is *Jhabwa*, his father's name is Laxman, caste *beldar*, a dweller of Bans-Bareilly, is aged around 25 years, and is engaged in the profession of grass-seller.

Q. Whose servant he was and where he was going?

R. He is a resident of Bans-Bareilly. When war broke out there, he was serving 'Aleem Allah Khan, *sawar*. When he met Rao Sahab at Kalpi, he too was with him. When he was with Rao Sahab, his salary was Rs. 2. When a battle was fought at Khajuria, Rao Sahab was defeated there. From then, they were separated from each other. He fell ill in a village. 'Aleem Allah Khan went with Rao Sahab.

Q. What goods he possessed?

R. He had one horse, one sword, one silver bracelet and a 10 rupee note. All these goods were taken by a villager. Now he holds nothing.

Q. Which village was that?

R. He does not know the name of the village. But it is at a distance of 5 to 6 cos from there.

Q. Were the Nawwabs in the company of Rao Sahab and whose armies were with him?

R. The armies of Nawwab Kamoliwala, Nawwab Bandawala and an English army were with him.

Q. Where were the battles fought?

R. The battles were fought at Tonk, Gwalior, Nathdwar, Patan, Bhilwara and Khajuria. He does not remember the names of other places.

Q. How many days he was in the army of the insurgents?

R. For the last 6 months.

Q. Where did Rao Sahab go and what was his future plan?

R. He does not know anything. He went on the other side of river Narmada.

PP 31-2. *Statement of Shiv Barat, the Insurgent, in the Presence of Saiyid Abbas Ali,* Thanadar *of Bamhuri.* States that his name is Shiv Barat, his father's name is Shiv Shankar, caste *dhamar*, a dweller of Gwalior, aged around 20 years, and is engaged in the profession of service.

Q. Who is he and from where did he come?

R. He was with Raghunath, *sawar* and a servant of Rao Sahab. The army of Rao Sahab had gone too far. They were at Jhaklone and were going behind them. They encamped in the mountains of *mauza* Dokri. They came in the village to get flour, etc. He was arrested by a *sawar* in a field of *juar*[17].

Q. Who was the chief of that army?

R. There was no chief of the army. These were the *sawars* of a *jamadar*.

Q. For how many days he was serving Raghunath.

R. For the last three months.

Q. Which place did he come in the forest in *mauza* Dokri?

R. He does not know the name of the place. But the place he came from is located 8 to 9 *cos* [18] away from this place.

PP 33-4. *Statement of Raghunath, the Insurgent, in the Presence of Saiyid Abbas Ali,* Thanadar *of Bamhuri.* States that his name is Raghunath, his father's name is Bhawani, a dweller of *mauza* Mukhra, *ilaqa* Lucknow, caste *kurmi*, is aged around 28 years, and is engaged in the profession of farming.

Q. From where he came and where was he going?

R. He was in the army of Peshwa. He was in the company of a *sawar* who was a Thakur. His name is not known to him. He was taking his meal with him. He marched with the army 4 days before. When he reached on the bank of a river in *mauza* Chhaner, the Thakur told him to keep the horse with him and walk slowly as he was coming after attending nature's call. He was walking slowly. Meanwhile, the army went too far. When he reached the village, the *sawars* shouted as to who he was. He fled in

17. Indian millet.

18. About 2 miles.

the direction of Bamhuri and saw that the forces were marching. He left the horse and hid in the field. He was seen by the armymen and thus, arrested by the *thanadar* and *tahsildar*. He does not know who took his horse.

Q. For how many days he was in the army?

R. He was in the army since the last 5 to 6 months when Gwalior was captured.

Q. Who was the chief of that army?

R. No one was the chief. It was only a combination of *sawars* and foot-soldiers.

Q. Where did this army go across Narmada?

R. He went upto 2 *curoh* towards Narmada and then he returned. He does not know where the army went.

Q. From which battlefield did this army flee?

R. After the defeat at Khorai, they fled.

Q. Where was he when the *sawars* of the insurgent forces were killed by the *sawars* of this government?

R. He was with the army in the mountains under the bushes. On that day, he came from Gayaspura.

P 35. *Ghulam Murtaza Khan to Nawwab Sikandar Begam.* Refers to the letter of Saiyid Abbas Ali, *thanadar* of Bamhuri, dated 21 *Rabi* II, 1275 AH, informing about the challan of Ganga Brahmin, captured at Bhagwanpur from amongst the insurgent forces, along with his statement. Informs that it was only the letter which was received in his office. After inquiry, it was heard that the challan of the captive was made through the office of *adalat-i faujdari* to Sehore. Information to this effect was a must which he did. The statement of the captive is also enclosed herewith. Dated 27 *Rabi* II, 1275 AH.

It contains the order that the letter and statement may be sent to Lala Paltu Lal, *muhafiz-i daftar-i insha*, for inclusion in the register and keeping in the *daftar*. A copy of the order may be sent to Bhawani Prasad, *wakil* to bring the matter into the notice of the Political Agent and his reply may be communicated to her. Dated 29 *Rabi* II, 1275 AH.

PP 37-8. *Statement of Ganga Misr, the Insurgent, in the Presence of Abbas Ali,* Thanadar. States that his name is Ganga Misr, his father's name is Sahaba Misr, a dweller of Leel Balra, district Patiala, caste Brahmin, engaged in the profession of service, and is aged 22 years.

Q. Who he served?

R. He was the servant of Rao Sahab Peshwa.

Q. When was he employed there?

R. In the month of *Jeth*, he joined him.

Q. What was his salary and what was his post?

R. He was a *sawar* there and his salary was Rs. 30.

Q. Where was he accompanying Rao Sahab in the loot of cities?

R. He did not accompany him anywhere in loot, as his horse was injured. Thus, he was not part of the loot.

Q. Where was he going then?

R. His intention was to part his way from the army. Now, he was going to Bhopal. He was not a servant of the British. He was a servant of Rao Sahab.

Q. Where was he injured?

R. It was a jungle where he got injured. It was not a village.

Q. How many personnel were in the group to which he was attached?

R. There were 400 to 500 *sawars* and foot-soldiers.

Q. Who was the chief of that group?

R. There was no prominent figure. One Rahimdad Khan, *risaldar*, who belonged to 5th Regiment, was their leader.

Q. Where was this group going?

R. They were going to join Rao Sahab, across the river Narmada.

Q. Was there any magazine in that group or not?

R. Some had magazine, others did not. Some had guns and some had spears.

Q. Why was Rao Sahab going across Narmada?

R. He does not know about this.

Q. How many battles did he fight along side Rao Sahab?

R. He was not in his company in any battle. But he had fought battles and had been in his company. He fought at Patan, Sironj, Rajgarh and Lalitpur.

Q. Where did he part his way from Rao Sahab?

R. It was the place where the British army appeared before them from a valley.

Q. How was he injured and how was he captured?

R. He was on the mountains. As he was hungry, so he came down. He was in a cornfield where he was injured by a *sawar*. He, anyhow went back to the mountains to the army. In the evening, they marched from there. He too was helped to sit on the horse. He was left behind the army. He was caught by the villagers, who snatched his horse and thrashed him.

P 39. *Ghulam Murtaza Khan to Nawwab Sikandar Begam.* Refers to the letter of Saiyid Abbas Ali, *thanadar* of Bamhuri, dated 20 *Rabi* II, 1275 AH, informing of the challan of three horses of the insurgents captured by the *sawars* of Jabar Singh, *jamadar*. Informs that it was only a letter without horse, which was received in his office. After inquiry, it was heard that the challan of the horses was made through the office of *adalat-i faujdari* to Sehore. Information to this effect was a must which he did. The letter of Saiyid Abbas Ali is also enclosed herewith. Dated 27 *Rabi* II, 1275 AH.

P 41. *Muhammad Abbas Ali,* Thanadar *of Bamhuri, to*

Ghulam Murtaza Khan, Kamdar, *Deorhi Khas.* Refers to the order of Bakhshi Murawwat Muhammad Khan to send the three horses captured from the insurgents by Jabar Singh, *jamadar* to the government. Informs that the challan of three horses and other goods, as per the details, is sent to him through the soldiers of *thana*. Dated 20 *Rabi* I, 1275 AH.

PP 43-4. *Abbas Ali,* Thanadar *of Bamhuri, to Nawwab Sikandar Begam.* Refers to her order, dated 4 *Rabi* II, 1275 AH, directing to send 6 horses of mandia brand and one big horse of the insurgents. Informs that he has already intimated about the meagreness of the horses. Due to this, one big mandia horse died on 1st *Rabi* I of the month and the other on 10th of the month. The other 4 small mandia horses were too weak to walk and were injured. So, these were auctioned before receiving her order. One big horse which too is very weak and injured, is being nourished. If saved, it would be kept by him by her order. His own mandia, big horse, purchased by him for his own use was injured by Tantia Tope, the insurgent. His personal belongings were too damaged by him. The information to this effect has already been sent to her. But the reply is not yet received. In view of the order to send the horses there, the big horse is being sent through Ghulam Murtaza Khan, *kamdar*, Deorhi Khas. The expenditure details of the dead mandia horse and the expenditure of big horse is sent herewith. Hopes for the order for disbursement of the said expenditure. Dated 28 *Rabi* II, 1275 AH.

It contains the order that the letter may be sent to Lala Paltu Lal, *muhafiz-i daftar-i insha*, for inclusion in the register and keeping in the *daftar*. A copy of the order may be sent to Ghulam Ali Khan, *thanadar* of Bamhuri, through Ghulam Murtaza Khan, communicating that Saiyid Abbas Ali, former *thanadar* of Bamhuri, who auctioned 4 horses of insurgents, should have deposited the amount of auction and then he should have asked for the payment of expenditure of food for the horses. Dated 5 *Jumada* I, 1275 AH.

PP 45-6. *Details of Food Expenditure of one Big Horse and the Expenditure of one Mandia Brand, Big Horse.* The expenditure includes the expenses of grass, gram, besides medicines, etc.

P 47. *Harsahai,* Tahsildar *of Bamhuri, to Nawwab Sikandar Begam.* Informs that neither the statement of the *sawar* or foot soldier was recorded nor was the register prepared there. The challan of duo-the *sawar* and the foot soldier, after their arrest was made to the government through *nazim-i mashriq* with proper security. He does not remember their names. However, the receipt obtained from the *nizamat* of the *sawar* and foot soldier is sent there. Dated 30 *Rabi* II, 1275 AH.

P 48. *Orders of the Nawwab as Recorded in the Letter of Harsahai,* Tahsildar *of Bamhuri, Dated 4* Rabi *II, 1275 AH.* Orders that the letter may be sent to Paltu Lal, *muhafiz-i daftar-i insha*, for inclusion in the register and keeping in the *daftar*. A copy of the order may be sent to Lala Harsahai, *tahsildar* of Bamhuri, through Ghulam Murtaza Khan, directing him to communicate the names of the *sawar* and foot soldier from among the insurgent forces who are arrested by him. Dated 9 *Rabi* II, 1275 AH.

PP 49-50. *Harsahai,* Tahsildar *of Bamhuri to Daulat Rai,* Nazim-i Mashriq. Informs that the receipt of the *parwana* of Nawwab, dated 4 *Rabi* II, 1275 AH, directing that if God gives him courage, he should send the challan of the arrested *sawar* of insurgent forces, to the government under proper security and in chain. Says, the challan of both the insurgents, the accused who were arrested there and the horse was already sent to him by the *thanadar* of Bamhuri before receiving the *parwana* of the Nawwab and that have been sent to the government. But from the *parwana* of the Nawwab, it appears that the said persons and the horse have not yet reached there. Requests that the challan of both the culprits and horse should be made to the government and a copy of their statement should also be sent to him as their statement was not recorded when they were arrested and then sent there. Dated 5 *Rabi* II, 1275 AH.

The letter bears an order that the letter may be returned to Harsahai, *tahsildar* of Bamhuri, communicating that the challan of both the persons and horse was made. Their statement was recorded which is sent to him. Dated 7 *Rabi* II, 1275 AH.

P 51. *Ghulam Murtaza Khan to Nawwab Sikandar Begam.* Informs that day, i.e. 1 *Jumada* I, 1275 AH, the challan of one horse, red colour of the insurgents was received from Abbas Ali, *thanadar*, carried by Pyare Singh and Phagwa Singh, the soldiers. The same is sent there. Dated 1 *Jumada* I, 1275 AH.

It contains the order that the letter may be sent to Lala Paltu Lal, *muhafiz-i daftar-i insha*, for inclusion in the register and keeping in the *daftar*. A copy of the order and horse of the insurgent may be sent to Muhammad Sa'd al-Din, *muhtamim*, *adalat-i faujdari*. Dated 5 *Jumada* I, 1275 AH.

File No. 304, A
Box No. 16
No. of Documents 20

News as Heard About the Encampment of the Insurgents in Basodah and Muhammad Garh, and Intending to Attack Siwans

PP 1-5. Contents

PP 7-8. *Ghulam Muhammad Khan,* Risaldar, *to Nawwab Sikandar Begam.* Informs that the previous day Udit, the informer, an employee of the battalion of Hattey Singh, *jamadar*, came and stated that he had gone to bring the news of the insurgents. When he arrived in *mauza* Chhotia, *ilaqa* Basodah, situating at a distance of two *curoh* from Bheglone, he found that Adil Muhammad Khan and his contingent of 1,000 *sawars* and foot-soldiers were making bread. When he arrived in *mauza* Tharka, he saw that 25 *wilayati* soldiers of that group were making bread. Says hearing this news, he immediately sent Bhim Singh, *jamadar*, to bring authentic news. He came back and reported that the news given by Udit was incorrect. There was no sign of Adil Muhammad Khan and his army. Informs the previous day, the battalion of Baldev Singh, *jamadar,* left for Siwans. Dated 21 *Rabi* I, 1275 AH.

It contains the order that the letter may be sent to Lala Paltu Lal, *muhafiz-i daftar-i insha*, for inclusion in the register and keeping in the *daftar*. A copy of the letter may be sent to Bhawani Prasad, *wakil*, to present it before the Political Agent and the reply received from him may be conveyed to her.

P 9. *Daulat Rai,* Nazim-i Mashriq*, to Nawwab Sikandar Begam*. Informs that day, a report from *thana* Siwans, dated 26 *Rabi* I, 1275 AH, day Thursday, was received. Kesri Kotwar of *mauza* Gopalpur, *jagir* of Karamat Khan, *jagirdar*, came to the *thana* and reported that Balahi sent by Lala Gappu Lal, a dweller of Muhammad Garh, met him and told to go to *thana* Siwans and report that night or the next night, as the insurgent forces might attack. There is a need to be careful and remain vigilant. Hearing this news, Ghanshyam Singh, soldier, and Lal Singh, peon, were sent to bring the authentic news. A report would be sent after their coming back. Says, he wrote to the *thanadar* of Siwans that there were too many forces in Siwans, the insurgents must be pursued. Dated 29 *Rabi* I, 1275 AH.

P 11. *News-Report from* Thana *Siwans Sent by Shaikh Nur Muhammad,* Thanadar*, Dated 26* Rabi *I, 1275 AH, Day Thursday*. Reports that Kesri Kotwar of *mauza* Gopalpur, *jagir* of Karamat Khan, *jagirdar* came to the *thana* and reported that Balahi sent by Lala Gappu Lal, a dweller of Muhammad Garh met him and stated that that night or the next, the insurgent forces might attack. Therefore, there is need to be careful and remain vigilant. Hearing the news, Ghanshyam Singh, soldier, and Lal Singh, peon, were sent to bring authentic news. A report would be sent after their coming back.

It contains the order of Daulat Rai, *nazim-i mashriq*, that the news-report may be sent to the government. A copy of the order may be sent to Shaikh Nur Muhammad, *thanadar*, communicating that there is a large force in Siwans. The insurgents must be pursued and dealt with firmly. Dated 29 *Rabi* I, 1275 AH.

P 13. *Daulat Rai,* Nazim-i Mashriq*, to Nawwab Sikandar Begam.* Sends the news-report received from *thana* Mahalpur, dated 3 *Rabi* II, 1275 AH, informing of the presence of insurgent forces in *mauzas* Bagrod, Basodah and Malthun, and about the devastation of *mauza* Basodah, as reported by Ratiram, informer. Dated 4 *Rabi* II, 1275 AH.

It contains the order that the letter and the news-report may be sent to Lala Paltu Lal, *muhafiz-i daftar-i insha*, for inclusion in the register and keeping in the *daftar*. A copy of the order may be sent to Daulat Rai, *nazim-i mashriq*, through *madar al-maham* that the informers should be instructed to adhere to report only the accurate and authentic news. Dated 5 *Rabi* II, 1275 AH.

PP 15-16. *News-Report from* Thana *Mahalpur Sent by Shahzad Rai,* Thanadar*, Dated 3* Rabi *II, 1275 AH.* Ratiram, informer of the *thana*, came and reported that, as ordered, he went to Bagrod and Basodah to know about the insurgent forces and that there was no insurgent. But he heard that a group of insurgents is in Malthun and that Basodah was not destroyed. He stayed one night in Bagrod. The report as sent by the informer is sent to him. Another informer, employed that day, has been sent to inquire further. A report will be sent once he comes back.

PP 17-18. *Bakhshi Murawwat Muhammad Khan to Nawwab Sikandar Begam.* Informs that day, i.e. 9th *Rabi*

II, 1275 AH, there was peace in the camp. Shaikh 'Abd al-Rahman, *thanadar* of Garhi, came after visiting the suburb of Garhi whom he asked about the insurgents, concerning whom he sent a report. He stated that an inhabitant of Garhi had gone to Basodah. Meanwhile, a person who was the companion of Adil Muhammad Khan came there. He stated what he has mentioned in his letter. Says, what he said to him was conveyed to the government. Dated 9 *Rabi* II, 1275 AH.

It contains the order that the letter may be sent to Lala Paltu Lal, *muhafiz-i daftar-i insha*, for inclusion in the register and keeping in the *daftar*. A copy of the order may be sent to Bakhshi Murawwat Muhammad Khan, communicating to send the companion of Adil Muhammad Khan to the government under security. Though his statement is not reliable, but he is from the group of insurgents. Also directs him to mention the name of such persons in his communique. Dated 14 *Rabi* II, 1275 AH.

P 19. *Daulat Rai*, Nazim-i Mashriq, *to Nawwab Sikandar Begam.* Sends the news-report received from *thana* Siwans, dated 11 *Rabi* II, 1275 AH, reporting that there was peace in the region. Dated 13 *Rabi* II, 1275 AH.

P 21. *News-Report from* Thana *Siwans Sent by Shaikh Nur Muhammad*, Thanadar, *Dated 11* Rabi *II, 1275 AH.* Reports, that day passed with calm in the entire *pargana*. There is no news of the insurgent forces.

P 23. *Muhammad Hasan Khan to Nawwab Sikandar Begam.* Informs that the previous day, i.e. 13 *Rabi* II, 1275 AH, passed with calm in the army camp stationed at Siwans. In the evening, it was heard that some insurgent forces have arrived in the plains and on the hills of Muhammad Garh. Says, it was then and there that a letter from *thana* Siwans was sent to the *thanadar* of Muhammad Garh to inquire about it. Informs that day, i.e. 14th *Rabi* II, 1275 AH, the reply of the *thanadar* of Muhammad Garh was received in the name of Nur

Muhammad, *thanadar* of Siwans, dated 13 *Rabi* II, 1275 AH, informing that the insurgent forces crossed the mountains of Muhammad Garh. Says, in the letter of the *thanadar* there were no details of the forces; about their number, their officers, their intention as to where they were going, about the date of their encampment and their march. So he sent Majid Khan, soldier to Pura Guna, to inquire about it. A report will be sent once he comes back from there. Assures that in case they enter the region, they would be dealt with firmly. Dated 14 *Rabi* II, 1275 AH.

PP 25-6. *Bakhshi Murawwat Muhammad Khan to Nawwab Sikandar Begam.* Informs that Bahadur Husain Khan took leave for four days to go to Basodah to meet his sister. He came back and stated that Satkunwar of *mauza* Doghra *pargana* Basodah came to him and said that the insurgent forces came there and many *sawars* were coming. Chhetan Rao, wine seller of Basodah, too gave similar news and that their intention was to attack Bhopal. Says, he then and there rided and marched to assess the situation. He ordered the army to be ready and the *sawars* and foot-soldiers of the *thana* were sent to know the reality. Also, a letter was sent to Raoji, the Commanding Officer at Ahmadpur. Mazbut Khan, soldier sent by Murtaza Khan, *jagirdar*, *mauza* Gondari, *pargana* Garhi came to Shaikh Abd al-Raman, *thanadar,* who was then sent to him. He stated that Siyagul and Jadun Mogha, dwellers of Basodah came to Ghulam Murtaza Khan and said that Adil Muhammad Khan and Aqil Muhammad Khan were encamping in *mauza* Doghra, *ilaqa* Basodah and a contingent of 600 *sawars* and foot-soldiers were with them. Thereafter, 600 more *sawars* joined them. Their intention seems to go to Pura Guna. Then, the letter of Hafiz Muhammad Hasan Khan arrived, giving similar information. The letter of Raoji too has the same information. Says, he wrote to them that the *sawars* who were arrested from them, stated that they were 300 *sawars*. But the figure given by them seems an exaggeration. They did not make an effort to go there and fight a battle with them. The informers who were sent by him brought similar news that the insurgent forces were 2,000 in number. The letters of Raoji and his reply to him are sent to her. Dated 14 *Rabi* II, 1275 AH.

P 27. *Bakhshi Murawwat Muhammad Khan to Raoji Dankar, Commanding Officer*. It is heard that the insurgent forces have gone from Inayatpur to Pura Guna. But they have not intimated anything about it. They are directed to know about it and inform him. Dated 13 *Rabi* II, 1275 AH.

P 29. *Bakhshi Murawwat Muhammad Khan to Raoji Dankar, Commanding Officer at Ahmadpur*. It is understood that the insurgents have entered in his jurisdiction but he has mentioned nothing in regard to how to deal with them. While the order of his government to him is that he should deal with the insurgents in concurrence with the forces of Bhilsa. If he is intending to fight with the insurgents, let him know so that he too may join him in the battle against them. Without intimation, he would not be able to join him. Dated 14 *Rabi* II, 1275 AH.

P 31. *Raoji Dankar to Bakhshi Murawwat Muhammad Khan*. Refers to his letter and says that he wrote him about the insurgent forces. This is true that the insurgent forces are 2,000, both the *sawars* and the foot-soldiers stationed at Pura. A letter has been sent to him in this regard early in the morning that day that might have been received by him. Dated 13 *Rabi* II, 1275 AH.

P 33. *Bakhshi Murawwat Muhammad Khan to Raoji Dankar, Commanding Officer at Ahmadpur.* Refers to his letter, informing of the arrival of 2,000 insurgent forces in Pura Guna. But the *sawars* of the insurgent forces who are arrested have described that they are 300 *sawars* and their chief is a *sawar* of the *risala* of Rahim Dad Khan, *risaldar* who was previously in the British army. He did not mention the name of the officer, besides the figure of the personnel given by him seems to be wrong. He also did not request to come and give a combined fight to the insurgent forces. Anyhow, there is no need to worry as there is full preparation on this side to fight with them. However, he too should remain alert and vigilant. Dated 14 *Rabi* II, 1275 AH.

PP 35-6. *Muhammad Hasan Khan to Bakhshi Murawwat Muhammad Khan*. Informs the previous day he came to hear an unauthentic news that a contingent of 2,000 armymen, both *sawars* and foot-soldiers are in the plains and on the mountains of Ghayaspur, Muhammad Garh and Bagrod. As he did not make investigation into this, therefore, he did not communicate this either to him or to the government. Now a man of confidence through the *thanadar* has been sent there to bring authentic news. A report will be sent once he comes back after assessing the situation. A *wilayati* soldier, besides two other soldiers, sent by him to the mountains of Tans to know the situation, came back and stated that there was no sign of the presence of insurgents in and around the said mountains. They have also mentioned the name of the *mauzas* they visited. The letter produced by him is sent to him. The soldier, due to tiredness, stayed there to rest for a while and soon will report to him.

P 37. *Raoji Dankar to Bakhshi Murawwat Muhammad Khan*. Informs that about 2,000 insurgent forces are encamping at Pura. There is a need to be alert and make provisions for *nakabandi*. Dated 13 *Rabi* II, 1275 AH.

PP 39-40. *Daulat Rai,* Nazim-i Mashriq*, to Nawwab Sikandar Begam.* Sends the news-report, dated 18 *Rabi* II, 1275 AH, received from *thana* Mahalpur as reported by Ratiram, informer, informing about the arrival of 3,000 insurgent forces in *mauza* Motia Chhari, *ilaqa* Basodah. Dated 19 *Rabi* II, 1275 AH.

P 41. *News-Report from* Thana *Mahalpur Sent by Shahzad Rai,* Thanadar, *Dated 18* Rabi *II, 1275 AH.* Reports that day, Ratiram, informer of the *thana*, came back and reported that he went to know about the insurgent forces and the previous day, he reached Jaitpur, 3 *curoh* away from Pura Guna, where he happened to meet a *sawar* and an informer sent by the *thanadar* of Garhi. They stated that about 3,000 insurgent forces were encamping at *mauza* Motia Chhari, *ilaqa* Basodah. They are also on move from there. He then returned back and stated what he heard from them. Informs that the statement of the informer is forwarded to him.

P 43. *News-Report from* Thana *Mahalpur, Dated 18* Rabi *II, 1275 AH, Sent by Shahzad Rai,* Thanadar, *Mahalpur, Day Thursday*. Reports that Ratiram, informer, came back and reported that he had gone to bring the news of insurgent forces and on previous day, he was 3 *curoh* away from Pura Guna at Jaitpur where he met one *sawar* and an informer sent by the *thanadar* of Garhi. He said that about 3,000 insurgent forces were at *mauza* Motia Chhari, *ilaqa* Basodah. Not only that, they had marched from there and were coming behind. Why he was going there, rather he should go back, they advised. Says, he returned from there. He stated what he heard. Says, what the informer reported the same was communicated. Ritu, wife of late Jamani Kajhi, reported that Hattey Singh, Jaitgarhwala was in Bheglone, *ilaqa* Bhilsa, adjacent to Lakhnauti. The same is sent to her. In the matter of Hattey Singh, orders have been issued. Also, reports that the *tahsildar* of Bamhuri wrote to him that the insurgent forces had arrived at Bamhuri and to deal with them, the *thanadar* had gone along with his contingent. He was blockading the road to Rajghati. As it was heard that insurgents were passing through Bamhuri, he came back to the *thana* to make arrangement there.

PP 45-7. *Statement of Mst. Ritu, Wife of Late Jamani Kajhi, a Dweller of Dehgaon,* Pargana *Mahalpur in the Presence of Shahzad Rai,* Thanadar, *Mahalpur.* States that her name is Mst. Ritu, wife of late Jamani Kajhi, a dweller of Dehgaon and a daily wage earner who is aged around 22 years. Further states that in the previous year, during the time of uprising, Jamani Kajhi, her husband, was in the service of Hattey Singh *Jaitgarhwala* at the Fort. He took her in his company from *mauza* Dehgaon and dropped her in *mauza* Lakhnauti, *pargana* Bhilsa, and went accompanying Jaitgarhwala. In recent times, he came in the company of Hattey Singh and stayed in *mauza* Begwan, adjacent to Lakhnauti. This is his place of residence. She went there to know about her husband. He told her that he was killed in the battle at Tahri. She asked him for her maintenance. But he refused to fulfill her demand. She is now helpless. She came to live in Dehgaon and requests for help. States that the day before yesterday, about 2,000 forces have arrived at Bagrod. The group which was at Pura Guna has gone from there.

File No. 304, B
Box No. 16
No. of Documents 24

PP 49-50. *Bakhshi Murawwat Muhammad Khan to Nawwab Sikandar Begam.* Refres to her order, dated 14 *Rabi* II, 1275 AH, as mentioned in his letter, directing him to send the person who was in the company of Adil Muhammad Khan and that he did not mention his name in his communiqué. Explains that he mentioned in his letter that the person accompanying Adil Muhammad Khan has reached Basodah. The *thanadar* of Garhi recorded his statement and sent it to the government. He communicated what was said to him. How could the companion of Adil Muhammad Khan be sent before her as the statement was sent from the *thana*? So he did not mention his name. Says, his name was Shamsher Khan, soldier. The companion of Adil Muhammad Khan did not tell his name. Dated 14 *Rabi* II, 1275 AH.

P 51. *Daulat Rai,* Nazim-i Mashriq, *to Nawwab Sikandar Begam.* Sends the news-report, dated 25 *Rabi* II, 1275 AH, received from *thana* Mahalpur reporting that there is no insurgent force anywhere, neither in Pura Guna nor in Basodah or Bagrod. Dated 27 *Rabi* II, 1275 AH.

P 53. *Shahzad Rai,* Thanadar, *Mahalpur, to Nawwab Sikandar Begam. News-Report From* Thana *Mahalpur Sent By Shahzad Rai,* Thanadar, *Day Thursday, Dated 25* Rabi *II, 1275 AH.* Reports that day Ganesh and Udit, the informers, who had gone to bring the news of the insurgents came back and reported that they went to Pura Guna, Basodah and upto Bagrod but found no sign of the insurgents anywhere and in Bagrod it was heard that they were encamping adjoining Sironj. Udit, the informer, also added that the British army, stationed at Bagrod proceeded to Bhilsa. Informs that what the informers stated, was communicated, without any omission.

P 55. *Daulat Rai,* Nazim-i Mashriq, *to Nawwab Sikandar Begam.* Sends the news-report, dated 11 *Jumada* I, 1275 AH, received from *thana* Siwans reporting that some insurgents are in the mountains of *mauza* Jharpona, *ilaqa* Sindhia, and that Lal Singh, peon of the *thana*, has been sent to find the fact of the news. Dated 14 *Jumada* I, 1275 AH.

It contains the order that the letter and news-report may be sent to Lala Paltu Lal, *muhafiz-i daftar-i insha*, for inclusion in the register and keeping in the *daftar*. A copy of these may be sent to Bhawani Prasad, *wakil* to present it before the Political Agent and his reply may be conveyed to her. Another copy may be sent to Lala Mansukh Rai to present it before James, Deputy Commissioner at Hoshangabad, and his reply may be conveyed to her. Dated 16 *Jumada* I, 1275 AH.

P 57. *News-Report from* Thana *Siwans*, *Sent by Nur Muhammad Khan,* Thanadar, *Dated 11 Jumada I, 1275 AH.* Reports that day, Nizam Ali Khan, *risaldar* communicated through a soldier that the insurgent forces were encamping in the mountains of *mauza* Jharpona, *ilaqa* Sindhia, situating at a distance of 3 *curoh* from there. Informs to find out the reality of the news Lal Singh, peon of the *thana*, has been sent. A report will be sent after his coming back. There is peace in the *pargana* and *qasba*.

P 59. *Husain Khan,* Muhtamim, Ta'mirat*, to Nawwab Sikandar Begam.* Informs of the translation of the letter of Bhawani Prasad, *wakil*, which he did for the Colonel who expressed his gratitude over it. The translation was regarding Tantia Tope's march from Khaljipur. Also informs of the letter of the Lieutenant encamping at Bhilsa to the Colonel regarding his deployment to deal with Muhammad, Garhiwala. He wrote that about 700 to 800 men of Adil Muhammad Khan devastated *mauza* Shakura and Jharpona, *ilaqa* Muhammad Garh, Basodah, and captured Patel of Jharpona and kept him in the mountains of Dhanpur situating at a distance of 15 *curoh* from Bhilsa. Dated 27 *Jumada* I, 1275 AH.

PP 61-2. *Muhammad Abd al-Rahman,* Thanadar, *Garhi Ambapani, to Nawwab Sikandar Begam.* Informs that day he sent a letter to the *nizamat,* informing the devastation of *mauza* Khunia, *ilaqa* Hinda and the arrest of Lally Patel of the said *mauza* by the insurgents. Meanwhile, the *balahi* of the said *mauza* came and said that Lally Patel who was arrested by the insurgents freed himself from their captivity and came to the village. Changi, *harkara*, who was sent by him and Puran and Dahan Singh, informers sent by the *bakhshi* to know about the insurgents in *mauza* Danbudhi, came back and stated that Bakhshi Amanat Khan along with an army of 700 to 800 was encamping on the hills lying in between *mauza* Raja Milan and Danbudhi, *ilaqa* Bhilsa. Adil Muhammad Khan along with an army of 700 to 800 was encamping in the mountains called Megannath lying in between *mauza* Ghokhra, *ilaqa* Basodah and *mauza* Midun, *ilaqa* Bhilsa. Previous day, while coming back from Danbudhi, he saw that Adil Muhammad Khan and his contingent had devastated *mauza* Saguria and *mauza* Jharpona, *ilaqa* Muhammad Garh, and was at that time in *mauza* Chopra. He and his companions were washing their hands and legs and were drinking water. He too drank water there. He asked him who he was and where he was going. He replied that he had gone to the market in *mauza* Sontia, *ilaqa* Bhilsa, and was going back to *mauza* Ghokhra to his house. He had a dagger and a silver bracelet in his hand. His eyes were red. His companions were calling him with the title of Nawwab Sahab. He asked one of his companions about their chief. He replied, he was known as Nawwab Garhiwala. Dated 28 *Jumada* I, 1275 AH.

It contains the order that the letter may be sent to Lala Paltu Lal, *muhafiz-i daftar-i insha*, for inclusion in the register and keeping in the *daftar*. A copy of the letter may be sent to Bhawani Prasad, *wakil* to present it before the Political Agent and his reply may be conveyed to her. Another copy of the letter may be sent to Lala Mansukh Rai to present it before Hutchinson, Deputy Commissioner at Hoshangabad, and his reply may be conveyed to her. Dated 3 *Jumada* II, 1275 AH.

PP 63-4. *Sardar Khan and Ghulam Muhammad Khan to Nawwab Sikandar Begam.* Informs that day, i.e. 13th *Sha'ban* 1275 AH, Chaturbhuj, barber and a dweller of Sangal Bardha who was sent to bring the news of Adil Muhammad Khan, came to the camp at Siwans and had wound of sword on his arm. He stated that, he started his journey on the 6th of *Sha'ban* from Siwans and on 7th of the month he reached Rampura, *ilaqa* of Maharaja, where the insurgents were encamping. At that very time, the armies of Nana Sahab, *Jhansiwali*, and Adil Muhammad Khan arrived. The total strength of the insurgent forces was around 8,000 which comprised of 1,000 *sawars* and 7,000 foot-soldiers. Amanat Khan, *bakhshi* of Adil Muhammad Khan, with a contingent of 250 or 300 *sawars* and foot-soldiers arrived at Ganj Basodah, situating at a distance of 12 *curoh* from Siwans. Adil Muhammad Khan and Aqil Muhammad Khan with 100 or 150 *sawars* and 3,000 foot-soldiers were encamping at Basodah. States that he too was moving with the insurgents and reached on the bank of river Ganj Basodah. He was then identified by an *ahir*, a dweller of *mauza* Shamshabad, and was brought before Adil Muhammad Khan. He was asked about Bhopal. He replied that he was an inhabitant of Sangal Bardha and was going to Bagrod for some work. But the *ahir* said, he was a servant of Bhopal government and was deputed as an informer. Adil Muhammad Khan ordered for his imprisonment and a guard was given the duty to keep a watch on him. At one time when the guard went to sleep, he let loose the rope around him and freed himself from the captivity. Meanwhile, the guard woke up and raised voice. Ultimately, he was captured by the soldier on guard. He ran after him and attacked with his sword and hence, he received wound on his arm. However, he reached Siwans. Says, he himself saw the wound on his right arm which had a finger's length. He gave him Re. 1 as reward and asked to purchase ointment to rub on the wound. Dated 13 *Sha'ban* 1275 AH.

It contains the order that the letter may be sent to Lala Paltu Lal, *muhafiz-i daftar-i insha*, for inclusion in the register and keeping in the *daftar*. A copy of the letter may be sent to Bhawani Prasad, *wakil* to present it before the Political Agent and his reply may be conveyed to her. Dated 18 *Sha'ban* 1275 AH.

P 65. *Muhammad Abd al-Rahman,* Thanadar *of Garhi Ambapani, to Nawwab Sikandar Begam.* Informs for the last two days, the news that Adil Muhammad Khan has arrived at Pura is heard. The previous day, Qaim Khan, *jagirdar* of *mauza* Bhanpur, communicated to him in reference to his brother, Hakim Mir Khan from Basodah, that an insurgent army marched from Basodah and reached Pura. Hearing the news he sent Alam Singh, soldier of the *thana*, along with Himmat Khan, soldier to Pura to know about the news. That day, Alam Singh came back from Pipilya, a place where his relatives live and *mauza* Pura is at a distance of one *curoh* from there.

He stated that 12 persons, the dwellers of Pipilya, who were the employees of Adil Muhammad Khan came to Pipilya and said that a contingent of 1,000 of Adil Muhammad Khan arrived at Pura. The rest would come that day along with Adil Muhammad Khan. The army of Adil Muhammad Khan was continuously pouring in Pura the whole night. Due to this, all roads were closed. Any unknown person was not allowed to enter, hence, he came back from Pipilya. The information to this effect was a must which he did. Dated 13 *Sha'ban* 1275 AH.

It contains the order that the letter may be sent to Lala Paltu Lal, *muhafiz-i daftar-i insha*, for inclusion in the register and keeping in the *daftar*. A copy of the letter may be sent to Bhawani Prasad, *wakil* to present it before the Political Agent and his reply may be conveyed to her. Dated 18 *Sha'ban* 1275 AH.

P 67. *Daulat Rai,* Nazim-i Mashriq, *to Nawwab Sikandar Begam.* Sends the news-report, dated *12 Sha'ban* 1275 AH, received from *thana* Siwans sent by Shaikh Nur Muhammad, *thanadar*, as reported by Chaturbhuj, barber, the informer about the insurgents. Dated 16 *Sha'ban* 1275 AH, from Raisen.

It contains the order that the letter and the news-report may be sent to Lala Paltu Lal, *muhafiz-i daftar-i insha*, for inclusion in the register and keeping in the *daftar*. A copy of the letter and the news-report may be sent to Bhawani Prasad, *wakil*, to present it before the Political Agent and his reply may be conveyed to her. Dated 18 *Sha'ban* 1275 AH.

P 69. *News-Report from* Thana *Siwans, Dated 12 Sha'ban 1275 AH, Day Friday, Sent by Shaikh Nur Muhammad,* Thanadar. Informs that on 6th of the month, Chaturbhuj, barber and an informer, went to bring the news of the insurgents. On 7th of the month, he stayed in the night at *mauza* Gayaraspur, *ilaqa* Sindhia, and in the morning he left for Agra Barkhera. On the way, he saw that Adil Muhammad Khan, Nana Sahab, *ilaqadar*, Rani

Jhansiwali along with 60, 000 forces and two cannon were encamping. They then marched into two groups from there. The informer also became their companion. Amanat Khan with 500 men was also encamping there. The rest marched and reached Basodah. Nana Sahab with two cannon and a contingent of 4,000 marched to Khorai, a British territory. Adil Muhammad Khan and Aqil Muhammad Khan along with a contingent of 3,000 were encamping at Basodah situating at a distance of 10 *curoh* from Siwans. The informer was identified by someone from amongst the insurgents and was arrested from the bank of river Ganj Basodah and kept in captivity in the army at Basodah. Next day, he managed to escape and freed himself from their captivity. He was attacked by sword and was slightly wounded in his arm. The royal army is quite alert and attentive.

P 71. *Nawwab Shahjahan Begam to Nawwab Sikandar Begam.* Sends the letter received from Muhammad 'Azeem Khan, *tahsildar*, and Durga Prasad, *thanadar* of Ghairatganj, dated 2 *Ramazan* 1275 AH along with the statement of Padam, *tarafdar-mustajir*, *mauza* Bhanpur, *pargana* Ghairatganj, which contains information about Adil Muhammad Khan. Dated 6 *Ramazan* 1275 AH.

It contains the order that the letter and statement of Padam, *mustajir*, may be sent to Lala Paltu Lal, *muhafiz-i daftar-i insha*, for inclusion in the register and keeping in the *daftar*. A copy of the letter and statement may be sent to Bhawani Prasad, *wakil* to present it before Cumming, Deputy Political Agent of Bhopal, and his reply may be conveyed to her. Dated 18 *Sha'ban* 1275 AH.

PP 73-4. *Muhammad 'Azeem Khan,* Tahsildar, *and Durga Prasad,* Thanadar *of Ghairatganj to Nawwab Shahjahan Begam.* Informs that Padam, *tarafdar-mustajir*, *mauza* Bhanpur, *pargana* Ghairatganj, was made captive by men of Adil Muhammad Khan from Nurja, *ilaqa* Basodah, and took him along. That day he came back from their captivity as he fled from there due to carelessness of the guards. What he described about Adil Muhammad Khan was recorded separately and sent to her. Dated 2 *Ramazan* 1275 AH.

It contains the order that the letter and statement of Padam, *mustajir*, may be sent to Muhammad Siddique Khan to include it in the register and keep in the *daftar*. A copy of the letter and statement may be sent to Nawwab Sikandar Begam. Dated 7 *Ramazan* 1275 AH.

PP 75-8. *Statement of Padam,* Tarafdar-Mustajir *of* Mauza *Bhanpur,* Pargana *Ghairatganj in the Presence of Muhammad 'Azeem Khan,* Tahsildar, *and Durga Prasad,* Thanadar. *Dated* 2 Ramazan 1275 AH. States that his name is Padam, *mustajir*, a dweller of Bhanpur, *pargana* Ghairatganj, and is aged around 20 years.

Q. Asked to tell as he was caught by men of Adil Muhammad Khan from Nurja, then how he got released from their captivity.

R. He had gone to Nurja. Suddenly, 10 to 15 *sawars* and foot-soldiers of the same number appeared, captured him and brought him in the camp. He remained there the whole night, guarded by a *risaldar*. He demanded Rs. 4,000. He said he would give Rs. 200. He did not agree and he was beaten mercilessly and then was presented before Adil Muhammad Khan. He said, that he was a rich man, he would take Rs. 4,000 from him. He said he would give Rs. 2,000. But he had nothing to pay. It was sheer fear and apprehension that he would be beaten so he stated so. He remained there for four days. The previous day, all armymen went to loot Sanchet and he was put under a guard to keep a watch on him. Once he found that the guard was sleeping, he secretly sneaked from there. When he found that he came too far from that place and nobody pursued him, he fled and reached there in their shelter.

Q. He was there for four days and he was also brought before Adil Muhammad Khan. He is asked to tell about the latter's army which was with him and where his camp was and from where he gets the *rasad* and what is his future plan?

R. His camp was in the middle of Ghokhra mountain called Aamwala, and Barwala Ghokhra. His army contingent had 200 *sawars*. There were 500 soldiers of Meena, Gond and Rajput tribes. They were the nomads of Rahti. Adil Muhammad Khan lived beneath a tree. The provisions were provided by village people who were paid for the provision. The people of Basodah were also providing them provision. They abused the people of Muhammad Garh. When they planned to loot any village in the night, they sent someone with the armymen. When he was there, they had looted the villages of Ghorasi and Sanchet. Their intention was to loot any village and capture the richmen of the village. Someone reported that Nawwab Sikandar Begam disbanded the army contingent. Adil Muhammad Khan became very happy upon receiving this news. Sweets were distributed. The companions were called and told that the disbanded contingent of Bhopal army had come and soon the army of Rao Sahab too would come. Then, they would fight with Bhopal. Some said that the Bhopal government was very strong. There would be too much fighting. But they did not have the courage to fight with Bhopal. A letter of a Raja came from across Narmada. He wrote to him to come to the mountains of Mahadev and make plan to loot the villages there. But the letter did not bear the name of the Raja. Adil Muhammad Khan called his *risaldar* and told him that they should cross river Narmada from any place. Some suggested via Chandpura. But if there will be some forces at Bari then it will not be possible. On the route through Sirmau, there is a contingent of Raja Sirmau. At Ghairatganj, there is less contingent. Then, he said that there were150 guns with the *thanadar* and 100 guns with the *tahsildar* along with four *risalas* of Bhanpur. If they reacted, they would be killed then. Bakhshi Amanat

Khan was too present there with 50 *sawars.*

Q. Where was that Ghokhra where they were staying? Is it possible to surround it by the royal forces?

R. He replied in affirmation and said that their check posts were at Ghokhra in Basodah, at Ganota, *ilaqa* Muhammad Garh and at Begwan, *ilaqa* Bhilsa. If the army cordones these three check posts, all men could easily be killed. There were 8 persons at every check post. Water in Ghokhra would last for only about 10 to 12 days.

Q. What was their future plan and which village they wanted to devastate?

R. It was not possible to know this as it discovered only after the return from loot. Their next plan was to loot Hardot. They had huge money with them.

P 79. *Daulat Rai,* Nazim-i Mashriq, *to Nawwab Sikandar Begam.* Sends the news-report, dated 16 *Ramazan* 1275 AH, received from Muhammad Abd al-Rahman, *thanadar* of Garhi, reporting about the encampment of insurgent forces in *mauza* Ghokhra, *ilaqa* Basodah. Dated 19 *Ramazan* 1275 AH.

It contains the order that the letter and news-report may be sent to Lala Paltu Lal, *muhafiz-i daftar-i insha*, for inclusion in the register and keeping in the *daftar*. A copy of the letter and news-report may be sent to Bhawani Prasad, *wakil*, to present it before William Cumming and his reply may be conveyed to her. Dated 22 *Ramazan* 1275 AH.

P 81. *News-Report from* Thana *Garhi Ambapani, Dated 16* Ramazan *1275 AH, Sent by Muhammad Abd al-Rahman*, Thanadar. Informs that day, by the graceness of God and with her blessings, there was calm in the *qasba* and in all the villages of the *ilaqa*. Reports that Jhakka, *harkara*, was sent to know about the insurgents. That day, he came back and stated that he went from there and reached *mauza* Ghokhra, *ilaqa* Basodah, and found that there were 700 insurgents in that area and in the mountains known as Siyariwala. This is the story as told by a gond of *mauza* Ghokhra who was captured by the insurgents, suspecting him an informer who anyhow fled from there and reached back to the village. In view of warnings of the *mustajir* of Ghokhra and due to fear of his life, he did not go to that point. About 400 persons were hiding in the bushes of Murjhari, *ilaqa* Bhilsa, adjacent to the Siyariwala range of mountains. The story is told by the gond and the *mustajir* of Ghokhra as well. At that time, two persons of caste *tiha* came from Pura Guna with their family members in *mauza* Ghokhra. But the *mustajir* did not allow them to stay in the vallage. Says, what the informer stated the same was reported without any omission or addition. The said informer has again been sent to see the reality from his own eyes and to report the same.

P 83. *Sardar Khan, Qila'dar, and Muhammad Khan from Siwans to Nawwab Sikandar Begam.* Informs that evening, Hari Singh, *katwar* of *mauza* Manipur *pargana* Garhi, came hurriedly to the camp and reported in reference to Khuba, *katwar* of *mauza* Dhamrohi, that an army of 8,000 of Chhatrasal, besides Raja Bhor and other insurgents were encamping at Hudya-Teghra, *ilaqa* Basodah, situating at a distance of 3 *curoh* from Siwans. This is the report, as given by *katwar* of *mauza* Mundla of the said *pargana,* and that he too should immediately convey the report to the camp and *thana*. He came in the camp to convey the report, as stated by *katwar* of *mauza* Dhamrohi about the arrival of the insurgents in *mauza* Hudya-Teghra. Dated 21 *Ramazan* 1275 AH.

It contains the order that the letter and news-report may be sent to Lala Paltu Lal, *muhafiz-i daftar-i insha*, for inclusion in the register and keeping in the *daftar*. A copy of the letter and news-report may be sent to Bhawani Prasad, *wakil*, to present it before William Cumming and his reply may be conveyed to her. Dated 22 *Ramazan* 1275 AH.

PP 85-6. *Muhammad Hasan Khan,* Naib Bakhshi, *and Mattu Khan,* Risaldar *to Nawwab Sikandar Begam.* Informs that 8th *Shawwal* 1275 AH, day Thursday, passed with calm in the camp. Mahna Singh and Laxman Singh, the soldiers of the battalion of Chhotey Ram, *jamadar*, who were sent to bring the news reported that Sarfraz Khan along with 300 *sawars* and foot-soldiers was encamping in the hills of Udaipura adjacent to Sanohta, *ilaqa* Ganj Badodah, and devastated the villages of Bhilsa and that Adil Muhammad Khan was still in Pura Guna. Amanat Khan, *bakhshi* of Adil Muhammad Khan, went the previous day with a contingent of 300 to 400 troops to meet Sarfraz Khan. That day, an informer reported that he died. Dated 8 *Shawwal* 1275 AH.

It contains the order that the letter may be sent to Lala Paltu Lal, *muhafiz-i daftar-i insha*, for inclusion in the register and keeping in the *daftar*. A copy of the letter may be sent to Bhawani Prasad, *wakil* to communicate it to the Political Agent and his reply may be conveyed to her. Dated 12 *Shawwal* 1275 AH.

P 87. *Nizam Ali Khan,* Bakhshi, Nizamat-i Mashriq, *to Nawwab Sikandar Begam.* Informs that day, the 18th *Shawwal* 1275 AH, from Chandan Singh, *kotha-dafadar*, battalion of Balwant Singh, *jamadar*, it was heard that a person of *mauza* Khadera, *ilaqa* Sarkar Buzurg, who had gone to Sironj to attend a marriage in *mauza* Ganjber said that Adil Muhammad Khan marched from Pura Guna and encamped in a garden in *mauza* Ranchera, *ilaqa* Ganj Basodah, and Amanat Khan, *bakhshi*, was buried in *mauza* Daulatpur situating at a distance of 3 *curoh* from the place of Adil Muhammad Khan. The British army was encamping at Ataya. Dated 18 *Shawwal* 1275 AH.

It contains the order that the letter may be sent to Lala Paltu Lal, *muhafiz-i daftar-i insha*, for inclusion in the register and keeping in the *daftar*. A copy of the letter may be sent to Bhawani Prasad, *wakil* to present it before James and his reply may be conveyed to her. Dated 19 *Shawwal* 1275 AH.

P 89. *Daulat Rai,* Nazim-i Mashriq, *to Nawwab Sikandar Begam.* Sends the news-report, dated 16 *Shawwal* 1275 AH, received from *thana* Siwans, reporting about the fleeing of insurgent forces due to fear of the British forces and taking shelter in the mountains of *ilaqa* Basodah. The defeat of the insurgent forces and their killing by the British forces, severe enjury to Amanat Khan *bakhshi* and fleeing of Adil Muhammad Khan would be known through the letter of Shahzad Rai, *thanadar,* Mahalpur. Says, this is the time to kill and arrest the insurgents. Requests for more army personnel to be deployed in the region. Dated 19 *Shawwal* 1275 AH.

It contains the order that the letter may be sent to Lala Paltu Lal, *muhafiz-i daftar-i insha*, for inclusion in the register and keeping in the *daftar*. A copy of the letter may be sent to Bhawani Prasad, *wakil*, to present it before James and his reply may be conveyed to her. Dated 20 *Shawwal* 1275 AH.

P 91. *News-Report from* Thana *Siwans, Dated 16* Shawwal *1275 AH, Day Friday, Sent by Khwaja Muhammad Daim,* Thanadar. Informs, that day there was calm in the *qasba*. The previous day, the 15th *Shawwal* 1275 AH, day Thursday, *katwar* of *mauza* Mundlabir, *pargana* Garhi and Bahadur, *sawar* guarding the said *mauza*, came to the *thana* and stated that the army of Adil Muhammad Khan, the insurgent, was encamping in the mountains of Jharya Beragi, the area bordering Bhopal State.

Hearing the news, he took over the command of the *sawars* of *thana,* besides Sardar Khan, *sipahsalar,* Faiz Muhammad Khan, son of Asif Muhammad Khan along with the battalion of Datar Singh, *jamadar* and some other *sawars* and reached hurriedly to the said *mauza* and sent Faiz Muhammad Khan with two *sawars* to know about the encampment of the insurgent forces. They came back and stated that the insurgent forces were encamping on the hills of *ilaqa* Basodah, nearby Jharya Beragi. Keeping in mind that *ilaqa* Basodah falls in other's territory and in view of safety and security of the inhabitants of *pargana* Garhi, he stayed for the night there and as per the royal order, dated 26 *Ramazan* 1275 AH, he brought the matter into the notice of Hafiz Muhammad Hasan Khan, *naib bakhshi*. The *naib bakhshi* and Mattu Khan, *risaldar*, with the contingent of Garhi, arrived in *mauza* Hardot, adjacent to *mauza* Bundla. That day with the consent of *sipahsalar,* two *sawars* and *katwar* of the village were sent to bring authentic news of the encampment of the insurgents. When they came back, they stated that the insurgents fled due to the fear of the British forces. Thereafter, he pacified the villagers and then came back to the *thana*.

It contains the order that the news-report may be sent to Lala Paltu Lal, *muhafiz-i daftar-i insha*, for inclusion in the register and keeping in the *daftar*. A copy of the news-report may be sent to Bhawani Prasad, *wakil*, to communicate to James and his reply may be conveyed to her. Dated 20 *Shawwal* 1275 AH.

PP 93-4. *Tikaram,* Muhtamim-i Karkhanajat, *to Nawwab Sikandar Begam.* Informs that, as ordered, he sent Udit and Ranjit, the informers to Pura Guna to bring the news of Adil Muhammad Khan. That day, he came back and stated that, as ordered he went to bring the news of Adil Muhammad Khan. On 12 *Ziqada* 1275 AH, they reached Raisen, on 13th of the month, they were at Garhi Ambapani, and on 14th, they were at Ghokhra, *ilaqa* Muhammad Garh, Basodah and found that the army of Adil Muhammad was lying here and there in the jungle of that *mauza*. The soldiers of the army entered *mauza* Ghokhra and demanded *saman-i rasad* from the Patel of that *mauza*. The Patel of the village was helpless before them. Whatever food-grains;

flour, pulses and gram were available in the *mauza*, were put on the shoulder of cobblers and the *zamindars* and brought in their camp. They too were arrested and a bag of flour was put on the head of Udit and a bag of pulse was put on the head of Ranjit and they went to their camp. They hoped that they would be able to see the camp of the army carrying bags on their heads towards their camp in the company of the Patel and the soldiers. They saw that an army of 4,000 of Adil Muhammad Khan was encamping here and there in the jungle. There were 1,000 *sawars*, 2 companies of Tilangas and rest were foot-soldiers. There were no cannon with them. They were interested to see their entire contingent, as they were distributing the food-grain among the armymen in their camp in the company of the Patel of *mauza* Ghokhra, carrying the bags of flour on their heads. Thus, they saw their entire army contingent. On the bank of river Sheerin, adjacent to *mauza* Ghokhra, they saw Adil Muhammad Khan sitting under a tree and hunting fish. 25 armed soldiers were standing around him, guarding him with full attention and promptness. At every step of 60 feet, the *sawars* were standing all around him. The horse of Adil Muhammad Khan was fully ready, standing nearby. The Patel of *mauza* Ghokhra appeared before Adil Muhammad Khan and said that whatever grain was available in the *mauza,* he brought it there and distributed amongst the armymnen. He said ok. They were all the time with the Patel as if they were forced labourers. They saw from their own eyes that Adil Muhammad Khan was in a white dress and a handkerchief was tied around his neck. Bakhshi Amanat Khan too was there. He had wound in his hand. Meanwhile, the commanders of the forces came and said that all the armymen had their lunch and they were fully ready. Adil Muhammad Khan then rode his horse and left for Pura Guna. Bakhshi Amanat Khan along with 1,000 or 1200 *sawars* and foot-soldiers went towards the mountain of Margannath situating at a distance of $1^{1/2}$ *curoh* from there.

In the afternoon, they returned to *mauza* Ghokhra and then arrived at Garhi Ambapani where they heard that Adil Muhammad Khan devastated *mauza* Bamhuri adjacent to *mauza* Aradmau and Jaitpura. Hearing the news, Hafiz Muhammad Hasan Khan, *naib bakhshi* of Bakhshi Murawwat Muhammad Khan, left with his army to fight with him. They came back and stated what they saw.

It contains the order that the letter may be sent to Lala Paltu Lal, *muhafiz-i daftar-i insha*, for inclusion in the register and keeping in the *daftar*. A copy of the letter may be sent to Bhawani Prasad, *wakil*, to communicate it to James and his reply may be conveyed to her. Dated 24 *Ziqa'da* 1275 AH.

P 95. *Daulat Rai,* Nazim-i Mashriq, *to Nawwab Sikandar Begam.* Sends the news-report, dated 15 *Zilhijja* 1275 AH, received from *Khwaja Muhammad Daim, thanadar* of *thana* Siwans. He has reported that Dungal Singh, son of Shankar Singh of *mauza* Anhaigarh, *ilaqa* Sindhia, with a contingent of 200 *sawars* and 300 foot-soldiers is encamping at *mauza* Kosua, *pargana* Basodah, as reported by Swami Ram. Dated 15 *Zilhijja* 1275 AH.

It contains the order that the letter and news-report may be sent to Lala Paltu Lal, *muhafiz-i daftar-i insha*, for inclusion in the register and keeping in the *daftar*. A copy of the letter and news-report may be sent to Bhawani Prasad, *wakil* to communicate it to the Political Agent and his reply may be conveyed to her.

PP 97-8. *News-Report From* Thana *Siwans Sent By Khwaja Muhammad Daim, Day Thursday, Dated 15* Zilhijja *1275 AH.* Reports that the previous day, he had sent Swami Ram to bring news about the insurgents. That day, he came back and stated that Dungal Singh, son of Shankar Singh of *mauza* Anhaigarh, *ilaqa* Sindhia, with a contingent of 200 *sawars* and 300 foot-soldiers was encamping at *mauza* Kosua, *pargana* Basodah, situating at a distance of $3/^{1/2}$ *curoh* from there. Rest every thing is okay in the entire *pargana* and *qasba*. Anything new, if happens , will be reported.

File No. 306
Box No. 16
No. of Documents 6

Management of Passages Across the Mountains Under the State of Bhopal to Prevent the Insurgents

PP 1-2. Contents

P 3. Parwana-i Ishtahari *of Nawwab Sikandar Begam Issued to her Three* Nazims. The management of the passages across the mountains under the *mahal*s in district south is a must. Therefore, the number of soldiers required to manage these passages may be communicated to the government along with the details of the passages.

P 5. *Daulat Rai,* Nazim-i Mashriq, *to Nawwab Sikandar Begam.* Informs that, as ordered, dated 29 *Rabi* I, 1275 AH, he wrote letters to the *thanadars* of the district directing them to provide details of the passages located in the mountains with the police personnel required to maintain and manage them. The *thanadars* have sent the list of the passages located under the mountains along with police personnel required to maintain them. A comprehensive list, in the light of those lists, has been prepared which is sent to her. The *thanadars* of all 60 *chaukis* have submitted the list of all the passages located in the mountains of their *mahals* of the district and for maintaining them, a contingent of 912 police personnel would be required. Says, it is not possible to deploy soldiers at every passage and expecting from them that they would fight with the insurgents as they might flee when such a situation arose under the pretext that they could not face them due to being less in number. Instead, in his opinion, a reliable person with some *sawars* and foot-soldiers should be deployed for petrolling throughout these passages and wherever any insurgent or a group of insurgent is noticed they should fight with them, kill or arrest them. In this way the insurgency would be prevented and also the passages would be maintained. Dated 18 *Rabi* II, 1275 AH.

PP 7-10. Yaddasht, *Containing Details of the Passages Under the Mountains in the* Mahals *of District East, Dated 18* Rabi *II, 1275 AH.*

P 11. *Muhammad Raza Husain,* Nazim-i Junub, *to Nawwab Sikandar Begam.* Refers to her *parwana,* dated 29 *Rabi* I, 1275 AH, directing him to inform about the number of soldiers required to maintain the passages across the mountains under the *mahal* of district south and also to communicate the total number of passages across the mountains. As ordered, a map of the passages, across the mountains under the *mahals* of the district was prepared with the help of those who were familiar of these routes and passages. Refers to his earlier letter, dated 23 *Rabi* I, 1275 AH, written during the early days whence the insurgents began passing through those passages requesting for soldiers to manage those passages. The proposal regarding the requirement of soldiers to maintain the passages lying across the mountains of Chhaner, Bharonda, Mardanpur, Bareilly and Udaipura may be kept pending. But the map of passages of one mountain situating in *pargana* Bari, Bareilly, Bamhuri and Mahalpur which is the bordering area of *pargana* Mardanpur, Tal and Jogigarh reflects that there are 22 passages under this mountain and by the management of these passages, the route of the insurgents to enter Mardanpur, whether from beneath the valley or from the upper part of valley, would be blocked. To manage these 22 passages, an estimation of a contingent of 376 soldiers would be required. In case, the proposal is not acceptable and if 4 or 5 battalions are provided, the *thandars* of *pargana* Bari and Jogigarh would be able to take care of the mountains and to prevent the insurgents. Dated 21 *Rabi* II, 1275 AH.

It contains the order that the letter, besides the map, may be sent to Lala Paltu Lal, *muhafiz-i daftar-i insha*, for inclusion in the register and keeping in the *daftar*. A copy of the order may be sent to Munshi Raza Husain through *madar al-maham*, communicating to him that for the management of the passages across the mountains of district south, a huge number of soldiers would be required. Now a large number of soldiers; both *sawars* and foot-soldiers have also been recruited. To manage these passages she would rather depend upon the Almighty. He should merely manage his own region through the contingent available with him. Dated 24 *Rabi* II, 1275 AH.

PP 13-17. *The Proposed Map of the Passages Under the Mountains of the* Mahals *of District South in the State of Bhopa, Dated 21* Rabi *II, 1275 AH.*

File No. 307
Box No. 16
No. of Documents 6

Investigation Into the Role of Wali Muhammad, Son of Nur Muhammad, Thanadar of Siwans, During the Uprising

P 1. Contents

P 3. *Bhawani Prasad to Nawwab Sikandar Begam.* Informs of the letter of the Political Agent, dated 8 October 1858, issued on the basis of the order from the office of the Collector, Muzaffarnagar, enquiring into the role of Wali Muhammad, son of Nur Muhammad, during the uprising who was with Nur Muhammad Khan at that time so that orders may be issued accordingly. Dated 1 *Rabi* I, 1275 AH/10 October 1858.

It contains the order that the letter along with the *parwana* of the Political Agent may be sent to Daulat Rai, *nazim-i mashriq*, through *madar al-maham*, directing him to inquire into the character of Wali Muhammad, son of Nur Muhammad, *thanadar* of Siwans and inform the government so that the same may be conveyed to the Political Agent.

P 5. *The Political Agent to Bhawani Prasad.* Directs him to inform about the role of Wali Muhammad, son of Nur Muhammad, husband of Mst. Aiman, *maafidar,* who during the uprising was with Nur Muhammad Khan, *tahsildar,* his father as per the orders issued from the office of the Collector, Muzaffarnagar, dated 23 September 1858. Dated 8 October 1858.

P 7. *Daulat Rai,* Nazim-i Mashriq, *to Nawwab Sikandar Begam.* Refers to the royal order, dated 3 *Rabi* I, 1275 AH, as recorded in the letter of Bhawani Prasad, *wakil*, asking about the character of Wali Muhammad, son of Nur Muhammad, *thanadar* of Siwans. Informs that he wrote a letter to Saiyid Waris Ali, *tahsildar* of Siwans, who is aware about him whereas he is not. In reply to that he informed him that Wali Muhammad, son of Nur Muhammad, was a thorough gentleman. He was never involved in insurgency nor was he an insurgent. His movement was restricted to the *thana* and the court. He was far away from the insurgents. Information to this effect was a must which he did by sending the letter of the *wakil* as well as the letter of the Political Agent. Dated 18 *Rabi* I, 1275 AH.

It contains the order that the letter besides the other letters may be sent to Lala Paltu Lal, *muhafiz-i daftar-i insha*, for inclusion in the register and keeping in the *daftar*. A copy of this and that of the *amil* of Siwans may be sent to Bhawani Prasad who may present it before the Political Agent and his reply may be communicated to her. Dated 3 *Rabi* II, 1275 AH.

PP 9-10. *Daulat Rai,* Nazim-i Mashriq, *to Saiyid Waris Ali,* Tahsildar. Sends him the letter of Bhawani Prasad, *wakil-i riyasat*, dated 1 *Rabi* I, 1275 AH which also contains a royal order besides the letter of the Political Agent. As a matter of fact, he and Shaikh Nur Muhammad, *thanadar*, were in the same place, hence, he would be well aware about the character of Wali Muhammad, son of Nur Muhammad. Directs him to inform about his character without any exaggeration so that the same may be communicated to the government. Dated 10 *Rabi* I, 1275 AH.

P 11. *Saiyid Waris Ali,* Tahsildar, *to Daulat Rai,* Nazim-i Mashriq. Informs about Wali Muhammad, son of Nur Muhammad, *thanadar,* what he knows that he is a thorough gentleman and a *Hafiz-i Quran* and a performer of five times' prayer. He has nothing to do with insurgency, what to talk of having connection with the insurgents. He stays either in his house or visits the *thana* or the court. He is far away from the elements of insurgents. He rarely visits the court of the *mahal*. He is more than that what he has described about his character and morality. Dated 10 *Rabi* I 1275 AH.

File No. 308
Box No. 16
No. of Documents 11

Circulatation of a Wrong Message that Adil Muhammad Khan, the Insurgent, is in Ichhawar or Kalyakhery or Anywhere in Bhopal

PP 1-2. Contents

P 3. *Muhammad Sa'd al-Din, Muhtamim, Adalat-i Faujdari, to Nawwab Sikandar Begam.* Informs, that day General Burton said, when *madar al-maham* and *mu'tamid al-maham* were also present, that the news was coming day and night, everyday from Ichhawar that some insurgents have reached there. Says, he immediately in compliance to the order of the General, wrote a letter to Khan Sahab, Disilva, *kamdar,* Deorhi Dulhan Sahaba. Also requests to issue orders to Dulhan Sahaba to send the news of Ichhawar day and night to him. Dated 22 *Rabi* I, 1275 AH.

It contains the order that the letter may be sent to Lala Paltu Lal, *muhafiz-i daftar-i insha*, for inclusion in the register and keeping in the *daftar*. The reply of the letter may be entered in the book of orders of the *adalat-i faujdari* and sent to the *muhtamim*, *adalat-i faujdari*. A copy of the letter addressed to Bibi Sahaba may be kept in the register. Dated 22 *Rabi* I, 1275 AH.

P 5. *Bibi Sahaba, Wife of Hakim Shahzad Masih, to Nawwab Sikandar Begam.* Informs that there is no insurgency in *qasba* Ichhawar which is her *jagir*. If there had been an insurgency, she would have come to know and it would have been communicated immediately as Hakim Khan Sahab Disilva is present in Ichhawar. Dated 22 *Rabi* I, 1275 AH.

It contains the order that the letter may be sent to Lala Paltu Lal, *muhafiz-i daftar-i insha*, for inclusion in the register and keeping in the *daftar*. The gist of the letter may be entered in the book of orders of the *adalat-i faujdari*. Dated 22 *Rabi* I, 1275 AH.

P 7. *The Gist of the Letter of Dulhan Sahaba*. There is no insurgency in Ichhawar, which is her *jagir*. The royal order, dated 22 *Rabi* I, 1275 AH, issued to enter in the book of orders of the *adalat-i faujdari* is that Muhammad Sa'd al-Din, *muhtamim, adalat-i faujdai*, should inform the British officer about the order.

PP 9-10. *News from Kalyakhery*. It is in English.

P 11. *An Urdu Translation of the English Letter*. Two camel riders left for Kalyakhery. One of them stayed in between Mehendwa and Bhojpur, and the other went to Kalyakhery. They returned to Bhopal in the night and informed that there was peace in Kalyakhery and that no insurgent was there. There was expectation of the arrival of a British army from Hoshangabad. This is recorded by Muhammad Farash, *rubkari* of Nawwab Sikandar Begam, who heard so from the camel rider. Dated 25 *Rabi* I, 1275 AH.

P 13. *Muhammad Sa'd al-Din, Muhtamim, Adalat-i Faujdari, to Nawwab Sikandar Begam*. Informs that day, i.e. 3 *Rabi* II, 1275 AH, a letter of Burton, addressed to him was received from the camp of the British through Maula Balahi, a dweller of Kalyakhery, from Hoshangabad. The British officer directed him to seek confirmation of the report from Munshi Muhammad Raza Husain, *nazim-i junub*, that Nawwab of Garhi entered Bhopal along with 4,000 forces. The said letter is sent to her, requesting for the reply to communicate further. Dated 3 *Rabi* II, 1275 AH.

It contains the order that the letter and a copy of the *parwana,* addressed to Muhammad Sa'd al-Din, *muhtamim*, *adalat-i faujdari,* may be sent to Lala Paltu Lal, *muhafiz-i daftar-i insha*, for inclusion in the register and keeping in the *daftar*.

P 15. *Burton to Muhammad Sa'd al-Din, Kotwal of City of Bhopal.* There is a confirmed news that Adil Muhammad Khan with an army of 3,000 to 4,000 has arrived in Bhopal or in the surroundings of Bhopal. He is directed, as desired by the Brigadier, to enquire as to where Adil Muhammad Khan is encamping by sending camel riders and other reliable persons and inform him the next day by evening. There should not be any kind of negligence or reluctance. Dated 8 November 1858.

PP 17-18. Parwana *of Nawwab Sikandar Begam to Muhammad Sa'd al-Din, Muhtamim.* Refers to his letter, dated 3 *Rabi* II, 1275 AH, along with the letter of Burton, dated 8 November 1858, addressed to him, asking about the entry of Adil Muhammad Khan in or around Bhopal. The letters received from Abd al-Rahman, *thanadar* of Garhi Ambapani, from Hafiz Muhammad Hasan Khan, *naib* Bakhshi from Raisen, and from Daulat Rai, *nazim-i mashriq,* describe that Adil Muhammad Khan and his forces did not yet enter Garhi Ambapani. Besides, the informers have also been sent to bring the news of the insurgents. The information to this effect would be communicated to the British officer after receiving the news. Brigadier Lucked has marched from Bhilsa and reached Gulgaon. Any information received further would be communicated first to the Brigadier. Some *sawars* and foot-soldiers of the army of TantiaTope came to this side from Pandorah *ghat*. Likewise, some *sawars* and foot-soldiers of the army of Adil Muhammad Khan who came from Bundelkhand were hiding in the mountains and caves of the *mahals* of district east. They were perturbed and heard that they were on the move, sometimes here and sometimes there. They did not assemble at one place. There is no report of the entry of Adil Muhammad Khan in Garhi Ambapani or accumulation of scattered insurgent forces at one place till the time of writing the *parwana* to him on the afternoon of 10 November 1858. Information to this effect must be communicated to Burton. Dated 3 *Rabi* II, 1275 AH.

PP 19-20. *Muhammad Raza Husain to Nawwab Sikandar Begam.* Informs that on 2nd *Rabi* I, he received a letter from Charles William Burton, addressed to Muhammad Sa'd al-Din, *muhtamim, adalat-i faujdari,* directing him to get the reply from him immediately. No sooner, he sent the letter to the *muhtamim*, *adalat-i faujdari.* The reply received from him was presented before the British officer who, thereafter, ordered the march of the forces to Siwanni. He was then given a letter in English, granting him leave and said that the General granted him leave. Major Lisbon with some force would remain there to report if Adil Muhammad Khan enters Bhopal. He also said that unless the army crossed river Narmada, he should remain there. Says, the previous day, he received a letter of Bansidhar, *mutasaddi-i mal* in the office of *madar al-maham,* desiring the replacement of the carts of *Bagh-i Farhat-i Afza*. He requested him for the replacement of the carts. He said no cart was being carried by him. He should ask the officer at Hoshangabad about the matter and convey his good wishes to the Nawwab. The British army has encamped on the other-side of river Narmada since then. He, as ordered, is staying in *mauza* Zarapur, executing the orders received from the officer of *sarbrah-i lashkar* for Bhopal and Bhilsa, and also to fulfill their need of green and soft grass and other necessities. Everyday, he goes to the other side of Narmada to meet them and in the evening comes back from there. Till then the arsenal, the godown and one *risala* of the British forces were in

Zarapur, waiting for orders to cross river Narmada. That day, a British officer with an army of 1,500 ; both *sawars* and foot-soldiers, came from Bhilsa. Captain Maine with his *risala* who was to return to Guna returned to Bhopal. That time, they were at *mauza* Joga. The time he received the letter of Bansidhar, *mutasaddi*, who is accompanying Colonal Benson from Hoshangabad, he is in search of carts for *Bagh-i Farhat-i Afza* for the army encamping on both sides of river Narmada. But he is yet to find the carts. 7 carts found in *pargana* Tal were changed with the carts of Hoshangabad. Dated 4 *Babi*II, 1275 AH.

It contains the order that the letter may be sent to Lala Paltu Lal, *muhafiz-i daftar-i insha*, for inclusion in the register and keeping in the *daftar*. A copy of the order may be sent to Rasul Khan, *darogha*, *Bagh-i Farhat-i Afza*, informing him that the carts and the bullocks of *Bagh-i Farhat-i Afza* which were in the company of the British army were coming back. He may be directed to report as to how many carts and bullocks are yet to come back. Dated 4 *Babi*II, 1275 AH.

P 21. *Paltu Lal to Nawwab Sikandar Begam.* Sends the letter of Muhammad Sa'd al-Din, *muhtamim, adalat-i faujdari*, Bhopal, dated 22 *Rabi* II, 1275 AH and the letter of Dulhan Sahaba and informs that on the question of insurgency in Ichhawar, neither any letter was written by the government for the month of *Rabi* I, 1275 AH nor was received any copy of such letter in the *daftar-i insha.* There is also no clue of any royal letter in reply to the letter of Dulhan Sahaba. Thus, he is unable to comply with the royal order to communicate the date of the letter of Muhammad Sa'd al-Din. The said letter is lying unattended for past 5 months. He made several attempts to clarify it but everytime he failed. It is a matter to understand that if there is no date written on the letter, how come he would bring the date and how come he would be able to intimate the same. Dated 21 *Sha'ban* 1275 AH.

It contains the order that the letter besides other two letters may be sent to Lala Paltu Lal, *muhafiz-i daftar-i insha,* directing him to copy the relevant content from the book of orders of *ilaqa* Deorhi Bibi Sahaba and keep it in the *daftar*. Dated 29 *Sha'ban* 1275 AH.

File No. 309
Box No. 16
No. of Documents 7

Search Operation of Adil Muhammad Khan by the British Forces

PP 1-2. Contents

P 3. *Hazrat Nur Khan to Nawwab Sikandar Begam*. The day the insurgents fled from *mauza* Rasla where the search operation was conducted by the British forces, a soldier of the insurgent forces reached *mauza* Tah, *ilaqa* Bheglone. Shahamat Khan, the soldier, an employee of the *zamindars,* noticed him as an insurgent who looked helpless. He thought that he should be followed and qustioned. Suddenly, he overpowered Shahamat Khan and fled. The Khan along with others of the village pursued him who entered in the forest. The insurgent threw his gun, etc. and ran away. All his belongings were captured and deposited in the *thana*. A list of the belongings is enclosed. The Khan desires that the goods should be given to him. Requests for orders to be followed. Dated 21 *Rabi* I, 1275 AH.

It contains the order that the letter and list of goods may be sent to Lala Paltu Lal, *muhafiz-i daftar-i insha*, for inclusion in the register and keeping in the *daftar*. A copy of the order may be sent to Hazrat Nur Khan, *amil* of Bheglone through Daulat Rai, *nazim-i mashriq,* directing him to send all the goods to the government. Had Shahamat Khan arrested the insurgent, the fugitive, orders for giving the goods to him would have been issued at that very moment. Dated 26 *Rabi* I, 1275 AH.

P 5. Yaddasht, *Containing List of Goods Found with an Insurgent Soldier*. The goods are: gun-1, sword-1, belt-1, etc.

P 7. *Daulat Rai,* Nazim-i Mashriq, *to Nawwab Sikandar Begam.* Sends the report received from Hazrat Nur Khan from Bheglone, dated 17 *Rabi* I, 1275 AH, reporting that Adil Muhammad Khan with an army of 8,000, comprising both *sawars* and foot-soldiers, fled from *mauza* Rasla where the search operation was conducted by the British forces, crossed river Banyan and encamped on the bank of the river in *mauza* Basraya and Chopra, situating at a distance of 9 *curoh* from Bheglone. Dated 25 *Rabi* I 1275 AH.

P 9. *Hazrat Nur Khan to Daulat Rai,* Nazim-i Mashriq. Informs that day, i.e. 17th *Rab*i I, 1275 AH, Beramchand, *zamindar* of *mauza* Chopra, came and described that the previous day, Adil Muhammad Khan fled from *mauza* Rasla where the search operation was conducted by the British forces, crossed river Banyan and encamped on the bank of the river in *mauza* Basraya and Chopra, situating at a distance of 9 *curoh* from Bheglone. He is carrying an army of 8,000, comprising, both the *sawars* and foot-soldiers. The places of *dak chaukis* have been identified from Bheglone to *mauza* Chopra to bring the news. Whatever the news arrives, would be communicated afterwards. Dated 17 *Rabi* I, 1275 AH.

PP 11-12. *Ghulam Muhammad Khan,* Risaldar, *to Nawwab Sikandar Begam.* Informs that day, i.e. 17 *Rabi* I, 1275 AH, Beramchand, *zamindar* of *mauza* Chopra, came and described that the previous day, Adil Muhammad Khan fled from *mauza* Rasla where the search operation was conducted by the British forces, crossed river Banyan and encamped on the bank of the river in *mauza* Chopra and Basraya, situating at a distance of 9 *curoh* from Bheglone. He is carrying an army of 8,000, comprising both the *sawars* and foot-soldiers. They did not harass the people of the village at all. If happens anything afterwards, would be communicated. Dated 17 *Rabi* I, 1275 AH.

It contains the order that the letter and report may be sent to Lala Paltu Lal, *muhafiz-i daftar-i insha*, for inclusion in the register and keeping in the *daftar*. A copy of the order may be sent to Ghulam Muhammad Khan, *risaldar,* informing him that his letter, dated 17 *Rabi* I, 1275 AH was received on 25 *Rabi* I, 1275 AH in the court. There is no report of further development in the region for the last 8 days. He is directed to report as to what was done to prevent the insurgents. Dated 26 *Rabi* I, 1275 AH.

P 13. *News-Report of Udit, the Informer, an Employee of Brother of Hattey Singh,* Jamadar. Reports that he had gone to *mauza* Piplai to bring the news of the insurgents, where he came to know that Adil Muhammad Khan is in *mauza* Gora and the army of Peshwa is at Lalitpur. The treasure of Muhip Singh Bundela, lying at Rampura, was destroyed by a British officer who came from Malthun. Another British officer arrived from Sagar at *mauza* Dungra, a dwelling place of Bundelas, and devastated it and many a rebels were hanged. Adil Muhammad Khan and other insurgents gathered at Lalitpur. But since the British troops were pursuing them, they fled from there and dispersed. Adil Muhammad Khan, having an army of 8,000 with him, crossed river Banyan at *ghat* Bhatson and encamped in between *mauza* Dalip Pur, a British territory, and *mauza* Basraya. Reports when he arrived at *mauza* Piplai, the Bundelas made him captive for five days suspecting him to be an informer. Dated 17 *Rabi* I 1275 AH.

File No. 310, A
Box No. 16
No. of Documents 24

Insurgency in Gathi and Crossing of River Narmada by Tantia Tope

PP 1-2. Contents

PP 3-4. *Saiyid Imtiaz Ali,* Thanadar, *and Rahim Bakhsh,* Tahsildar *of Jogigarh, to Muhammad Raza Husain.* Informs that before midnight, Shaikh Chand, soldier at *thana* Mahalpur, and Najaf Khan of Chandpura who had gone with Chandulal, *tahsildar* of Garhi Ambapani, came back. They stated that that day the insurgents reached Garhi Ambapani and caused devastation and destruction there. The *thanadar* and *tahsildar* both fled. Thereafter, the insurgents on that very day, i.e. 19th *Rabi* I, 1275 AH, day Thursday, marched from there and encamped at Dehgaon. The two informers, through the routes of mountains, hurriedly reached Bhalaria, situating at a distance of 1/4 *curoh* from Mahalpur. Chunnilal, son of Bhog Chand, *qanungoi* of Mahalpur, told them that the insurgents devastated Mahalpur and arrested the *thanadar* and *tahsildar* and asked him where he was going. They came back. It is not known as to where the insurgents went after capturing Mahalpur. They expressed what they saw or heard. To inform him and the Nawwab was a must which they did. A letter addressed to the Nawwab in the matter is enclosed which may immediately be sent to her. Dated 20 *Rabi* I, 1275 AH.

The letter, contains the order that this along with a copy of the letter, dated 19 *Rabi* I, 1275 AH addressed to Nawwab Sikandar Begam, may be sent to Lalaji Lal, *muhafiz-i daftar-i insha*, for inclusion in the register and keeping in the *daftar*. One copy of the order may be sent to Saiyid Imtiaz Ali, *thanadar,* and Rahim Bakhsh, *tahsildar* of *pargana* Jogigarh, informing that at the moment from amongst the soldiers posted at different *chaukis* and from soldiers of the *jagirdars,* 50 soldiers are sent to be posted at Chandpur. They may also be directed to deal with the insurgents firmly and to prevent them. The reliable informers may be deputed to provide the actual news of the insurgents i.e. about their encampment and about the actual number of their forces everyday and send to the government their suggestions in the matter everyday. Dated 19 *Rabi* I, 1275 AH.

PP 5-6. *Muhammad Raza Husain to Nawwab Sikandar Begam.* Informs about a letter received from the *thanadar* of *pargana* Jogigarh, dated 19 *Rabi* I, 1275 AH, which is regarding the destruction of Garhi Ambapani and Mahalpur by the insurgents along with a letter addressed to her which was immediately sent to her through the post. As they did not write about the number of troops of the insurgents or the place where they encamped, he sent another 5 informers from Kalyakhery to bring the news of the insurgents on a regular basis. A copy of the letter written in reply to the letter of the *thanadar* and *tahsildar* of *pargana* Jogigarh is sent to her and that a contingent of 50 soldiers has been sent to Chandpur from amongst the soldiers posted at *chaukis* and from amongst the soldiers of the *jagirdars*. Since *parganas* of Tal, Jogigarh and Udaipura are in district south of *mahal* Mahalpur while the others are in the *mahals* of district east, he himself is contemplating to go to Jogigarh after receiving the report from there. New soldiers, if needed, would be recruited only after receiving her order to deploy them at the *mahals* of Tal, Jogigarh or in other *mahals*. Hopes for orders in regard to the number of recruits so that he may then approach the peasants and farmers and get them recruited. To manage day-to-day administration, it is a must that the amount of expenses should be provided to them before the end of the month. It is also to be noticed that there are gunners in every *mahal* apart from the new recruits, who would require food. The quantum of food which is1 *anna* per diam would be reasonable. Dated 19 *Rabi* I, 1275 AH.

PP 7-8. *Madho Kishan, Amil, and Muhammad Ali,* Thanadar *of Udaipura, to Muhammad Raza Husain.* Refers to a letter received from the *thanadar* and *tahsildar* of Bamhuri, informing about the devastation of *mauza* Aradmau and Jaitpur by the insurgents, as communicated to him by the *tahsildar* and *thanadar* of Garhi Ambapani through their letters, who sought help by sending troops of the *thana* and *mahal.* Informs that all the forces of the *thana* and *mahal* were sent there, besides 20 soldiers from *mahal* Udaipura to maintain and manage *mahal* Bamhuri and 20 soldiers from amongst the soldiers of *malguzars* were also sent to manage and maintain the *chaukis* of guard of *mahal* Bamhuri.

Informs that day Shaikh Karim Khan and soldiers of the office of purchasing horses for the British government, had gone to Bhilsa for purchasing horses. They came back and said that the British army had reached in the adjoining region of Bhilsa, and from other side the army of the insurgents had taken their position. Now in Bhilsa, except the two armies, nobody was there as all others had fled. Thereafter, he reached Garhi Ambapani where he saw that the insurgent forces were devastating Garhi Ambapani and the houses and *thanas* were being burnt. The insurgent forces would have comprised of 2,000 *sawars* besides the foot-soldiers. In such a situation, the dwellers of the villages of the *mahal* were intending to flee here and there due to the harassment and difficulties. However, they were trying their best to pacify them and requesting them not to panic. Informs that by the grace of Almighty, they would not show any reluctance in carrying their responsibilities. Information to this effect was a must which they did, so that if any instruction is to be given to them they may do so. Besides, a letter for information to the Nawwab about the situation is enclosed which may be sent to the Nawwab by post if he opines so. Dated 19 *Rabi* I, 1275 AH.

PP 9-10. *Daulat Rai,* Nazim-i Mashriq, *to Muhammad Raza Husain.* Refers to his letter, dated 21 *Rabi* I, 1275 AH, informing that the insurgents are in Garhi Ambapani, Mahalpur and Dehgaon. Says, it was 17th of this month when the insurgent forces suddenly entered Jaitpur and Aradmau in the afternoon and stayed for the night there and a report to this effect reached Garhi from Aradmau. Hearing the news, Saiyid 'Abd al-Ali, former *tahsildar,* Chandulal, present *tahsildar* and Shaikh Abd al-Rahman, *thanadar*, took round of the *qasba* the whole night. In the morning, the insurgent forces reached Garhi and devastated it. Saiyid Abd al-Ali, former *tahsildar* Chandulal, present *tahsildar* and Shaikh Abd al-Rahman, *thanadar*, and Shahzad Rai, *thanadar,* informed that the insurgents entered Garhi and

Lala Chaturbhuj, *mutasaddi* in the office of *madar al-maham,* just getting the news of the insurgents entering Garhi left for Raisen. The insurgents followed them and arrested Saiyid 'Abd al-Ali from *mauza* Mondiakhera and the rest of them from *mauza* Dehgaon. All their belongings, whether clothes or weapons were taken away. The following day, Saiyid 'Abd al-Ali and Lala Chaturbhuj were freed. The others were made captive and taken along to *mahal* Bamhuri. From them it was heard that the insurgent forces were 6,000 to 7,000 or even more in strength, and intending to go to Bamhuri and Udaipura to destroy it. Hopes that he too would be careful in his region. The British forces have reached from Bhopal to Raisen that day and would pursue the insurgents. The insurgents have also destroyed *mauza* Dehgaon. It is heard that the insurgents would stay in Bamhuri that day. The insurgents are spreading the rumour, through the *balahis* and the *begars* (forced labour), that the Bhopal army are coming to pursue them. The insurgents are in English *kurtis* and *patloons* and most of them are *wilayatis*. They have more *sawars* than foot-soldiers. Dated 21 *Rabi* I, 1275 AH.

P 11. *Muhammad,* Tahsildar, *to Muhammad Raza Husain.* Refers to his letter, dated 21 *Rabi* I 1275 AH, addressed to the Nawwab which is regarding the insurgency and requests that the same may soon be sent to the Nawwab.

PP 13-14. *Muhammad Mustaqim to Muhammad Raza Husain.* Refers to his letter, dated 21 *Rabi* I, 1275 AH, informing the arrival of insurgent forces in *qasba* Bamhuri and their intention to come to Bareilly, dispersing of the inhabitants, and requesting help him. Says that day, i.e. 22nd of the month, the insurgent forces have marched from Bamhuri and have the intention to pass through this region and Udaipura and to cross river Narmada at the *ghat* situating in *mauza* Patrora, *ilaqa* Udaipura. It is heard that they would go to Hoshangabad. The forces that crossed the river were 6,000 in strength. It is also heard that the remaining forces of the insurgents would cross river Narmada either through this or the other route. If an army comparable to that of the insurgent army is provided to him, the insurgents could easily be suppressed. Dated 23 *Rabi* I, 1275 AH.

PP 15-16. *Muhammad Jamal al-Din,* Madar al-Maham, *to Muhammad Raza Husain.* Refers to his letter, dated 21 *Rabi* I, 1275 AH, informing that the insurgents have reached Mahalpur and nearby *mahal* Chandpura under *pargana nizamat-i junub,* fearing the destruction of *daftar* and *malkhana,* as the roads and lanes are damaged, the movement of bullock carriers is hindered, and elephants to carry the goods of *malkhana* to Bhopal are far away. Informs that the matter, as mentioned, was conveyed to the Nawwab. In reply, an order is received, conveying that half of the force of the *nizamat* under the command of his *naib* may be sent to Chhaner and he himself along with rest of the force may go to Kalyakheri to make arrangement of *rasad* for the British forces who are coming to Bhopal and make the best possible arrangement of *sarbrah-i rasad* and to ensure that the posts which come from Kalyakhery to Bhopal should reach fast and promptly. Also to see that everyday news of all the happenings, particularly the movements of insurgents wherever they go and encamp, should be reported explicitly and elaborately. A *parwana* of the Nawwab in his name to this effect has also been received which is sent to him. Dated 21 *Rabi* I, 1275 AH.

PP 17-18. *Muhammad Raza Husain to Nawwab Sikandar Begam.* Acknowledges the receipt of her *parwana* in reply of his letter, dated 21 *Rabi* I, 1275 AH, desiring full information about the insurgents, i.e. about their encampment and the crime, committed by them. Informs there is no doubt about it that a group of insurgents has assembled in *mahal* Bareilly, in between *pargana* Udaipura and Bari on the bank of river Narmada. This is quite clear from the letter of the *tahsildar* and *thanadar* of Mardanpur. The same has been sent to her. It is also clear that the insurgents, if they found it possible to cross river Narmada, they would cross it. Otherwise, they would spread across all over the *mahal* around the *ghat*. But in the mountaineous range, lying in between *pargana* Bari and other *mahals* situating in district south from the bank of river Narmada upto Bari there are two or three *ghats* from where the bullock carts could easily cross. Otherwise, the rest are the *pagdandis* from where even the *sawars* could cross with great difficulty. If it is possible to make arrangement at all the *ghats* by deputing one or two soldiers at every point, the insurgents could easily be prevented from entering Jogigarh, Tal and and Mardanpur. In this way, *mahal* Sardanda and Chhaner would automatically become safe.

Informs that five days before he had sent 6 informers to bring the news of the march of the insurgents, their encampment and about their actual number. They are yet to come back. However, one of them brought the news of the arrival of insurgents at Bamhuri Kondani, day before yesterday. Information to this effect has been sent along with the letters of the *tahsildars* and *thanadars* of Jogigarh. Informs that day, two other informers are sent to Bareilly. The people of the district are so hopeless that inspite of government orders to destroy the goods of insurgents and inspite of best efforts of the *tahsildar* and *thanadar* to pacify them, they are fleeing from their villages. Now it has been decided to appoint *balahis* from this place upto the encampment of the insurgents. Whatever news they give, the same would be supplied to the government. The army of the General is yet to arrive to guide them about the routes and ways. Dated 23 *Rabi* I, 1275 AH.

P 19. *Saiyid Inayat Ali,* Thanadar *of Mardanpur, to Muhammad Raza Husain.* Sends a letter addressed to the Nawwab informing that the insurgents, after hearing the news of the arrival of the British forces, fled to the mountains known as Mahadev. Requests to send it to the Nawwab after going through it. Dated 24 *Rabi* I, 1275 AH.

PP 21-2. *Muhammad Raza Husain, Nazim-i Junub, to Daulat Rai,* Nazim-i Mashriq. Refers to his letter, dated 21 *Rabi* I, 1275 AH, informing about the insurgency and disturbances created by the insurgents in Garhi Ambapani and Mahalpur, and then their march to Baṃhuri. Says, thereafter, no authentic news about them was heard. The information given by the *tahsildar* and *thanadar* of *pargana* Jogigarh and Bareilly has been sent to the Nawwab. Urges him to give authentic news of the insurgents as it is heard that they have gathered in Garhi Ambapani and Bamhuri along with cannon and magazine. Dated 24 *Rabi* I, 1275 AH.

PP 23-4. *Notification Issued in the Name of Muhammad Raza Husain, Nazim-i* Junub. It is time for all the employees of the government that wherever they are and whatever might they have, they should fight with the insurgents. If they die for the cause of the government, it is good because one day everyone has to leave this world so where is the need to worry and why to become a cause of anger for his master. If he is an officer and makes an excuse, then there is no hope from a soldier except to flee. This is not worth bravery if he is an army officer or he is a *thanadar* or *tahsildar* or *nazim* or *risaldar* or *jamadar* that he should seek ways to free himself if falls prey in the hands of insurgents. It is strange that a man who is a *thanadar* or *tahsildar* or *risaldar* or *jamadar* or *nazim* becomes captive without giving a fight or without killing the enemy. Dated 24 *Rabi* I, 1275 AH.

It contains the order that the above order may be sent to Muhammad Naem Ashraf, his *naib*, directing him to communicate to all the *tahsildars* and *thanadars* of the district that they themselves execute the order and others too should be made aware about it. Dated 25 *Rabi* I, 1275 AH.

P 25. *Saiyid Inayat Ali,* Thanadar *of Mardanpur, to Muhammad Raza Husain.* Sends a letter addressed to the Nawwab informing of 19 cannon fires in Hoshangabad on the occasion of fleeing of the insurgents and arresting of 6 of them and their execution. Requests to send it to the Nawwab after going through it. Dated 25 *Rabi* I 1275 AH.

P 27. *Saiyid Inayat Ali,* Thanadar *of Mardanpur, to Muhammad Raza Husain.* Sends a letter addressed to the Nawwab informing of the well-being in *pargana* Mardanpur till the writing of this letter and fleeing of the insurgents to the mountain known as Mahadev. Requests to send it to the Nawwab after going through it. Dated 25 *Rabi* I, 1275 AH.

P 29. *Muhammad Ali,* Muhtamim Chaukiyat, *to Muhammad Raza Husain.* Informs that although *ghatbandi* (blockading of river passes) has been done but it is not as effective as it should have been as on 21 *Rabi* I, 1275 AH, day Monday, the insurgent forces which were 6,000 to 7,000 in number, some say they were 10, 000 inclusive of both cavalry and artillery, crossed from the *ghat,* situating in *mauza* Patrora, *ilaqa* Udaipura, and *mauza* Sandia situating on the bank of river Narmada falling under the British territory which was devastated and looted. All the employees and inhabitants, due to fear, fled to the forests and mountains. They arrested Saiyid Abbas Ali, *thanadar* of Bamhuri, and took him along and after two-three days he managed to flee from captivity. The army of Adil Muhammad Khan is behind them. Informs that his place of duty is nearby to that, but by his blessings there is peace in the region. Dated 23 *Rabi* I, 1275 AH.

P 31. Thanadar *to Muhammad Raza Husain.* Sends a letter, addressed to the Nawwab informing of the arrival of insurgents and then their flight across river Narmada. The letter would make everything clear. Says he is busy in providing *rasad* to the army. Dated 25 *Rabi* I, 1275 AH.

PP 33-4. *Rahim Bakhsh and Saiyid Imtiaz Ali to Muhammad Raza Husain.* Informs of the letter received from Lala Chandulal, *tahsildar*, Garhi Ambapani, dated 7 *Rabi* II, 1275 AH, along with the letters of Harsahai, *tahsildar*, and Saiyid Abbas Ali, *thanadar, pargana* Bamhuri, informing to take precaution and remain alert as the army of Adil Muhammad Khan, rebel of two governments, has marched from Chehla and is intending to launch attack upon *qasba* Bamhuri that day or the next day. The same is presented to him for his perusal. Further adds that, as ordered by the Nawwab, the arrangement of *dak* has been made upto Bhopal. Dated 8 *Rabi* II, 1275 AH.

P 35. *Lala Chandulal,* Tahsildar *of Garhi Ambapani, to Shaikh Rahim Bakhsh,* Tahsildar*, and Saiyid Imtiaz Ali,* Thanadar *of* Pargana *Jogigarh*. Refers to a letter, received from Harsahai, *tahsildar* and Saiyid Abbas Ali, *thanadar* of Bamhuri, dated 6 *Rabi* II, 1275 AH, informing that from the letter of *naib patwari* of Ushapur, it has come to the notice that Gadmu Patel, who was in the army of Adil Muhammad Khan and knew the condition of the people of Pura Guna said to him that, that day or the next day, an army of 6,000 to 7,000 under Adil Muhammad Khan would launch attack on Bamhuri. The said army has been divided into two groups-one group would come through the *ghati* of Balwali and the other group would come via Shahgarh. It is a must to take precaution and block the river *ghats* and roads and remain alert. As mentioned in the letter, it is desired to act accordingly. Dated 7 *Rabi* II, 1275 AH.

P 37. *Letter of Lala Harsahai,* Tahsildar, *and Saiyid Abbas Ali*, Thanadar. Refers to a letter received from *naib patwari*, *mauza* Ushapur, situated in this *pargana* informing that Gadmu of this region who was well aware of the condition of the people of Pura Guna and about the army of Adil Muhammad Khan told him to be aware as 8,000 or 7,000 forces of Adil Muhammad

Khan would attack Bamhuri on that very day or the next day. The army would be divided into two groups; one group would come through the *ghati* of Balwali and the other group via Shahgarh. He said that he came from the army to communicate to them and to remain alert and aware. He said so, and then returned. It is in the interest of the government that one should remain alert. Thus, it is a must for them to be aware and make arrangement on the roads, posts and *ghats*. Dated 7 *Rabi* II, 1275 AH.

P 39. *Order of Nawwab Sikandar Begam to Muhammad Raza Husain.* The letter may be sent to Paltu Lal, *muhafiz-i daftar-i insha*, for inclusion in the register and keeping in the *daftar*. A copy of the order may be sent to Muhammad Raza Husain, *nazim-i junub*, through *madar al-maham,* directing him to send Nazar Muhammad Khan of the *risala* Jang Baz Khan, *risaldar,* to bring the news of *pargana* Bareilly. It is a must for him that only authentic news of *pargana* Bareilly and other *parganas* of district south should be reported. What is the use of sending news of *pargana* Bamhuri, situating in district east, based on hearsay? It is a must that only authentic news of *parganas* of district *junub* should be reported. Dated 3 *Rabi* II, 1275 AH.

P 41. *Shaikh Khuda Bakhsh, Deputy* Thanadar *of Udaipura, to Muhammad Raza Husain.* Reports that night Amanat Ali, *sawar* deployed at *chauki* Dandah, *mauza* Bamhuri under this *thana*, came and stated that he had gone to *mauza* Chhaner for inspection where he heard that some *sawars* of the insurgent forces who had gone to the other side of Narmada fought a battle there. Two soldiers were sent to Hyder Muhammad Khan, *jamadar*, to know the reality. They came back with a letter in Hindi from the *jamadar* in his name. The *jamadar* informed him that the *sawars* were taking rounds along with him. Someone saw them, who suspected them and reported the same which spread to other places. Dated 11 *Rabi* II, 1275 AH.

P 43. *Shaikh Khuda Bakhsh, Deputy* Thanadar *of Udaipura, to Muhammad Raza Husain.* Informs that as reported by Amanat Ali, *sawar* deputed at *chauki* Bamhuri, who had gone to Chhaner and returned to Udaipura told that the insurgent forces crossed river Narmada and fought a battle in *mauza* Patrora. The said *sawar*, although did not see this from his own eyes, but reported as he heard from Chhaner that five *sawars* went to Patrora to bring the booty. Dated 10 *Rabi* II, 1275 AH.

P 45. *Karam Ali Husain, Thanadar of* Pargana *Bari, to Muhammad Raza Husain.* Informs of a letter of Raja Mardan Shah, dated 5 *Rabi* II, 1275 AH, in reply to his letter, whom he asked about the arrival of insurgent forces and Adil Muhammad Khan. The Raja in his letter has written that, the previous day he had sent his men to bring the news of insurgents and that day he informed that Adil Muhammad Khan along with an army of 8,000 was at Bagrod, *ilaqa* Bhilsa, situating in between Rahatgarh and Gayaraspur and was in distress. Information to this effect was a must which he did as per the letter of Lala Sahab Chandulal. Dated 6 *Rabi* II, 1275 AH.

P 47. *Karam Ali Husain*, Thanadar *of* Pargana *Bari, to Muhammad Raza Husain.* Informs of a letter of Mustqim Khan, *thanadar* of Bareilly, dated 3 *Rabi* II, 1275 AH, in reply to his letter whom he asked about the arrival of insurgent forces and Adil Muhammad Khan. The *thanadar* informed that there was no news of the arrival of Adil Muhammad Khan or any other insurgent in the region. Information to this effect was a must which he did. Dated 6 *Rabi* II, 1275 AH.

PP 49-50. *Rahim Bakhsh,* Tahsildar, *to Muhammad Raza Husain.* Refers to his letter from Zarapur, dated 3 *Rabi* II, 1275 AH, informing about the arrival of Adil Muhammad Khan, the rebel of the two governments, in Garhi Ambapani and the instructions to deal with him firmly and to report the news in detail. Says he at that very moment sent two soldiers with his letter to the *thanadar* and *tahsildar* of Mahalpur to inquire into the matter. Informs that the *tahsildar* and Shahzad Rai, *thanadar*, wrote to him on the basis of the report of the *thanadar,* Garhi Ambapani and also on the basis of the report of informers that no insurgent was found anywhere in the areas of Garhi, Basodah and Bagroda. If they are on the hills or in the forests, it is only known to God. The letter of the *thanadar* and *tahsildar* is sent to him, as it would make things clear. Dated 6 *Rabi* II, 1275 AH.

File No. 310, B
Box aNo. 16
No. of Documents 26

P 51. *Rahim Bakhsh,* Tahsildar, *to the* Tahsildar, Thanadar *and Lala Shahzad Rai.* Informs that, as directed by Muhammad Raza Husain, *nazim-i junub,* the accurate report about the encampment of Adil Muhammad Khan and the number of his armymen may be sent to him so that the same may be sent to the *nazim-i junub*. The *nazim* who is in Mirzapur to make arrangement for the British army would communicate them about it. Dated 24 *Rabi* II, 1275 AH.

P 52. *The* Tahsildar, Thanadar *and Shahzad Rai to Rahim Bakhsh*. Refer to his letter and inform that, as described by the informers and as written by the *thanadar* of Garhi, no insurgent is found anywhere in the vicinity of Garhi, Basodah and Bagrod. There is no information if they are hiding in the hills. Further, the informers have been sent to other regions. The news received from there would be communicated accordingly. Dated 5 *Rabi* II, 1275 AH.

P 53. *Shaikh Khuda Bakhsh to Muhammad Raza Husain, Nazim-i Junub.* Informs that presently, there is no insurgent in this region. But it is heard that on 23 *Rabi* I, 1275 AH, about 12,000 forces comprising of both *sawars* and foot-soldiers were in *mauza* Chhuwarah and in the morning they marched to *mauza* Patrora falling under this *thana*, crossed river Narmada and went to the south. Village Chhuwarah and other villages were totally devastated. The dwellers of this region like the dwellers of Udaipura and Chhaner, due to fear, were fleeing to other regions. The insurgents destroyed the houses of the mahajans with whom the dwellers hid their *nishan zar-i mal* and their houses. Some dwellers destroyed those houses which were vacant. An investigation is under process. Dated 1 *Rabi* II, 1275 AH.

P 55. *Saiyid Imtiaz Ali,* Thanadar, *and Rahim Bakhsh,* Tahsildar *of Jogigarh, to Muhammad Raza Husain, Nazim-i Junub.* Informs that day Mansukh, *kahar* of *mauza* Sangal, *pargana* Mahalpur, sent by Moti Ram, *mustajir* of Sangal, to *mauza* Siwanni which is under this *pargana* amd under his *mustajari*. He came back and stated that, that night two soldiers from Bhilsa came to the house of Bijay Ram Seth, a dweller of Sangal, and said that the army of 12,000 of Peshwa came to Bhilsa. Harcharan Tirath was there. They did not destroy Bhilsa but demanded *sarbrah.* The officer of Bhilsa provided them *sarbrah-i rasad,* as demanded by them. He suggested him that he too should go to Bhilsa to provide *sarbrah-i rasad* to them. So the said Seth, at that very moment in the night, left for Bhilsa. Patel of Sangal has informed him of the matter. Dated 14 *Rabi* II, 1275 AH.

P 57. *Raja Mardan, Bariwala, to Muhammad Raza Husain, Nazim-i Junub.* Refers to his letter, dated 3 *Rabi* II, that Adil Muhammad Khan along with his forces is roaming around Garhi Ambapani and Bari, etc. therefore, he should be ready to deal with them along with his forces and inform him about the details in this regard. It is informed that it is an authentic news that Adil Muhammad Khan along with his forces did not yet arrive in Garhi or Solwani or Siwans or Bari. However, with the receipt of this letter, he immediately sent soldiers to all those places. The news coming thereafter would be communicated and he too would make efforts to deal with the insurgents. As half of the forces or even more than that were sent on 3rd of this month with Sa'adat Khan, *jamadar* to Kalyakheri and only 25 soldier are left with him, the soldiers which are at Kalyakheri may be returned to him. Dated 4 *Rabi* II, 1275 AH.

P 59. *Madho Kishan, Amil of Udaipura, to Muhammad Raza Husain*. Informs that, as reported by Durga Prasad, *thanadar* of Ghairatganj through his letter, that the insurgent forces were at Bagrod and Khurai, he deployed 2-3 informers at different places to bring the news. It is heard that insurgents are at *ghat* Malthun. Dated 6 *Rabi* II, 1275 AH.

P 61. *Karam Ali Husain, Deputy* Thanadar *of* Pargana *Bari, to Muhammad Raza Husain*. Sends the letter received from Raja Mardan, *jagirdar* of *pargana* Bari. Hopes that everything will become clear about the movement of insurgent forces after going through it. Dated 8 *Rabi* II, 1275 AH.

P 63. *Raja Mardan To Karam Ali Husain,* Thanadar *of Pargana Bari*. Informs that Afzal Khan, soldier, was sent to Bamhuri Solawani to bring the news about the insurgents. He came back and stated as told him the *tahsildar* of Bamhuri, that 10, 000 to 12,000 forces are at Khorai Khimlasa. Previous day, the British were in the camp of Solwani. It is heard that the British, who are coming from Sagar, would go to Solwani. Dated 7 *Rabi* II, 1275 AH.

P 65. *Nanak Chand,* Tahsildar, *to Muhammad Raza Husain*. Sends the letter received from Raja Mardan, dated 25 *Rabi* I. It is clear that the insurgent forces are at *mauza* Ubardha, *ilaqa* Hoshangabad, and some forces are at Garhi. Dated 26 *Rabi* I, 1275 AH.

P 67. *Raja Mardan to Nanak Chand,* Tahsildar *of Pargana Bari*. Informs that the forces from Bamhuri via Utiya Chapara crossed at the *ghat* Patrora and Kiloghan. Some forces are at Garhi, and as heard that they too would cross Narmada. The forces which crossed

Narmada have reached Umardha that night. However, the dwellers of Bamhuri, Jamghar and Utiya, due to fear, have fled towards the mountains. Dated 24 *Rabi* I, 1275 AH.

P 69. Tahsildar *to Muhammad Raza Husain*. Refers to the letter of the *tahsildar* of *pargana* Bamhuri, dated 15 *Rabi* II, informing that 2,500 insurgent forces including both *sawars* and foot-soldiers and one elephant have arrived in *mauza* Pura Guna, *ilaqa* Bhilsa, while the other forces are in the mountains of Barkhera Bagda in the vicinity of Muhammad Garh, Basodah. It is must to have a good arrangement under his region for not allowing the insurgents to pass from there. A letter addressed to the Nawwab is enclosed herewith which may be sent after going through it. Dated 15 *Rabi* II, 1275 AH.

P 71. *Letter of Muhammad Raza Husain to the Commanding Officer of the British Forces Led by General Patrick at Hoshangabad*. Refers to the letter of Shaikh Muhammad Lal, *tahsildar* of *pargana* Bamhuri, dated 15 *Rabi* II, in reference to the letter of the *tahsildar* of *pargana* Bamhuri, informing that about 500 *sawar* and foot-soldiers with one elephant are at Pura Guna, *ilaqa* Bhilsa, while some other forces are in the mountains of Barkhera adjoining to Muhammad Garh Basodah. A copy of the letter is sent to him as directed by General Patrick when he was leaving Hoshangabad that the Major who is in Hoshangabad with some British and Indian forces should be informed as and when he receives any information about the insurgent forces entering Bhopal. The news, as sent, seems accurate as per the reports of the informers. The region of Pura Guna and the mountains of Muhammad Garh, Basodah are under the territory of Bhopal government. Dated 23 November 1858/16 *Rabi* II, 1275 AH.

P 73. *Muhammad Raza Husain to Nawwab Sikandar Begam*. Informs that night he received a letter of Shaikh

Muhammad Lal, *tahsildar* of *pargana* Bareilly, dated 15 *Rabi* II, in reference to the letter of the *tahsildar* of *pargana* Bamhuri informing that about 2,500 insurgent forces, both *sawars* and foot-soldiers with one elephant are at Pura Guna, *ilaqa* Bhilsa, besides another group of insurgent forces which is in the mountains adjoining Barkhera and in the vicinity of Muhammad Garh, Basodah. The same was sent to her at the very moment through the post and everything will become clear after going through it. A copy of the letter of the *tahsildar* is sent to General Patrick, the Commanding Officer of the British forces, encamping at Hoshangabad, who had said to him while leaving Hoshangabad that whenever was news of the coming of insurgents in thc tcrritory of Bhopal it should be sent to the Commanding Officer of the British and the Indian forces encamping at Hoshangabad.

P 75. *Daulat Rai,* Nazim-i Mashriq, *to Muhammad Raza Husain*. Informs as stated by Lala Shahzad Rai, *thanadar* of Mahalpur, that around 1,000 insurgent forces including both *sawars* and foot-soldiers are encampimg at Pura Guna and they intend to go to the other side of Narmada via Budaganj, *Pargana* Ghairatganj, and they might cross Narmada in between *ilaqa* Ganj and Solwani via Udaipura and Bareilly. Requests him to make arrangement on the *ghats* on the river Narmada and kill or arrest the insurgents. The insurgents should not be allowed to cross Narmada at any cost. The information has also been sent to the Nawwab. Dated 17 *Rabi* II, 1275 AH.

P 77. *Muhammad Raza Husain to General Patrick, the Commanding Officer of the British Forces*. Refers to his letter, dated 23 November 1858, along with the letter of Shaikh Muhammad Lal, *tahsildar* of *pargana* Bareilly, informing about the presence of insurgents at Pura Guna, *ilaqa* Bhilsa, situating at a distance of three *curoh* from Ambapani under the State of Bhopal. Informs that day he received a letter from Daulat Rai, dated 17 *Rabi* II, informing about the intention of the insurgents encamping at Pura Guna to cross the river Narmada. The same is sent to him for information. Dated 24 November 1858/18 *Rabi* II, 1275 AH.

P 79. *Muhammad Raza Husain to Nawwab Sikandar Begam*. Refers to a letter of Daulat Rai, dated 17 *Rabi* II, informing about the intention of the insurgents who are around 1,000 in strength, inclusive of both *sawars* and foot-soldiers, encamping at Pura Guna to cross the river Narmada from places in Bareilly and Udaipura and also informing that the information has also been communicated to the government. Informs that he immediately informed the *tahsildar* and *thanadar* of *pargana* Bareilly and Udaipura to pursue and kill or make the insurgents captive, having with them 25 *sawars* deployed at Chhaner, and information to this affect has been given to the Commanding Officer of the forces under the company of General Patrick, encamping at Hoshangabad, and a copy of that letter is sent to her for information. Dated 18 *Rabi* II, 1275 AH.

P 81. *Jang Yar Khan,* Risaldar, *to Muhammad Raza Husain*. Refers to the royal order, dated 3 *Rabi* II, directing that Nazar Muhammad Khan of *risala* Jang Yar Khan, *risaldar,* may be sent to *pargana* Bareilly to bring news. He should only report such news which is seen by him in *pargana* Bareilly and other *mahals* of district south. There is no use of reporting news of *pargana* Bamhuri on hearsay basis. Informs that Nazar Muhammad Khan did not yet arrive there nor knew where he is to communicate him the royal order to execute it. Requests that wherever he is, he may be communicated about the royal order through the *thanadar* of that *mahal*. He himself would implement the royal order. If Nazar Muhammad Khan arrives there, he would be communicated about the royal order. Dated 19 *Rabi* II, 1275 AH.

P 83. *Orders of Nawwab Sikandar Begam as Recorded in the Letter of Muhammad Raza Husain*. The Nawwab orders that the letter may be sent to Paltu Lal, *muhafiz-i daftar-i insha*, for inclusion in the register and keeping in the *daftar*. A copy of the order may be sent to Muhammad Raza Husain, communicating that whenever there is an authentic news about the insurgents, only such news may be sent to the Officer Commander at Hoshangabad as per the order of General Patrick. Any unauthentic news should not be sent to him at any cost. Dated 17 *Rabi* II, 1275 AH.

P 85. *Letter of Muhammad Mughal,* Amil *of Bareilly, to the Government*. Informs that some peons of Jamghar came there who were called to *mahal* Bamhuri as directed by the *tahsildar* and *thanadar* of Bamhuri.

P 87. *Nanak Chand,* Tahsildar, *to Muhammad Raza Husain*. Informs about the letter of Muhammad Mustaqim Khan, *thanadar* of Bareilly, in the name of Saiyid Khan, Ali Husain, Deputy *Thanadar*, dated 15 *Rabi* II, communicating that from the letter of Lala Harsahai, *tahsildar* of Bamhuri, addressed to Muhammad Mughal, *tahsildar* of Bareilly, it is clear that 2,500 insurgent forces, both *sawars* and foot-soldiers with one elephant are in Pura Guna, *ilaqa* Bhilsa. Other group of insurgents is in the mountains of *mauza* Barkhera, *ilaqa* Muhammad Garh. The same is sent to him. Dated 17 *Rabi* II, 1275 AH.

P 89. *Diyanat Khan, Dafadar, and Nazar Muhammad Khan to Muhammad Raza Husain*. Informs that, as ordered, he went to Chhaner to take a round of Audhora and from Chhaner to Audhora. Besides, 25 *sawars* under Haider Khan, *jamadar, risala* Jang Yar Khan, *risaldar,* were sent to Channer to take a round there. Everyday news of the insurgents from all corners with details of *ghats* on river Narmada reach which are sent to him. Today, i.e. on 15 *Rabi* II, Gulsher Khan, a *sawar*, has come with a royal order for taking rounds. Abbas

Ali, the *thanadar* has sent him a letter and also to the *risaldar,* requesting to come with *sawars* as Nathuram Chaudhary of *mauza* Sangpuri has informed that 1,500 insurgent forces are in the valley of *mauza* Sawakhera. But to enter in an area falling in other *nizamat* is a matter of concern while the government has deployed *sawars* in district south to take rounds of the area. Request for orders in this regard.

P 91. *Shaikh Khuda Bakhsh, Deputy* Thanadar *of Udaipura, to Muhammad Raza Husain.* Informs that there is calm in the *pargana.* Informs about a letter of Lala Chandulal, *tahsildar* of Garhi Ambapani to Lala Madho Kishan, *tahsildar* of Udaipura, informing that a large number of insurgent forces are at Pura Guna. Says, to know the reality, he sent 5 *sawars* and 4-5 soldiers of the *thana,* besides the informers. They did not yet come back. The information received from them would be communicated. Dated 16 *Rabi* II, 1275 AH.

P 93. *Shaikh Khuda Baksh, Deputy* Thanadar *of Udaipura, to Muhammad Raza Husain.* Refers to his letter, dated 13 *Rabi* II, informing that it is heard that a group of insurgents crossed river Narmada and inspite of the instructions, he did not report anything, and directing that with the receipt of the letter, he himself should go to inquire about the number of *sawars,* the insurgents and the passage crossed by them and communicate the details to him, otherwise it will not be good for him. Informs that in this *pargana,* the soldiers and *sawars* are deployed at Chhaner who took regular rounds upto Deori, Bareilly, Bhopal and Solwani but found no sign of insurgents anywhere. Dated 16 *Rabi* II, 1275 AH.

PP 95-6. *Nanak Chand,* Tahsildar *of* Pargana *Bari, to Muhammad Raza Husain.* Refers to a letter received from Gobind, *harkara,* posted at Bamhuri to bring the news of insurgent forces, and informing that the *tahsildar* and *thanadar* of Bamhuri with their soldiers and *sawars* went to fight with the insurgents in the valley of Sewagarh. They arrested three insurgents, killed one and another one was wounded and three horses of the insurgents were also captured. The soldiers then went on the hills to make arrangement. Says as it is not clear that where Sewagarh is situated, therefore, an inquiry is being made into the matter. A report will be sent thereafter. Dated 18 *Rabi* II, 1275 AH.

PP 97-8. *Shaikh Khuda Bakhsh, Deputy* Thanadar *of Udaipura, to Muhammad Raza Husain*. Refers to a letter received from Shaikh Sultan, soldier of *mahal* Udaipura, besides the letter of Amrit Lal, *patwari* of *mauza* Chhaṇer, addressed to Lala Madho Kishan, *tahsildar,* informing that the insurgent forces have reached near Garhi Ambapani as mentioned in a letter arrived from Bari to the shop of Seth Nandram. Says, the matter was further enquired from the *dafadar* and *sawar*, posted at Chhaner. Besides, two *sawars* were also sent to Bamhuri. Amanat Ali and Hamid Ali, *sawars,* posted at *chauki* Danda, *mauza* Bamhuri have reported that everything is well. Although some insurgents are at Khorai. Anything, if heard further, would be communicated. A letter in this respect, along with the translation of that letter, has been sent to the government. Dated 13 *Rabi* II, 1275 AH.

P 99. *Nanak Chand,* Tahsildar *of* Pargana *Bari, to Muhammad Raza Husain.* Sends the two letters brought by Gobind, *harkara*, besides the letter of Raja Mardan of Bariwala, dated 19 *Rabi* II. All three letters tell the story that the insurgent forces are in *Pargana* Bari and that another group of insurgents has crossed the river Narmada. Dated 20 *Rabi* II, 1275 AH.

File No. 310, C
Box No. 16
No. of Documents 25

P 101. *Madho Kishan,* Amil *of Udaipura, to Muhammad Raza Husain*. Informs that on 17 *Rabi* II, 1275 AH, about 1,000 foot-soldiers and 500 *sawars* of the insurgents who were at Sewagarh valley, *ilaqa* Ghairatganj, crossed Narmada from *ghat* Patrora falling on the route of *thana*

Chhaner. Hearing the news, Khuda Bakhsh, *thanadar*, along with 25 soldiers pursued them and he himself remained alert with the remaining forces at the *mahal* and also pacified the dwellers. The insurgent forces, however, made 16 soldiers and 8 horses captive. The latter belonged to the *sawars* of *risala* Jangyar Khan, *risaldar*, who were encamping at Chhaner. Further informs of a letter of Durga Prasad, *thanadar* of Ganj, informing that as heard from an informer that about 2, 000 insurgent forces are at Pura Guna and some forces are at Khorai intending to cross the river Narmada. Thus, in accordance to the information of the *thanadar,* an arrangement has been made. Other information, as received would be communicated. Invites attention towards the less number of soldiers there and as the route of insurgent forces falls under this region it would be good if some forces with one or two canon are sent to Chhaner. Dated 17 *Rabi* II, 1275 AH.

P 103. *Muhammad Akbar Ali,* Tahsildar, *to Muhammad Raza Husain*. Informs that day, the British forces with 1,500 Turk *sawars* have marched but the destination where they have gone is not known. If information is received, it will be communicated. Dated 18 *Rabi* II, 1275 AH.

P 105. *Karam Ali Husain to Muhammad Raza Husain.* Informs about the letter of Muhammad Amir Khan, *thanadar*, dated 25 November 1881, informing that the insurgent forces crossed river Narmada at Patrora *ghat* in the Hoshangabad region. The same is sent to him. Dated 19 *Rabi* II, 1275 AH.

P 107. *Muhammad Ali,* Thanadar, *to Muhammad Raza Husain*. Refers to his earlier letter informing that the insurgent forces are in the hills of Barkhera, Pura Guna and Muhammad Garh Basodah.

P 109. *Diyanat Khan and Nazar Muhammad Khan to Muhammad Raza Husain.* Inform that day, i.e. 25 *Rabi* II, from the letter of *thanadar* of Ghairatganj, it came to notice that the insurgent forces have gone to Basodah. But from the report of the *thanadar* of Bamhuri it came to the notice that on the day of market in Bamhuri, people who came from the side of Basodah and Garhi Ambapani, when asked, did not say anything about the insurgent forces.

P 111. *Diyanat Khan, Dafadar and Nazar Muhammad Khan to Muhammad Raza Husain.* Inform that day, i.e. 23rd *Rabi* II, it is clear from the letter of Chandulal, *tahsildar* of Garhi Ambapani, and Madho Kishan, *tahsildar* of *mahal* Udaipura, that around 6,000 *sawars* of the insurgent forces have reached near Garhi Ambapani who are ready to take on battle and it is a must for tham that they should be ready for the battle. Inform that since the day the insurgent forces passed through this region and reached the other side of Narmada, they are fully ready and alert, day and night. It is also clear that the intention of the rest of the insurgent forces is to cross the river Narmada.

P 113. *Karam Ali Husain to Muhammad Raza Husain.* Informs about the order of the *nizamat-i junub,* issued in accordance to the royal *parwana,* dated 15 *Rabi* II, directing that one copy each of the order may be sent to all the *thanadars* of the district, instructing them that except the soldiers posted at *chaukis* enroute to the English posts, all other soldiers of the *chaukis* should assemble at the *thana* so that whenever the insurgents enter the region they should be dealt with firmly and they are to be killed. Dated 17 *Rabi* II, 1275 AH.

P 115. *Nanak Chand,* Tahsildar, *to Muhammad Raza Husain.* Refers to the letter of Lala Ramden, *peshdast wakil*, dated 24 *Ziqada* 1275, instructing that whatever news is sent to the government it should be first verified. Assures that the order would be taken into consideration, in letter and spirit. Dated 14 *Rabi* II, 1275 AH.

P 117. *Nanak Chand,* Tahsildar, *to Muhammad Raza Husain.* Informs that the previous day, i.e. 18th *Rabi* II,

125, he received a letter of Muhammad Amir Khan, *thanadar* of Hoshangabad, addressed to Karam Ali Husain, Deputy *Thanadar* of Bari, informing that on 24 November 1858, the insurgent forces crossed Narmada at *ghat* Patrora, situating in the said *mauza* and arrived in *mauza* Sandiya. The same is sent to him for information. Dated 19 *Rabi* II, 1275 AH.

P 119. *Karam Ali Husain to Muhammad Raza Husain.* Refers to the royal order, dated 20 *Rabi* I, as recorded in the letter of the *nizamat*, that wherever the royal forces are, no other force would be provided; to recruit soldiers from the dwellers; and request to meet the necessity of food for the soldiers; instructions for these have been sent to the *amils* and *thanadars* by the government. It is also instructed several times that if the insurgent forces are more in number that can not be dealt with, the dwellers should be kept ready and alert. There is no information, what has been destroyed of the dwellers from the hands of insurgents. Assures that the royal order would be taken into notice, in letter and spirit. Dated 7 *Rabi* II, 1275.

P 123. *Nanak Chand,* Tahsildar, *to Muhammad Raza Husain*. Sends a letter to the government in reply to the notification issued from the office of the government that relates to make an effort to arrest Tantiya Tope and Rao Sahab, nephew of Nana Peshwa. Hopes that the letter would be sent to the Nawwab. Dated 19 *Rabi* II, 1275 AH.

P 125. *Karam Ali Husain, Deputy* Thanadar, *to Muhammad Raza Husain*. Informs about the receipt of the letter of Gobind, *harkara*, in the name of Nanak Chand, *tahsildar* of *pargana* Bari, who is posted in Bamhuri to report about the insurgent forces, dated 7 *Rabi* I. Informs that the insurgent forces are in the hills and the British forces are arriving soon in *mahal* Bareilly and other *mahals*; *rasad* is being sent to the British forces; and 1,000 soldiers of the government with 4 cannon have gone to Garhi. The movement of insurgents is so much that soldiers are ready everytime. He should take care of his *mahal.* The report is worthless as the *harkara* has not mentioned anything about the insurgents as to where in the mountains they station, although he is all the time busy in making arrangements against the insurgents. To inform him in the matter was a necessity which he did. Dated 10 *Rabi* II, 1275 AH.

P 127. *Karam Ali Husain to Muhammad Raza Husain.* Refers to the notification issued by the government, dated 24 *Rabi* I, in the name of the *Nazim* of district South which contains the order for execution. As per the notification, all officials and soldiers of the government would fight with the insurgents with all might. If someone losses his life for the cause of the government, it is good. But it is sad that the officials at the time of fighting flee and none of the insurgents is killed. Informs that, as per the order of the government, information as per the notification has been given to Annu Khan, *jamadar*, and soldiers of the *mahal.* Their signatures have been obtained assuring that they would follow the order.

P 129. *Orders Issued to Muhammad Raza Husain.* There is no need to wait for a while for her order or that of a British, but he should do whatever he may deem suitable and what the time demands in regard to kill and suppress the insurgents and the miscreants. The only thing is that the information should be sent to her. If there will be any delay or negligence in dealing with them, it will not be good for him.

P 131. *Saiyid Inayat Ali,* Thanadar *of Mardanpur, to Muhammad Raza Husain.* Informs about the receipt of a copy of letter of Qasim al-Din Ahmad, *tahsildar* of *pargana* Harda, district Hoshangabad, through a letter of Saiyid Inayat Ali, *thanadar* of *pargana* Bharonda which is regarding the victory of British forces over the insurgent forces. The same is sent to him to inform the *thanadars* of Mardanpur and Bharonda for informing the employees. Dated 1 *Jumada* I, 1275 AH.

PP 133-4, 139-40 & 161-2. *Letter of Qasim al-Din Ahmad Khan,* Tahsildar *of Harda, Dated 26 November 1858*. To the same effect as the foregoing.

P 135. *Letter of Saiyid Inayat Ali,* Thanadar *of* Pargana *Bharonda, to the* Thanadar *of Mardanpur*. Refers to a letter received from the *tahsildar* of *pargana* Harda sent by Ahmad Allah Khan, *thanadar* of Chhaner, which is in regard to the victory of British forces over the insurgent forces for informing the Nawwab. Says firstly, it was sent for calligraphy, and after that it will be communicated to the *thanadar* of Mardanpur so that others may come to know of the news of victory. Dated 30 *Rabi* II, 1275 AH.

P 137. *Saiyid Inayat Ali to Muhammad Raza Husain*. Informs about the receipt of a letter from Harda, district Hoshangabad, informing of the victory of the British forces and defeat of the insurgent forces. According to that a letter is sent to the Nawwab and copy of that is sent to *thanadar* of Mardanpur and also to him. Dated 30 *Rabi* II, 1275 AH.

P 141. *Karam Ali Husain to Muhammad Raza Husain*. Informs that day, at noon, 16 soldiers along with *jamadar* went to Ramgarh to take care of *danda*[19] of the *pargana*. Dated 21 *Rabi* II, 1275 AH.

P 143. *Saiyid Inayat Ali,* Thanadar *of Mardanpur, to Muhammad Raza Husain.* Informs about the receipt of the letter of Saiyid Karam Ali Husain, Deputy *Thanadar* of Bari, informing that Raja Mardan, *jagirdar* of villages in *pargana* Bari, has informed that on the 16th of the month, around 1,000 or 1,200 *sawars* and foot-soldiers of the insurgent forces encamped at Sewaghati and on 17th of the month, 200 *sawars* via Chhaner and the rest via *mauza* Songa crossed the river Narmada at *ghat*

19. Boundary line.

Patrora. From Bhilsawala, who is encamping at Bari, it is heard that the insurgents who were at Pura Guna came to this side. In Bhilsa, it was also heard that around 4,000 forces wherein Adil Muhammad Khan was also present, arrived at Manik chowk, adjoining Dondada. Says an informer has been sent to Hoshangabad to know whether they crossed *ghat* Patrora on Narmada or at some other place, and he himself is alert along with his forces. Dated 21 *Rabi* II, 1275 AH.

P 145. *Orders of Nawwab Sikandar Begam as Recorded in the Letter of Daulat Rai.* Orders that the letter may be sent to Paltu Lal, *muhafiz-i daftar-i insha*, for inclusion and keeping in the *daftar.* A copy of the order may be sent to Daulat Rai, communicating that the insurgents have destroyed the dwellers and he is writing for the safety of the dwellers. Skirmishes are going on with the insurgents which is clearly a matter of befooling her. It is not the time to take care of the dwellers but to attack the insurgents and suppress them. The forces which are at Raisen should be kept ready and attack the insurgents at the time, when they are at rest and the dwellers should be ready to destroy the forces of insurgents. If it is not possible for him then Wazir Khan, *qila'dar*, should reach there with the forces which are at Siwans. Dated 20 *Rabi* II, 1275 AH.

P 147. ...*to Muhammad Raza Husain.* Refers to the royal order as recorded in his letter and the order of Hazrat Nur Khan, *amil* of Bheglone, dated 21 *Zilhijja*, that the moment Adil Muhammad Khan and Aqil Muhammad Khan pass through the territory of Bhopal State, there should not be any reluctance in dealing with them and to assassinate them. Assures that whenever Adil Muhammad Khan and Aqil Muhammad Khan would enter in the region, they would be dealt as per the royal order. Dated 16 *Rabi* II, 1275 AH.

P 149. *Nanak Chand,* Tahsildar, *to Muhammad Raza Husain.* Refers to the royal order, dated 13 *Rabi* II, as recorded in the letter of Bhawani Prasad, *wakil*, instructing to capture bullocks of *banjaras* as *sarbarah* for the British army. Assures that the royal order would be executed in letter and spirit. Dated 24 *Rabi* II, 1275 AH.

File No. 310, D
Box No. 16
No. of Documents 16

P 151 & 153. *Nanak Chand,* Tahsildar, *to Muhammad Raza Husain*. Informs about a letter of Lala Durga Parsad to Saiyid Karam Ali, *thanadar* of Bari, informing that around 8,000 insurgent forces entered Ganj Basodah, Pura Guna, Bhilsa, Chopra and Bamhuri and through the mountains in Manik Chowk and that the news of insurgent forces is coming regularly. It is not known that from where these forces would cross Narmada. It is for information so that extra vigil be observed in this region. Dated 25 *Rabi* II, 1275 AH.

P 155. *Karam Ali Husain to Muhammad Raza Husain.* Informs that he received the news from two persons, belonging to caste Gond and dwellers of *mauza* Gondwana, that the insurgents along with some forces and two cannon are encampimg at Manik Chowk or Ramgarh and Pura Guna. Hearing the news, he immediately sent one soldier to inquire into the matter. The report received from him, after his return, would be sent to him and would try his best to prevent the insurgents. Requests for an order to Raja Mardan of Bariwala to meet him and suppress the insurgents by giving his company to him. Dated 26 *Rabi* II, 1275 AH.

P 157. *Nanak Chand to Muhammad Raza Husain*. Informs that on 3 *Jumada* I, he received a letter of Karam Ali Husain, *thanadar,* informing that Dharam Das Niranjan and Shaikh Sa'adat were sent to bring the news of the insurgents. They came and stated that from the grass sellers it was heard that, around 2,000 *sawars* and foot-soldiers led by Adil Muhammad Khan were at Satparha. From some other persons, it was heard that at Balabhat, *ilaqa* Chanderi, and at Manik Chowk,

150 *wilayati* soldiers were encampimg. To know the truth there is a need to send some soldiers there. The information is sent to him as described in the letter of *thanadar*. Dated 4 *Jumada* I, 1275 AH.

P 159. *Ram Prasad,* Tahsildar, *to Muhammad Raza Husain.* Informs that day, he received a letter of Ahmad Allah Khan, *thanadar* of *pargana* Chhaner along with the copy of letter of Qasim al-Din Ahmad, *tahsildar* of *pargana* Harda, informing about the victory of British forces and the defeat of insurgents. The said letter is sent to him. Dated 30 *Rabi* II, 1275 AH.

PP 161-2. *Qasim al-Din Ahmad,* Tahsildar *of* Pargana *Harda.* Informs that Shamsher Khan, *sawar* who was captured by the insurgents, freed himself from the captivity of the insurgents at Harda. He stated that thereafter they went to Lutangli Chauki where they looted the goods of the merchants. They captured Marmorwala and his men. They also captured a cook who was ill and killed him. They went further and reached Swarajpur and stayed there for the night. On 25th of the month, they marched from there and were making loot on the way. In the meantime, 150 to 200 British soldiers and 40 to 50 bullock *sawars* and a platoon of riflemen appeared and fought with the insurgents. Once, the insurgents fired cannon and killed many. Then, they lost the battle and fled. In this battle, atleast 2,000 to 2,500 men of the insurgents were killed. The British forces emerged victorious. Dated 26 November 1858.

P 163. *Saiyid Burhan al-Din,* Tahsildar *of Chhaner, to Muhammad Raza Husain.* Informs of a letter of Ali Bhai, *thanadar* of *pargana* Harda under the British territory, dated 9 December 1858, informing of the news of the arrival of 500 *sawars* of insurgents from Botul to the mountains of Kalibhat, *ilaqa* Harda, situating at a distance of 20 *curoh* from Harda; besides the news of coming of other groups of insurgents, and giving information of coming of 3,000 British forces, the previous day under the command of Colonel Major at Nayamgarh, *ilaqa* Khandwa, pursuing the insurgent forces, besides the arrival of British forces at Charwa, situating at a distance of 10-12 *curoh* from Harda, and going of *sawars* and deputy *tahsildar* for the arrangement of *sabrah i- rasad,* besides the report of present scenario sent through Burhan al-Din, informer employed at *thana* by Ahmad Allah Khan, *thanadar* of Chhaner. The said *thanadar* has sent the letter to government. A copy of the letter is sent to him. Dated 7 *Jumada* I, 1275 AH.

P 165. *Ali Bhai,* Thanadar *of* Pargana *Harda, to Ahmad Allah Khan,* Thanadar *of* Pargana *Chhaner*. Expresses his concern for not receiving letters since long. May Allah keep him well. Says that he has sent 2-3 letters earlier to him asking about the insurgents but has recieved no reply pertaining to the whereabouts of the insurgents, their numbers, and whether they are making loot there, whether they carry gun powder and magazine with them, what is their position of encampment and the distance of one camp to another camp from where from they get their food or they are totally confined to one specific region. From the letter of Ram Charan, *barqandaz* deployed at chowki Gadrapur, it is learnt that some provisions are accumulated at Murdanpur, Bharonda and Rehti and the insurgents would pass through that road. After going through the said letter, he was told to inform the *thanadar* of Chhaner through a letter, communicating about the matter of insurgents in the region of Bhopal, Mardanpur, Rehti and Chhaner as heard by him through any letter or friend or employee or from any outside source. The situation in the region is that merely 500 insurgent *sawars* are hiding in the mountains of Kalibhatt, *ilaqa* Harda, situating at a distance of 20 *curoh* from Harda towards south. Besides this, 500 *sawars* of other group of insurgents are also arriving there. The British forces who are 3,000 under the command of Colonel Major are coming to suppress these insurgents. The previous day, they were at

Pahamgarh, *ilaqa* Khadua. That day, they have marched to Kharwa Chauharda situating at a distance of 10-12 *curoh* from there or they would be at Gangabat. To make arrangement of provisions for them, some *sawars* and few horses and the Deputy *Tahsildar* have gone there. Ramaji, a wine seller, is being sent to him. Whatever the situation is there, it may be communicated to him through Ramaji or through Shaikh Salim. Dated 9 December 1858.

P 167. *Nanak Chand,* Tahsildar, *to Muhammad Raza Husain*. Sends the letter of Karam Ali Khan, Deputy *Thanadar* of *pargana* Bari. Dated 5 *Jumada* I, 1275 AH along with the letter of Gobind Ram, *harkara* at Bamhuri, dated 4 *Jumada* I, which are in regard to the insurgent forces addressed to him. Dated 7 *Jumada* I, 1275 AH.

P 169. *Karam Ali Husain to Nanak Chand.* Sends the letter received from Gobind, *harkara.* From his letter it is learnt that the insurgent forces are at Bagrod. Their number is 2,500, both *sawars* and foot soldiers, who will march to Chandpura. To know about them one Gond and one soldier have been sent to Bagrod. The information will be sent once they return. It is a must that he should remain alert and the information about the situation in Bhopal and Hoshangabad should be sent to him. Dated 5 *Jumada* I, 1275 AH.

P 171. *Gobind Ram to Ali Bhai,* Thanadar. Informs that he was at Garhi, *pargana* Mahalpur, but found no sign of insurgents in those places. The forces which are at Bagrod, it is not known where they will go further. If ordered he may proceed, if not, he would remain there.

PP 173-4. *Madho Kishan,* Amil *of Udaipura, to Muhammad Raza Husain*. Refers to the royal *parwana*, dated 3 *Rabi* II, in regard to not receiving the letter of *amil* and *thanadar* of Udaipura from the day, the insurgent forces crossed from the *ghat* in *mauza* Harda. Informs that on 20 *Rabi* I, day Thursday, just after getting the news of the coming of insurgent forces through Haider Muhammad, *jamadar* of *thana* Garhi Ambapani and Dehgaon, a letter was sent to the Nawwab and to him through Rustam Khan by paying him Rs. 2. Thereafter, on 21st, day Friday, the letters of Faqir Khan and Rahim Khan, soldiers were received from *mahal* Bamhuri who said that the previous day, at noon, the insurgent forces reached Bamhuri and devastated it. The *tahsildar* fled from there and the *thanadar* was arrested by them, and that they would come to this place thereafter. Getting the news everyone fled. He sent all the men and foot-soldiers who were with him, to Basodah and Bamhuri, situating at a distance of half a *curoh* from Udaipura in south and by distributing cartridges and gunpowder to the soldiers present at the *mahal*, they decided to fight with the insurgents. Some soldiers, who were the employees of *malguzars* and *mahal*, after getting the cartridges and gun powder hid themselves. News about the arrival of insurgent forces at *mauza* Chhapara and by the evening or in the noon their arrival to Udaipura was heard. After this news, 5-6 soldiers were sent to fight with them. After getting letters from there, the insurgents were cordoned in between Bamhuri to *mahal* and upto river Narmada and 6 *chaukis* of coast guards were established. The soldiers and *sawars* deployed on the way and in the villages, and due to fear of getting themselves arrested it was difficult to write them and send letters. Thereafter from 22nd till 23rd, the informers and *sawars* of the insurgents were in search of *amil* and *thanadar* of the *mahal*. There was also news of the arrival of other group of insurgents. In view of this, people of the house were sent to *mauza* Sarsari across the river Narmada. From there a letter is being sent through Chand Khan, *Ajoradar* who was sent by Munshi Dhar. There is no news worth mentioning. Dated 9 *Rabi* 1275.

P 175. *Madho Kishan,* Amil, *to Muhammad Raza Husain*. Informs that the previous day at night, Shaikh Sultan, soldier deployed at Chhaner came back and reported the coming back of insurgent forces from across river Narmada and sending two *sawars* to bring news at the site of *ghat* Narmada and demanding help from the *thana* and *mahal*. Thus, at the very moment a reply with the letter to Diyanat Khan, *dafadar*, arrived asking him to inquire about the perfect news and the intention of the arrival of these forces to the site and to bring back those who are captive there and to vacate the house of *mahal* and requesting for help from *Bakhshi* to deal with the insurgents at Bamhuri.

PP 177-8. …*to Muhammad Raza Husain*. Refers to the letter of Diyanat Khan, *dafadar*, and Nazar Muhammad Khan, *sais* posted at Chhaner, requesting to help the *tahsildar* and *thanadar* of Udaipura which contains his comments that he is not cooperating with the *sawars* in arresting the insurgents which is not good. It is a must that he should pursue and prevent the insurgents and kill and arrest them. Explains that on the arrival of the letter of *dafadar* and *sais* on 17 *Rabi* II, 1275 AH, the *thanadar* along with the forces of the *thana* and *mahal* went to assist the *sawars* and he himself was alert at the *mahal* as that day news of another group of insurgents was being heard. He along with the forces of *mahal*, on the advice of the companions who had come to write the news-report, remained alert and attentive. On 19 *Rabi* II, 1275, the news of coming back of insurgents was heard. In reply to that, he had informed him that after getting authentic news the same would soon be conveyed. If the insurgent forces come back, the forces would go to deal with them. In this regard, he had informed that the place of *mahal* was not safe for the insurgents.

P 179. *Nanak Chand,* Tahsildar *of* Pargana *Bari, to Muhammad Raza Husain*. Refers to the royal order, dated 24 *Rabi* II, 1275 AH, as recorded in the letter of Lala Madho Kishan, *tahsildar* of Udaipura, directing him to assist the *amils* and *thanadars* those days in one way or the other, as the insurgents pass through one direction.

Presently, the insurgents move in all directions, it is a must that the forces of *mahal* and *thana* posted at any *pargana* should remain posted there and the soldiers of *mahal* should do the work of *tahsil* and the forces of *thana* should pursue and attack the insurgents and arrest them. Assures that he would follow the order in letter and spirit. Dated 7 *Jumada* I, 1275 AH.

P 181. *Nanak Chand,* Tahsildar *of* Pargana *Bari, to Muhammad Raza Husain*. Refers to the order, received from the office of *nizamat-i junub*, dated 19 *Rabi* II, 1275 AH, as recorded on the letter of Shaikh Khuda Bakhsh, deputy *thanadar* of Udaipura, directing him to search and arrest the insurgents. Assures he would follow the order in letter and spirit. Dated 7 *Jumada* I, 1275 AH.

File No. 311
Box No. 16
No. of Documents 15

Orders of Nawwab Sikandar Begam on the Rubakar of Amir Muhammad Khan, the Suspended Risaldar, Issued by the Criminal Court of Bhopal, which is in Regard to the Insurgency in Hoshangabad, Dated 4 Safar 1275 AH

PP 1-5. From the *rubakar,* it emanates that Amir Muhammad Khan, the suspended *risaldar,* as ordered by Nawwab Baqi Muhammad Khan, went to persuade and provoke the miscreants of the *risala* and the army of Bhopal; his involvement with other miscreant forces of Bhopal, who were demanding *zar-i lane* and *domaha*; not putting his seal by himself on the papers of insurgency in Hoshangabad; the attestation by Murtaza Khan to inscribe his statement on the letters of insurgency in Hoshangabad; keeping his seal with Amir Ali Khan, *nishanchi*, issuing orders for the *risala,* who was his *bargir,* and a native of the suspended *risaldar,* Ghulam Nabi Khan; the presence of Amir Ali Khan with Amir Muhammad Khan, *risaldar*, till the victory at Garhi Ambapani and then his disappearance without taking his outstanding amount from the government till his dismissal, even without informing Amir Muhammad Khan, *risaldar*; not providing evidences by Amir

Muhammad Khan to the witnesses like Shamsher Khan, Kale Khan, Raj Ali Khan, Dost Ali Khan, *dafadar*, *risala*, red uniform, in regard to putting seal by Amir Ali Khan, *nishanchi,* on his behalf on the papers of insurgency in Hoshangabad; not informing any matter, either through letter or verbally to the government; taking back the seal from *nishanchi* after hearing the order of his dismissal; coming back from Garhi Ambapani but not enquiring from the *nishanchi* about the affixing of the seals on the papers of insurgency in Hoshangabad; not putting Amir Ali Khan, *nishanchi,* in custody for interrogation in the matters of putting seal and then helping him in his disappearance; expressing inability to disclose the names of those sent by Ghulam Nabi Khan, *risaldar*, to bring him in their company; intimating Ghulam Nabi Khan that the Sikhs were with him, in demanding *zar-e lane* and *domaha* and sending *wilayatis* by Ghulam Nabi Khan, *risaldar*, to kill the Sikhs as per the information of Amir Muhammad Khan, *risaldar*; and lastly, his refusal and non-cooperation in disclosing the names of those *wilayatis* and the officers who were with him.

All these allegations are labelled against him and these are established facts. Taking cognizance of the crime committed by Amir Muhammad Khan, *risaldar,* the accused, while in service is a prove that he had a bad intention against the government and he is liable to be killed. But in view of a good deed done by him in his lifetime, as appeared in the orders of Major William Henry Richards, the Political Agent of Bhopal, that he was sent to Indore to serve there before the eruption of uprising and there is no adverse report against him while serving in Indore and that he faithfully helped Henry Durand, Deputy Agent to the Governor-General, Centrel India, reach Hoshangabad from Sehore. There is no report of disloyalty against him, although the soldiers generally became disloyal those days. Nawwab Baqi Muhammad Khan and other officers of the government urged not to kill him sighting this work as an example of his loyalty. Amir Muhammad Khan is father-in-law of Baqi Muhammad Khan. Thus, Amir Muhammad Khan is sentenced to life imprisonment.

Notwithstanding, the statement of Amir Muhammad Khan, *risaldar*, that he kept his seal with Amir Ali Khan, *nishanchi*, because he was a native of Ghulam Nabi Khan and that he might have put his seal on the papers of insurgency of Hoshangabad, does not seem true, hence it is not to be accepted. Keeping seal by Amir Muhammad Khan, *risaldar,* with Amir Ali Khan, *nishanchi,* clearly indicates that he had given him full authority to use his seal as he may like. According to the statement of Amir Muhammad Khan, after the suppression of insurgency, the said *nishanchi* was there for two to four months but Amir Muhammad Khan neither inquired from him about the matter of putting seals on the papers of insurgency in Hoshangabad nor did he take back his seal from him and it remained with him as usual inspite of his knowing that Amir Ali Khan, *nishanchi*, is a native of Ghulam Nabi Khan, *risaldar*, who has been dismissed. When Amir Muhammad Khan saw that the secrets were being disclosed and orders of his dismissal were issued, he took back the seal from the *nishanchi* and after 2 to 3 days, he helped him via his confidant to flee so that secrets might not be disclosed. Dated 5 *Rabi* I, 1275 AH.

PP 9-22. *Proceedings of a Criminal Case Executed in the* Rubakari *of Nawwab Sikandar Begam by Munshi Muhammad Jamal al-Din Khan,* Madar al-Maham, *Diwan Kishan Ram,* Mu'tamid al-Maham, *and Muhammad Sa'd al-Din,* Muhtamim, Adalat-i Faujdari, *Dated 4* Safar *1275 AH.* The papers of the case exchanged between the government and Amir Muhammad Khan, *risaldar,* indicate that the *muhtamim, adalat-i faujdari*, was ordered to examine the petition of Amir Muhammad Khan, *risaldar,* dated 30 *Sha'ban* 1274 AH, and give judgement with appropriate suggestion to the government. The petitioner in his petition argues that, he was in the bungalow at Jahangirabad and was sick when the uprising erupted in the contingent of state army. To enquire the reason of the resentment in the *risala,* he met Umrao Daulah and told him that the personnel of the *risala* are demanding the implemention of *domaha* rules and *zar-i lane*, and the Nawwab told him to have patience. But the miscreants who were behind them sparked the issue. As a result, they assembled at the bungalow of Jahangirabad and, thus, the insurgency erupted. Thereafter, Ghulam Ali Khan, *jamadar, risala*, red uniform, and Ghulam Nabi Khan, *risaldar, risala* IV, black uniform took all the *sawars* of red uniform in their company and came at the bungalow. The *jamadar* held talk with them and then he met him demanding his participation. He replied that neither he would go to the *kothi* nor would dare to participate in the uprising. He persuaded him to come to the *kothi*, accompanying the *risala*, black uniform, to demand *domaha and zar-i lane*. He tried to prevail upon him for not raising the banner of revolt. He thought that it is better for him to sit in the bungalow and the salary would automatically arrive there. Says that he sent Shamsher Khan, *sawar*, before the Nawwab to describe the situation but he did not turn up. He also explained the matter to Husain Khan, *muhtamim-i ta'mirat*. The *muhtamim* warned him through the *sawar* that he should not participate in the insurgency and should sit in the bungalow. The matter of insurgency would be brought forth to the government. Some persons were sent to him by Ghulam Nabi Khan, *risaldar*, and Ghulam Ali Khan, *jamadar*, communicating to go to the *kothi* in their company but he refused. The bearers of the letter became harsh and said they would carry him by force, as they were ordered by Ghulam Nabi Khan and Ghulam Ali Khan. To get rid from them, he agreed to become part of their company and said to the *sawars* of red uniform and the dwellers of the city that he was with them in the demand of *domaha* and *Zar-i lane* but he would not be a part of the miscreants.

Meanwhile, Ghulam Nabi Khan and Muhammad Ali Khan, *risaldar*, sent some *wilayatis* to kill the Sikhs. He expressed his resentment if they committed such crime and conveyed the *risaldar* that such heinous crime would create conflict between him and them. It would also invite anxiety of the government and the consequences would be bad. The Sikhs came to him and expressed their solidarity with him. This message was given to Ghulam Nabi Khan and Muhammad Ali Khan.

Thereafter, they sent some papers to put his seal upon them. After going through those papers, he conveyed that the content of the papers was not good. It would only invite the anxiety of the government and thus, he refused to put his seal on those papers. If they like they may put their own seals. As far as the demand of *zar-i lane* and *domaha* is concerned, he is with them. But so far as the other matters are concerned, he does not agree at all with them. The other demands were:

i. Bakhshi Murawwat Muhammad Khan should not hold the post of *Bakhshigiri*.

ii. There should not be a change of colour of horses.

iii. English monthly distribution system should be stopped.

iv. One who passes away, his son or his brother should be given employment on compassionate ground and not the others.

v. Anyone selected by them as an officer should get due recognition by the government.

vi. Wherever they go, they would go unitedly.

Thereafter, another set of papers was sent. The content pertained to:

i. Demand of *zar-i lane.*

ii. Withdrawal of the order of the changes of colour of horses.

iii. Cease of English monthly system.

Atlast, he put his seal on the paper. The miscreants, although got *zar-i lane* and *domaha,* still they went on the path of insurgency. He requested Nawwab Umrao Daulah that the miscreants should be dealt with firmly. He said that after one hour he would issue the order. The miscreants hearing the news, dispersed. Thereafter, *chobdar* of the Nawwab, and the Major of uniform came to order them to perform the duty of weekly salute. But they faced stiff resistance from them. Meanwhile, a royal order was received by him, directing him to present all armymen for giving the salute. As ordered, he persuaded Muhammad Ali Khan and Ghulam Nabi Khan, *risaldar*, to get ready for the salute but they did not agree. This information was given to Nawwab Umrao Daulah. He ordered that at any cost, they should be brought. He, then in the company of some armed soldiers, went to Jahangirabad, sat in his bungalow and sent a message to the miscreants threatening them that if they would hesitate in performing the salute to the government it would not be good for them.

Ghulam Nabi Khan and Muhammad Ali Khan, when they received this message, came to him. He persuaded and presented them before the government. After defusing the crisis he left for Sihore, as ordered to him, to serve there. The services which he rendered there are known to Bhawani Prasad and Muhammad Hasan Khan. The time when everyone present at Sihore refused to accompany the Britishers to Hoshangabad, he volunteered himself and through the *naib bakhshi* conveyed that he was ready to give company to the Britishers to Hoshangabad. His loyalty is known to all as expressed by the Britishers to Husain Khan, *muhtamim*, *ta'mirat*, that his loyalty is such that they would communicate it to the Nawwab. He also received the *parwana* of his loyalty from them through Husain Khan, *muhtamim, ta'mirat*. When he came back from Hoshangabad and presented himself before the Nawwab, he was bestowed with awards and a *parwana* of appreciation by her. It is a fact that he was never lebelled with the charges of disloyalty. During the uprising, he never indulged in any conspiracy. He is ready for any inquiry and if found guilty, he must be punished.

An examination of all three letters issued to create insurgency in Hoshangabad reveals that all three letters have the same content, they bear the seal of Amir Muhammad Khan, *risaldar,* and these are addressed to [a] officers, *subadars*, *jamadars* and soldiers of platoon; [b] to the *subadars*, *jamadars*, *hawaldars* and musketeers; and [c] to the *risaldars*, *jamadars* like Mir Farzand Ali, Mir Wali Shah, Rahim Khan, Mir Inayat Husain, and to all other officers-big or small, of the former disbanded contingent of Sehore.

The said *risaldar* was directed to explain it. The reply received from him reveals that the army of Bhopal, both cavalry and infantry, agreed upon and took an oath that they would surely go to Hoshangabad to loot the huge wealth which was lying there and then, with their consent, they would go to Delhi. In the third paper, this much is also added that the forces which are at the *kothi* of Nawwab Umrao Daulah at Jahangirabad should be informed.

The statement of Amir Muhammad Khan is that he did not put his seal on any of the papers, sent here and there by the insurgents during the uprising. However, he put his seal on the paper which was received from Nawwab Umrao Daulah and the letter which was presented by the armymen to the government. Since his seal was with Amir Ali Khan, *nishanchi,* a dweller and a native of Ghulam Nabi Khan, *risaldar,* it is not beyond doubt that he would have affixed his seal and now he is absconding. When the government called him back from Garhi Ambapani, where he was deployed and was dismissed, the *nishanchi* too was in his company and reached there but without telling him anything he escaped. Where he is now, he does not know. Why he was upset and why he absconded without interrogation is also not clear. From the prevailing condition it seems that since he affixed his seal on the papers of insurgency, hence, he absconded. Since he was performing the duty of *kotha-dafadari,* he thought that it would be better if he keeps his seal with him, as during the last three years he experienced the missing of seal on several occasions. It was a lesson for him that he should hold the seal and it should not have been handed over to others. All three papers, which bear his seal, were seen by him and he has also heard about this. But surely, he swears that neither does he know anything about the drafting of these letters nor did he affix his seal on them.

Amir Ali Khan affixed his seal in the presence of Shamsher Khan, Kale Khan, Raj Ali Khan, *sawars*, and Dost Ali Khan, *dafadar*, *risala* II, red uniform. But neither he is aware about it nor does he know as to why Amir Ali Khan used his seal. All these witnesses were under the command of Abd al-Aziz Khan, *risaldar*.

Thereafter, on 13 *Zilhijja* 1274 AH, a questionnaire was issued to Shamser Khan and others from this office in the name of *Bakhshi* to obtain reply of the questionnaire from them. On 20th *Muharram*, a letter of *Bakhshi* addressed to him was received. The statements of Kale Khan, Shamsher Khan, Raj Ali Khan, Dost Ali Khan, the witnesses, are similar to the statement of Amir Muhammad Khan, *risaldar.* Amir Ali Khan, *nishanchi*, used the horse of Amir Muhammad Khan, *risalda,* to carry the business of grain and grass. The seal of the *risaldar* was with him from the day he was brought in *risala* II from *risala* IV, red uniform, and it was with him till his dismissal. No letter was ever drafted in their presence. The letter related to insurgency in Hoshangabad was neither drafted nor was the seal of the *risaldar* affixed on those papers in their presence. They are not aware of this incident.

The nutshell of the statement of Amir Muhammad Khan, *risaldar,* dated 22 *Muharram* 1275 AH, is that when he was removed from Garhi Ambapani in the month of *Ramazan* or *Shawwal* 1274, he directly came there. Shamsher Khan, Kale Khan, Raj Ali Khan, and Dost Ali Khan said to him about affixing of his seal on the papers of insurgency in the presence by Amir Ali Khan, *nishanchi*, at his house where Sardar Khan, son of Wazir Khan, *qila'dar*, was also present. By that time, Amir Ali Khan had fled. After his coming from Garhi Ambapani, he came to know about affixing of his seal on the papers of insurgency which led to his dismissal. By that time he had brought back his seal from Amir Ali Khan. The day, Ghulam Nabi Khan, *risaldar*, and Ghulam Ali Khan, *jamadar* sent some soldiers to bring him even forcibly, he was sitting in his bungalow lane and Shamsher Khan, Ghulam Haider Khan, Shaikh Faqir Muhammad, *sawars*, and Dost Ali Khan, *lais dafadar*, *risala* 2, red uniform, were present. Names of the soldiers who were sent by Ghulam Nabi Khan are not known to him. The *wilayatis* who came to kill the Sikhs were persuaded not to commit such a crime. Their names and the name of their officers are not known to him. Through 'Abd al-Karim Khan, *sawar,* he conveyed to Ghulam Nabi Khan and Ghulam Ali Khan to desist from committing such a crime, as it will be a matter of anxiety for the government and it will not be good for them. He was sitting, as per the royal order, in his bungalow lane when the Sikhs approached him out of fear and for the safety of their lives. He, by a Sikh whose name he forgot, conveyed Ghulam Nabi Khan and Muhammad Ali Khan, *risaldar*s, that he was with them in the matter of *domaha* and *zar-i lane* but he was not party with them in any other matter.

The two letters written by the officers of insurgents had different clauses-one of the two was returned due to fear of the government as the matter mentioned in it was against the government. But on the other paper, he affixed his seal due to fear on his life by the insurgents. It was Hakim Faqir al-Din who had come to him with those papers and then he returned back with those papers. He did not become part of their conspiracy. At the time of the uprising, Ghulam Ali Khan, *jamadar*, had come to his bungalow with some *sawars* to persuade him to join them but he bluntly refused their offer. At that time, Shamsher Khan, *sawar*, and Ghulam Ali Khan, *jamadar*, were also present there. Through Shamsher Khan he brought all the matters into the notice of the government and through Husain Khan, *muhtamim, ta'mirat*. If Ghulam Nabi Khan refuses, the sending of the soldiers to call him or to kill the Sikhs, might be his exigency. The fact is that what he has written is exactly the same as it had happened.

Amir Muhammad Khan, *risaldar*, has enclosed the royal *parwana,* dated 21 *Ziqada* 1273 AH, addressed to him, which shows the pleasure of the government. Similarly, Colonel Durand, Deputy Agent to the Governor-General, in his letter, dated 9 July 1857 addressed to him expressed that in his journey to Hoshangabad, he was deeply impressed with the loyalty and behaviour of Amir Muhammad Khan, *risaldar*, and his *sawars*. This shows his extreme loyalty and fedility. The *parwana* and the letter certify his loyalty and his sacrifices.

Then the letter of Munshi Husain Khan, *muhtamim, ta'mirat,* dated 25 *Muharram* was received in the office of *adalat-i faujdari*. The contant of the letter is that during the time of uprising, Shamsher Khan, *sawar* of the *risala* of Amir Muhammad Khan, *risaldar*, came in the evening and said that he was sent by the *risaldar* to communicate that Ghulam Ali Khan, *jamadar*, sent some soldiers to bring him in their company. But he refused to follow him. He said that the *risaldar* did well by not going from the bungalow to *kothi*. He asked to convey him, after *salam*, that he would never become part of the insurgents nor would go to the *kothi* or allow the *sawars* of his *risala* to join the insurgents. The next day in the morning, Bahadur Khan, *dafadar* met him at Moti Mahal and said the *risaldar* conveyed to him that all the *sawars* went from lane to *kothi* and he was alone in the bungalow. He conveyed the message to the government. He was told to request Nawwab Umrao Daulah and follow what he says. He came outside and told the *dafadar* about the royal order. He then left for the *deorhi* of Nawwab.

The crux of the statement of Ghulam Nabi Khan, the suspended *risaldar*, is that he did not send anyone to bring Amir Muhammad Khan, *risaldar*. He neither sent any officer along with the *wilayatis* to kill the Sikhs nor did he convey anything to Amir Muhammad Khan by anyone. The information of the *risaldar* is false. The Sikhs were not his partners. But it was said that all the armymen were together. Since he did not send any paper to Amir Muhammad Khan, *risaldar*, so he is unable to tell the name of the bearer. He does not know as to where Amir Muhammad Khan was at that time when those letters were being drafted. He does not know whether he was involved in the process of advising or not. It was heard that the seal of the *risaldar* was affixed on the papers in his bungalow itself.

Thereafter, on 29 *Muharram*, a questionnaire was sent to Sardar Khan. On 3 *Safar*, a letter of Wazir Khan, *qila'dar* from Raisen, along with the reply of Sardar Khan was received. The same has been included in the register. The gist of the letter of Sardar Khan, son of Wazir Khan, *qila'dar*, is that Shamsher Khan, Kale Khan, Raj Ali Khan and Dost Ali Khan never mentioned about any paper of insurgency at the time of uprising nor about putting of seal by Amir Muhammad Khan, *risaldar*, on any paper. But one day he himself asked them whether Amir Muhammad Khan, *risaldar*, ever put his seal on those papers. They replied that *risaldar* did not affix his seal. But since his seal was in the possession of Amir Ali Khan, *nishanchi*, the latter might have used his seal. The letter of Wazir Ali Khan, *qila'dar*, and the orders of the government, dated 19 *Sha'ban* 1974, are included in the register which carries a note that it is strange that on the basis of statements of some petitioners, Amir Muhammad Khan, *risaldar*, was suspended, whereas during interrogation he did not come across any crime which might justify his dismissal. Thus, it was heard that the seal of the *risaldar* was affixed on any paper of insurgency. If so, the *risaldar* under pressure of some rebel armymen would have handed over his seal to someone of his confidence to remove doubts from their minds and to carry out the official business in a peaceful manner. He was not involved in any matter of insurgency. If he had been involved, he would have niether pleaded nor requested for a thorough investigation. The case needs a thorough investigation.

The gist of the statement of Murtaza Khan *Bakhshi*, the scribe of the letter of insurgeny of Hoshangabad, is that he is not aware of affixing of seal by the *risaldar* on any paper in his presence. The seals of Ghulam Nabi Khan, Muhammad Ali Khan, *risaldars*, and Imam Ali Khan and Ahmad Khan, *jamadars*, were affixed. Thereafter, the letters were handed over to Ghulam Nabi Khan, *risaldar*, and then he returned to his house.

From the proceedings of the case, it is found that the seal of Amir Muhammad Khan was found affixed on all the three papers of insurgency of Hoshangabad. The crime of affixing seal on the said paper is a proven fact on the accused as the *risaldar* who made Shamsher Khan, Kale Khan, Raj Ali Khan and Dost Ali Khan witnesses of affixing of seal by Amir Ali Khan, *nishanchi,* but the witnesses in their statements refused having any knowledge in the matter. However, Sardar Ali Khan's statement is different from the statement of others. Thus, how come the statement of the accused is to be accepted in the absence of any authentic prove that

Amir Ali Khan, *nishanchi*, might have used his seal in affixing seal on the papers of insurgency.

From the statements of all four witnesses, this much is clear that the seal was kept with Amir Ali Khan, *nishanchi*. But how far it would be correct to accept that he used his seal without having informed him- there is no prove of it. If Amir Ali Khan, *nishanchi*, was not a confidant of the *risaldar*, then why he was allowed to affix his seal on routine matters? Keeping aside these assertions, why the *risaldar* did not keep his seal in his possession as it was the time of insurgency. Apart from this, the seal of *risaldar* was found affixed on six other papers of insurgency which were related to *domaha* and *zar-i lane*. In such circumstances, the refusal of the accused seems worthless. Other issues sighted by the *risaldar* such as that he was not a part of the insurgents or carrying a *parwana* of his faithfulness is not related to this case and it is a different matter. If the *risaldar*, at any stage, came to know about affixing his seal by the *nishanchi* on any such papers of insurgency why he did not bring the matter into the notice of the government. He himself has confessed of his fault of not communicating this to the government. Now Amir Ali Khan, *nishanchi,* is traceless and a fugitive, otherwise a face-to-face examination of the case would have been conducted. As the *nishanchi* is absconding, whatever assertion is made by the *risaldar* against the *nishanchi* is meaningless. Whereas the other accused in the case, the proceedings of everyone prepared separately and they were examined and the court came to the conclusion that they were the culprits. Since the case is very sensitive, as it is related to Hoshangabad court of the British government, it seems fit to send the *rubakar* of this office to William Richards, the Political Agent, through the *wakil* and let him decide and issue the judgement regarding the punishment to the accused. But as the accused was holding a coveted post of *risaldari* under this government, it would be fit to dismiss him from the services for the entire life in view of the friendship between the two governments.

It contains an order that the case may be sent to the government for final decision.

P 25. *Opinions of the Army Officers in the Case of Amir Muhammad Khan,* Risaldar, *the Accused for Putting his Seal on the Papers of Insurgency.*

Name of the Officer-Bakhshi Murawwat Muhammad Khan.

From the proceedings of the case pertaining to putting of seal on the papers of insurgency by Amir Muhammad Khan, *risaldar*, and his connection with the rebel armymen, whether willingly or unwillingly, is proven. His statement that his seal was with Amir Ali Khan, *nishanchi*, who might have used his seal without his knowledge is also baseless and liable for harsh punishment. But taking into consideration his past services, he might be dismissed from the services with one year's imprisonment that would be a lesson for him and for others too.

P 27. *Opinion of Nawwab Baqi Muhammad Khan on the* Rubakar *of Amir Muhammad Khan,* Risaldar. In view of good deeds of Amir Muhammad Khan, *risaldar*, as he dared to accompany Major Durand in the early days of uprising and brought him safely to Hoshangabad and received a letter of appreciation. Similarly, he prevented the armymen from spreading insurgency. Amir Muhammad Khan, *risaldar*, was one of those who accepted 21 days' salary formula when the rebel armymen had refused to accept the said formula and also prevailed upon them to accept the formula and not to go on the path of insurgency. His courage and bravery was beyond doubt when he captured Sitaram, the culprit, and presented him before the government. But from the proceedings of the case in regard to putting seal on the papers of insurgency either by Muhammad Ali Khan, *nishanchi*, or by the *risaldar* himself, and the recommendations of *madar al-maham,* Jamal al-Din, *mu'tamid al-maham*, Diwan Kishan Ram and *muhtamim, adalat-i faujdari*, Maulawi Muhammad Sa'd al-Din are also correct. The final decision lies upon her. Dated 9 *Safar* 1275 AH.

P 29. *Ghulam Husain Khan, Red Uniform*. The recommendation of Maulawi Muhammad Sa'd al-Din, *muhtamim, adalat-i faujdari*, in the case of putting seal on papers of insurgency by Amir Muhammad Khan, *risaldar*, seems reasonable.

P 31. *The Recommendation of Diwan Kishan Ram,* Mu'tamid al-Maham, *in the Case of Affixing Seal By Amir Muhammad Khan On The Papers of Insurgency and Writing Letters of Insurgency to the Armymen To Devastate Hoshangabad*. From the proceedings of the case, the seal was found affixed on all three papers of insurgency in Hoshangabad, and the involvement with other insurgent armymen of Bhopal army on the pretext of demanding *zar-i lane* and *domaha* formula who had assembled at Jahangirabad, is a proven and established that Amir Muhammad Khan was involved in the conspiracy of affixing seal on the papers of insurgency in Hoshangabad like other insurgents of the Bhopal army and his opinion that he is liable for life long imprisonment like other insurgents. But looking into his past services and faithfulness to the governmnet as he and other *sawars* dared to escort Colonel Durand, Deputy Agent to the Governor General, Central India, and other British offficals who had come from Indore to Hoshangabad when the uprising had just erupted and the insurgency had spread in the army of Bhopal and the British officers had issued a letter of appreciation to him on 9 July 1857 which was produced in the government, if some relaxation is given to him in his punishment, it would be good. Dated 14 *Safar* 1275 AH.

P 33. *Opinion of Sikandar Khan, Agenty II, an Army Officer in the Case of Amir Muhammad Khan,* Risaldar, *an Accused in Affixing Seal on the Papers of Insurgency.* From the proceedings of the case, the crime of affixing seal on papers of insurgency in Hoshangabad by Amir Muhammad Khan, *risaldar*, the accused is established and proven. His denial of his crime by asserting that his seal was with Amir Ali Khan, *nishanchi*, who might have used his seal without his knowledge cannot exonerate him from the crime. In view of this, the opinion of *muhtamim, adalat-i faujdari*, of his dismissal from the service and his exile from the State of Bhopal and even putting him in jail for one or two years seems justifiable. Dated 15 *Safar* 1275 AH.

P 35. *Opinion of Madar al-Maham, Jamal al-Din Khan, on the* Rubakar *of Amir Muhammad Khan,* Risaldar. From the *rubakar,* the doubt of commiting the crime by Amir Muhammad Khan and that the *nishanchi* is the main culprit gets strengthened. The *risaldar's* arguement is that he was performing his duty in lane so he kept his seal with the *nishanchi* during the uprising who secretly used his seal. Later on, he took back his seal from him but did not put the *nishanchi* in prison inspite of knowing that his dismissal was due to that seal which was kept with *nishanchi*. If the *risaldar'*s role in escorting Colonel Durand to Hoshangabad and a letter of appreciation was not issued to him by the British officer, he too would have recommended the punishment as was recommended for Ghulam Nabi Khan but he considers the punishment as recommended by *muhtamim, adalat-i faujdari*, justifiable. Dated 17 *Safar* 1275 AH.

A notification should be made in the entire State of Bhopal that the seal of Amir Muhammad Khan was found affixed on the papers of insurgency of Hoshangabad and was liable for capital punishment. But in view of his past services and his faithfulness to the government, as he executed an order of the Nawwab during the uprising when there was insurgency in the army contingent of Bhopal, he dared to escort General

Durand, Deputy Agent to the Governor-General, Central India, to Hoshangabad and obtained a letter of appreciation in his name from the British officer his exemplary punishment is removed. For the crime of keeping his seal with the *nishanchi*, who used his seal illegally should be imprisoned, and the *risaldar* should never be allowed to serve the government in future. The purpose of this notification is that the other insurgents should keep themselves away from committing such a crime and always think to serve the British government faithfully.

P 37. *Opinion of Muhammad 'Abd al-Karim, Agenty III, an Army Officer in the Case of Amir Muhammad Khan,* Risaldar, *an Accused in Affixing Seal on the Papers of Insurgency*. From the proceedings of the case, the crime of affixing seal on papers of insurgency in Hoshangabad by Amir Muhammad Khan, *risaldar*, is well established and proven. He cannot be exonerated of his crime by merely saying that his seal was with Amir Ali Khan, *nishanchi*, who without his permission used it. Such a statement is merely an eyewash as nobody ever gives his seal to any other person. If suppose, anyone gives his seal to anyone else he must be his trustworthy and a trustworthy never commits treachery with his master. So the statement is nothing but befooling the others. It is a crime which demands punishment. But in view of his past good deeds as he volunteered himself at a time when there was open rebellion in the army contingent of Bhopal State he escorted Major Durand, Deputy Agent to the Governor-General to Hoshangabad who came from Indore-a good deed which attracted the attention of the British officer and issued an appreciation letter in his favour, besides his help in arresting Sitaram, the chief accused who engineered conspiracy of insurgency in the army, his opinion is that he should be removed from the services for the entire life. Such a treatment would be more humiliating for a respectful person than to kill him. Dated 20 *Safar* 1275 AH.

P 39. *Opinion of Muhammad Hasan Khan,* Naib Bakhshi, *an Army Officer in the Case of Amir Muhammad Khan, the Suspended Risaldar.* The crime of affixing seal of Amir Muhammad Khan, the suspended *risaldar,* whether by Amir Muhammad Khan himself or by Amir Ali Khan, *nishanchi,* a fugitive, on the papers of insurgency in Hoshangabad has been proved by the circumstantial evidences and through the evidences in the *rubakar*, besides the opinion of *madar-al- maham*, Munshi Jamal al-Din, which is based on reason. The lament excuse of Amir Muhammad Khan that he did not affix the seal by his own hand, and that it was done by Amir Ali Khan whereas the witnesses make the accused a culprit. But in view of his past good deeds like his help in getting Sitaram arrested and taking salary of 21 days along with other *sawars* and obtaining a letter of appreciation by serving Major Durand- the punishment of his offence of affixing seal on the papers of insurgency and his involvement with other insurgents of the armymen at Jahangirabd should be as suggested by *madar al-maham* and Bakhshi Murawwat Muhammad Khan, he opines Dated 20 *Safar* 1275 AH.

P 41. *Denanath to Paltu Lal, Muhafiz-i Daftar-i Insha*. Refers to his letter, dated 20 *Ramazan* 1285, in reference to the royal order, dated 16 *Ramazan* 1285 that after going through all the papers, the required papers may be traced from among the papers of the time of uprising. Thus, the papers relating to the case of Amir Muhammad Khan, *risaldar,* the accused in regard to putting seal on the papers of insurgency in Hoshangabad may be searched in all the relevant registers and sent to this office or give an appropriate reply. Dated 30 *Shawwal* 1286 AH.

P 42. *Paltu Lal to Denanath*. Refers to his letter and explains that the paper referred to in the letter is not available in the *daftar,* whereas all other papers are available. If there is any letter which is still with Amir

Muhammad Khan, it should be obtained from him and entered in the register. Dated 3 *Muharram* 1275 AH.

PP 43-4. *Gist of the Letter of Bhawani Prasad,* Wakil. A royal order, dated 28 *Sha'ban* 1274 AH, recorded in his letter of 20 *Sha'ban* 1274 AH is that Amir Muhammad Khan, *risaldar*, like others should be imprisoned. But before that she should send a *yaddasht* to the Political Agent. As and when she receives the reply of the Political Agent, he would be imprisoned. Says, all the matters were brought to the notice of the Political Agent who said that all such persons should be imprisoned. This is what his opinion is.

The letter contains the order of the Nawwab that it may be sent to Paltu Lal, *muhafiz-i daftar-i insha*, for inclusion in the register and keeping in the *daftar*. Bhawani Prasad may be conveyed that after the victory of Gwalior, Amir Muhammad Khan and the suspended Mama Qahar Khan would be imprisoned. At the moment, he being the relative and a confidant of Baqi Muhammad Khan, precaution is being taken. Dated 6 *Ziqada*1274 AH.

P 45. *Statement of Shaikh Jiwan*. States that his name is Shaikh Jiwan, son of Khuda Bakhsh, a dweller of Bhopal, and a government employee. On the question as to where Amir Muhammad Khan, the former *risaldar* is and his reply that Amir Muhammad, *risaldar*, died one year ago. Dated 8 *Muharram* 1289 AH.

PP 49-53. *Muhammad Siddiq Hasan Khan to Nawwab Shahjahan Begam.* Says that in the case of Amir Muhammad Khan, *risaldar*, *risala* II, red uniform, who put his seal on the papers of insurgency and went to Hoshangabad and the case was subsequently referred to the office of *faujdari* wherein he came to know that earlier, a stricture was passed by the government that it may be submitted with the opinions of the army officers, the *mu'tamid al-maham*, *madar al-maham,* and Nawwab Umrao Daulah. The case was then settled by Nawwab Sikandar Begam. Thereafter, the case was reffered to his office as instructed to Raja Kishan, *mu'tamid al-maham*, dated 20 *Jumada* II, 1289 AH, that there were some papers of Amir Muhammad Khan which needed thorough investigation. He is directed to collect all the papers and after comparing with the old ones, they may be sent to the government for issuing orders. Amir Muhammad Khan, *risaldar*, has also given a petition to him. That petition which bears her orders 'should also be included for consideration.' On that basis two letters were sent to Paltu Lal, *muhafiz-i daftar-i insha*, for obtaining **that** letter which was obtained from there.

The crux of the case is that Amir Muhammad Khan may be communicated that he would not be able to serve the Bhopal State for his entire life and need not to send petitions everytime. His saying that it was a mistake which he committed is worthless. Whereas the stricture has been passed against him. It is enough that he is not put behind the bar or killed. It is due to taking into consideration the opinion of Nawwab Umrao Daulah. Otherwise, he too would have been dealt with at par the other rebels and insurgents. Paltu Lal wrote that Amir Muhammad Khan should be sent a reply on the address available there. Hence, a reply was sent to him as all the papers were available in the relevant register of the case.

Now this office has been asked to examine the case once again. It is learnt that Amir Muhammad Khan has already died one year ago. Now it is useless to keep the case pending for further investigation. The same is sent so that the office of *daftar-i kul* may keep it among registers of the time of uprising. Dated 9 *Muharram* 1289 AH.

File No. 312
Box No. 16
No. of Documents 5

Recruitment of the Risala of Kunwar Mohan Singh, Berasiawala, in the Bhopal Army as New Recruitment

P 1. Contents

PP 3-4...*To Lala Thakur Prasad*. Informs about his well-being and hopes for the well-being of everyone. Refers to his letter in reference to the orders of the Nawwab demanding army personnel and foot-soldiers. In accordance to that, the letter of Thakur Nirbhay Singh addressed to the Nawwab is sent to him. Requests that after going through the terms and conditions, put forward in regard to the timing and condition of his arrival, if it is feasible the same may be presented to the Nawwab through Balmukund Maharaj, the bearer of this letter, and also send him a reply of it. Assures that the army personnel would be supplied, as and when demanded by the government. But before that there should be a formal discussion in the matters of salary of the armymen and about the rank and position of Kunwar Mohan Singh. Refers to the copies of orders of the Nawwab, sent to him again and again by Baijnath, which was not required as the reply in compliance to has already been given.

Further informs that on 6 *Muharram* 1274 AH, the government accommodation of Kamdar Khan Munshi due to his misbehavior was withdrawn and shifted to the *haveli* of chaudhuries made of brick. The guarding and management of *chauki* is being done by the personal soldiers of chaudhuries and the soldiers of Narsingarh and Pons, as the officer is staying there for the last 16 days. He is attending the officer, day and night. On 27 September 1857, two campanies and 30 *sawars* of the army contingent of Bhopal arrived and Kamdar Khan and Yar Muhammad Khan, the two brothers, left for Kalarah. Hearing the news of their fleeing, the *sawars* were sent to pursue them and both of them were caught. The camel riders of carriers and three gunmen were arrested and produced before the Officer. Their belongings were searched and a bag full of documents was recovered. There was also a letter signed by Yar

Muhammad Khan, younger brother of Kamdar Khan, which contains the information that 400 gunmen may be sent to him at Berasia to conduct a secret attack to help get the Munshi released. The officer went through this and the letters of Chhatrasal Agrawala. Harnath Singh Gadhawala and found that all the documents were leading to conspiracy. All these were sent to the Political Agent. It is heard that Kamdar Khan and Yar Muhammad Khan are residing at Patan. Shaikh Hasan Khan and other insurgents and their children and Kamdar Khan have fled to Piprarnagar. The Munshi has not yet given orders for the arrest of the insurgents and miscreants. Perhaps the *subadars* have the excuse of the arrival of cannon from Bhopal. Mian Khan who was sent by Mardan Singh, Banpur Chanderiwala, was in *mauza* Sai. When the armymen got the news, he was arrested by them and produced before the Munshi. He was carrying letters in the name of the Maharaja of Indore and the Nawwab of Bhopal and a *hukmnama* addressed to the army officials of Indore, Bhopal and Hoshangabad which contained that by the grace of God, the King has succeeded. Now it is a must upon them that, wherever the Britishers are found and seen, they should be killed and that all should come to him. From there they would launch an attack upon Sagar and Hoshangabad. Such a *hukmnama* was also recovered from Fazil Muhammad Khan that was addressed to the army officers. The Munshi sent him to Sehore under the security of two persons along with all the letters. The letters of *sahus* of Jaipur addressed to the treasurer of Sehore, containing the news of the victory of the British gave him pleasure. Requests that Yasin Khan, famous as *Peer Sahab* and one of the five brothers of Kamdar Khan, serving in Jahangirabad *risala* with 4 horses should be informed of the news of Kamdar Khan. Dated 4 October 1857.

P 5. *Thakur Nirbhay Singh Chaudhury,* Pargana *Berasia, to Nawwab Sikamdar Begam*. It is the prime and foremost duty of a loyal servant of the government that no insurgency ever erupts and the disloyal and dishonest persons are always eliminated. No doubt, that he is an old, and loyal to the government of Bhopal and desires from the core of his heart that Kunwar Mohan Singh, whose bravery is well established, should report to her with 50 soldiers, comprising of both cavalry and infantry and get a chance to serve her and to prove his loyalty. It is his firm belief that his bravery and sacrifices would get recognition if he gets a chance to do so. Reiterates that he is an old loyalist and the most obedient servant to the government of Bhopal. It is still his earnest desire that he should remain so as it is beneficial for him. Dated 4 October 1857.

It contains the order that the letter may be sent to Lala Paltu Lal, *muhafiz-i daftar-i insha*, for inclusion in the register and keeping in the *daftar*. A copy of the order may also be sent through Munshi Bhawani Prasad and Baijnath to Nirbhay Singh Chaudhury of Berasia directing him to explain as to how many *sawars* and foot-soldiers would be accompanying Kunwar Mohan Singh as it is not mentioned in his letter. An official order would be issued only after this clarification.

P 7. *Thakur Nirbhay Singh Chaudhury, Pargana Berasia, to Nawwab Sikandar Begam.* Refers to her order as recorded on his letter, dated 4 October 1857, asking him about the number of cavalry and infantry that will be accompanying Kunwar Mohan Singh. Informs presently, there are 25 *sawars* and 50 foot-soldiers who will report to her and after their settlement and after the nourishment of Kunwar, the contingent as much as required by the government, would be provided. Surely, Kunwar Mohan Singh would not leave any stone unturned in proving his loyalty and fedility. Adds that one of the sons of Lala Kalyan Rai, a very capable and wise person of his *karkhana,* would also be acompanying Kunwar Mohan Singh. Hopes that in view of his fidelity and loyalty, Kunwar Mohan Singh would be bestowed with all happiness so also will be the son of the Lala, who too would prove his capability while executing any official order and managing all affairs assigned to him. Dated 1 *Rabi* I, 1274 AH.

It contains the order that the letter may be sent to Lala Paltu Lal, *muhafiz-i daftar-i insha*, for inclusion in the register and keeping in the *daftar*. A copy of the order may also be sent to Nirbhay Singh Chaudhury of Berasia, directing him to send 100 foot-soldiers and 50 *sawars* for their formal recruitment under the army contingent of Bhopal and to be deployed in the *parganas* and villages to deal with the miscreants. Dated 6 *Rabi* I, 1274 AH.

P 9. *Baijnath, Deputy Assistant of the Political Agent, Bhopal, to Nawwab Sikandar Begam.* Refers to her order, dated 18 *Safar* 1274 AH, to Chaudhury Nirbhay Singh enquiring about the number of cavalry and infantry accompanying Kunwar Mohan Singh. Says, he immediately conveyed the message to Chaudhury Nirbhay Singh. Presently, he would be sending 75 soldiers and 35 *sawars* in the company of Kunwar Mohan Singh. There is no doubt that the Chaudhuries of Beresia are nourished by her. The honor and respect they have in the eyes of the government since past is very clear upon her. Not only this, but their respect and honor in the eyes of the British government is also well established as in the eyes of the Bhopal government. Now the said Kunwar along with his *mu'tamid*, Pyarelal, son of Kalyan Rai, *gumashta* of Chaudhury, would seek her blessings. The said Kunwar is a man of credibility and would remain firm in his loyalty. Hopes that he would get due recognition of his deeds, what he would execute. Dated 22 *Rabi* I, 1274 AH.

It contains the order that the letter mey be sent to Lala Paltu Lal, *muhafiz-i daftar-i insha*, for inclusion in the register and keeping in the *daftar*. A copy of the letter may also be sent through Bakhshi Murawwat

Muhammad Khan to Lala Chain Rai, *munib*, *daftar-i bakhshigari*, directing him to recruit new foot-soldiers and *sawars* as fresh employees as mentioned in the letter. Dated 29 *Rabi* I, 1274 AH.

ILLUSTRATIONS

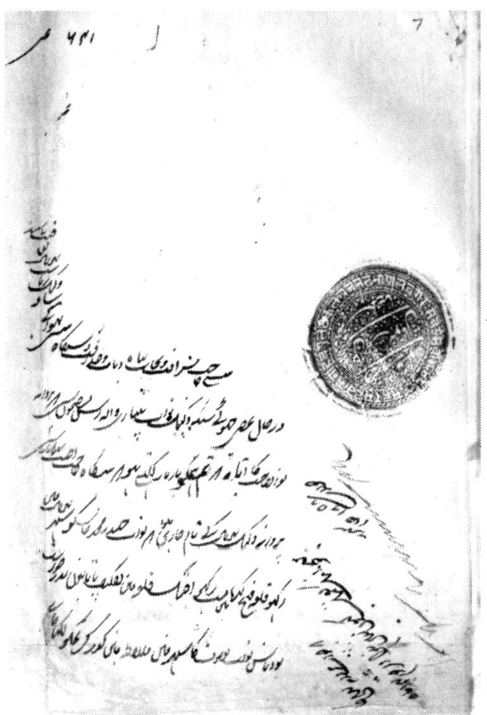

The Political Agent asks Bhawani Prasad wakil that why his order was not executed in regard to keeping Nawab Hyder Khan in the city of Bhopal and not in the fort of Fatahgarh. (F. No. 261, P-7)

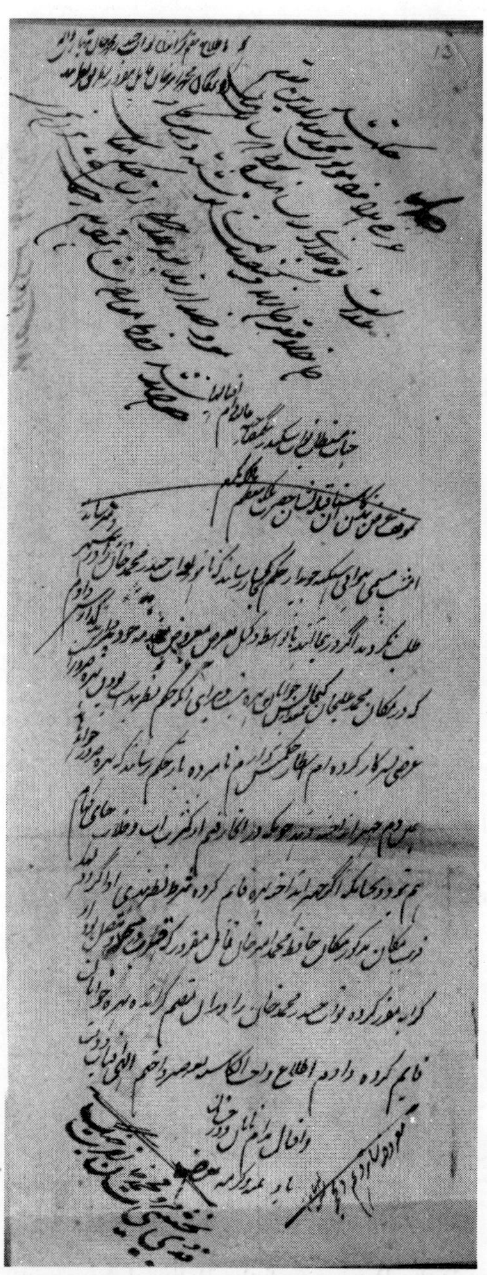

Bakhshi Murawwat Muhammad Khan informs Nawwab Sikandar Begam that the house of Muhammad Ali Khan is not too big to accommodate the guards of Jamadar. (F. No. 261, P-13)

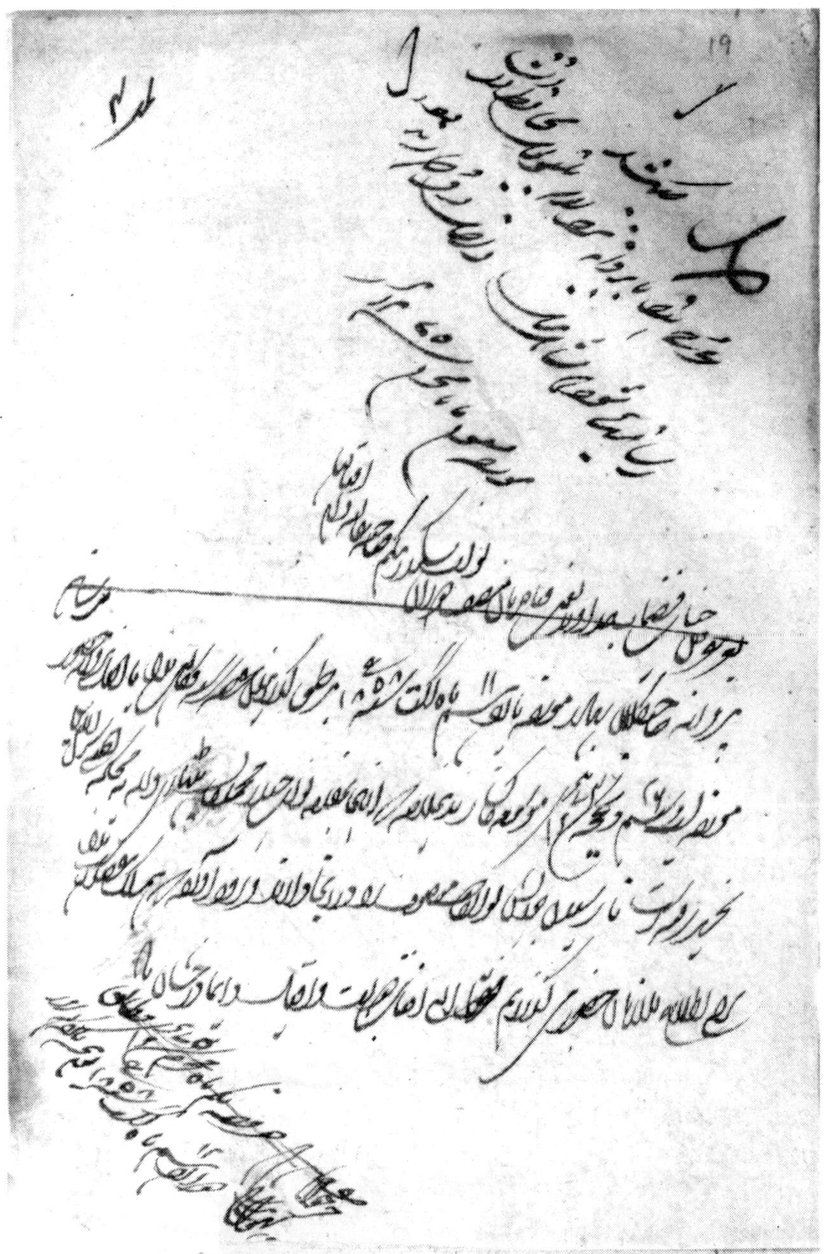

Bhawani Prasad sends the Parwana of the Political Agent, informing that until a reply is received from the office of the Agent to the Central India, Nawwab Hyder Khan should be kept in Bhopal. (F. No. 261, P-19)

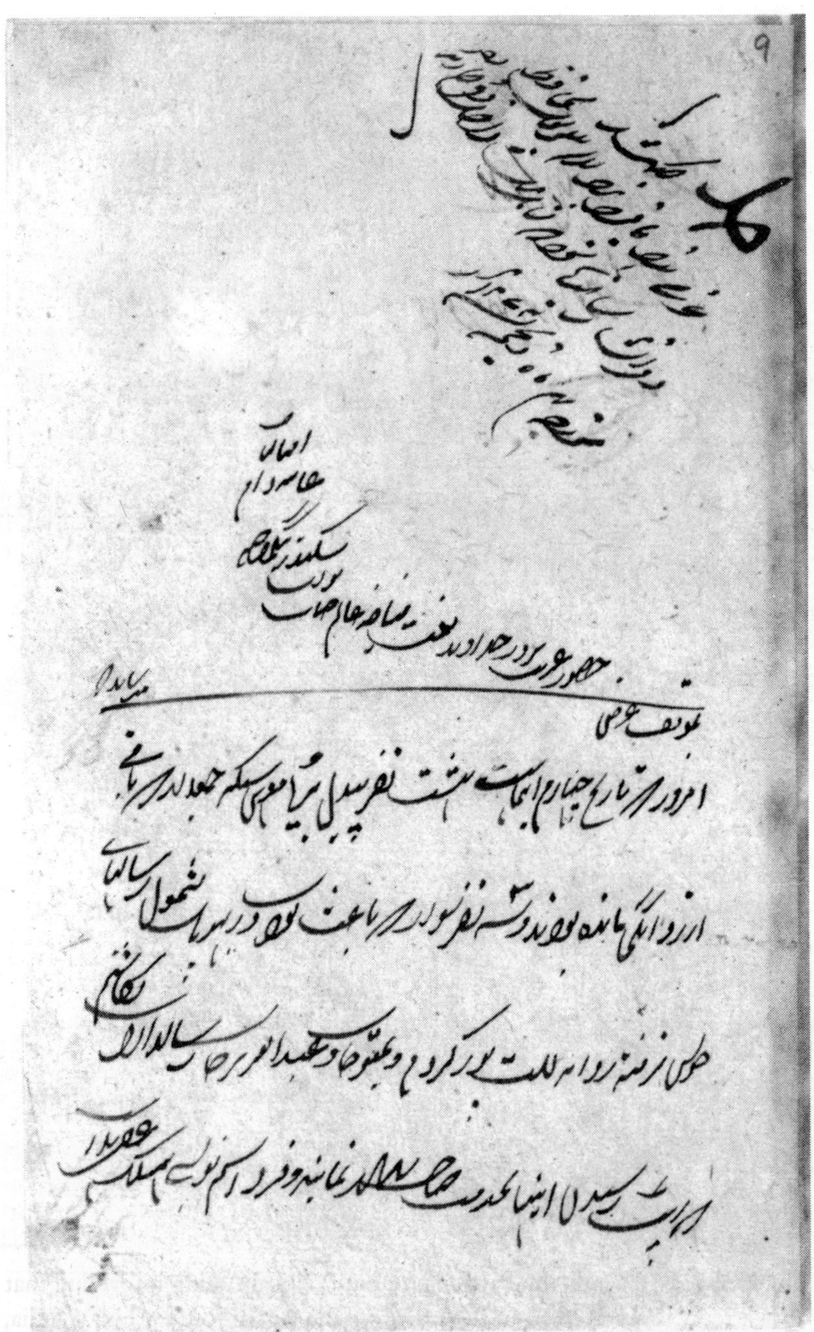

Muhammad Hasan Khan informs Nawwab Sikandar Begam that 8 foot-soldiers aned 3 sawars who left behind, were send to Lalitpur.
(F. No. 262, P-9)

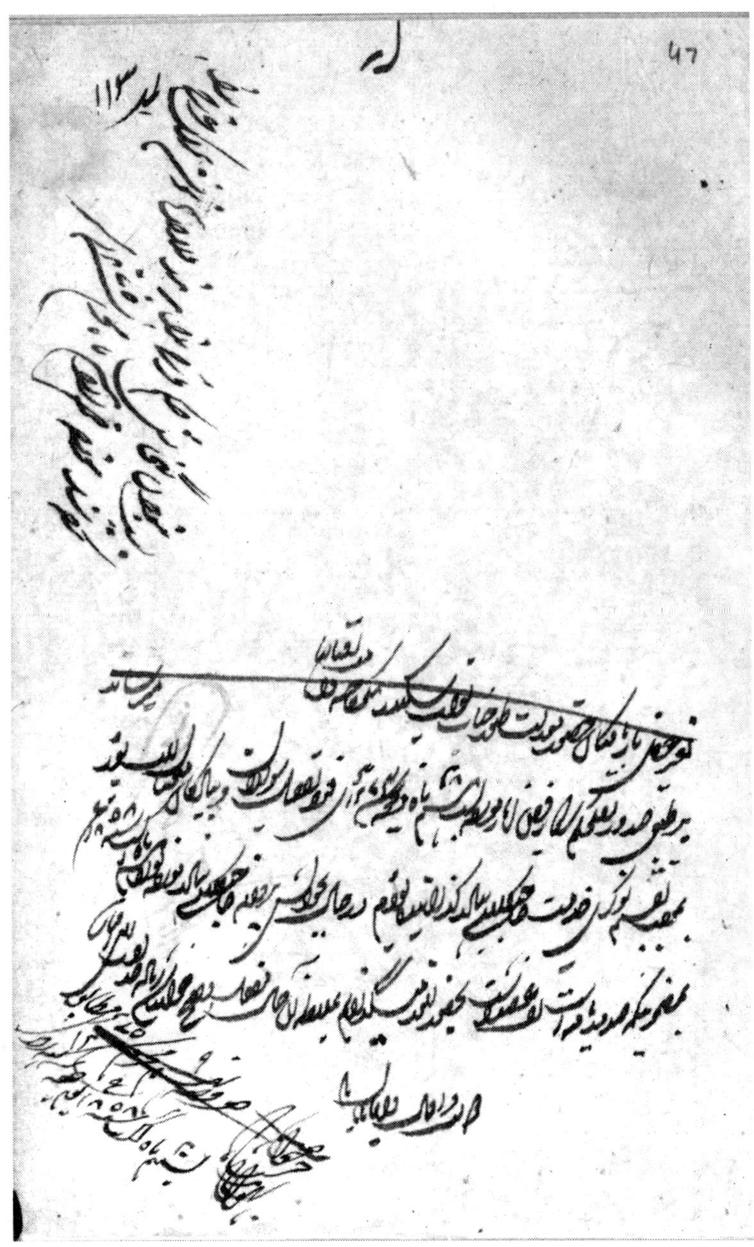

Bhawani Prasad informs Nawwab Sikandar Begam that he put before the Political Agent the details of sawars and artillery deployed at Lalitpur. (F. No. 262, P-47)

Nawwab Sikandar Begam orders her officials that if Adil Muhammad Khan and Aqil Muhammad Khan or any insurgent enter in the State of Bhopal, there should not be any reluctance in dealing with them. (F. No. 270, P-27)

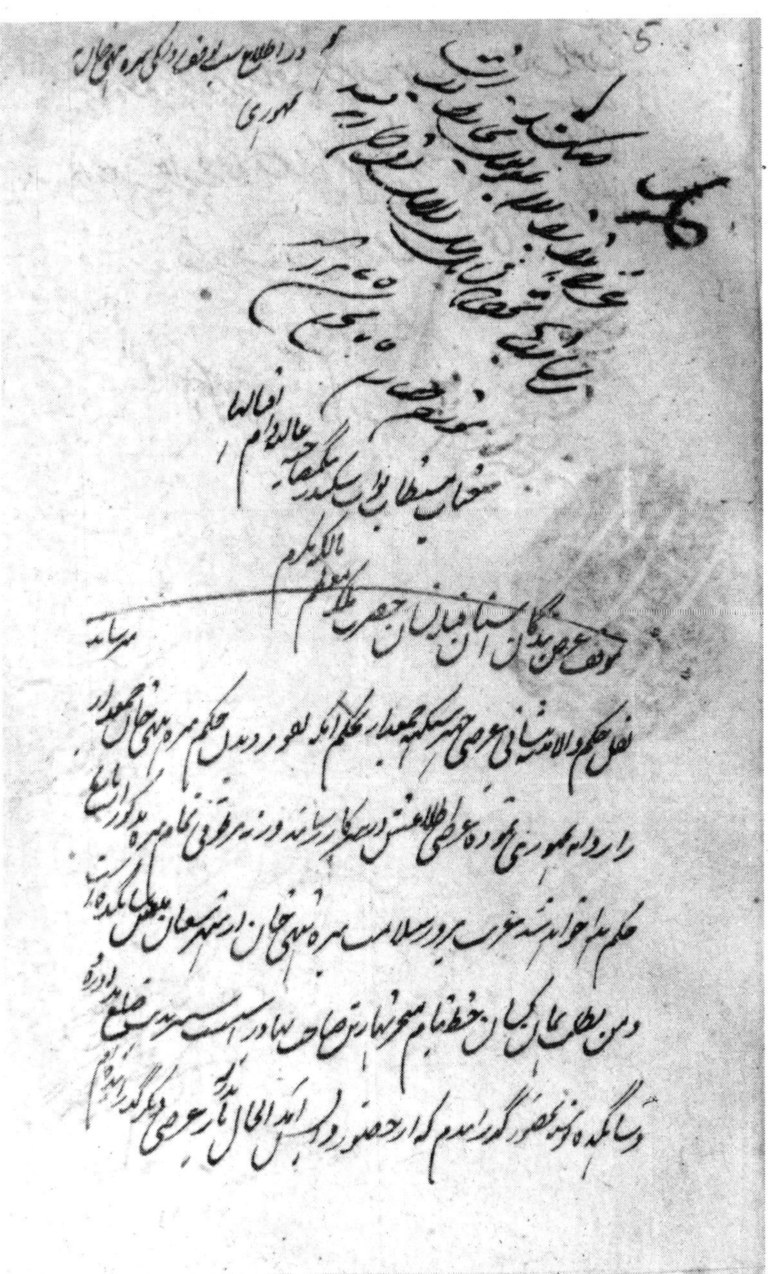

Murawwat Muhammad Khan informs Nawwab Sikandar Begam theat the battalion of Nanhay Khan is in Shahgarh and as soon as it comes back, it would be deployed at Bamhuri. (F. No. 273, P-5)

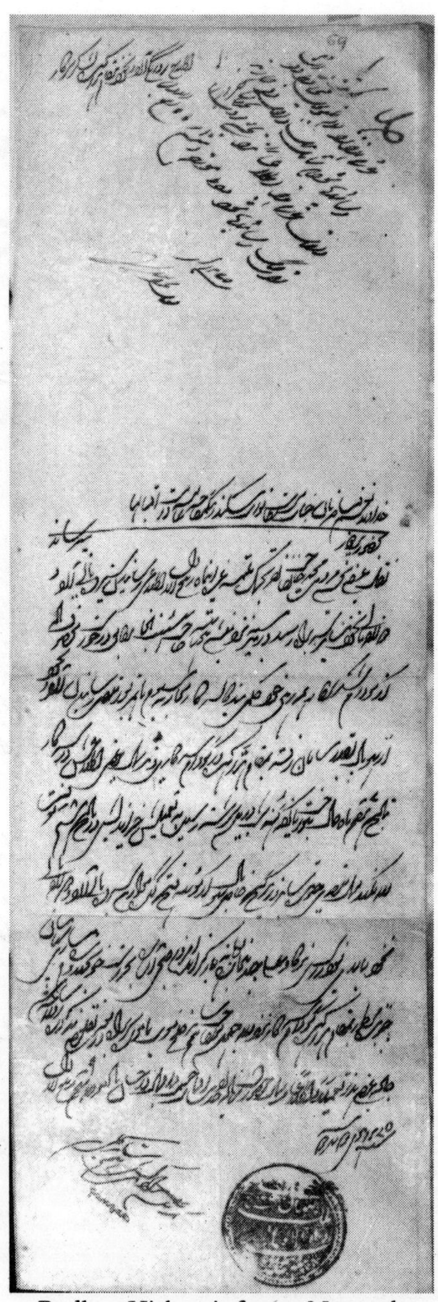

Radhey Kishan informs Nawwab Sikandar Begam that 13 maund flour and 12 maund gram, sarbrah-i rasad were sent to Berasia. (F. No. 275, P-59)

Bhawani Prasad sends the Parwana of the Political Agent to Nawwab Sikandar Begam, infarming that keeping one in captivity for the sake of others is unlawful. (F. No. 278, P-3)

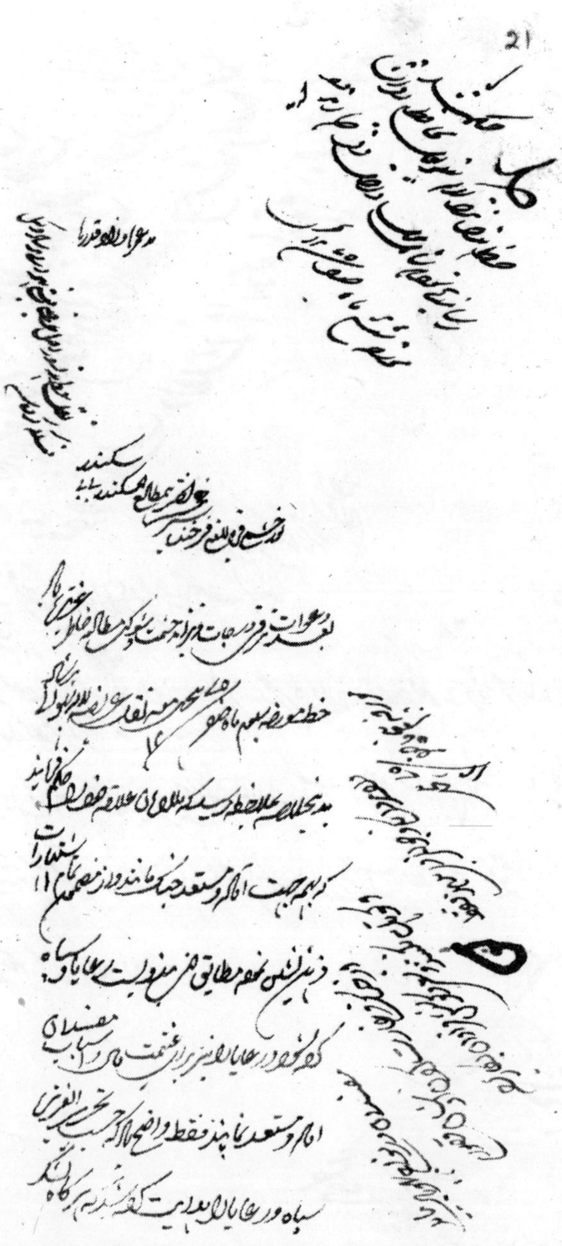

Nawwab Qudsia Begam informs Nawwab Sikandar Begam that the public and army have been informed that whenever the insurgents enter in the territory of Bhopal State, they should leave no stone unturned in fighting with them and destroying them.
(F. No. 281, P-21)